MATTER

An Earth Science

Concepts in Science

NEWTON EDITION

MATTER

An Earth Science

Paul F. Brandwein
Daniel J. Brovey
Arthur W. Greenstone
Warren E. Yasso

Harcourt Brace Jovanovich
New York Chicago San Francisco Atlanta Dallas *and* London

THE AUTHORS

Paul F. Brandwein, Adjunct Professor, Conservation and Education, University of Pittsburgh; Director, School Department, Harcourt Brace Jovanovich, Inc.; formerly Director, The Pinchot Institute for Conservation Studies, Milford, Pennsylvania; formerly chairman of department and teacher, now consultant to schools on curriculum and instruction.

Daniel J. Brovey, Associate Professor of Education, Queens College, City University of New York, New York, New York.

Arthur W. Greenstone, Pima College, Tucson, Arizona; formerly Chairman, Physical Science Department, Bayside High School, New York, New York.

Warren E. Yasso, Associate Professor of Science Education, Teachers College, Columbia University, New York, New York; formerly Assistant Professor, Department of Geology, Virginia Polytechnic Institute, Blacksburg, Virginia.

WITH THE ASSISTANCE OF

Violet R. Strahler, Author of the Teacher's Manual and Searchbook; Executive Director of Curriculum Development and Director of Science Centers, formerly Supervisor of Science, Mathematics, and Curriculum Publications, and formerly teacher, general science and chemistry, Dayton Public Schools, Dayton, Ohio

William A. Nierenberg, Director, Scripps Institution of Oceanography, La Jolla, California.

Acknowledgements: For permission to reprint copyrighted material, grateful acknowledgment is made to the following publishers:

Page 80, Dover Publications, Inc.: From *The Birth and Development of the Geological Sciences* by Frank D. Adams, New York, 1954.

Page 240, D. Van Nostrand Company, Inc.: From *The Global Sea* by Harris B. Stewart, Jr., © 1963 by Litton Educational Publishing, Inc.

Photograph, page 73, Fritz Goro, *Life* Magazine © Time Inc.

Map, page 97, Adapted from "The Origin of the Oceans" by Sir Edward Bullard. Copyright © 1969 by Scientific American, Inc. All rights reserved.

FRONT COVER: Lichen on Volcanic Rock by Philip Hyde from SLICKROCK, Sierra Club.
BACK COVER: Skylab Photograph of Colorado River, NASA.

PRINTED IN THE UNITED STATES OF AMERICA

ISBN 0-15-365901-7

CONTENTS

UNIT THREE

UNIT SIX

Introduction

This book is about matter. Everything you can touch is made of matter, of course. But some things you cannot touch are matter as well—the sun, for example. This book deals with chunks of matter of all shapes and sizes; huge chunks, such as stars; small chunks, such as rocks; and tiny chunks, such as crystals. (1) In these chunks of matter we shall try to find "hidden likenesses." Is there anything about stars, moons, rocks, crystals, and drops of water that is a likeness, a likeness that perhaps we cannot see, or touch? Yes, there is—but now we're getting ahead of the story.

We who study science use two powerful tools. The first tool consists of *verified and organized knowledge;* it is therefore reliable knowledge. The second tool is *a way of acquiring, verifying, and organizing new knowledge,* a way of adding to knowledge of the world in which we live. As you shall see, both tools are important.

(1)

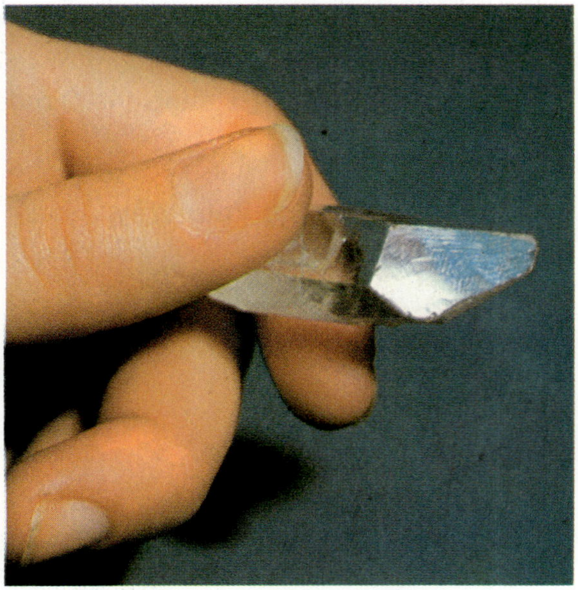

Verified and organized knowledge is also cumulative knowledge. When Isaac Newton, the great English scientist, said that if he saw further than other men it was because he stood on the shoulders of giants, he meant that he could go further in his work because of the verified reliable knowledge accumulated by others.

We know more about the moon than did Galileo; we know more about forces than did Boyle, more about gravitation than Newton; we know more about the nature of disease than did Pasteur, more about the atom than the chemist, John Dalton, and more about the nature of the Earth than the geologist, Lyell. For each scientist builds on the accuracy of the work of those who went before him; he does indeed stand on the shoulders of other scientists. Scientific work is cumulative: it builds one discovery on another.

For example, men once believed the earth was the center of the universe. Ptolemy proposed that the sun and all the planets moved in perfect circles around the earth. Centuries later Copernicus proposed that the sun was the center of the universe and that the earth and other planets moved around the sun in circular orbits. It remained for Kepler, starting with Tycho Brahe's accurate observations of Mars, to determine that the orbits of the planets were not circles—indeed, they were ellipses. But he could do this only because of men who came before him.

In building upon the work of others, scientists use certain processes of investigation. A great scientist, the physicist Percy Bridgman, called these processes "the methods of intelligence." These methods include reading what other scientists have done, making accurate observations, carefully designing investigations (including experiments), developing theories, and the like. This book will give you many opportunities to use the processes of the scientist as you do your own investigations.

This book brings to you some of the cumulative work of the scientists who have investigated matter. Among them are geologists, chemists, and meteorologists. Does this book bring you all the scientific knowledge concerned with matter, all the knowledge accumulated over centuries? No! It would be impossible—and it is even unnecessary at this point in your studies.

What cumulative knowledge does the book bring you? Why have we selected this knowledge from all the knowledge available? We have good reasons for our selection. You will agree that we could not include all scientific knowledge in this book, even if we wished to. Some ninety percent of all scientists are alive and at work today; someone has calculated that every hour they produce enough knowledge to fill a book the size of an encyclopedia volume. So we must select from this great collection of knowledge—but on what basis? There is a way in which we can organize knowledge in useful patterns. These are patterns of knowledge, or *concepts*, as we call them. A few examples will show how the organization of knowledge under concepts can be of use to you.

Examine this structure. ❶ Does it belong to a fish? A reptile? It belongs to a bird, you say. In that case, you probably have a concept of "birdness." From one structure, a feather, you have constructed a whole animal, a bird. Furthermore, having this concept of a bird enables you to recognize as a bird any of the millions of animals with feathers.

Take this example. ❷ If you recognize a magnet at work, then you probably have a concept of magnetism. Now examine this. ❸ What do you see? You see a different type of magnet in action. Once you have a concept of magnetism, you are able to recognize different magnets.

A book organized around concepts, therefore, is able to organize a great deal of knowledge. This is what we have done in this book. Because this book is organized around concepts, you will find it easier to learn from. Science, however, is not learned only through

❶

2

3

reading. Concepts in science are attained through experience, through investigation, through exploration. The scientist has developed an art of investigation that enables him to add to knowledge. As you form science concepts with the help of this book, you will also learn how to investigate, to inquire into the way the world works.

How is this book organized to help you learn something of the art of investigation? On page 10 you will find a section called **A Note on the Art of Investigation.** There you will see for yourself the opportunities for learning to learn through investigation.

Unit One

A PROBE INTO PLANET EARTH

Almost 500 years ago, a Genoese explorer, Christopher Columbus, found a new world across an uncharted ocean. Since then, many things have been discovered about our planet. Explorers have charted the seas, the polar ice caps, the deserts, the jungles. People have even gone beneath the surface of our planet. The piece of malachite you see on the opposite page was found under the surface of the earth.

But we study our planet for much more than the treasures it may hold. There is still another kind of exploration; and you will make it. In fact, the exploration of the planet you live on is the work of this year—and of this book. Turn the page and begin.

1

Spheres of Planet Earth

You are in a spaceship, approaching a strange planet. (1) The conditions of the planet have been studied very carefully. You know the atmosphere of the planet is thick. The spaceship must pass through the atmosphere at a shallow angle or burn up before it reaches the surface.

You may know that seventy percent of the planet is covered with water. So there is a good chance that you will land in a body of water. Other data indicate that six percent of the planet is hot, barren land. Another three percent is covered by glaciers and sheets of ice. Temperatures in these regions occasionally fall as low as 100 degrees below freezing. The remainder of the land, twenty-one percent, has moderate temperatures. Some of these areas are covered with forests and are inhabited by many kinds of living things—both plants and animals.

(1)

Finally, volcanic activity is still in evidence in some areas. This activity indicates that the interior of the planet is hot and molten. Do you recognize this planet?

You are already there. Are you surprised? How much do we really know about planet Earth? Air, water, and land—all pieces of Earth. They don't seem to be alike at first, yet they are all alike in certain ways.

2

1. EARTH SPHERES

The earth is not just a sphere of solid matter, even though we usually think of it that way. The earth is actually three spheres, one within another. You have only to look at a globe to realize that this is so.

The first sphere is made up of the solid matter of the earth. We live on the wrinkled surface of this solid sphere. Since it is made of rock, this sphere is called the **lithosphere,** which means "rocky sphere." You will learn more about the lithosphere in Chapter 5.

Look at the globe; a layer of water is wrapped around the lithosphere. 2 This layer of liquid, fortunately for us, is broken in places by the lithosphere. Yet if you turn the globe, you will see that the liquid layer still forms a sphere. This sphere of water is called the earth's **hydrosphere,** the "watery sphere." Living on land as we do, we tend to think of the lithosphere as the main part of the earth. Actually, about three-fourths of the lithosphere is covered by the hydrosphere.

If you were observing the earth from a spaceship high above the place where you are now, you would notice another sphere. Wrapped around the lithosphere and the hydrosphere is a third sphere made up of the mixture of gases we call air—the earth's **atmosphere,** the "vapor sphere."

Beyond the atmosphere is cold, airless space. Where does the atmosphere end; where does it begin? What do we know about our atmosphere, the invisible sphere of matter? Let's examine it—from the bottom up.

The Atmosphere

We think of the boundary between the lithosphere and the hydrosphere, and between the hydrosphere and the atmosphere, as being sharp and clear—but, in fact, the spheres overlap. Some of the water of the hydrosphere, for example, penetrates into rocks in the earth's crust. Some rock, although it looks as solid as rock is supposed to be, is riddled with very tiny holes through which water can pass. Some of the water of the hydrosphere is also present in the atmosphere, as water vapor, and helps to produce what we refer to as weather.

The air you are breathing right now is a tiny sample of the atmosphere. Is the rest of the atmosphere like the sample you are using? Oddly enough, the answer is no. If you could arrange to ascend through the atmosphere, taking samples as you go, you would find that

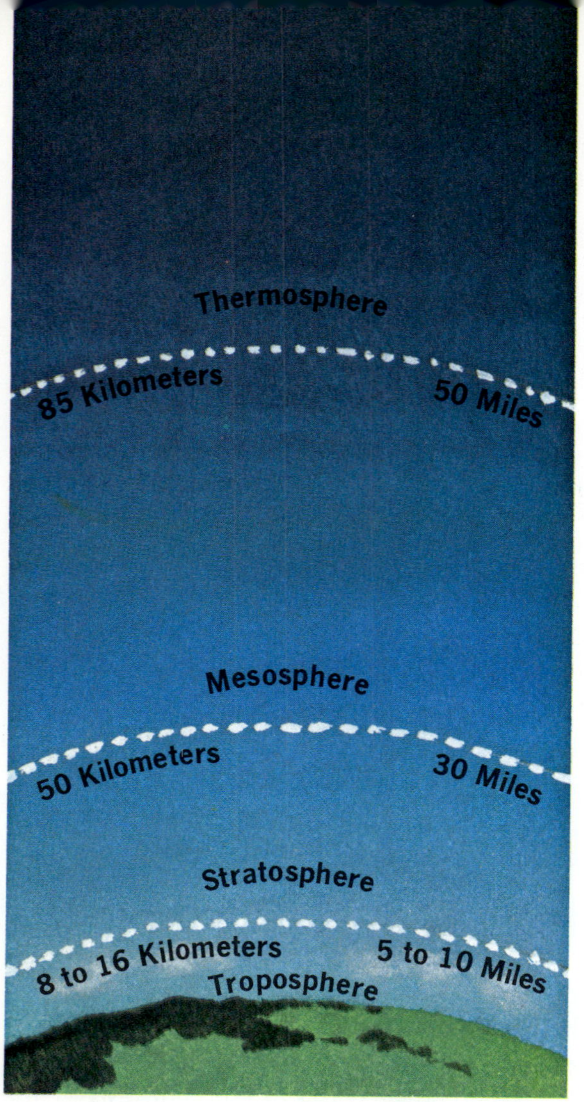

1

the atmosphere seems to be made up of different layers. 1 Observe in the diagram that the height of the various layers is shown in miles at the right, and in kilometers at the left. (Note that both *miles* and *kilometers* are used in the diagram. Why? Take time at this point to study **A Note on Measurement,** page 12.)

The lowest layer of the atmosphere, the layer in which you live, is the densest layer. This lowest level is the **troposphere.** Although the height of the troposphere varies from place to place, it is a fairly narrow region of the atmosphere. This layer might be called the "weathersphere," for it is here that the phenomena we call weather take place—winds, humidity, clouds, fog, rain, and snow. Our word "troposphere" comes from the Greek *tropos,* for "turning." This suggests how changeable weather is.

The higher one goes in the troposphere, the colder the air becomes. The temperature of the air around a high-flying jet plane, for instance, is about −40°. Strangely enough, however, the temperature does not continue to drop as one goes higher. The temperature suddenly holds steady with increasing height. This is a sign that a new layer of the atmosphere is at hand, the **stratosphere.** The stratosphere layer is about twice as thick as the troposphere. Since air movement is mainly horizontal in the stratosphere, it is well suited for air travel. The absence of large upward or downward air currents means that there is very little air mixing to cause marked changes in temperature or weather.

Toward the top of the stratosphere, solar radiation causes some of the oxygen gas to change to a form of oxygen known as **ozone.** Oxygen is odorless, but ozone has a sharp, slightly metallic odor. You may have detected the odor of ozone after an electrical discharge has taken place from a sparking electric motor, or in a thunderstorm.

Ozone, unlike oxygen, absorbs ultraviolet radiation, which is harmful to living things. This turns out to be of some importance to us. The sun sends out an enormous flow of radiant energy, including ultraviolet radiation. A very small fraction of this radiation is directed at the earth, but if it reached the surface of the earth, most forms of life as we know it could not exist. It is the concentration of ozone toward the top of the stratosphere that prevents too much ultraviolet radiation from reaching the surface of the earth. Life depends on this ozone layer.

At the top of the stratosphere the temperature, which has risen gradually, takes a sudden drop. The third layer of the atmosphere, the **mesosphere,** begins where this sudden change in temperature occurs. Although the word mesosphere comes from the Greek *mesos,* for "intermediate," the temperature drops steadily in this layer. In fact at the top of the mesosphere, the temperature is lower than in any other part of the atmosphere.

In the upper part of the mesosphere, the particles of extremely thin air are bombarded by electromagnetic radiation from the sun and by cosmic radiation from space. As a result, the particles become electrically charged particles, or **ions.** These ions are important to hearing your favorite radio program, as you will soon see.

Extending upward into space from the mesosphere is another layer, the **thermosphere.** Here air particles are few and far between, compared with their crowded condition at the earth's surface. Although the temperature rises steadily in the thermosphere, the relatively few particles do not tend to heat up objects in this layer. However, satellites in this region do become hot by absorbing solar radiation.

The upper part of this layer is sometimes considered as a special region called the **exosphere.** Satellites can orbit in this region and beyond with practically no friction to slow them down. Where does the exosphere end? No one knows. Some scientists hold the view that this outermost layer of the earth's atmosphere extends all the way to the sun—and that the sun's atmosphere likewise extends all the way to the earth.

The Ionosphere

Let's return in our trip through the atmosphere to the upper region of the mesosphere where charged particles, or ions, are produced. Today scientists know that there is a whole ionized region in the atmosphere extending upward from the mesosphere. Within this region, which is known as the **ionosphere,** are several layers of ionized gas. These layers of ions block some of the sun's radiation and some of the cosmic radiation.

More remarkable still, the layers of the ionosphere allow us to communicate with people in other parts of our globe. These layers of ions reflect radio waves. Radio waves that would travel out into space are bounced back to earth by the ionosphere. **2** In this way we can communicate by radio around the curve of the earth's surface.

2

The Magnetosphere

You know that the earth behaves as a giant magnet. Perhaps you are familiar with the shape of the magnetic field of a bar magnet. ① The earth has a magnetic field that extends through its whole atmosphere and far beyond the ionosphere. The region in space that encloses the earth's magnetic field is the **magnetosphere.** ②

Trapped within the upper part of the magnetosphere, between 650 and 67,000 kilometers —that is, about 400 to 40,000 miles—above the earth's surface, is a collection of electrically charged particles. This roughly doughnut-shaped belt of particles was discovered in 1958 by a team of American space scientists led by Dr. James Van Allen. It is known as the Van Allen belt.

Beyond the Van Allen belt is the earth's outer magnetosphere, enclosing a zone shaped like an enormously elongated teardrop. ② What is the cause of the peculiar lengthening of one end? Notice the direction of the solar wind, which seems to push the magnetosphere away from the sun. Just as comets have tails blown away from their heads by the solar wind, the earth has a tail that is blown away by the solar wind. The earth's tail is made up of very thin ionized gas bounded by the outer magnetosphere.

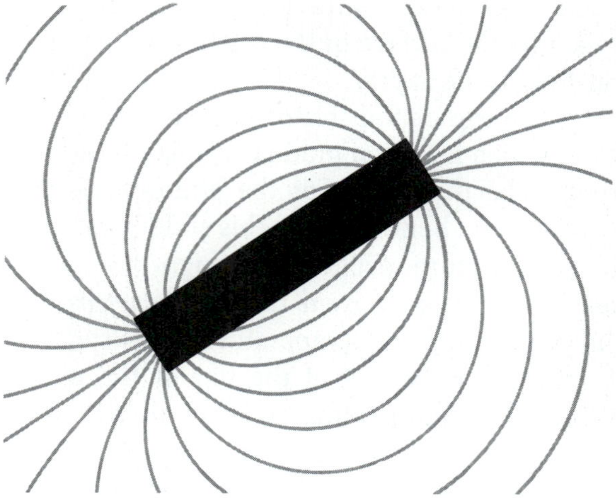
①

②
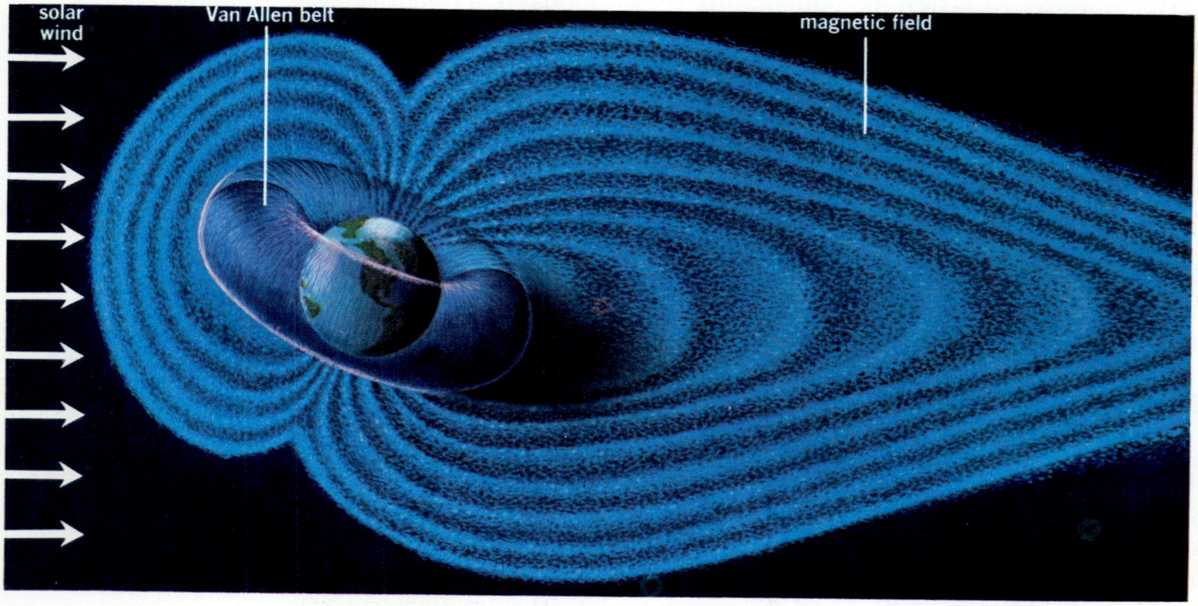

3

4

No matter where it is in its orbit around the sun, a comet's tail is always streaming away from the sun. 3 The same is true of the earth's tail. As the earth travels its orbit, its outer magnetosphere is lengthened on the side away from the sun.

The tail thus formed is at least 200,000 kilometers, or 120,000 miles long. Its shape has been determined by a satellite that mapped the shape by repeated crossings. If the tail extends as far as the solar wind is known to blow, as some scientists think it does, then it may extend between 10 and 160 times as far as the distance from the earth to the sun. If the solar wind is actually a thinned-out extension of the sun's corona, as it may be, then we might say that the orbit of the earth lies within the sun's atmosphere.

Interplanetary space between the earth and the sun is not so empty after all.

Solar Radiation

Look outside. Is it a bright sunny day; is it foggy and gray? You know that no matter what kind of day it is, energy is radiating from the sun. To reach us this energy, or solar radiation, must travel about 150 million kilometers (93 million miles). What happens to the solar radiation when it reaches our atmosphere? Three things happen. Particles in the atmosphere reflect some energy back into space. Some energy is absorbed by gases of the atmosphere and by the earth. And finally, some energy produces charged particles in the gases of the atmosphere, for example, in the ionosphere.

About 30 percent of the *in*coming *sol*ar radi*ation*, or **insolation,** is reflected back into space. Another 15 to 19 percent of insolation is absorbed by the atmosphere. The remainder reaches the earth and is absorbed.

When this radiation strikes the earth, the earth is heated. Some of the heat is radiated from the ground back into the atmosphere as infrared radiation, but it does not pass out into space again. The carbon dioxide and water vapor in the atmosphere absorb this energy, and trap it. This is sometimes called the "greenhouse effect." 4 Energy from the sun passes easily through the glass into a greenhouse—but, when reradiated, energy is absorbed by the moist air within. The energy is trapped. Let's investigate this process. But before we do, let's look at the art of investigation itself. ■

A Note on the Art of Investigation

One learns to investigate by investigating, just as one learns to paint by painting, or to do anything by doing it. Of course, learning certain aspects of the art of investigation may be made easier by instruction, making it possible for you to do simple investigations, then more difficult ones, with the aim of enabling you to investigate on your own.

The investigations that you will have the opportunity to do will be of three kinds.

1. The first, which we will call **An Apprentice Investigation,** will be found throughout the text. It is intended to give you opportunities to engage in observing, measuring, analyzing, planning, designing experiments and their controls, and searching out references. You will, in short, be engaged in learning how to use the processes of science. These apprentice investigations will be illustrated with photographs (or drawings) so that you may see how the investigation is done—even as you do it. You will find an example of this kind of investigation on page 11.

2. Having "seen"—through the apprentice investigation—how an investigation may be done, you may then proceed to do **An Investigation On Your Own.** A question is asked, but few directions (if any) are given. The solution to the on-your-own problem is generally not to be found in this text. This is an invitation to investigate in your own way. This may be done in the classroom, the laboratory, or at home. You will find investigations of this kind just after the apprentice investigations.

3. Another kind of investigation is included in the last section of each chapter, under the heading **Extending the Concepts.** These are research investigations. Some may be completed within an hour or so. Some may take weeks or even months to complete. You are again on your own. Your ability to complete the investigation depends somewhat upon your understanding of the processes of investigating discussed in the Apprentice Investigations. You will find examples of this kind of investigation on page 21.

Throughout you will find an enormous number of investigations that will interest you. Some of them will surely arouse your curiosity. No doubt you will want to probe further on your own—beyond the investigations suggested.

■ AN APPRENTICE INVESTIGATION into the Greenhouse Effect

Make two small stands of modeling clay to support two thermometers in an upright position. Be sure the clay does not touch the bulbs of the thermometers. ❶

Place both thermometers in sunlight, a few inches apart. Place the thermometers so they receive the same amount of radiation. When the liquid in the thermometers stops rising, read the thermometers. These readings were obtained during one trial. ❷

How do the readings compare? How do you explain this?

Now put one thermometer in a glass jar and cap the jar tightly. (The thermometer should not touch the sides of the jar.) Return the thermometer (in the jar) to its former place, so that it receives the same amount of radiation as the other thermometer.

After a time, compare the temperature of the thermometer in the jar with the temperature of the thermometer outside the jar. These readings were obtained during one trial. ❸ How can you explain what happens to the temperature in the glass jar?

An Investigation On Your Own

Which thermometer will *lose* heat more rapidly? Why? How can you find out?

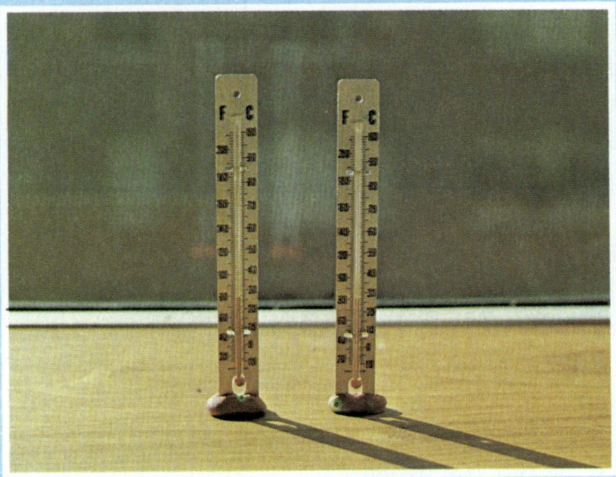
❶

❷

❸

In your investigation, you saw that the temperature of the air inside the glass jar was higher than the temperature outside. Energy from the sun passes through the glass to warm the air inside the jar. Once inside, the energy is absorbed by the air, and increases the temperature inside the jar.

Did you find that the air in the jar *lost* heat more slowly than the outside air?

REVIEW

1. Describe the planet earth in terms of three spheres.

2. Name and describe briefly each of the layers of the atmosphere.

3. What is the magnetosphere? Briefly describe how the magnetic field of the earth is affected by the solar wind.

4. The space between the earth and the sun is not entirely empty. Explain.

5. What is the greenhouse effect?

NEW VIEW

1. Skylab is a huge space laboratory orbiting the earth. Find out at what distance from the earth it orbits. What layer of the atmosphere is it in? Explain why it is found there.

2. How are living things on earth protected from the greater part of the deadly radiation that enters our atmosphere?

3. Why is knowledge of the Van Allen belt of great importance in planning space flights?

4. Particles of dust and water droplets create many interesting atmospheric effects. Find out how rainbows and mirages are produced. Do you think you can photograph these phenomena?

5. Do other planets have atmospheres like ours? Find out what Pioneer 10 has discovered about the atmosphere of Jupiter.

A Note on Measurement

Scientists and most other people throughout the world use the metric system of measurement. It is probable that in the United States we shall change from our present English system to the metric system, or more precisely to the International System, abbreviated SI.

In most places in this textbook, you will find measurements of length, volume, weight (mass), and temperature given in metric values, followed by the approximate English equivalent in parentheses.

Perhaps you have studied the metric system in your earlier work in science and mathematics and know how to convert measurements from one system to another. If not, you will find the tables below useful. In using the metric system, several prefixes are important:

prefix		
kilo	=	thousand (1000)
centi	=	hundredth (0.01)
milli	=	thousandth (0.001)

example		
1 kilogram	=	1000 grams
1 centimeter	=	0.01 meter
1 milliliter	=	0.001 liter

METRIC UNITS OF LENGTH

1 kilometer (km)	=	1000 meters (m)
1 meter (m)	=	standard of length
1 centimeter (cm)	=	0.01 meter (m)
1 millimeter (mm)	=	0.001 meter (m)

METRIC UNITS OF WEIGHT (MASS)*

1 kilogram (kg)	=	standard of mass
1 gram (g)	=	0.001 kilogram (kg)
1 centigram (cg)	=	0.01 gram (g)
1 milligram (mg)	=	0.001 gram (g)

METRIC UNITS OF VOLUME

1 liter (l)	=	standard of liquid volume
1 milliliter (ml)	=	0.001 liter

UNITS OF TEMPERATURE

0° Celsius (C)	=	freezing point of water
100° Celsius (C)	=	boiling point of water

ENGLISH—METRIC EQUIVALENTS

1 inch (in)	=	2.54 centimeters (cm)
1 yard (yd)	=	0.914 meter (m)
1 mile (mi)	=	1.61 kilometers (km)
1 pound (lb)	=	454 grams (g)
1 ounce (oz)	=	28.35 grams (g)
1 quart (qt)	=	0.946 liter (l)
32° Fahrenheit (F)	=	0° Celsius (C)
212° Fahrenheit (F)	=	100° Celsius (C)

METRIC—ENGLISH EQUIVALENTS

1 centimeter (cm)	=	0.394 inch (in)
1 meter (m)	=	39.4 inches (in)
1 kilometer (km)	=	0.621 mile (mi)
1 kilogram	=	2.205 pounds (lb)
1 gram (g)	=	0.035 ounce (oz)
1 liter (l)	=	1.06 quarts (qt)
0° Celsius (C)	=	32° Fahrenheit (F)
100° Celsius (C)	=	212° Fahrenheit (F)

To convert quickly from one system to the other, you may find the following Conversion Tables useful.

CONVERSION TABLE FOR APPROXIMATE VALUES

English to Metric

inches to centimeters	–	multiply by 2.5
feet to centimeters	–	multiply by 30
yards to meters	–	multiply by 0.9
miles to kilometers	–	multiply by 1.6
pounds to kilograms	–	multiply by 0.45
quarts to liters	–	multiply by 0.95
° Celsius to ° Fahrenheit	–	(9/5 x ° C) + 32

CONVERSION TABLE FOR APPROXIMATE VALUES

Metric to English

centimeters to inches	–	multiply by 0.4
meters to feet	–	multiply by 3.3
meters to yards	–	multiply by 1.1
kilometers to miles	–	multiply by 0.6
kilograms to pounds	–	multiply by 2.2
liters to quarts	–	multiply by 1.06
° Fahrenheit to ° Celsius	–	(° F – 32) x 5/9

---

* Although weight and mass are not equivalent, the metric unit of mass is usually used as the unit of weight, except in technical work.

■ **AN APPRENTICE INVESTIGATION into the Composition of Water**

❶ 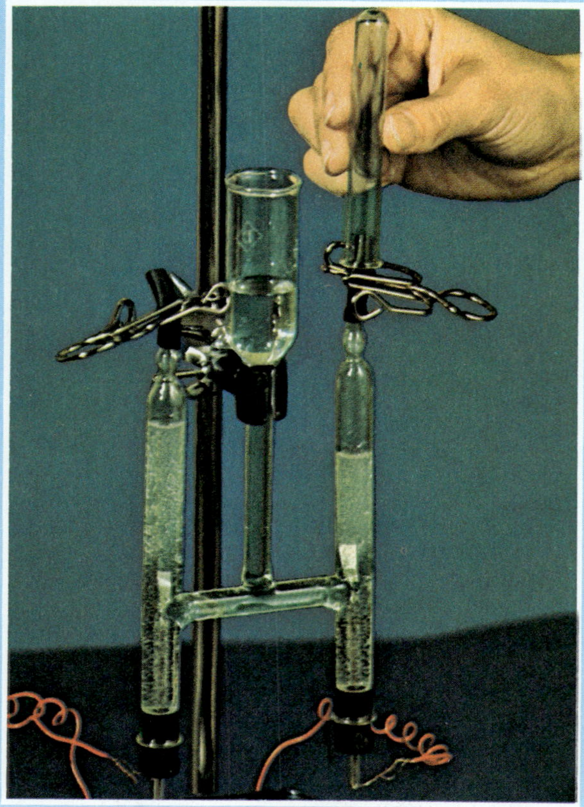

Water molecules can be separated into simpler substances by passing an electric current through the water in a special apparatus. ❶ A little sulfuric acid in the water helps conduct the current. Turn on the electric current. What happens? Bubbles of gas rise in the tubes. How much gas collects in each tube? What are these gases?

You can find out by testing the gases in both tubes. Place a Pyrex or Kimax test tube over the gas tube containing the *smaller* amount of gas. Let out enough gas to fill one test tube. Thrust a glowing splint into the tube. What is the result?

Now place a test tube over the other gas tube. Fill this second test tube with gas. (Be sure this tube is dry.) Place a burning splint near the mouth of this tube. What happens? Examine the tube to see what substance forms.

An Investigation On Your Own

Repeat the investigation using distilled water. Are your results different in any way? Explain.

2. OUR WORLD OF WATER

About three-fourths of our planet is covered by a liquid—water. We are so familiar with water that we rarely stop to analyze it. We swim in the water of lakes and oceans, we drink water and we wash in water. But what exactly is water? If your school laboratory has an apparatus like the one shown here, you can find out. ■

The electric current that passed through the water broke the water apart. The liquid water disappeared, and in its place two gases appeared. What were these gases? When a *burning* wooden splint is brought close to one tube of gas a slight (harmless) explosion with a "popping" sound occurs. This test identifies the gas as **hydrogen.** When a *glowing* wooden splint is brought close to a tube of the second gas, the splint bursts into flame. This test identifies the gas as **oxygen.** If you kept the current on until all the water disappeared, you would find that you had collected only these two gases.

You probably noticed that you collect twice as much hydrogen as oxygen. All samples of water will give you the same results. Since no other substances appear, water must be made up of two forms of matter—the gases hydrogen and oxygen. And we have learned something else. In water the hydrogen and oxygen exist in a definite proportion—2 parts hydrogen to 1 part oxygen.

You know we can break down water into two different gases. Suppose you tried a similar procedure with these gases. You would find it impossible to break down the hydrogen and the oxygen into simpler substances. A substance that cannot be broken down into other substances is an **element.** Hydrogen and oxygen, the components of water, are elements. Substances, like water, that are made up of two or more elements are **compounds.**

You saw that twice as much hydrogen as oxygen was formed when water was broken down. You could repeat the procedure many times and you could use sea water or pure water, but you will always get the same result. The elements hydrogen and oxygen are present in water in a definite proportion. In a certain compound, the same elements are always found in the same proportion.

Another Look at Water

While we and other air-breathers normally keep our heads above water, crabs, snails, and other animals live under water. Water is to them what air is to us. Just as we are surrounded by air, they are surrounded by water.

What does natural water contain that allows certain animals to live in it? Try the next investigation. ■

■ AN APPRENTICE INVESTIGATION into Substances in Natural Water

Collect some water from the sea, a lake, river, pond, or an aquarium. Pour the water into a clean Pyrex or Kimax beaker. Heat the water until it is nearly all boiled away. Turn off the flame and allow the rest of the water to evaporate completely.

The whitish and grayish material left on the sides and bottom of the beaker consists of solid substances that were dissolved in the water. Scrape some of this solid residue from the beaker and pick it up with a wire loop. Hold the loop in a flame. What do you observe? Here is what happened in one trial with the solid left from the evaporation of sea water. ❶

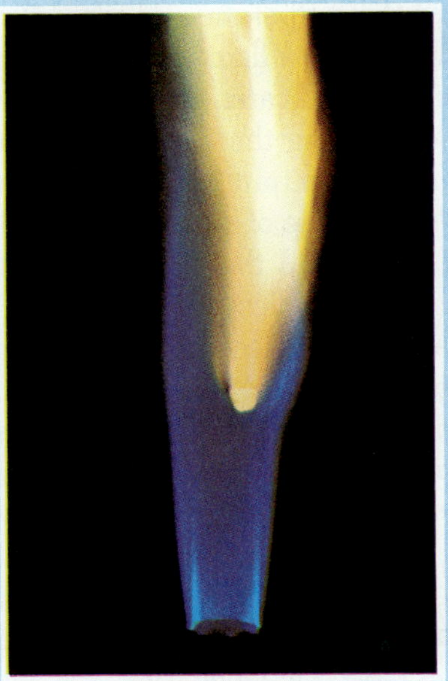
❶

Dissolve another bit of the solid residue in a little water in a test tube. Add a few drops of silver nitrate solution. What do you see? ❶ Allow this sample to stand a few minutes, and observe again. ❷

An Investigation On Your Own

Try these tests with water from different sources. Include tap water as well as natural waters you did not use before.

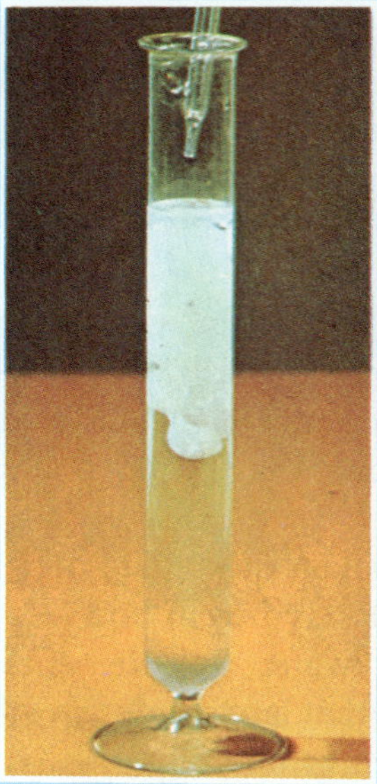

❶

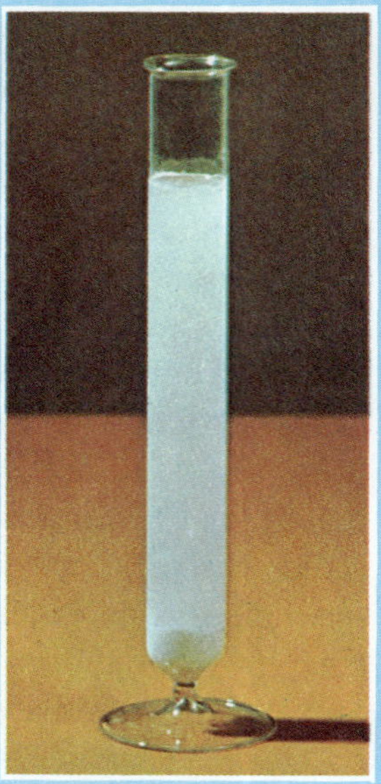

❷

Solids and Salts in Sea Water

In your investigation, you saw that a solid left after the evaporation of sea water imparts a yellow color to a flame. Chemists have found that this test indicates the presence of a compound containing the element sodium.

When silver nitrate was added to the originally clear sample of sea water a solid material formed. Any solid that forms when two clear liquids react is called a **precipitate.** On standing, the precipitate settled to the bottom of the test tube. This formation of a precipitate with silver nitrate is evidence that the water contained a chloride—a salt containing the element chlorine. All chlorides react this way with silver nitrate. One of the most common chlorides is sodium chloride, familiar to you as table salt.

From the flame test and the silver nitrate test, we have evidence that the water contained the compound sodium chloride. A chemist's complete analysis of water from oceans, lakes, streams, and other sources uses the same procedures as those in your investigation. One chemical analysis of the dissolved solids in sea water indicated the presence of the following substances.

SOME SUBSTANCES IN SEA WATER

Compounds	*Elements in the compounds*
sodium chloride	sodium, chlorine
magnesium chloride	magnesium, chlorine
calcium sulfate	calcium, sulfur, oxygen
potassium sulfate	potassium, sulfur, oxygen
potassium chloride	potassium, chlorine
magnesium bromide	magnesium, bromine
calcium bicarbonate	calcium, hydrogen, carbon, oxygen
magnesium sulfate	magnesium, sulfur, oxygen
sodium iodide	sodium, iodine

Suppose you let another sample of sea water stand in a warm place for about half an hour. Bubbles collect on the inside of the container. These bubbles contain gases that are dissolved in the water. In one chemical analysis of sea water, these gases were found: oxygen, nitrogen, carbon dioxide, argon, helium, and neon. There is about twice as much nitrogen as oxygen, almost equal amounts of oxygen and carbon dioxide, and tiny amounts of argon, helium, and neon.

The amounts of dissolved solids are very nearly the same throughout the sea. But the percentages of dissolved gases vary in different parts of the sea and under different conditions. In the next section, we shall see that these gases are also present in the air, but the relative amount of each is different in the atmosphere.

REVIEW

1. Define the term element. Give two examples of elements.

2. Name several compounds found in sea water.

3. Suppose that you have a sample of sea water. How would you test for the presence of sodium chloride?

4. Describe what happens when an electric current is passed through water. What are the products?

NEW VIEW

1. You have probably heard people refer to water as "H-two-oh." Explain this phrase in the light of the apprentice investigation into the composition of water?

2. Fuel cells used in spacecrafts combine oxygen and hydrogen to produce electrical energy and water. How is this similar to the apprentice investigation into the composition of water?

3. SAMPLING ANOTHER EARTH MATERIAL

You are living at the bottom of a sea of air. You know that your life depends on the air you breathe. You also know that air is matter—it takes up space and has mass. What kind of matter is air? Let's find out.

Air—A Mixture

There was a time when people thought air was a single substance; but chemists soon found that air was not one but several substances. Some of these substances are elements, for example, hydrogen and oxygen; other substances are compounds, such as carbon dioxide (CO_2). Air, in fact, is a **mixture** of these substances.

What is a mixture? In the investigation on the composition of water, you collected a tube of hydrogen and a tube of oxygen. Suppose you then placed the tubes together, mouth to mouth, and shook them. Will the atoms in hydrogen and oxygen come together to form water again? No, not until a flame provides the energy to cause the atoms to unite. In shaking the oxygen and hydrogen together, you have merely mixed the elements. You have produced a *mixture* of two different gases. If you mix carbon dioxide, a compound of carbon and oxygen with these gases, you have a mixture of three gases.

A mixture has no definite chemical composition; it cannot be described by writing a formula. Vegetable soup, for example, is clearly a mixture. The amount of each element, each compound, and each ingredient varies, depending upon who makes the soup. Air, sea water, and many rocks are mixtures too.

Analyzing Air

If you were asked to name the substances in air, you would very likely begin with oxy-

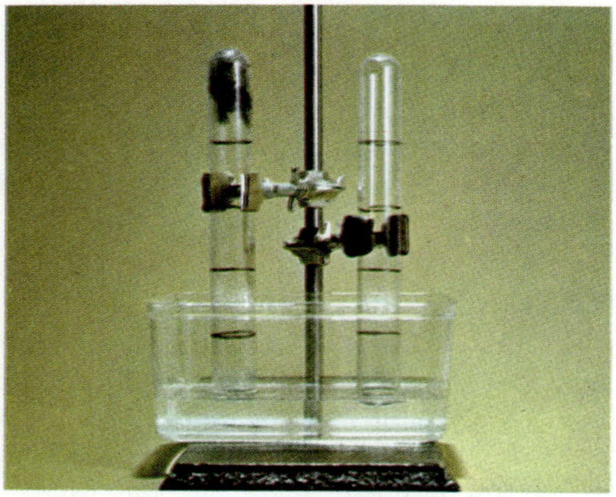

①

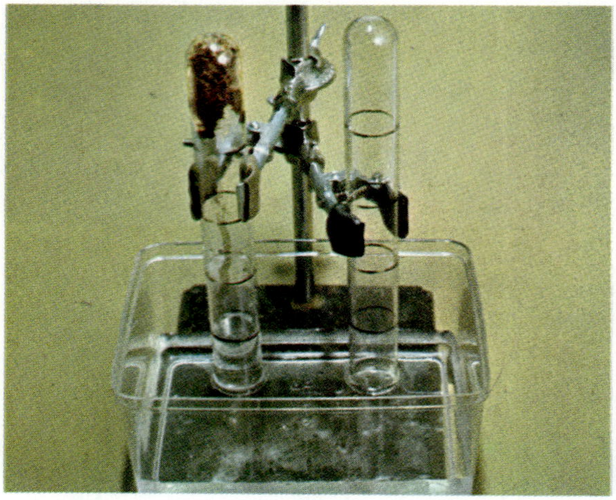

②

gen. Yet oxygen, important as it is, is not the most abundant substance in the air. What evidence is there to support this statement?

Suppose you wet the inside of a test tube, and stuff some steel wool into it. Mark the test tube off into 5 equal parts and then place the tube upside-down in water. At the same time, place a control tube, one containing no steel wool, in the water.① As the iron in the steel wool rusts, water rises in the tube until the volume of air in the tube decreases by about $\frac{1}{5}$.②

Is there a way to explain this behavior? There is. Rust is a compound made up of two elements, iron and oxygen. The iron in the test tube combined with the oxygen in the air within the test tube. The volume of air in the tube decreased by the amount of oxygen taken from the air. Whenever oxygen combines with another element, an **oxidation** reaction takes place. The oxidation reaction that took place in the tube used up about $\frac{1}{5}$ of the air in the tube. So it would seem likely that the air is about $\frac{1}{5}$ oxygen.

SUBSTANCES IN AIR

Element or Compound	*Percentage by volume (clean, dry air)*
nitrogen	78.0
oxygen	21.0
argon	1.0
carbon dioxide	.03
neon	.002
krypton	(less than neon)
xenon	(less than neon)

❸

Of course this single example does not prove that air is $\frac{1}{5}$ oxygen. But chemists have analyzed air often with these same results.

As you see in the table, nitrogen, not oxygen, is the most abundant substance in the air. The element nitrogen makes up almost $\frac{4}{5}$ of the air. Nitrogen does not react (take part) in our breathing, nor in most chemical changes in nature. However, compounds containing nitrogen are essential to all living things.

The air you are breathing is mainly a mixture of nitrogen and oxygen. After oxygen, the most abundant element in the air is argon. Argon, neon, krypton, and xenon do not enter into the composition of living things, in breathing or in any other way.

There is not much carbon dioxide in the air, but carbon dioxide is essential to living things. Plants use the compound carbon dioxide in food making, and we depend on plants for food.

What else is in the air? The heading "clean, dry air" in the table gives us a clue. Most air is not perfectly dry. Air usually contains some water. The amount of water in the air varies from time to time, and from place to place. On the average, water makes up only about 1.2 percent of the air. But this water is vital for living things.

When it comes to substances that make air dirty, the list is almost endless. Air pollution is an increasing problem. ❸ But even if all the particles of air pollution were analyzed, we can be sure they contain only the elements we already know. Unfortunately, some of these elements are harmful to living things and we must take precautions to remove them from our "breathing space."

REVIEW

1. What is a mixture? How is it different from an element, from a compound?

2. Name the gases that make up the air. Which gas is most abundant? Which is essential to living things?

NEW VIEW

1. Take a deep breath. What substances did you take into your lungs? Find out what happens to these substances when you exhale.

2. How does "clean, dry air" differ from the air of the atmosphere?

4. RELATING THE CONCEPTS

Matter is the stuff our world is made of—it makes up the earth we walk on, the food we eat, the air we breathe. These, and all the other forms of matter in our everyday surroundings, are made up of elements and compounds.

Right now you are breathing in elements and compounds of the air. You are sitting in a chair made up of elements and compounds. Your body is digesting compounds in the food you ate. As your body oxidizes some of this food, it releases energy as heat and as energy of motion.

The earth is composed of elements and compounds in solid, liquid, and gaseous states. The earth's solid part is the lithosphere. The earth's liquid part is the hydrosphere. The earth's gaseous part is the atmosphere. These spheres interact and affect one another: solids and liquids are found in the air; gases and solids are dissolved in liquids; liquids and gases penetrate into solids.

Land, water, air. Man depends on all of these earth materials in order to survive. Decisions we make concerning our environment will always depend upon carefully collected facts about land, water, and air. In this chapter, you began collecting some of this data of earth. More data will become available as you continue your study.

Reviewing the Concepts

► *Matter takes up space and has mass.* Everything in our environment that has mass and occupies space is matter. Thus, air, land, and water are matter. The bodies of all living things, including ourselves, are matter. And rocks, planets, stars, and all the countless other kinds of objects on earth and throughout the universe are matter. Though their differences are great, all kinds of matter are alike in that they occupy space and have mass.

► *The earth is composed of matter in solid, liquid, and gaseous states.* The lithosphere is solid; the hydrosphere is liquid; and the atmosphere is gaseous.

► *The earth's atmosphere has a structure of definable layers.* Each layer—troposphere, stratosphere, mesosphere, thermosphere, ionosphere, and exosphere—has its own characteristics. The magnetosphere pervades the whole atmosphere and extends far beyond it into outer space.

► *Samples of matter are classified as elements, compounds, or mixtures.* A substance that cannot be broken down chemically into other substances is an element. Substances that are made up of two or more elements are compounds. Mixtures are combinations of elements or compounds that are not chemically united.

Testing Yourself

1. The ionosphere, troposphere, stratosphere, mesosphere, and exosphere are all layers of the atmosphere. Arrange these in the correct order, beginning with the layer nearest the earth's surface, and state an important characteristic of each.

2. What is (a) the Van Allen belt? (b) the magnetosphere?

3. Describe what happens to solar radiation when it reaches the atmosphere of the earth.

4. Suppose you were given an unknown white solid that looked like table salt. Describe how you could determine in the laboratory whether or not the substance contained sodium chloride.

5. Suppose you were given two corked test tubes that looked empty. You are told that both contain the same gas. You suspect it is not air.

How could you determine if it is hydrogen or oxygen?

6. What gases make up the air? What gases are dissolved in sea water? How do the amounts of these gases differ in the sea and air?

7. Salt, sugar, and iodine are dissolved in the same beaker of water. Do you have a mixture, a compound, or an element? Explain your answer.

8. Suppose you have passed an electric current through a quantity of water. Explain what happens. What can you determine about the composition of water?

Extending the Concepts

Investigation 1. To find the area of a rectangular table top, we use the formula $A = l \times w$; area equals length times width. To find the surface area of a sphere, we use the formula $S.A. = 4\pi r^2$.

The earth is a sphere with a radius of about 6,700 kilometers (4,000 miles). Using the formula for surface area, find the surface area of the earth. How much of the earth is covered with water? with land?

Investigation 2. Using an almanac, find how many square kilometers (or miles) of land there are in various countries. Which is the largest? the smallest? How many people are there in these countries? How many people are there per square kilometer? (or per square mile?)

Suggested Reading

Lapp, Ralph E., and the editors of LIFE, *Matter* (Life Science Library), New York, Time Inc., 1963. A beautifully illustrated book about man's sources of matter and the uses he makes of this matter.

Matthews, William H., *Introducing the Earth*, New York, Dodd, 1972. This book shows you the earth through the eyes of a geologist. See the discussion on the three spheres of the earth.

2

The Smallest Part

Imagine you have a tiny drop of water on a glass slide. 1 Suppose you were to divide the tiny drop in half, divide the half into half again, and so on until the particle you had left could no longer be divided and still be a particle of water. What would that particle be?

1

1. PARTICLES OF MATTER

Think about the smallest particle of a substance in this way. Suppose a test tube of red dye were poured into the ocean and allowed to spread through all the oceans of the earth. Years later a glass of ocean water dipped up from any place in any of the oceans would contain thousands of particles of the red dye. Imagine how many particles were in the original test tube! These particles must be very small indeed. But each of these tiny particles has the properties of the red dye. Scientists call these particles **molecules.** One molecule of water is the smallest particle with the properties of water.

Recall what happened when you sent an electric current through water. You broke up the molecules of water. You found that water is made up of two other substances, oxygen and hydrogen; water is a compound. You also found that oxygen and hydrogen could not be broken down into simpler substances. They are elements. An element, then, is composed of only one type of matter. If we could divide a sample of an element an infinite number of times, we would eventually arrive at the

■ AN APPRENTICE INVESTIGATION into a Chemical Reaction

Light the candle and allow some wax to collect on the bottom of the beaker. Set the candle in the soft wax and cover the beaker with the Petri dish lid. ❶

Watch what happens. Droplets of a liquid form on the inside of the lid. What do you think this liquid is?

Wait until the candle goes out. Lift the lid slightly and pour in some limewater. ❷ Gently swirl the beaker. How does the limewater change? What substance must be present to turn the limewater milky? What substances are produced when the candle burns?

An Investigation On Your Own

Do you think candle wax and gas from a stove are similar? Design an investigation to find out.

❶

❷

smallest part of the element—the **atom.** Because an element is composed of only one type of matter, all the atoms of an element are of one kind. Thus, all the atoms of the element oxygen are oxygen atoms.

The smallest part of water that still has all the properties of water is one *molecule* of water. When you split the molecule of water, you produced *atoms* of hydrogen and oxygen.

Chemical Symbols

To split water into oxygen and hydrogen, we passed electric energy through the water. This process is called **electrolysis.** The electrolysis of water can be expressed by a word equation.

$$\text{water} + \text{energy} \longrightarrow \text{hydrogen} + \text{oxygen}$$

This is how you read the word equation: "Water plus energy yields hydrogen plus oxygen." The arrow in the equation means "yields" or "produces." The substance entering into the chemical reaction (water) is called the *reactant;* and the substances formed are called (hydrogen and oxygen) the *products.*

Electrolysis is only one type of chemical reaction which can be expressed by a word equation. Let's investigate another. ■

1

Carbon dioxide and water are the products of the reaction. Did you know what the reactants were? Candle wax is made from compounds called paraffins. When a paraffin burns, it combines with the oxygen of the air. You know this reaction as oxidation. Now let's write the word equation.

paraffin + oxygen ⟶ carbon dioxide + water

A word equation, recall, states the name of each element or compound in a reaction. But chemists, as you probably know, also use **symbols** to shorten their work. They write H for hydrogen, for instance, and Cu for copper. Each symbol consists of a capital letter or a capital letter and a small letter. When you use chemical shorthand, it is important to write chemical symbols correctly. Be sure to capitalize only the first letter of a symbol. For example, C stands for carbon, but Cl stands for chlorine. Some symbols such as Fe for iron, come from foreign languages. The Latin name for iron is "ferrum."

A Model of a Compound

The expression H_2O stands for a molecule of water. The subscript 2 after the H means that water is composed of two atoms of hydrogen joined to one atom of oxygen. Notice that there is no subscript after the symbol O. The absence of a subscript after the O means that water has just one atom of oxygen. The formula for carbon dioxide is CO_2. What do the symbols stand for? Here are models of H_2O and CO_2. 1

Many common compounds consist of molecules. Just as the symbol of an element stands for one atom of that element, the **formula** for a compound, such as water, stands for one molecule of that compound. A chemical formula represents atoms that are joined together. Let's try to write the formula of another compound.

Here is a way to make the compound magnesium oxide. Rub a small strip of magnesium ribbon with sandpaper or steel wool until it is clean and shiny. Observe that the ribbon is silvery in color and bends easily. 2 With

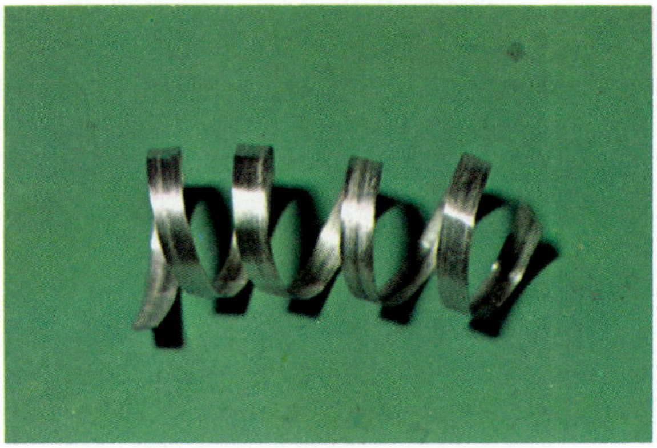

2

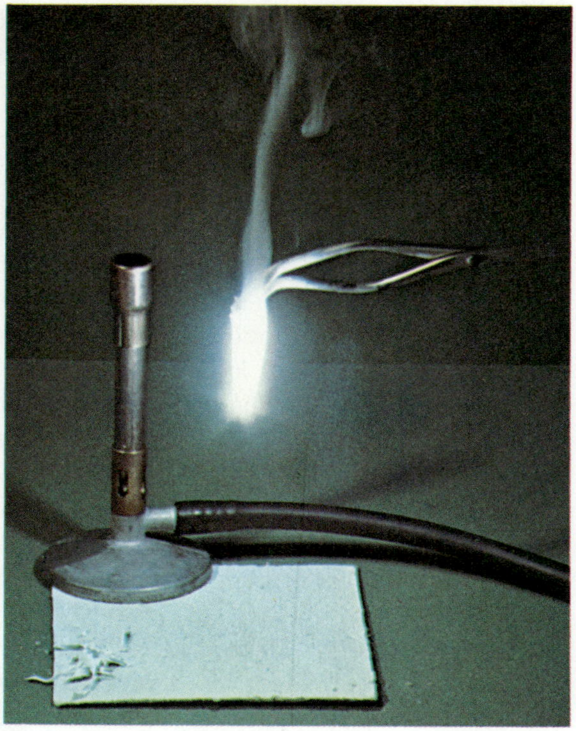

3

tweezers, hold the magnesium in a flame. 3 (*Caution:* Set the burner on asbestos and do not look directly at the flame as the metal burns.)

The magnesium burns with a brilliant light. The shiny, silver colored ribbon turns into a dull white powder. This powder is the magnesium oxide. The chemical formula of this compound is MgO. In the case of magnesium oxide, the product is not a molecule. However, the formula still represents atoms that are joined together. Later you will learn more about the ways in which atoms combine.

REVIEW

1. Describe the smallest unit of the compound water.

2. Write the word equation for the electrolysis of water.

3. What products are formed when a candle burns?

4. Write the chemical formula for water, carbon dioxide, and magnesium oxide.

NEW VIEW

1. One atom of carbon combines with 2 atoms of oxygen to produce one molecule of carbon dioxide. Write the word equation for this reaction. Write the equation using symbols.

2. A certain amount of water is broken down into oxygen and hydrogen. Then the two elements are recombined. Write the word equations for the two chemical changes that take place.

2. STATES OF MATTER ON EARTH

Matter on earth exists in three states: solid, liquid, and gas. Let's take a close look at these three states of matter. How do they differ? Can matter change from one state to another?

Change of State

This is a crystal of iodine. 4 Suppose we place the iodine in a large Florence flask and heat it very gently on a hotplate. What happens to the crystal?

4

1 

Very likely, the crystal turns into a purple gas. 1 (Under special conditions, heated iodine may first turn into a liquid, but usually it changes directly from a solid into the gas.) Heat makes the bit of matter called iodine change its state from a solid to a gas. The gaseous state of a substance that usually exists as a solid or a liquid is known as a **vapor.** Notice that a large volume of iodine vapor is produced by a small volume of solid iodine.

Iodine in the solid state can become a vapor —that is, vaporize—without the use of a hotplate. Suppose we place a few crystals of iodine in a stoppered test tube and leave them there for a day or two. You will observe iodine vapor in the tube. Where does the heat needed to vaporize the crystals come from? It comes from their surroundings: from the air around the crystals, for example. If the iodine vapor is cooled, it will return to the solid state and become gray crystals again.

As you may have noticed, solid iodine does not usually melt when heated, but turns directly to the gaseous state. Although pure liquid iodine can be prepared under certain conditions, the brown, liquid iodine sometimes used as an antiseptic is a *solution* made by dissolving crystals of iodine in alcohol.

It appears that heat has something to do with the changes of state of matter. To see how heat is involved in such changes, let's investigate another change of state, but in such a way that we can follow the part that heat plays in it. Try the investigation on the next two pages. ■

Here is a mystery. Heat is added to a solid substance. As we expect, the temperature of the substance rises. Suddenly the temperature stops rising and remains unchanged for several minutes although heat is being added to the substance all the time. Then the temperature begins to rise again.

One more observation must be noted, however. While the temperature of the substance being heated was behaving in this way, a *change of state* was taking place in the substance. The water in its solid state, ice, changed to liquid water. In fact, the ice was melting while the temperature remained unchanged. When all the ice had changed to water, the temperature began to rise again.

In other words, heat absorbed by the ice before it began to melt raised the temperature. Heat absorbed by the water after the ice melted raised the temperature. But heat absorbed while the ice melted did not raise the temperature. Instead, this heat seems to have been used somehow to change the state of the water from solid to liquid.

■ AN APPRENTICE INVESTIGATION into Changes of State

Set a thermometer with both Celsius and Fahrenheit scales in a Pyrex or Kimax beaker of water. The thermometer bulb must be just under the surface of the water but not in contact with the bottom of the beaker.❶

Place the beaker in a freezer so that the water becomes solid ice. Let the ice remain in the freezer until its temperature is between 15 and 30 degrees below the freezing point of water, 0°C (32°F).❷

Have ready a hotplate and a watch with a second hand. Remove the beaker from the freezer and place it on the hotplate turned to its lowest setting, so that the ice is being heated *very gently*.❸ Read the thermometer in the

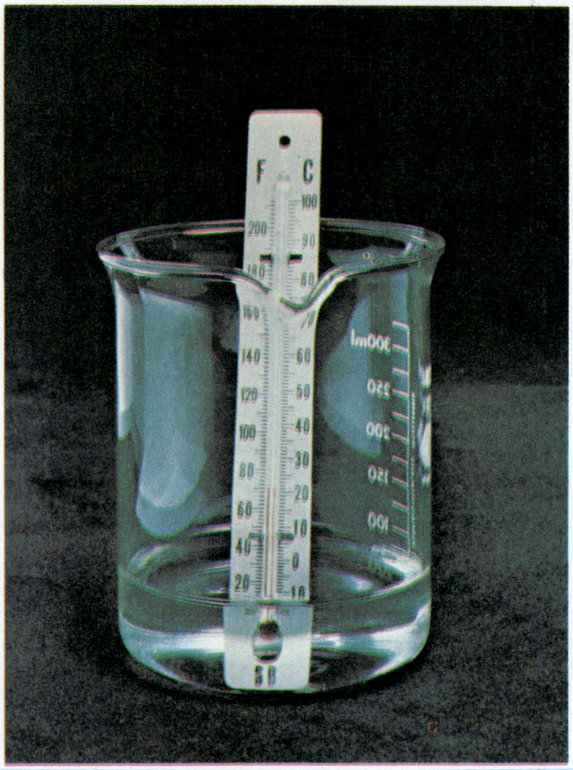

❶

❸

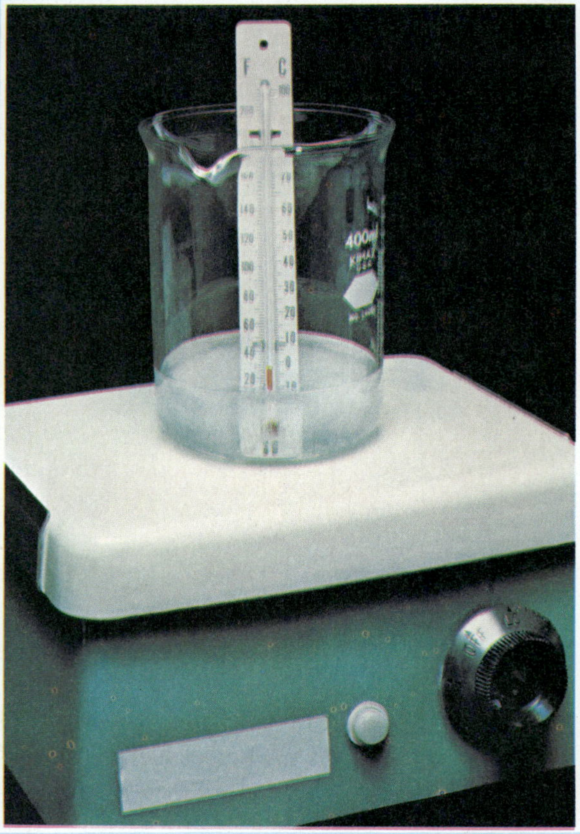

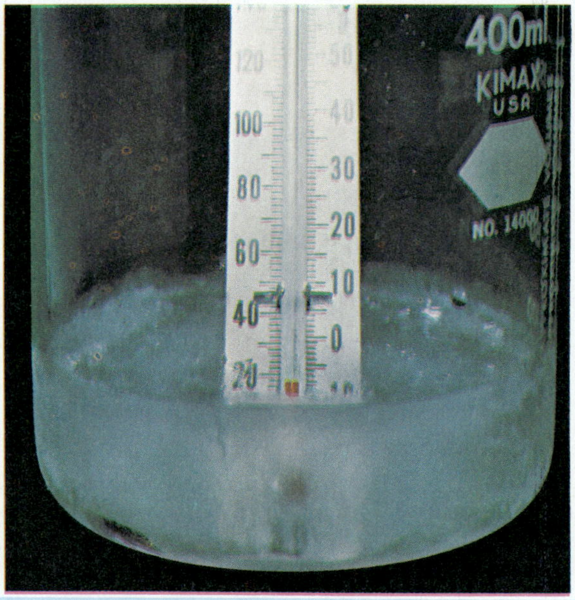

❷

❶ 

OBSERVATIONS: THERMOMETER IN ICE

Time in minutes	*Temperature in* °C	°F	*Time in minutes*	*Temperature in* °C	°F
0	−12	10	15	1	34
1	− 7	20	16	2	36
2	− 4	25	17	3	37
3	− 2	28	18	1.6	35
4	0	32	19	1	34
5	0	32	20	1.6	35
6	0	32	21	2	36
7	0	32	22	4	39
8	0	32	23	7	44
9	0	32	24	10	50
10	0	32	25	11.6	53
11	0	32	26	13	56
12	0	32	27	20	68
13	0	32	28	21	71
14	0.5	33	29	23	74

ice and record the temperature indicated. Make a prediction: What do you think will happen to the temperature of the ice as heat is applied and the change of state takes place? Read and record the temperature indicated by the thermometer every 60 seconds. ❶ Above are the readings observed during one trial.

What happened to the temperature (a) as the ice was heated, (b) as the ice changed to water, (c) when all the ice had changed to water?

What part does heat play in a change of state? What happens to a substance during a change of state? To answer these questions we may use models of molecules (or ions, as the case may be) of the matter that is changing. Let's see how this is done to explain the behavior of iodine and of water when they undergo changes of state.

Molecules and Changes of State

A molecule of iodine is made up of two atoms of iodine joined together as in this model. ❶

❶ 

❷ 

A molecule of water has two atoms of hydrogen joined to one of oxygen, as in this model. ❷

Here is a model of an iodine crystal. The iodine molecules are packed closely and held together in an orderly, definite form. ❸

3

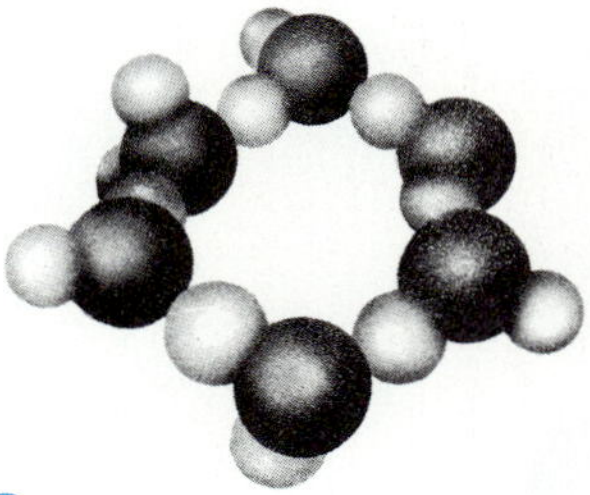

4

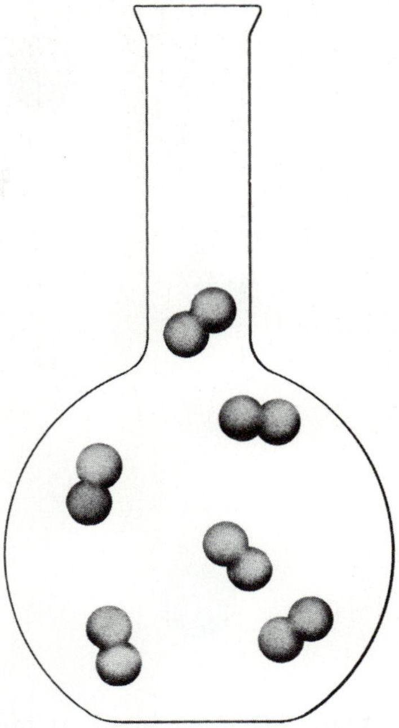

5

Now let's look at ice, water in the solid state. Its molecules are also close together and have a definite and orderly pattern, as you can see in this model. 4

These solids are rigid and keep their shape because their molecules attract one another strongly. Molecules in a solid are in motion—they vibrate, but not enough to move apart from one another.

Iodine or ice is warmed when heat is supplied to the molecules. This heat is transformed into energy of motion of the molecules. The molecules vibrate more rapidly. They now have enough motion to move apart from one another. Their fixed and orderly arrangement breaks down: the molecules can slide around and over each other. The substance becomes a liquid.

A liquid can flow because its molecules have enough energy to move freely: the attraction between the molecules is less than in the solid. The molecules still attract one another, however. In water, for instance, the attraction is strong enough to hold a drop of water together.

When a liquid is heated to the boiling point, the molecules vibrate so vigorously that they move much farther away from one another. Now the molecules have far more energy of motion than they had in the solid state or the liquid state. The molecules move far apart from one another, leaving a great deal of space between them. They have become a gas, a vapor. In the vapor state, the molecules of a substance move freely enough to fill any container.

Here is a model of iodine vapor. 5 If we were to enlarge the model to make the spaces between the molecules to scale, they would be much too far apart to fit on the page.

1

2

You must also imagine much larger spaces between the molecules than it is possible to show on the page in this model of water vapor. 1

Adding heat to a solid can make the solid change its state to a liquid, and make a liquid change its state to a gas. We explain these changes of state by means of molecular models. It seems that the added heat is transformed into energy of motion of the molecules, making them move both faster and farther apart.

However, as you have seen in the case of iodine, a solid may go directly into the gaseous, or vapor, state without first becoming a liquid. Snow, for another example, often changes directly from the solid state of water to the gaseous state.

How does a substance evaporate? Some of the molecules in solid or liquid water, for example, have more energy than others. These molecules move faster and can better overcome the attracting forces that pull them toward other molecules. Some of these high-energy molecules at the surface of the water may "leap" from the surface and escape. In an open container some of the molecules that leap from the surface fall back again. Those that escape are in the vapor state. 2

Solids may change to liquids and to gases. The change of state may go the other way, as you know: liquids may change to solids, gases may change to liquids or solids. Whichever way a change of state proceeds, however, heat energy is involved. To change a solid to a liquid, or a liquid to a gas, heat energy must be supplied. To change a liquid to a solid, or a gas to a liquid, heat energy must be taken away.

We explain these changes of state by two statements. One is included in the concept that matter is made up of minute particles. We suppose that the molecules of a molecular solid (such as iodine or ice) are pretty well fixed in place (although vibrating a little), while the molecules of a liquid are free to move around each other, and the molecules of a gas are still more free. The other statement is that heat energy can be changed into another sort of energy, the energy of motion. We suppose that the heat energy supplied to ice as it changes state is transformed into energy of motion of the molecules, so that they move faster. So far this explanation has stood up well to the tests that it has been subjected to, and has turned out to be very useful in other ways, as will be seen.

Solid, liquid, and gas: these are the three states of matter on this planet we call earth. The three layers of matter of the planet earth are solid, liquid, and gas, too: lithosphere, hydrosphere, and atmosphere. And these spheres consist of an astonishing variety of substances.

Let's continue the study of our planet by looking at the smallest unit of any substance.

REVIEW

1. Why does a solid keep its shape while a liquid or a gas flows?

2. Using iodine or ice as an example, explain what happens when a solid changes to a liquid; when a liquid changes to a gas.

3. Cite evidence for this statement: When matter changes from the solid state to the liquid state, its molecules absorb energy.

NEW VIEW

1. A solid has its own definite shape, and a liquid takes the shape of the bottom of any vessel you pour it into. What is the shape of a gas? Explain your answer.

2. Iodine exists as **diatomic** molecules. Make sketches of a possible model of:

a. solid iodine   b. iodine vapor

3. What is the difference between the molecules in a cloud and the molecules in water vapor?

3. INSIDE THE ATOM

You began your study of the earth by examining a common liquid, water, and a common gas, air. Both of these substances introduced you to the basic units from which all matter is made—the basic units we have called elements. You will not be surprised to learn, then, that all solids are combinations of these elements. In solids, elements have come together in a variety of ways to produce some marvelous samples of earth's materials. 3 How do elements come together to form so many different materials? To find out, let's continue our probe of an element's smallest part, the *atom*.

In about 1800, the English scientist John Dalton suggested that elements were composed of tiny particles called atoms. According to his theory, atoms were solid, indivisible, and extremely small. Although we still agree with part of Dalton's theory, our picture of the atom has changed considerably.

3

Another Model of the Atom

For years scientists investigated the atom. After they had gathered a great deal of evidence, they were able to propose new atomic models. They discovered that although the atom was too small to be seen with the most powerful microscope, it was composed of still smaller particles.

What are the particles that make up the atom? How are these particles arranged? Experiments have shown that there are three particles—**electrons** and **protons** that carry electrical charges, and **neutrons** that have no charge. Scientists know that most samples of matter are electrically neutral, so they developed a model to account for this property.

PARTICLES IN ATOMS

Particles	*Charge*	*Symbol*
proton	positive	P
neutron	neutral	N
electron	negative	e

Today one model of the atom is something like a miniature solar system. 1 The *negatively* charged electrons spin in orbits around a *positively* charged **nucleus.** The protons, which carry the positive charge, and the neutrons, which are neutral, make up the nucleus. So as you can see, atoms are not solid spheres as Dalton had imagined. In fact, much of the atom is empty space!

1

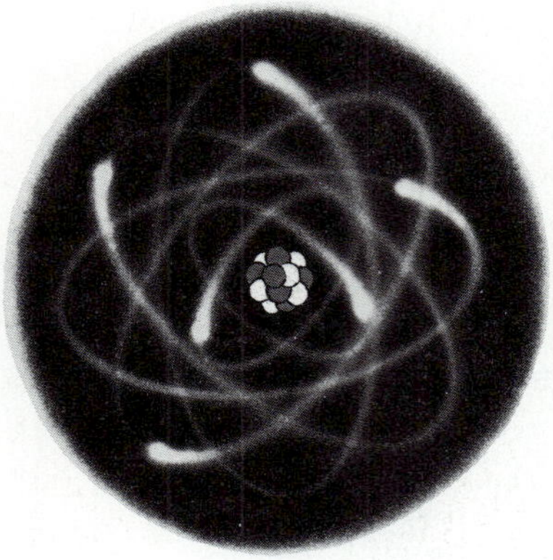

2

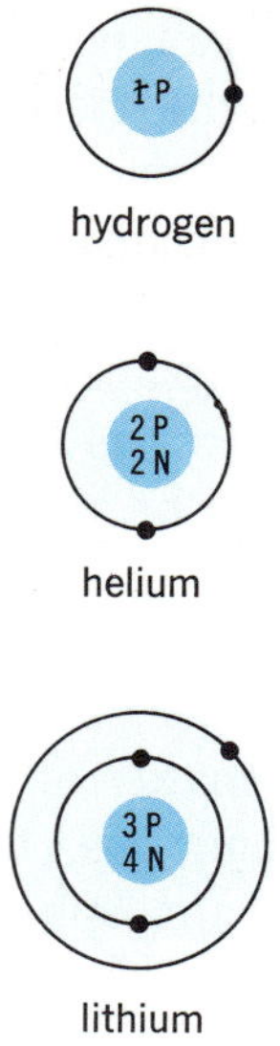

Atoms and Elements

If all atoms are composed of the same types of particles, how do atoms of the various elements differ? Look at the diagrams of three atoms. 2 These are **electron-shell diagrams.** Electron-shell diagrams are useful because they show how the atomic particles are arranged in each element. Notice that each element has a different number of atomic particles.

Hydrogen, the simplest of all atoms, consists of 1 proton in its nucleus and 1 electron around the nucleus. An atom of helium has 2 protons and 2 neutrons in its nucleus—and 2 electrons around its nucleus. The third element, lithium, is slightly more complex. An atom of lithium has 3 protons and 4 neutrons in its nucleus. How many electrons does an atom of lithium have?

Atomic Diagrams and Data

Element	Symbol	Atomic number	Diagram	Protons	Neutrons	Electrons	Mass number	Atomic weight
Hydrogen	**H**	1		1	0	1	1	1
Oxygen	**O**	8	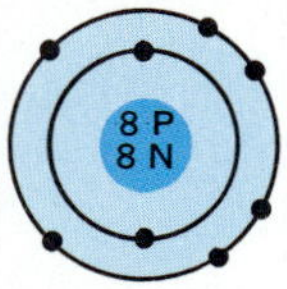	8	8	8	16	16
Sodium	**Na**	11	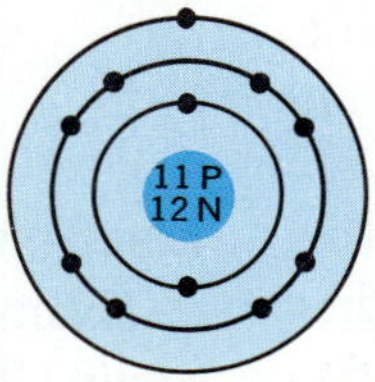	11	12	11	23	23

Now examine the diagrams of other atoms in the chart on this page. Do you see any relationship between the number of protons and electrons?

As you know, protons are positively charged and electrons are negatively charged. In an atom, the number of protons is the same as the number of electrons. Equal numbers of positive and negative charges cancel each other so that the atom as a whole is neutral. This is why most of the matter around us is electrically neutral.

Weighing an Atom

Examine the data in the chart for sodium. A sodium atom has 11 protons and 11 electrons. Notice that the number 11 also appears in the column headed **atomic number.** The atomic number of an element is equal to the number of protons (or the number of electrons) in an atom of that element.

Just as each element has its atomic number, each element also has its **atomic weight** (mass). Scientists have determined experimentally the mass of each atomic particle. As these weights in grams are extremely small, the weights are usually given in atomic mass units, abbreviated **amu.** Scientists find the atomic weight of an element by adding the weights of all the protons, neutrons, and electrons in an atom of that element.

The approximate atomic weight of both a proton and a neutron is 1 amu. The mass of an electron is only 1/1,836 the mass of a proton. Since electrons have such a small mass, we disregard them in determining the approximate atomic weight of an element. To find the approximate atomic weight of an element, just add the number of protons and the number of neutrons. Predict the atomic weight of an element whose atoms have 11 protons and 12 neutrons. Check the last column in the chart. Did you predict correctly an atomic weight of 23 amu for sodium? Scientists usually drop the amu, and give the atomic weight of sodium as 23.

❶

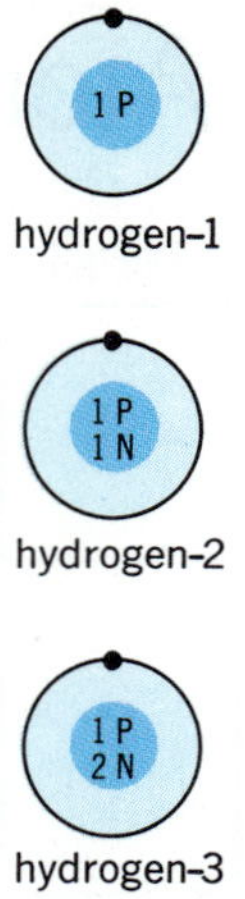

Isotopes

In 1912, scientists were surprised to find that some atoms of neon had an atomic weight of 20, while others had an atomic weight of 22. They also found different kinds of uranium atoms, chlorine atoms, and even different kinds of hydrogen atoms. How could this be?

Not all atoms of hydrogen have an atomic weight of 1. Some hydrogen atoms have an atomic weight of 2, and some even have an atomic weight of 3. Today these atoms of the same element with different atomic weights are called **isotopes.** Hydrogen then, has three isotopes; neon has two. How are these isotopes identified?

Look at the chart again. If you add the number of neutrons to the number of protons, you find the **mass number** of each element. *The mass number is equal to the number of protons plus the number of neutrons in the nucleus of an atom.* Check the chart to see that the mass number of hydrogen is 1, of oxygen is 16, and of sodium is 23. Chemists write these as hydrogen-1, oxygen-16, and sodium-23.

But not all atoms of hydrogen have a mass number of 1. Hydrogen has three isotopes with mass numbers 1, 2, and 3: hydrogen-1, hydrogen-2, and hydrogen-3. Isotopes, then, are identified by their mass numbers. Isotopes of hydrogen, like all isotopes, are atoms of an element with the same number of protons but a different number of neutrons. All hydrogen atoms have 1 proton, but while hydrogen-1 (ordinary hydrogen) has no neutrons, hydrogen-2 has 1 neutron and hydrogen-3 has 2 neutrons. ❶

Electron Shells

Examine the diagrams in the chart once again. The electrons surround the nucleus in circles that represent electron shells. The first shell of an atom is filled to capacity when it has 2 electrons. No atom ever has more than 2 electrons in this first shell. There is, of course, just one possible kind of atom—an atom of hydrogen—in which the first shell is not completely filled.* In all other kinds of atoms the first shell contains 2 electrons.

In atoms with more than one shell, there are never more than 8 electrons in the second shell. Some atoms, of course, may have fewer than 8 electrons in the second shell. The second shell can hold up to 8 electrons, but no more.

What happens when there are more than 10 electrons—2 in the first shell and 8 in the second shell? The first shell is filled to capacity with 2 electrons. The second shell is filled to capacity with 8 electrons. So the eleventh

* Hydrogen has only 1 electron because it has only 1 proton, and the number of electrons must be equal to the number of protons for the atom to be neutral.

2

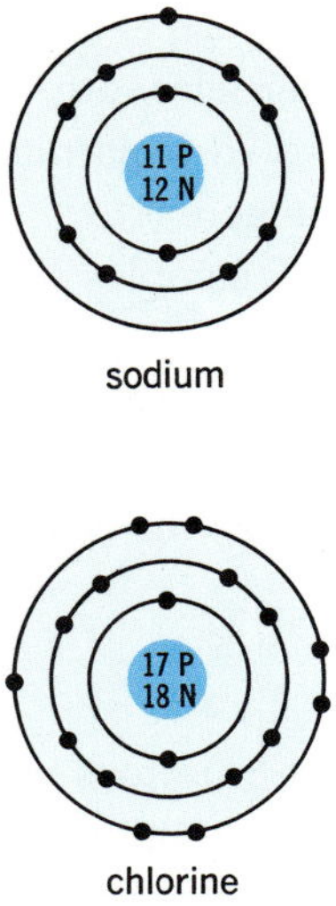

3

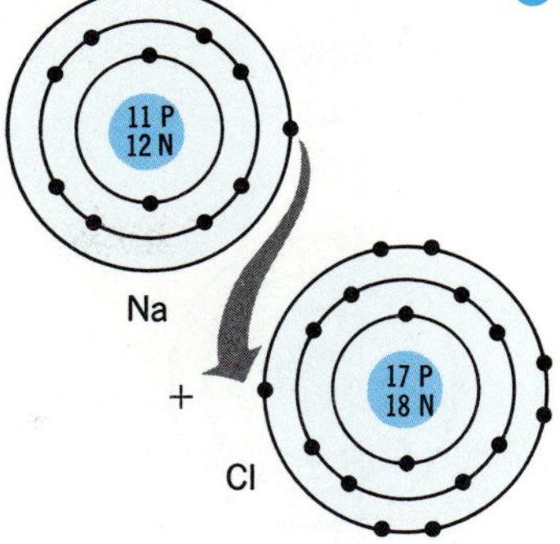

electron goes into a third shell. Remember that the first shell of electrons around the nucleus of an atom holds no more than 2 electrons, and the second shell no more than 8 electrons. Additional electrons go into shells beyond the second shell.

Bonding by Transfer

Electron-shell diagrams are useful tools to see how atoms combine. Chemists call this combining of atoms **chemical bonding.** In general, bonding occurs in two ways: bonding by *transfer* and bonding by *sharing*.

The outer shell of any atom (except hydrogen and helium) can hold up to 8 electrons. Chlorine has 7 electrons in its outer shell; thus, it needs 1 electron to fill this shell. Sodium has only 1 electron in its outer shell. ② What happens when sodium chloride, table salt, is formed?

The chlorine atom *borrows* 1 electron from the sodium atom. ③ Or you could say that the sodium atom *lends* 1 electron to the chlorine atom. In other words, the atoms combine by the transfer of electrons. But the chlorine atom now has 17 protons (+17) in its nucleus and 18 electrons (−18) in its electron shells. The chlorine atom now has 1 more electron than proton. The extra electron gives the chlorine atom a negative charge. Chemists call an electrically charged atom an **ion.** A charged atom of chlorine is a chloride ion. Since the chloride ion has one more negative charge than positive charge, the chloride ion has a charge of −1, Cl^-.

The nucleus of the sodium ion has 11 protons (+11) and the electron shells contain a total of 10 electrons (−10). The sodium ion has a charge of plus one (+1), Na^+. Because of the opposite charges of the sodium ions and the chloride ions, these particles are attracted to one another. The chemical bonds between these ions are **ionic bonds.** A compound consisting of positive ions and negative ions is called an **ionic compound.** ④ All ionic compounds are formed by ***bonding by transfer.***

4

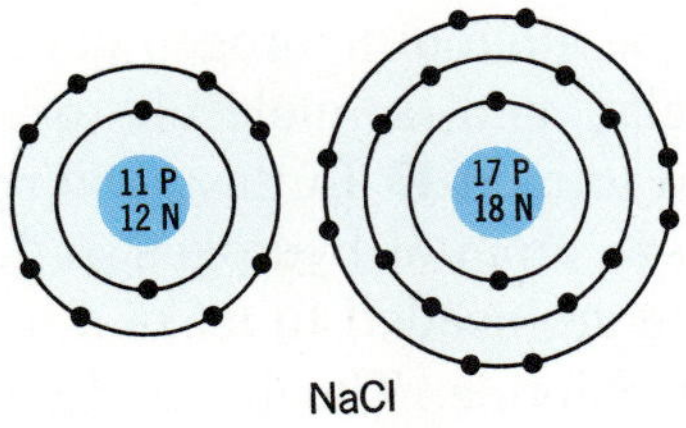

1

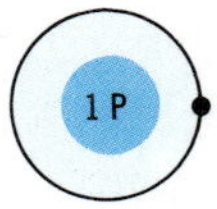

H

2

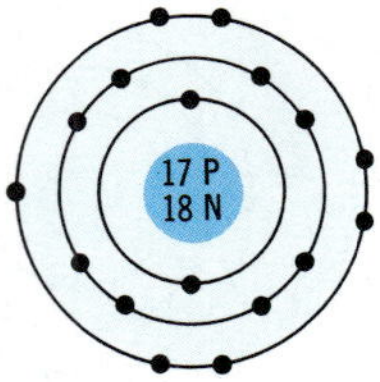

Cl

3

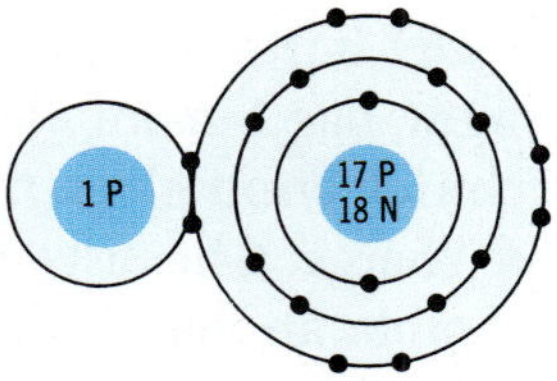

HCl

Bonding by Sharing

Not all compounds are composed of ions. In fact, most compounds are composed of molecules. Water, hydrogen chloride, and carbon dioxide are just a few of the many **molecular compounds.** Let's see how molecular compounds are formed.

A hydrogen atom has just 1 proton and 1 electron. 1 Chlorine has 17 protons and 17 electrons. 2 As you have seen, with 7 electrons in its outer shell, chlorine needs 1 electron to fill this shell. An atom of hydrogen also needs 1 electron to fill its outer shell. Where might each atom get the electron it needs? One atom of hydrogen *shares* an electron with one atom of chlorine. As a result, both the atom of chlorine and the atom of hydrogen have complete outer shells, and a molecule of hydrogen chloride is formed. 3 In this *bonding by sharing,* just one atom of hydrogen and one atom of chlorine are needed to make a molecule of hydrogen chloride. The bonds formed when atoms share electrons are **molecular bonds.**

REVIEW

1. Of what particles are atoms composed? What charge does each particle carry? How are the particles arranged?

2. Why are most samples of matter electrically neutral?

3. Define the terms isotope, ion, mass number, atomic number.

4. Briefly describe the ways in which atoms combine.

NEW VIEW

1. An atom has 8 protons and 9 neutrons.
   a. What is its atomic number?
   b. How many electrons does it have?
   c. What is its mass number?
   d. Draw its electron-shell diagram.

2. The mass number of copper is 64 and its atomic number is 29. How many neutrons are in an atom of copper? Explain.

3. All atoms except hydrogen have a nucleus containing at least one neutron and one proton. A neutron has 1 weight unit, and a proton has 1 weight unit.

The nucleus of an atom of the element lithium has 7 weight units. Using P for proton and N for neutron, draw two possible nuclei of lithium. Can there be any other combinations? Explain.

4. The following formulas represent two compounds of carbon with oxygen: CO_2 (carbon dioxide), and CO (carbon monoxide). How do you know that these are different compounds and not different formulas for the same compound?

4. RELATING THE CONCEPTS

Through more than 2,000 years our concept of the atom has changed. Today, as a result of the work of many men and women we have a useful model of the atom. You have seen how a theory is developed to explain the known facts. And you have seen how new theories attempt to explain newly discovered facts. Because scientists constantly ask questions concerning natural phenomena, then continually make new observations. Other scientists add more new observations. Eventually, Dalton's concept of solid atoms was no longer satisfactory. A new model replaced the Dalton model.

Was Dalton wrong? No. For his time, and for his observations, he was "correct." But for our time, with the facts we have available, Dalton's atom is unacceptable, and other models of the atom are more nearly "correct." Our model is simply this: matter is made up of tiny particles called atoms. The atoms are made up of even smaller particles. The main kinds of particles in atoms of all elements are protons, electrons, and neutrons.

Scientists have developed a system for measuring the weights (or masses) of the particles. This system, like any system of measurement, is relative to a convenient standard. The present standard for measuring weights of individual particles and atomic weights in amu is the isotope carbon-12. Isotopes are atoms of the same element with different atomic weights.

Reviewing the Concepts

► *Atoms are made up of particles, mainly protons, electrons, and neutrons.* This concept is of fundamental importance for a modern model of the atom. We saw that elements and compounds are made up of the tiny particles we call atoms. We find that these atoms, in turn, are made up of even smaller particles. The main particles are the protons, electrons, and neutrons.

► *When atoms combine with other atoms in chemical change, they combine as wholes and in definite proportions.* When atoms of hydrogen and oxygen, for example, combine to form water, there are always 2 atoms of hydrogen and 1 atom of oxygen in the compound H_2O. And, since atoms of each kind have definite weights, there are always certain proportions by weight of hydrogen and oxygen combining to form water.

► *Matter is particulate.* The matter around us is made of atoms; and an atom, in turn, is made up of electrons circling around a nucleus made up of protons and neutrons. All atoms of the same element have the same number of protons and electrons but not the same number of neutrons. Isotopes of the same element have different numbers of neutrons.

► *Each kind of atom has a definite number of electrons arranged in a definite pattern in shells around the nucleus.* In an atom of oxygen, for example, there are 8 electrons, 2 in the first shell and 6 in the outermost shell. Thus, an atom of oxygen does not have a complete outer shell, which has a capacity of 8 electrons.

► *Each element has a different atomic weight.* Chemists base the system of relative weights, or atomic weights, on the isotope carbon-12. The approximate atomic weight of an element can be determined by combining the weights of the protons, neutrons, and electrons in an atom of the main isotope. The atomic weight is usually "rounded off" to the nearest whole number, but the presence of isotopes accounts in large part for the fact that accurate atomic weights are fractional weights.

Testing Yourself

1. List six different changes of state, such as the change from solid to liquid, and give an example of each (example: melting ice).

2. Describe the arrangement and motion of the molecules of water in the solid, liquid, and gaseous states.

3. What characteristics do all forms of matter have in common?

4. How would you distinguish between an element and a compound?

5. Complete this word equation:

$$\text{water} + \text{energy} \longrightarrow ? + ?$$

What are the substances on the left side of the arrow called? the right side?

6. Explain what the expression H_2O means.

7. A certain atom has 13 electrons. Draw an electron-shell diagram to show how these electrons are arranged.

8. An atom of sulfur has 16 protons, 16 neutrons, and 16 electrons. Find the mass number, the atomic number, and the approximate atomic weight of sulfur.

9. Hydrogen-1, hydrogen-2, and hydrogen-3 are isotopes of the element hydrogen. How are they alike? How are they different?

Extending the Concepts

Investigation 1. New investigations of the structure of the atom, especially the atomic nucleus, are constantly under way. Chemists can usually confine their attention to the three main particles within atoms: electrons, protons, and neutrons. But a number of other particles, such as positrons, neutrinos, and mesons, enter into new concepts about the nuclei of atoms. To investigate nuclear structure, begin with a modern high-school physical science text.

Investigation 2. Matter in our environment of earth, air, and water ordinarily consists mainly of protons, electrons, and neutrons organized into atoms. In some other parts of the universe —such as our sun—matter normally is not organized into complete atoms. Even on earth some matter exists as separate subatomic particles. Free neutrons, for example, sometimes pass through the air around you and even into your body.

Where do these particles come from? What is matter like on the sun and in other stars? Why? You might look first into Chapter 8 of this book to begin your investigation of matter in other parts of the universe. Go to the library for advanced additional information.

Suggested Reading

Esterer, Arnulf, *Your Career in Chemistry,* New York, Julian Messner, 1964. Describes the work of chemists and chemical engineers. Information on the education you will need if you are interested in a career in the field.

Smith, Richard Furnald, *Chemistry for the Million,* New York, Scribners, 1972. A description of the development of chemistry from alchemy, and some interesting sidelights into the history of science.

3

The Crystals of Earth

The earth is a giant chemical laboratory. Elements are the main components. You are familiar with some elements: copper, iron, gold, and silver. Other elements you may not know: germanium, scandium, actinium.

Elements in the earth's crust come together to form common compounds like table salt (sodium chloride). Some elements come together to form marvelous compounds, like this magnificent ruby—one of the largest "star" rubies on earth. (1) But common or unusual, most of the solid earth is made up of compounds called **minerals.** A mineral, in fact, is any naturally occurring solid substance in the earth's crust.

1. IDENTIFYING MINERALS

Over 2,000 different minerals are known. This is another way of saying that a few elements have combined to form minerals in over 2,000 different ways. We say a few elements since only about eight elements make up almost all of the minerals found in earth. And 47 percent of the weight of the crust is just one element, oxygen. You know that the oxygen of the air is a gas, so the fact that solid minerals contain oxygen may surprise you. Yet oxygen, when combined chemically with other elements usually forms solid substances.

Imagine 2,000 different minerals! Surely it would be difficult to be familiar with so many. Fortunately, some minerals are much more common than others. Scientists have found that about 10 minerals make up about 99 percent

(1)

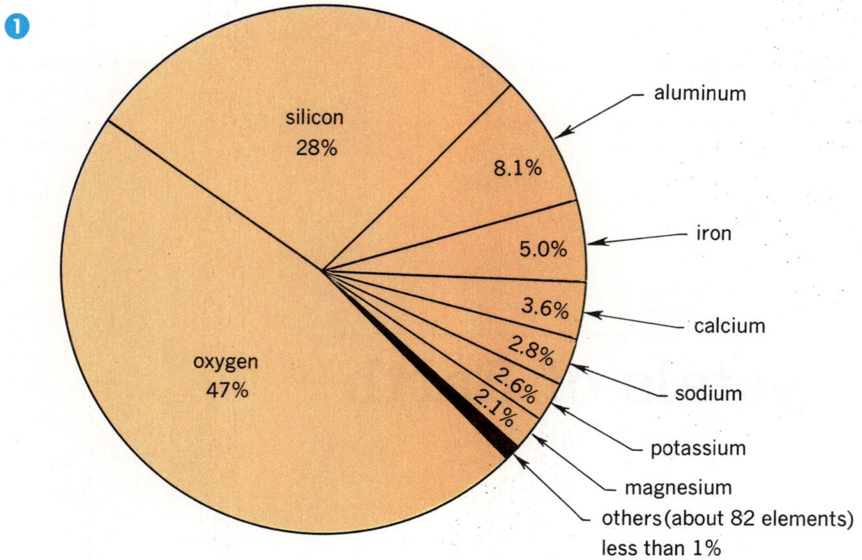

of the rocks of the earth's crust. ❶ Let's take a closer look at some samples.

Investigating Physical Properties

Suppose you have a little chunk of a mineral you want to identify. How would you go about doing this? Perhaps it is an attractive specimen you would like to keep, as well as know its name and chemical make-up. If so, it will be useful if you can test the properties of the specimen without destroying it. Properties observed in this way, without changing the chemical make-up of the substance, are the **physical properties** of a substance.

Color, luster, streak, hardness, specific gravity, and crystal shape are among the physical properties you can observe for any mineral. As you learn how to investigate these characteristics, apply the tests to whatever specimens of minerals you have on hand.

COLOR: The variety and beauty of colors of the minerals are characteristics that make them desirable collector's items.

Color is an important clue to the identity of a mineral, but sometimes minerals of almost the same chemical make-up can exist in several different colors. Why is this so?

Naturally occurring substances have varying amounts of different impurities. Each substance gives to the mineral a specific color. Fluorite, for example, may be green, white, blue, violet, or other colors, depending on what impurities are mixed with the calcium fluoride, which is mainly what fluorite consists of. So you can't identify fluorite by color alone. For minerals of metals like copper, color is a more reliable guide to identity.

LUSTER: Does the mineral have a shiny appearance? If so, this is because its surface reflects light, somewhat the way mirrors do. When a substance is shiny, it has luster. Dark, opaque minerals, such as graphite, galena, and iron pyrite, may have a *metallic* luster. Lighter-colored minerals, with transparent edges, such as sulfur, diamond, asbestos, and mica, may show *nonmetallic* luster.

STREAK: If a mineral is ground to a fine powder, it has a particular color. However, some minerals are difficult to grind into a fine powder. One good way to form a small amount of fine powder is to rub the mineral

MOHS' SCALE OF HARDNESS OF MINERALS

Hardness	*Example*	*Test for hardness*
1	talc (from which talcum powder is made)	can be scratched easily with fingernail
2	gypsum (from which chalk and plaster of Paris are made)	can be scratched with fingernail, but less easily
3	calcite	can be just scratched with a copper penny
4	fluorite	can be scratched easily with a knife, but will not scratch glass
5	apatite	can be scratched with a knife (with difficulty)
6	feldspar	cannot be scratched with a knife; can be scratched by a file
7	quartz	scratches glass easily
8	topaz	scratches quartz easily
9	corundum (ruby, sapphire, etc.)	scratches topaz easily
10	diamond	scratches other materials, can be scratched only with another diamond

across an unglazed porcelain plate. The mark a mineral makes on this "streak plate" is its streak. Some minerals have streaks of characteristic colors that help to identify them. Here is the streak made by iron pyrite. ❷

HARDNESS: Hardness is a physical property; it is an important one that helps us distinguish among minerals. Different minerals offer different degrees of resistance to being scratched. For instance, a knife will scratch certain minerals but not others.

To determine a mineral's hardness, refer to the Mohs' scale of hardness shown above. The softest minerals have a hardness of 1 on the hardness scale, and the hardest a hardness of 10.

Each mineral on the scale will scratch those of a lower number of hardness, and can be scratched by all those of a higher number of hardness. You may use either the minerals themselves or the equivalent instruments (fingernail, penny, knife, glass, file) to determine hardness.

SPECIFIC GRAVITY: A given mineral usually has a certain **specific gravity,** or weight compared with the weight of an equal volume of water. You can determine the specific gravity of a mineral for yourself. ■

❷

■ AN APPRENTICE INVESTIGATION into Determining Specific Gravity

❶

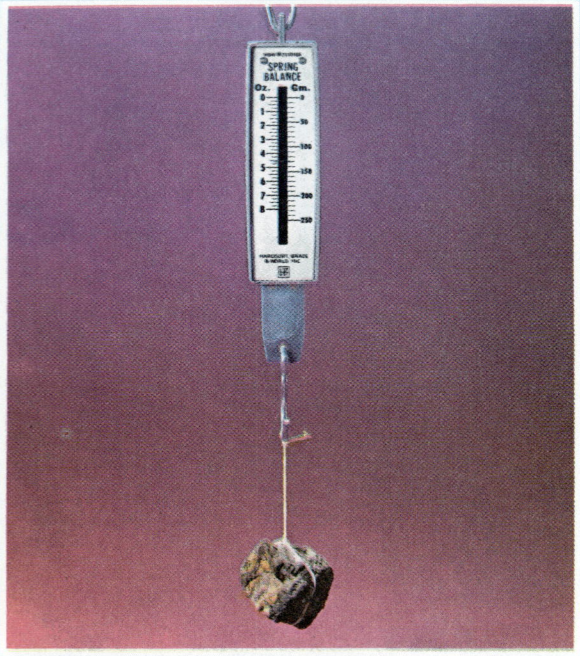

❷

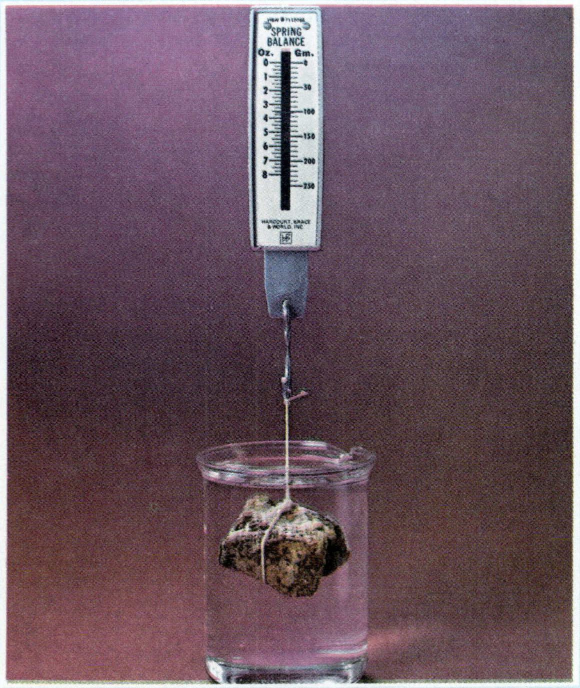

Tie a string around a mineral sample and put a loop into the loose end of the string so you can weigh the sample on a spring scale. Weigh the sample in air and record the results.❶ The data below were collected by one student.

Fill a container with water to a depth that covers the sample completely. Lower the sample into the water. When the sample is completely submerged, read the weight of the sample in water.❷

Find the weight lost in water by subtracting the weight of the sample in water from its weight in air. Then divide the weight in air by the weight lost in water. The result is the specific gravity of the sample:

$$\text{specific gravity} = \frac{\text{weight of object in air}}{\text{loss of weight in water}}$$

Study the sample calculations of specific gravity made by the student.

weight in air	=	129 grams
weight in water	=	104 grams
loss of weight in water	=	25 grams
$\frac{\text{weight of object in air}}{\text{loss of weight in water}}$	=	$\frac{129 \text{ grams}}{25 \text{ grams}}$
specific gravity	=	5.1

Now determine the specific gravity of your mineral sample using grams and ounces.

An Investigation On Your Own

A hydrometer is a floating tube used to determine the specific gravity of liquids. Obtain a hydrometer and determine the specific gravity of salt water, tap water, and alcohol. In which does the hydrometer float higher? Why?

Using clues such as color, streak, hardness, and luster, you can identify many common minerals. In addition to these physical properties, mineralogists also use chemical tests.

Investigating Chemical Properties

Think back to the results of the "chloride test" in your investigation into the substances found in natural water (see p. 15). In that investigation, you changed some of the sodium chloride into another substance (a precipitate) by chemical reaction with silver nitrate. This reaction is an example of a **chemical property** of sodium chloride. This chemical property of a chloride can be used to identify the chloride. The element sodium was identified by means of a flame test. Other metallic elements can also be identified by flame tests.

FLAME TESTS

Name of element	*Color of flame*
barium	yellow-green
calcium	orange-red
copper	emerald green
lithium	crimson
potassium	violet
sodium	yellow
strontium	scarlet

First hold a mounted nichrome or platinum wire loop in a flame until the flame has no color other than its normal blue. If the wire is not clean, this procedure will burn away any substance that would interfere with the test.

Scrape off a small amount of the rock or mineral you want to test and pick up some of the material with the wire loop. Hold the loop in the flame. Compare the color you see with those in the table and the photograph below. ❶ Notice that flame tests for some elements give almost the same color. How might a chemist tell these elements apart? (See the investigation on page 151.)

Other Tests

How do minerals affect the passage of light? Some minerals allow light to pass through them. To test for this property, mineralogists need a very thin sample. This may be difficult to obtain, but there may be a very thin section at one edge. Some minerals break in such a way that a sharp, feathery edge is formed and can be used to test the passage of light. If objects can be seen through the specimen, the specimen is composed of a transparent material. Mica is a transparent mineral, for example. If objects cannot be seen through the specimen, yet light passes through, the specimen is translucent. Clear quartz is transparent; cloudy quartz is translucent.

❶

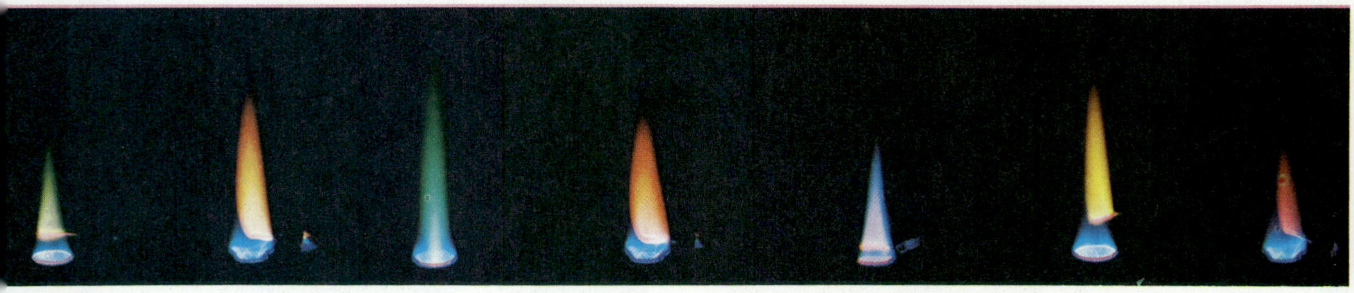

Barium Calcium Copper Lithium Potassium Sodium Strontium

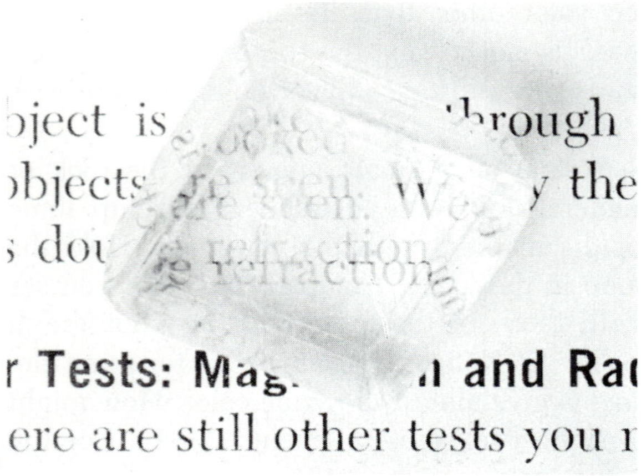

❶

Most minerals are opaque: light cannot pass through them. A piece of coal, for instance, is opaque. Most minerals do not have the ability to transmit light. A few minerals, however, can be identified by the way they affect transmitted light. For example, Iceland spar, a form of calcite, is transparent. ❶ When an object is looked at through this crystal, *two* objects are seen. We say the crystal produces double refraction.

There are still other tests you may apply to minerals. These tests identify only a few specimens, but may be of help at times. Bring a magnet in contact with the specimen: is it attracted? Magnetite, a form of iron oxide, is attracted by a magnet. It is best to use a powerful magnet in this test; an Alnico magnet is small but powerful.

REVIEW

1. What are some physical properties that can be used to identify minerals? Explain why color or shape is not enough to identify a mineral?

2. Describe the Mohs' scale of hardness. What is the hardest mineral on this scale? the softest?

3. What chemical property of sodium chloride can be used to identify this mineral?

4. What is specific gravity? How can it be used to distinguish mineral samples?

NEW VIEW

1. In a handbook of chemistry, find the chemical names and formulas for these minerals:

a. iron pyrite b. apatite c. gypsum

2. To answer the following, refer to the hardness scale on page 41.

a. Suppose you have a sample of a mineral that you can scratch with a copper penny. Can the same sample be scratched with a piece of feldspar?

b. Can you use your fingernail to scratch calcite? Explain.

c. The synthetic substance *borazon* has the same hardness as diamond. Suggest some industrial uses for borazon.

2. CRYSTALS

Look at a mineral sample. ❷ What is the first thing you notice? Is it the shape? This solid with a naturally formed, regular geometric shape is called **a crystal.** Every mineral has a characteristic crystal structure. However, special conditions in the earth's crust are needed before well-shaped crystals can grow. Since these special conditions are found in very few places, fine crystal specimens are rare—and treasured when they are found.

❷

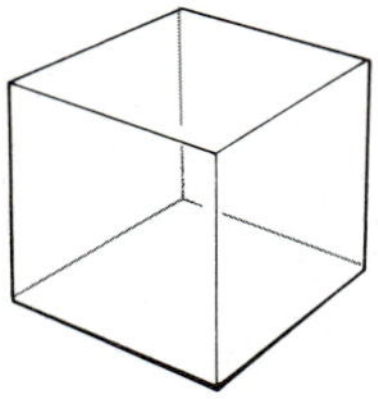

cubic crystal
(example: halite)

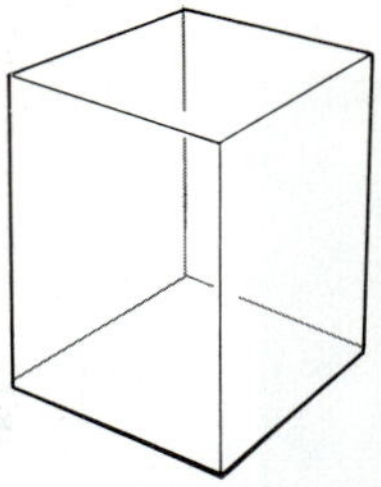

tetragonal crystal
(example: zircon)

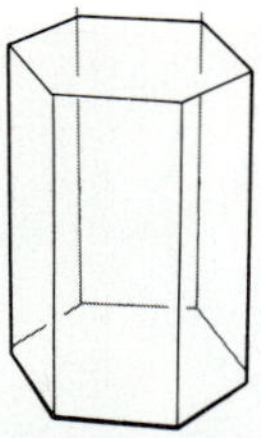

hexagonal crystal
(example: quartz)

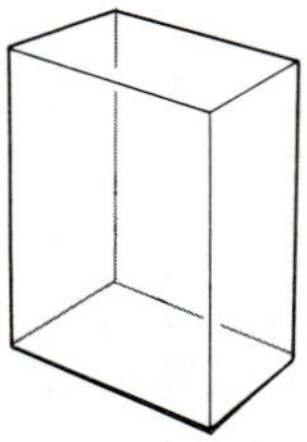

orthorhombic crystal
(example: sulfur)

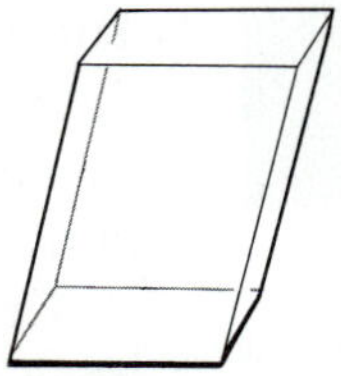

monoclinic crystal
(example: gypsum)

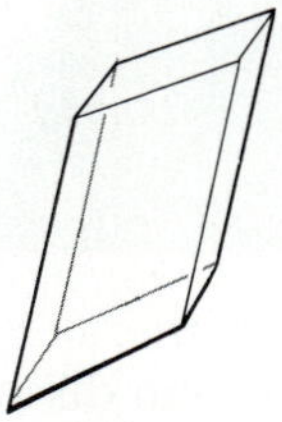

triclinic crystal
(example: feldspar) 3

Crystal Structure of Minerals

As a clue to the structure of a mineral, shape is one of the most important physical properties to use for identification. Notice the different crystal shapes. 3 Because every mineral has a definite crystal structure, it has a characteristic shape.

One good way to investigate the crystalline structure of minerals is to grow a few crystals of your own. When crystals are to be "made to order," you start with a solution of the substance whose crystals you want. To grow large crystals, you will do well to start with a solution that contains as much solid as will dissolve in a certain amount of water. How is such a solution prepared?

Making Solutions

To make a solution you usually mix a soluble solid, such as salt, with a liquid, such as water, and stir until the solid disappears in the liquid. Try this with a teaspoonful of salt in a glass of water. Does this solution contain the greatest amount of salt that will dissolve in the water? It is easy to find out. Add a few more grains of salt to the clear solution. Notice how these added grains dissolve if you again stir the mixture. Clearly a glassful of water will dissolve more than just a teaspoonful of salt. But is it only a few grains more? How do you determine the largest amount of salt that will dissolve in the water?

Suppose we try a procedure in which we measure the water and salt accurately. This is how a chemist determines the amount of a substance that will dissolve in a given amount of a liquid. Let's add 1 tablespoonful of salt to 100 milliliters (ml) of water. Stir and warm the mixture. Most of the salt dissolves, but some remains undissolved. Let the mixture stand until it reaches room temperature and the undissolved salt settles.

Now suppose we pour off some of the clear solution into a test tube. Make a prediction:

1

Will this solution dissolve any more salt? How can we test the prediction? Let's add a small amount of salt (not more than a dozen grains) to the clear solution. This is what happens. 1

In the test tube we have a solution that would not dissolve any extra salt. What does this mean? Before we added the extra salt, we already had a solution that contained as much salt as can dissolve in 100 milliliters of water (at room temperature). A solution of this kind is a **saturated solution.**

For every soluble substance there is a certain weight of the solid that can dissolve in 100 grams (or 100 milliliters) of water at a given temperature. A saturated solution of a substance contains a certain weight of the dissolved substance. What is this weight for sodium chloride?

If we look up the solubility of sodium chloride in a handbook of chemistry, we find that the solubility of sodium chloride is given as 36.0 grams per 100 grams of water at 21°C.

The Structure of Crystals

Suppose we produced crystals of sodium chloride from a saturated solution by evaporating the water. They would look like little cubes. 2 Whether we observe the tiny crystals from a salt shaker or the larger ones made from a saturated solution, they are still cubic crystals.

Very large cubes of salt form in nature. These natural sodium chloride crystals are known by their mineral name, halite. 3 Have you noticed a strange thing? Sodium chloride crystals are *cubic* in shape regardless of their size. This is true of all mineral crystals: each substance forms crystals of a certain shape, and regardless of the size, the shape is the same. That shape is not always cubic, but it is always the *same* for a given substance.

Crystals, as you know, differ in shape. Now make some crystals for yourself to study another crystal shape. ■

2

3

■ AN APPRENTICE INVESTIGATION into Crystallization

Mix and stir about 65 grams of powdered copper sulfate in 100 ml of hot water. (*Caution:* Copper sulfate is a poison. Wash your hands after working with it.) Cool the solution. What evidence is there that you have a saturated solution? ❶

Pour about 25 ml of the clear saturated solution of copper sulfate into each of two watch glasses. Let one watch glass stand at room temperature until its contents have evaporated to dryness. Heat the other over boiling water until its contents are dry, as shown. ❷

Compare the crystals that were formed slowly with those that were formed rapidly. ❸ Which ones are larger? Make a sketch to show the shape of the crystals.

Carry out the same procedure with a clear saturated solution of sodium chloride. (How many grams of sodium chloride will you need in 100 ml of hot water?) Which crystals are larger? Sketch their shape.

An Investigation On Your Own

Find out what is meant by a *supersaturated* solution. Make crystals from some supersaturated solutions. One substance that is good for this purpose is photographer's hypo (sodium thiosulfate).

❶

❷
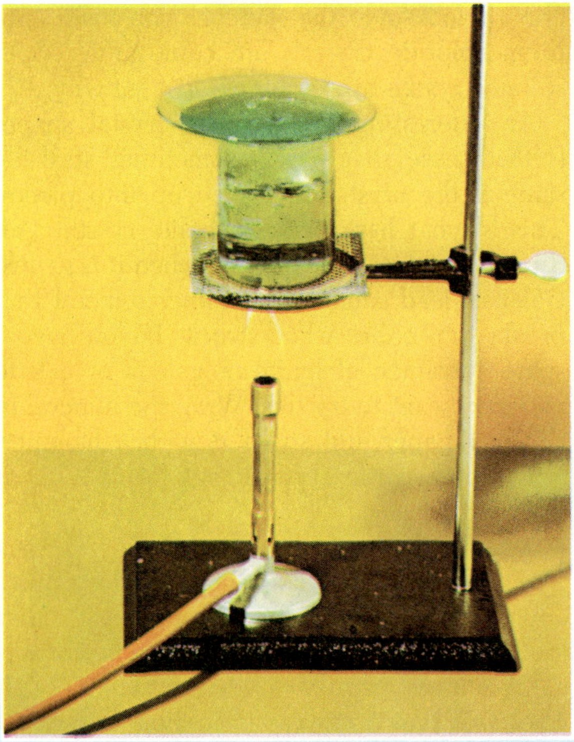

❸
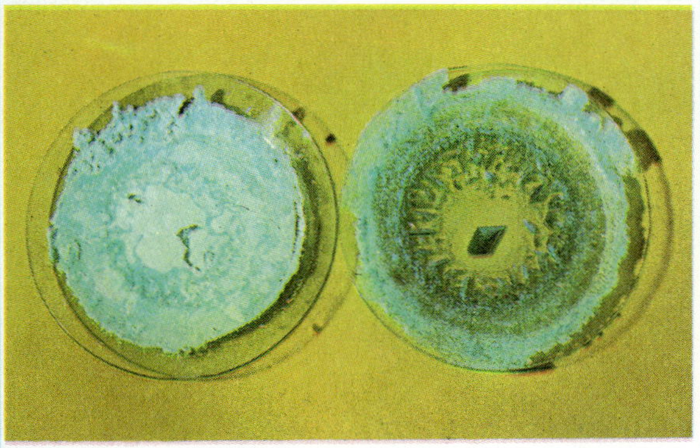

1

Crystal Properties

Look over the records of your observations in these investigations and notice the relationship between the time it takes for a crystal to form and the size of the crystal. It seems that, in general, the longer it takes for crystals to form, the larger they grow.

Now look over the sketches you made. Sodium chloride crystals are cubic and copper sulfate crystals are triclinic. Let's see why.

An interesting thing about crystal shapes is that these shapes will sometimes stay the same if the crystal is broken up into pieces. This is what happens to a halite crystal (sodium chloride), for example, when it is struck. Galena (lead sulfide) is another mineral that breaks into cubes when struck. If you have a spare specimen of halite or galena or calcite you may want to try this. Wrap the mineral in cloth or paper and strike it with a hammer. Observe the little crystals that form. What is their shape?

The breaking up of a mineral when struck is called **cleavage.** Halite and galena have cubic cleavage. Other minerals have other kinds of cleavage. Mica, for example, breaks along planes parallel to the crystal faces. (1) The cleavage of mica is in just one direction, unlike the three-dimensional cleavage of halite. If you have some mica, pick at it with a pin. It will cleave into flakes. These flakes can be picked again and again into thinner and thinner flakes.

Not all minerals show cleavage. If you strike some minerals, such as flint, they do not break along the cleavage surface. (2) Mineralogists say that such minerals **fracture.**

Why do minerals have cleavage? Men have known about mineral cleavage for centuries, and as long as 300 years ago they began to suspect the reason for it. They speculated that somehow a mineral was composed of many tiny units identical in shape. From an understanding of cleavage, men have proceeded to an understanding of the arrangements of atoms in a crystal.

Atoms in a Crystal

You already have much more knowledge of science than men had 300 years ago. What men speculated about then is something we have solid evidence for now. For instance, you know that all elements and compounds are composed of atoms, and that all minerals are elements or compounds. If a crystal is

2

3

made up of units, we know these units must owe their shape to orderly arrangements of particles within the solid. This photograph, taken by placing a crystal of sodium chloride in the path of an X-ray beam, shows that the structure of a crystal is determined by the arrangement of its particles. 3

As you know, sodium chloride has the formula NaCl. This means that for every ion of sodium in the compound, there is one ion of chlorine. The sodium and chloride ions have opposite electric charges. The sodium ion has a positive charge and the chloride ion has a negative charge. These ions can be represented as spheres.

The force of attraction between their opposite charges holds these ions together. In a way, this model is too simple, however, for it has only one sodium ion and one chloride ion. In any actual amount of sodium chloride—even a single grain from a salt shaker—there are billions and billions of positive and negative ions.

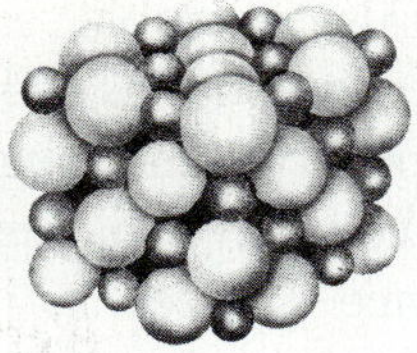

The ions here are arranged as they are in a small part of a crystal of sodium chloride. In the "ball-and-stick" type of model, you can clearly see that each sodium ion is surrounded by ions of chlorine, and each chloride ion is surrounded by ions of sodium.

When many ions are grouped together, they make a **space lattice** like this.

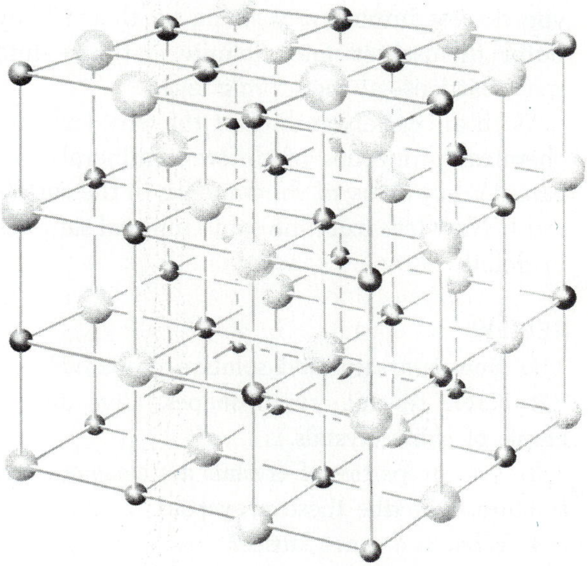

All together, the ions in this model make a tiny cube. In this model you can see that the same kinds of atoms, arranged in the same orderly way, repeat themselves over and over. Thus the structure of the crystal follows an orderly pattern of its own.

Most minerals resemble sodium chloride in being ionic compounds. That is, they are made up of positive and negative ions. For this reason, they have patterns of ions arranged in space lattices as their "building blocks." The lattices account for the orderly patterns that appear when crystals are cleaved.

The theory of crystal lattices is, like any good theory, useful in explaining more than just our observations about the cleavage of minerals and crystals. The theory also accounts for other observations, for instance, those we make about crystal growth. When you grow crystals of sodium chloride, alum, copper sulfate, or any ionic compound from solutions (as in your investigation on p. 47), you do not impose any shape on them. They build themselves into definite patterns—into space lattices—at the atomic level.

With an understanding of the physical and chemical properties of different minerals, we can identify many of the minerals in the earth's crust. Now let's examine some mineral samples in detail.

REVIEW

1. How is a saturated solution prepared?

2. Name several crystal shapes. Give an example of cubic crystals.

3. Two properties of crystals are cleavage and fracture. Describe these properties.

4. What is a space lattice?

5. Briefly describe the arrangement of a crystal of sodium chloride.

NEW VIEW

1. Potassium chloride is an ionic compound. Its crystals are cubic. How does its structure at the ionic level determine the crystal shape?

2. Find out how scientists have used X-ray diffraction studies to confirm the view that crystals are made up of atoms arranged into space lattices.

3. MINERAL GROUPS

Suppose you had 2,000 different coins you were trying to identify. What is the first thing you might do? Right, arrange them in several groups. Similarly, geologists classify different minerals into three groups: **rock-forming** minerals, **metal-bearing** minerals, and **nonmetallic** minerals. Rock-forming minerals, as the name suggests, are commonly found in rocks. Metal-bearing minerals contain metallic elements, such as iron, aluminum, or copper. Nonmetallic minerals contain nonmetallic elements, such as sulfur or carbon. Perhaps you already have mineral samples that belong in these groups. Let's find out.

A Rock-forming Mineral: Quartz

You know that oxygen is the most abundant element in the earth's crust. Are you surprised to learn that the second most abundant element is silicon? Atoms of these two elements combine in various ways to produce many rock-forming minerals. **Quartz** is one of the simplest minerals formed from silicon and oxygen.

Scientists have investigated the structure of compounds consisting of only silicon and oxygen atoms. They find that each silicon atom joins with four oxygen atoms in the shape of a pyramid. (1) Because the silicon atom is so small, it can fit in the center of a pyramid formed by four oxygen atoms, each bonded with silicon. In this pyramid the one silicon atom has four bonds with four oxygen atoms. But a single pyramid forms only a part of the model of the molecule. In the actual molecule

1

2

3

one pyramid is joined to another by bonds between the silicon and oxygen atoms. 2

If we enlarge the model further, we get a three-dimensional effect. 3 In this model there are two oxygen atoms for every silicon atom. What we have modeled here is part of a macromolecule—a huge molecule of silica, as it occurs in sand and in quartz. The chemical name for silica is silicon dioxide.

Quartz is a common mineral found in most rocks. Because it is hard and durable, quartz tends to resist wear better than other minerals. For this reason, many beach sands contain abundant samples of quartz.

Quartz may be found as large, clear, single crystals or in small groups. At Crystal Spring, Arkansas, many fine quartz crystals are found. Some of these crystals may weigh over 45 kilograms (100 pounds). 4

Quartz occurs in many varieties. Large crystalline types include rock crystal, as well as milky, rose, yellow, and smoky quartz. These types differ in color and in their ability to transmit light. A purple variety of quartz, called **amethyst,** is frequently used as a semiprecious stone. 5

Extremely tiny crystals of quartz produce additional forms: **Agate** is a form of quartz that has natural bands of different colors. 6 A variety of agate, called **onyx,** is used in jewelry.

4

5

6

(1)

Flint is another form of quartz. Because flint produces an extremely sharp cutting edge when it is fractured, many primitive tribes used it for making weapons and tools.(1)

Other Rock-forming Minerals

Although quartz is the best known rock-forming mineral, many other minerals are included in this category. Most important among these are the silicates.

SILICATE MINERALS: Silicate minerals are compounds containing silicon, oxygen, and atoms of other elements, mainly metals. One of these metals, aluminum, is the most abundant *metal* in the earth's crust.

There are three main types of silicate structures. In all these, silicon-oxygen bonds form the basic framework of the mineral.

One type of silicate mineral has a chainlike structure.(2) The bonds within the chain are much stronger than those between adjacent chains. Minerals with this structure have the type of crystal that cleaves into needlelike slivers, like these fibers of asbestos.(3)

Silicon-oxygen pyramids can also join together in sheets.(4) The bonds that hold the sheets together are strong, but those between the sheets are weak. Minerals with this structure have the type of crystal that cleaves into thin plates, as in mica.(5)

Mica is a very common mineral often recognized by its one perfect cleavage plane. This property makes it possible to split crystals of mica into thin transparent, flexible sheets. Occurring in several colors, small or large crystals of mica are found in granites.

In the third type of silicate minerals, atoms are arranged in a three-dimensional network.(6) Because of their strong bonds in three directions, silicates of the network type do not cleave easily. Among these minerals are the feldspars, a sample of which is pictured here.(7)

Feldspars are found in more types of rock than any other mineral. They are found in all granite rocks. Feldspars have a glassy luster and range in color from whitish to pink, but may be yellow or gray.

(2)

3

Hornblende, olivine, garnet, and talc are rock-forming silicates that contain the metals iron and magnesium. (See the Appendix for more information on these minerals.)

CALCITE AND MAGNETITE: **Calcite,** a common mineral found in limestone and marble rocks, is the compound calcium carbonate, $CaCO_3$. In its pure form calcite may be quite transparent. As you know, it has the property of double refraction, and may occur in a variety of colors. **Magnetite** is another common rock-forming mineral. Magnetite, a compound of iron and oxygen, is naturally magnetic. Deposits of magnetite are an important source of iron.

4

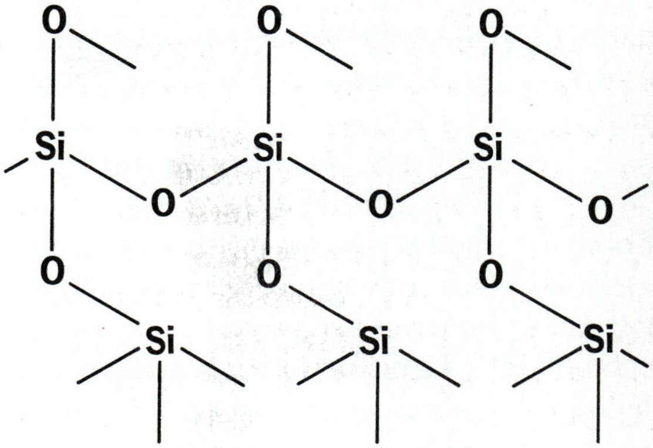

5

6

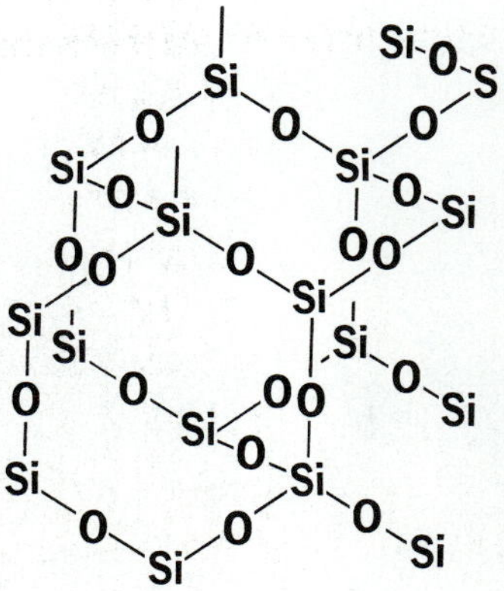

7

1

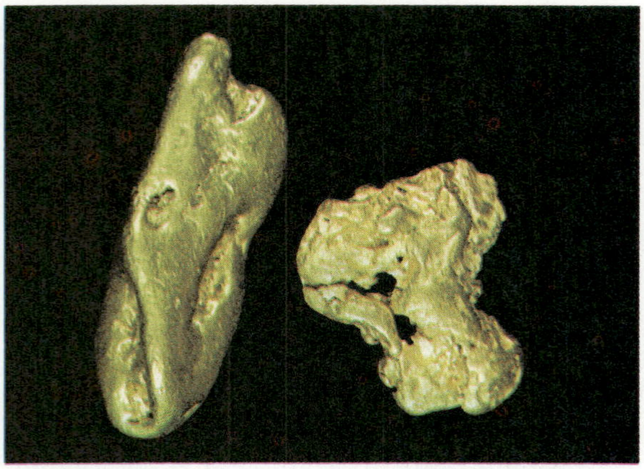

3

Metal-bearing Minerals

A few metals are found in pure, or elemental, form.(1) Among these are copper, silver, gold, and iron. You may be lucky enough to find one of these, but it is more likely that you will pick up a specimen of an **ore.** An ore is a mineral from which an element, usually a metal, is obtained.

Hematite, bauxite, and **sphalerite** are ores from which iron, aluminum, and zinc, respectively, are obtained. Hematite is the most important source of iron.(2) It is found in many places in the United States, with large deposits in Alabama and the Great Lakes region.

A specimen consisting of grains and claylike masses, with color ranging from white to yellow or reddish-brown, may be a chunk of bauxite, an ore of the metal aluminum.(3) In the United States bauxite is most often found in Alabama, Arkansas, or Tennessee.

One type of zinc ore is sphalerite. It is found in many places and is usually associated with lead. Sphalerite is grainy or fibrous, and may be found in layered masses. Sphalerite, which has a cubic crystal structure, is yellow-brown to black in color.

Here are two other metal-bearing minerals, **galena** and **malachite.** Deposits of galena are widespread throughout the United States.(4)

2

4

Galena is gray in color and has a characteristic property: cubic cleavage. Lead is the metal obtained from galena.

Malachite, a carbonate of copper, is the only carbonate that is green.(5) The distinctive color is a way to identify this mineral. Malachite is both an ornamental stone and a source of copper.

Nonmetallic Minerals

The nonmetallic minerals are frequently subdivided into two groups: the *industrial minerals* and the *gem-bearing* minerals. Sulfur, graphite, halite, and gypsum are examples of industrial minerals. Diamond, corundum, and beryl are samples of the gem-bearing minerals. Let's take a closer look at these minerals.

SULFUR: **Sulfur** is a soft, yellow mineral that gives a white streak.(6) Deposits of sulfur are found in regions of recent volcanic activity and in areas of the Texas-Louisiana gulf coast. Sulfur is a vital industrial chemical; it is used mainly in making sulfuric acid.

GRAPHITE: **Graphite** is a soft, greasy-feeling, black mineral composed of the element carbon.(7) Mixed with clay, graphite forms a substance you are very familiar with—the "lead" in your pencil.

HALITE: **Halite** is the mineral name for naturally occurring salt, NaCl. The characteristic salty taste makes halite easy to identify. Halite is deposited in extensive beds as sea water evaporates.

GYPSUM: **Gypsum** is a compound containing calcium, sulfur, oxygen, and hydrogen. Three varieties of gypsum are found in nature: *satin spar* is a fiber type; *selenite* is a transparent crystalline type: *rock gypsum* is a grainy type. Gypsum is used primarily in the con-

1

struction industry for plaster of Paris, wallboard, and roofing tines. Like halite, gypsum is deposited as salt water evaporates. 1

DIAMOND: **Diamond** is a naturally occurring crystal of the element carbon. 2 (Compare this form of carbon with graphite.) Diamond is the hardest known mineral; it is capable of scratching all other minerals.

Diamonds are commonly found in "pipes" or chimneys of extinct volcanoes. The diamond mines of South Africa are the most famous source of diamonds, yielding occasional samples worth over three million dollars. Only the best diamonds are used in gems. Those containing impurities are used for cutting tools on wheels, drills, and saws. By subjecting graphite to heat and pressure, "industrial" diamonds can now be made in the laboratory.

2

CORUNDUM: **Corundum** is the compound aluminum oxide—Al_2O_3. Blue-colored crystals of corundum are *sapphires;* red crystals are *rubies.* Sapphires and rubies can be as valuable as diamonds.

BERYL: **Beryl** is a complex aluminum compound containing other metals, particularly chromium. Green-colored crystals of beryl are called *emeralds.* Pale-blue or light green varieties of beryl are called *aquamarine.*

Mineral identification comes with practice. Collect mineral samples on a field trip or study some provided by your teacher. With the information in the section on IDENTIFICATION OF MINERALS and the tables in the Appendix you can greatly improve your skill.

In the next chapter you will see how a knowledge of minerals forms the basis of our understanding of the earth's rocks.

REVIEW

1. Name the three classifications of minerals and give an example of each.

2. Briefly describe three structures of silicate minerals and give an example of each.

3. What are two minerals composed only of carbon? How are their properties alike or different?

4. Name three minerals that are sources of metals.

NEW VIEW

1. Many beach sands contain abundant samples of quartz. Using reference books, find out what other mineral is common to the beaches from Cape Cod to South Carolina; what mineral is most common in the sands of Florida; what material forms the beaches along the coasts of Oregon and Washington.

2. Semi-precious stones and gems are varieties of common minerals. What is your "birthstone"? What substance is it composed of?

IDENTIFICATION OF MINERALS

If you found a mineral while on a field trip or if your school has a mineral collection, why not try to identify some minerals? The photographs and information here and in the tables in the Appendix will help.

Calcite, in its pure form, may be quite transparent (left). ❸ It has the property of double refraction, and may occur in a variety of colors. Calcite has a hardness of 3, a specific gravity of 2.7, and reacts to the hydrochloric acid test.

Mica, a very common mineral, is recognizable by the ease with which it is split into thin sheets (center). There are several colors and several types of mica; six-sided crystals typify its structure. It may be found in granites as tiny or very large crystals.

The feldspar shown is one of several types (right). It is a common mineral in granites, gneisses, and lava. The hardness of feldspar is approximately 6, and its specific gravity is about 2.6. Feldspars have a glassy luster. The color is usually whitish to pink, but it may be yellow or gray.

Here are some other rock-forming minerals: quartz, gypsum, hornblende. ❹ You are most likely to find quartz (left), which has a hardness of 7. In contrast, gypsum (center) has a hardness of 2. Both range in color from white to amber, from gray to pink.

Hornblende, as you see, is dark in color (right). Usually it is found in hexagonal crystal form. Its hardness is rated at 5.5 and its specific gravity as 3.2. You can find hornblende in many rocks, such as granites.

There are some minerals that constitute ores. (An ore, as you now know, is a mineral from which an element—usually a metal—is obtained.) A metal is usually obtained from a compound that includes the metal and (frequently) oxygen. Some few metals are occasionally found in pure or elemental forms. Among these metals are native copper, silver, gold, and iron. You may be lucky enough to find one of these, but it is more likely that you will pick up a specimen of an ore of these or other metals.

These three ores—hematite, bauxite, and sphalerite—are sources of iron, aluminum, and zinc. ❺ Hematite (left) is the most important ore of our most important metal, iron. This mineral has an earthy appearance, a red to brown streak, no cleavage, and a hardness of about 6. It is found in many places in the United States, with large deposits in Alabama and the Great Lakes region.

❸

❹

❺

If a specimen consists of grains or claylike masses, has a hardness of between 1 and 3, a specific gravity of 2.5, with color ranging from white to yellow or reddish-brown, it may be a chunk of bauxite (center), an ore of the metal aluminum. In the United States bauxite is most usually found in Alabama, Arkansas, and the Tennessee region.

Zinc ore, one type of which is sphalerite (right), is found in many places and is usually associated with lead. Sphalerite is grainy or fibrous in texture, and may be in the form of layered masses. Sometimes it is found in crystal form as well. The crystal structure of sphalerite is cubic. It is yellow-brown to black in color, has a specific gravity of 4, a hardness of 3.5, a resinous luster, and a streak test will produce a light yellow or brownish color.

Here is another group of ores: magnetite, galena, malachite. ❶ The ore magnetite (left) is an important source of iron. Galena (center) is an important source of lead, and malachite (right) is a source of copper—a fact which was known to the early Egyptians.

Magnetite has the unusual property of being naturally magnetic. It has a hardness of 6, a specific gravity of 5.8, and its streak as well as its color is black. Being a metallic ore, magnetite has a metallic luster.

❶

Galena (center) has a conspicuous characteristic: cubic cleavage. It has a gray, metallic luster and its weight may surprise you, for its specific gravity is 7.5. Streak and color match, both being gray. However, galena's hardness is low on the scale, about 2.5. Although deposits of galena vary in value, it is a widespread mineral, being found to some extent in each of the United States.

Malachite (right) is a good source of the metal copper. Perhaps malachite's most conspicuous characteristic is its color, green. It is usually found in separate small masses, although crystals occasionally appear. Malachite is rated at 3.5 on the hardness scale; its specific gravity is 4; and its streak is a lighter green. Its luster may vary from silky to dull metallic. Another interesting property of malachite, one which makes identification more certain, is that it reacts with hydrochloric acid. Malachite is the only carbonate that is green in color.

4. RELATING THE CONCEPTS

We have looked at matter as it occurs in tiny bits—atoms, ions, and molecules. Atoms of elements combine to form compounds. In the solid part of the earth, these compounds are called minerals. In fact, a mineral is defined as any naturally occurring solid substance in the earth's crust.

Although there are over 2,000 different minerals, less than a dozen make up 99 percent of the solid rock of the crust. These rock-forming minerals include quartz, feldspar, mica, and calcite.

In addition to rock-forming minerals, there are metal-bearing minerals and nonmetallic minerals. Metal-bearing minerals include those found in pure or elemental form: copper, silver, gold. Metal-bearing minerals also include metallic ores, those minerals from which a metal can be obtained. Hematite and bauxite are metallic ores from which the metals iron and aluminum are obtained.

Minerals are identified by various physical and chemical properties. Color, luster, streak, hardness, specific gravity, and crystal shape are physical properties. Tests for chemical properties include reactions to produce a precipitate and flame tests. Other tests include a minerals reaction to light and magnetism.

Reviewing the Concepts

► *The slower the rate of crystallization of a substance, the larger the crystal.* Many crystals form in nature by the evaporation of solutions of the mineral substances. Halite, made up of cubic sodium chloride crystals, is one common example. We can grow crystals in a similar way in the laboratory. There we discover that the more slowly the crystals are allowed to form, the larger they will be. But no matter how rapidly or slowly the crystals grow, the crystalline form for a given mineral is always the same. Crystals of halite, for instance, are always cubic in form.

► *The amount of a substance that must be dissolved at a given temperature to make a saturated solution is fixed.* One identifying property of some minerals is their solubility in water. The degree of solubility varies from substance to substance and with temperature. When a given amount of water contains as much of the substance as will dissolve at a given temperature, we have prepared a saturated solution of the substance. Crystals are often grown from saturated solutions.

► *The orderly arrangement of the atoms, ions, or molecules that make up a crystal determines the form of the crystal.* For a given substance, such as halite, there is just one way in which its particles (ions of sodium and chloride) arrange themselves in the basic pattern known as a unit cell of that substance. For halite, many unit cells grow together into a space lattice with a cubic pattern. No matter how many unit cells there are in a given space lattice, the shape of the whole is a cube. Small crystals of halite, then, are little cubes; large crystals of halite are big cubes.

Testing Yourself

1. In the scale of hardness, we find the following: talc 1, gypsum 2, calcite 3. What is the significance of these numbers?

2. Suppose you have a sample of a mineral with a cubic crystalline form, and you suspect it may be sodium chloride. If the sample is sodium chloride,

a. what physical properties (besides shape) would help you identify it?

b. what would be the result of a flame test?

3. How is the size of a crystal of copper sulfate related to the rate at which the crystal forms from an evaporating solution?

4. How are the ions of sodium and chlorine arranged in the space lattice of sodium chloride?

5. Suppose you have a mineral sample you want to identify. Outline a procedure for its identification.

6. What test can you apply to a solution of copper sulfate to determine whether or not the solution is saturated? Explain the result of the test (a) if it is positive, and (b) if it is negative.

7. Why do large cubic salt crystals cleave into small cubes?

8. There are three main types of silicate structures. Briefly describe them and give an example of each.

9. Name two general subdivisions of nonmetallic minerals and give examples of each.

Extending the Concepts

Investigation. Crush a blue crystal of copper sulfate and heat it in a Pyrex or Kimax test tube. What do you observe? Why do chemists call blue copper sulfate a *hydrate?* Try the same procedure on gypsum, one of the many minerals that are hydrates. Look up the formula for hydrated copper sulfate and for gypsum.

Is there a definite weight of water of hydration in blue copper sulfate? Devise a way to find out, and check your results in a textbook.

Suggested Reading

Fay, Gordon, *The Rockhound's Manual,* New York, Harper, 1972. Information on how minerals form, how to identify them, and where to find them.

Nicolay, H. H. and A. V. Stone, *Rocks and Minerals,* Cranbury, New Jersey, A. S. Barnes, 1967.

Pearl, Richard M., *American Gem Trails,* New York, McGraw-Hill, 1964. A guide to identifying gems and where they may be found in each of the 50 states.

Sinkankas, John, *Mineralogy for Amateurs,* Princeton, Van Nostrand, 1964.

See also the Suggested Reading for Chapter 4.

4

The Rocks of Earth

What is a rock? We usually think of a rock as a "medium-sized" chunk of matter, such as this piece of granite. ① But what sort of matter is rock?

When a geologist uses the word "rock," he means almost everything solid in the earth's crust. Not only the large masses of stony matter that make up the earth's crust, but sand, clay, gravel, and soil are also "rock"—that is, derived from rock.

1. ROCK MATERIAL

Examine one or more rocks with a magnifying glass to see what kinds of particles they seem to be made of. If you can crush the rock, you will see its make-up more clearly. In a piece of granite, for instance, you may recognize as many as three different minerals: quartz, feldspar, and black mica. This is evidence that at least one rock, granite, is a bundle or collection of several minerals. If you can, examine several other rocks the same way to see if this evidence is confirmed.

Analyzing a Rock

There is another way we can investigate the make-up of a rock—by studying its chemical properties. Suppose our rock sample is the one shown in this photograph. ② This rock is *smithsonite*. What is smithsonite made of? ■

①

②

■ AN APPRENTICE INVESTIGATION into Substances in a Rock

Take a piece of the rock smithsonite. (If smithsonite is not available, you can use zinc carbonate.) Use a file to remove small particles from the smithsonite.❶ Place these particles in a Pyrex or Kimax test tube until the test tube contains about 1 centimeter (one-third inch) of smithsonite.

Now place a one-hole rubber stopper containing a piece of bent glass tubing in the test tube.❷ Attach the test tube to a ring stand. Insert the other end of the glass tubing into a test tube of limewater. Using a Bunsen burner, gently heat the first test tube. After a short time, what has happened in the second test tube?❸

Do you observe bubbles of gas in the test tube? Does the limewater become milky? From your previous work in science, you know that limewater becomes milky in the presence of carbon dioxide.

Continue heating the test tube a little longer. What happens? No matter how long you continue to heat the test tube, a substance remains in it. This substance is mainly zinc oxide, but it also contains a few impurities found in the smithsonite.

❶
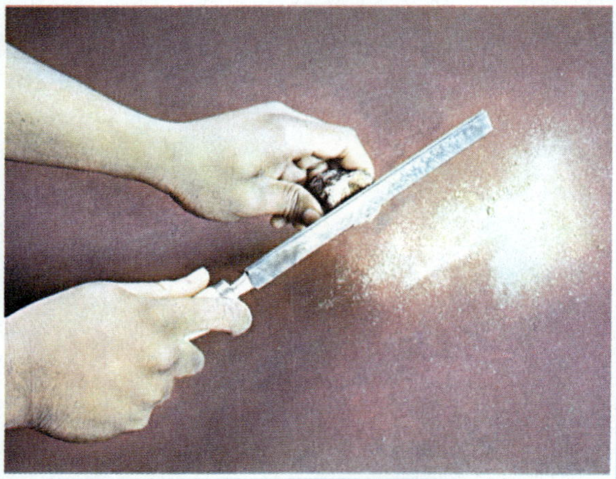

An Investigation On Your Own

Repeat the investigation, but this time heat the smithsonite (or zinc carbonate) until all the carbon dioxide is removed and the limewater becomes clear again. Why does the limewater become clear? Prove that the substance remaining in the test tube contains zinc.

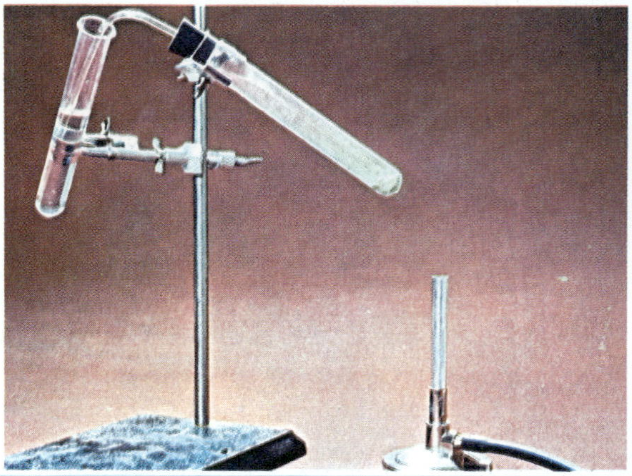
❷

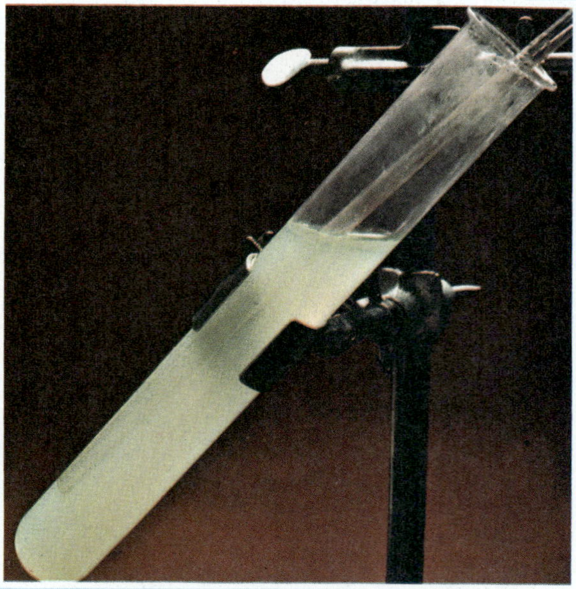
❸

What does this investigation show? It seems as if smithsonite contains at least three elements: zinc, carbon, and oxygen. With the right kind of apparatus, a chemist can analyze the smithsonite, that is, break it down more completely into the elements of which it is composed. The analysis can identify traces of other elements you could not find. Using special methods of analysis, the chemist finds evidence of the presence of all these elements in smithsonite:

zinc	manganese	cadmium
carbon	magnesium	cobalt
oxygen	copper	lead
iron	calcium	

One way to describe what is in smithsonite, then, is to list the elements it contains.

To identify rocks, however, you do not need to "test" for every element present. Recall from the previous chapter that elements may combine to form minerals. Hence, you can analyze a rock for the minerals it does or does not contain. For example, if you place a small piece of limestone in a beaker and add several drops of dilute hydrochloric acid, only part of the rock dissolves. Some of the material in the limestone does not react with the acid. Another mineral, then, is mixed with the one that does dissolve. The mineral calcite (calcium carbonate) reacts with hydrochloric acid. Calcite is the main mineral in limestone. Yet since a part of the rock does not behave like calcite, we know there is at least one other mineral in limestone.

This is one of the major differences between minerals and most rocks: a mineral is always a fairly pure element or compound, and a rock is usually a *mixture* of substances. The physical and chemical properties of any mineral differ from those of any other mineral. In a rock, then, the presence of more than one set of properties, such as different colors, different degrees of hardness, or different reactions with an acid, indicates the presence of more than one mineral.

Another difference between minerals and rocks is that we may write chemical formulas for minerals, but (usually) not for rocks. A chemical formula, such as $CaCO_3$ (for calcite), shows that the mineral has a definite composition: 1 atom of calcium is combined with 1 atom of carbon and 3 atoms of oxygen. Every piece of pure calcite has this same chemical composition. Limestone, however, varies in its composition. Different specimens of the rock we call limestone contain varying amounts of calcite and varying amounts of one or more other substances.

Sometimes a rock is made up of a single mineral, for example, quartz. Usually, however, many crystals of various minerals are found together in a rock. Therefore, we usually define a rock as a mixture, or bundle, of minerals.

Classifying Rocks

Look at the rocks in any collection you choose. Perhaps there is a collection in your school, or you can start one of your own. Most rock samples can be found in **rock outcrops.** Rock outcrops are places such as mountains, stream valleys, or highway cuts where the underlying rock mass is exposed. These places should supply you with many interesting rock samples.

How would you go about grouping the rocks into different kinds? You might try to classify them according to their color, texture, mineral content, the places where they were found, and so on. Geologists have discovered, however, that the most useful way to classify rocks is according to their origin.

A rock looks solid and stable enough, but every rock is different now from what it once was. One rock in your collection may have come from a hot liquid substance that cooled and solidified. Geologists call a rock like this **igneous,** which means "fire-formed." Another rock in the collection may have formed when many solid particles settled (usually in water) and became pressed and stuck together. This kind of rock is **sedimentary,** which means "settled." Still another kind of rock can form when one of the first two kinds undergoes a change in its form. This class of rocks is called **metamorphic,** which means "changed form."

Igneous, sedimentary, and metamorphic are the three main classes of rocks. Let's look at some characteristics and examples of each.

REVIEW

1. In general, how is a rock different from a mineral?

2. A rock is treated with dilute HCl, and a gas is given off. What is one mineral in this rock?

3. Name the three classes of rocks.

4. How do geologists classify rocks?

NEW VIEW

1. Bricks, concrete, and macadam are a type of rock. What are these substances and how are they formed?

2. From a textbook or another source, find the relationship among calcium carbonate, limestone, dolomite, and marble. What do they have in common? How do they differ?

2. IGNEOUS ROCKS

The earth seems very solid, doesn't it? But deep below the surface, the temperature of the earth is so great that rocks melt. Geysers and hot springs give us some clue to these high temperatures in the earth. Do you need direct proof? Imagine yourself in this picture.① Standing on the rim of this volcano, you can actually see pools of melted rock below!

①

Molten material below the surface is called **magma.** All igneous rocks begin as hot, liquid magma. Some of this molten mixture may solidify while still under the earth's surface. Cooling slowly, the magma produces coarse-grained rocks. This coarse-grained texture is easily seen in this igneous rock, **gabbro.**② Gabbro, and other coarse-grained igneous rocks that cool slowly underground are called **plutonic,** or **intrusive,** igneous rocks. The word plutonic comes from Pluto, the name of an ancient god of the underworld.

②

Some of the molten mixture may find its way to the surface and pour out of the earth's crust. This molten mixture cools quickly, producing fine-grained rocks. **Basalt** is one example of fine-grained igneous rock.(3) Basalt and other igneous rocks that cool at the surface are **volcanic**, or **extrusive**, igneous rocks.

Finally, some of the molten mixture may explode onto the surface, cooling rapidly. This rapid cooling produces igneous rocks in which no crystalline structure is apparent. A solid that contains no apparent orderly arrangement of its atoms is called a **glass. Obsidian** is an example of an igneous glass.(4) If steam and other gases are present in the exploding material, the mixture may solidify into a "frothy" mass. **Pumice** is an example of an igneous froth.(5)

Based on texture, then, we can identify two large classes of igneous rocks: plutonic, or intrusive, rocks; and volcanic, or extrusive, rocks. There are several types of plutonic rocks and several types of volcanic rocks. These types differ because of the different minerals they contain. Let's see what these minerals are.

Minerals in a Molten Mixture

Seven minerals are commonly found in most igneous rocks. Three of these minerals are light-colored: **quartz,** and two **feldspars.** The four common dark minerals include **hornblende, pyroxene, mica,** and **olivine.** In various combinations, these seven minerals make up most of the coarse-grained and fine-grained igneous rocks.

Granite is a coarse-grained, intrusive rock composed mostly of quartz, a feldspar, hornblende, and mica. Great quantities of granite are present in the earth's crust. Mountain-building processes bring these granite masses into view. Stone Mountain, Georgia, at the southern end of the Appalachian Mountains

(3)

(4)

(5)

1

3

is made of granite. So are the Sierra Nevada Mountains. Yosemite Valley, carved out of the Sierra Nevada Mountains, shows spectacular granite masses. 1

Rhyolite is a fine-grained igneous rock that contains the same minerals as granite; it ranges in color from tan to red. 2 Rhyolite is formed as **lava** pours slowly out over the surface of the ground. Lava is the name given to the molten material that flows out onto the surface of the earth. While underground, the molten material is, as you remember, called magma.

You learned earlier that gabbro is a coarse-grained intrusive rock. Gabbro is composed of a feldspar, pyroxene, and olivine; but it does not contain quartz. Gabbro is not found in great masses like granite, but in smaller igneous features. It is the rock that forms the Palisade cliffs along the Hudson River. 3 Above and below these gabbro cliffs are layers of red sandstone. In Chapter 5, you will learn how these cliffs were formed.

Basalt is a fine-grained, igneous rock that contains the same minerals as gabbro. A dense rock, gray to black in color, basalt is the common igneous rock formed as lava flows harden. Many of these lava flows cover large areas of land. The Columbia Plateau of northwestern United States is an excellent example of this type of igneous activity. 4

2

4

REVIEW

1. How are igneous rocks formed?

2. Distinguish between plutonic and volcanic igneous rocks. Give an example of each.

3. Name the seven most common minerals of igneous rock.

4. How does the rate of cooling affect the formation of a rock? Use examples in your answer.

NEW VIEW

1. The earth's very first rocks may be considered as igneous. Why is this a reasonable guess?

2. Igneous rocks form by crystallization of molten material instead of by crystallization from solution. Why would a plutonic igneous rock, such as granite, be coarser grained than a volcanic rock, such as pumice?

5

6

3. SEDIMENTARY ROCK

Deep under the ground, rocks melt and become magma. Propelled by its dissolved gases, the magma flows to a new location under the surface or above it. Then it solidifies, forming new rock. Just as surely as magma has in the past formed new igneous rock, geologists predict that it will continue to do so in the future.

Another thing geologists predict is that igneous rocks exposed to the weather will slowly wear away, and that erosion will wash particles of their component minerals down to lower ground and the sea. The processes of weathering and erosion have been going on for billions of years. You can see their effects yourself if you observe, over a few months' time, rock exposed to the action of wind and water.

Weathering affects all rocks, not only igneous rocks. The particles of rock that are worn off are often washed into bodies of water, where they settle and become sediment. This sediment turns into sedimentary rock. How does this come about?

The Making of Sedimentary Rock

Sand, clay, and gravel are three kinds of materials that may become sediments. 5 Compare a pile of sand, a pile of clay, and a pile of gravel with these three rocks: shale, sandstone, and conglomerate. 6 Can you match each rock with the kind of sediment from which it was formed? How does a sediment change before we can call it a rock?

❶ 

 ❷

When the material in a sediment is cemented together and compressed by the weight of water and new sediment above it, the particles become firmly stuck together. This process is called **lithification,** which means "turning into rock."

Rocks that come from the lithification of fragments and grains of other rocks are *clastic* sedimentary rocks. Sandstone, shale, and conglomerate are all clastic rocks.

Sandstone is made up mostly of particles of quartz cemented together. Because of the spaces between the particles, sandstone is a porous rock that often holds underground deposits of oil or water. When deposits of clay are put under pressure, shale is formed. Unlike sandstone, shale is not porous, and it breaks easily into thin layers. Conglomerate is a coarse-grained rock made up of rounded pebbles or even small boulders.

Sediments may also be formed from living things. Rocks from such sediments are therefore said to have an organic origin. Coquina, for example, is a limestone that clearly reveals its animal origin. ❶ Another organic sedimentary rock is coal. Pieces of plant materials, transformed by bacterial action and compression, turn into coal. The dark brown or black color of coal reveals that the element carbon is its main mineral. ❷

Bog iron, a kind of iron ore found in Michigan, is believed to be another sedimentary rock of organic origin. Certain bacteria, as a result of their body functions, may assist in forming vast deposits of bog iron.

Some sedimentary rocks are of chemical origin. To see how chemical sediments form, try this investigation. ■

The precipitate that forms in this chemical change is calcium carbonate. You can see the calcium carbonate settle to the bottom of the test tube. In somewhat the same way, calcium carbonate formed by chemical action in natural waters becomes a sediment. When sediments of calcium carbonate are changed into rock, limestone is formed.

Many—but not all—limestones are of chemical origin. Some are organic. Fossils, the remains of ancient living things, are commonly found in sedimentary rock, as you probably know.

These fossils represent the preserved remains of living plants and animals. ❸ The fossils of marine plants and animals are especially abundant near the margins of ocean basins. When the organisms die, their remains

■ AN APPRENTICE INVESTIGATION into a Chemical Sediment

Dissolve about 1 gram of sodium carbonate ("washing soda") in 10 milliliters of water in a test tube. In a second test tube, dissolve about 1 gram of calcium chloride. Each solution should be clear and colorless. Next, pour the contents of the two tubes together. What happens? ❶

Here is the word equation for this reaction. ❷ The downward arrow written next to a product in a reaction means that the substance is a precipitate.

An Investigation On Your Own

Using the methods of filtration and evaporation, separate the two products of the reaction. Then identify both products, using their physical and chemical properties as your clues.

❶

❷ sodium carbonate + calcium chloride ⟶ sodium chloride + calcium carbonate ↓

❸

settle to the bottom of the ocean basin. There they are quickly buried by the sediment that pours into these basins. The layers of sediment become thicker and thicker, applying more and more pressure on the lower layers. These lower layers eventually form sedimentary rock. The shells or bones of the organisms trapped in the airless layers of sediment form the fossilized remains that we see. For this reason sedimentary rock is particularly useful to biologists for investigating ancient forms of life.

In one sense of the word, sedimentary rocks are truly "settled"; but geologists predict that they will not stay as they are. For one thing, a sedimentary rock that is raised above water is sure to be crumbled into bits again as it is exposed to weather. Washed away by erosion, the particles form new sediments, and eventually, these are lithified into new sedimentary rocks.

Some sedimentary rocks, however, have a different fate. They become metamorphic rock. How does this come about?

REVIEW

1. What are two types of sedimentary rock? Give examples of each.
2. Why is sedimentary rock of interest to biologists?
3. Describe how a sedimentary rock can be formed by chemical action.
4. Briefly describe how fossils are formed in layers of rock.

NEW VIEW

1. Gravel, sand, silt, and clay are names given to different sizes of particles. Arrange these particles in order of increasing size. From a textbook or other source, find the type of sedimentary rock that forms from each size particle.
2. Why are we more likely to find fossils preserved in sedimentary rocks than in any other kind of rock?

4. METAMORPHIC ROCKS

You have probably seen a colorful patio or pathway. ❶ The flat sheets of red, gray, or green rock are firm and durable. But what is this colorful rock? At first glance, it appears to be shale—a sedimentary rock we have already examined. This rock, however, is different. For example, it is much harder than shale. Perhaps some of you already know the name of this rock; it is **slate.** Slate resembles shale. Is it possible that one has been changed into the other? Yes, it is.

❶

Rocks that have undergone changes from their first forms are metamorphic rocks. High pressure, heat, gases, or water solutions may change any type of rock into a "new" type of rock. Metamorphic or "changed" rocks are not formed from molten material. Rather, changes occur in the solid rock: bands of minerals may form, large crystals may grow; new minerals may be produced, a layering or flakiness may develop.

Simple and Complex Rocks

Depending upon how much they have been changed, some metamorphic rocks have features that resemble the original rock. Slate, marble, and quartzite are three of these simple metamorphic rocks. ❷

Slate results from the metamorphism of shale. Although slate has a wide range of colors, blue, green, gray, brown, and red, it usually resembles shale enough to be recognized easily. Slate is a type of *foliated* rock. Foliated rock breaks into layers. Because it

2

3

breaks easily into durable sheets, it is often used for roofing tiles or "flagstone" walks.

Marble is formed from limestone. A simple test shows they are related. (3) Drop a little acid on a bit of each rock. The same thing happens to both—bubbles of carbon dioxide are formed. This chemical test means that both rocks are made up mainly of the mineral calcite (calcium carbonate, $CaCO_3$). Limestone that is subjected to heat and pressure becomes marble. The limestone changes form but retains the same chemical make-up. Marble is an *unfoliated* rock; it does not form sheets or layers when broken.

Quartzite results from the metamorphism of sandstone or conglomerates. Quartzite is a hard, durable rock. Many sharp mountain ridges are composed of this rock, which is not easily worn away.

Schist and **Gneiss** (pronounced nice) are two complex metamorphic rocks. Schist represents rock, perhaps a shale or slate, that has undergone severe metamorphism. In the process, new minerals such as garnet or tiny flat crystalline plates of mica may form.

Gneiss is the most complex metamorphic rock. It may form from any type of igneous or sedimentary rock. It is easy to identify, however, as mineral bands are almost always present.

Any igneous or sedimentary rock, then, may be metamorphosed by heat and pressure. Even metamorphic rock may be further changed by the same forces. For example, hard coal (anthracite) forms when soft coal (bituminous) is metamorphosed. When hard coal is metamorphosed, graphite, a nearly pure form of carbon is formed. Then graphite may be metamorphosed further into diamond. If the temperature and pressure are great enough, metamorphic rock changes further by melting into magma.

Cycle of the Rocks

When we speak of metamorphic rock melting to make magma, we have come full circle. All the successive changes that may result from the formation of magma begin again. Magma becomes igneous rock, which may weather to form sediment. Sediment is lithified into sedimentary rock, and this in turn may be transformed into metamorphic rock.

[1]

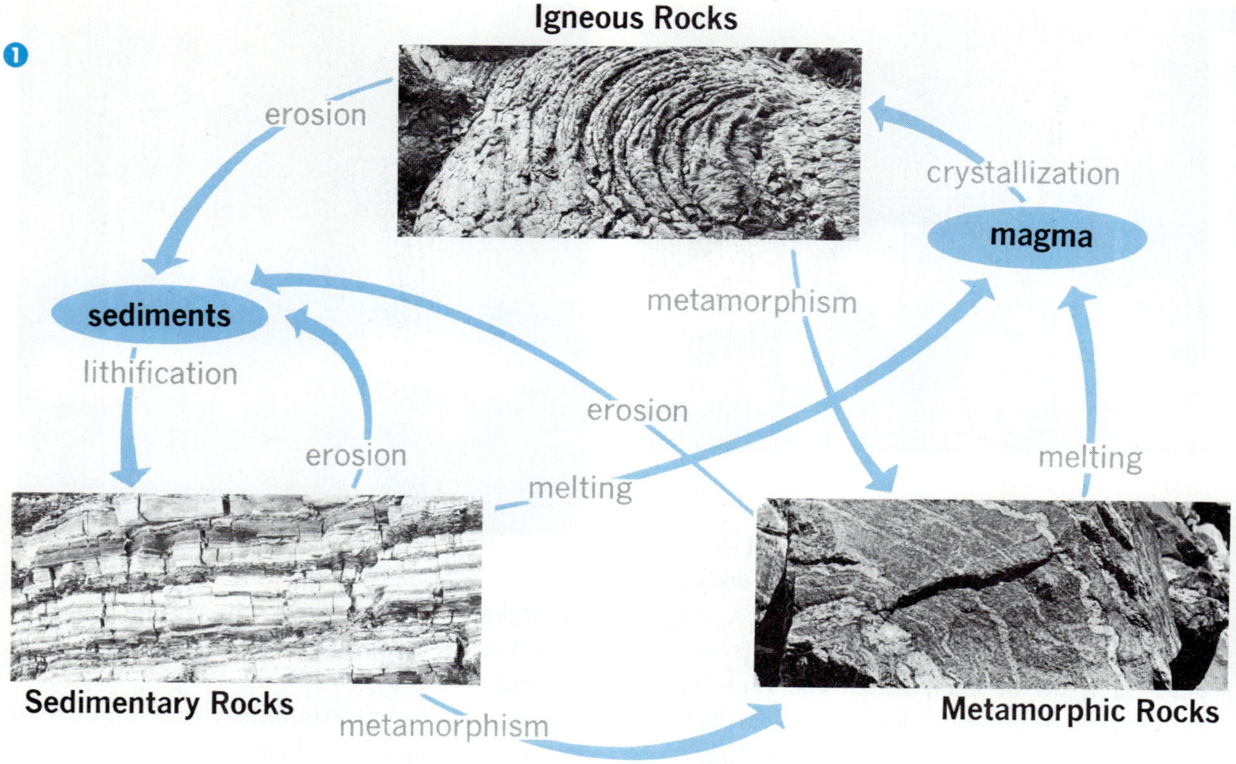

The melting of the metamorphic rocks again produces magma. This is the cycle of the rocks on the earth. [1]

Moon Rocks

Does a similar cycle of rocks take place on the moon? Scientists throughout the world are investigating the rock samples brought back from the moon in an attempt to learn how they were formed. Thus far, the rocks seem to be mainly igneous rocks.

When Armstrong and Aldrin stepped onto the moon, they reported that its surface was slippery. Study of the soil samples they brought back indicates that the moon, or at least the portion on which they walked, is paved with tiny, glasslike beads. If you could observe moon dust under the microscope, you would see beads of glass mixed with rock fragments. [2] The surface was covered with this moon soil and with breccias (brech′ē·əz). [3] On earth, breccia is an igneous rock composed of slivers of volcanic glass, pumice, mineral fragments, and fragments of volcanic rock cemented together. Rock 13, brought to earth by the astronauts of Apollo 12, appears to be a breccia.

The basaltic rocks from the surface layer are similar, yet different, from those on earth. The igneous rocks contain the same elements, mainly silicon, oxygen, aluminum, iron, titanium, calcium, and magnesium; but the properties of these elements are different. The minerals found in these rocks, for example, feldspar and olivine, are typical of basalt on

2

4

3

5

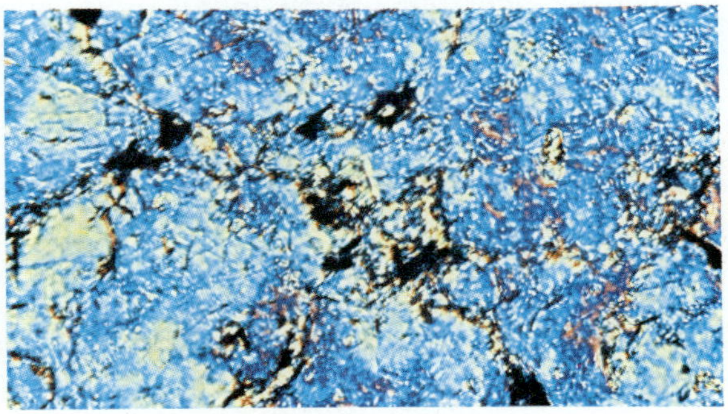

earth. Other basaltic moon rock is porous. 4 This pumice-like rock indicates that the rock cooled very quickly somewhere near the moon's surface.

About 10 percent of the rocks gathered by the Apollo 11 astronauts are not basalt. They are the igneous rock ***anorthosite*** (an·ôr'thə·sīt), a rock composed of feldspar, rich in calcium and chromium, and somewhat less dense than basalt. 5

As you follow studies of the moon, as scientist-astronauts analyze more information about the moon, you may hear more of this rock—especially if the hypothesis of some scientists that the highlands of the moon have a thick layer, or crust, of anorthosite turns out to be correct.

REVIEW

1. What are four factors that contribute to changing the form of a rock?
2. Name and describe some simple metamorphic rocks.
3. What are the types of rocks found on the moon? How do they compare with rocks on earth?
4. What is the difference between foliated and unfoliated rock?

NEW VIEW

1. Describe the changes that take place for material from a mountain top to change and eventually become metamorphic rock.
2. How might metamorphic rocks become sedimentary rocks?

IDENTIFICATION OF ROCKS

If you have collected a rock specimen, what is it? What can be observed in the specimen to suggest its classification? Consider the texture of your rock. Does the surface appear to contain crystal-like particles? Then it is probably a plutonic rock, formed by heat but cooled slowly below the surface of the earth. Does the texture have a glassy or an extremely fine appearance? If so, the rock is probably volcanic, formed by heat but cooled rapidly—probably on the surface of the earth. In either case, the rock is igneous in origin.

Can you observe particles in the texture which seem to be separate parts of the rock? The particles may perhaps rub off, or they may be large pebbles and small stones embedded in the mass. Perhaps you can see shell fragments in the rock. Or are there fossil imprints? Does the rock seem likely to break into layers? If your sample has any of these features, it is probably a rock of sedimentary origin.

Perhaps your rock belongs to the third group, metamorphic rocks. Does it have stripes or veins of different colors? Is it hard but tends to break into layers? Some sedimentary rocks retain their layer structure when they are metamorphosed. For example, metamorphosed shale becomes slate; both shale and slate tend to break into layers. Other layered sedimentary rock merely retains indications of the original layers as stripes or veins in the metamorphosed rock.

There is still more evidence available to help in identifying the origin of a rock sample. The testing you do can gives you additional information about your specimen. You can also compare your specimen with pictures and descriptions in books. Matching your specimen with samples in a museum can be most helpful. Now look at your specimen again and compare its features with the descriptions and photographs here.

Igneous rocks of the plutonic type are illustrated here. ❶ The first sample is a typical granite. Granites always contain quartz and feldspar, and may be almost any shade of gray, brown, or red. Felsite, the second specimen, is composed mostly of feldspar, and its crystals are microscopic. All felsites have a light tone. Gabbro, the third specimen, is a dark-colored rock. Its crystals are coarse and give the rock a rough texture.

This picture is of volcanic rocks: basalt, pumice, and obsidian. ❷ Basalt is a heavy, fine-grained dark rock that may contain many holes or pockets. Pumice is very porous in appearance. It is usually pale gray and is light enough to float. Obsidian is "volcanic glass" that is usually dark brown or black. It is very hard but brittle, and it breaks easily with a shell-like fracture, yielding smooth pieces with sharp edges.

❶

❷

❸

❹

Sedimentary rocks of the clastic type are illustrated here.❸ Sandstone (at the right) is rough and gritty and is largely grains of quartz cemented together. However, as these grains are not closely packed, sandstone is porous. It may be red, white, gray, or brown. Shale (in the center) is composed of fine particles of clay. The spaces between these particles are so small that shale is nonporous. It is fairly soft, easily broken, and frequently gray in color. Conglomerate (at the left) is the most coarse-grained of all clastic rocks. It frequently contains fairly large, rounded pebbles cemented in a mass of sand grains.

Limestone, which is organic or chemical in origin, is at the left.❹ It may have various colors, depending on the shells or particles from which it formed. It has a dense appearance, is smooth when touched, and reacts to hydrochloric acid. Coquina (at the right) has an organic origin. In coquina, bits and fragments of animal shells are cemented together but rather loosely packed. Individual shell fragments are often still distinct.

Metamorphic rocks of the unfoliated type are illustrated here.❺ Marble (at the left) is some type of metamorphosed calcium carbonate. Marble is found in a range of colors; and like other calcite reacts to hydrochloric acid. Quartzite (in the center) results from the application of great heat and pressure to sandstone. It is so firmly compacted that it is among the hardest common rocks. Anthracite, or hard coal, is metamorphosed soft coal. It originated from plant life, and the carbon in anthracite gives it a black color.

Here is a group of foliated metamorphic rocks.❻ Slate (at the left) is metamorphosed shale. It may be green, red, gray, or black, and it splits into neat layers. Schist (in the center) is very highly metamorphosed shale. It is fairly easy to break, and tends to break along parallel lines. Gneiss (at the right) may be formed from many different rocks, such as granite or sandstone. The minerals in gneiss give it a typical banding of colors.

❺

❻

5. RELATING THE CONCEPTS

You have begun your study of the lithosphere, the solid layer of the earth, where matter comes in medium-sized chunks—rocks. Just as you learned about an organism by identifying the different cells that make it up, so you learned something about the surface of the earth by identifying the rocks that make it up.

A rock is made up of one or more minerals. We can tell by their appearance that many rocks, such as granites, are mixtures of several minerals; and we identify rocks by the properties of the minerals that make them up.

How do sedimentary, igneous, and metamorphic rocks form? The outline of the story is rather simple.

Sediment continually rains down on the ocean floor and sedimentary rocks form. Magma flows, pushes, and escapes, forming plutonic and volcanic igneous rocks. Sedimentary and igneous rocks metamorphose as they are crushed and chemically changed.

The formation of rocks hints of great changes taking place on and in the earth. What are these changes?

Reviewing the Concepts

► *The origins of igneous, sedimentary, and metamorphic rocks are reflected in their structure, texture, and mineral composition.* Geologists study the characteristics of rocks and the forms of the land in which rocks of different kinds are found. From these clues, geologists can determine how the rocks originate. A rock is more than a collection of minerals: every rock has a history and has undergone change. Classifying a rock as igneous, sedimentary, or metamorphic emphasizes the rock's past and helps us to understand our earth in terms of how its lithosphere came to be.

► *Igneous rock forms when magma cools and solidifies.* When heat from radioactive sources melts rock within the earth's crust and upper mantle, magma is formed. Igneous rocks of two main kinds come into being when this magma cools: plutonic igneous rocks solidify below the earth's surface, and volcanic igneous rocks solidify on the earth's surface.

► *Sedimentary rock forms when sediments of rock-forming minerals lithify.* Rocks on the earth's surface, including those at the tops of the highest mountains, continually erode. As a result, particles of sediment are produced. This sediment consists of tiny chips of old rocks. After it is transported into the sea, the sediment is eventually lithified (turned into rock) as its layers are pressed and cemented together.

► *Metamorphic rock forms when igneous or sedimentary rock is changed by heat and pressure.* Rock of either igneous or sedimentary origin is sometimes changed into new forms by being heated and compressed deep within the earth. Limestone, for example, can metamorphose into marble, and soft coal can metamorphose into hard coal. Changes such as these take place gradually over many millions of years.

► *Igneous, sedimentary, and metamorphic rocks are continually, though slowly, changing into one another.* This broad concept, which we have called the cycle of the rocks, expresses how the three main classes of rocks are related to each other by origin. Understanding each of the three preceding concepts, which state how rocks of each class originate, is part of understanding the rock cycle.

Testing Yourself

1. Granite is a rock, and quartz is a mineral. Using these examples, explain the difference between a rock and a mineral.

2. What classes of rock are formed in each of these ways?

a. Liquid rock cools and solidifies.
b. Particles are compacted and cemented together.
c. Pre-existing rock is changed by heat and pressure.

3. What is the difference between magma and lava?

4. How are limestone and coal different from clastic sedimentary rock?

5. Describe how fossils can come to be found in sedimentary rock.

6. What is the difference between a froth, a glass, a fine-grained rock, and a coarse-grained rock?

7. Rock 13, brought back from the moon, appears to be a breccia. What is a breccia?

8. Name the minerals that are commonly found in most igneous rocks.

9. Describe one type of organic sedimentary rock.

Extending the Concepts

Investigation 1. What substances are in sandstone? Collect one or more samples of sandstone and devise a method of separating the particles of which it is composed. Compare them for physical characteristics such as shape, size, and color. Plan a procedure for identifying the kinds of particles.

Investigation 2. Undertake a detailed investigation of rocks. You might start a life-long hobby by preparing a rock collection. Where will you collect your specimens? How will you obtain and identify them?

Roadcuts, quarries, mine dumps, excavations, hills, mountains, and streams usually offer good opportunities for collecting. But go only where you are permitted to go and where it is safe.

Determine the size of specimen that will best serve your purpose. Pieces that measure 5 to 10 centimeters (2 to 4 inches) are practical, but smaller pieces can be useful, too. Select a fresh-looking surface. If you use your hammer and chisel (remember to protect your eyes), you can cut to size a specimen that will have at least one fresh, clean surface.

Record in your notebook information about the specimen such as date found, where, under what conditions. Give your notebook entry a number, and label your specimen to match the number of the notebook entry. It is most important to get *all* the information you will need at the time you find the specimen because you may never return to that particular spot.

Store your specimens in such a way that you can get at each one when you want to. Display a specimen so that its best qualities are emphasized and clearly visible. Obtain reference books that will help you identify specimens. You may want to buy books you find most helpful. A few useful books are listed at the end of this section.

Suggested Reading

Deeson, A. F. L. (editor), *The Collector's Encyclopedia of Rocks and Minerals*, New York, Crown, 1973.

Fenton, C. L., and M. A. Fenton, *The Rock Book*, New York, Doubleday, 1940.

Zim, Herbert, and Paul Shaffer, *Rocks and Minerals*, New York, Golden Press, 1957.

See also the Suggested Reading for Chapter 3.

Unit Two
THE EARTH'S LAND

As you stand at the rim of the Grand Canyon and look down, you see a truly magnificent sight—layers upon layers of rock, in many hues and colors, in an array of patterns, forming an enormously deep canyon.

When you look at the rock at the bottom of the canyon, you are looking at rock more than 100,000,000 years old. Then, if you look slowly back up to the top, you are "reading" part of the long history of the earth.

How did the Grand Canyon form? What forces change the face of the earth? Let's see.

5

The Restless Earth

About 1,900 years ago a Roman named Seneca described the interior of the earth as people then believed it to be. ❶

"Be assured," Seneca wrote, "that there exists below [the surface of the earth], everything that you see above. There are vast caverns, immense recesses, and vacant spaces with mountains overhanging on either hand. There are yawning gulfs, stretching down into the abyss, which have often swallowed up cities that have fallen into them. These retreats are filled with air, for nowhere is there a vacuum in nature; through their ample spaces stretch marshes over which darkness ever broods. Animals are also produced in them, but they are slow-paced and shapeless. . . ." Sometimes the air in these "dark and clammy" caverns inside the earth rushed about with great violence, and was the cause of earthquakes, Seneca wrote.

People believed in this picture of the interior of the earth for many centuries after Seneca. Today, as you know, we have a rather different picture—but not because we have

❶

penetrated into the earth's interior. The deepest hole we have drilled has reached down only a few kilometers: the distance to the center of the earth is about 6,700 kilometers (4,000 miles).

We have barely scratched the surface of our planet. However, scientists have managed to collect some indirect evidence as to what is inside the earth. Let's look at some of this indirect evidence and what it suggests about the inside of this planet.

1. THE LITHOSPHERE AND BELOW

From where you are now, it is about 6,700 kilometers (4,000 miles) to the center of the earth, straight down. Unless you happen to be located on bare rock, there is some soil under you and around you. Important as soil is to us, it is hardly worth mentioning here. Soil is usually not more than 6 meters (20 feet) deep, and much less than that on the average. It is hardly a layer of dust on this planet, so to speak.

Dig down through the soil, where there is any, and you will sooner or later hit solid rock —the **bedrock** that lies below the soil. You might think, when this happens, that you have now reached the very stuff of which our planet is made. But not so. This hard bedrock is only a skin, somewhat like the skin on an orange. However, the earth's skin is considerably thinner than an orange's skin, size for size. This skin is called the earth's **crust.** 2

The crust is no more than 67 kilometers (40 miles) thick at most, and only 5 or 6 kilometers (3 or 4 miles) thick in some spots. In general, the crust is thickest under continents and thinnest under seas. It is made up of rock of various kinds.

What's underneath the hard, thin crust? The evidence at hand suggests that below the

2

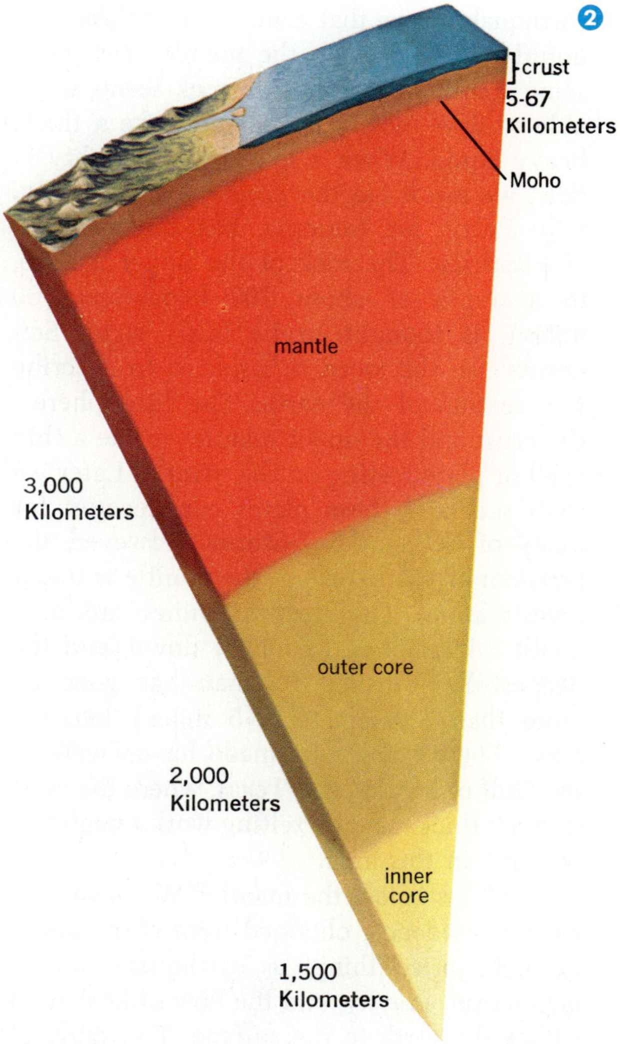

crust is a layer of the earth where the rock has some properties of a solid but can also bend or flow. This layer is called the **mantle.** 2

Notice the line labeled "Moho" between the lithosphere and the mantle. The Moho is not a layer: it is the boundary where the crust ends and the mantle begins. It was named after its discoverer, the Yugoslavian scientist Andrija Mohorovicic.

The mantle is about 3,000 kilometers (1,800 miles) thick. It is certainly solid, for a kind of earthquake wave that cannot travel through a liquid travels through the mantle. Yet under some conditions the mantle rock seems to be able to flow—slowly, to be sure—like a thick, heavy liquid. When a solid has the ability to flow, we say it has the property of **plasticity.** Silly Putty, for example, has the property of plasticity. The rock of the upper mantle, to a depth of about 100 kilometers (60 miles), is thought to be fairly rigid. Scientists use the word *lithosphere* to describe this section of the earth. The lithosphere—the crust and the upper mantle—is like a thin shell or plate resting on the mantle. Later we shall see how these plates can account for many of the earth's features. However, the problem of the nature of the mantle is under investigation. The deepest mines are only about 3 kilometers (2 miles) down, and the deepest hole drilled by man has gone no more than 8 kilometers (5 miles) into the crust. These holes were made for oil wells in the Gulf of Mexico and Texas, where the crust is quick thick. Much exciting work remains to be done in this area.

What lies below the mantle? We have only indirect evidence, obtained from observations of such varied things as earthquake waves, magnetism, gravity, and the flow of heat from within the earth to the surface. The study of earthquake waves, for example, provides information about the density of the matter deep in the earth. The overall density of the interior of the earth is about 5.5 g/cc. This is an average, however; the density varies at different depths. Moreover, the density varies in such a way that we know there are layers inside the earth.

Since the density of the earth's interior varies in this way, we conclude that below the mantle there must be a different substance, forming what we call the **core** of the earth.

DENSITIES AT VARIOUS DEPTHS WITHIN THE EARTH

Approximate depth in kilometers	*Average density in grams per cubic centimeter*	*Layer*
5 to 67	2.7	crust
67 to 3000	5.5	mantle
3000 to 5000	10.0	outer core
5000 to 7000	14.5 or more	inner core

The outer core, about 2,000 kilometers (1,300 miles) thick, may be mainly iron. The inner core, with a radius of about 1,500 kilometers (900 miles), has an even higher density than the outer core: The inner core may be iron mixed with some nickel and cobalt. This kind of core would also agree with the earth's magnetism. But the pressure in the core must be tremendous.

So far we have had to rely on indirect evidence about the nature of the earth's interior. The study of earthquakes provides much of this evidence. Let's see what earthquakes tell us about the earth.

REVIEW

1. Name the layers of the earth's interior and briefly describe each layer.

2. What is meant by plasticity? Which layer of the earth's interior has this property?

3. Is the density of the earth uniform? If not, how does it vary?

4. What evidence do we have for our model of the earth?

NEW VIEW

1. In about 200 B.C., the Greek philosopher Eratosthenes determined that the circumference of the earth was about 40,000 kilometers (25,000 miles). Using his calculations, find the distance from the surface of the earth to the center. Compare this figure with present-day values.

2. How have scientists determined the thicknesses of the layers of the earth?

2. THE EARTH QUAKES

"The mountains seemed to walk," wrote an eye-witness of the great earthquake in the Shenshi province of China. The year was 1556. Whole villages, and with them over 800,000 people, were buried. Since man first began to record his history there have been many stories of disastrous earthquakes.

Big earthquakes have occurred recently. The San Francisco quake of 1906, the Anchorage, Alaska quake of 1964, the Managua, Nicaragua quake of 1972, were among the most destructive earthquakes of this century.

Most earthquakes, however, are not major disasters. Over the earth there is, somewhere, an earthquake every few minutes. Many of them occur in places like New England, but they do not even rattle a glass on a table. If these gentle earthquakes can't even be felt, how do we know they occur?

Detecting Earthquakes

Scientists have invented delicate instruments able to respond to even the slightest movement within the crust of the earth. The most common type of earthquake detection depends on one of Newton's laws of motion, the law of inertia. Let's see how.

Suppose you hang a lead weight on the end of a string about 60 centimeters (2 feet) long. Attach the string to a support and you have a pendulum.(1) If you now jerk the base of the support quickly across the table, you will observe that the weight remains fixed. We may explain what happens this way. According to the law of inertia, an object at rest tends to remain at rest. Due to its inertia, the weighted pendulum, which is at rest, tends to stand still when the base is jerked beneath it.

1

The instrument used to detect vibrations in the earth has a pendulum that works on the same principle. This time, however, the pendulum is mounted horizontally, and there is a pen attached to the weight.(2) We call this instrument a **seismograph.**

2

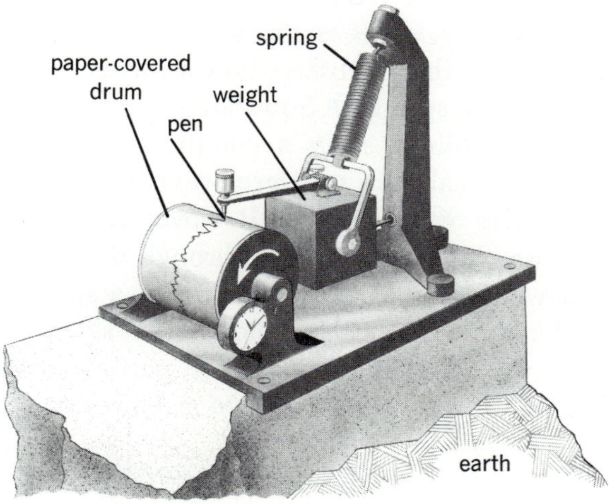

1

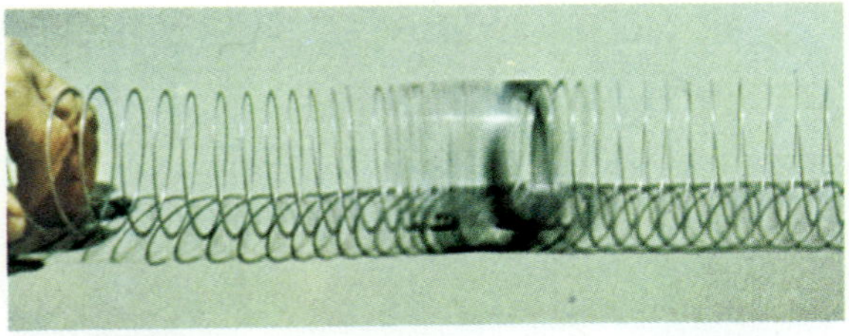

When the earth vibrates, the base of the seismograph moves from side to side, but the weight stands still. If both the earth and the weight are still, the pen writes a continuous straight line on a paper-covered drum. If the earth (and the drum with it) vibrates, the stationary pen makes a more or less wiggly line, depending on the strength of the vibrations.

Studying the lines made by seismographs, scientists have discovered that movements in the earth's crust produce several kinds of waves. These waves are called **seismic waves.** You have seen (in the picture of the seismograph) the kind of record that seismic waves make on a seismograph. You cannot see the waves themselves, but you can investigate them with models.

Seismic Waves

Suppose you lay a Slinky spring straight out on the floor. While a friend holds one end of the Slinky, squeeze together several coils; then release them. Observe how a wave travels through the spring. 1 Squeezing some of the coils in a Slinky starts a compression wave, sometimes called a **pressure wave.**

Pressure waves, called P waves for short by seismologists, can move through the earth somewhat the way they do through a spring.

Think of the earth's solid matter as composed of particles. Suppose the particles are spaced like this before a wave arrives.

As a P wave passes through, the particles are squeezed together and pushed apart.

Sound energy is also carried by compression waves. Sound, like P waves, travels especially well through solid materials. (Just put your ear to the wall while a friend taps a message from the other end of the room, and you will see how readily sound waves move through a solid.)

The number of vibrations per second is the **frequency** of a compression wave. Sound waves have frequencies that range from about 20 to 20,000 vibrations per second. This, then, is the difference between P waves and sound waves: unlike sound waves, P waves move with frequencies usually only about 2 or 3 times per second, frequencies much too low to be heard.

P waves of unusually low frequency, one vibration in 20 to 54 minutes, were discovered by the use of very delicate new seismographs during the Chilean earthquake of 1960. During these waves, the whole earth vibrates, "ringing" like a bell at about 20 octaves below middle C. This is, of course, far too low to hear. Nor would you feel the vibrations from these waves, since they barely move the surface of the ground. But seismographs show that the waves continue for weeks after a major quake.

Another kind of earthquake wave behaves differently from a P wave. This is a seismic wave called a **shear wave,** or S wave, for short. Shear waves twist, shake, and distort solid substances as they pass through. Suppose that before an S wave passes through, the particles of earth are arranged like this.

An S wave causes the particles to slide past each other crosswise.

One difference, then, between P waves and S waves is in the way they affect the material they pass through. P waves compress, and S waves twist.

Another difference between P waves and S waves is their speed. P waves travel faster from their source than S waves do. When a movement in the rocks occurs somewhere on earth, P waves and S waves are both produced. At a seismograph some distance away from the source of a quake, the P waves are detected first. The S waves, traveling more slowly, come later. Because of the difference in their speeds and arrival times, P waves are sometimes called "primary waves" and S waves are called "secondary waves."

All over the earth, seismographic stations keep their instruments operating all the time. By timing the arrival of P waves and S waves, scientists at each station can determine the distance of their station from the source of any earthquake. This distance is used as the radius of a circle around the station on a map of the world. By comparing the distance from several seismographic stations, seismologists are able to locate the earthquake's center. 2

Seismic Studies of the Earth's Interior

From the way in which seismic waves travel through different substances, scientists have learned a great deal about the nature of the inside of the earth itself. Careful measurement with sensitive instruments has shown that P waves travel through solids, liquids, and

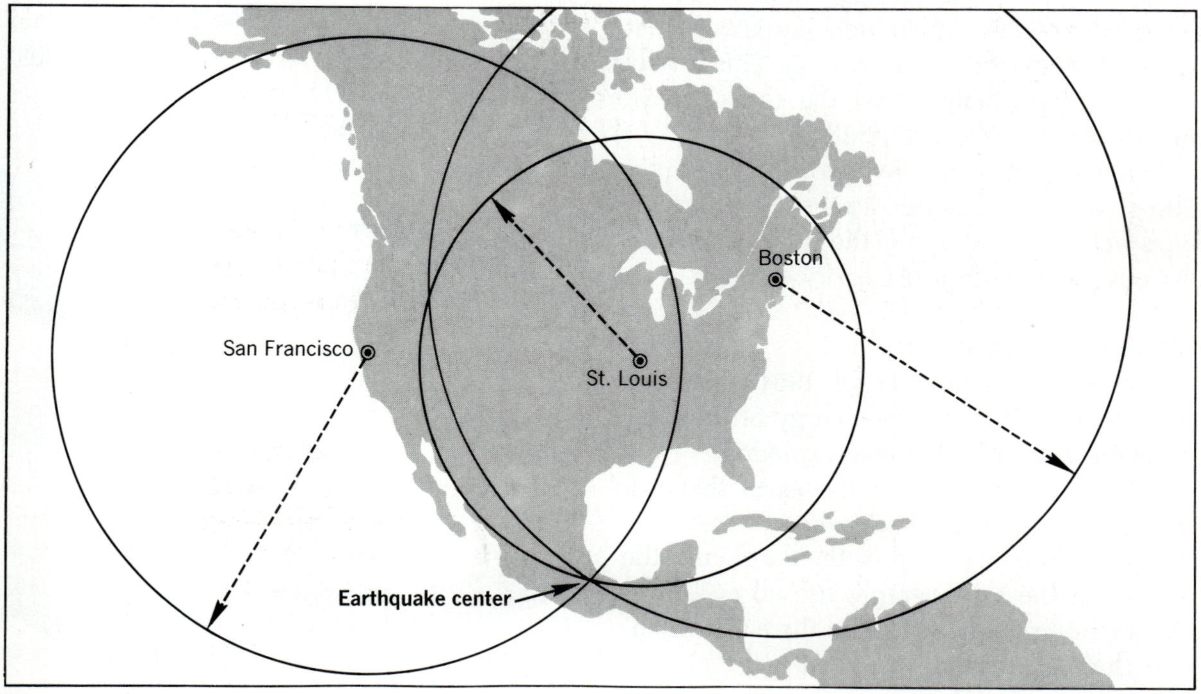

2

1

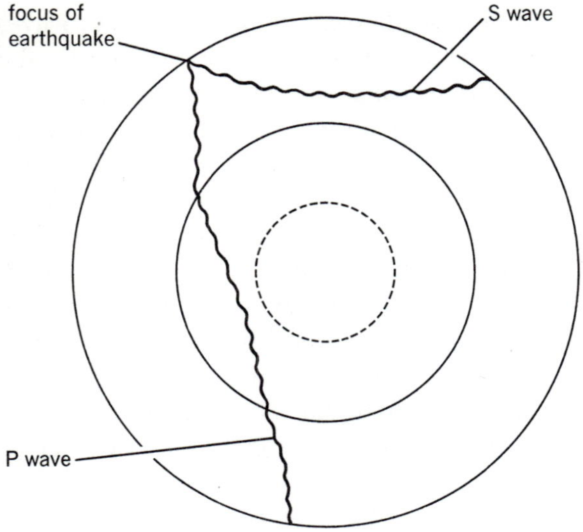

gases; S waves travel only through solids or very dense, glassy liquids.

By studying the way in which S waves and P waves are received at stations around the globe during strong earthquakes, seismologists have collected evidence that S waves, which do not travel through liquids, do not travel through the earth's core. (1) This is why some scientists believe that the core, at least in its outer portion, is liquidlike.

The patterns made by earthquake waves also give evidence of the depths of the borderlines between layers and the densities of the various layers within the earth.

Faults in the Rock

The Alaska earthquake of 1964 unleashed more than 2,000 times the energy of the most powerful nuclear bomb ever exploded!

What are the forces in the earth that can produce such tremendous energy? The rumbling and bursting open of the earth, and the records of the seismographs are all evidences of something going on within the earth whenever there is a quake. Just what is it that happens? Scientists do not all agree on a theory, but in the main this is what they think.

When rocks in the earth's crust are subjected to pressure, they tend to bend under the strain. There is a limit, however, to how far the earth's rock layers can bend before they break. Great pressure from the weight of overlying rock, or from the push of magma from below, can produce a crack known as a **fault** in layers of rock. (2) Faulting sets the stage for the slippage of rocks that starts earthquakes. For example, studies of the San

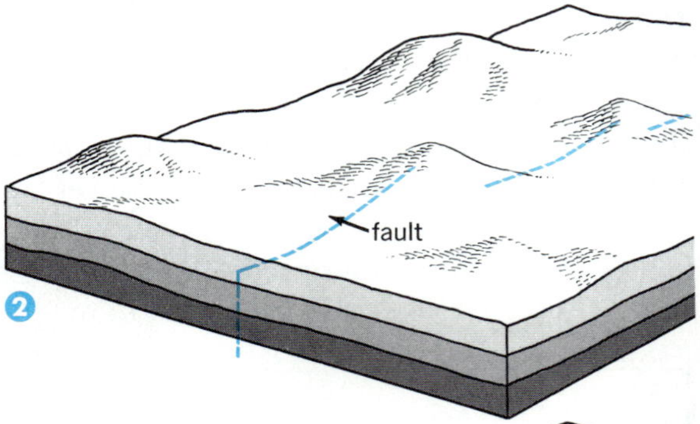

2

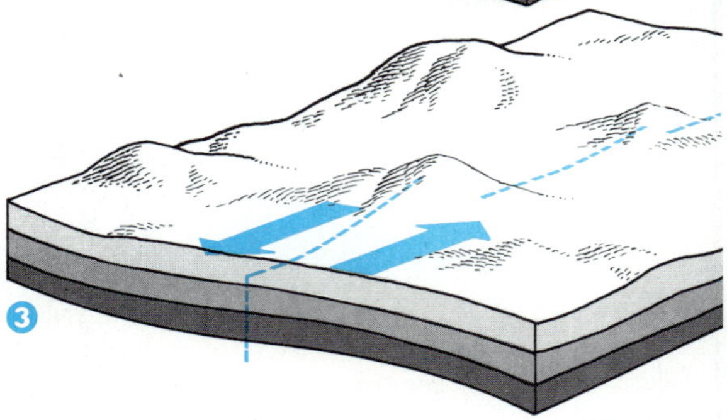

3

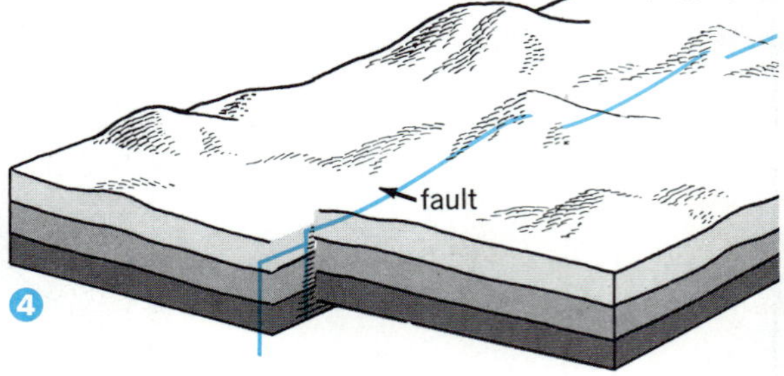

4

Andreas fault in California, where many quakes occur, provide evidence for a relationship between faulting and earthquakes.

For some time before a quake, the pressure within the earth builds up strain in the rock on either side of a fault. ③ Energy is stored somewhat the way it is in a coiled spring. If the tension on the spring is relaxed, the spring rebounds, releasing the stored energy.

In a similar way, tension is relaxed when rock finally yields to the strain along a fault and breaks. ④ The movement of snapping back, the rock's rebound, releases stored energy. This energy is transformed into shock waves or vibrations, P and S waves, and other kinds of seismic waves.

If the rocks shift under the ocean floor during an earthquake, large ocean waves may be produced. These are called seismic sea waves, or **tsunamis** (tsōō·näm'ēz), which you will study more about in Chapter 12. If the earthquake occurs under the shallower parts of the ocean that extend far out from the shore, the sediment there may be loosened. The sediment may then flow rapidly downward toward the deep ocean floor. The sediment flows in deep channels, just like the channels of streams on land. These channels are called **submarine canyons.** The sediment flows very rapidly, and it can widen and deepen the submarine canyons or make new ones. These flows have been known to cut through underwater telephone and telegraph cables that lie in their path.

Perhaps you have heard that earthquakes and volcanic eruptions sometimes happen together. This suggests that their causes are somehow related. It is true that both earthquakes and volcanoes are usually located in the same "belt," as you can see on the map. ⑤

⑤

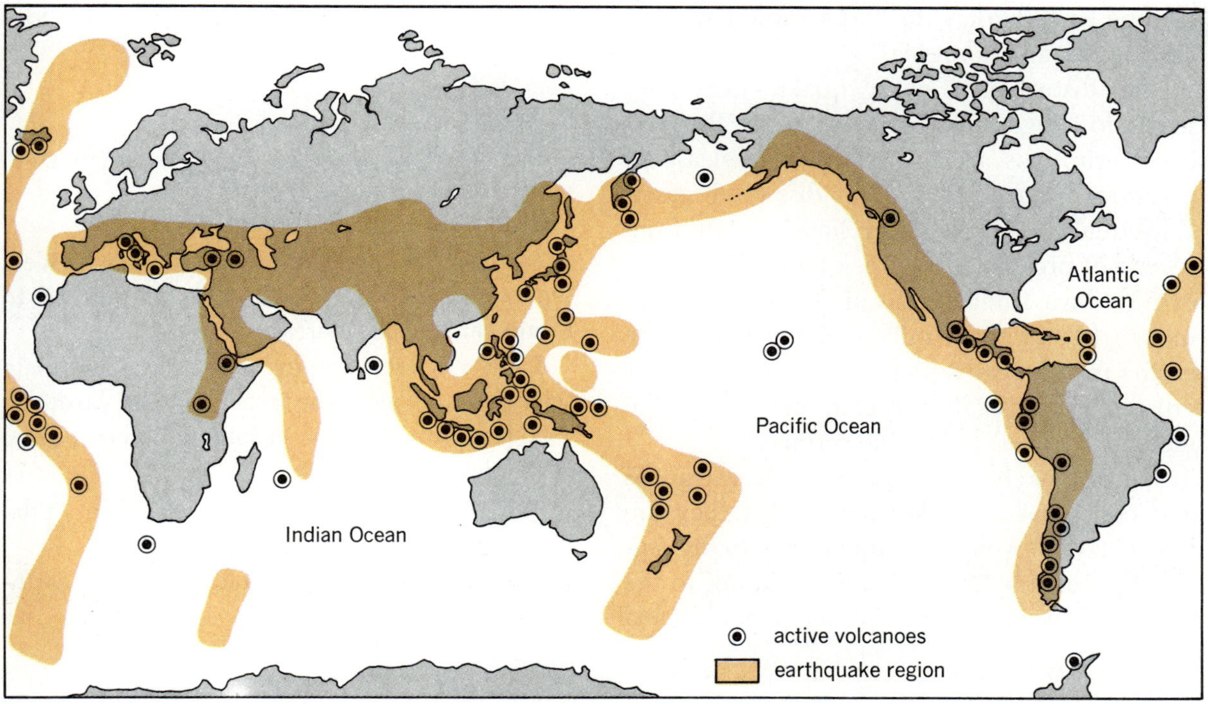

1

Notice that the belt is made up of two zones. Because of the frequency of earth movements, these areas are known as **mobile zones.** The main mobile zone, the Circum-Pacific Belt, almost surrounds the Pacific Ocean. Most major earthquakes occur here. The same region has been called the "circle of fire" because of its numerous volcanoes. Another mobile zone, the Mediterranean Belt, extends from Europe and Turkey to India, and joins the Pacific Belt in Indonesia.

The disturbance of a quake sometimes seems to trigger a volcanic eruption. But volcanic eruptions are caused by the release of pressure on magma and its dissolved gases. Earthquakes, on the other hand, result from release of pressure along rock faults. Volcanoes extrude lava from depths of 67 or more kilometers (40 or more miles), down within the earth's mantle; earthquakes occur in the earth's crust and are usually centered less than 8 kilometers (5 miles) below the surface.

We are likely to think of both volcanoes and earthquakes as destructive, yet they are beneficial as well. Volcanoes eventually enrich the earth by bringing new minerals to the surface. Volcanic earth, formed from eroded lava, is usually very rich in minerals needed for plant growth. In Hawaii, for example, the soil is enriched by volcanic materials. 1 Earthquakes may also bring valuable minerals to the surface as shifting ground exposes new rocks.

Very little is known yet about the earth's interior. The study of earthquake waves gives us information. A study of the heat that flows from the earth, as we shall see, provides another source of information.

REVIEW

1. What do P waves and S waves have in common? How are they different?
2. Explain how a seismograph operates.
3. Make a simple diagram to show how widely separated seismological stations work together to locate earthquake sources.
4. How does the study of seismic waves help scientists to explore the interior of the earth?
5. How are volcanic eruptions different from earthquakes?
6. A tsunami is sometimes called a "tidal wave." Why is this name misleading?
7. In what ways are volcanoes and earthquakes beneficial to man?

NEW VIEW

1. Man has not yet learned how to predict earthquakes, but the time of the arrival of seismic sea waves in Hawaii can often be determined several hours in advance. How is this possible?

2. One of the first instruments that man landed on the moon was a seismograph. What was it to tell us about the moon?

3. From recent newspaper and magazine accounts of moon exploration, find out what evidence there is (if any) of volcanic activity on the moon.

4. Earthquakes differ greatly in intensity. Find out how seismologists rate earthquakes on intensity scales.

3. THE EARTH'S NUCLEAR FURNACE

As every spelunker (cave explorer) knows, it is not usually warm just below the earth's surface. On a hot summer day it may even be refreshingly cool in a cave a few meters underground. If the spelunker goes deeper underground, however, he will begin to notice a rise in temperature, whatever the temperature at the surface may be; and the deeper he goes, the warmer it gets. This means that in a shaft 2 kilometers deep the temperature may well be 82°C. You can see why powerful cooling and ventilating fans are used in mines. But where does the heat come from?

Heating the Earth's Interior

Can the source of this heat within the earth's crust be the sun? Think a moment about the spelunker in the cave. If soil and rock carried the sun's heat into the crust from the surface, he would find caves just below the surface to be about as warm as the surface. He would find the temperature decreasing as he went further below the surface. But this is not what happens. Therefore it cannot be the sun that warms the interior of the earth. It must be some kind of "furnace" within the earth.

Here is another bit of evidence that the earth has an internal furnace. When a volcano erupts, molten rock may pour out. This molten rock, or lava, may be as hot as 1,100°C. The lava is formed at the lower part of the crust, and the upper part of the mantle, from solid rock. Where does the great heat needed to melt this rock come from? There must be heat inside the earth. But what is the source of this heat?

One answer to this question begins by assuming that when the earth was formed it was very hot and completely molten. It has cooled enough from the outside to become solid, but still has some of its original heat inside. This hypothesis was widely believed for a time, but most scientists no longer accept it. Why? Assume that the earth is at least 5 billion years old. (There is a good deal of evidence for this assumption, as you will see later.) If the earth were completely molten to begin with, calculations show that by now it would be far colder than it actually is. The evidence is against the old hypothesis.

What is the source of the heat within the earth, then? Most scientists now accept the hypothesis that this heat is being produced by certain kinds of atoms that are breaking down within the earth and radiating energy as they do so. This energy is the source of heat for the earth's furnace.

Energy from an Atom's Nucleus

Certain elements give off radiation. It is the breaking down of the nucleus that releases the radiation. Elements whose atoms change in this mysterious fashion are radioactive. We say mysterious, for we do not know what makes a particular atom's nucleus break apart, or **decay.** Nor do we know anything that affects the rate at which decay takes place in a group of such atoms.

When radioactive elements deep within the earth decay, part of the radiation they give off is in the form of heat, and a part is converted into heat as the radiation is absorbed by the substance around it. Of course the amount of heat produced by a decaying nucleus in this way is small indeed. It does add up, however, as billions of atoms decay over billions of years.

What is this radiation like? One of the first things observed was that it seemed to be of three kinds. At the beginning of the twentieth century, an English scientist, Ernest Rutherford, gave them the names alpha, beta, and gamma radiation, using the first three letters in the Greek alphabet. The original names that Rutherford chose have stuck, even though scientists now know what these radiations really are.

Alpha radiation is a stream of particles, called alpha particles. An alpha particle is composed of 2 protons and 2 neutrons. Since a proton has a positive charge, and a neutron has no charge, the alpha particle is positively charged.

alpha particle

Beta radiation is a stream of particles too. A beta particle is a high-speed electron. Like other electrons, a beta particle has a negative charge. Unlike other electrons, a beta particle does not come from the outer shell of electrons in an atom: A beta particle comes from the nucleus of an atom.

This is strange. A nucleus ordinarily contains protons and neutrons but no electrons. Somehow, when the nucleus of a radioactive atom decays, it seems as if a neutron might break down into a proton and an electron. The electron formed is then shot forth from the nucleus as a beta particle—or so it would appear at present.

As some kinds of atomic nuclei decay they throw off **gamma radiation** along with alpha and beta particles. Gamma radiation is a form of energy similar to X rays. Both gamma radiation and X rays are very penetrating forms of energy. However, sooner or later gamma radiation is absorbed by the substance through which it is traveling, if there is enough of the substance. When this happens, the gamma radiation is converted into heat.

When either an alpha or a beta particle is thrown out of a decaying nucleus, a tiny bit of the mass of the nucleus is changed into energy. The amount of energy can be determined from the equation, $E = mc^2$. The energy is given off partly as motion of the particles hurtling out of the radioactive atom, and partly as heat and other radiations.

There are, then, three kinds of radiation that come from radioactive atoms.

Kind of radiation	*Composition*
alpha particle	2 protons + 2 neutrons
beta particle	1 electron
gamma radiation	radiant energy

It is the decay of the nuclei of radioactive elements that produces heat in the mantle and crust of the earth. This heat helps warm the oceans, causes volcanoes to erupt, and even helps to raise mountains, as you will learn later on.

Radioactivity and Isotopes

To understand what goes on in a radioactive atom when it decays, let's look at a model of an atom again. As we saw in Chapter 2, a diagram of any atom can be made if the number of protons, neutrons, and electrons in the atom is known. Let's take the element potassium.

Most atoms of potassium have 19 protons, 19 electrons, and 20 neutrons. The mass number (the number of protons and neutrons) is 39. Potassium-39, however, is not the only isotope of potassium. Another isotope of potassium has 19 protons, 19 electrons, and 21 neutrons; it is potassium-40. Here are diagrams of both isotopes. ❶ Notice once again that isotopes of the same element differ only in the number of neutrons in the nucleus.

Chemically speaking, isotopes behave alike. Their only difference is in their weight. However, it turns out that some isotopes are radioactive: their nuclei decay. Other isotopes are not radioactive: their nuclei are **stable,** that is, they do not break down. To give you some idea of the variety of isotopes, radioactive and stable, there are some examples in the table on the next page. Almost every element has at least two isotopes, although some isotopes are very unstable and decay very quickly. The time it takes for *half* of the atoms in a sample to decay is called the **half-life** of that substance.

Now consider the element uranium. There are 14 isotopes of uranium; that is, there are 14 different kinds of uranium nuclei, the differences between them being the number of neutrons in each. Three of these are listed in the table. Each of these three (and the other eleven, too) has the same number of protons, 92. But one uranium isotope has 143 neutrons, which makes its mass number 235. We name it uranium-235. Another uranium isotope has

❶

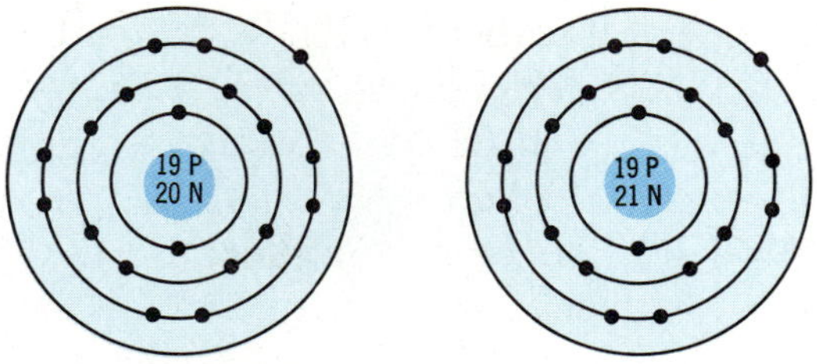

potassium-39 potassium-40

146 neutrons, which makes it uranium-238. The third uranium isotope listed has 147 neutrons and is uranium-239.

Changing the number of neutrons changes the mass number (and the weight) of the atom—but it is still the same element. Changing the number of protons, however, makes a different element. If you could manage to take away 2 of the 92 protons in a uranium nucleus, you would have a different element, thorium, which has 90 protons.

Notice that all of the isotopes of uranium listed in the table happen to be radioactive. And so are all the other uranium isotopes. This is true for only a few elements, however. Most elements have one or more stable, or nonradioactive, isotopes.

However, we are interested in the radioactive isotopes, the fuel for the earth's internal furnace. Let's see what goes on when a radioactive isotope decays. If your teacher has a cloud chamber available, you can actually observe this process. ❷

❷

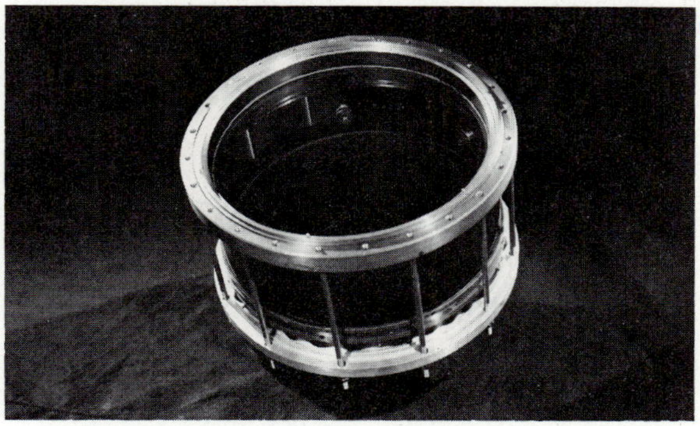

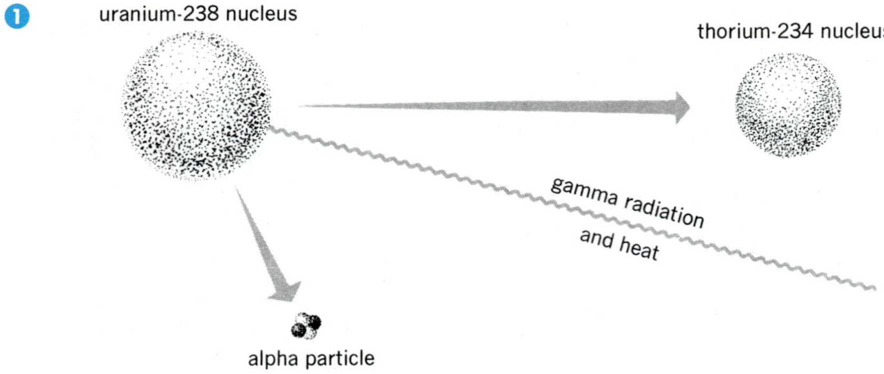

The Decay of Radioactive Isotopes

In the nucleus of uranium-238 there are 92 protons and 146 neutrons. What happens to them when, for reasons unknown, the nucleus suddenly comes apart? Here is what happens when a uranium-238 nucleus decays. 1

As the uranium-238 nucleus decays, it gives off an alpha particle. The alpha particle takes 2 protons and 2 neutrons from the nucleus. What is left, then, is a nucleus containing 90 protons and 144 neutrons—and this is no longer a nucleus of uranium. It is the nucleus of an atom of a different element, thorium. It is the nucleus of the isotope of thorium known as thorium-234. Thus, when uranium atoms decay, they not only give off alpha particles, heat, and gamma radiation, they turn into atoms of another element.

SOME ISOTOPES OF SOME ELEMENTS

Name of isotope	*Number of protons*	*Number of neutrons*	*Number of electrons*	*Mass number*	*Stable or radioactive*
hydrogen-1	1	0	1	1	stable
hydrogen-2	1	1	1	2	stable
hydrogen-3	1	2	1	3	radioactive
carbon-12	6	6	6	12	stable
carbon-14	6	8	6	14	radioactive
potassium-39	19	20	19	39	stable
potassium-40	19	21	19	40	radioactive
thorium-230	90	140	90	230	radioactive
thorium-234	90	144	90	234	radioactive
radium-222	88	134	88	222	radioactive
radium-226	88	138	88	226	radioactive
uranium-235	92	143	92	235	radioactive
uranium-238	92	146	92	238	radioactive
uranium-239	92	147	92	239	radioactive
lead-204	82	122	82	204	stable
lead-206	82	124	82	206	stable
lead-208	82	126	82	208	stable

Decay does not stop here. The thorium-234 decays. In fact a long and complex chain of radioactive breakdowns follows. The radioactive decay ends when an atom of lead-206 is formed. This isotope is stable.

The amount of heat given off by one decaying atom is unimaginably small, to be sure. But there are billions of radioactive atoms in rock, and the rock in which decaying atoms are locked does not carry the heat away readily. Rock is a poor conductor of heat, and so the heat builds up within the earth's crust and mantle. Thus, in time, enough heat can collect to account for the earth's warming from within.

Men have believed since ancient times that there was a fire in the center of the earth. (How else were volcanoes to be accounted for?) As to what kind of fire it was, men invented some strange hypotheses. Yet perhaps none of these hypotheses was so strange as what does produce heat within the earth: the sudden, unexplained, and unpredictable breakdown of the nuclei of atoms.

REVIEW

1. What are the major differences between an alpha particle and a beta particle?

2. How does gamma radiation differ from beta radiation?

3. How do we account for the heat in the mantle and crust?

4. What is meant by the isotopes of an element?

5. What is the distinction between a stable isotope of an element and a radioactive isotope?

NEW VIEW

1. What is the difference in the cause of heat on the sun and within the earth's crust?

2. What is the similarity in the cause of heat on the sun and within the earth's crust?

4. MAGNETISM—ANOTHER CLUE

You are familiar with the shape of the magnetic field of a bar magnet. You also know that the earth has a magnetic field. The earth acts like a huge magnet with its magnetic poles located near the North and South Poles. The earth's magnetic field extends through the earth and far out into the atmosphere. The region in space that encloses this field, recall, is the magnetosphere.

How does the earth's magnetic field affect the earth's material? When we answer this question, we will have another clue to the earth's interior.

Paleomagnetism

One of the newest fields in the study of the earth is **paleomagnetism,** or the study of "early magnetism" in the rocks of the earth. You know that iron is magnetic, and that rocks containing iron-rich minerals are also magnetic.

When these rocks were formed, the iron-rich minerals aligned themselves with the direction of the earth's magnetic field. Or we could say the direction of the magnetic field was "frozen" into the rocks. If the rock mass, or even the entire continent, moved after the rocks were formed, the direction of the magnetic field "frozen" into the rocks moved with them.

From the direction of these magnetic fields, scientists have attempted to reconstruct the previous location of the earth's magnetic poles. Strangely enough, *the rocks of the same age* on the various continents do not point to the same location. Therefore, geologists reason, it appears that the continents changed their positions with respect to each other after these early rocks were formed. The continents have moved! This evidence from paleomagnetism supports a theory that was suggested many years ago—the theory of continental drift.

Continental Drift

A map of the ocean floor of the North Atlantic region appears on pages 244 and 245. Study this map. Observe that there is a kind of groove along the Mid-Atlantic Ridge. This groove is a steep-walled valley that runs along the top of the ridge, a valley 30 to 50 kilometers (20 to 30 miles) wide and as much as 1,800 meters (6,000 feet) below the mountain tops on each side. What could account for such a valley? In an attempt to answer this question, scientists have considered several theories of the origin of the continents and the ocean floor.

Much of the discussion has been about the theory of **continental drift**—the theory that the continents were originally joined together and in time past broke up and slowly drifted apart. This theory of continental drift, or the idea that the continents have not always been in the same relative position and same distance from each other, was developed in detail by Alfred Wegener of Germany around 1915. A few years before he had been studying a map of the world. He was impressed by the fact that because of the shapes of their coastlines, the continents bordering the Atlantic Ocean seemed to fit together like the pieces in a jigsaw puzzle. Wegener also knew that fossils of closely related plants as well as animals were found on the southern continents. Wegener believed that the separation or drifting of continents away from one another sometime in the past explained why similar fossils were found on the continents separated by vast areas of ocean water.

Wegener's earliest theory of continental drift assumed that all land masses had once been connected to form a supercontinent, which he called Pangaea. Later he revised his theory to suggest that there were originally two supercontinents, Laurasia (Europe, Asia, and North America) and Gondwanaland

1

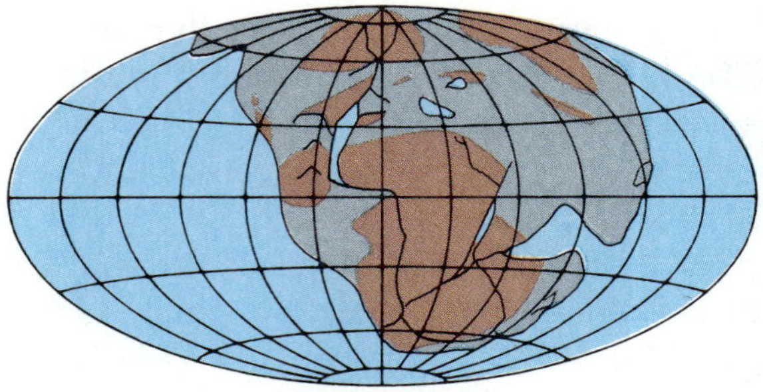

GONDWANALAND

(Africa, Australia, India, Antarctica, and South America). Now study Wegener's map of the world for 300 million years ago. 1 The areas in brown are land masses, the areas in gray-blue are land masses once covered by shallow seas, and the areas in blue are, of course, the oceans.

Wegener was convinced that the continents were moved around like giant granite "icebergs" on a "sea" of solid basalt. But he could not explain how the continental blocks, which are mainly granite, broke up and drifted over the basalt rock of the ocean crust. Yet recent data from paleomagnetism support the idea that the continents have moved. But how?

Sea-Floor Spreading

A second important fact geologists have learned about the Mid-Atlantic Ridge is that its valley walls are spreading apart very gradually. In other parts of the mid-ocean ridge system, there are many other smaller valleys that are also widening. The rate of **sea-floor spreading,** the spreading apart of the mid-ocean ridge system, is about 1 to 3.8 centimeters (0.4 to 1.5 inches) a year. Apparently, molten material from below the surface of the earth is moving into the ocean valleys, causing the ocean floor to move apart.

Evidence for this sea-floor spreading also comes from paleomagnetism. Geologists have observed a difference in the direction of the

2

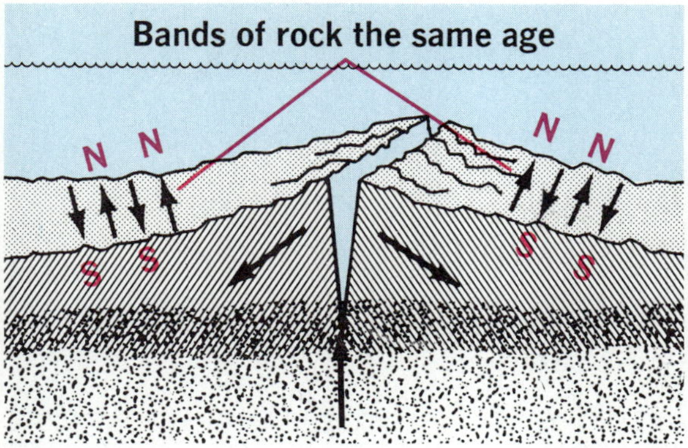

magnetic fields in minerals in basalt rock deposited *during different times* in the earth's history. Moreover, they have evidence that the earth's magnetic field has changed its direction, or reversed itself, many times in the past. Yes, the north magnetic pole has become the south magnetic pole, and vice versa, at irregular intervals many times over thousands and millions of years.

The direction of the magnetic poles is preserved in the basalt rocks as they spread out from the mid-ocean ridges. 2 Assume that two geologists could move outward in either direction along the ocean floor from the mid-ocean ridge. They would find bands of rock in which the magnetic poles were in one direction alternating with bands where the direction was reversed. By using rock-dating techniques, geologists can calculate the age of these rocks. Then, knowing the distance of these rocks from the center of the mid-ocean ridge, they can calculate the rate of sea-floor spreading.

The sea floor is spreading. Material from deep in the earth is spreading apart the valley walls of mid-ocean ridges. But if the sea floor is moving outward from the mid-ocean ridges, what is happening to the continents? Are they moving? Let's probe this question.

Rigid Pieces of Earth

Were there originally only two supercontinents? Did they separate and move apart to form the face of the earth as we know it today? We still can't answer these questions. But today many geologists believe that they have a model that can explain *how* continents can move. They call this model **plate tectonics.**

Geologists use plate tectonics to describe how the movement of pieces of the earth's crust shape the continents and the ocean basins of the earth. 3 Using this model, scientists say some startling things. The Atlantic Ocean is growing wider. The Pacific Ocean is getting

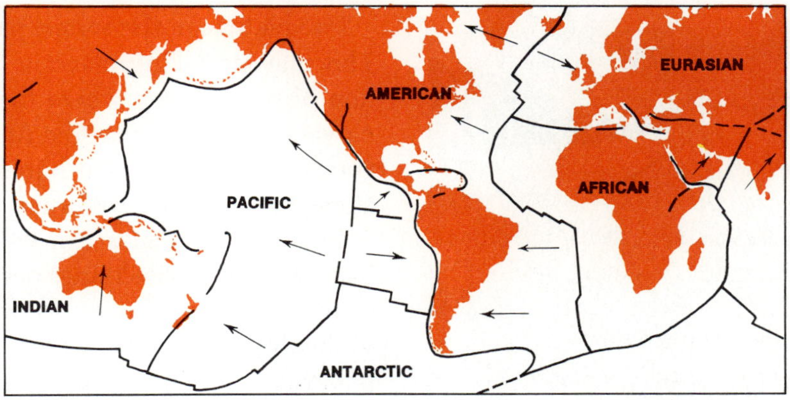

3

1 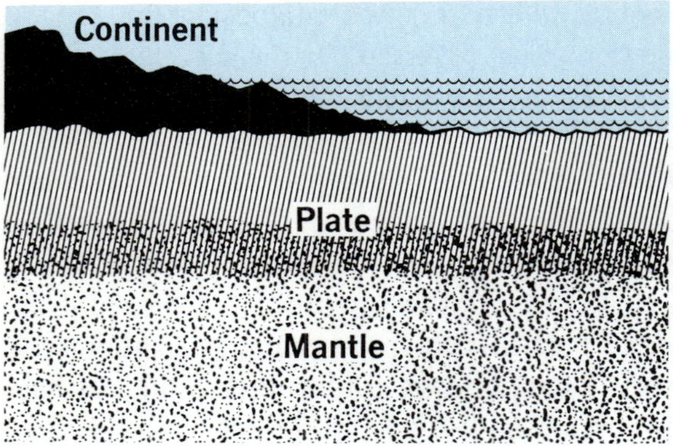

3

smaller. Los Angeles may someday be north of San Francisco! Do they have evidence for these statements? Let's see.

Picture the crust of the earth as being divided into six to eight rigid sections called **plates.** The outlines of several of these plates can be seen in the diagram on page 95. A cross section of a plate might look like this. 1 Notice that the ocean floor and rigid upper section of the mantle are components of the plate. This plate, about 100 kilometers (60 miles) thick, moves over the "plastic" mantle. Recall that this section of the earth is called the lithosphere. It is the lithosphere that is divided into several plates. The continents are carried along, much like passengers, on the backs of the moving plates.

2 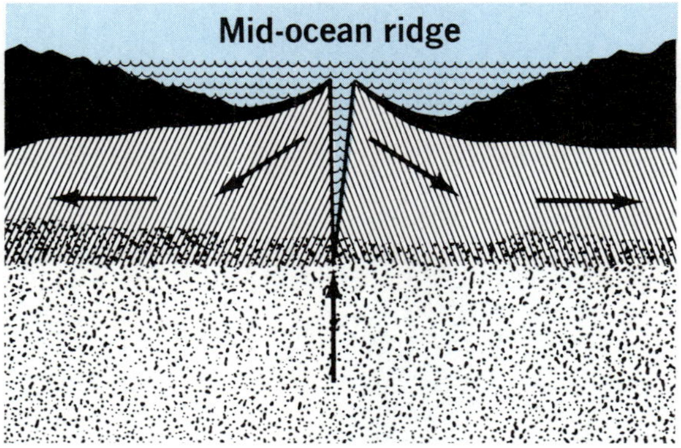

In what ways can these plates move? Let's see what would happen if they do move. Two plates can move apart from a mid-ocean ridge. 2 When this happens, volcanic material oozes up, creating a new ocean floor. In this plate tectonic model, the material added in the ocean valleys is an *effect* of plates moving apart. In the sea-floor spreading model, the material added to the ocean valleys is the *cause* of the ocean floor moving apart.

Volcanic activity and earthquakes take place in these mobile areas. Along the Mid-Atlantic Ridge, the American plate is separating from the European and Asian plates. And here we do find both volcanoes and earthquakes. In fact, the Island of Surtsey, atop the northern part of the ridge, has had a dramatic history of volcanic eruptions. 3

Two plates can also scrape past each other. 4 This may be taking place in the western section of our country where the Pacific plate is moving northward past the American plate. As you probably know, earthquakes are common along the coast of California.

Finally, two plates can collide. When this happens, one of two things occurs. If the plates come together slowly, mountains can be pushed up. Many scientists believe the Appalachian mountains were formed this way. If

4

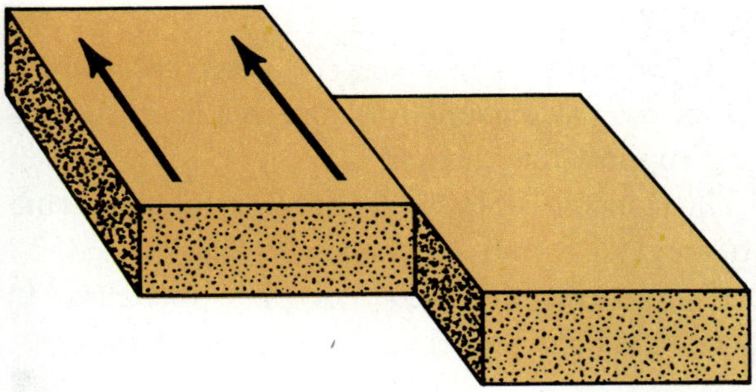

the plates come together rapidly, one plate may slide under the other, forming deep ocean trenches and volcanic islands. 5 This situation exists wherever deep ocean trenches are found.

Scientists are not certain about what causes the movement of plates in the earth. Yet there is much evidence that North America separated from Europe and Asia about 250 million years ago, and the Africa and South America separated about 150 million years ago. 6 Apparently, Africa then separated from the other Gondwanaland continents about 110 million years ago. And only about 40 million years ago Australia separated from Antarctica. Within the last few million years, Arabia has separated from Africa to form the Gulf of Aden, and Baja California has separated from Mexico to form the Gulf of California. New data needs to be collected and new theories formulated to explain the everchanging nature of the face of the earth. As more evidence is being collected, a new concept of the earth's interior is being developed.

Convection Currents

Just what causes the plates to spread outward from a mid-ocean ridge? When oceanographers began to measure the flow of heat from the ocean floor, they discovered that the flow of heat was greatest on or near the mid-ocean ridges and smallest near the continents. They hypothesized that since the ocean crust is very thin, the heat must come from the earth's mantle. And this heat, which results from the decay of radioactive isotopes, causes the rock in the mantle to become plastic—and even flow.

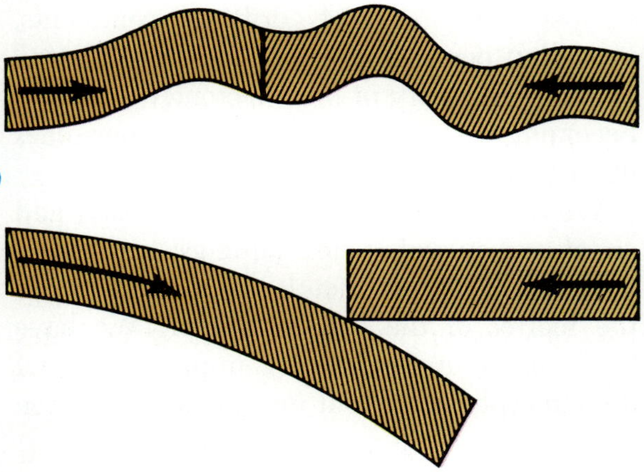

5

6

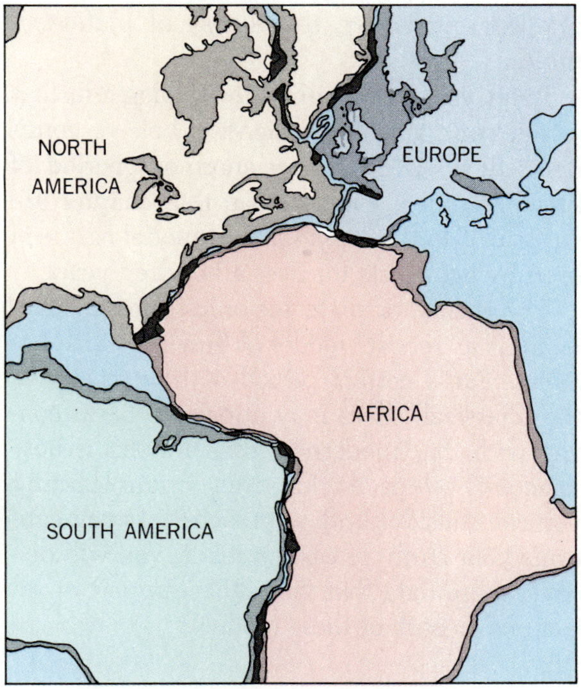

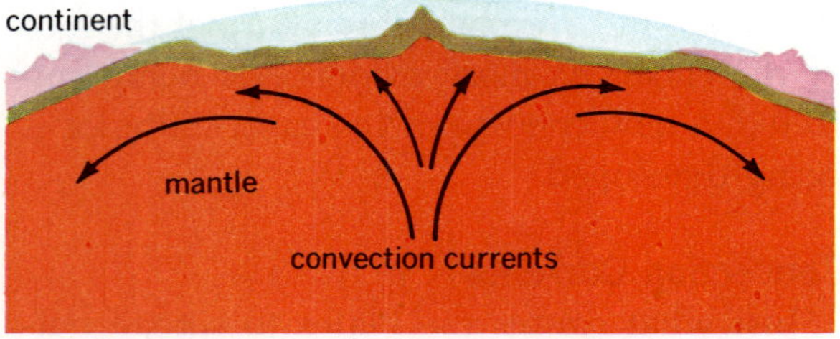

According to one widely held hypothesis, the hot rock of the mantle rises under a mid-ocean ridge, and flows outward. (1) As this plastic rock flows outward, the rock cools, becomes denser and sinks. These movements, or currents, in the upper mantle are called **convection currents.** These, as all convection currents, are caused by a change in temperature.

As the plastic mantle rock flows toward the land, it may *drag the plates with it.* In this way, convection currents in the mantle of the earth may explain both continental drift and sea-floor spreading, the theory of plate tectonics.

Later you will examine the geologic history of our continent, how scientists believe continents developed over an enormous period of time. The ideas suggested in that chapter are "classical" in the sense that the model has been used by geologists for over a hundred years.

The theory of plate tectonics, on the other hand, is a "recent" model of how the earth behaves. For a certain period of time, many of the "classical" ideas may appear to be in conflict with the "modern" ideas. But this is how science develops. At this stage of your learning you can consider both approaches. As you continue your study of earth science, you will discover more data that will either support or reject one or both of these models.

REVIEW

1. Describe the theory of continental drift. How do paleomagnetism and sea-floor spreading support this theory?
2. How do convection currents explain continental drift and sea-floor spreading?
3. Describe the theory of plate tectonics. In what possible ways can the continents move?

NEW VIEW

Many books and articles have been written on the topics of plate tectonics, continental drift, sea-floor spreading. Write a brief report on any aspect of these theories that interests you.

5. RELATING THE CONCEPTS

How could you find out what is inside a sealed box if you couldn't see into it or reach inside? This problem is similar to the one earth scientists face as they attempt to study the inside of the earth. Data can be gathered only by indirect methods.

Using the evidence provided by earthquakes, heat flow, and magnetism, scientists have developed a model of the interior of the earth. In this model, the solid earth is arranged in layers—crust, mantle, outer core, inner core.

Changes deep within the earth cause changes on the surface. Models have been developed that support drifting continents, spreading ocean floors, and moving "plates." In fact, the theory of plate tectonics is rapidly becoming one of the fundamental cornerstones of earth science.

We've taken a look at the land, water, and air of our everyday surroundings, and examined the results of scientists' investigations of the matter of the earth's interior. We have taken an excursion into the upper reaches of the atmosphere and out into the airless region that is becoming familiar "territory" to the space explorer. Thus, our probing of the earth has been both below and above our immediate environment.

Reviewing the Concepts

▶ *The earth's interior has a layered structure.* The evidence indicates that under the crust our planet has layers made up of different forms of matter. These layers are the mantle, outer core, and inner core.

▶ *Movements of the earth's crust result in seismic waves which travel through the earth.* Seismic waves bring about the seismic shocks we call earthquakes. A seismograph can detect earthquakes too mild to be felt, as well as those strong enough to split the ground and destroy buildings. The study of different types of seismic waves has enabled scientists to investigate the interior of the earth.

▶ *Radioactivity produces heat within the earth's crust.* As radioactive atoms within rock break down, some heat is released directly. Some gamma radiation absorbed by rock is converted into additional heat.

▶ The following is a hypothetical concept: *The earth's continents may once have been united but have now drifted apart.* If the earth's mantle is made of rock in the plastic state, and therefore capable of flowing, then the theory of continental drift may be an accurate explanation of the origin of the earth's present "map"—the structure of its continents and oceans, and their relationships with one another. Geologists see evidence that supports continental drift in the structure of the mid-oceanic ridges in both the Atlantic and Pacific oceans, in the widening of the valleys in these ridges, in paleomagnetism, in sea-floor spreading, and in convection currents. The theory of plate tectonics continues to develop as the model that best explains the evidence.

Testing Yourself

1. Define the terms Moho, mantle, core, and plasticity.

2. What is a fault in the earth's crust? How does faulting relate to the occurrence of earthquakes?

3. What evidence is there that volcanoes and earthquakes may be related?

4. What is the composition of each of the three kinds of radiation from atomic nuclei: (a) alpha; (b) beta; (c) gamma?

5. Potassium-39 and potassium-40 are atoms of the same element.

a. How are they alike?

b. How are they different?

6. The half-life of uranium-238 is about $4\frac{1}{2}$ billion years. What prediction can you make from this statement?

7. Describe some important features of the sea bottom that you might encounter during an imaginary walk across the floor of the Atlantic Ocean.

8. What is one hypothesis that explains the groove along the Mid-Atlantic Ridge? Describe the hypothesis briefly.

9. What is continental drift? What evidence has been discovered recently to make the theory more acceptable to scientists?

10. Explain how the theory of plate tectonics explains continental drift and sea-floor spreading.

Extending the Concepts

Investigation 1. If you can borrow a Geiger counter from your school or some other source, such as your local civil defense unit, explore your environment for background radiation. Collect rocks and minerals and test them for radioactivity. Or test the rock and mineral collection in your school. How will you determine (a) the background count? (b) the count due to your sample?

Investigation 2. The state of matter on the sun is called *plasma.* Plasma is a kind of gas in which the atoms are stripped of their electrons and it exists only at very high temperatures. Scientists have made a plasma torch with a temperature 5 times that of the sun's surface —and they expect to go higher. *Scientific American* has reported on this research. Consult an index of this magazine and report on the uses man may make of the plasma state.

Suggested Reading

Clark, Sydney P., *Structure of the Earth,* Englewood Cliffs, Prentice-Hall, 1971. For students with a good science background, this is an interesting discussion on the latest developments in seismology and plate tectonics.

Gamov, George, *A Planet Called Earth,* New York, Viking, 1963. The earth's biography, past, present, and future, told by a well-known scientist and science writer. For students with a good science background.

Lauber, Patricia, *Earthquakes: New Scientific Ideas about How and Why the Earth Shakes,* New York, Random, 1972. Well-illustrated and interesting explanation of earthquakes.

6

Raising the Land

Look at any building near you—no doubt it is made of brick, glass, wood, or steel. These materials are arranged in a certain design. And we can usually identify the purpose of the building from this design. ① Some structures, of course, are so unusual that it is difficult to identify the purpose for which they were built. ② (What do you think is the purpose of this building?*)

For the moment, consider planet earth to be a building. What do you know about the earth by looking at its structure? In the first unit of this book you examined the earth's materials—its igneous, sedimentary, and metamorphic rocks. Yet if most of these materials are formed underground, why do we find them in high mountains? If the earth is continually being worn down, why do any places of high elevation remain? Some answers to these questions are found in the arrangement, the structure, of the rock layers themselves. Now, let's look closely at these rock layers.

①

②

* This is a nondenominational chapel at the Massachusetts Institute of Technology, Cambridge, Massachusetts.

1 

1. THE STRUCTURE OF SEDIMENTARY ROCKS

Layer upon layer of loose sediment deposited in shallow ocean basins hardens into sedimentary rock. Thus most sedimentary rock is originally arranged in horizontal layers of different thickness. Certain rock layers forming the walls of the Grand Canyon are sedimentary rocks. 1 These rock layers have been pushed high above the shallow ocean basins where they were formed. Notice, however, that these sedimentary layers in the Grand Canyon are still horizontal.

2 

Folded Rocks

In many places, however, we find layers of sedimentary rock that are not horizontal, but are bent and folded. 2 The upfolds in such rock layers are called **anticlines.** The downfolds are called **synclines.** The shape of an anticline can be thought of as the crest of a wave; the shape of a syncline resembles the trough of a wave.

Let's examine a simple model to illustrate one condition necessary for the formation of anticlines and synclines. 3 The photograph shows several layers of colored cloth. Each colored cloth layer represents a layer of horizontal sedimentary rock. When you apply pressure from the side, you create miniature anticlines and synclines. 4

In nature, of course, such folding occurs deep underground. The source of this great "sideways" force may be the moving plates you examined in Chapter 5. As the plates move together, the rock layers deposited in ocean basins may crumble and fold. Other forces may later raise the entire mass of folded rock into mountains and highlands.

Don't forget—folded rock layers are still hard, solid rock. But it is possible for these solid rocks to be bent permanently into the many deformed shapes in which we find them. We have already mentioned one factor necessary to bend solid rocks: the exertion of force, perhaps by moving plates. Scientists believe three other factors are necessary: high temperature, a confining pressure from above, and a long period of time over which these conditions

3

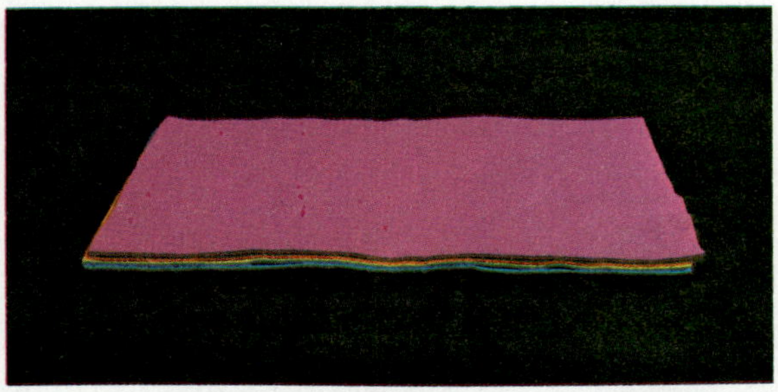

4

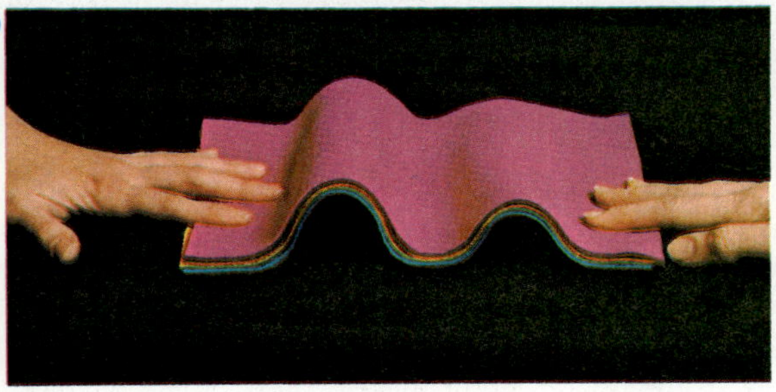

are present. High temperature and confining pressure exist deep underground, and the history of the earth is measured in millions of years.

Broken Rocks: Faults

If a force is exerted on a mass of rock over a short period of time, the rock does not bend —it breaks. Such breaks, as you know, are called faults. In the diagram you can identify the fault by noting the separation occurring across the layers of horizontal rock. 5 Note that along the left side of the fault line, the rock layers are lower than the same layers along the right side of the fault line. Find the fault line in the diagram and trace the broken layers across the fault.

In many areas of the world where earthquakes are common, faults are produced. You have already seen how faults and earthquakes are related (p. 86). A mass of rock can move upward relative to another part of the rock mass. Where this happens, the exposed edges of the uplifted rock produce a small cliff. 6 A river flowing over this cliff can form a waterfall. The vertical movement of rock is direct evidence that land is being raised from below, that mountains are being formed! Even in areas where the uplift is only centimeters per century, the result over a long period of time is enormous. In the western United States, for example, very careful measurements show that the land is rising at a rate of about 50 centimeters (20 inches) in 100 years. How high would the land be in a geologically short period of time—say a million years?

5

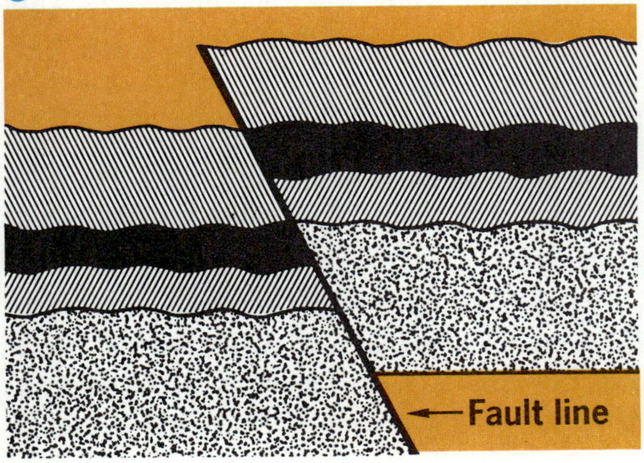

6

1

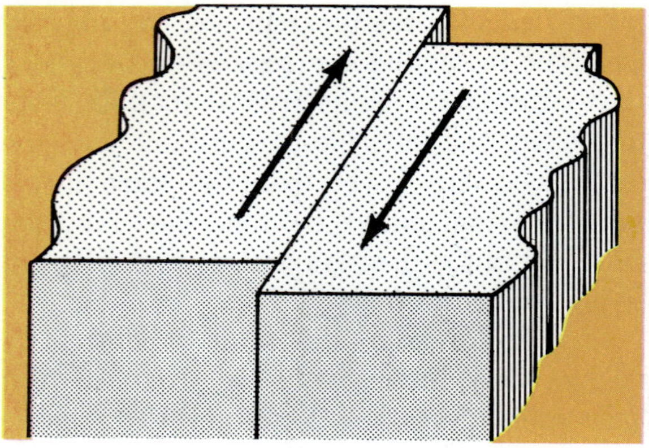

3

Rock layers are sometimes broken as they move *vertically* past each other. Layers of rock are also broken as they slide *horizontally* past each other. The diagram shows blocks of rock moving in opposite directions along a fault line. 1 The famous San Andreas fault is an example of such horizontal motion. 2 Apparently, the land mass west of the fault is on a plate moving north in relation to the land east of the fault line. The city of San Francisco is situated east of the fault line. Los Angeles, located south of San Francisco, is on the plate that is moving north. If this movement continues, some day Los Angeles may be north of San Francisco!

2

Raising the Land—More Evidence

Folded and faulted rock support the theory that rocks can move. Precise measurements show that this movement is vertical, producing mountains, as well as horizontal. Fossils also provide evidence that the land moves. Fossils, formed in the sedimentary rock of ocean basins, are often found on the tops of mountains.

In some coastal regions, flat areas have been carved in the rock by breaking waves. These features, called **marine terraces,** are found in a series of steps high above the tide line. 3 You might very well ask: Was the ocean once this high? All the oceans of the world are connected. If the water was once high enough to carve these features, then marine terraces should be found at the same height in many parts of the world. But they are not. This is further evidence supporting our theory that land can be pushed up from below.

REVIEW

1. What are the conditions necessary for the formation of anticlines and synclines?

2. Describe a fault. How can rock masses move along a fault line?

3. Marine terraces provide evidence that the earth is pushed up from below. Explain.

NEW VIEW

1. Today many scientists are involved in a study of the San Andreas fault. What is happening along this fault? Find out why some scientists predict that the city of San Francisco may someday slip into the sea.

2. Rock formations can be found as horizontal layers and as folded or tilted rocks. Are there sections of the United States where only horizontal rock layers are found? If so, where? Are there sections where only folded or tilted rock layers are found? If so, where?

2. ANOTHER WAY TO RAISE THE LAND

Before November, 1963, the sea in this spot not far off the coast of Iceland was deep and unbroken. Then the volcanic island Surtsey (in the foreground) was born. Three years later, just as a second island, Syrtlinger, was pushing its way through the sea, an eyewitness made this picture. 4

Erupting Volcanoes

Although few people ever see a volcano's birth, in the past 400 years some 500 new volcanoes have burst from the earth Most volcanoes build up gradually over a period of years, remain active for some time, and eventually "die" or seem to become extinct.

Many volcanoes produce cone-shaped hills or mountains at spots where the earth was once flat. In the ocean, a volcano may produce a **seamount,** a kind of underwater mountain that rises from the ocean floor. The top of a seamount is under water. If the top of an undersea mountain breaks through the water's surface, it forms an island.

An erupting volcano sends out quantities of hot gas. This is largely composed of steam,

4

[1]

which can be seen as it condenses into clouds. Along with the steam come other gases: these may include carbon monoxide, nitrogen, chlorine, hydrogen, and vapors of sulfur (which solidify into sulfur deposits upon cooling).

Then there usually comes **lava,** molten rock. Some of the lava may solidify before it reaches the air. In this case, the lava doesn't pour out, but is hurled forth as pieces of rock. These rocky fragments vary in size from dustlike "ashes" to stonelike "bombs."

Where does all this matter come from? It originates in the depths of the earth, in the substance we call magma.

Origin of Magma

Geologists cannot as yet give a very complete account of how magma forms, but they have some clues. They have discovered that the interior of the earth is very hot, as you may recall. At a depth of 50 kilometers (30 miles), for instance, the temperature is about 1,200°C—hot enough to melt rock. It would seem, at first glance, that this is simply how magma comes to be, for magma is fluid rock. Yet the evidence is that the earth 50 kilometers down is solid. Why, if the temperature is so high, does the rock stay solid and not melt? And what *does* cause rock to melt, for clearly some rock must somehow melt. Otherwise, we wouldn't see lava flowing out of volcanoes. [1]

Most rocks, like other solid substances, expand when they are heated. This means that the molecules or ions that make up the solid tend to move apart from each other, so that the whole mass of material takes up more space. When the temperature reaches the melting point of the particular solid being heated, the particles it is made of move far enough apart for the substance to change into a liquid.

Suppose, now, that at the same time the molecules are getting enough heat to move apart, there is an outside force that tends to push them closer together. Air pressure is an outside force that acts this way whenever we heat something at the earth's surface. Heat a piece of butter in a pan on a stove, for instance. In order for the butter to melt, its molecules have to have enough energy to overcome the pressure of the air above the pan. How much is the air pressure?

To melt anything at the earth's surface we have to heat it enough to overcome a force of 1 kilogram per square centimeter (14.7 pounds per square inch), the average air pressure of the atmosphere. Because matter in the earth is so much heavier than air, pressures within the earth are much greater than they are at the surface. Scientists think that the pressure at a depth of 50 kilometers (30 miles) is 20,000 times that at the surface. So to melt rock at this depth in the earth, we would have to heat it enough to overcome 20,000 times the pressure at the surface.

Now we have the answer to the question of why the rocks 50 kilometers down stay solid.

Although their temperature is so high that they would melt if they were on the surface, very high pressure keeps the molecules or ions of rock from moving apart.

This leaves our other question to be answered, however. That is, what *does* happen that permits some of the rock to melt, and thus to form magma?

For one thing, geologists believe that at certain spots in the deep, hot rock layers, the temperature can rise even higher—high enough for particles in the rocks to gain enough energy to overcome the tremendous pressure. These places are the areas where radioactive elements are concentrated. Because the heat produced by radioactive decay is not conducted away from one spot very fast, radiation might build up an especially high temperature in a certain spot. In this way, scientists think, a small amount of magma might form as the rock in a certain spot reaches an intense degree of heat.

Another way in which deep rocks might melt to form magma would be for the pressure in certain places to be lowered. When overlying rocks bend and break, the high pressure they normally exert might be reduced enough to allow melting of the rocks beneath them.

Some geologists think that lava originates in the earth's upper mantle, about 100 kilometers (60 miles) below the surface. In this region the rock is very firm and solid, but it is a peculiar sort of plasticlike solid with some liquidlike properties. If in some way the pressure on such plasticlike solid rock decreases, it might then melt into the truly liquid state of magma.

How Magma Comes to the Surface

Have you ever opened a bottle of soda just after shaking it? If you have, then you know how the release of pressure affects a liquid that has a gas dissolved in it. When you remove the bottle cap you lower the pressure on the fluid within. The gas, carbon dioxide, bubbles out of solution, and both liquid and gas shoot out of the mouth of the bottle.

If you can, shake and then remove the cap of a bottle of a warm soft drink that is *not* carbonated. This time nothing happens. Without the energy of the escaping gas the liquid does not bubble out at all.

The molecules of a gas have much more energy of motion than do those of a liquid. It is the enormous energy of escaping gases, when the pressure on the mixture is released, that supplies the force that carries the liquid along.

All magma contains gases dissolved in the liquid rock. When some change reduces the pressure on magma and its dissolved gases, the mixture begins to move. Aided by the force of its escaping gases, the magma can flow into cracks in other rocks. Sometimes it forces its way up to the surface and becomes lava, the molten rock that flows from openings at the base or on the sides of a volcano. When lava cools, it solidifies into various volcanic rocks.

One common type of volcanic rock, often sold in drugstores, is pumice. Place a piece of pumice in water and notice that it floats. A rock that floats on water has an unusually low density for a rock. Why is the density of pumice so low? It is for the same reason that raised bread is light. When bread dough is left in a warm place to rise, the yeast in the dough releases carbon dioxide gas. The gas in the dough expands and escapes, leaving air holes that make the bread porous and light. Pumice has air holes, too, left by gases that expand and escape through hot lava before it solidifies.

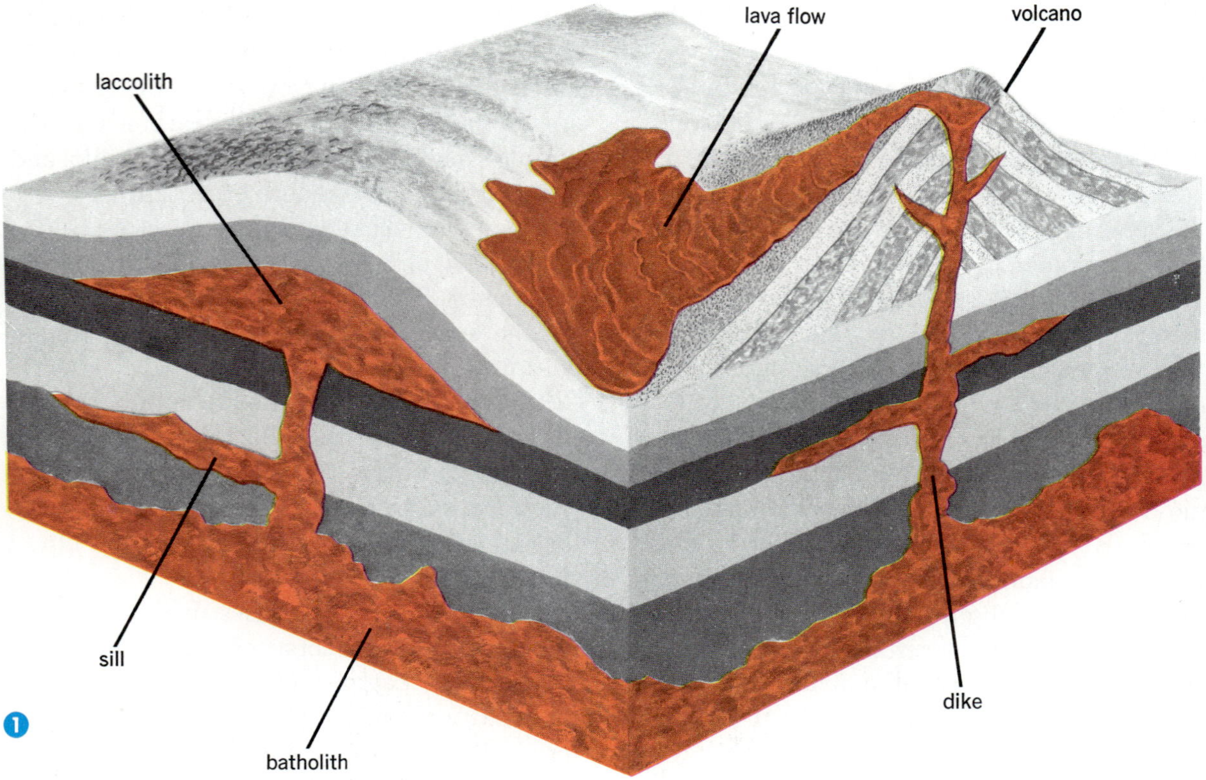

❶

Volcanic Mountains and Lava Plateaus

Most volcanoes produce mountains. One kind of volcanic mountain consists of alternating layers of lava flow and volcanic ash, as shown in the diagram. ❶ The dark layers in the diagram represent layers of hardened lava. The light layers are made up of volcanic "ash," or cinder, which forms when escaping gases break up lava into pieces. A volcano with large amounts of ash is a *cinder cone*. This kind of volcano has a steep cone, often very beautifully shaped. Mount Fujiyama in Japan, and Mount Shasta in California are volcanic mountains that have this kind of layered structure.

Some volcanoes do not build mountains, but pour out their lava quietly over widespread flat areas. Layer after layer of these lava flows build enormous plateaus, such as the Columbia River plateau that underlies central Oregon and parts of the states next to Oregon. The Columbia River plateau covers over 520,000 square kilometers (200,000 square miles).

Underground Activity of Magma

Magma that becomes lava and flows out on the ground is an exception to the rule. Most magma never comes to the surface. Instead, it invades nearby underground rocks, melting and dissolving them as it moves into and between them. Igneous rocks that form from such underground activity are called plutons, as you may recall.

In the diagram you can see several different kinds of plutonic rock formations and how they can be related to one another. ❶ **Batholiths,** the largest plutonic formations, are massive. In central Idaho, for instance, one batholith spreads over 42,000 square kilometers (16,000 square miles). Other batholiths are at the heart of mountain ranges such as the Rockies and the Sierra Nevadas.

Here and there erosion has exposed parts of a batholith, making it accessible to dating with a geologic "clock." Some have proved to be relatively young, others old. This means that batholiths may play a part in the continual rebuilding of the earth's crust from the magma underneath.

Notice the other kinds of plutons in the diagram. The **laccolith** takes a mushroomlike or blisterlike shape under the earth's surface. In a laccolith the magma seems to have spread between the rock layers of the crust and lifted those above it into a dome. Some of these domes are as much as 300 meters (1,000 feet) in height and 16 kilometers (10 miles) in width.

From the description of batholiths and laccoliths, you may get the impression that magma generally follows lines of least resistance. Often it does just that. Once magma begins to flow, or a batholith has begun to form, sheetlike branches of molten rock may follow joints and cracks beneath the surface. When lava cuts across existing layers of rock, a **dike** is formed. The upper part of a dike may spread horizontally, making a tablelike formation. Some fine examples of dikes exposed by erosion can be seen at Shiprock, New Mexico, and Spanish Peaks, Colorado.

If an underground flow of magma moves somewhat parallel with the existing layers, the result is a **sill,** as you can see in the diagram. Magma that forms a sill shoulders its way between layers of rock. Sometimes, when the earth's crust is displaced by crustal movements, the earth's rock layers are tilted. When a tilted layer is exposed, a sill may come to view, as it has along the Hudson River in a region known as the Palisades.

REVIEW

1. What keeps rocks from liquefying at a depth of 50 kilometers (30 miles)?

2. What do volcanoes give off in addition to liquid rock?

3. Why does pumice have a low density?

4. In what way is a batholith like a laccolith? In what way are they different?

5. Describe how dikes and sills are formed.

NEW VIEW

1. A great deal of sulfur is often found near old volcanoes. Are its crystals large or small? Why?

2. Imagine that you are climbing a mountain. What would you look for to decide whether or not it is an old, partly eroded volcano?

3. MOUNTAINS, PLATEAUS, PLAINS

Masses of igneous, sedimentary, and metamorphic rock were formed deep underground. Yet they are now found as raised platforms of land high above the ocean waters. The heights of these land masses, of course, are continually changing. As quickly as the land is raised, it is being worn down. So the features we see today —the mountains, plains, and plateaus—are only temporary ones. The temporary height of the land across the United States is shown on maps

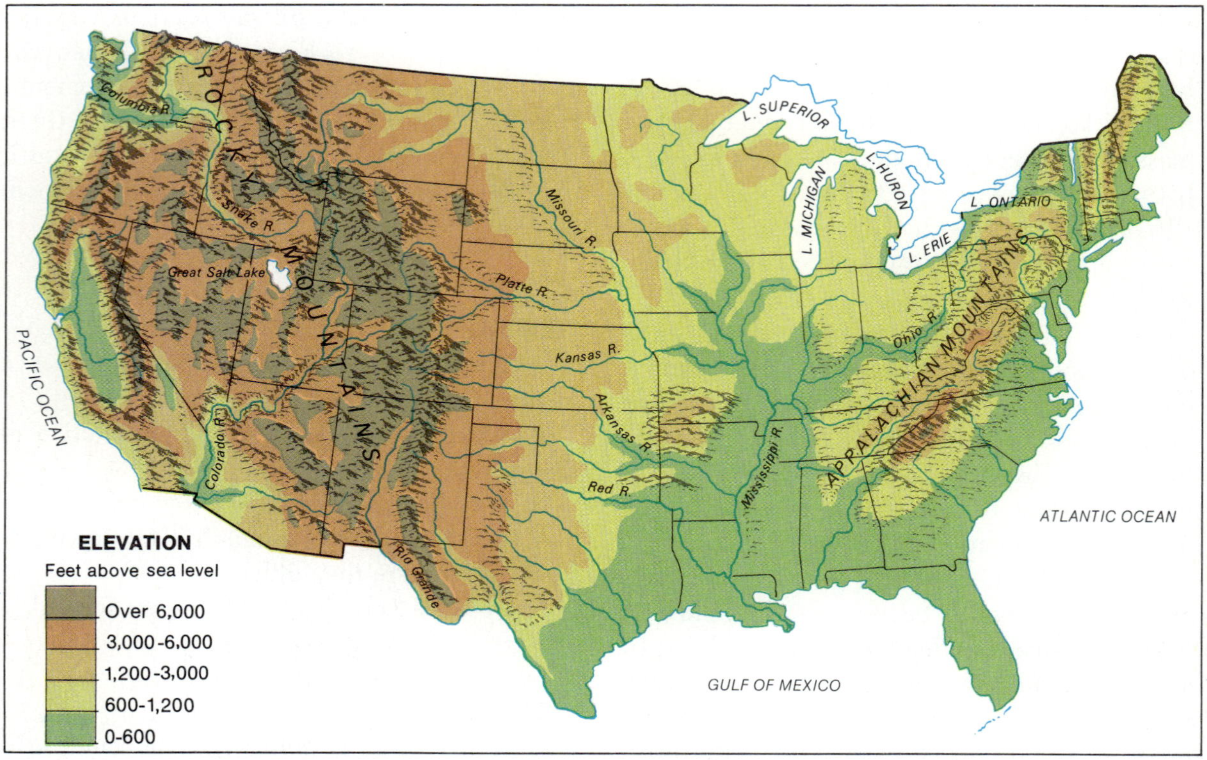

❶

similar to this one.❶ What is the average height of the land where you live?

Mountains

Mountains, of course, are elevated sections of the land. The rock mass of a mountain is generally highly folded and faulted, or formed from the lava of erupting volcanoes. About one-fifth of our country is mountainous. Among these mountains are the Appalachian Mountain chain in the East, and the Rockies, Coast Ranges, and Sierra Nevada Mountains in the West.

All mountains are not the same. Some mountains are higher than others and are always covered with snow. Some mountains are covered with heavy forest; others are barren. Some have jagged peaks; others are rounded. Geologists, however, describe mountains in a different way. They classify mountains into four main types: **fold, fault-block, volcanic,** and **dome.** Let's go through the country and find examples of these types of mountains.

A Look at the Landscape

Fold mountains are long belts of highly bent and broken rocks. The Appalachian Mountain chain, for example, is over 2,500 kilometers (1,500 miles) long.❷ Beginning in Alabama, it extends northward to Nova Scotia where it disappears beneath the Atlantic.

From east to west across the belt, the material of the rocks as well as the structure of the rocks vary. In the eastern part, the rock mass is

2

3

mainly metamorphic rock; slates, schists, and gneisses as well as masses of granite. The upper layer of sedimentary rock has long been weathered away, exposing these deeply-formed rocks. Stone Mountain, Georgia, is a good example of these granite masses.

In the western part of the Appalachians, the folding is much less intense and the rock type is mostly sedimentary. In fact, many of the sedimentary rocks, sandstones, shales, and limestones, are still in a horizontal position. Such raised areas of horizontal rock layers are **plateaus.** Next to the Appalachian Mountains is the Appalachian Plateau.

Fold mountains and plateaus are also found in the western part of our country. The Rocky Mountains are fold mountains. West of the northern Rocky Mountains is the vast Columbia Plateau built of layer upon layer of lava flows. West of the Southern Rocky Mountains is the Colorado Plateau, a region of horizontal rocks over 1,500 meters (5,000 feet) high. 3 The Grand Canyon is carved into this plateau. Where much of the material of plateaus has been washed away, small elevated land areas may remain. These hills are called **mesas** or **buttes.** In general, the width and length of a mesa is greater than its height. A butte is usually as high as it is wide. Plateaus, however, may be many kilometers long but only a few hundred meters high.

Fault-block mountains are formed as large masses of rock are broken by faults. The result is a series of elevated and lowered masses of rock. 4 The elevated portions form *ranges;* the lowered portions form *basins*. The Basin and Range area of southwestern United States is the principal region of fault-block landforms.

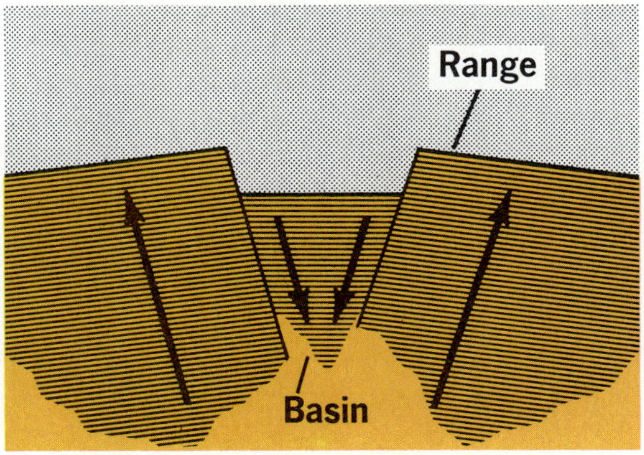

4

1

The Sierra Nevada Mountains represent the upturned edge of a faulted block of granite. 1 The beautiful Yosemite Valley is carved into the westward sloping part of this block.

Volcanic mountains, of course, are formed from the accumulation of volcanic material. Along the Pacific Coast of the United States, volcanic mountains form the 800-kilometer (500-mile) long Cascade Range of Oregon and Washington. Along the top of this chain are found some of our highest peaks—Mount Ranier, Mount Hood, and Mount Shasta.

Dome mountains are special types of fold mountains. Rock layers are gently folded over a local area of uplift. As the central portion of the rock layers are worn away, the edges of the more resistant rock form circular mountain ridges. The Adirondack Mountains in New York are examples of dome mountains. 2

2

Up and Down—Across the Country

Mountains and plateaus are regions of high elevations. These features cover fifty percent of the land in the United States. Plains, regions of low elevation, make up the remaining fifty percent.

The rock structure of plains, like that of plateaus, is generally horizontal. The central part of the United States is a vast plain. One of the most productive agricultural areas in the world is found in this area. The Atlantic and Gulf Coastal Plains are other examples of this type of land feature.

This map is called a *profile.* 3 It shows the various elevations of our country as if we were looking at it from the side. Notice the lower elevations in the east and across the central United States. Look how rapidly the land rises to the Rockies. Notice how the western part of our country appears rugged. Platforms of land stand above sea level. How did they come to be that way?

REVIEW

1. Describe the three major land features.
2. What are the four main types of mountains? Briefly describe each type.
3. Define plains, plateaus, butte, and mesa.

NEW VIEW

The United States can be divided into *physiographic provinces.* Find out what these provinces are. What province do you live in; what are the characteristics of your province; what types of landforms are common?

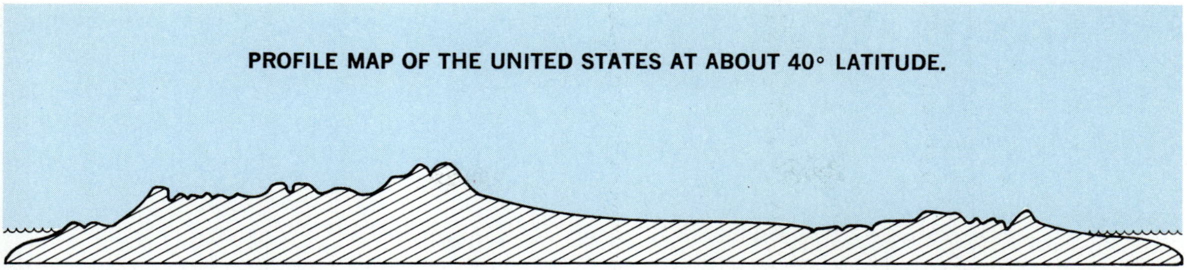

4. MOUNTAINS YOUNG AND OLD

The different mountains we see now are at different stages of their life cycles, some in their youth and some in their old age. From a human point of view, of course, all mountains seem old. As parts of the earth, though, some mountains are young. Remember that the geologic clock has placed the age of the earth at about $5\frac{1}{2}$ billion years. By comparison, the Rockies, the Andes, the Alps, and the Himalayas are young mountains—no more than 60 million years old. Young mountains like these have jagged peaks. 4

In time, weathering and erosion wear down the sharp edges of young mountains. When the mountains become rounded, like those of

4

1

the Appalachians, they are really old. 1 The age of the Appalachians is estimated as 200 million years, over three times that of the Rockies. Even more worn down are the Ozarks of Arkansas and Missouri, and the Arbuckles of Oklahoma.

The forces of weathering and erosion that round off the tops of mountains eventually wear them down completely. For example, the gently rolling Penokee Hills in Wisconsin are remnants of the once mighty Killarneyan Mountains that ranged through Wisconsin, Minnesota, and southern Canada. The Killarneyans were at least 800 million years old. Weathering and erosion reduced their size, transporting them almost entirely into the sea. Given enough time, the forces that level mountains can be powerful indeed.

The Killarneyans, for the most part, are now transformed into sedimentary rock. But sedimentary rock does not accumulate forever. Sooner or later it is uplifted, and that lifting process also takes time. The great Killarneyan Mountain Range probably took 25 million years to rise, from sediments that had accumulated for 200 million years.

It is well to keep in mind the importance of long, long periods of time as we consider the theory of mountain building; the changes during mountain building are generally too slow for us to notice. But as you have learned, *evidence* of changes in mountains is easily seen.

How Mountains Begin

A mighty mountain range may have its beginning in a shallow sea just off the coast of a continent. Sediment that is removed from the land piles up in a kind of depression or trough, at the bottom of the shallow sea. 2 Such a trough in the earth's crust is known as a **geosyncline.** As times goes by, more and more sediment falls into the geosyncline.

The geosyncline, which is usually parallel to the shore and hundreds of kilometers long, gradually sinks as thousands of meters of sediment pile up in it. The pressure of the sediment on top helps turn the lower layers into sedimentary rock.

When the sediment becomes at least 9,000 meters (30,000 feet) thick, an important change takes place. According to the theory, pressure from both sides, or horizontal compression, pushes on the sedimentary rock in the geosyncline. (3) One effect of pressure on rocks is, as you know, the kind of breaking known as faulting. If solid rock is subjected to pressure over a long enough period of time it may fault. On the other hand, the rock may be pushed out of shape without breaking. That is, the rock may buckle and fold. The pressure on either side of the geosyncline produces much folding and faulting, and the whole geosyncline is gradually uplifted, or elevated.

In time, the bottom of the geosyncline pushes down into the hotter part of the earth's crust. In this region of high temperature, some of the sedimentary rock is under enough pressure to change to metamorphic rock. At the lowest part of the geosyncline, where heat and pressure are greatest, some of the rock may even get hot enough to melt and turn into magma. Here a great mass of hot magma, which may come partly from the melted rock and partly from the underlying mantle layer, forces its way up into the geosyncline. (4) As it cools underground, the magma becomes a batholith, or core, of granite, an igneous rock. The sedimentary rock near the top doesn't change at all.

In this way, the theory accounts for layers of both metamorphic and igneous rock, mixed with layers of sedimentary rock, that we see in mountains. Mountain-building forces lift all these kinds of rocks together.

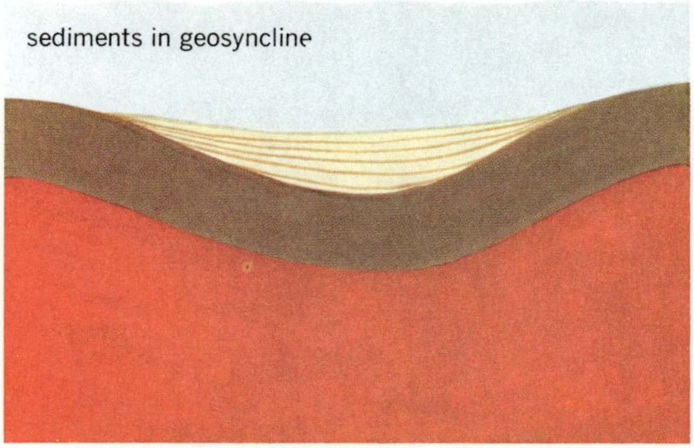

2

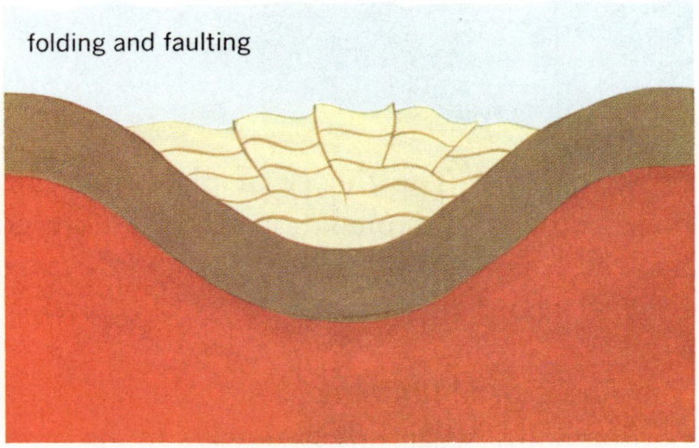

3

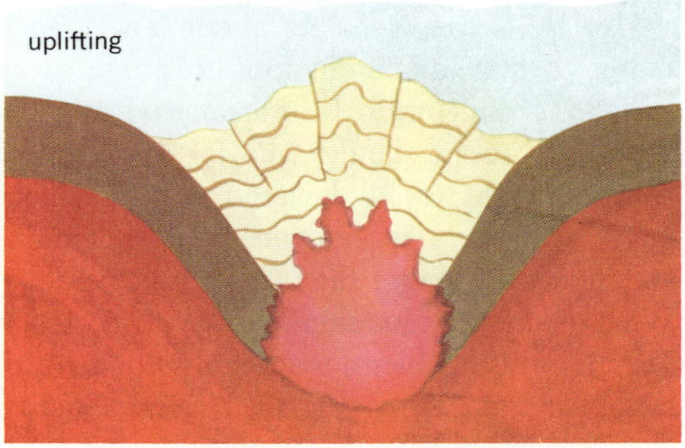

4

What forces can do the uplifting; what causes the vertical rise of the mountain? Geologists really do not know. The pressure of heated, expanded rocks and the elevation resulting from the folding and faulting of large rock masses seem, however, to be at least part

1

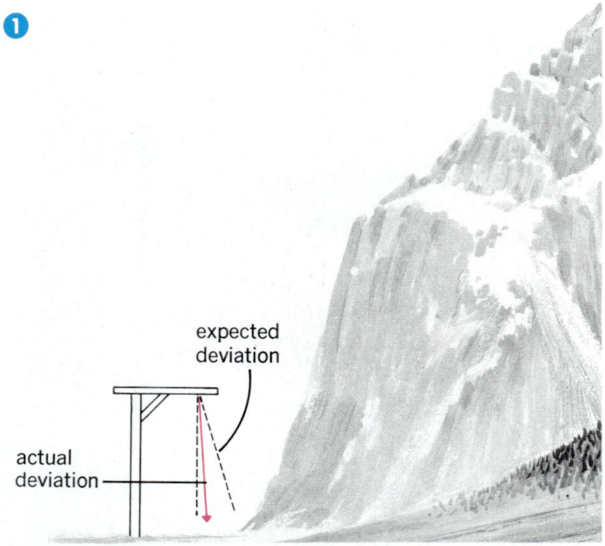

of the answer. The theory of plate tectonics may also be an explanation. If you like, go back to Chapter 5 and review what you have learned about this theory.

The Roots of Mountains

Mountains wear down slowly, to be sure. *Too* slowly, in a way, geologists think. Why?

Geologists can calculate about how long it ought to take mountain tops to erode away and the sediments to be transported into the sea. The time it should take for a peak of a certain height to be lowered can be calculated. But there is evidence that mountains stay up much longer than this predicted time. What makes the mountains stay up so long? To solve this problem, we begin with a bit of evidence from a hanging lead weight known as a "plumb bob."

Suppose you suspend a plumb bob out in the middle of a flat area on the earth. As the earth's enormous gravitational force pulls on it, the bob hangs straight down. Now suppose you move the plumb bob near a sizable mountain and suspend it as before. The earth still pulls the bob down, but the mass of the mountain is big enough to pull the bob a bit sideways, as well. 1

If we know the kind of rock in the mountain, we can calculate its mass from the known density of that kind of rock. Knowing the mountain's mass, then, the degree it should deflect a plumb bob can be calculated. The calculation is based on Newton's Law of Gravitation, which relates the pull between objects to their masses.

When scientists made these calculations for Mount Everest, they predicted that the plumb bob would slant a certain amount. When they actually measured the slanting of the bob, however, it turned out to be only a third as much as expected. 1 The same experiment was tried on many other mountains, with the same kind of results. The mountains were all acting as though they were lighter than thought to be. Why?

Geologists have just one explanation that seems satisfactory: the mountains have roots. These roots and the mountain itself are made of rock of lower density than that of the rock surrounding the roots. Study the diagram to see how this can be. 2

2

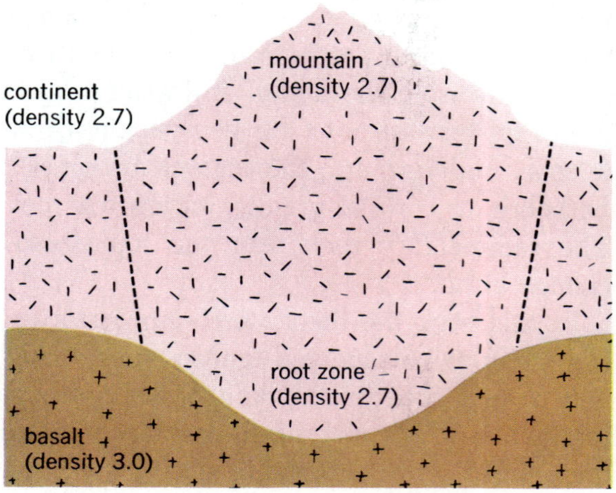

In the diagram, notice that the mountain mass, including its root, is made of granite, which has a density of 2.7 g/cc. The root is sunk into a deeper layer of basalt, with a density of 3.0 g/cc.

This means that the whole mass of the mountain, including its granite root, is less than it would be if the space taken up by the root were filled with basalt.

This mountain of rock is, in a way, like an iceberg. An iceberg is a solid with a density of about $\frac{9}{10}$ that of water. Because of its lower density, the iceberg floats in the ocean with just $\frac{1}{10}$ of its mass above the surface. The other $\frac{9}{10}$ might be "rooted" in the water if the water did not flow so freely. In a similar way, the granite mountain "floats" in an "ocean" of basalt.

You can make a model of a floating mountain and see for yourself what happens when its top erodes away. Place several blocks of wood of different sizes in a pan of water. Observe that the larger blocks have deeper "roots" in the water than the smaller blocks do. In a similar way, taller mountains on the earth have deeper roots than eroded mountains do.

Let one of the larger blocks represent a mountain. Pile sawdust on top of it. ❸ To represent the erosion process, remove the sawdust little by little. Observe how the block rises a bit each time you remove some of the sawdust. ❹ The "mountain" is wearing away, and yet it remains for a time at the same height.

In the same way, granite mountains "floating" in basalt are believed to rise as their tops wear down. This is why it takes much longer for the mountain to wear all the way down than it would if this rising did not take place.

❸

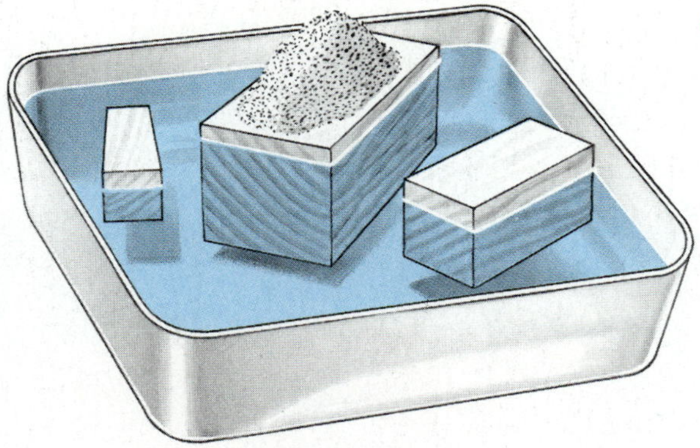

❹

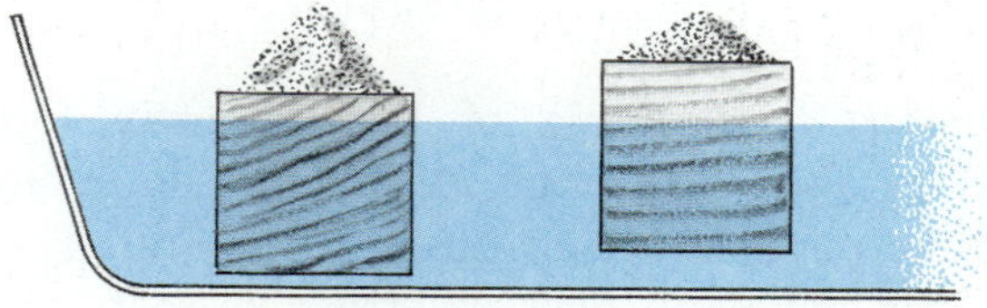

The Floating Continents

It is now generally accepted among geologists that the layer of basalt that forms the earth's crust under the oceans completely encircles the earth. And the mountains, as well as the flatlands of the continents, are composed mainly of granite floating on this basaltic rock. Evidence from seismic waves indicates that the basalt layer of the crust under the ocean is an average of 5 to 6 kilometers (3 to 4 miles) thick. Under the continents, however, the crust, which is composed of granite floating on the basalt, may be about 5 times as thick, on the average.

The behavior of the earth's crust is one manifestation of **isostasy** (which means "equal standing"), the theory that the earth maintains a balance among its parts. Parts of the earth's crust move up or move down whenever some change upsets the earth's balance—its isostasy.

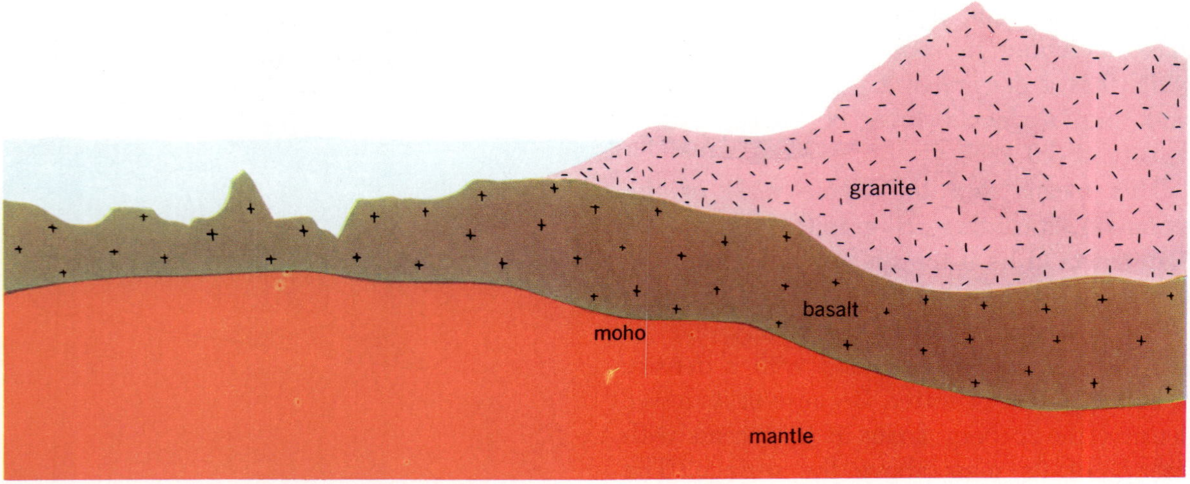

❶

Since the eroding of the mountain tops brings about a change in balance, the rising of the mountain is an isostatic rebound. That is, the mountain goes up, from its root, precisely because it wears down from its top! In fact, isostasy probably accounts in part for the vertical uplift of developing mountains. ❶

As the earth moves to maintain its isostasy, the mountains nevertheless wear down. If you finally remove all the sawdust from the blocks in the model, the tops of the blocks are left quite flat. Unless new mountains heaved up from the sea floor, our earth would have long ago been left smooth and flat all over. As the sediments reach the sea, however, new mountains are already in the making. No matter how slowly they build up, new mountains will rise. The earth's crust is in constant change.

REVIEW

1. How did the Penokees come to be?

2. How would you account for the presence in mountain ranges of (a) sedimentary rock? (b) igneous rock? (c) metamorphic rock?

3. Describe a sequence that you accept as useful in explaining the rise of mountains.

4. How is the floating of a mountain like the floating of an iceberg?

5. What is isostasy? Cite two kinds of evidence that support the view that the earth's crust has isostasy.

NEW VIEW

1. There is evidence that a plain near the seacoast was once covered with a thick ice sheet. A change in climate caused the ice sheet to melt and, as a result, the level of the land was raised slightly. Explain.

2. What is the role of *convection currents,* caused by heat in the earth's crust, in one modern hypothesis of mountain-building? (Consult a reference book.)

3. Mountains lifted from a sediment-filled geosyncline grow very slowly. What kind of mountains on the earth can grow very rapidly?

4. We have no evidence that there were ever any real seas on the moon. And the lack of an atmosphere means there is probably no weathering or erosion on the moon, as there is on earth. Yet the moon has mountains. How could they have originated?

5. RELATING THE CONCEPTS

At first glance, the earth seems stable, doesn't it? Your house, the walk, the road remain seemingly unaltered from day to day. But if you look here and there you see changes: paint peels, bricks crumble, the sidewalk curb flakes and breaks, the road develops cracks and holes. So too the earth, the seemingly stable lithosphere, changes.

The most obvious evidence that the earth changes is found in the arrangement of the rock layers themselves. This arrangement, the structure of the rock, shows rock layers are folded and faulted—evidence that rocks have been squeezed, pushed, and broken by great forces. Such evidence exists for you to see in any mountain, plain, or plateau.

The changes in the lithosphere are sometimes sudden and dramatic. Rocks crack, volcanoes flare, and the earth quakes. So even though the earth's inhabitants usually think of their planet as a stable place, the view that *the earth is in continual change* is more accurate.

Reviewing the Concepts

► *The structure of rock provides evidence for motion of the earth's crust.* Folded and faulted rock indicate that great forces are continually changing the landscape.

► *Volcanic activity produces many distinct landforms.* Volcanic mountains, lava plateaus, batholiths, laccoliths, sills, and dikes are typical igneous structures.

► *The earth's mountain ranges are in continuous change.* It may take hundreds of millions of years for a mountain range to be raised. And it may take hundreds of millions of years more for the same mountain range to be leveled again. Slow as these changes seem to be, the evidence is that they happen now just as they have happened during billions of years of the earth's past ages.

What causes mountains to rise? Scientists believe part of the answer is pressure. Bends and breaks caused by pressure result in folding and faulting, and these in turn play their part in mountain building. We have good theories to account for some mountain-building processes. But we do not yet understand completely the uplift of mountains. As for what causes the mountains to get lower and lower until they flatten completely, it seems that the powerful forces of erosion play a major role.

► *The earth's crust tends to maintain an isostatic balance among its parts.* This is a statement of the concept of isostasy ("equal standing") of the earth's mountains, flatlands, and ocean basins. The hypothesis that these parts of the earth's crust are all "floating" on a kind of "ocean" of plastic rock helps to explain the earth's isostatic balance.

Testing Yourself

1. Take an imaginary walk from west to east across the country. Describe the features that you find along the way. Give specific examples of each feature.

2. What do scientists believe to be the origin of lava?

3. How does lava get to the vent of an erupting volcano? What are some other products (besides lava) of volcanic action?

4. What evidence do we have that rock layers can be pushed up from below?

5. How are faults related to earthquakes and volcanic activity?

6. Describe the geologic changes occurring along the San Andreas fault.

7. How can you tell a relatively young mountain from an older one? Why do young and old mountains differ in this way?

8. How might a mountain range have its beginning in a geosyncline under the sea?

9. How is pressure within the earth probably related to mountain building?

Extending the Concepts

Investigation. Make a three-dimensional model of the land in an area near where you live, or of some place that has particularly interesting landforms. To do this, first obtain a contour map from your town or city engineer, your state agricultural department, or the U.S. Geodetic Survey. The lines on the map are formed by connecting points of the same elevation.

As a base for your model, use the contour map itself, or trace the map's lines onto a piece of paper. Use clay or papier-mâché for your modeling material. You can save modeling material and make your map lighter and easier to handle if you use crumpled paper as the base for hills and mountains.

Suggested Reading

Calder, Nigel, *The Restless Earth,* New York, Viking, 1972. An introduction into the processes that build up and break down the earth's crust.

Roberts, Elliott, *Our Quaking Earth,* Boston, Little, Brown and Company, 1963.

Williams, Howel, "Volcanoes," *Scientific American,* November, 1951. (Reprint no. 822 by W. H. Freeman and Co., San Francisco.) Written by an authority on volcanoes, with excellent illustrations.

7

Shaping the Land

Dynamite is carefully set into the side of the mountain. With a giant, shuddering blast, the explosion shatters the rock mass. Man moves mountains, lowering the high places and filling in the lower places, shaping the surface of the earth. Raised land is also being worn down by natural agents, changing the landscape in a variety of ways. The scheme of this shaping is rather simple: Material is eroded from one place and deposited in another. The agent responsible for the movement may be ground water or surface water (streams), wind, glaciers, or waves and currents. The results are the familiar landscape we see all about us. (1) Now let's see how these agents shape the land.

1. FROM ROCK TO ROCK DEBRIS

Before rock material can be moved, the hard solid mass of rock must be broken down into smaller pieces. The breaking down of most

(1)

1 

rock masses begins by the formation of natural cracks, or joints. 1 Joints are formed where material covering the rock mass is removed, relieving pressure and allowing the rock to expand slightly. In these joints, the natural points of weakness in the rock, the primary breakdown of rock masses begins.

2 

3 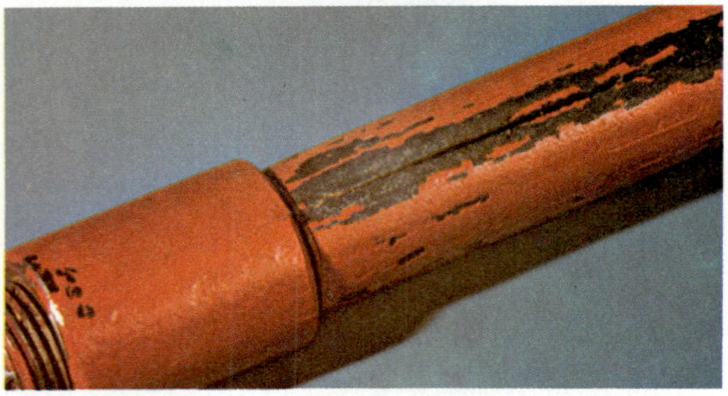

If water enters the joints, the water may freeze and expand, splitting the rock into smaller fragments. Let's see how.

Here is a hollow tube of cast iron with thick walls. 2 Now it is completely filled with water, leaving no air spaces within, and the plug is screwed in place. The tube is put in a freezer so that the water inside turns to ice. Here is the result. 3 What do you observe? When water freezes, it expands, and the force of expansion can be great. To see how much freezing water expands, try the investigation on the next page. ■

When water freezes it expands by about $\frac{1}{10}$ of its original volume. Water that seeps into a crack in a rock may freeze during a cold night and, as the freezing water expands, it may enlarge the crack a little. As this expansion takes place night after night, the surface layer of the rock slowly splits off. There is some evidence that water is also absorbed by certain minerals in the rock. As the minerals take in water they expand, causing more of the rock surface to split off. Finally, the rock may even split apart.

This breaking down of rock due to exposure to the atmosphere is one example of **weathering.** Weathering may seem to be a

■ AN APPRENTICE INVESTIGATION into the Expansion of Freezing Water

Fill a Pyrex or Kimax graduated cylinder about $\frac{2}{3}$ full of water. Mark the level of the water with a wax pencil or a label.❶ Set the cylinder upright in a freezer. When the water has frozen, remove the cylinder and observe its contents. How does the level of the ice compare with the water level? Here is the result of one trial.❷

By what fraction of its original volume did the water expand? Repeat the investigation with cylinders of different sizes.

An Investigation On Your Own

Do other liquids behave this same way when they freeze? Investigate the change in volume of various substances such as milk, rubbing alcohol, liquid detergent, salt solution, ink, or other liquids you may find at home. How do your results compare with the observation made with water? If possible, repeat the procedure with distilled water as a control.

It may surprise you to learn that substances that contain no water generally do not expand but contract when they change from the liquid to the solid state. Devise your own way to investigate the change in volume of a liquid that contains no water, such as melted wax, when it solidifies.

How is the behavior of water when it solidifies explained? How is the different behavior of wax when it solidifies explained? (Consult advanced texts and references.)

❶

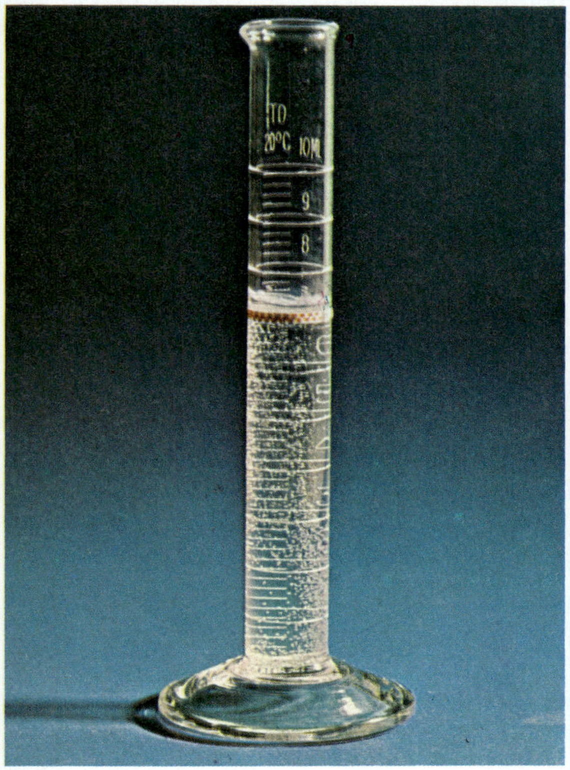

❷

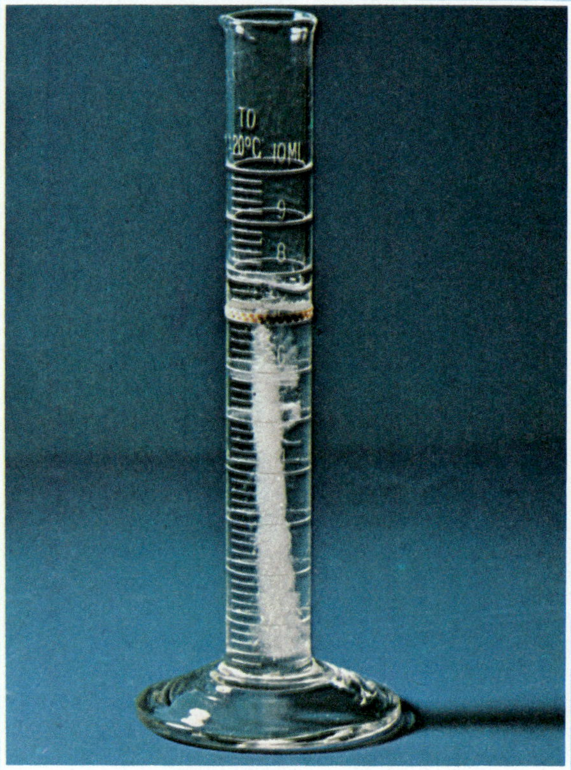

1

2

slow process, but since it goes on day after day, year after year, century after century, it is effective just the same. Notice the splinters and pieces of rock, called **talus,** that have collected on the side of this mountain. 1

The appearance of the talus suggests one of the most important effects of weathering—the formation of soil. Without soil, there would be no anchorage or water supply for the roots of plants. Weathering, as you know, also plays an important part in the leveling of mountains and the transformation of landscapes everywhere. The kind of weathering caused by water freezing in rocks is known as *mechanical* weathering.

Plants can cause weathering, too. A seed that falls into a crack in a rock may be able to grow there. As it grows, the roots of the plant may exert a force that enlarges the crack, a process called **root-pry.** You may have seen root-pry taking place on a sidewalk. 2 This prying action, like the action of expanding water, is a kind of mechanical weathering.

Chemical Weathering

Plants also cause *chemical* weathering. Plant roots may produce acids that can dissolve rock by chemical change. If the acids enter the rock, it may break down from within, cracking and peeling off in layers. Plants without roots, such as the lichens, can grow on bare rock. 3 They produce acids that slowly crumble the rock.

The greatest amount of chemical weathering, however, is due to acids formed from the mixture of atmospheric and volcanic gases with water. These acids can increase the solvent action of water considerably. The rate at which weathering goes on depends, as you might expect, on the type of rock and the

3

4

climate. This stone is decomposing rapidly in the acid-loaded atmosphere of New York City. 4

Weathering, then, is a process that transforms the land, perhaps slowly but none the less surely. More accurately, weathering *starts* the transforming of the land, and another process completes it. What is this process? We will examine it next.

REVIEW

1. Explain the process of chemical weathering.
2. What is mechanical weathering? Give two specific examples.
3. What is an important effect of weathering?
4. Describe the action of freezing water on rock.

NEW VIEW

Scientists sometimes speak of three classes of weathering: chemical, physical, and biological. Do research to find examples of each kind.

2. REMOVING THE WEATHERED ROCK

Has it ever occurred to you that our atmosphere is a tremendous reservoir? We often wish that the release of water from the reservoir could be controlled, and perhaps in time, as our knowledge of precipitation increases, it will be. What happens to the water that is released from the reservoir of the atmosphere?

Rain falls. Raindrops strike the ground, and the earth is worn away—a little bit. Rain falls and streams form. The earth is moved downhill, and the continents are lowered—a little bit. Bit by little bit, land is removed from one place and deposited in another place. Bit by little bit, the earth's surface is being shaped into the forms we see today.

1

Water has a slow but awesome effect in shaping the face of the earth. 1 Water and other agents remove, transport, and deposit rock debris, that is, cause **erosion.** And water is by far the most powerful agent of erosion.

Water in the Ground

As you know from your own observations, some of the water that falls on the ground may run off the surface, and some may sink in. As you'd expect, the proportions vary with the nature of the ground. Water sinking down through soil soon encounters what we usually think of as "solid" rock.

Often enough, however, rock is not solid but porous: it is riddled with tiny cavities, as is this piece of sandstone. 2 The cavities may form a network of tiny tunnels, so that water may not only enter porous rock but flow through it—though the rate of flow will be pretty slow, of course. Materials, such as sandstone and gravel, through which water passes readily, are *permeable.* A good part of the water that falls on the earth's surface makes its way through the permeable rock layers into the *impermeable* layers beneath. Impermeable rock layers through which water cannot pass may be shale or almost any igneous or metamorphic rock.

The water that collects in permeable rock layers is known as **ground water.** As a rule ground water is not evenly spread through a permeable rock layer, but tends to collect at the bottom of the layer, where it fills the holes with water and saturates the rock there. The level at which saturation begins is called the **water table.** 3

Above the water table the pores in the rock are lined with only a thin film of water, and air fills the rest of the space. As you can see in the illustration, a well drilled into water-bearing rock must reach below the water table to get water. The height of the water table varies with the amount of water in the rock. In a dry season the level of the water table may fall so far that a well goes dry.

A great amount of water, however, is stored in the earth's permeable rock layers, and travels considerable distances through these layers. Where the water table cuts the surface on the side of a hill, a spring may form. 3 Unseen and slow-moving as it is below the earth's surface, ground water is indeed an important part of our water supply.

2

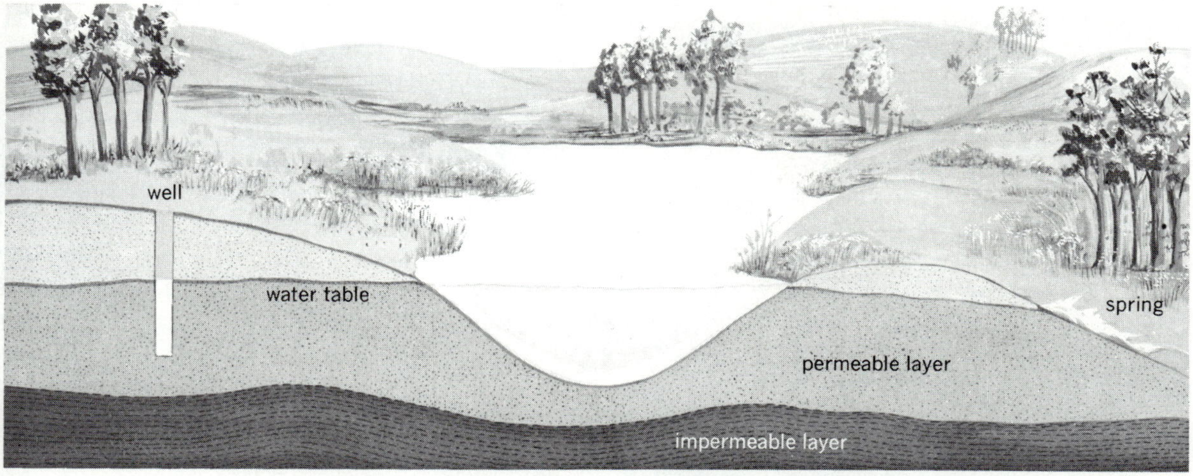

Underground Water Comes to the Surface

Ground water usually stays near the *average* yearly temperature of the area where it is found. Therefore, water from springs is usually cool in summer. Occasionally, ground water passes through regions of igneous rock where lava activity has occurred fairly recently. The water flowing over this lava comes to the surface as hot springs.

In a very few places, hot spring water reaches the surface in a more spectacular way. From time to time, some hot springs give off their water as a fountain. Such erupting hot springs are called **geysers.** One of our most famous geysers is Old Faithful in Yellowstone National Park. 4 It erupts about once every 65 minutes.

Geologists are not certain about what causes geysers. They think the ground water collects in a narrow, pipelike opening that extends many feet into the hot rock. Here a process similar to that in a pressure cooker takes place. Water usually boils at 100°C; but if the pressure is increased, it boils at a higher temperature. The water at the bottom of the pipe is under great pressure, so it boils at a temperature well above its usual boiling point. In time, the boiling water changes to steam, expands further, and forces the water above it out of the pipe in a violent eruption. After the eruption, water again seeps into the pipe, and the whole cycle begins again.

Occasionally, hot spring water comes to the surface through soft, delicately colored clays.

1

2

These clays result from the weathering of volcanic rocks. If you have been to Yellowstone National Park, you may have seen some of these thick, bubbling regions, which are appropriately called *"paint pots."* 1

In a few volcanic regions, you may find steam and hot gases escaping steadily from cracks or holes in the earth's surface. 2 These openings from which the steam and gases escape are called **fumaroles.** In some areas of the world, the steam from fumaroles has been used for heat and even to produce electricity.

Work of Underground Water

Have you ever visited Carlsbad Cavern in New Mexico or Mammoth Cave in Kentucky? 3 If so, you've seen another wonderful sight that results from the slow, steady action of ground water. Although limestone is not porous, cracks may appear in it. Water containing dissolved carbon dioxide from the air and decaying animal matter runs into these cracks. Over thousands of years the ground water containing the carbon dioxide dissolves the limestone (calcium carbonate) and hollows it out to form caves.

If you have visited some of the more beautiful caves, you know that "icicles" of calcium carbonate hang down from the ceiling while other more rounded deposits point up from the floor. How are these icicle-like **stalactites**

3

and more rounded **stalagmites** formed? Sometime ground water containing dissolved limestone drips from the roof of the cave. As the water evaporates, the calcium carbonate may be deposited on the roof of the cave as stalactites. When drops fall to the floor of the cave and evaporate, stalagmites are formed. Occasionally, stalactites and stalagmites meet and form columns.

The surface of the land in limestone areas is also changed as a result of rock dissolving underground. Small basins, called **sink holes,** are often formed. 4 Although surface water may drain through these sink holes, they may become blocked and form ponds.

4

Work of Surface Water

Some of the water that falls on the land as rain soaks into the ground, but some of it becomes what is called **surface runoff.** As this surface runoff moves, it moves some of the land with it. It may carry away some soil, for example. To be concerned about the amount of soil that a raindrop can carry away seems overly cautious, at first—until you find out that a heavy rainstorm may remove in one hour the soil that it took a thousand years to produce.

Have you noticed large boulders like these in the bed of a stream? 5 They are evidence of the carrying power of running water. You'd

5

expect that the faster a stream flows, the bigger the rocks it can roll along. What you might not expect is *how* big the rocks may be. There is evidence to show that if the velocity of the stream is doubled, the size of the rock it can move is not merely doubled—it is 2^6 or 64 times as big.

Remember, too, that material running water is bearing along may be used to knock loose still more material from the land, as well as to grind it all into very small pieces. You will then begin to realize the part that running water plays in the process of erosion.

Work of a Stream

Running water on the side of a mountain finds a course, and a rivulet is formed. The rivulet cuts into the rock of the mountain, over millions of years, deeper and deeper, and becomes a stream. Other rivulets on the mountain have cut their way down and become streams, so have rivulets on other mountains. The rivulets become streams, the streams become rivers.

Young rivers rushing down steep slopes cut deep into the bedrock, so that the valley walls of a young river are shaped like a V. (1) These

1

stream canyons are among the most spectacular of all land forms. The Grand Canyon, a stream canyon over 300 kilometers long and more than 2 kilometers deep in places, was cut by the Colorado River! (2)

In the upper part of a new stream, other landscape features are found. Rapids and waterfalls are formed as the stream passes over resistant rock that has not yet worn away. (3) As the stream "ages" and the landscape is worn down, however, these features disappear.

2

As the river makes its way to the sea, the erosion of the stream floor decreases. Passing onto a flat area, the stream frequently overflows its confined channel, eroding material across a wide area. A **flood plain** is thus produced. Some of these channels may be cut off from the main flow of water and form features called **ox-bow lakes.** (4) Flood plains and ox-bow lakes are features of a river in "old age."

The river flows slowly onward to the ocean basins. Here, it finally deposits the tremendous load of sediment it has been carrying. **Deltas,** fan-shaped deposits, are the features of the landscape that result from this deposition—the final activity of the stream in wearing down and shaping the land. (5) The Mississippi Delta has added more than 16 kilometers (10 miles) of land to the Gulf Coast since the beginning of the Civil War.

(3)

(4)

(5)

REVIEW

1. What is meant by the water table?
2. How are stalactites and stalagmites formed in underground caves?
3. How are geysers and fumaroles similar? How are they different?
4. What features of the landscape are produced by running water?

NEW VIEW

1. A young mountain has the shape in cross section of a **Λ**. An older mountain has the shape of a **∩**. The valley of a young river has a shape approaching a **V**. An older river valley has a wider |_| shape. Account for the shapes of young mountains and rivers by applying what you know of the action of water.
2. Could any of the canyons in the continental shelf have been formed the way the Grand Canyon was formed? Explain your answer.

1

3. THE WORK OF GLACIERS

High up on this mountain the snow falls very heavily during winter. 1 As it piles up, the snow below is compressed by the growing weight of snow above. Have you ever squeezed a handful of snow? If you have, you know that squeezed snow can turn to ice. Something of this sort happens on the mountain side—as more snow falls, and more weight is added, the lower layers of snow become ice. As more snow falls, the mass of ice grows larger—and *moves.* The ice moves down the mountain side, pulled by gravity, into the valley below. It moves through the valley, as more ice forms and comes down.

Thus a mass of moving ice, a glacier, is formed. This glacier pours into the sea, where chunks of ice break off and float away as icebergs. But, we don't think of ice as able to move, usually. How can this happen?

Flowing Ice

You may recall that so solid a substance as the rock under the earth's crust, the magma, can flow when great pressure is applied to it. Under pressure, ice can flow too. The pressure is applied by the weight of ice and snow above the lowest layers. Under pressure, ice can become somewhat plastic, and the crystals that make it up can move about.

Ice tends to melt under pressure, too, and to freeze again when the pressure is relieved by moving to another position. So the mass of ice that is a glacier can move under the pull of gravity, can creep down a mountain side and through valleys like a river in slow motion. Stakes driven into the ice of a glacier, in a straight line across it, change position and show that the middle of the ice river moves more rapidly than the sides, where friction slows down the flow just as it does in a river of water.

The rate of flow of glaciers varies. Some glaciers move as little as 12 meters (40 feet) in a year, others as much as 120 meters (400 feet) in a day. Since the surface of a glacier is not under pressure, it is brittle, rough, and uneven, and breaks into deep cracks or crevasses. ❷

The glacier shown on page 132 is flowing through a valley and is called a **valley glacier.** Its direction of movement has been set by the valley, which was there before the glacier was.

A **continental glacier,** on the other hand, is a vast sheet of ice that spreads in all directions, like pancake batter being poured on a griddle. The ice of a continental glacier is much thicker than that of a valley glacier.

As you may imagine, a huge mass of ice (whether a continental or a valley glacier) moving across the land is likely to make some changes in the land. Let's examine some of these changes.

Glaciers Change the Land

As a glacier moves down a valley, twisting and turning, it tends to widen and deepen the valley and give it a U-shaped cross-section. The moving river of ice loosens and scrapes material from the valley walls and makes them into steep cliffs. Some of this material falls on the surface of the glacier and is carried along there. In the glacier shown on page 132, the dark bands you see on the ice are just such material. There is still more material inside, of course.

At the head of the glacier, up on the mountain side, the forming and moving ice tends to pluck pieces of rock out of the mountain, making a circular basin called a **cirque.** The pieces of rock from the cirque are carried down in the ice, too, so the interior of a glacier is a huge collection of pieces of rock and other material that acts like a giant rasp on the land over which the ice passes.

Moreover, the front of the glacier tends to behave like a bulldozer, piling up material. A valley glacier, then, tends to deepen and make more rugged the land it moves through. A continental glacier, however, since it spreads over the whole landscape, tends to flatten and round off the land.

❷

When a glacier melts and retreats, it leaves behind the materials it was carrying. These mixtures of gravel, sand, sediment, rocks and boulders that a glacier deposits are called **moraines.** When it retreats, the front of a glacier may leave a crescent-shaped ridge of debris, which is called a **terminal moraine.**

Some geologists think that Long Island, about 200 kilometers long (118 miles), is partially a terminal moraine heaped up by the last continental glacier—which may give you some idea of the scale on which a continental glacier works. Specimens of rock from northern regions are found on Long Island, having been dumped there some 11,000 years ago when a great continental glacier spread down from the Arctic region. It covered almost all of Canada and moved into what is now the United States. (You will study more about this in Chapter 16.) A similar sheet moved into Northern Europe. The glacier covered much of the land and then retreated. Today glaciers cover 10 percent of our land mass, but there is evidence that they once covered three times as much.

Continental glaciers move by spreading out in all directions from the center of greatest concentration of the ice. As they flow outward they level land, pushing debris before them. The Great Lakes were scooped out, as were the Finger Lakes of New York. As the glacier melted, the lake basins filled with water. Material deposited by the melting ice made the land near these lakes very fertile.

In Wisconsin and other Midwestern states, as well as in New York, Massachusetts, and parts of Canada, the debris from the retreating glacier sometimes takes the form of loaf-shaped hills, called **drumlins.** The Cape Cod area in Massachusetts is made up of debris pushed and carried down to the sea by glacial ice and its melting. The sandbars south of the

1

New England coast are also the result of glacial action. Rocks that dot the Canadian flatlands are remnants of a vast continental glacier.

The glacier carried huge boulders from the north and deposited them. Here sits one of these rocks, quite unlike anything around it. 1 The glacier leaves its marks behind it, too. All over Canada and the northern region of the United States, preserved in hard rock surfaces, are long thin scratches called **striae** made by rocks that were once imbedded in the underside of the glacier. These striae tell us the direction in which the glacier moved.

The Earth's Ice Ages

Geologists have found evidence that during the past two million years the earth has had four ice ages. During these ice ages continental glaciers advanced and retreated.

When does a glacier advance? When the glacial ice is forming faster than it is melting, the glacier grows and spreads. Now, for more ice to form, there must be more snow. For more snow to fall, there must be more water in the atmosphere. For more water in the atmosphere, there must be more evaporation, from the sea. What would make for a higher rate of evaporation? If the sea water became warmer, that would increase the rate of evaporation, certainly. If this chain of reasoning is correct, then, the water in the Arctic must at some time have been warmer than it is now —strange as that may seem to us.

Is this hypothesis an accurate explanation for those ice ages we know have taken place? Still more evidence is needed, and is being gathered. If this hypothesis is correct, however, we are now in a period when the Arctic Ocean is beginning to get warmer, and more open, the start of the melting part of the cycle.

Other explanations have been suggested. Perhaps the advance and retreat of a continental glacier is due to changes in the heat released by the sun. If at certain times the sun radiates less energy, then the earth would get colder, and poles would gather ice. If the sun radiated more energy at other times, the poles would get warmer and the ice would melt. But evidence for such changes in the sun's heat production has not yet been found.

Wind and Waves

Wind and waves are two other natural agents that can erode material from one place and deposit it in another place. Their effect on shaping the land, however, is limited. Wind is most effective in dry areas covered by loose materials. Hence, we look to deserts or beaches to find the most dramatic work of wind. The geologic work of waves, on the other hand, occurs mostly at the shorelines of the oceans. (2)

2

3

The principal feature produced by the wind is a landform called a **blowout.** These blowouts are shallow basins produced by the removal of loose particles. (3) Blowing over a dry surface, the wind can pick up the smallest sized particles—clay and silt—and carries them high in the air. The larger sand grains are moved only small distances, usually by rolling or bouncing along the surface. The still larger rock fragments—the pebbles and gravel—may not be moved at all. In some places, the wind has sorted the materials very effectively, leaving behind a surface covered only with pebbles and larger rock pieces.

1

2

Dunes are deposits of sand formed and shaped by the wind. Depending on the strength and direction of the wind, the type and amount of sediment, and the quantity of vegetation, dunes may take many forms. 1

Features formed by waves are particularly dramatic where a steeply sloping land surface descends into the water. As waves chew away at such a land mass, a **seacliff** is formed. 2 In a rock mass that extends into the water, the waves can etch out **sea caves, sea arches,** and **sea stacks.** 3 In time, however, these features are worn away, and a beach is formed in front of the headland.

In several areas of the United States, especially along the Atlantic and Gulf Coasts, **barrier islands** are found. These barrier islands are sand masses separated from the shore, and

3

4

are usually several kilometers long and wide, and 30 meters (100 feet) or more high. Many of our most famous beaches such as Jones Beach or Atlantic City, are located on barrier islands. 4

Water, wind, waves, and glacial ice continually shape the land. Removing material from one place and depositing it in another is one of the simple themes that dominate our study of the ever-changing earth.

REVIEW

1. Explain the flow of a glacier.
2. How does a glacier produce erosion?
3. Distinguish between valley glaciers and continental glaciers.
4. Account for the formation of drumlins and terminal moraines.
5. Account for the formation of icebergs.
6. On a world map or globe locate the places where glaciers exist now.
7. Describe how wind and waves cause erosion.

NEW VIEW

1. A terminal moraine is found in Long Island. What is the sequence of events that may have produced it?
2. Glacial lake deposits often contain layered deposits of coarse, dark-colored material alternating with fine, light-colored material. Find out how these deposits, called *varves*, can be used to tell time.
3. What is the evidence (if any) that the North Pole was once tropical?

4. RELATING THE CONCEPTS

You live on the crust of the earth in contact with two "oceans," the atmosphere and the hydrosphere. Both are related in many ways to one another, and to the lithosphere under your feet. Evaporation of water from the sea and the ground results in water vapor in the air. This water vapor in turn condenses to form raindrops, streams, rivers, and glaciers whose movements carry away land and build it up. In time, the action of water levels majestic mountains, carves deep canyons in rock, and lays down huge quantities of sediment. The earth's water changes the earth's land, even as you read this.

Water also shapes the land along our coasts. The continuous action of waves build up and break down the land, producing a variety of landforms.

Water frozen into glaciers also shapes the land. The effects of modern glaciers provide evidence to support the theory that there have been many ice ages in the past.

An understanding of the concepts that underlie the behavior of water in the atmosphere, in precipitation and in erosion, brings us a clearer understanding of a planet in continuous change.

Reviewing the Concepts

► *The surface of the earth is in continual change.* The face of the earth is not fixed and unchanging. The change is slow, taking place over what we regard as long periods of time, but the change is drastic.

► *The earth's crust is being worn down and built up.* The material that is the result of the processes of weathering and erosion can be carried away by moving water, wind, and ice, and laid down elsewhere. Thus in some places the land is being worn down, in other places built up.

► *Various landforms are produced by the action of water moving over the surface of the earth.* Water, still or moving, underground or on the surface, in the form of rain or ice, is the most powerful agent of erosion.

Testing Yourself

1. What part does weathering play in shaping the land?

2. How are underground caves formed?

3. What causes a geyser to erupt?

4. What is ground water? How does it affect the water table?

5. How is the location of a spring related to the water table?

6. What is a valley glacier, and how does it form?

7. What do glaciers do to the face of the earth?

8. Describe how blowouts and dunes are formed.

9. What is a terminal moraine? Why do some geologists think that Long Island may be an example?

10. How is a continental glacier different from a valley glacier?

11. Describe the effects of waves on the landscape.

12. Briefly describe several landscape features that can be produced by running water.

Extending the Concepts

Investigation 1. You know that there is water in ponds, lakes, and streams. Is there also water in surface soil? Why not find out?

Place a sample of seemingly dry soil in the bottom of a clean, dry test tube or a junior-size baby food jar. Place a loose-fitting cover over the top. Then very gently warm the bottom of the container so that the soil is slightly warmed. Observe the inside of the jar. Is there any evidence of condensation there? If there is condensation, where do you think the moisture comes from?

Investigation 2. How does moving water (in a river, for instance) affect soil? You can learn a lot by being observant during, or just after, a rain storm by examining miniature rivers or river beds. Find a sandy place in a roadside gutter, or where rain-water runoff has taken place. Observation will probably show you canyon, gullies, rapids, flood plains, and deltas formed by the action of the running water. They are much the same as those formed by large rivers. Observe the particle sizes of the soil in the different sections you have observed. How do you account for what you see? You may want to photograph your observations.

Suggested Reading

Dyson, James L., *The World of Ice,* New York, Knopf, 1962. All aspects of glaciers and their study.

Harrington, John W., *To See A World,* St. Louis, Mosby, 1973. An introduction to geology with a special section on historical geology.

Ley, Willy, and the editors of LIFE, *The Poles* (Life Nature Library), Time, Inc., 1962. The geology and biology of the earth's ice-bound poles. Many illustrations.

Unit Three

THE EARTH IN THE UNIVERSE

Look at the stars on a clear night. For thousands of years, people have looked at the sky in the same way. With their unaided eyes, they saw and described thousands of stars. To our unaided eyes, the look of the universe hasn't changed much. To our minds, the universe has changed a great deal. We can see beyond the closest stars. We can discover such things as the Great Nebula in the constellation Orion.

Today we know more about the universe than people of old, watching the sky, ever dreamed of. What have we discovered about the universe? How have we made these discoveries?

8

Our Star, the Sun

The year is 1609. In Florence, Italy, a man is writing a letter to his brother-in-law.

"You must know, then, that some two months ago the word spread here that in Flanders Count Maurice had been presented with an eyeglass fashioned with such cunning that it made things which were most distant appear very near, so that a man very far off could clearly be seen. This seemed to me so wonderful a result that I began to ponder on it; and as I was of the opinion it was based on the science of perspective, I turned my thoughts to its construction, which I finally achieved and with such perfection, that one of those I have fashioned far exceeds the reputation of the one in Flanders. . . ."

1

1. WITH THE ASTRONOMER

Perhaps you have guessed that the man writing the letter was Galileo. Using his knowledge of the "science of perspective"—we would say "science of optics"—Galileo had made a simple telescope. (1)

Galileo was not content, however, to watch distant men or far-off ships with the fascinating new instrument. He turned his telescope to the night sky. And so began the astonishing and revolutionary discoveries about the universe that the telescope has made possible.

We can hardly imagine astronomy without telescopes. All the stars we can see at night with the unaided eye are so far away that they are tiny points of light. Beyond them, so far away that they are not visible at all, are many more stars. How does a telescope bring into view stars we cannot see?

Collecting Light

The Hale telescope perched on Mount Palomar in California is the largest of its kind in the world.❷ Its main part is a huge mirror almost 5 meters (17 feet) in diameter. This mirror is curved inward, so that light from a star is reflected to a single point in front of the mirror. This point is called the *focus* of the mirror. If you held a piece of white paper at the focus when the mirror is pointed at a star, you would see on the paper an image of the star formed by the curved mirror.❸

The image of the star on the paper would be very bright. Can you see why? The huge mirror gathers far more light from the star than your eye does. The larger the reflecting surface of the mirror, the greater the amount of light it can gather.

❷

❸
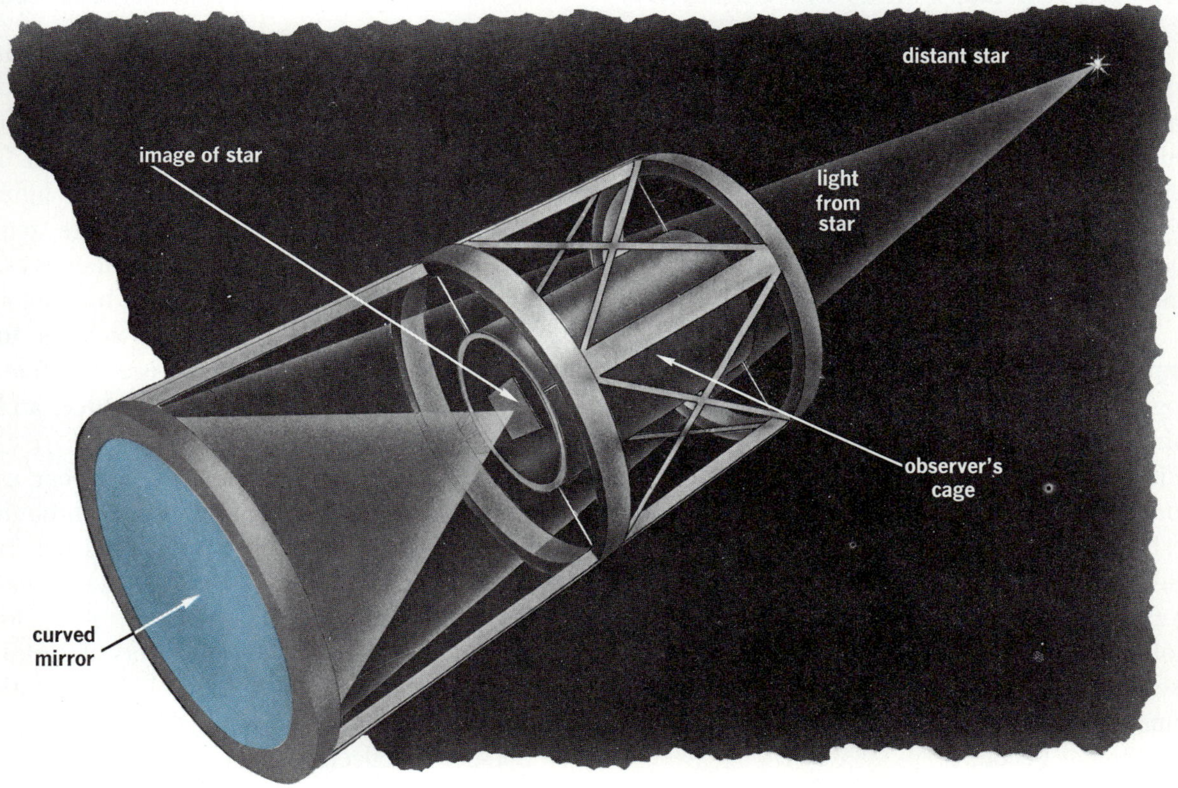

❶ 

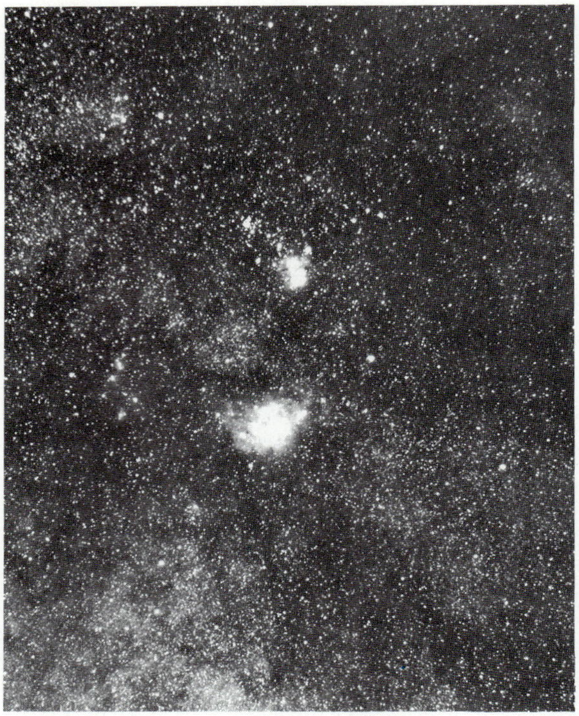 ❷

If the mirror is pointed at a part of the sky where there are many stars, it will form an image of those stars. You could examine this image with a magnifying eyepiece. But an astronomer would probably prefer to make a photograph. For one thing, a photograph is a permanent record of an observation. For another, a time exposure can be used.

To see what the gathering of light by time exposure can reveal, look at these two photographs of the same section of the sky. The photograph on the left was exposed for 10 minutes. ❶ The one on the right was exposed for 45 minutes. ❷

Notice how the bright stars near the center seem to grow brighter as the exposure time gets longer. Of course the stars themselves do not become brighter. Photographic film collects light; the longer the film is exposed, the more light it collects, and the brighter the star image becomes.

Observe that some stars not visible at all in the first photograph appear in the second one. How do we explain this? So little light from these stars reaches the telescope that a longer time is needed to collect enough light to make them visible. Each star's image gets brighter as the time of exposure increases. Thus, by making use of the ability of photographic film to "store" light as well as to collect it, the astronomer can use his telescope to make faint stars seem brighter, and invisible stars visible.

Stars are much too far away to appear as anything but points of light, even through the largest telescope in the world. It is not its magnifying power that makes the Hale telescope the world's most powerful; it is its power to gather light. Astronomers describe the size of a reflecting telescope by the width of its mirror, so they call the Hale telescope a "200-inch" reflector.

3

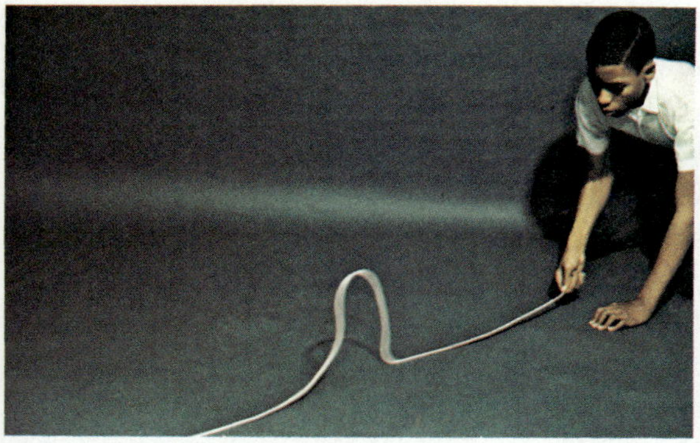

4

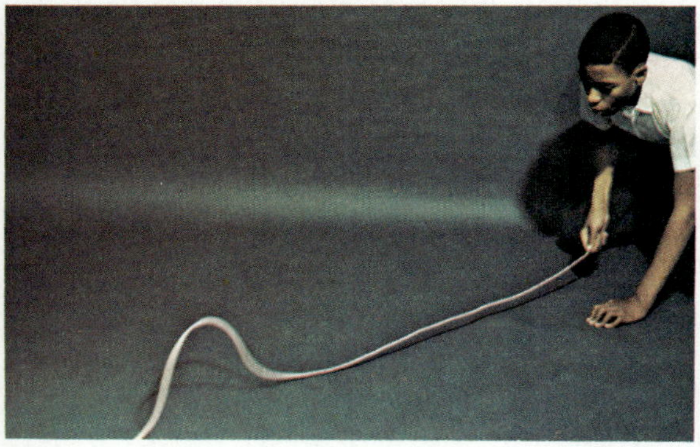

The world's fifth largest reflecting telescope, a "100-inch" reflector, stands on Mount Wilson, near Mount Palomar. Reflectors of many sizes are in use in observatories throughout the world. The larger the reflecting surface of the mirror, the more light it can gather. This is why the "200-inch" mirror of the Hale telescope reveals objects in space too dim to be seen with any other instrument.

Energy in Waves

Lay a length of clothesline along the floor. Set a pencil across one end of the rope. Give the other end of the rope a quick up-and-down flip. 3 If you put enough energy into it, a loop will travel the length of the rope and throw off the pencil. 4 You have demonstrated that energy can travel in the form of a wave.

If you flip the rope end several times without stopping, you can send a series of waves along the rope, sending out as much energy as you like. And you will find that if you vary the speed at which you flip the rope, you can send out waves whose crests, or tops, are closer together, or farther apart. In other words, you can send out waves of different lengths, the **wavelength** being the distance from the crest of one wave to the crest of the next.

So you have shown that energy can be sent out in waves of different lengths. You have also made a model of how light energy reaches us from the stars.

Starlight, including the kind we usually call sunlight, is energy traveling in the form of waves. These waves are of different lengths, moreover, for each star (including our sun) radiates energy of many different wavelengths. As you know from your earlier work in science, when sunlight is passed through a prism it breaks up into a spectrum of colors. Each color is made up of a range of wavelengths. Scientists are able to measure the wavelengths of each color.

Color	*Wavelength*
violet	1/26,000 of a centimeter (1/65,000 of an inch)
blue	
green	
yellow	wavelength decreases
orange	
red	1/12,000 of a centimeter (1/30,000 of an inch)

Perhaps you recall that at each end of this visible spectrum there is some invisible radiation. Just beyond the violet wavelengths are still shorter wavelengths of radiant energy which we call ultraviolet. Anyone who has had a sunburn knows what ultraviolet waves from a star (the sun) can do. Ultraviolet light also kills bacteria in the air and aids the production of vitamin D in the skin.

At the other end of the visible spectrum, just beyond the red wavelengths we see, is a still longer group of wavelengths we don't see, called infrared radiation. Infrared radiation is the main source of heat in the total amount of radiation we receive from the sun. Matter is warmed when it is struck by infrared radiation—as by radiation from the visible part of the spectrum.

If you feel that we have about reached the end of the list of waves that a star radiates, you are in for a surprise. The fact is that stars give off energy through a tremendous range of different wavelengths. The wavelengths of visible light are given in the table on page 145. Other waves can be several kilometers long. Ultraviolet, visible light, and infrared radiation are just a small part of the energy spectrum, as you can see here. ❶

Light, gamma radiation, X rays, ultraviolet, infrared, and radio—these are the names we give to different wavelengths of this radiant energy. Except for light, these waves are not visible to us. However, we know these invisible forms of energy by their effects.

Cosmic radiation, for instance, can be detected by its effect on a Geiger counter. Cosmic radiation comes to us from outer space and forms part of the background radiation that makes a Geiger counter click. **Gamma radiation** also makes a Geiger counter click. You are right if you guess that radioactive substances give off gamma radiation. Waves of cosmic radiation and gamma radiation are shortest of all.

Next to gamma radiation in wavelengths are X rays. The wavelength of X rays are so small that 3 million X-ray waves can be contained in the length of one line on this page. When your teeth are X-rayed you do not see or feel these waves, but you can see their effect on photographic film. As you see in the diagram, the bands named gamma radiation and X rays overlap, as do other bands throughout the spectrum.

Beyond visible light and the infrared waves, there are the waves of radio energy. Radio waves have the longest wavelengths in the energy spectrum. No doubt radio waves are passing around you and through you as you read these words, but you need a radio receiver to make their effects audible.

In many different wavelengths, energy is being radiated from the stars. All of these different wavelengths of radiant energy are

❶

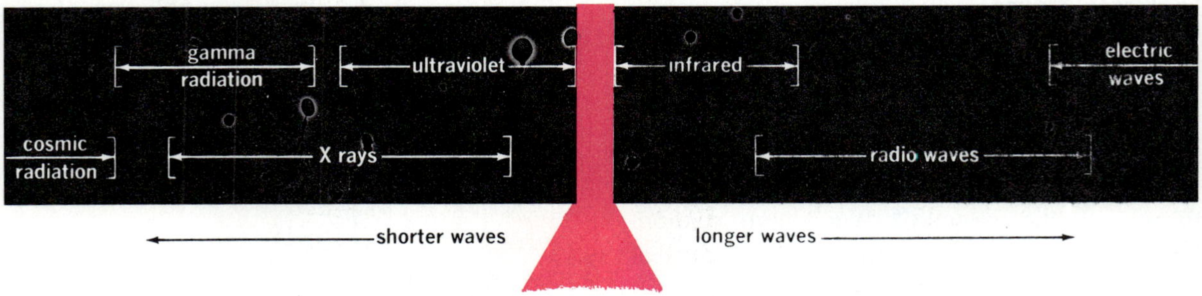

❷

both electric and magnetic in nature. They are known as **electromagnetic waves,** therefore. The whole array of electromagnetic waves spread out in the diagram on page 146 is called the **electromagnetic spectrum.**

Next time you look at a star, think of it as a sphere of matter pouring out energy, a ball of matter-energy. Think of the waves it is pouring forth that you do *not* see.

Windows on Space

The sun and the other stars send out electromagnetic radiation of many wavelengths. But fortunately for us, not all of these waves can penetrate the earth's atmosphere. Some that can't get through our atmosphere are deadly to living things. The parts of the electromagnetic spectrum that can get through our atmosphere are windows into space, so to speak, for through them we can find out what is going on outside the earth.

There are two main windows: astronomers call them the "visible window" and the "radio window." An optical telescope, like the Hale reflector, for instance, collects radiation in the form of light through the "visible window" into space. But only recently have astronomers discovered that there is a "radio window," as well as a "visible window," through which they could observe some totally unexpected events in space.

The discovery of the radio window came about as things sometimes do in science—unexpectedly. A young American physicist named Karl Jansky was looking for the cause of radio static that made a soft but steady hiss in even the best radio receivers. Jansky made an astonishing discovery with his odd-looking radio antenna. ❷ The hiss was being caused by radio waves coming from outer space—in fact, the radio waves were coming from outside the solar system.

1

Jansky reported his sensational discovery in 1932. The newspapers picked up the story and Jansky became famous for a time. But oddly enough, nothing else happened right away. No other physicist or astronomer followed up Jansky's discovery to see where it led.

A radio ham named Grote Reber, however, read Jansky's original reports and determined to find out more about these mysterious radio waves from outer space. Reber made for himself what turned out to be the first radio telescope, and began to explore the Milky Way with it in 1937. Thus a kind of radio window, through which especially strong sources of radio waves of certain wavelength are received on earth, was found and put to use. Astronomers began building radio telescopes as well as optical ones.

An optical telescope collects light waves; a radio telescope collects radio waves. 1 The curved reflector, called a "dish" by astronomers, is made of fine wire mesh. (In some radio telescopes the dish is made of sheet metal.) The mirror of an optical telescope reflects light waves to a focus. The dish of a radio telescope reflects radio waves so that they focus on the radio antenna in front of the dish.

The reflector of a radio telescope has to be very much larger than that of an optical telescope. The "200-inch" mirror of the Hale telescope on Palomar is dwarfed by the "1,000-foot" dish of the radio telescope at Arecibo in Puerto Rico.

In the next chapter we will take a look through the astronomer's radio window into space, through which we have received much valuable—and some unexpected—information. But first let's look again through the visible window and see how the visible spectrum has enabled astronomers to tell what the stars are made of. This is one way that we learn something of the forms of matter in the universe, and their changes.

REVIEW

1. A student notes the colors of the visible spectrum as violet, green, blue, orange, yellow, and red. He has them in the wrong order. List them in the correct order, beginning with the color that has the shortest wavelength. Also add infrared and ultraviolet radiations.

2. What was the work each of these men did to help modern astronomers look farther into space?

a. Galileo b. Jansky c. Reber

3. What two advantages does photography have in astronomical observation?

4. How are all kinds of electromagnetic radiations alike? How do they differ from each other?

5. What is meant by the "visible window" into space? the "radio window"?

6. Tell how we can detect each of the following invisible radiations:

a. X rays b. infrared c. gamma

NEW VIEW

1. Which telescope has more working hours in the day, the Hale telescope or the radio telescope? Explain your answer.

2. X rays, ultraviolet radiation, and much of the infrared radiation from the sun and other stars are screened out by the earth's atmosphere. How, then, do scientists know that these radiations are present beyond our earth's atmosphere?

3. Why are some stars we cannot see called radio stars?

4. Black and white are two "colors" that do not appear in the spectrum. Explain the origin of each.

2. WAVELENGTHS AND ELEMENTS

In the year 1825 a noted philosopher pointed out that there were limits to what men could know. There were some kinds of knowledge that men could never obtain because there was no imaginable way of obtaining it. For example, he confidently said, men could never hope to find out what the distant stars are made of.

It was not a good example. Less than ten years later scientists were finding out what elements there are in stars. And how was this unimaginable thing done? With colored light, strangely enough.

To find out what elements there are on the earth, the chemist analyzes bits of the earth's matter. To find out what elements there are in a star, the astronomer analyzes the light sent out by the star. These may seem very different sorts of analyses, yet both chemist and astronomer use the same basic method.

Suppose that a chemist suspects that a certain bit of the earth's matter contains the element sodium. He performs a flame test. He puts the bit of matter in a colorless flame. If sodium is present, the flame turns a yellow color. In other words, certain wavelengths of light characteristic of the element sodium are given off. 2

For greater accuracy, the chemist may look at the yellow flame through a **spectroscope,** an instrument that separates light into the wavelengths that make it up. The spectroscope allows him to identify the wavelengths more exactly. He compares his observation with earlier ones, and is thus able to say that the bit of matter in the flame is giving off just the wavelengths of light that show the presence of sodium.

Notice that it is light that gives the chemist this information. Even if the light comes from a distant star, the spectroscope can separate it into its wavelengths, and the scientist can compare these with wavelengths obtained from elements in the laboratory. The astronomer can use the same tool as the chemist to find out what elements there are in the stars.

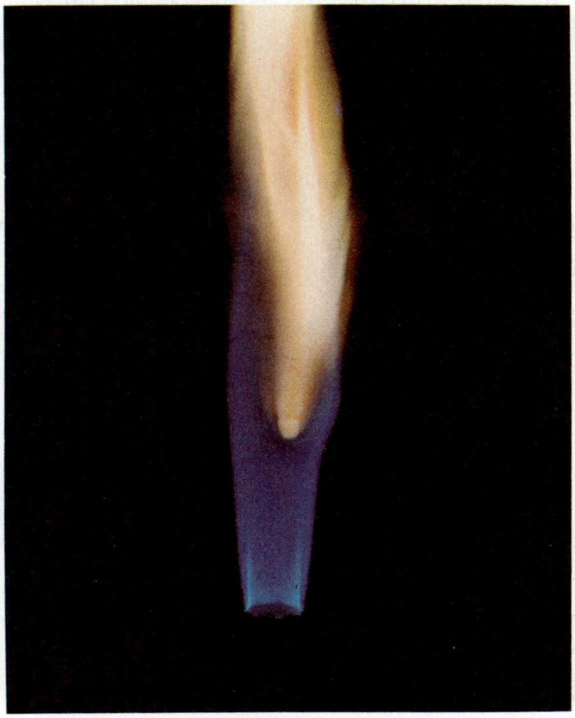

2

Exploring with a Spectroscope

You can make a spectroscope for yourself. As you know, a prism can separate light into different wavelengths; many spectroscopes are made with prisms, but you can more easily use a **diffraction grating,** which does the same thing. A diffraction grating is a piece of transparent plastic with very fine parallel lines on it. The lines are very close together—there may be 15,000 of them in a space one-third as long as this line. They form a sort of grating of very tiny slits. The slits are far too small to see, but you can readily see their effect on light. If you look through the grating at a light bulb, you will discover a spectrum off to one side of the light. (You may find several spectra.) The diffraction grating, like a prism, sorts out light into wavelengths. ■

Spectrum Analysis

Simple as your homemade spectroscope is, it allows you to observe two basic kinds of spectra.

A **continuous spectrum** is a smooth rainbow of colors: red, orange, yellow, green, blue, violet. Light of every visible wavelength is present. Every glowing solid produces a continuous spectrum. ❶

A **bright-line spectrum** is made up of colored lines against a dark background: some wavelengths of light are present, but not all. The bright-line spectrum consists of certain parts of the continuous spectrum. A glowing gas produces a bright-line spectrum. Here is the spectrum of gaseous mercury. ❷

A third kind of spectrum is called a **dark-line spectrum.** ❸ The darkline spectrum looks like a continuous spectrum cut by dark lines. A glowing gaseous mass like the sun, or any other star, produces this kind of spectrum. The spectrum shown is the sun's.

The dark lines in this spectrum show that certain wavelengths of light are absent. When these dark lines appear in a spectrum, it means that certain wavelengths are being absorbed by a cooler substance that surrounds a glowing mass that gives off a continuous spectrum. The inside of the sun, for example, gives off a continuous spectrum of light wavelengths. But cooler gases in the outer part of the sun absorb certain wavelengths of the continuous spectrum. So the spectrum we receive from the sun has dark lines in it.

You have seen that a glowing gas gives a spectrum of bright lines, and that different

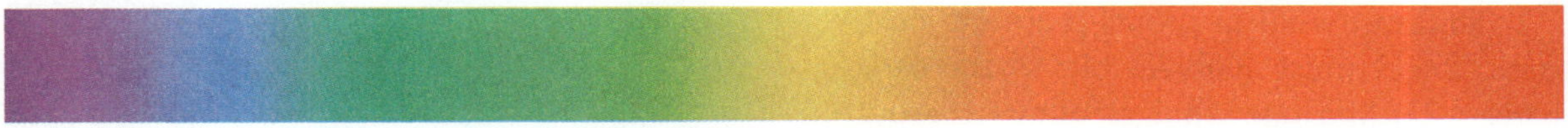
❶

❷

❸

■ AN APPRENTICE INVESTIGATION into Spectra

Cut a hole about 1 centimeter ($\frac{1}{2}$ inch) in diameter at each end of a shoebox. Over the hole at one end, tape a piece of aluminum foil. Then make a narrow vertical slit in the foil.

Look through a diffraction grating at a light source. Turn the grating until the spectra are horizontal. Tape the grating in this position over the hole at the other end of the box.❶

To use the spectroscope, look through the grating end while aiming the slit end at a light source. ***(Caution: Do not aim the spectroscope at the sun. Serious damage to the eyes can result.)*** When light source, grating, and slit are properly lined up, a spectrum will be seen to either side of the slit.

1. Aim the spectroscope at a light bulb. Here are the spectra seen in one trial.❷ What colors are seen? What is the order of the colors? Do the colors blend, or are they separated?

2. The filament of an electric light bulb is a glowing solid. Now examine a glowing gas. Get a partner to hold some sodium chloride at the tip of a spoon in a Bunsen flame. The heat of the flame turns the solid salt into a gas that colors the flame yellow. Look at the yellow flame with the spectroscope. How does this spectrum compare with the spectrum of the incandescent bulb, a glowing solid? Here is the observation made in one trial.❸

3. Take your spectroscope out one evening and examine the light from a neon sign. A red neon sign contains glowing neon gas. Here is one observation of glowing neon gas.❹

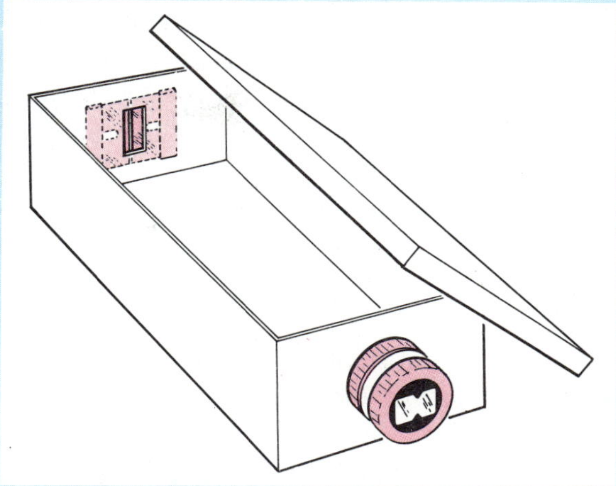
❶

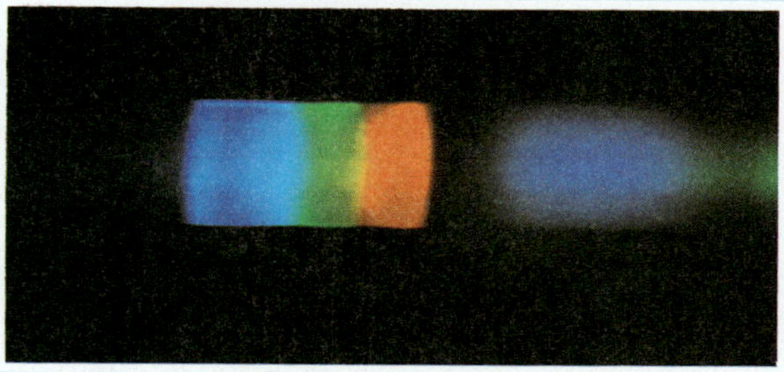
❷

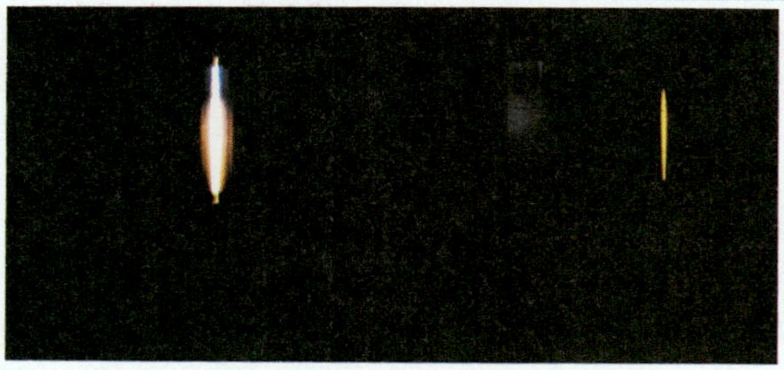
❸

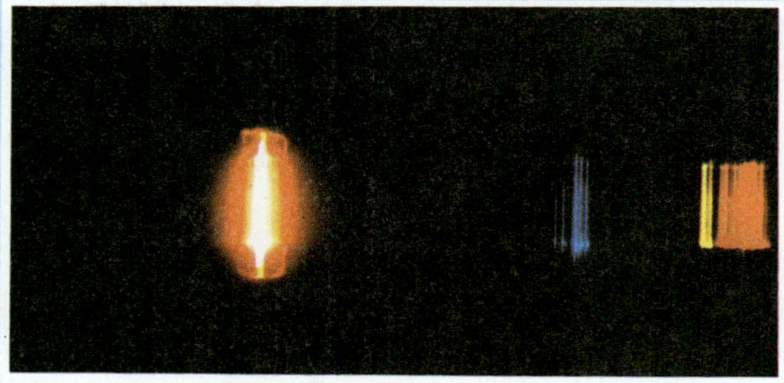
❹

An Investigation On Your Own

Observe the spectra of blue and green light from neon signs. Observe the light from a mercury-vapor street lamp if one is available. What do the observations suggest about the spectrum from a glowing gas?

gases—such as sodium and neon—give different bright-line spectra. Now the astonishing fact is this: Each element produces a spectrum of its own. When an element is heated to a glowing gas, the pattern of bright lines it makes in a spectroscope is different from the pattern made by any other element.

The spectrum of each element is like a fingerprint, in other words. A person can be identified by his fingerprint; an element can be identified by its spectrum. Notice, by the way, that the *location* of the lines along the spectrum shows the presence of particular wavelengths of light. The colors themselves are not necessary for "fingerprinting" the elements.

Why do atoms of a certain element produce certain wavelengths of light? It is because that element is made up of a certain kind of atom, which has a certain number and arrangement of electrons. When those electrons move from outer to inner shells in the heated atoms, they give off certain wavelengths of light. An atom of another element, with a different arrangement and number of electrons, gives off other wavelengths of light when heated. Since no two elements have the same structure of atoms, the pattern of lines in a spectrum is different for each element.

So it is the pattern of lines in an element's spectrum that identifies the element, wherever it may be—on the earth, on our star the sun, or on other stars. The spectroscope can be used to analyze matter throughout the universe. Let's see how this is done.

1

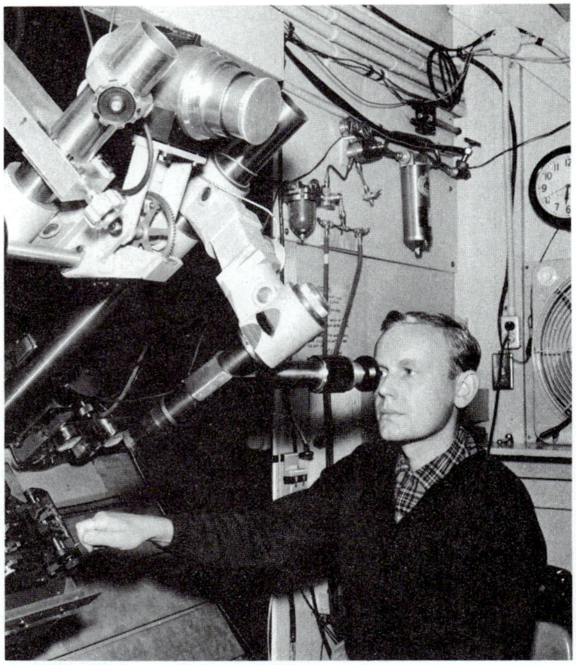

Spectroscopes on Telescopes

Here is a telescope with a spectroscope attached to it. 1 Suppose that the astronomer wishes to observe the spectrum of the star called HD193182. (So many stars have been identified that astronomers assign numbers, rather than names, to most of them.) He aims the telescope at the star. The telescope mirror or lens collects light from star HD193182 and sends it through the spectroscope. The spectroscope separates the various wavelengths of the star's light into a spectrum. The lines of the spectrum are recorded on a photographic film. 2 The film is on a glass plate rather than flexible plastic, so astronomers refer to photographic plates.

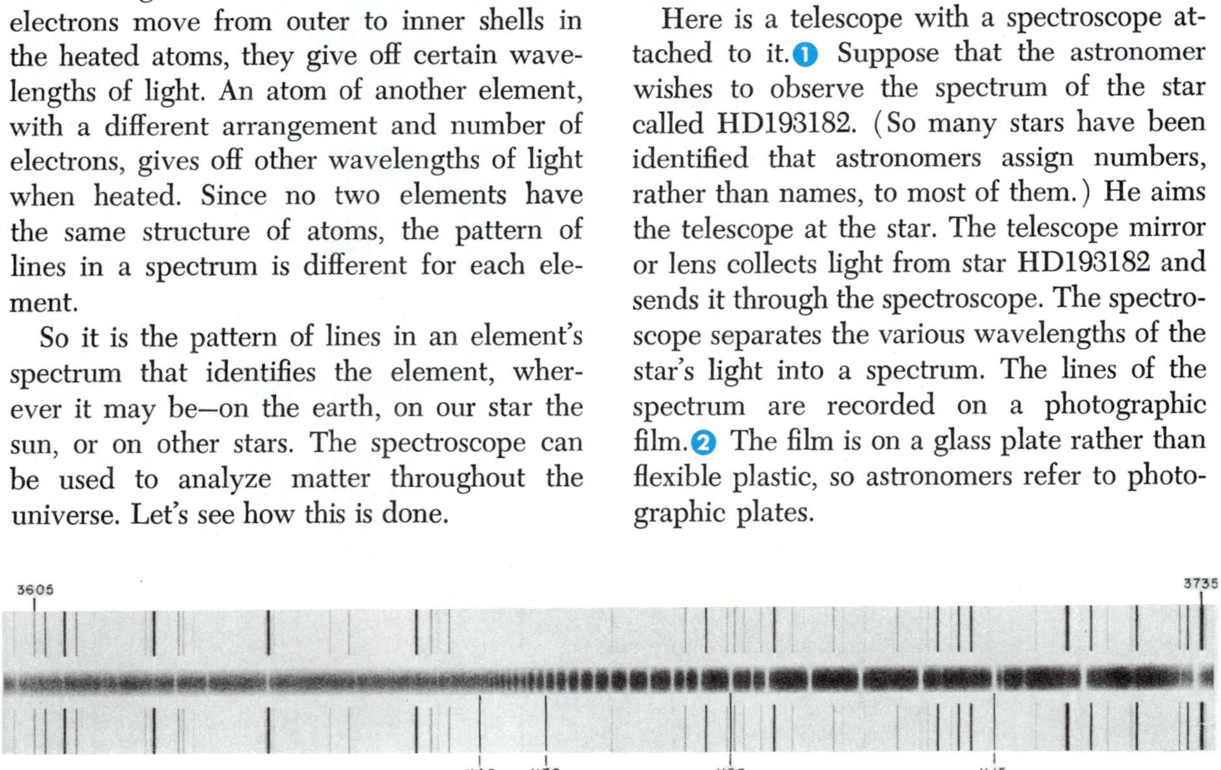

2

As you can see, a great number of different wavelengths have fallen on the photographic plate, many more than the number produced by any one element. Evidently the star is composed of a number of different elements. However, scientists who specialize in the analysis of spectra are experts at sorting out the combination of elements in a spectrum. They can even tell something about the amount of each element present from the intensity of the lines.

For example, here is a photograph of the spectrum of the element iron.③ This is iron's fingerprint; no other element has a spectrum just like this. Actually, there are *two* spectra of iron shown here, with the spectrum of the sun in between. Observe that there are dark lines in the sun's spectrum that match exactly iron's bright-line spectrum. This means that there is iron in the sun. More exactly, it means that in the gaseous outside of the sun there is iron vapor which is absorbing certain wavelengths of light.

The Chemical Make-up of Stars

By analyzing the light from a star, the astronomer can tell what elements the star contains. What has the astronomer found out, then? Is our sun different in its chemical make-up from other stars? How does the chemical make-up of the sun and stars compare with that of the earth? The table below will tell you the story.

Evidence provided by the spectroscope shows that in general the sun and other stars are made of the same kinds of elements as the earth. For thousands of years men believed just the opposite: that the sun and stars must be totally different from our earth. They believed that the earth must be the only thing of its kind in the universe. The spectroscope says otherwise.

It will hardly surprise you that the percentage of elements is very different in the earth and the sun. The sun is plainly very different from the earth. But it may surprise you that other stars have the same elements, in

SOME ELEMENTS IN THE EARTH, SUN, AND STARS

Elements	*Earth*	*Sun*	*Other stars (average)*
hydrogen	less than 1%	nearly 50%	nearly 50%
helium	less than 1%	nearly 50%	nearly 50%
oxygen silicon aluminum iron (and 97 other elements)	99%	1%	1%

about the same amounts as the sun. It is plain to see that our sun is really just one more star.

If the sun is like the other stars in chemical make-up, is it like them in size? in brightness? in hotness? We have other evidence that the sun is indeed an "average" kind of star. You will see some of that evidence in Chapter 10. Meanwhile you may want to keep in mind that what you find out in the next section about the sun is very probably true for countless other stars in the universe.

REVIEW

1. In what way does the bright-line spectrum of a substance resemble the dark-line spectrum of the same substance? What is the difference in the way these two kinds of spectra are produced?

2. Why does each element have its own "fingerprint," that is, its characteristic pattern of spectral lines?

3. How is a continuous spectrum produced?

4. What is a spectroscope?

NEW VIEW

1. Helium is an element whose name comes from the Greek *helios,* meaning "sun." This element was discovered on the sun before it was found on the earth. Explain how this discovery was possible.

2. Suppose the light from a newly discovered star is analyzed and found to contain a pattern of spectral lines never seen before. What are some possible explanations for this? Suggest at least two.

3. The radio portion of the electromagnetic spectrum has waves of many different wavelengths. How is this fact used in radio broadcasting? How might it be used in radio telescopes?

4. How does the chemical make-up of the sun compare with that of other stars? How does it compare with that of the earth?

3. THE SUN'S MATTER AND ENERGY

The sun's disk darkens as the moon blots it from view. Then, at the moment of total eclipse of the sun, the **corona** appears. The corona is astonishingly beautiful—an eerie crown with faint, brushlike streamers. It is a phenomenon that astronomers have studied eagerly for many years, and are still studying.

What is this phenomenon? The corona is the outer part of the sun's atmosphere. Just above the sun's surface, clouds of hot gas surge up in its atmosphere, sometimes as high as 340,000 kilometers (200,000 miles) and more. This gas forms hot, glowing tongues called **prominences.** ❶ The prominences curve high above the sun's surface. Then they seem to rain back onto the surface.

What is the sun's surface like? Here is a photograph made with a special telescope. ❷ The surface of the sun has a grainy look due to formations known as *granules.* A granule is a kind of bubble of hot gas rising to the surface from the sun's interior.

The dark patches among the granules are known as **sunspots.** Astronomers think that sunspots are eruptions of the sun's surface. They look dark because they are not as hot as their surroundings. If you could view a sunspot without seeing the rest of the sun, however, the spot would look bright.

Sometimes intensely bright spots appear near the dark sunspots. These bright spots are called **solar flares.** ❸ They release enormous amounts of energy. About one day after a strong solar flare appears, there is an unusually intense shower of atomic particles on the earth, from space. The shower consists mainly of protons and electrons. It seems to be a "gust" of a more or less constant **solar wind.** So the sun sends out not only energy but particles of its matter as well.

1

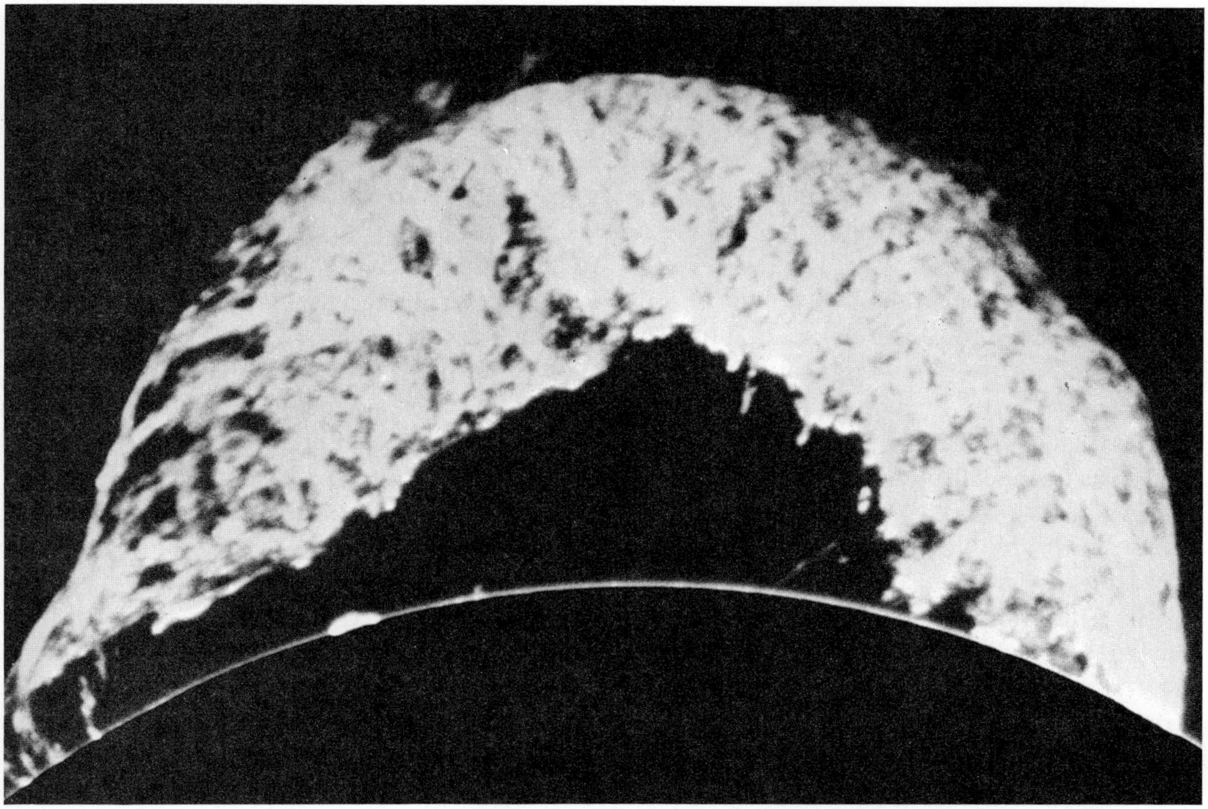

2

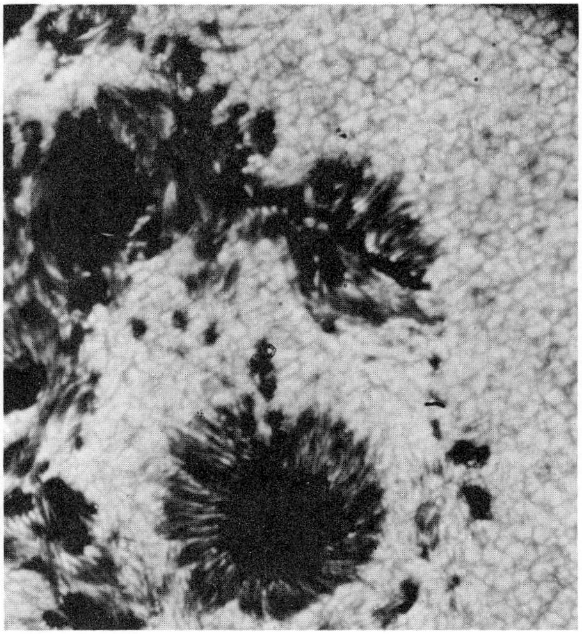

3

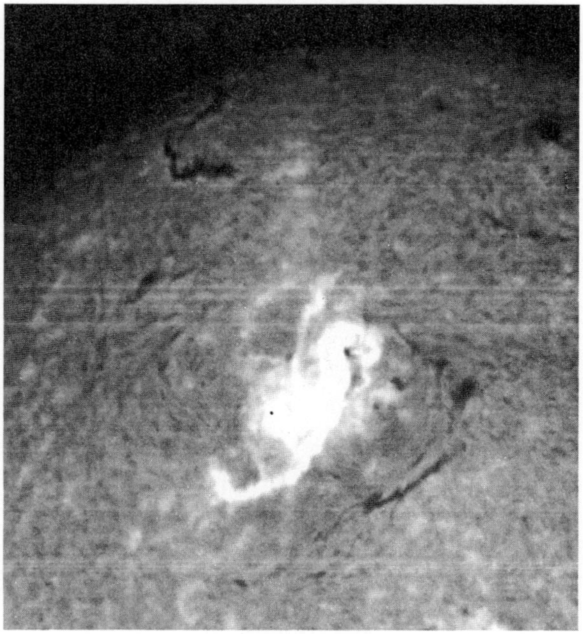

The Mystery of "Coronium"

When scientists first studied the spectrum of the sun's corona, they saw spectral lines that did not fit any element they knew. They decided that the corona must be composed of a substance present on the sun but not on the earth. They christened the mysterious substance "coronium." In 1940, however, a Swedish physicist named Bengt Edlén suggested that there was no such substance and offered an alternate explanation.

Edlén put forth a new hypothesis. He suggested that the strange spectrum of the corona was produced by atoms of ordinary elements, mostly atoms of iron and calcium. To explain why the spectral lines were not the same as for iron and calcium atoms on earth, Edlén said that the atoms had been drastically changed by conditions in the sun. He proposed that the atoms had been stripped of about half of their outer electrons.

Compare a model of an ordinary atom of iron with that of a "stripped" atom of iron. (1) In the stripped iron atom, half of the normal 26 electrons are missing. Since it is the motion of electrons in the outer shells of an atom that determines the atom's spectrum, it is reasonable to expect that an atom which has lost many of its outer electrons will give a different spectrum.

Edlén's hypothesis has withstood the tests applied to it by other scientists, and is now accepted.

(1)

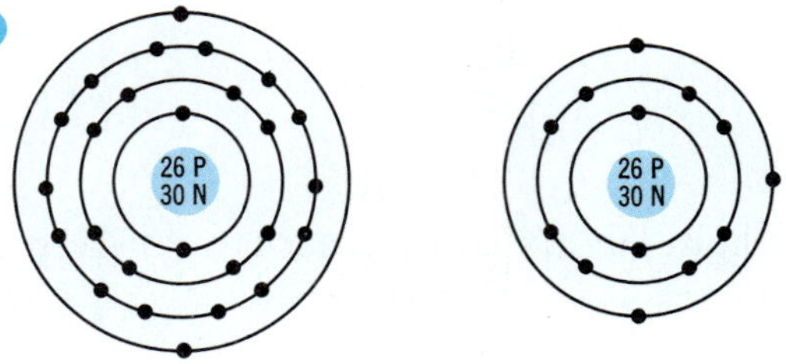

iron atom   "stripped" iron atom

The Sun's Energy

The energy we receive from the sun supports life on the earth. Green plants capture some of the sun's energy and use it to make food and other things which we use.

We use the sun's energy in the form of chemical energy stored in oil and coal by organisms that lived long ago. According to one theory, oil began as the stored fat of tiny one-celled animals that fed on tiny one-celled green plants. Coal was once the wood of fernlike trees flourishing in forests on the earth some 600 million years ago.

For how long has the earth been receiving energy from the sun? The earth has been receiving energy from the sun for probably several billion years. So we know that the sun has furnished the earth with a tremendous amount of energy through ages of time. Yet this energy that the earth has received is but a tiny fraction of the sun's whole energy. Only about one billionth of the sun's total energy output reaches the earth. The sun's energy output is enormous.

How long is this energy to last? We have evidence that the sun's huge energy production is likely to continue for many more billions of years.

How is the sun able to produce this incredible amount of energy? The main explanation is the nature of the sun's fuel. This fuel is not oil or coal. The sun's fuel is hydrogen—but hydrogen used in a special way, unlike our ordinary fuels on earth.

Fuels on the Earth

When we use the word "fuel," we usually mean a substance that *burns* to produce heat and light energy. Wood, coal, gasoline, kerosene, oil, and gas are all fuels.

What do we mean by "burn"? We mean a kind of chemical action, a chemical action in

2

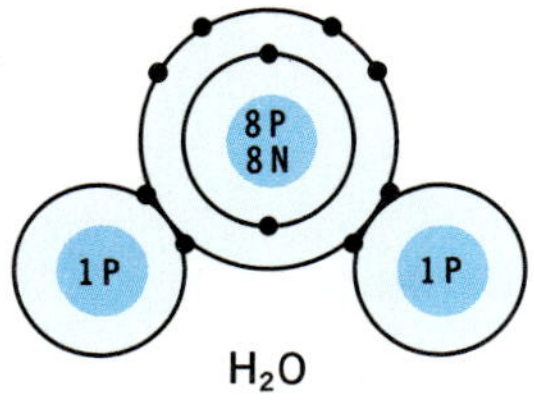

which atoms of fuel combine with atoms of oxygen and give off energy in the process. Oxidation takes place, in other words. For example, hydrogen is a fuel that can be burned, or oxidized. Hydrogen atoms combine with oxygen atoms, energy is given off, and water is formed as a result.

$$\text{hydrogen} + \text{oxygen} \longrightarrow \text{water} + \text{energy}$$

When hydrogen and oxygen atoms combine, only the electrons in their outer shells are involved. Notice that the nucleus of each atom is not affected at all by this change. 2 Only the outer electrons of the atoms are affected. This holds true for any ordinary chemical change: only the electrons in the outer shells of the atoms are involved.

There is another thing that holds true for this chemical reaction, as it does for all ordinary chemical reactions. As far as a chemist is able to measure it, the same amount of matter comes out of the reaction as was put in. Let's take the balanced chemical equation and do some bookkeeping. (It's worth doing here because we'll find a striking difference in the sun's fuel reaction.)

$$\begin{array}{l} \text{hydrogen} + \text{oxygen} \longrightarrow \text{water} + \text{energy} \\ \quad 2H_2 \quad + \quad O_2 \quad \longrightarrow 2H_2O + \text{energy} \end{array}$$

Let's add up the weight of atoms on each side of the equation. The atomic weight of hydrogen is 1.008 atomic mass units, and of oxygen is 15.999 atomic mass units. (You have used atomic weights that were rounded off to whole numbers before.) On the left side are two molecules of hydrogen and one molecule of oxygen. They form two molecules of water, on the right side. But we are interested in the atoms. There are 4 atoms of hydrogen and 2 atoms of oxygen on the left side, and exactly the same number on the right. So to find the total weight, we multiply 4 times the weight of one hydrogen atom and 2 times the weight of one oxygen atom.

$$\begin{array}{c} (4 \times 1.008) + (2 \times 15.999) \\ = (4 \times 1.008) + (2 \times 15.999) \\ 36.030 \text{ amu} = 36.030 \text{ amu} \end{array}$$

Chemists have weighed the reactants and the products as accurately as possible, and they have found that the same amount of matter is indeed present in the product as in the reactants. The atoms are only recombined, not changed into other kinds of atoms. In this ordinary chemical reaction, as in all ordinary chemical reactions, matter is neither created nor destroyed. Matter is conserved, in other words. You have met the concept of conservation of matter before.

What of the heat: Where did it come from? Before the reaction the energy was stored in the hydrogen and oxygen as chemical energy. The energy was released as heat when the hydrogen and oxygen combined to form water.

When any fuel is oxidized, these two concepts hold true:

(1) The outer shell of electrons of the atom is affected, but the nucleus of the atom is not changed.

(2) Chemical energy stored in the reactants is transformed into heat and light.

We have taken a quick look at how heat and light are ordinarily produced on the earth —by burning. Now we are better equipped to tackle the question of how heat and light are produced by the sun.

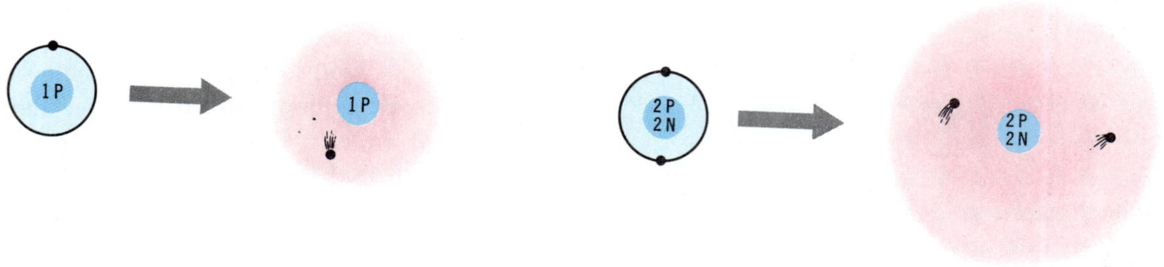

1

Fuel in the Sun

During an eclipse, when the sun seemed to be going out, the Ojibway Indians used to shoot flaming arrows at the sun to light it again. The idea that the sun is burning must have occurred to men many ages ago.

You know, however, that the sun is made mostly of hydrogen and helium, with very little of anything else. The spectroscope has shown that only 1 percent of the sun's matter consists of elements other than hydrogen and helium. So there cannot be enough oxygen to make oxidation a likely source of the sun's heat. Unlike the air around the earth, the atmosphere of the sun is not a source of oxygen that could be used for burning hydrogen. Something different from ordinary chemical burning must happen in the sun.

Furthermore, the huge amount of energy being produced by the sun's fuel has to be accounted for. Scientists have deduced that the temperature inside the sun goes as high as 20 million °C, in the center of the sun where the heat, light, and other forms of radiant energy are produced.

To make such high temperatures by ordinary burning would, if possible at all, take immense amounts of fuel. If burning hydrogen were the source of the sun's energy, the sun would have run out of fuel long ago. Actually the sun uses only a tiny fraction of its hydrogen each day. This is another reason to conclude that the sun's heat cannot come from the ordinary burning of hydrogen. Some other process must be releasing energy in the sun.

A physicist named Hans Bethe, working at Cornell University, first proposed the theory which scientists accept as the explanation of the sun's energy. Bethe's theory is that some of the hydrogen in the sun is always being changed to helium.

Scientists can make a reasonable assumption as to how this happens, for they have managed to make a similar reaction occur on the earth during the explosion of a hydrogen bomb, in which a very large amount of energy is released. This reaction is called a **thermonuclear reaction.** "Thermo," meaning heat, refers to the very high temperature; "nuclear" refers to the fact that the reaction occurs between the nuclei of the atoms. This is no ordinary chemical reaction, then, involving only the outer electrons of atoms, but a **nuclear reaction** involving the nuclei of atoms. The temperature in the sun is so high that the atoms have been stripped of their electrons. A temperature of 1 million °C or more strips the hydrogen atoms of their single electrons, and the helium atoms of their two electrons. So the hydrogen and helium atoms are naked nuclei. The hydrogen nucleus is just a proton. The helium nucleus contains two protons and two neutrons. The electrons that the nuclei would have around them at a lower temperature are floating about freely in the sun. ❶

Ordinary chemical reactions, like burning hydrogen in oxygen, are due to the sharing of outer electrons. They do not change the make-up of the nuclei. In the thermonuclear reactions within the sun, however, it is the nuclei that react. The protons and neutrons are involved in changes. Let's see what these changes are like, and how they produce the sun's extraordinary energy.

Nuclear Fusion

What happens is simply this. As a result of a series of reactions, four hydrogen nuclei come together and combine. When the four hydrogen nuclei join together, or fuse, they become a helium nucleus, and a very large amount of energy is released. This process is called **fusion.**

During fusion, then, the nucleus of one kind of atom becomes the nucleus of another kind of atom. Hydrogen becomes helium.

Fifty years ago no chemist would have believed such a thing possible.

There is another surprise as well. When the weights of hydrogen and helium in the nuclear reaction are compared, something unusual turns up.

The weight of a helium-4 nucleus is 4.003 amu. The weight of a hydrogen-1 nucleus is 1.008 amu.

$$\begin{array}{ccc} 4\,\mathrm{H} & \longrightarrow \quad \mathrm{He} & (+\ \text{energy}) \\ 4 \times 1.008\ \text{amu} & 4.003\ \text{amu} & \end{array}$$

But 4 times 1.008 is 4.032. This does *not* equal 4.003.

The weight difference is $4.032 - 4.003$, or 0.029 amu. Somehow 0.029 amu of matter has been lost. This loss cannot be put down to defects in the measuring instruments or experimental errors: it is too large for that. We must account for this loss of matter.

There is yet another surprise in this nuclear fusion reaction, and it also needs to be explained. The fusion of atomic nuclei releases energy, as we said. But the energy released is about half a million times as great as it would be in a chemical combination.

It is this conversion of matter into energy that is the source of the sun's energy. Since a very small amount of matter can be changed into a very large amount of energy, the sun can produce a tremendous amount of energy from its huge supply of matter. In fact, scientists have calculated that the sun would use up only 1 billionth of 1 percent of its mass if it produced radiant energy for 100 years, at its present rate. The mass of the sun is enormous.

What happens in an exploding hydrogen bomb is similar to what is happening now in the sun. There is one big difference, however, in the rate at which the nuclear fusion reaction goes on in a bomb and in the sun. In a bomb, huge amounts of energy are suddenly released, and are enormously destructive. In the sun, hydrogen is regularly and steadily converted into helium, yielding energy on which life on the earth depends.

The Conservation of Matter and Energy

Scientists used to believe that energy was unchangeable and indestructible. They believed that if a certain amount of energy was put into a reaction, exactly the same amount of energy would come out. Energy was conserved, in other words. This broad concept was the Law of Conservation of Energy. But scientists had to change their concept. This is no surprise, really: science is, in a way, organized for the ready change of concepts.

1 

Scientists discovered that matter can be changed into energy—and energy can be changed into matter, too. Energy was not, after all, unchangeable. This being so, the Law of Conservation of Energy was no longer true. Let's consider this further.

Albert Einstein, the German-born American scientist who died in 1955, was one of the most creative scientists of all time. 1 One of the many important things he accomplished in theoretical physics is his discovery of the relationship between matter and energy. This is summed up in the equation $E = mc^2$. What does this equation say?

The symbols in the equation stand for energy (E), mass (m), and the velocity of light (c). In effect, $E = mc^2$ says that the resulting energy (E) is equal to the change in mass (m) multiplied by the square of the velocity of light (c). In Einstein's equation c is equal to 30,000,000,000 (30 billion) centimeters per second, and c^2 is equal to 900,000,000,000,000,000,000 centimeters per second. This, you will no doubt agree, is a huge number.

When the value of c^2 is multiplied by the change in mass (m), the result is a fantastically large value for the energy released. What Einstein's equation means, then, is that a small amount of matter can be converted into an enormous amount of energy. In the fusion of hydrogen-1 to form helium, for example, the amount of mass changed into energy is small—just 0.029 gram of mass are "lost" when 4.032 grams of hydrogen-1 are fused. At the same time, the production of energy, as we would expect, is very large—some 580 million calories (a unit of heat) are released.

From this and many other nuclear reactions, scientists have confirmed that the amounts of matter and energy in a nuclear equation do not stay the same. However, there is something in the reaction that does stay the same. The *sum* of the matter and energy put in is the same as the *sum* of matter and energy that comes out. The matter that is "lost" appears as energy. A certain amount of matter disappears: a certain amount of energy appears. The total amount of matter and energy before the reaction is the same as the total amount of matter and energy after the reaction.

In a very simple way, Einstein's equation expresses the concept of the conservation of matter-energy, or, as it is often called, the conservation of mass-energy: *Matter can be changed into energy but the total amount of matter and energy in the universe remains constant.*

So we have a new Law of Conservation of Matter and Energy:

The sum of matter and energy is conserved.

The old law of conservation of energy has not been thrown away, you may notice. It has become part of a larger concept, a concept so vast it will help to anchor other concepts. This is the way of science.

REVIEW

1. Describe the nature of (a) sunspots, and (b) solar flares.

2. How did the work of Edlén and Bethe help explain the nature of the sun?

3. What are the differences between an oxidation reaction and a nuclear reaction?

4. What is the significance of the equation $E = mc^2$ in the nuclear reaction in the sun?

NEW VIEW

1. If hydrogen continues to be converted into helium on the sun, what will be the fate of matter and energy on the sun in millions of years?

2. The sun's matter is described as gaseous. Another name for the sun's "gas" is *plasma*. How does plasma differ from gases on the earth?

3. Astronomers list 5 classes of solar prominences: (1) active (2) eruptive (3) sunspot (4) tornado (5) quiescent. In a reference book, locate photographs and information on these kinds of prominences. Write a brief report, including descriptions and illustrations.

4. RELATING THE CONCEPTS

When we compare the make-up of matter on earth with the make-up of matter in other parts of the universe, we find that the same elements are present everywhere. The amounts of the various elements differ, however, among different bodies in space. For example, less than 1 percent of the earth's matter consists of the two lightest elements, hydrogen and helium; but these elements make up 99 percent of the sun's matter.

When we compare the reactions of matter on earth with the reactions of matter in the sun, we find that the sun produces its radiant energy by nuclear fusion, a process that does not naturally occur on earth. And the oxidation of fuels on earth, a chemical change, is a process that does not occur on the sun. Yet *in both kinds of reactions, nuclear and chemical, the sum of matter and energy remains constant.*

Reviewing the Concepts

► *Radiant energy is given off by the sun and other stars.* Radiant energy is made up of radiations in many different wavelengths. Energy of all the wavelengths together make up the electromagnetic spectrum. The parts of this spectrum of radiant energy that can penetrate our atmosphere are our windows into space. Through the visible window, optical telescopes receive light energy of all the wavelengths within the visible spectrum. And through the radio window, radio telescopes receive waves of radio energy.

► *The spectrum of a given element is unique for that element.* From the spectrum of a luminous substance on earth or in space, the elements it contains can be identified by scientists. The spectrum of each element is unique because it has a pattern of lines characteristic of that element. For example, the pattern of lines for iron is different from that for potassium.

► *In chemical reactions, matter is neither created nor destroyed.* Once again we meet this basic concept of the conservation of matter. In the burning of hydrogen on earth, for example, the total number of atoms that enter the reaction is the same as the total number of atoms in the product. The nuclei of the atoms remain unchanged, but the electrons in outer shells are rearranged and, as a result, the atoms themselves are rearranged to form new molecules. We have the same *kinds* of atoms—hydrogen and oxygen atoms—in the product, water, as we had in the reactants.

▶ *In nuclear changes, matter can be changed into energy; the sum of matter and energy remains constant.* The fusion of hydrogen into helium in the sun, for example, is a nuclear change, for the nuclei of atoms are involved. In this change, the identity of the atoms is not the same at the end of the reaction as it was at the beginning: hydrogen atoms become helium atoms. In this reaction a significant amount of matter is changed into energy, and compared to the amount of matter "lost," the amount of energy released is tremendous. Yet, scientists have discovered that the energy released is equivalent to the matter that is destroyed; $E = mc^2$. So we may call this concept of nuclear changes in matter the Conservation of Matter and Energy.

Testing Yourself

1. What are the basic characteristics of electromagnetic radiations?

2. Explain briefly what is meant by the electromagnetic spectrum.

3. Why do certain sections of the electromagnetic spectrum have a label, such as "visible" or "radio"?

4. Why does each element have its own pattern of spectral lines different from that of every other element?

5. What are the basic likenesses and differences between the kinds of matter on the earth and on the sun?

6. How does the process of energy production on the sun differ from ordinary burning (oxidation) on the earth?

7. What are some of the kinds of radiations that come from the sun and other stars?

8. Why can life continue on the earth although some kinds of radiation from the sun are deadly to living things?

9. How is Einstein's equation related to the Law of Conservation of Mass-Energy?

Extending the Concepts

Investigation 1. Heated objects give off invisible infrared radiations that you can detect photographically even in the dark. To do this, you will need a special film, sensitive to infrared radiation. This film is quite expensive, so you may want to organize a group of classmates to plan an investigation and share the costs. If you cannot get the film from a local photographic supply house, they may order one from their supplier; or you may write directly to Eastman Kodak Co., Rochester, New York. They will also furnish you with helpful information and instructions.

Investigation 2. Sunspot activity varies from year to year in a pattern that is known as the sunspot cycle. What is the significance of this cycle? Make a graph of the sunspot activity that has been recorded over a period of 40 or more years. (Use one or more of the references listed at the end of this chapter.) Can the graph be used to predict future occurrences of sunspots?

Suggested Reading

Gamow, George, *A Star Called the Sun*, New York, Viking, 1964. An excellent book to own. It tells many facts and theories about the sun, and is well illustrated. This book is also available in a paperback edition.

Woodbury, David O., *The Glass Giant of Palomar*, New York, Dodd, 1953. This book tells how the world's largest telescope was designed and constructed.

Beiser, Germaine and Arthur, *The Story of Cosmic Rays*, New York, Dutton, 1962. This book tells what cosmic rays are, how they are studied, and how they affect us.

9

Place and Position

How many stars are in the sky? When the night is dark and clear, astronomers say the "seeing" is good. With good seeing, from any one place on earth, about 3,000 stars are visible with the eyes alone.

With ordinary binoculars the number of visible stars increases greatly: you can see about 30,000 stars. With a "4-inch" telescope about 2 million stars are visible. With a "100-inch" telescope the number of visible stars is in the billions. The "200-inch" Hale telescope brings into view an almost limitless number of stars. With the instruments of modern astronomy the stars become truly "countless."

1. A SKY FULL OF STARS

Where does one begin to map countless stars? The system that modern astronomers use is built on the ancient plan of dividing the sky, as seen with the unaided eye, into **constellations.** A constellation is a pattern of stars visible to the naked eye in a small area of sky. Each of the 48 constellations catalogued by the early Greeks was named for a living thing, an everyday object, or a god or hero from mythology. (Modern astronomers have named 88 constellations.)

Constellations

Here is an old picture of the constellation called Orion.[1] The ancients imagined a man's figure around this pattern of stars, the figure of Orion, the hunter. On the hunter's shoulder is the bright reddish star named Betelgeuse. On his ankle is the white star Rigel. Three prominent stars, close together in a row, make up his belt. You may find it

1

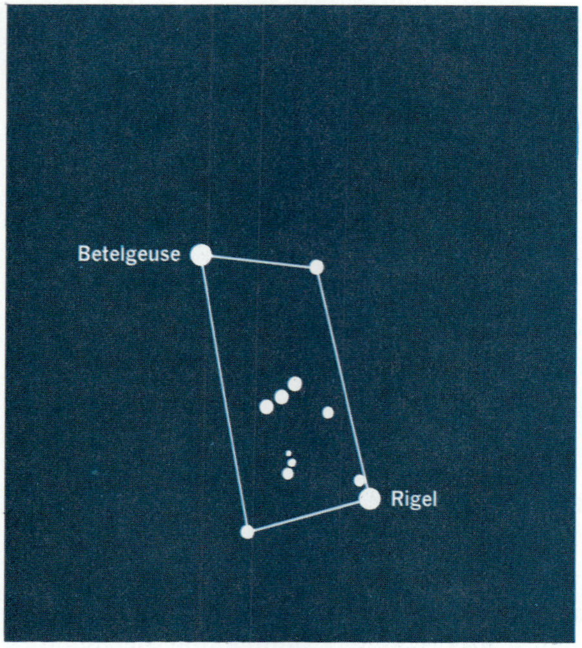

easier to see the pattern of the main stars in the constellation of Orion as they appear on a modern star map. ❶

Perhaps you would like to investigate some constellations in the night sky. If you have never identified constellations before, you can start with a simplified star map. ■

Polaris is the end star in the handle of the constellation called the Little Dipper. Polaris is not especially bright, yet it is one of the easiest stars to find, and it will help you get your bearings when you want to locate other stars or constellations. You can always see Polaris directly north (if you do not live very far south in the United States). The Big Dipper and the Little Dipper change position as they wheel around Polaris, but they can always be found in the night sky (provided that the seeing is good).

Most constellations are visible only at certain seasons. This means that to find Orion and other constellations, you must use a star map that is right for the season of the year. If you want to identify other stars and constellations, see pages 193–196 at the end of the chapter. There you will find star maps and instructions for using them.

Stars in Pairs and Clusters

The stars in a constellation seem to be close together in space, yet in reality they may be widely separated. However, astronomers have learned that groups of stars that are close together do exist.

The star called Algol is in the constellation called Perseus. ❷ Algol can be seen with the unaided eye. If you watch Algol every night for a week, you will see something odd: Algol changes in brightness. Every two days and 21 hours the star changes from dim to bright to dim again. The cycle goes over and over. The Arabs observed this blinking star centuries ago, and called it "the demon," *al gol.*

Why does Algol's brightness change? Astronomers have found that Algol is actually

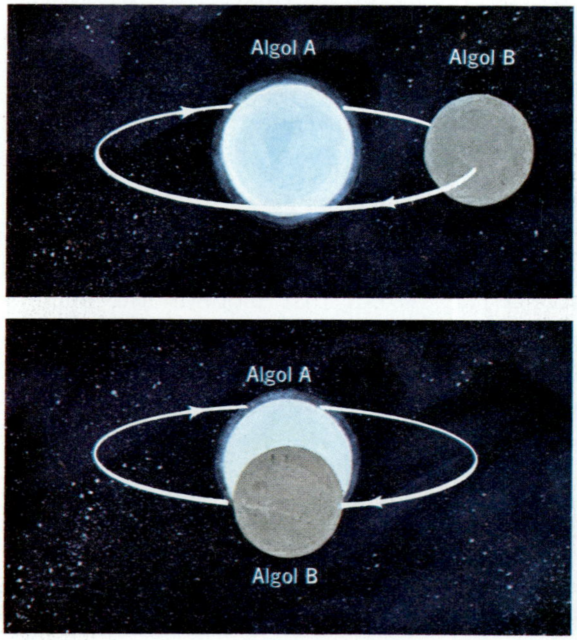

■ AN APPRENTICE INVESTIGATION into Constellations

On a clear, moonless night, look for the seven bright stars of the constellation called the Big Dipper, as shown on this map. ❶ If necessary, rotate the map until the Big Dipper appears to be in the same position on the map as in the sky. Extend a line, as shown, from the last two stars in the bowl of the Big Dipper. The first bright star along this line is Polaris, the North Star.

An Investigation On Your Own

Identify several other constellations in the same part of the sky, known as the North Polar area. Some of these are: Cassiopeia, Cepheus, Lacerta, Draco, and Lynx.

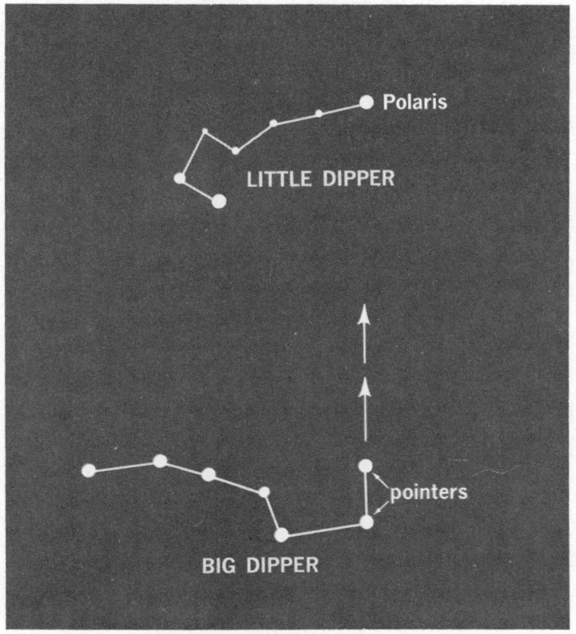

❶

❸

a pair of stars, which they have named Algol A and Algol B. Algol A is brighter than Algol B, and they circle around each other.

When Algol B, the dim star, moves between Algol A and the earth, it eclipses Algol A, the bright star. When Algol B is not eclipsing Algol A, the bright star is again visible from the earth. To the unaided eye Algol A and Algol B seem to be one star with a regular change in brightness. Double stars of this kind are called **eclipsing binaries.**

Our eyes can detect some large clusters of stars, as well as single stars and eclipsing binaries. One type of **star cluster** looks like a dim star to the unaided eye, but a telescope reveals it as a group of some 50,000 to 100,000 stars. There is a cluster of this kind in the constellation Hercules. ❸ More than half of all the stars near us are in pairs or in clusters.

Clouds in Space

Telescopes have helped us to see that a great deal of the matter in the universe exists as huge clouds of dust and gas. Such a cloud is known as a **nebula.** A nebula may be visible in one of two ways.

If a nebula happens to be near a bright star, the nebula will glow with reflected starlight. Or it may give off light of its own, like the beautiful Great Nebula in Orion. ①

If a nebula is not near a bright star, it may stand out as a dark cloud against a bright background of distant stars. It is then called a dark nebula. The famous Horsehead Nebula, also in Orion, is a dark nebula. ②

Distances Between Stars

Suppose you open a camera's shutter to snap a picture in sunlight. At what time did the light that strikes your film leave the sun? The sun is about 150,000,000 kilometers (93,000,000 miles) away. The speed of light is 300,000 kilometers (186,000 miles) per second.

$$\frac{150{,}000{,}000 \text{ kilometers}}{300{,}000 \text{ kilometers/second}} = 500 \text{ seconds}$$

So the sun's light takes 500 seconds, or about 8 minutes, to reach the earth.

This method is the astronomer's way of measuring the star's distance from the earth. The sun is about 8 light-minutes away from the earth, that is, it takes light 8 minutes to travel the distance between sun and earth.

Only the sun is near enoungh for light-minutes to be a convenient unit of measure. Distances to other stars are so great that we use **light-years** to measure them. Light travels about 10 trillion kilometers (6 trillion miles) in a year. One light-year, then, is equivalent to this distance.

Next to the sun, our nearest star is Alpha Centauri, which is 4.3 light-years away. If Alpha Centauri were to explode tonight and disappear, you would continue to see it for about four and a third years more.

Antares is a huge star 390 light-years away. The light of Antares takes 390 years to reach us. The distance to Antares seems large when compared to the distance to Alpha Centauri, 4.3 light-years. But these distances are tiny when we compare them to the dimensions of a **galaxy**, for example, the huge group of stars and nebulae in which we are located.

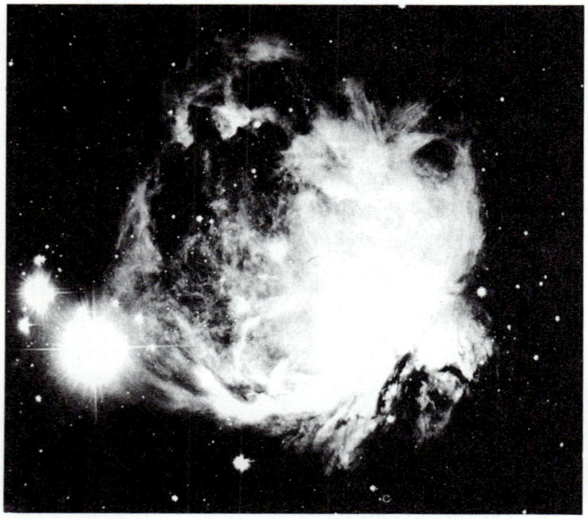

①

②

3

Our Galaxy

Look up at the sky on a clear, moonless night, away from lights, and you will see the faint band of light that the ancient Greeks named the Milky Way. A photograph of the Milky Way through a telescope reveals that, actually, it is made up of a great many stars. 3 (It was Galileo who made this discovery with his telescope.) These stars of the Milky Way are part of our galaxy, which has about 100 billion stars altogether. The stars make up about half the total mass of our galaxy. The other half consists mostly of nebulae, clouds of dust and gas.

Using radio telescopes, astronomers have been able to map our Milky Way galaxy with considerable accuracy. If we could get outside our galaxy, we would see it as a huge swirling pinwheel with a bulge in the center and thin spirals at the edges. 4

Imagine yourself in the position marked "solar system." Can you see why the Milky Way is only a band and does not cover the whole sky? The distance to the nearest edge

4

❶

of the galaxy is about 25,000 light-years. The distance across the galaxy is 100,000 light-years. At its thickest, the center of the galaxy measures about 20,000 light-years, and the edges are between 2,000 and 3,000 light-years in thickness.

The entire pinwheel of the galaxy is revolving in such a way that our sun travels through space at the rate of 227 kilometers (136 miles) per second. Even at this speed, it takes the solar system 200 million years to make one complete trip around the center of the galaxy.

When you look up at a star-studded sky, what you generally see are the stars of our galaxy. This is a very small bit of the universe, however. Our galaxy is only 1 of about 1,000,000,000 galaxies visible with the Hale telescope. It happens that ours is a fairly large galaxy, but even average galaxies contain a billion or more stars. How far away are other galaxies, and what do they look like?

Other Galaxies

In the constellation Andromeda there is a faint, fuzzy spot that looks much like the cluster of stars in the constellation Hercules (p. 165). The cluster in Hercules is within our galaxy, which has a diameter of 100,000 light-years. The blur of light in Andromeda, however, is approximately 2.2 million light-years away. Think about this distance. One light-year is the distance light travels in one year. Over 2 million times *this* figure is the distance to Andromeda, the nearest major galaxy.

When the surprised astronomers discovered that the spot of light in Andromeda was so very far away, they realized they were looking at another galaxy. Here is a photograph of the Andromeda galaxy. ❶ The galaxy seems to be more oval and somewhat larger than our own Milky Way galaxy. Many billions of these huge islandlike collections of stars, separated by vast reaches of space, seem to make up the universe. ❷

2

How can we get some idea of the vastness of the universe? Compared to our galaxy, the earth is an incredibly tiny speck of matter, spinning with 8 other planets around an average-size star. If the stars were counted at the rate of 1 each second, it would take 6,000 years to finish the job for our galaxy alone, with no time to eat or sleep. And you would not have begun to count any of the millions of other galaxies!

REVIEW

1. About how many stars are visible with the unaided eye? with the Hale telescope?

2. We never see any object in the night sky as it is, but only as it was. Explain.

3. If a star is at the very edge of the Milky Way galaxy, how many light-years is it from the center of the galaxy?

4. The galaxy nearest our own galaxy is a small one, called the Clouds of Magellan, 150,000 light-years away. How many miles is this? What is this distance in kilometers?

5. When examined by the "200-inch" telescope, three fuzzy spots of light turn out to be three different objects: a nebula, a galaxy, and a star cluster. Describe what each of these objects is.

6. Why does Algol change in brightness?

NEW VIEW

1. Why do radio telescopes make possible a more complete map of the Milky Way than do optical telescopes alone?

2. Radio waves travel at the same speed as light, about 300,000 kilometers (186,000 miles) per second. At a certain point in its orbit, when the moon is near its apogee (point of greatest distance from the earth), it takes a radio signal 2.7 seconds to travel to the moon, bounce off, and travel back to the earth. How far away is the moon at the time of the signal?

2. OUR STAR, GIANTS, AND DWARFS

To us the sun seems to be the biggest, brightest, and hottest of the stars. In reality our sun is merely an average star, as stars go. It is a medium-size star, with medium brightness and medium temperature. How do astronomers know these things? As usual in astronomical matters, the story begins with the ancients.

Magnitude and Luminosity

Ptolemy was a Greek mathematician-astronomer-geographer who lived and worked in Alexandria, Egypt, over 1,800 years ago. The night sky looked to him about as it does to us now. He decided to put the stars in order—in one kind of order, at any rate. What Ptolemy did was to classify the stars he could see on the basis of brightness. He devised a system that had six different degrees of brightness, called **magnitudes.** Stars of the first magnitude were the brightest ones. Stars of the sixth magnitude were the dimmest ones that could be seen. For star maps and catalogues, astronomers today use a scale of magitudes based on this ancient system. The North Star, for instance, is a second magnitude star.

After the invention of the telescope many stars became visible that were dimmer than those of the sixth magnitude. Thus, the brightness scale had to be extended to include these newly seen stars. Stars as faint as the twenty-third magnitude can be seen with the Hale telescope.

The modern brightness scale is not only much longer than the ancient one, it also has some zero and negative magnitudes. Some stars that the ancients classed as first magnitude are so bright that we assign them a still lower number—zero. A few even brighter stars have negative magnitudes. The brightest star, not counting the sun, is Sirius with a magnitude of −1.6. The magnitude of the sun itself is −26.7.

Notice that the degree of magnitude describes how bright a star *appears* to be. Thus it is more accurate to speak of the **apparent magnitude** of a star, meaning its brightness to an observer on earth. Star maps may note a star's apparent magnitude as a clue to identifying the star.

Apparent magnitude is also an important clue to finding out how far away a star is. Imagine that you are on a dark football field at night. You are standing by a goal post at one end. Two friends with identical flashlights are standing out on the field. One friend is on the 10-yard line; and the other friend is at the 50-yard line. Could you tell

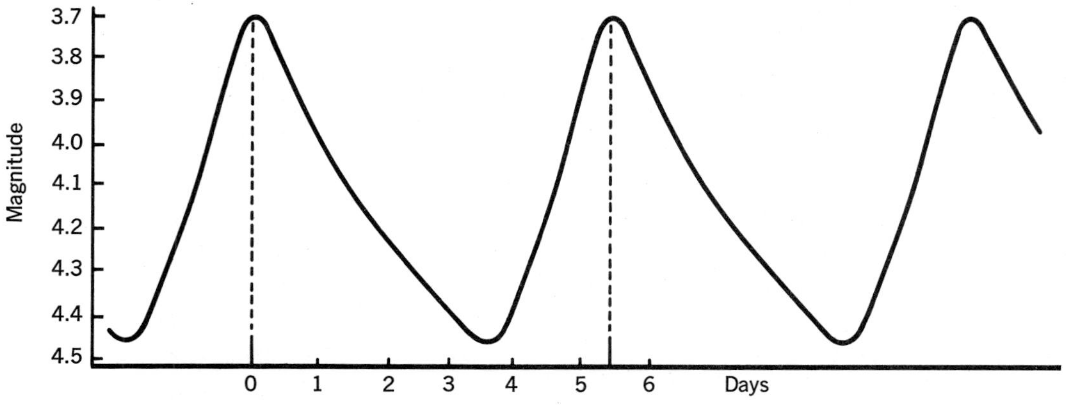

1

■ AN APPRENTICE INVESTIGATION into Apparent Magnitudes

In a large, darkened room, compare the apparent brightness of a flashlight at different distances. Here is an observation at 3 meters (10 feet).❶ At 9 meters (30 feet).❷ At 15 meters (50 feet).❸ What happens to the apparent magnitude of the light as the distance to the light increases? What happens to the luminosity?

Take two lights of different luminosities—a large flashlight and a pencil-size flashlight. How must they be placed if the light of smaller luminosity is to have the *same* apparent magnitude as the light of greater luminosity?

Arrange the lights so the light of smaller luminosity has a *greater* apparent magnitude than the light of greater luminosity.

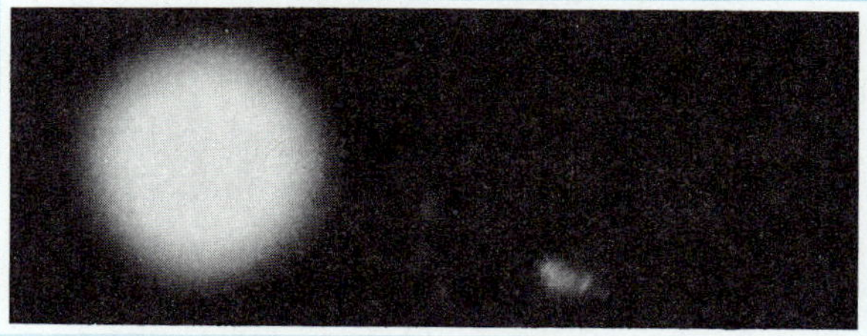
❶

❷

❸

which one is nearer? Yes, since you know that the real brightness of the two lights is the same. The nearer light would *seem* brighter.

Every flashlight, star, or any other source of light has a certain real brightness, a certain intensity of light it is actually giving off. This real brightness is called **luminosity.**

We must consider the luminosity (how much light the flashlight or the star actually gives off) as well as the apparent magnitude (how much light the flashlight or star seems to give off) when we set out to tell how far away it is. See for yourself the effect of distance on the apparent brightness of light. ■

The apparent magnitude of a light source depends on two things: its luminosity and its distance. The distant flashlight with high luminosity may seem dimmer than the nearer one with low luminosity. The more distant, larger, star with high luminosity may seem dimmer than the nearer star with low luminosity. The reverse may also be true—a star that seems to be very bright may actually have a low luminosity. Astronomers measure the luminosity of a star by comparing it with the luminosity of the sun.

Henrietta Leavitt's Discovery

Look at the star named Delta Cephei, in the constellation Cepheus, and you will see a star that changes in apparent magnitude from night to night. If you see Delta Cephei one night at its brightest, then it will be at its dimmest $3\frac{1}{2}$ days later. The star will again appear at its brightest $5\frac{1}{3}$ days from your first observation. Then the cycle repeats. It takes Delta Cephei $5\frac{1}{3}$ days to complete one cycle, as you can see in the graph.❶ This length of time is known as the *period* of the star.

Delta Cephei is not an eclipsing binary like Algol. Algol is actually two stars, one bright and one dim. Delta Cephei is a single star that really does change its luminosity. There are many stars of this kind. Stars that vary like Delta Cephei are called **cepheid variables.** Astronomers do not yet know why the output of energy of a cepheid variable changes. But they do find cepheid variables very useful, thanks to a woman astronomer.

During the year 1912 Henrietta Leavitt, an astronomer at Harvard University, studied some cepheid variables. Miss Leavitt found that the least luminous cepheid variables had periods of about one-half day. And more luminous variables had longer periods. Henrietta Leavitt discovered that the longer the period, the greater the star's luminosity.

This discovery turned out to be very useful. A cepheid variable's period can be observed and measured. Then the star's luminosity can be calculated, using its period. This is how astronomers have learned the luminosities of many stars. And it turns out that the luminosity of some stars is 10,000 times as great as that of our sun, and the luminosity of other stars is 1/10,000 as great.

Astronomers have also found Henrietta Leavitt's discovery useful in another important way. Once the luminosity of a star has been calculated, that luminosity can be used, along with the apparent magnitude, to calculate the *distance* to the star! Thus modern astronomy was provided with one of its most important and powerful tools: the ability to measure distances to the stars.

The Color of a Star

Now let's see how the colors of the stars also lead to some unexpected and valuable knowledge of the universe.

Look up at the night sky and you can see for yourself that stars differ in color. Some stars are red, like Antares. Others are white, like Canopus. Can it be that a red star is "red hot," and a white one is "white hot"?

Use pliers to hold one end of a pin in a Bunsen flame. Observe how the heated metal turns red, then yellow, and then white, as it gets hotter. Star colors and temperatures are related in the same way. Yellow stars are hotter than red stars, white stars are hotter than yellow stars, and blue-white stars are hotter than white ones. By studying the spectrum of a star and observing the wavelengths of light given off, astronomers can determine the star's temperature as well as its composition.

Light from a blue-white star produces a spectrum with strong lines in the blue part of the spectrum. Light from a red star produces strong wavelengths at the red end of the spectrum.

Actually, stars of all colors can be seen: white, blue, green, yellow, orange, and red. The sun, for instance, is a yellow star. Its most intense radiation is in the yellow part of the spectrum. The sun's temperature is between that of a red star and a blue-white star.

Next time you go star-gazing, see if you can find some of these stars. Their colors are easily seen with the unaided eye.

Star	*Color*	*Surface temperature (°C)*
Rigel	blue-white	12,300
Sirius	blue-white	10,700
Canopus	white	8,200
Sun	yellow	5,530
Capella	yellow	5,200
Arcturus	orange	4,230
Antares	red	3,200

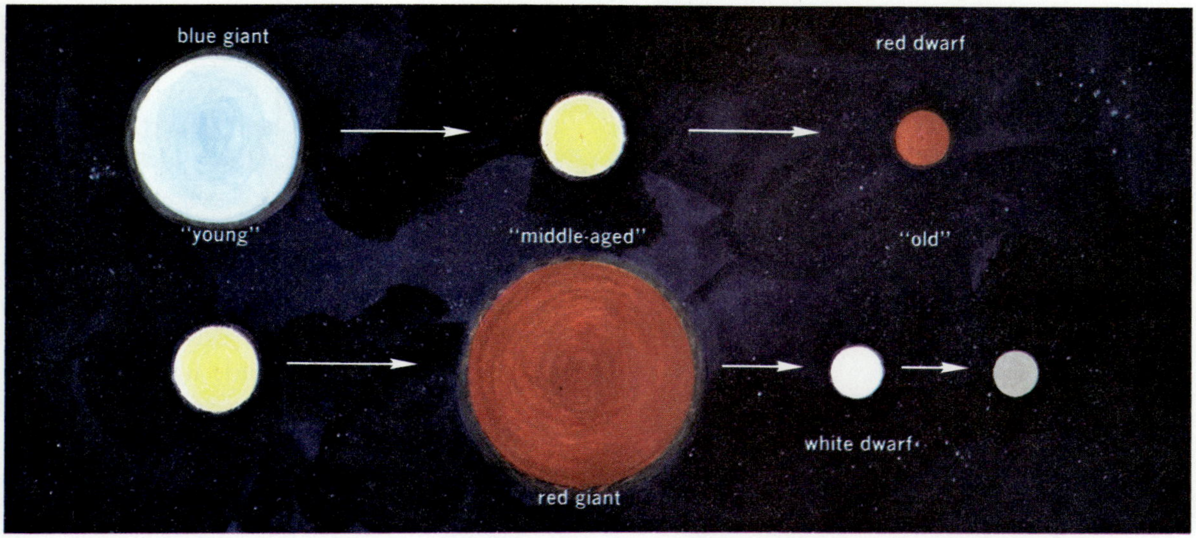

1

Observing the color of a star gives a general idea of its temperature. A more accurate temperature can be calculated from the pattern of the lines in a star's spectrum. The temperatures in the table were calculated from the stars' spectra.

Red and Blue Giants Among the Stars

The sun has a surface temperature of about 5,530°C. The red star Antares has a surface temperature of about 3,200°C, only about half that of the sun. Yet the luminosity of Antares is nearly 2,000 times greater than that of the sun. How is this possible?

Suppose Antares and the sun had the same diameter. Then Antares, with a temperature half that of the sun, could give off much less energy than the sun. For the energy produced by Antares to be as great as it is, Antares must have a much greater diameter than the sun.

In fact, astronomers can calculate the diameter of any star from the star's luminosity and surface temperature. The diameter of Antares has been calculated, and turns out to be about 390 times the diameter of the sun.

Betelgeuse is even larger than Antares. These stars are called **red giants,** and are truly giants among giants. Other large red stars like Beta Pegasi (113 sun-diameters) and Aldebaran (35 sun-diameters) are smaller than Antares and Betelgeuse, but they are still giants compared with our sun.

Another kind of star with a large diameter is the **blue giant.** As you can tell by its color, a blue giant is hotter and brighter than a red giant. Rigel is an example of a blue giant.

Why do stars differ in size and color?

A Star's History

One hypothesis is that a blue giant is a young star. As the young star ages, it consumes its fuel more slowly, becomes cooler, and shrinks. As a "middle-aged" star, it turns yellow and resembles our sun. This yellow star then shrinks still further and turns into a **red dwarf** star. Red dwarf stars are faint, cool, and small. If this hypothesis is correct, red dwarfs are old stars. 1 Lacaille 9352 is the name of one red dwarf star. Our sun may have begun its life as a blue giant and may end as a red dwarf.

Another hypothesis, however, is that a middle-sized yellow star gets hotter and larger, not cooler and smaller. It then swells further to become a red giant. When the red giant's nuclear fuel is used up, the star shrinks and turns into a **white dwarf** star as shown in the diagram on page 173. A white dwarf is very hot at first, as you would expect, but cools off and becomes dark. Some white dwarfs are as small as some planets in our solar system.

Something else can happen to a star, however. It may become a **nova,** a star that suddenly flares up and becomes perhaps a thousand times brighter than before. Then the nova slowly fades away.

An unusually brilliant flare-up of a large star is called a **supernova.** In the year 1054 the Chinese observed a star that became as bright as the planet Jupiter. The star must have been a supernova. Today, more than 900 years later, what remains of that 1054 supernova is a mass of scattered dust and gas called the Crab Nebula. 1

1

Where Did the Elements Begin?

All the evidence we have indicates that the same kinds of elements are present throughout the universe, although they are not evenly distributed. How did the elements begin? No one knows for certain, but scientists have developed some interesting hypotheses. Let's look at one of them.

Scientists think that our solar system probably began as a cloud of dust and gas. This cloud must have been made up of all the elements now present in the solar system. But where did the substances in the cloud come from? The evidence suggests that elements may be manufactured, in a spectacular way, during the explosion that creates a nova or supernova.

In many stars, like the sun, hydrogen undergoes fusion into helium. But if, for some unknown reason, a star becomes a nova or a supernova, the immense heat of the exploding star creates *other* fusion reactions. Scientists suspect that all the heavier elements may form during these fusion reactions in a nova. Just as helium results from the fusion of the lighter element hydrogen, it may be that carbon, oxygen, nitrogen, iron, sodium, and the rest of the heavier elements are formed by the fusion of lighter elements.

At the same time that the nova is producing the necessary heat for manufacturing elements, it is exploding. So the nova not only makes elements but scatters them into space. These elements may then be attracted by gravitation to form a gaseous cloud. If our solar system was once a gaseous cloud, it could have received the heavier elements in this way. More evidence is needed, however, to confirm (or to contradict) this hypothesis.

As men venture into space they will find new evidence on the origin of the elements that may solve this puzzle.

2

The Movements of Stars and Galaxies

The sun *seems* to rise and set each day, but this movement is an illusion caused by the earth's rotation. Yet the sun does move, along with all the other stars in our galaxy. We do not see the sun's real motion, for as it speeds through space the sun takes its whole family along with it. That includes us: where our star goes, we follow.

We do not notice the real motion of the other stars, either, but for a different reason.

The ancients believed that the stars were fastened to the "dome" of the sky. 2 This dome was thought to be the inside of a hollow sphere which revolved around the earth. Thus the rising and setting of the stars was explained: it was the dome of the sky that moved, not the stars. The stars were fixed in unchanging positions, so far as men could observe. But after men learned to observe better, the notion of fixed stars gave way.

One of the triumphs of modern astronomy has been the observation that the positions of stars *do* change. Astronomers call these changes the **proper motions** of the stars. Even for Barnard's Star, the fastest-moving star

1

2

known, the amount of proper motion—its apparent motion—is small. The picture at the left was made 22 years before the one at the right. (1) Barnard's Star is marked with an arrow in both pictures. Notice that it has moved, compared with the other stars. (2)

If you could watch Barnard's Star for 180 years, its position would seem to change by only the diameter of the moon. Furthermore, Barnard's Star is a 10th-magnitude star, visible only with a telescope. The fastest star that can be seen with the unaided eye has but 1/100 as much proper motion as Barnard's Star.

No wonder the ancients thought the stars were fixed in position. Only over many thousands of years would the stars' proper motions change the patterns seen in the sky.

How do we explain the fact that these observed proper motions of stars are so small? It is mainly because the stars are so extremely far away. Yet scientists have managed to find ways of measuring the motion of a star. Let's see next how they can tell how fast a star is moving and the direction of its motion.

Red and Blue Shifts

A spectroscope separates the light from a star into different wavelengths. The pattern of colored lines formed by the spectroscope, the spectrum, reveals the chemical composition of the star. However, this pattern can reveal something more. It can show us the motion of the star. For a clue to how the motion of a star may be revealed by its light waves, you can observe the behavior of water waves. ■

As you can see, if the source of water waves, the vibrating hand, stays in one position, it sends out evenly spaced waves on each side. But when the source of the waves changes position, the waves ahead of the source are squeezed closer together. The wavelength of the waves ahead of the moving source becomes shorter, in other words. The waves behind the moving wave-source are stretched farther apart, and so their wavelength becomes longer.

This change in wavelength caused by motion of the wave source is called the **Doppler effect.** (It is named after an Austrian physicist, Christian Doppler, who explained it.) The Doppler effect can be observed in sound waves as well as in water waves. Have you ever heard the pitch of an automobile horn drop quickly as the car went by? Have you heard the roar of a jet plane's engine drop suddenly to a lower note as the plane streaked

■ AN APPRENTICE INVESTIGATION into the Behavior of Waves

A stretch of water at least 1 meter (3 or 4 feet) long is best for this investigation (try it in a bathtub rather than a fishbowl). A strong beam of light directed at the water will make waves stand out more clearly, if necessary.

Dip your hand, fingers together, in the water. Vibrate your hand with a regular and even motion, back and forth, to make evenly spaced waves. Notice the wavelength. ❶

Now, continue to vibrate your hand and make waves as before, but move your vibrating hand very slowly and evenly forward. (If you go too fast, your hand will overtake the waves it is sending out and spoil the effect.) What happens to the wavelength of the waves ahead of the moving hand? ❷

The next behavior is more difficult to observe, but not impossible. Move your vibrating hand *very* slowly in the opposite direction. What happens to the length of the waves behind the moving hand? ❸

❶

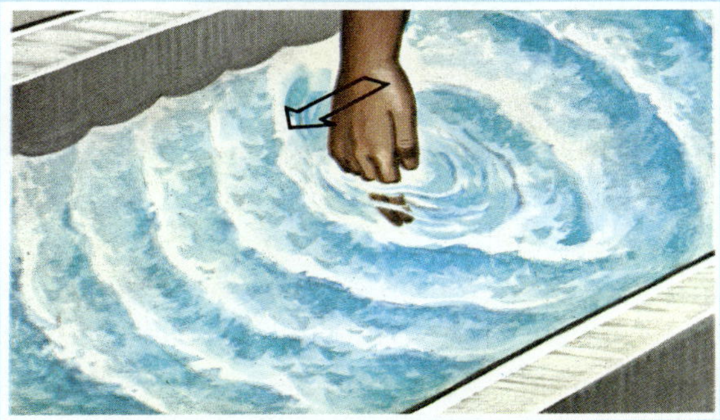

❷

❸

An Investigation On Your Own

Using a tuning fork and your arm, can you demonstrate the Doppler effect with sound?

across the sky? If you have, you have heard the Doppler effect.

It occurred to Doppler that this effect ought to happen with light waves as well. He suggested that if a star were moving toward the earth, its light would seem to have shorter wavelengths than normal. The star's color should then seem to us more blue than it really is. On the other hand, if a star were moving away from the earth, its light wavelengths would seem to be stretched out. That star's light, Doppler suggested, would appear to us more red than it actually is.

Doppler had an excellent idea, but unfortunately it turned out that the change in color of a star that occurs because the star is moving is too small to be observed with the eye. Some time later, however, a French physicist showed that this change in color could be observed very nicely with a spectroscope. (This is a good example, by the way, of how one scientist builds on the work of another.)

Seen through a spectroscope, the spectrum of a star that is moving toward the earth is shifted toward the blue end of the spectrum, where the wavelengths are shorter. But if a star is moving away from us, the light waves that reach us on earth seem longer, and the star's spectrum is shifted toward the red end of the spectrum.

You may recall that Algol A, a bright star, circles around Algol B, a dim star (p. 164). This means that Algol A is moving toward the earth at one time, and away from the earth at another. When Algol A is moving toward us, its spectrum shows a blue shift. When it is moving away from us, its spectrum shows a red shift.

Thus the Doppler effect tells us whether a star is moving toward the earth or away from it. Moreover, the faster a star is moving, toward or away from us, the greater the shift of its spectrum.

In the same way, by the Doppler effect, the spectrum of a distant galaxy reveals the motion of the galaxy. And here we find two striking observations. First, every galaxy has a red shift—every galaxy is moving away from us. Second, the farther away a galaxy is from us, the faster it is moving.

A galaxy in the constellation Virgo, for example, is some 43 million light-years distant from the earth, and is moving away from us at the speed of 1,250 kilometers (750 miles) each second. Notice the two dark lines (above the arrow) in its spectrum. 1 Another galaxy, in the constellation Ursa Major, is some 560 million light-years away, and is moving away from us at 15,500 kilometers (9,300 miles) per second. The two dark lines in its spectrum have shifted towards the right. 2 (In these spectra, the blue end is at the left and the red end at the right.)

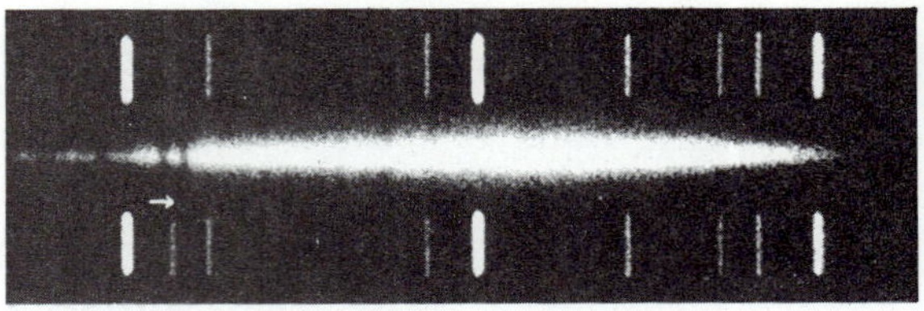

1

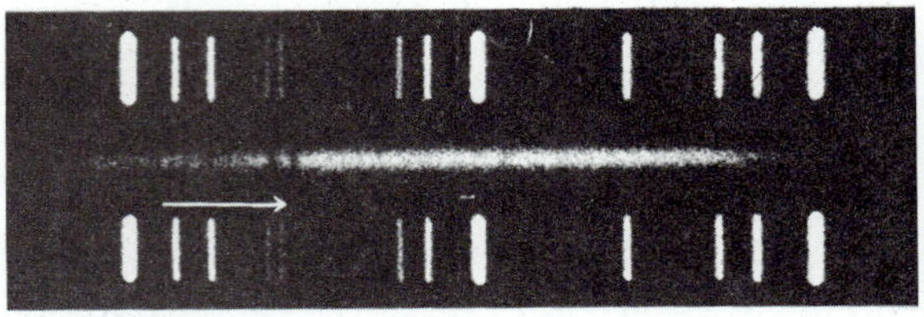

2

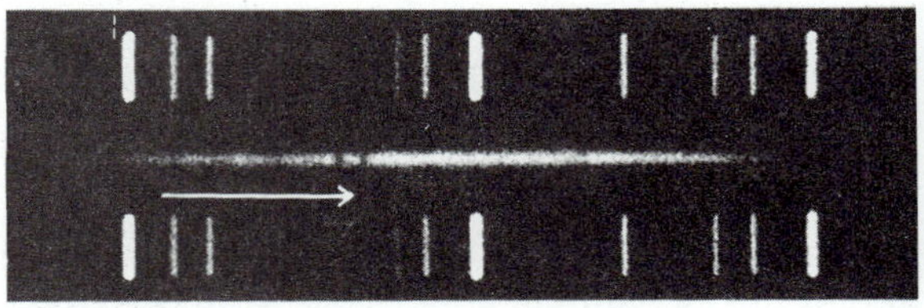

3

A third galaxy, in the constellation Corona Borealis, is some 720 million light-years away, and it is moving away from us at 22,300 kilometers (13,400 miles) per second. Notice how the two dark lines in its spectrum have shifted even farther towards the red end. 3

Every galaxy that we examine seems to be moving away from us. Do you see what that means? It means that the universe is expanding. Every part of the universe seems to be moving away from every other part.

You might think that if every galaxy beyond our own is moving away from us, we must be in the center of the universe. Not necessarily! Imagine a bag of popcorn suddenly exploding so that the pieces of popcorn fly all over the room. If you were small enough to ride on one of those flying pieces (and calm enough to make the observation), you would see that the pieces of popcorn around you were all getting farther away. This would be so no matter where you happened to be in the cloud of flying popcorn.

We cannot say that because every other galaxy is moving away from us we are in the center of the universe. We can only say that the universe is expanding.

Quasars and the Big Bang

The speeds and distances of the galaxies in the universe are remarkable, to put it mildly. Yet only a few years ago astronomers discovered some entirely unexpected and even more remarkable objects in the universe. These newly found objects are far more luminous, farther away, and faster than the most distant ordinary galaxy. The reason no one suspected the existence of these objects is that their discovery had to wait for the invention of the radio telescope.

When astronomers discover a powerful source of radio energy in the sky, by means of a radio telescope, they then examine that part of the sky with an optical telescope. In this way they have found that many radio energy sources are stars in distant galaxies.

However, some of the radio sources, although they look like very distant blue stars, have turned out to be something quite different. They give off quantities of energy perhaps millions of times greater than any ordinary star. Yet compared with ordinary stars they are remarkably small in size. These very powerful radio sources cannot be ordinary stars. Astronomers have christened them **quasars.**

These quasars are by far the most distant objects in our universe, as well as the speediest and the most energetic. Some are billions of light-years away. They shine with the light of 50 to 100 ordinary galaxies like the Milky Way. The speed at which quasars are moving away, as measured by the red shift, ranges from about 155,000 kilometers per second to 248,000 kilometers per second (93,000 to 149,000 miles per second).

The discovery of quasars furnishes important new evidence that may help scientists decide on a theory of the origin and history of the universe. The most generally accepted theory is that the universe began billions of years ago with a vast explosion. Hence this theory is known as the Big-bang theory. Since the universe is now expanding, the theory goes, there must have been a time in the past when all the matter now expanding was close together. An explosion of some sort started to form the galaxies, and gave them enough energy to move away from each other.

Where do quasars fit into the Big-bang theory? Some scientists think that a galaxy comes into being with a giant explosion, and that a quasar is just such an explosion—the birth of a galaxy. The quasar later becomes an ordinary galaxy.

Astronomers have seen a quasar 9 billion light-years away. Think what this means. It means that astronomers have seen something that happened 9 billion years ago. So astronomers looking at a quasar may be looking back at the birth of the universe itself! However, more information must be gathered. Perhaps some very different theory will come out of the work astronomers are now doing.

This much we do know. Quasars, galaxies, our own Milky Way, the stars, our sun, and the earth, in orbit around the sun, are all in motion. Stars, bright or dim, cool or hot, blue, yellow, or red, are changing—changing size, changing color, and changing luminosity. Galaxies are changing, too. The universe of which we are a part is always changing.

REVIEW

1. Can two stars with the same luminosity have different apparent magnitudes? Explain.

2. Aldebaran is a red giant whose apparent magnitude is 1.1.

a. Can this star be seen without a telescope?

b. Could this star have a luminosity 100 times as great as the luminosity of the sun? Explain.

3. A certain star grows dim every 4 days and 10 hours. What are two possible explanations for this?

4. One of two stars has a reddish color, and the other is yellowish. Which is hotter? What is your reasoning?

5. Describe the Doppler effect in waves of water, sound waves, and light waves.

6. Why do scientists think the universe is expanding?

7. Describe the Big-bang theory briefly.

8. Modern astronomers have discovered that the stars move at great speeds through space. Why, then, did men believe for thousands of years that the stars were fixed?

NEW VIEW

1. The moon has an apparent magnitude of −12.7, and the planet Mars an apparent magnitude of −2.8. About how many times brighter than Mars is the moon? Use a reference.

2. The drawing at the left below shows the present shape of the Big Dipper. (1) The drawing on the right shows how the Big Dipper will appear thousands of years from now. (2) Why will the shape change?

3. What kind of evidence would help astronomers tell an eclipsing binary from a cepheid variable?

4. How do satellites and other spacecraft add to our knowledge of the universe?

3. OUR SPECK OF MATTER

In November of 1971, Mariner 9 was launched on its way to the planet Mars. (3) On the thirteenth day of November, it became the first artificial object to orbit another planet. Between that time and October 27, 1972, Mariner took 7,329 photographs of the Martian surface. These photographs, radioed back to earth, enabled scientists to study features of Mars that had never been seen before. And from them, they put together the first detailed map of another planet. (4) Its mission accom-

(1)
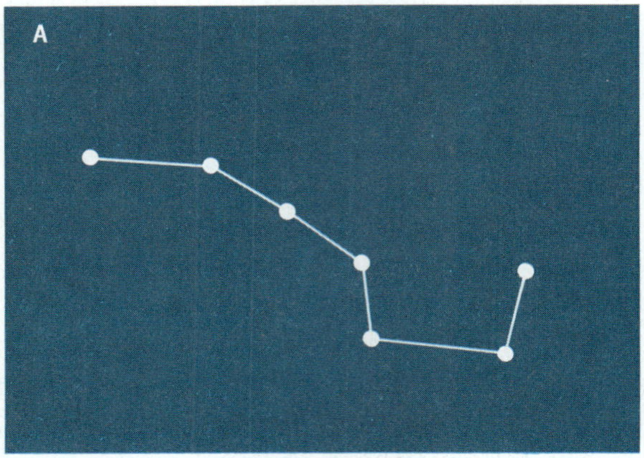

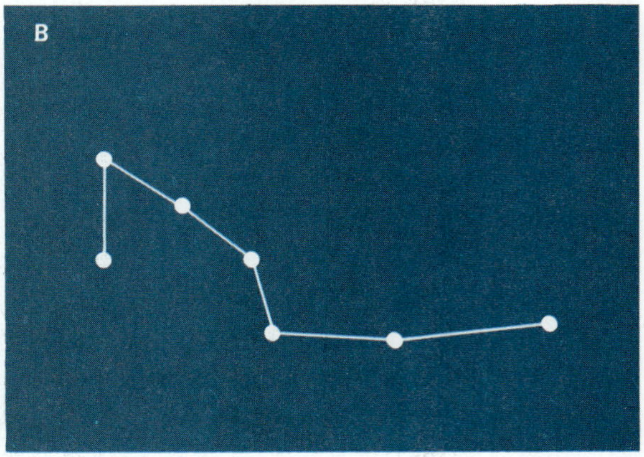

(2)

3

4

plished, Mariner 9 remains for a time in orbit around Mars.

Mariner 9's journey is just one of many probes we have sent into space. However, it would be more accurate to call Mariner 9 a "solar-system shot" than a "space shot." None of our space probes has left the solar system.

Maps of Space

It took precise knowledge of the orbits of the earth and other planets to make the Mariner 9 shot possible. An accurate map of the solar system was needed, and was available. It took men a long time to map the universe and to account for the motions of the bright objects they saw in the sky.

What did ancient men see? By day, of course, they saw the sun. By night they saw the moon, which seemed to move around the earth as the sun did. The sun seemed to revolve around the earth once in 24 hours. The moon seemed to take 25 hours to revolve once around the earth. The stars, fixed in their places, revolved around the earth once in 24 hours, like the sun.

Against the apparently unchanging background of the stars, however, there were five bodies that did *not* take a steady and regular course across the night sky. Seen against the fixed pattern of the stars, these bodies seemed to wander about. So the Greeks called these bodies **planets,** which means "wanderers."

The motions of the sun, the moon, and the stars were not hard to account for. The sun, moon, and stars seemed to revolve around the earth. But to account for the motions of the wanderers—Mercury, Venus, Mars, Jupiter, and Saturn—was difficult. For example, the path of Mars is sometimes like this. 5

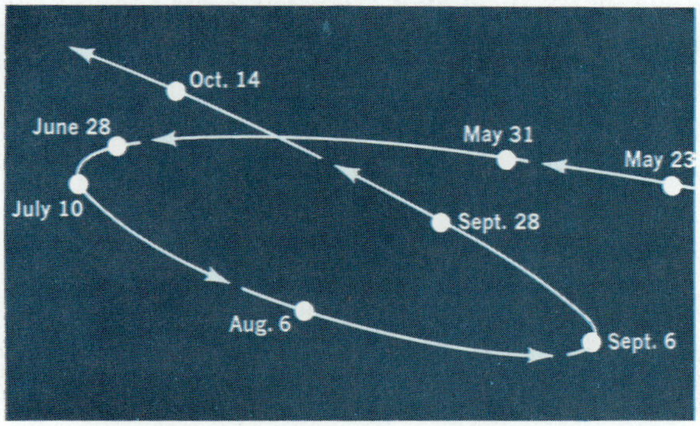

5

❶

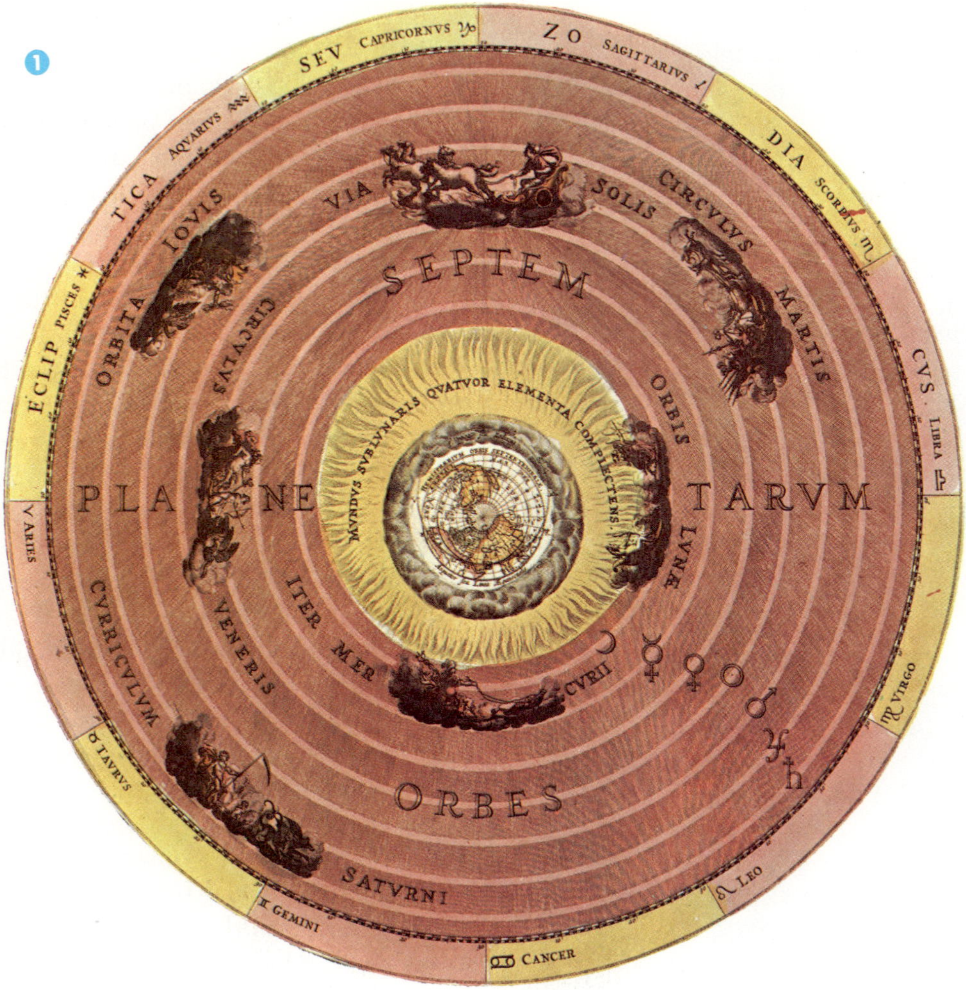

In 150 A.D.—Ptolemy's Map

About the year 150, Ptolemy again made a contribution to astronomy—he published a map of the universe. It was based chiefly on work done some 300 years earlier by another Greek astronomer, Hipparchus. Through Ptolemy's treatise, however, it became famous as the Ptolemaic system.

Ptolemy's map of the universe was based on a very simple idea. Ptolemy believed that the circle was the perfect shape and that all the bodies in the heavens had to move in circles. As Ptolemy said, his aim was "to demonstrate that all the phenomena in the sky are produced by uniform and circular motion." He placed the earth at the center of the universe. Then around the earth, in perfect circles, revolved the sun, the moon, Mercury, Venus, Mars, Jupiter, and Saturn. And beyond Saturn, the stars fixed in their sphere revolved around the earth. ❶

How were the irregular motions of the wanderers, the planets, accounted for? Mars, for example, sometimes moved in an S-shaped curve and sometimes seemed to move backward! How could this be explained by "uniform and circular motion"? The Ptolemaic system explained this observation by placing

Mars on the circumference of a small circle whose center moved along Mars' large circular orbit. ❷

The small circle is called an **epicycle.** The large circle is called a **deferent.** The beauty of this system of epicycle and deferent is that by choosing the right diameter and speed for the epicycle path, a fair approximation of Mars' observed motion can be obtained.

In fact, by varying the ratio of the diameters of epicycle and deferent, and the speeds, an astonishing variety of curves can be made. You may get some idea of how this works by drawing a circle several inches in diameter on a piece of paper. Then around one point on the circumference of this large circle, move your pencil in a continuous small circle. Go on making this small circle, but move your hand so that the center of the small circle moves along the large circle. You will find that varying the diameter of the epicycle and its speed along the deferent will produce a variety of figures.

In the Ptolemaic system, all of the planets had epicycles as well as large, circular orbits, or deferents. To account for the observed motions of the sun, moon, and the five planets,

❷

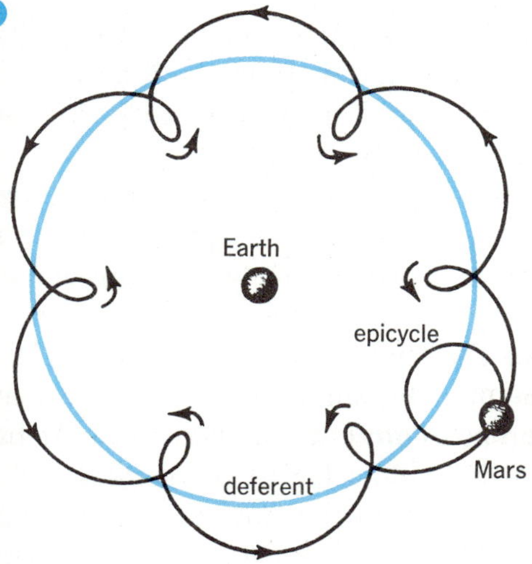

39 epicycles and deferents were needed. It was a somewhat complicated system, as you can imagine! However, it did preserve the Greek idea that the bodies in the heavens were perfect, and must therefore move in circles, the perfect motion.

Ptolemy placed the earth at the center of his map of the universe. Long before Ptolemy, a Greek astronomer named Aristarchus of Samos had proposed that the earth was not at the center of the universe. Aristarchus argued that the earth and the planets moved around the sun. He could not find enough evidence to make this hypothesis convincing, however. And people did not want to give up the belief that the earth was the center of the universe.

The Ptolemaic system did seem to fit the facts, and so Ptolemy's map of the universe was accepted for more than a thousand years. With time, though, the observations and calculations of astronomers became more accurate. Objections to Ptolemy's system began to accumulate. For example, there was the problem of the stars in the Ptolemaic system. According to Ptolemy, the stars were circling the earth fixed in a sphere beyond the orbit of the planet Saturn. They formed the background against which the motions of the planets were observed. New evidence was found which suggested that the stars were much further away than the Ptolemaic system supposed. This posed a problem. How could the stars so far away move fast enough to go around the earth in 24 hours?

This problem, and others, could not be solved by astronomers using the Ptolemaic system. At last, some 14 centuries after Ptolemy, a Polish astronomer named Nicholaus Copernicus proposed a "new" hypothesis. Copernicus proposed a different map of the universe.

[1]

1543 A.D.—The Map of Copernicus

It was not new evidence about the motions of the heavenly bodies that caused Copernicus to question the Ptolemaic system. It was that Ptolemy had not been able to do what he set out to do: "to demonstrate that all the phenomena in the sky are produced by uniform and circular motion." The planets moved in circles in Ptolemy's system, but their motion was not uniform.

Copernicus set out to correct this defect. If he assumed that the sun, not the earth, was at the center of the universe, then "this very difficult and almost insoluble problem" was solved. So the Copernican system placed the sun at the center of the circular orbits of the five planets and made the earth one more planet circling the sun. [1]

Notice that the orbits of the planets were still perfect circles, and epicycles were still needed to account for wandering motions. But the number of epicycles needed was reduced. The backward motion of Mars, for example, was explained as due to the earth's motion in an orbit around the sun. Sometimes the earth would seem to be overtaking Mars; sometimes the earth would seem to be falling behind Mars, because of the earth's motion.

This sun-centered universe was an exciting idea (Aristarchus of Samos had been forgotten long ago). Yet Nicholaus Copernicus was reluctant to make it known. He did write out a brief outline of his system, which passed from one scholar to another and gave him a kind of underground fame. For many years, however, he would not consent to publish the book he had written about his system. When he did at last consent, it was late. Seventy years old, he died a few hours after a copy reached him from the printer's. But his book, *On the Revolutions of the Heavenly Spheres,* published in 1543, laid a foundation for modern astronomy.

Copernicus had pictured the orbits of the planets as perfect circles, as had Ptolemy. The complicated movements of epicycles were still needed. It was the astronomical genius of Johannes Kepler that finally did away with epicycles and made plain the true orbits of the planets. 2

2

Kepler and the Planetary Orbits

"Who would have thought it possible? This hypothesis, which so closely agrees with the observed oppositions, is nevertheless false . . . ." With these words Kepler admitted that six years of work and 900 pages of tedious calculations had contradicted, instead of confirmed, the hypothesis that these planets move in perfect circles.

Kepler had been given the job of working out the circular orbit of the planet Mars, using observations made by his master, the astronomer Tycho Brahe. In other words, Kepler had to locate Mars' path in space. It was a difficult job, but Kepler kept at it. Then, just when he thought he had succeeded in describing Mars' orbit, he found some observations of Mars' position that did not fit in.

Earlier astronomers might have ignored these inconvenient observations as errors of the instruments. Kepler had too high an opinion of the accuracy of Brahe's work to do that. He knew that Brahe was an observer without equal. So Kepler reasoned that it was the hypothesis that was false, not the observations.

He wrote, "The conclusion is quite simply that the planet's path is not a circle—it curves inward on both sides and outward again at opposite ends. Such a curve is called an oval. The orbit is not a circle, but an oval figure."

The orbit of a planet is *not* a circle, said Kepler. More than 1,000 years of astronomy stood contradicted. It was not only the ancients, with their earth-centered Ptolemaic map, who believed the planets had to move in perfect circles. Even Copernicus, with his sun-centered map, had not questioned the old Greek notion that the planets must have perfectly circular orbits.

The orbit of Mars is an oval, Kepler claimed. But what sort of an oval? Kepler wrestled with this problem for years. He

1

made mistakes, took wrong turns, explored blind alleys, got lost, found his way again. At last he came upon the solution: *The orbit of Mars is an ellipse.* The complicated epicycles disappeared. The true path of the planets was known at last.

If you are not well acquainted with ellipses, you can make some for yourself in this way. Pin a large piece of paper to a drawing board or heavy cardboard. Stick two thumbtacks a short distance apart near the middle of the paper.(1) Tie the ends of a string 45 centimeters (18 inches) long to make a loop. Place the loop over the tacks and pull it tight with a pencil. Draw a line using the string loop to guide the pencil as shown. The resulting shape is an ellipse.

The points where the thumbtacks are located are called the **foci** of the ellipse. An ellipse has two foci: see what happens to the shape of the ellipse when the distance between the two foci is changed. (How do you make an ellipse that is nearly a circle? How do you make a long, narrow ellipse?)

What Kepler found true of Mars is true of the other planets—the orbits of the planets are ellipses. They are not long and narrow ellipses, though; they are nearly circles. The sun is at one focus of each ellipse.

Kepler calculated that the speed of a planet varies in such a way that a line drawn from the planet to the sun covers equal areas in equal times.(2) He also worked out how the speed of a planet is related to the distance of the planet from the sun. Thus, Kepler's Laws of Planetary Motion, as they are called, helped astronomers to draw the map of the solar system (and the universe) that we use today.

A Model of the Solar System

Copernicus knew of 6 planets moving in orbits around the sun, including the earth.

2

3

Putting in epicycles as needed, he tried hard to show that the planets must move with uniform circular motion. Kepler knew of the same 6 planets, but showed that the motion was not uniform, not circular, and did away with the epicycles. Today's map of the solar system includes the 9 known planets, each with an elliptical orbit. 3

1 

Moons, Asteroids, Meteors, and Comets

Suppose you were a visitor from another solar system, entering our solar system in a spaceship. What would you see? You could see the planets revolving around the sun. You would discover the earth's natural satellite, and find that the earth is not the only planet with a moon. You'd observe that Mars has 2 moons, Neptune has 2, Uranus has 5, Saturn has 10, and Jupiter has 12—a total of 32 moons.

You would also find, in orbit between Mars and Jupiter, a swarm of little **asteroids,** or tiny planets. There might be as many as 50,000 asteroids. More than 150 asteroids have been photographed from the earth.

On your imaginary journey you might be endangered by smaller bits of stone and metal moving through space. Such pieces of space matter are **meteoroids.** Most meteoroids would be harmless: they are merely bits of dust. If a meteoroid plunges into the atmosphere of the earth, friction heats the meteoroid until it glows. Then it is known as a **meteor.** Meteors appear in the night sky as "shooting stars," making streaks of light as they disintegrate in the upper atmosphere.

Sometimes a meteor may be so big a chunk of metal or rock that it does not disintegrate completely, but hits the surface of the earth. A **meteorite** is a meteor that hits the earth. The largest meteorite on display is in the American Museum of Natural History. 1

On your way through our solar system, you might see a **comet.** A comet appears to be a kind of "flying gravel bank," a collection of small particles. Some of the dust-size bits break away and turn into meteoroids. A comet does not give off its own light. It becomes visible as it nears the sun and reflects sunlight. The comet tail grows as some of the finest particles stream away from the comet head. 2 As a comet moves through the solar system, its thin tail of gas and dust streams away from the sun. The tail is pushed partly by the force of radiation from the sun and partly by the force of the particles of matter making up the solar wind.

2 

One of the most impressive sights men have seen in the sky is Halley's comet, last seen in 1910 and due to return in 1986. Not all comets return. Comets that return have become a part of our solar system, and have predictable orbits. The orbit of Halley's comet is a long and rather narrow ellipse, with the sun at one of the foci. 3 The long, narrow shape of the comet's orbit explains why we see Halley's comet only once every 75 or 76 years.

Your Neighbors in Space

What would you find if you could explore some of the other planets in our solar system? Man's exploration of space by means of artificial satellites began in 1957, and has already added greatly to our knowledge of the solar system. In the table on the next two pages you can sample some of this knowledge.

REVIEW

1. How did Copernicus' map differ from Ptolemy's map? How did Kepler's ideas improve upon those of Copernicus?

2. Mars sometimes seems to move backward in the sky.

a. How did the Ptolemaic system account for this?

b. How did Kepler's ideas account for the same fact?

3. Suppose star Y is 1.5 light-years from star X. What is the distance in miles from X to Y?

4. Where would you be likely to see each of these: a meteoroid, a meteor, and a meteorite? Explain your answers.

5. In what way are comets and asteroids similar? How are they different?

6. How does a comet resemble a planet? How does it differ from a planet?

7. When will Halley's comet again be seen?

NEW VIEW

Use the chart of the planets on the next two pages to answer these questions.

a. What is the relationship between the speed of a planet's revolution around the sun and its distance from the sun?

b. On which planet would day and night be most like it is on earth? Why?

c. What information in the table makes it unlikely that life as we know it exists on Venus?

3

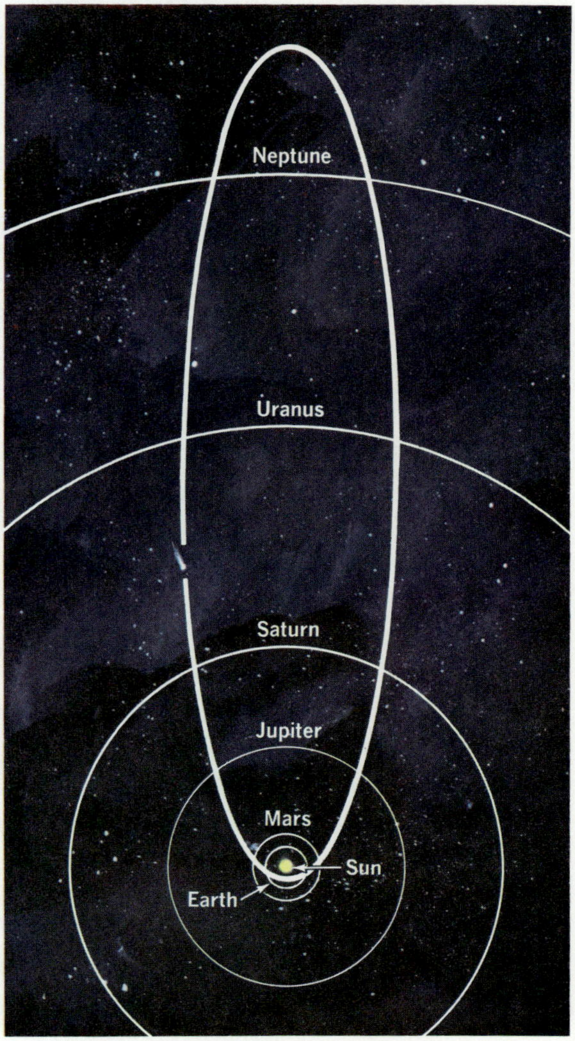

Some Data on the Planets

	diameter	distance from sun	average surface temperature
Mercury	5,030 km 3,020 miles	0.39 AU	425°C 800°F (sunlit side)
Venus	12,700 km 7,600 miles	0.72 AU	355°C 670°F
Earth	13,197 km 7,918 miles	1.0 AU	15°C 57°F
Mars	6,970 km 4,180 miles	1.52 AU	12°C 54°F
Jupiter	143,000 km 86,000 miles	5.2 AU	–143°C –226°F
Saturn	117,000 km 70,000 miles	9.5 AU	–148°C –234°F
Uranus	50,000 km 30,000 miles	19.2 AU	–207°C –341°F
Neptune	47,000 km 28,000 miles	30.1 AU	?
Pluto	13,000 km 8,000 miles	39.5 AU	?

period of rotation*	period of revolution	number of moons	mass compared to earth	substances observed in atmosphere
88 days	88 days	0	.05	none
247 days	224.7 days	0	.8	carbon dioxide (CO_2)
23 hours, 56.07 min.	365.26 days	1	1.0	nitrogen (N_2) oxygen (O_2) water (H_2O) carbon dioxide (CO_2) and others
24 hours, 37.4 min.	687 days	2	0.1	carbon dioxide (CO_2) water (H_2O)
9 hours, 55 min.	11.86 years	12	318	hydrogen (H_2) ammonia (NH_3) methane (CH_4)
10 hours, 30 min.	29.46 years	10 and 3 rings	95	hydrogen (H_2) ammonia (NH_3) methane (CH_4)
10 hours, 50 min.	84.02 years	5	14	hydrogen (H_2) methane (CH_4)
16 hours	164.8 years	2	17	hydrogen (H_2) methane (CH_4)
6.4 days	248.4 years	0	?	?

*Periods of rotation and revolution are given in terms of days and years on earth.

4. RELATING THE CONCEPTS

Our concept of the universe today differs greatly from that of Ptolemy. In the ancient Ptolemaic system the earth was the center of a small, almost cosy universe. Today we know our universe, in which the earth is but one of many planets in an average-sized galaxy, to be large beyond the farthest stretch of imagination.

Space is the environment of the planet earth. Our planet's place is in a solar system centered upon a medium-sized yellow star, the sun. The sun's place is among billions of other stars in the Milky Way Galaxy. The galaxy itself is just one among billions of galaxies in a universe we are just beginning to explore.

This universe is always changing. The planets whirl around our modest star; comets hurtle through the solar system; meteoroids dart through space, to burn out in our atmosphere as meteors or hit the earth as meteorites. Our sun, too, is in continual motion, in a galaxy that whirls like a magnificent pinwheel. The galaxies rush away from each other at immense speeds in a universe that seems to be expanding.

So we have traveled a long way from the "cosy" universe of Ptolemy with the earth at its center. We are, because of science, acquiring a new concept of the universe. We are acquiring not just a new concept of the universe, but a new concept of *our* place in the universe. We are acquiring a new concept of what men are—and what men may become.

We have traveled a long way, yet the road ahead looks more exciting still.

In earlier chapters of this book we have thought mainly about the forms and changes of matter in terms of tiny bits or particles—molecules, atoms, protons, electrons, neutrons. In this chapter we have been mainly concerned with the forms and changes of matter on a different scale—matter in the form of huge chunks: the planets of our solar system, the star around which they revolve, and the myriads of stars that make up the huge number of galaxies in the universe.

A concept that is true about matter in huge chunks is this: *The universe is in continuous change.* This concept is a broad one, in some way served by each of the concepts to follow.

Reviewing the Concepts

► *The universe is made up of a great many galaxies separated by great distances.* Because of these distances, we may say the universe is mostly space. And if, as astronomers generally believe, *the universe is expanding,* the galaxies which are now so far apart are all moving even farther away from one another. Each galaxy consists of billions of stars in motion around a center.

► *Stars of different sizes and energy output are in different stages of their life history.* Astronomers believe that this concept is a reasonable interpretation of a great deal of evidence of many kinds. The study of the changeable stars known as cepheid variables, for example, reveals that the longer the period of variation of the star, the greater its *true* brightness.

► *The sun is a medium-sized star with average luminosity and temperature.* Knowledge of the luminosities of other stars supports this concept about our sun.

► *The solar system consists of the sun and nine planets moving in definite orbits about the sun.* In addition to nine planets, the sun's family also contains many smaller bodies—asteroids, moons, meteoroids, comets.

Investigating the Constellations

THE NORTH POLAR CONSTELLATIONS

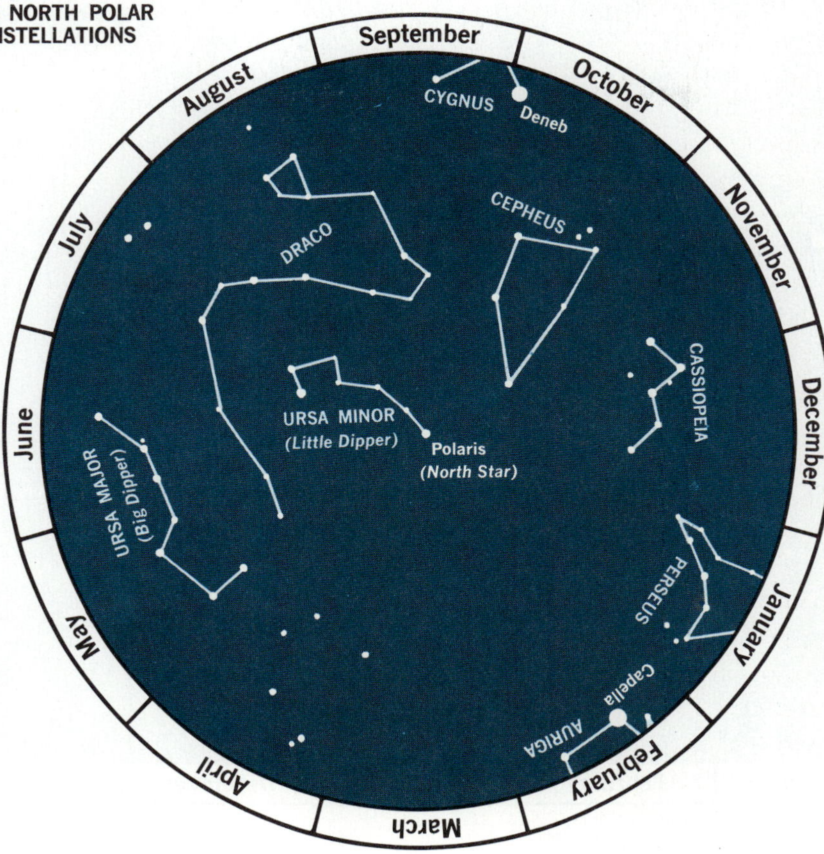

North Polar Star Map

In the Apprentice Investigation on page 165 you saw how to locate the Big and Little Dippers and the North Star. To learn more about the map of the sky, use the star maps on this and the next three pages.

First, hold the North Polar Star Map (above) at arm's length, pointing toward the North Star. Rotate the map so that the right month is on top. If the standard time is about 8:00 P.M., the map should agree with what you see in the sky. For example, at 8:00 P.M. in November the Big Dipper will appear almost directly below the North Star. Then you may expect to find the M-shaped constellation Cassiopeia the Queen high in the northeast. Cepheus the King will appear to be upside down high in the northwest.

If the time is earlier than 8:00 P.M., first hold the map with the proper month on top and then rotate it clockwise by 15 degrees per hour. Thus, for example, at 7:00 P.M. in November, Cassiopeia will appear farther northeast than it does at 8:00 P.M., and Cepheus will appear to be more nearly above the North Star than it does at 8:00 P.M. (Suppose the time is later than 8:00 P.M. How should you rotate the map? Why?)

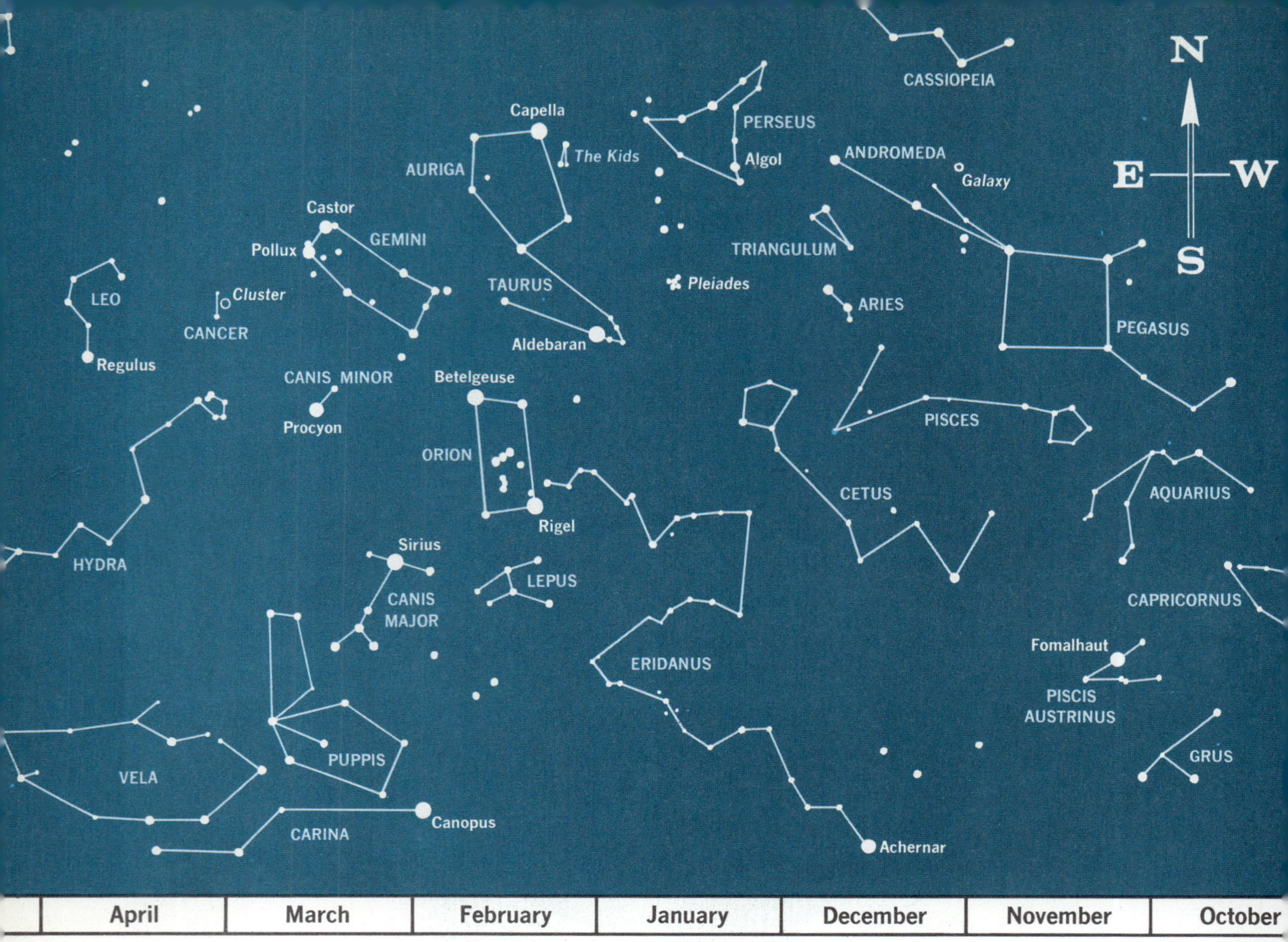

Seasonal Star Maps

The maps on these two pages show the prominent stars and constellations you will see if you look toward the south from the continental United States. Hold the map in front of you as you face south. Suppose you are observing at 8:00 P.M., standard time. Then the stars south of you appear above the proper month written at the bottom of the map. (What should you do if the time is earlier or later than 8:00 P.M.?)

The constellations low in the southern sky are near the bottom of the map. In August, for example, one of these would be Scorpius the Scorpion. And in September, Sagittarius the Archer is prominent in the lower part of the southern sky. Almost over your head are the constellations near the top of the map. In September, for example, one of these would be Aquila the Eagle. Past the overhead point, in the northern sky, are the constellations at the top of the map. In January, for example, one of these would be Perseus the Hero.

Since to our modern eyes the constellations do not seem to have the shapes of the names assigned to them by the ancients (who used their imagination a good deal), you may find the following descriptions helpful.

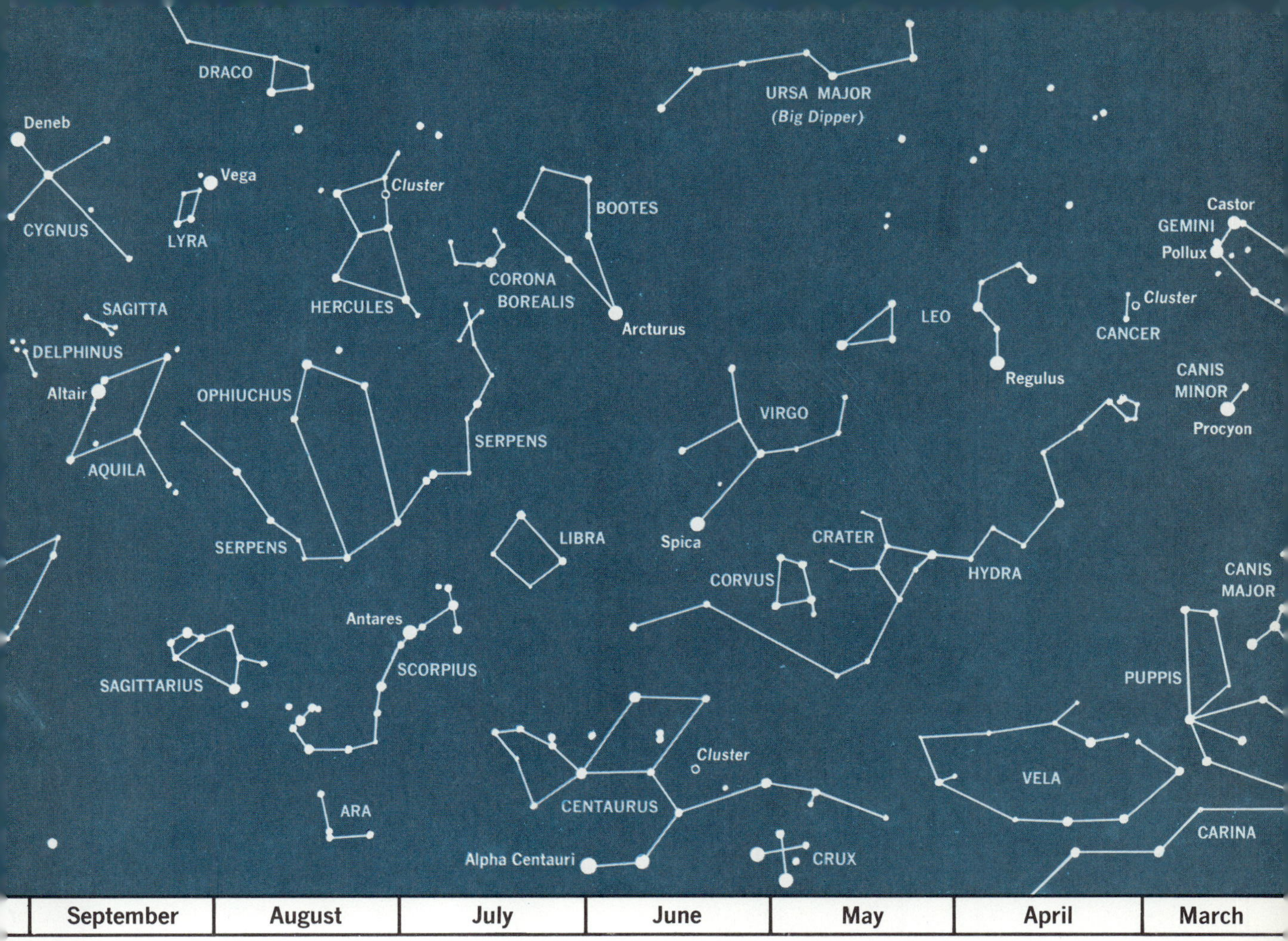

In April and May, for example, Leo the Lion is outstanding. Its eastern part is a triangle, with the bright star Regulus at the end. Corvus the Crow, another spring constellation, resembles the mainsail of a boat. In June there is Bootes the Herdsman, a kite-shaped group with the bright orange star Arcturus at its base.

Gemini the Twins, seen in March, is a rectangle with the bright stars Castor and Pollux (who were twin brothers in Greek mythology) together at one end. Two other March constellations are Canis Major and Canis Minor—Canis Major the Greater Dog contains Sirius, the brightest star in the sky; and Canis Minor the Lesser Dog is made up of just two stars, one of them the bright star Procyon.

Visible in August and September is Lyra the Lyre, made up of a parallelogram to which is attached a small triangle with the prominent star Vega at one point. In September and October there is Cygnus the Swan, sometimes called the Northern Cross because of its crosslike shape. Orion the Hunter, seen in January and February, has a rectangular shape, with Betelgeuse at his right shoulder, Rigel at his left ankle, and three bright stars making up his belt.

THE SOUTH POLAR CONSTELLATIONS

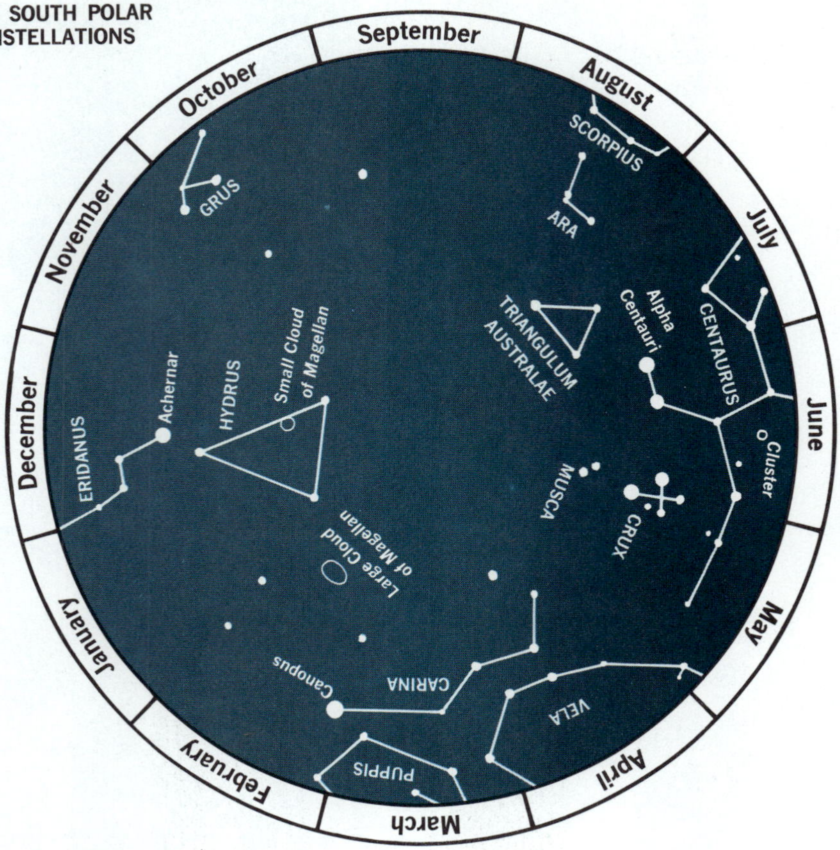

South Polar Star Map

The stars in the North Polar Map (page 193) and the Seasonal Map (pages 194–195) are all shown as they would appear from latitudes within the continental United States. But to see all the stars in the South Polar Map on this page you would have to be located south of the earth's equator.

Perhaps the best-known of the south polar constellations is Crux the Cross, commonly called the Southern Cross, whose four brightest stars are arranged in a crosslike shape. Another prominent constellation is Triangulum Australae the Southern Triangle. Then there are the earth's "satellite galaxies": the large and the small Clouds of Magellan.

On these star maps there are 35 constellations (out of 88 that astronomers have named) and some of the brightest, most easily seen stars. After you have become familiar with them, you may want to go further on your own with the references below.

Moore, Patrick, *Naked Eye Astronomy*, New York, W. W. Norton Co., 1965. This book is a complete guide to astronomy, for beginners without a telescope.

Bernhard, Hubert J., and others, *New Handbook of the Heavens*, New York, McGraw-Hill, 1948. This well-known and widely used guide to astronomy is available in a paperback edition (New York, Signet, 1962).

Testing Yourself

1. Astronomers believe the Milky Way Galaxy is 100,000 light-years in diameter.

a. What is meant by a light-year?

b. How many miles are equivalent to one light-year?

2. How does a galaxy differ from a nebula?

3. What is meant by the magnitude of a star? How does a star's magnitude differ from its luminosity?

4. The sun is a yellow star, Aldebaran is red, Arcturus is orange, and Sirius is blue-white. Arrange these stars in order of their surface temperatures, beginning with the one with the greatest temperature.

5. The sun is a medium-sized star with average luminosity. What evidence is there to support this statement?

6. How does the Doppler effect support the view that the universe is expanding?

7. Why was the Ptolemaic system accepted for many centuries?

8. Why did the map of Copernicus replace Ptolemy's map?

Extending the Concepts

Investigation 1. Read about the so-called UFO's (Unidentified Flying Objects), which some people think are "visitors" from outer space. What do you think? Find out what astronomers think and why. Give reasons for your opinion.

Investigation 2. What hypothesis about the origin of the universe is currently most favored by scientists? You have read about the Big Bang hypothesis. The hypothesis of Continuous Creation, sometimes called the Steady-state Universe, is another important view of the possible origin of the universe. Where would you find more about these hypotheses? Try a periodical like *The Scientific American,* if it is in your school library, or a recent edition of an encyclopedia.

Investigation 3. You have learned about the use of light-years in astronomical measurement. But astronomers also use other units of measurement for distances in the universe. One such unit is the *parsec.* The parsec is a unit related to the angle formed by two straight lines that cross at the center of a circle, so that they cut off arcs of the circle measured in seconds. In a reference book, read about parsecs and how they are used. One book you may try is *Modern Space Science,* by Frederick Trinklein and Charles Huffer, Rinehart and Winston, 1961.

Suggested Reading

Mayall, Newton, and others, *The Sky Observers' Guide,* A Handbook for Amateur Astronomers, New York, Golden Press, 1965. This book is richly illustrated with maps and pictures.

Armitage, Angus, *William Herschel,* New York, Fernhill, 1962. Biography of a famous astronomer who discovered the planet Uranus in 1781.

Alter, Dinsmore, and others, *Pictorial Astronomy,* 3rd. ed., New York, Crowell, 1969. Contains sections on the earth, moon, eclipses, planets, comets, meteors, stars, and nebulae.

Muirden, James, *Amateur Astronomer's Handbook,* New York, Crowell, 1968. A more advanced book for the student who is more than a beginner in astronomy.

Texereau, Jean, *How to Make a Telescope,* New York, Doubleday, 1968. The author of this book built his first 10-inch telescope at the age of 20.

Moore, Patrick (editor), *1973 Yearbook of Astronomy,* New York, Norton, 1972.

10

Origin and Orbit

The earth is a planet moving in orbit around the sun. It is not the sun's only planet. There are other planets, in other orbits, moving around the sun. All these planets, including the earth, move in the same direction around the sun. All the orbits lie in nearly the same plane—except the outermost orbit (Pluto's), which is tilted.

How did this remarkable collection of moving objects get this way? How did the objects come to have orbits in nearly the same plane? Did the solar system come together bit by bit from different directions in space, at different times? Or did it have a single origin? If it had a single origin, how did it develop?

Let's examine some hypotheses that scientists have devised to answer these questions.

1. A CLOUD OF DUST AND GAS

Immanuel Kant, a famous German philosopher, and Pierre de Laplace, a great French mathematician, both lived during the eighteenth century. Both concerned themselves with the same problem—how did the solar system begin? And both developed, independently, the same hypothesis: the solar system began as a cloud of dust and gas in space, a nebula. Their concept has been called the **nebular hypothesis.**

The Hypothesis of Kant and Laplace

Imagine that particles of dust and gas in a nebula are at first widely separated, spread out fairly evenly, and the nebula is slowly rotating. ❶

Imagine that as the cloud rotates, its particles come closer together. In other words, the cloud condenses. As it condenses, the cloud forms a huge central bulge surrounded by a flat ring of dust and gas. ❷

In time, the rotating flat ring splits into several rings, which move away from the central bulge. ❸

The material in each ring condenses further and forms a planet. The material in the central bulge forms the sun. Each planet continues to revolve around the sun in the plane of the ring it came from. ❹

Was the birth of the solar system like this? What is the evidence? The Kant-Laplace nebular hypothesis is supported by at least two observations. First, clouds of dust and gas nebulae do exist in space. Indeed, the gas and dust in our galaxy make up as much mass as all the galaxy's stars put together.

Second, according to the nebular hypothesis the planets ought to rotate in the same direction, in nearly circular orbits, and in nearly the same plane. Observations show that, in the main, these things are so. There are two differences, however. Venus spins in the opposite direction from the other planets, and Pluto's orbit is not in the same plane as the others. Scientists think these observations can be explained in a way that does not upset the main hypothesis.

A serious weakness of the nebular hypothesis, however, was that its inventors did not back it up with accurate data and mathematical verification. For this reason, the nebular hypothesis was soon challenged.

The Nebular Hypothesis is Challenged

The challenge to the Kant-Laplace hypothesis came from an English physicist and mathematician, James Clerk Maxwell. Maxwell studied the rings of the planet Saturn. In 1859 he showed that the rings were not solid, but collections of particles—like those in the nebular hypothesis. Why did the rings of Saturn not form planets? Maxwell asked. If the rings of Saturn did not form planets, he reasoned, then the rings described in the Kant-Laplace hypothesis would not have formed planets either. Instead of planets, there would have been a huge sun surrounded forever by Saturnlike rings.

Maxwell's criticism gained support in 1902 from the calculations made by two Americans, Thomas Chamberlin and Forest Moulton. Chamberlin and Moulton tested the nebular hypothesis mathematically and found several defects in it. If the Kant-Laplace hypothesis were correct, they reasoned, the sun would rotate very rapidly and the planets would be practically motionless. Just the opposite is true, however: The sun rotates very

1

2

3

4

slowly, while the planets have a good deal of motion.

Chamberlin and Moulton proposed a hypothesis of their own. It was based upon the idea that the sun already existed as a star before there were any planets. During the early twentieth century a number of scientists proposed new hypotheses built upon this same basic idea. One of these hypotheses was that another star came near the sun, and pulled several giant streamers of matter from the sun as it passed. (1) These streamers later condensed into planets, according to this hypothesis.

Another hypothesis was that our sun collided with or "sideswiped" another star. The result was that the other star knocked from the sun some matter that later became the planets. This hypothesis was known as the **collision hypothesis.**

However, these hypotheses proved to be unsatisfactory for a number of reasons. For one thing, they did not account for the fact that the orbits of the planets are nearly circular and in nearly the same plane. If the masses that became planets were violently pulled out of the sun, their orbits would have been long narrow ellipses, and each orbit would probably be in a different plane.

(1)

Another objection is that astronomers have not found any star that could have met with the sun at about the time that the earth was formed. Here is an instance of how observations can upset a hypothesis. Scientists demand that hypotheses fit the facts.

Modern Theories

Since 1940, hypotheses about the origin of the planets have been based on the assumption that the sun and planets were formed together. Many new observations were at hand when Carl von Weizäcker, a German physicist, proposed a return to the basic concept of the nebular hypothesis. The objections that had been made to the nebular hypothesis were removed by modifying some of the ideas of Kant and Laplace.

Some of the new facts were about the chemical make-up of objects in space.

About 99% of the matter making up the sun and other stars is a mixture of the light gaseous elements hydrogen and helium. The other 1% of the matter in stars consists of the heavier elements—oxygen, iron, aluminum, nitrogen, and others.

Only about 1% of the earth's matter consists of the lighter elements.

The other inner planets—Mercury, Venus, and Mars—resemble the earth in their chemical make-up: they all consist of about 99% of the heavier elements.

The outer planets—Jupiter, Saturn, Uranus, and Neptune—contain a great deal of the lighter element hydrogen and relatively small amounts of the heavier elements. (The chemical make-up of Pluto is not yet known.)

Weizäcker suggested that these facts could be accounted for this way. At first there was a huge nebula that was 99 percent hydrogen gas and helium gas. The other 1 percent of the nebula was made up of heavier elements in the form of dust particles floating in the mixture of gases. As the nebula slowly rotated, the dust particles collided with one another, generating great heat. During these collisions some particles began to stick together. Gradually these clusters grew into larger and larger solid bodies, eventually becoming the planets.

"First Planets"

An American astronomer, Gerard Kuiper, advanced a more recent version of the Kant-Laplace theory in the 1950's. According to Kuiper, each body of condensed matter that was to be a planet first formed a **protoplanet.** Around each protoplanet was a thick atmosphere. ❷

As the protoplanets continued to condense, they became very hot. The more they condensed, the hotter they became. When the hot protoplanets eventually stopped condensing, they began to cool.

Meanwhile, the largest condensation of all was in the center of what had been the original nebula. What formed there was a protostar, destined to become our sun. ❸

As this protostar condensed, it became very much hotter than the protoplanets. Since the protostar was much larger than the protoplanets, it could condense a great deal more and thus generate more heat. In fact, the protostar's temperature went up to some 12 to 15 million °C. This temperature is high enough to start a fusion reaction, the conversion of hydrogen into helium. As you know, this nuclear reaction produces vast amounts of electromagnetic energy, including light

❷

❸

❹

and other radiation. Thus the protostar became a star, our sun, the source of a continuing supply of energy.

Once the sun started producing its own energy, the pressure of that energy, known as **radiation pressure,** and the solar wind from the sun began to drive away the gaseous atmospheres of the protoplanets. The protoplanets slowly began to turn into the bodies we know as planets. ❹

The pressure of the sun's radiations is very slight, but if kept up for millions of years the effect can be substantial. Thus, it is possible that after some 100 million years the sun's radiation pressure completely drove away the gaseous atmosphere of Mercury, the planet nearest the sun. Only the bare rocky kernel of Mercury was left.

Venus, Mars, and the earth had practically all of their hydrogen and helium driven away by the sun's radiations. These three planets have been left with thin atmospheres over their rocky kernels. The outer planets—Saturn, Jupiter, Uranus and Neptune—still have thick atmospheres that contain considerable amounts of hydrogen. Since they were farthest away from the sun, they were least affected by radiation pressure as protoplanets.

The idea of radiation pressure affecting the thickness of a planet's atmosphere may not apply to Pluto, however. Pluto, the planet farthest away, is believed to be small and rocky. Pluto may have little or no atmosphere, like the other small planets nearest the sun. But scientists aren't sure. More information about Pluto is needed. Meanwhile, scientists assume that Pluto was formed later than the other planets.

Other members of the solar system—our moon, other moons, comets, meteoroids, and asteroids—must also have been formed later in some other way.

However, our exploration of space is constantly furnishing us with new facts about the solar system. Many of these facts are not accounted for by the nebular hypothesis in its present form. So the search for a satisfactory hypothesis, one that explains all the observations, continues. Meanwhile, the hypothesis that the sun and the planets were formed out of an original cloud of dust and gas is generally accepted by scientists.

REVIEW

1. How did the nebular hypothesis account for the fact that the planets generally revolve around the sun in the same direction and the same plane?
2. What was the Moulton-Chamberlin objection to the Kant-Laplace hypothesis?
3. What are two objections to the assumption that the sun existed before the planets?
4. What observations does the protoplanet hypothesis leave unexplained?
5. What basic theory of the origin of the solar system is accepted by most scientists?

NEW VIEW

1. What makes the idea of protoplanets a theory? When may a theory change?
2. How does the modern theory of our sun's origin suggest that planets similar to the earth may exist outside our own solar system?
3. Propose a hypothesis for the origin of the many natural satellites (including the earth's moon) found in the solar system.
4. Propose hypotheses for the origin of (a) asteroids, (b) comets, (c) meteoroids.

2. ROTATION AND REVOLUTION AT A.U. 1

We are, you might agree, conveniently situated. The earth is about 150,000,000 kilometers (93 million miles) from the sun—one **astronomical unit** (A.U.) as the astronomers say. But suppose the earth were at some other distance than 1 A.U. from the sun, so that we received more or less of the sun's energy than we do. For instance, if the earth were moved to 0.8 A.U. from the sun, only the polar regions would be cool enough to support life as we know it. At 1.6 A.U. from the sun, only the equator would be warm enough to support life as we know it.

■ AN APPRENTICE INVESTIGATION into a Model of a Planet in Orbit

Let an electric bulb represent the sun. Let a small ball stand for an imaginary planet that moves in orbit around the model sun. Mark an **X** on one side of the model planet. Place the model planet so that light from the model sun falls on the **X**.

Move the model planet in orbit around the model sun as shown, so that the **X** is always toward the "sun." Observe that when the model planet has made one complete revolution around the "sun," the model planet has rotated just once on its own axis. ❶

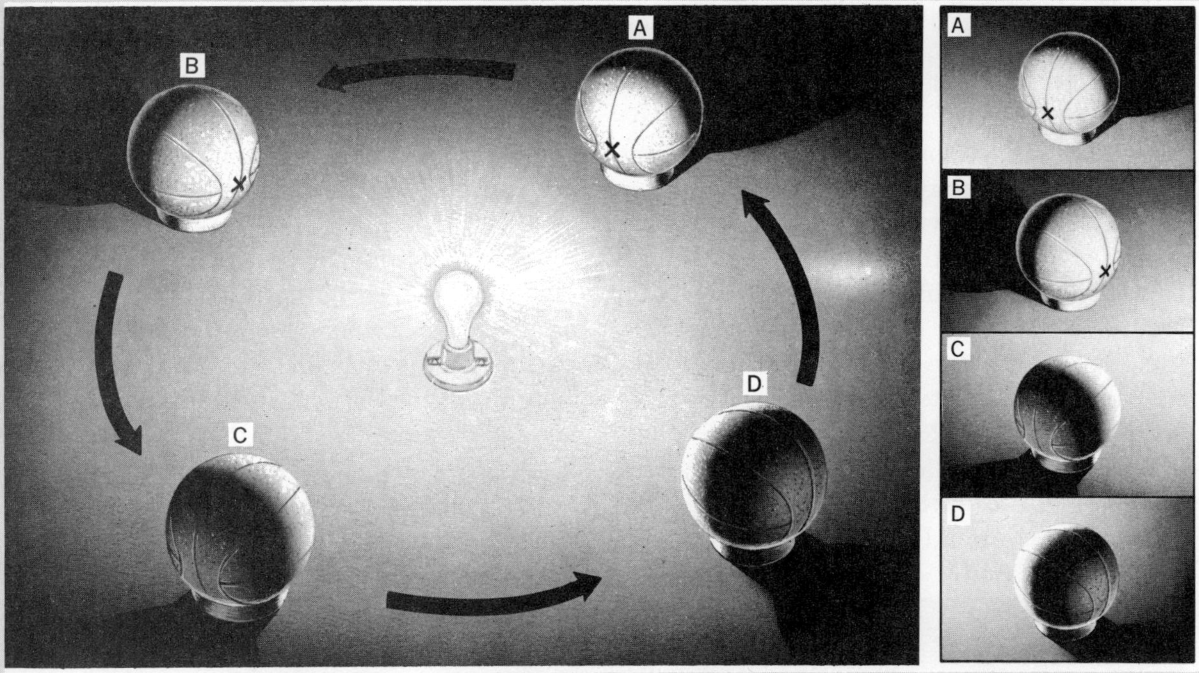

❶

Day and Night

Being the distance we are from the sun is one reason why we receive what seems to us to be the "right" amount of the sun's energy. Another reason our supply of the sun's radiation seems "right" to us is that our planet has day and night. Under what conditions would a planet *not* have day and night? ■

For any imaginary people living on the X side of this imaginary planet, it is always day. The other side of the planet is always night. There could be a planet without day and night if the planet rotated so that it always kept the same side toward the sun.

Unlike the imaginary inhabitants of this imaginary planet, people living on the earth do experience day and night. We happen to be on a planet that is spinning rather rapidly on its own axis as it moves in orbit around the sun. The earth makes a complete revolution around the sun in about 365 days, and makes a complete rotation on its own axis every 24 hours. So most (but not all) of the people who live on this planet experience day and night every 24 hours.

Days and nights do vary in length, however. We know that in summer the days are longer and the nights shorter; in winter the days are shorter and the nights longer. We may suspect, then, that there is some link between the varying length of days and nights, and the seasons. What is the link?

Winter and Summer

In some parts of the United States, daylight may last as long as 16 hours on some summer days. Yet daylight may last as little as 6 hours on some winter days. We can discover why the length of day differs at different seasons by examining the earth's orbit around the sun. (1)

Notice that as the earth moves around the sun, the earth is tilted. The earth's axis is at an angle of about 23.5 degrees to the plane of its orbit. The tilt of the earth stays at the same angle, and in the same direction, as the earth moves around the sun. One way we know this is so is that the North Pole of the earth always points toward the North Star.

Notice that on certain dates the earth is always at certain places in its orbit. On December 22, for instance, the earth is at the place in its orbit where the North Pole is tilted away from the sun. On June 21, the earth is at a place in its orbit where its North Pole is tilted toward the sun.

The movement of the earth around the sun is very regular indeed. As the saying goes, you could set your clock by it. And in fact this is just what men have done for thousands of years. They have set their clocks—and their calendars, too—by the regular motion of the earth in its orbit.

Let's look more closely at the position of the earth in its orbit on June 21. (2) This is the time of year when the North Pole is tilted toward the sun, and now you will see how important the tilt is. Remember that the earth is rotating on its axis, that imaginary line from the North Pole to the South Pole. Observe that just one half of the earth is in darkness, on the side away from the sun.

(1)

Suppose that you happen to be living at point A, near the North Pole. ② You will have 24 hours of daylight and no night at all, thanks to the tilt. If you are at point A, the rotation of the earth will not carry you into the dark. ③

Observe what happens if you live at point B, which is more likely. You will have day and night, for the rotation of the earth will carry you into the dark. ③ What of the lengths of day and night, though? Compare the time spent in daylight with the time spent in darkness. More time is spent in daylight than in darkness: the days are longer than the nights.

Let's examine the earth at the other side of its orbit, on December 22. ④ At this time the North Pole is tilted away from the sun. Point A now has 24 hours of night, and no day. The rotation of the earth does not carry point A into the light. Point B still has day and night, but the nights are longer than the days.

What happens as the earth moves along its orbit from December 22 to June 21? Most of us in the northern hemisphere live nearer to point B than to point A. For most of us, then, the hours of daylight increase, day by day, as the earth goes from winter to summer. Then from June 21 to December 22 the number of hours of daylight in our northern hemisphere decrease day by day. For the few hardy souls at the North Pole, six months of daylight are followed by six months of darkness. Meanwhile, what is happening to day and night in the southern hemisphere?

In the southern hemisphere just the opposite happens. The days get longer from June 21 to December 22, and shorter from December to June. December 22 is the longest day of the year in the southern hemisphere.

②

③

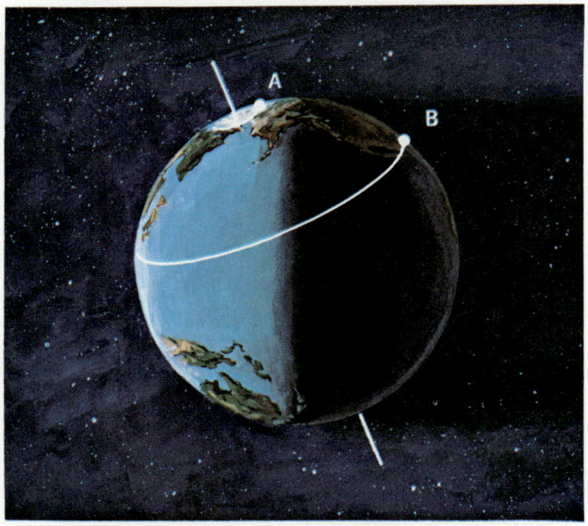

④

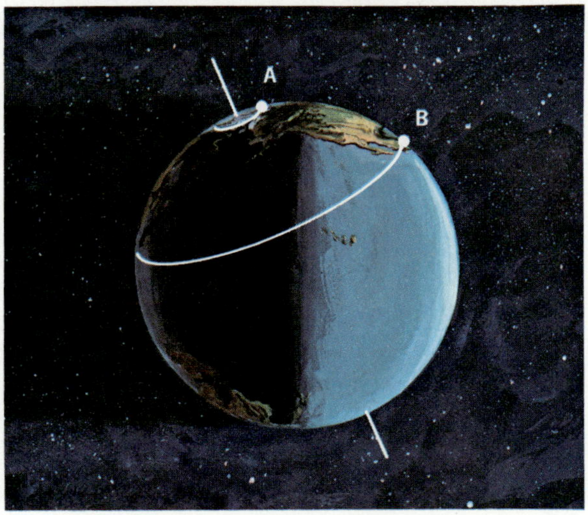

1

For the northern hemisphere, June 21 is the longest day of the year. This day is called the **summer solstice.** December 22, the shortest day of the year, is called the **winter solstice.** On March 20 and September 22, day and night are of equal length. These dates are known as the **spring equinox** and the **fall equinox.** The dates of the solstices and equinoxes are not always the same in every year, but may vary by one or two days from those in our example. The reason for this is that our calendar does not reflect precisely the earth's movement around the sun. (Can you think of another way in which our calendar is not perfect?)

It is the tilt of the earth's axis, then, that causes the length of day to change as the seasons change. Something else changes with the seasons, however. It's warmer in summer and colder in winter. Why does the average daily temperature change from one season to the next?

Seasonal Changes in Temperature

A July day is likely to be much warmer than a January day, in the northern hemisphere. The earth's tilt is having an effect here, too.

For one thing, the tilt of the earth's axis causes the length of day to vary, as you have seen. In summer there are more hours of daylight for the ground to absorb the sun's energy than in winter.

The earth's tilt also affects the way in which the sun's rays strike the ground. This is another cause of temperature variations. ■

A beam of light striking a surface at a slant covers a larger area than the same beam striking the same surface at right angles. But the light at the surface is brighter when the beam is at right angles. The greater the slant, the dimmer the light on the surface. Why? The beam of light has a certain amount of energy, no more. At a slant, that energy is spread over a large area. At right angles, that energy is concentrated in a small area.

In the same way, the ground receives less energy when the sun's rays strike it at a slant than when they strike it at a right angle.

2

3

■ AN APPRENTICE INVESTIGATION into the Angle of Light Falling on a Surface

Hold a flat piece of cardboard at right angles to the beam of a flashlight. Draw a line around the spot of light made by the beam, to show the area. ❶ Notice the brightness of the spot of light.

Now, keeping the cardboard at about the same distance from the flashlight, tilt the flashlight (or the cardboard) so that the light strikes at a slant. ❷

What happens to the brightness of the spot of light? What happens to the area of the spot?

An Investigation On Your Own

Can you devise a way of using a photographer's light meter to show how the intensity of light varies under these circumstances?

❶

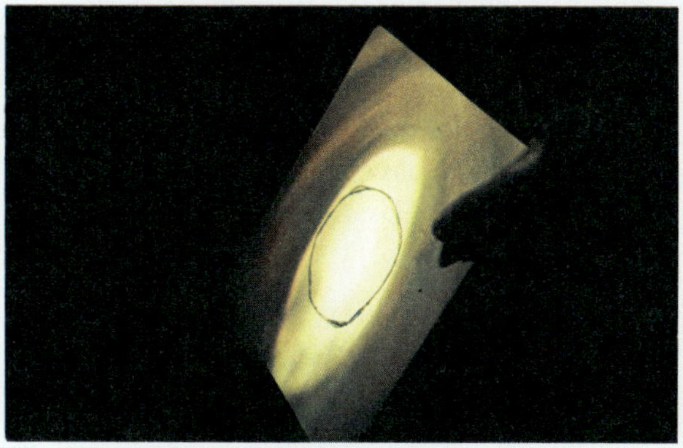

❷

Due to the curve of the earth's surface, the sun's rays strike the surface most directly near the equator, and are more slanted toward the poles. ❶ But the angle at which the sun's rays strike the earth at any one place changes as the seasons change. For example, on December 22 in New York City, the angle of the sun's rays with the ground is about 27 degrees at noon. ❷ On June 21, same place, same time, the angle is about 72 degrees. ❸ You don't have to go to New York City to know which angle produces more heat.

The angle at which the sun's rays hit the earth changes with the seasons because the earth's axis is tilted toward the sun during one half of its orbit, and away from the sun during the other half. It is the earth's tilt that causes seasonal changes. It is the earth's motion, as well as its tilt, that regulates how much energy we receive. We see and feel the effects of our planet's rotation on its axis and revolution around the sun every day.

REVIEW

1. What might happen if the earth moved from A.U. 1.0 to A.U. 0.8? to A.U. 1.6?
2. What evidence is there that the earth's axis points to the Pole Star?
3. Why does the length of day vary?
4. What is meant by an equinox? a solstice?
5. How does the angle of the sun's rays striking the earth affect the earth's temperature?

NEW VIEW

1. In the continental United States, December 22 is the shortest day of the year and marks the first day of winter. In Argentina, December 22 is the longest day of the same year and marks the first day of summer. Explain fully.

2. What would happen if:

a. the earth did not rotate on its axis but continued to revolve in its orbit?

b. the earth rotated just once in 365 days?

3. Suppose the earth's axis were not tilted. What would be the effects on the part of the earth where you live?

4. The axis of the planet Mars is tilted 24.9 degrees. Mars rotates on its axis once in 24½ hours, and revolves around the sun once in 687 days. Does Mars have seasons? Explain.

5. How many A.U.'s are equivalent to 1 light-year?

3. NEWTON AND THE UNIVERSE

Kepler, with his pages of calculations, showed that the planets move in ellipses, not in circles, around the sun. Why do the planets move as they do? Kepler believed, as men had believed for centuries, that to keep a moving body moving, a force was necessary. So he speculated that the sun had invisible "spokes" stretching out from it. As the sun rotated, its spokes swept the planets around in their orbits. As for the question of why the planets stay around the sun, Kepler suspected that some sort of magnetism was involved.

But Galileo showed that a force is *not* necessary to keep a moving body moving. He contradicted the belief of centuries. A body in motion tends to keep moving, said Galileo. The tendency of a body in motion to keep moving, or of a body at rest to stay at rest, is its **inertia**. Like all other bodies, the planets have inertia. Therefore the planets need no force to keep them going. As for the question of why the planets stay around the sun, Galileo believed (contrary to Kepler) that the planets moved in circles because he thought that was "the natural way" for a moving body to move. Galileo had not questioned this ancient idea of the Greeks.

An eminent French scientist, Descartes, added yet another contradiction. Descartes showed that a body in motion tends to move in a straight line, not in a circle. This was contrary to Galileo's idea, of course.

So the situation was somewhat confused. It took the powerful mind of a man named Newton to straighten it out.

A Falling Apple

Isaac Newton was born the same year that Galileo died, 1642. He was only 24 years old when he solved the problem of what holds the solar system together. The story, as you probably know, is that a falling apple set Newton thinking in the right direction. It was not the question of why the apple fell that interested him. Everyone knew that gravity pulled things toward the earth. Gravity made the apple fall, of course.

The question that probably popped into Newton's mind was, Is the moon possibly falling, too, like an apple? And rushing into his mind after this wild question came others. Is it possible that gravitation reaches beyond the earth, to the moon? Is it possible that the force of gravitation links the earth and the moon together? Is it possible that gravitational force links the sun and planets together?

Now let's catch our breath and go back to the first question. The idea that the moon is falling seems absurd, to be sure. If the moon is falling toward the earth, pulled by gravitation, why doesn't the moon get nearer? Why

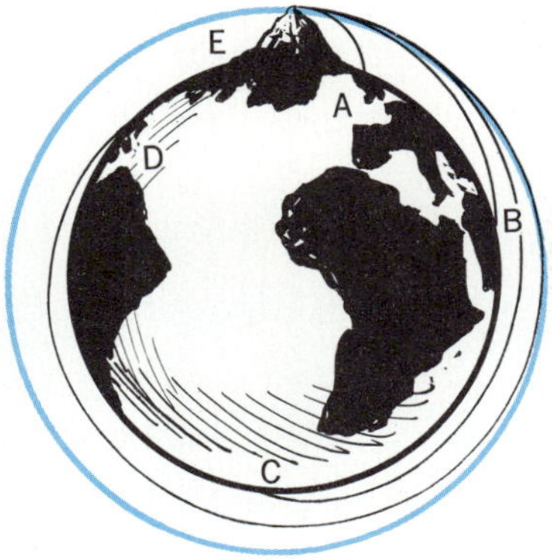

❶

doesn't it hit the earth? Isaac Newton worked out an ingenious answer to these questions.

Newton used a diagram much like this one.❶ Imagine a cannon on top of the highest mountain on earth. It is firing cannonballs horizontally. The first cannonball fired follows path A. As the cannonball moves, gravity pulls it down, and it soon hits the ground. Now the velocity with which each succeeding cannonball is fired is increased. Cannonball B goes farther than cannonball A. So do cannonballs C and D, although each is being pulled by gravity toward the earth all the time. The last cannonball, E, is fired with such tremendous velocity that it goes completely around the earth. It returns to the mountaintop and continues around the earth again and again. The cannonball's inertia causes it to continue in motion indefinitely, in orbit around the earth.

Newton imagined an artificial satellite, in orbit around the earth, about 300 years before men managed to put a satellite in orbit.

Now notice that this imaginary cannonball speeding around the earth is being pulled all the time by gravity. It is actually falling toward the earth. It never reaches the earth, however. The earth's surface curves away from the cannonball as fast as the cannonball falls toward the earth.

This, said Newton, is how the moon moves in orbit around the earth. The moon keeps moving because of inertia. It is steered around the earth by the pull of gravitation. Moreover, the planets are steered around the sun in the same fashion, by the same force that pulls down apples—gravitation.❷

The Force of Gravitation

It was a breathtaking hypothesis. Newton set out to show mathematically that there was evidence to support it. He described how the force of gravitation behaves. The force of gravitation exists between any two bodies. The amount of the force pulling the bodies together depends on two things: the mass of the bodies and the distance between them. The greater the mass of the two bodies, the greater the gravitational pull between them. The greater the distance between the bodies, the smaller the gravitational pull between them.

Newton put his description of the force of gravitation into a mathematical formula. He substituted values in the formula for the mass of the earth and the mass of the moon, and for the distance between the earth and the moon. He found that the results agreed

❷

1

2

"pretty nearly" with the orbit of the moon. The calculated force of gravitation between the moon and the earth was about what it should be to make the moon go around the earth as it does.

Newton did not publish these results, however. Perhaps "pretty nearly" was not good enough for him. He dropped the problem for almost 20 years. Then Edmund Halley, a friend and fellow scientist, persuaded Newton to take up the problem again. With more accurate data, which had been collected meanwhile, Newton showed that the calculated gravitational force between the earth and the moon could produce the moon's motion around the earth.

Newton went on to calculate the gravitational forces between the sun and the planets. He showed that the orbits of the planets have to be ellipses because of the way gravitational force behaves.

So Newton tied together not just the solar system but the entire universe with gravitation. Hence his well-established hypothesis is now called Newton's Universal Law of Gravitation. Let's look, now, at a familiar phenomenon on earth that universal gravitation explains—the tides of the oceans.

Gravitation and Tides

If you live near the ocean or visit the seashore, you have surely seen the tide come in and go out, or flow and ebb, as we say. About twice a day (once in every $12\frac{1}{2}$ hours) the tide flows and ebbs. In some places the difference between high and low tide may be very great. At low tide in the Bay of Fundy, in Canada, this pier seems to be on dry land. 1 At high tide, the water has risen some 12 meters (40 feet). 2 Tides in the Bay of Fundy are greater than anywhere else in the world.

What makes the tides? You can imagine that men must have puzzled over this question for thousands of years. So far as we know, a man named Pytheas, watching the rise and fall of water along the shores of the English Channel, was the first to suggest that the tides were caused by the moon. That was

3

in the fourth century B.C. *How* the moon caused the tides was explained some 2,000 years later by Isaac Newton.

In his book on universal gravitation, Newton explained how tides are caused. They are caused by the gravitational pull of both the moon and the sun on the earth. The mass of the sun is much larger than that of the moon, but the moon is much nearer to the earth than the sun, so the moon's effect on tides is more than twice as much as the sun's.

At the time of the new moon, for instance, the sun and the moon are in line and pull in the same direction on the earth. (3) Their gravitational pull causes the water on opposite sides of the earth to bulge out. The tides are at their highest and lowest levels, and are called **spring tides.** Despite the name, spring tides occur all year round.

It is easy to see why the water on the side of the earth nearest the moon bulges toward the moon. The water on that side of the earth is nearer the moon than the bulk of the earth. Gravitational pull varies with distance. So the water on that side of the earth is pulled more strongly toward the moon than the earth is.

But why does the water on the opposite side of the earth bulge out? Why does the moon cause two tidal bulges? Oddly enough, distance from the moon is the cause here, too. In this case, though, the bulk of the earth is nearer the moon than is the water on the far side of the earth. The gravitational pull of the moon is stronger on the earth than on the water on the far side. In a way, the earth is pulled away from the water on the far side, making the water bulge.

What happens to the tides when the moon and the sun are in different positions around the earth? As we've seen, spring tides occur when the moon and the sun are pulling in the same line on the same side of the earth. (3) When the moon is on the opposite side of the earth from the sun, the sun and the moon are pulling in the same line again, and spring tides occur again. (4)

4

1

When the moon and the sun make a right angle with the earth, their gravitational pulls tend to work against each other. (1) At this time, the tides are moderately high and moderately low. They are called **neap tides.** Neap tides occur when the moon is in the opposite position as well.

According to this explanation of the tides, then, the water *away* from the shore must be rising and falling. So it is, but observers in a ship at sea do not notice this tidal motion because the ship itself moves up and down with the tides.

In the same way, we do not notice the tides that occur in the solid part of the earth, in the ground beneath our feet. We do not feel tides in the ground as we go up and down with them, but instruments can detect these earth tides. The difference between high tide and low tide may be as much as 50 centimeters (20 inches) for an earth tide. There is also a twice-a-day tide in the earth's atmosphere.

Some Preparations for Space Travel

For almost 2,000 years men assumed that a moving object in the heavens had to be pushed to keep moving, and that it tended to move in a circle. Men didn't realize, of course, that these assumptions were hindering their understanding.

The discoveries of how a body in motion (or at rest) actually behaves revolutionized men's view of the universe. Newton summed them up precisely and compactly in three Laws of Motion. Here is one of the laws, the Law of Inertia:

> A body at rest remains at rest, and a body in motion remains in motion in a straight line with constant speed unless acted on by an unbalanced force.

To us today this seems only common sense. A bowling ball at rest tends to remain at rest. We have to apply a force to the ball to make it move. Once we get the bowling ball moving, though, we know it tends to keep on moving. It takes an external force to stop the ball: some of it provided by the pins, if all goes well, and some by the padded stop. If we have not added an external force on the ball in the shape of a spin, the ball goes in a straight line. The ball has mass; mass has inertia; inertia makes the ball behave this way.

The Law of Inertia, Newton's other laws of motion, and his Law of Universal Gravitation can all be used to account for the behavior of a bowling ball speeding down an alley. The astonishing thing is that they also account for the behavior of a space vehicle speeding around an orbit.

Look again at Newton's diagram (p. 209). Each cannonball fired from the cannon on the mountaintop goes farther than the one before. Each cannonball, then, is fired faster than the one before. The faster a cannonball leaves the cannon, the farther it goes. How fast does the cannonball have to be going to orbit the earth? The cannonball must be moving with a speed of 29,200 kilometers (17,500 miles) per hour. Calculations show that any

■ AN APPRENTICE INVESTIGATION into a Model of a Satellite in Orbit

A bowl with sides that curve upward smoothly is necessary. Put a small marble in the bottom of the bowl. Flick the marble with a finger so that it climbs the side of the bowl and rolls back to the bottom. The marble is behaving somewhat like a ball that is thrown upward and then falls back to the earth under the influence of gravitation. The bottom of the bowl represents the earth.

Now to put the marble in orbit around the "earth." Give the bowl a gentle circular motion with your hands, so that the marble races around the sides of the bowl.❶ With a little practice you should be able to keep the marble going steadily at a certain height around the sides. The marble is "in orbit."

Observe the speed of the marble in orbit. Then replace the small marble with a larger one.❷ Does the increase in mass make any difference to the speed in that orbit?

❶

❷

An Investigation On Your Own

Your impression of the speed of the orbiting marble may be unreliable. Can you measure the speed of the marbles in any way?

speed below this will allow the cannonball to be pulled to the ground.

Oddly enough, speed is the important thing here. The mass of the cannonball does not matter: it can weigh any amount. You can glimpse this concept with the help of some marbles and a bowl. ■

To stay in orbit around the sides of a bowl, a marble must reach a certain speed. The mass of the marble makes no difference: it does not affect the speed. To stay in orbit around the earth, an object must have a minimum speed of 29,200 kilometers (17,500 miles) per hour, whatever its mass. To reach this speed was beyond man's power until the rocket engine was developed.

Here again Isaac Newton's thinking helped. One of Newton's laws of motion described how an action produces a reaction, and how action and reaction are related to each other. For every action, says Newton's Third Law of Motion, there is an equal and opposite reaction. It happens that the rocket engine is a reaction engine.

The rocket engine is simply an enormously powerful gas generator. It turns solid or liquid fuel into gases, at an unbelievable rate, and pushes the gases away. As the engine pushes the gases away, however, the gases push the engine away, with equal force—but in the opposite direction. This is the reaction. 1 Action and reaction are equal, but in opposite directions, as Newton described them.

When rocket engines made the necessary speed of 29,200 kilometers (17,500 miles) per hour available, and the necessary energy to get high enough as well, men managed to put an object into an orbit around the earth. On October 4, 1957, Russian scientists and engineers put Sputnik 1 (which means satellite) into orbit. The greatest distance of its orbit from the earth, or its **apogee**, was about 847 kilometers (508 miles). The low point, or **perigee**, of its orbit was 237 kilometers (142 miles) from the earth. Because its orbit was low, Sputnik 1 was gradually slowed down by air resistance. After three months in orbit it re-entered the earth's atmosphere and burned up.

1

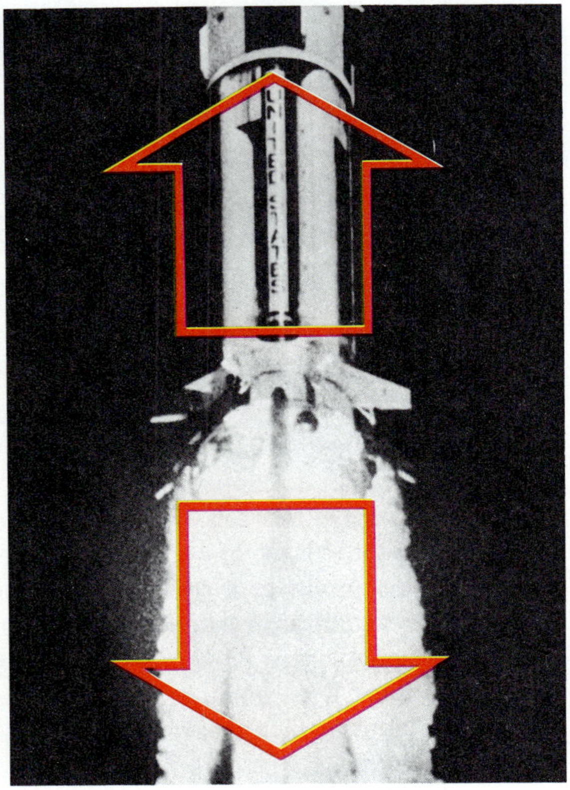

Since then, as you know, we have put many satellites into orbit, all of them carrying instruments, and some carrying men. There are now hundreds of these artificial satellites looping around our planet, collecting scientific data of various kinds, relaying television and radio signals from one part of the earth to another, taking global weather photographs, observing the sun, and performing other tasks.

We have taken a further step into space, however. We have managed to send spacecraft away from the earth altogether.

Orbit Beyond the Earth

Toss a ball straight up: gravitational force quickly brings it down. Give the ball all the energy you can: throw it as hard as you can. It goes higher and stays up longer, but it comes down. The force of gravitation has overcome the ball's upward motion again. Is it possible to give the ball enough energy to overcome the force of gravitation? It is, but it takes a mighty hard throw, so to speak. You must get the ball, or whatever it is that you want to send away from the earth, moving at a speed of at least 39,026 kilometers (24,250 miles) per hour. This **escape velocity** is the minimum speed required to escape from the earth into space, approximately twice the speed needed for an orbit of the earth.

What are we doing with our ability to put spacecraft into space beyond the earth? Some spacecraft have been sent to the moon, where they have landed. Here is the path of

2

Ranger X to the moon. 2 We are probing space, exploring, searching for knowledge by sending spacecraft beyond the moon. Some of our space probes have flown around the planets Venus and Mars, and have radioed photographs and other data back to earth, across millions of miles of space. Eventually these "fly-bys" go into orbit around the sun. 3 As our rocket engines and guidance systems improve, we will probe farther into

3

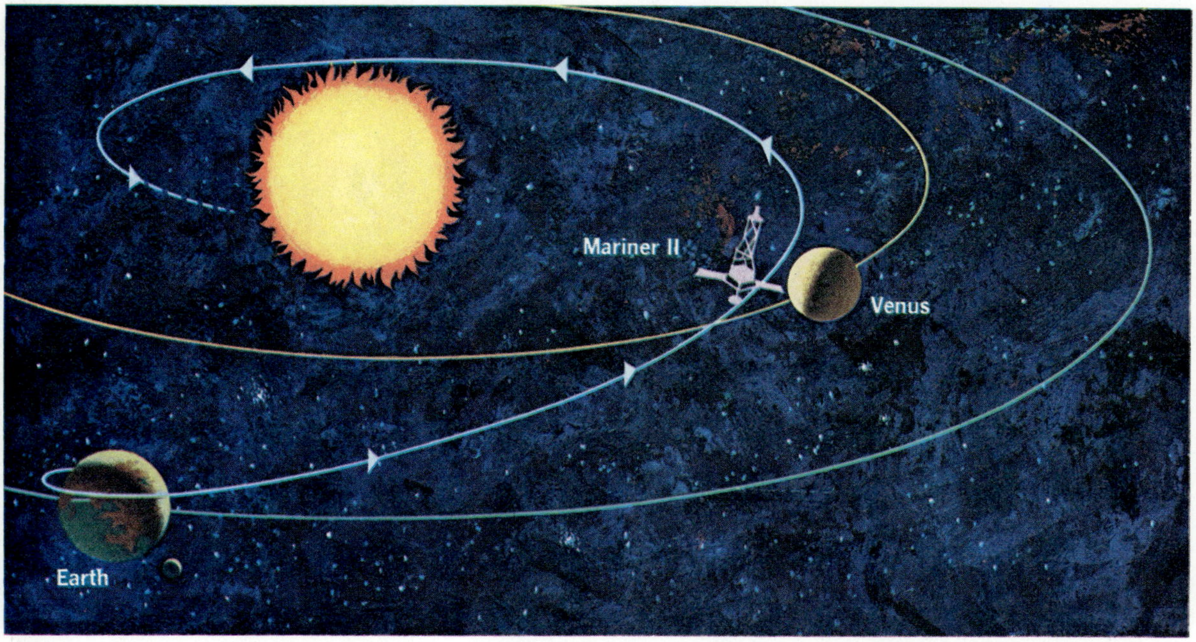

space with our instruments. And men will follow: the mighty Saturn rocket has already taken men to the moon (see Chapter 11). 1

Without Newton's work our exploration of space would not be possible. Without the work of other scientists, Newton's work would not have been possible. As Newton himself said, "If I have seen farther than other men, it is because I have stood on the shoulders of giants." Two such giants were Kepler and Galileo. The achievements of science have been possible because scientists build on the work of other scientists.

REVIEW

1. What views about force and motion were held by each of the following?

a. Galileo b. Kepler c. Newton

2. Any earth satellite, natural or artificial, is said to be constantly falling toward the earth.

a. Why do most satellites not land even though they continue to fall?

b. Under what circumstances will a satellite land?

3. Suppose a certain planet has $\frac{1}{3}$ the surface gravity of the earth. If 3 atoms of uranium find their way to this planet, how will their weight be affected? How will their mass be affected?

4. What determines whether a spacecraft will go into an orbital flight?

5. Why is the moon said to control the tides? How does the sun affect the tides?

6. Explain the relation of the Law of Action and Reaction (Newton's Third Law of Motion) to the firing of a rocket.

7. Upon what two quantities does the amount of gravitational force between two objects depend?

8. Draw diagrams to show the relative positions of the earth, sun, and moon (a) at spring tide (b) neap tide.

NEW VIEW

1. What force held together the dust and gas in the nebula from which our solar system originated? What keeps all the stars and interstellar matter of a galaxy together?

2. How does the escape velocity on (a) Jupiter and (b) Mars compare with the escape velocity on the earth? Explain your reasoning.

3. The orbits of the planets are not perfect ellipses, but have slightly irregular motions known as perturbations. These motions can be explained by Newton's Law of Gravitation. Can you explain how?

4. Why are there two high tides daily and two spring tides monthly?

5. To operate a jet space gun, an astronaut "shoots" to the left when he wants to move to the right. Explain.

1

4. RELATING THE CONCEPTS

We believe that the earth, its fellow planets, and the sun originated together, and that the force of gravitation keeps them together. All the members of the sun's family, to which our earth belongs, keep moving in a way described by Newton's Laws of Motion. These laws, and other concepts that help us to understand the earth's origin and orbit, are all related to a familiar major concept about the large chunks of matter in space: *The universe is in continuous change.*

Reviewing the Concepts

► *The sun, the earth, and other members of the solar system have a common origin.* The chemical make-up of the sun and the planets furnishes us with one piece of evidence that all the members of the solar system may have come from an original cloud of dust and gas—a nebula. The motions and orbits of the earth and its fellow planets provide us with further evidence of their common origin.

► *The earth is in orbit at a position of about 150,000,000 kilometers (93 million miles, 1 A.U.) from the sun.* The earth's orbiting motion is known as its revolution around the sun. Together with the earth's rotation on its tilted axis, the earth's revolution accounts for the changes of day and night, and for the seasons—both of which are very important features of our environment on earth.

► Newton's Law of Universal Gravitation states that *every object attracts every other object in the universe by a force known as gravitation.* This is one of the concepts that helps us understand and predict the paths of orbiting bodies, such as planets, moons, and artificial satellites.

► Newton's Law of Inertia also helps us to predict orbits: *An object at rest remains at rest and an object in motion continues in motion in a straight line at constant speed unless acted upon by an unbalanced force.* This concept helps us understand why a satellite may be pulled off course. If an artificial satellite traveling in a straight line comes close to a large body in space, that body's gravitational pull will alter the satellite's course.

► Another one of Newton's laws states: *For every action, there is an equal and opposite reaction.* This law describes the principles upon which rocket engines depend.

Testing Yourself

1. Would it have been possible for the earth to have originated at a time other than the time of origin of the other planets? What are your reasons?
2. Why did von Weizäcker's theory replace the Kant-Laplace theory of the origin of the solar system? What new observations did not fit the Kant-Laplace theory?
3. Describe the effects of the earth's periods of rotation and revolution on our immediate environment. What would happen if these periods were the same?
4. Describe the effect on our immediate environment of the earth's tilt on its axis.
5. Explain why the moon does not fall to the earth.
6. Why do theories change over the years?
7. What was Newton's discovery about gravitation? How did it help explain the motions of the planets and their satellites?
8. What determines the gravitational force between any two objects? How does this principle help explain variations in the tides?
9. On what principle does a rocket engine operate?

Extending the Concepts

Investigation. Inertia is described as the resistance of an object to any change in its motion. To a scientist, the mass of an object is a measure of its inertia—the greater the mass of an object, the more force is required to produce a given change in its motion.

If you have an electric train, roller skates, or simply a ball suspended on a string, you can investigate inertia. Try some of these suggestions, or invent your own procedures.

1. Stand a tube from a roll of paper towels on end on a flatcar of your train set, or use a roller skate for a cart. Allow the loaded cart to roll down a slight ramp and run into an obstruction, such as a book placed flat on the table. What happens to the cart? to the tube? How do you account for your observations?

2. Attach a string to the cart loaded with the tube. Be sure the cart and tube are motionless; then jerk the string to set the cart in motion. What happens to the tube? What did the cart do? Explain.

3. Set up a circular track for your electric train. Place the engine on the track and couple a flatcar to it. Use a flatcar with no rails or stakes on the sides. Stand the cardboard tube on end on the flatcar. Start the train and gradually increase its speed. What eventually happens to the tube? Describe all your observations—the direction in which the tube moved, how long it traveled, and the like.

4. Repeat investigation 3, but use a tennis ball or rubber ball in place of the cardboard tube. Be sure there is no obstruction on the flatcar that will prevent the ball from reacting to forces exerted upon it. Record all of your observations and explain them.

5. Spin a ball in a circle around your hand by means of a string attached to the ball. Release the string at different points of the ball's orbit. (Of course, you will do this in a safe place.) Observe the motion of the released ball and make a diagram to show the motion. Why does the ball return to the surface of the earth? How fast would you have to spin it to put it into orbit?

Suggested Reading

Ronan, Colin, *Astronomers Royal,* New York, Doubleday, 1969. Contributions of famous astronomers over the last four centuries.

Dille, J., and P. S. Hopkins, *Americans in Space,* New York, Harper & Row, 1965. A collection of stories and photographs of the exciting history of man's adventures into space.

Stumbler, Irwin, *Project Mariner,* New York, Putnam, 1965. The dramatic story of Mariner II, and its voyage to Venus.

Hoyt, Mary Finch, *American Women of the Space Age,* New York, Atheneum, 1966. The role of women scientists and engineers at work in U.S. space programs.

11

The Moon, Earth's Natural Satellite

For thousands of years people believed that the moon was a smooth, perfect sphere. It was so smooth, they thought, that its surface reflected the irregularities of the earth's surface like a mirror.

Then Galileo turned his telescope on the moon. His report created a sensation: ". . . the surface of the moon is not perfectly smooth, free of inequalities and exactly spherical, as a large school of philosophers contends. . . . on the contrary, it is uneven, full of irregularities, hollows, and protuberances, just like the surface of the earth itself. . . ."

Since Galileo peered through his "optick tube" at the moon in 1609, we have probed the moon with telescopes, spectroscopes, radar, man-made satellites, and spacecraft.

The next step was to go to the moon. The knowledge we have gained by going to the moon will help us solve many puzzles about the origin and nature of the universe But first let's look at the moon, as people have for thousands of years, with our own unaided eyes.

1. THE MOON'S MOTION

If you kept a careful watch on the moon night after night for several weeks, you would see the moon rise in the east, like the sun. It would move across the sky, against the background of the stars, and set in the west. Each night the moon would rise about 50 minutes later. Each night the shape of the moon would appear to change a little. You would find that these changes in the apparent shape of the moon—the phases of the moon—occur in a cycle that takes about $29\frac{1}{2}$ days to complete. (1) (Hence our word month: "moonth.")

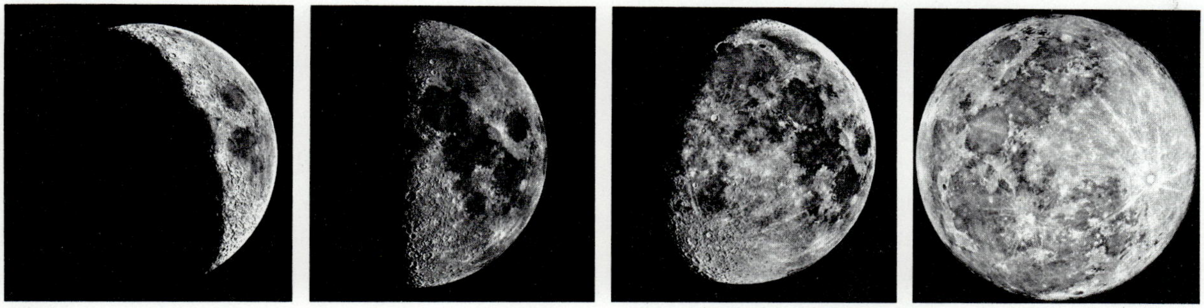
(1)

The Face of the Moon

Although the early telescopes were not very good by our standards, early astronomers began to draw maps of the face of the moon. These observers mapped such features as seas, lakes, swamps, and oceans, as well as mountains and craters. It was not until telescopes were much improved that the nature of the moon's surface began to be understood. Yet, in spite of the fact that man has stepped on the moon, we still use many of the old names that the early observers gave to the moon's features. Large, dark, flat-looking areas are called "seas." One of these is the Sea of Tranquility. 1 Why is it famous? We know now that if there is water in any form on the moon, it is *not* in the seas. (Nor is there water in the moon's so-called lakes.)

The light-colored regions in this photograph of the moon have rough textures and contain mountains. Some mountains are near the bowl-like depressions known as craters; others look like the mountains on earth.

Notice how the southern part of the moon is covered with craters of all sizes. The largest crater on the moon is about 240 kilometers (146 miles) across. The crater Copernicus is about one-third this size. 1 Like Copernicus, some craters have mountains rising from the floor inside the crater. Other craters have flat floors. However, almost all craters have a floor that is *below* the level of the land outside the crater. (The crater floor of a volcano on earth is usually above the surrounding land.)

How the moon's craters were formed has been the subject of much argument among scientists. One hypothesis is that the moon, with its cold, solid core, was bombarded by meteors that formed craters as they crashed into the moon's surface. Meteor Crater in Arizona was formed in this way. 2 Another hypothesis is that material from the molten core of the moon welled up through cracks and fissures in the moon's surface and formed craters and mountains. These craters on the Isle of Maui, Hawaii, were formed as the result of such volcanic action. 3 Yet another hypothesis is that gases inside the moon made the surface swell up in places; then the swelling collapsed and left craters. Our explorations of the moon have not yet settled these arguments. The moon's history is, perhaps, more complex than even these arguments suppose. It seems clear that the moon has had a longer history than scientists had thought.

Selenologists (sel′ə·nol′ə·jists), the scientists who study the moon, need more evidence. At present, our knowledge is limited to the smooth lunar basins. These have fewer craters than the higher areas—the highlands. Nevertheless, there seems to be little doubt that a large number of craters of the moon are the result of bombardment by meteorites. But are any of the moon's craters the result of volcanic action? Or we might ask, is the interior of the moon hot? The interior of the earth is hot, you know.

Whatever caused the craters on the moon, the rocks brought back from the moon are clearly from material that was once molten. (You may want to read about moon rocks again, page 72.) Intense heat is necessary to melt

2

3

❶ 

material to produce such rocks. Could it have been heat from the moon's molten interior? Could it have been heat produced by the impact of bombarding meteorites?

We need come to no conclusion at this moment. Now there is a stronger possibility that more facts will soon be available. After all, no theory is stronger than the facts it explains.

The Moon's Phases

Turn on a single bright lamp in a darkened room. Hold a tennis ball at arm's length between you and the lamp. ❶ Turn slowly on your heel to the left, so that the ball moves in a complete circle around you. Observe how the lighted part of the ball changes shape.

You will see that the changes are like the phases of the moon. The lamp represents the sun, your head represents the earth, and the tennis ball represents the moon moving around the earth in the sun's light.

When the lighted part of the ball is turned away from you, it is a model of the position of the moon between the earth and the sun. In this position the moon is called a new moon. ❶ The new moon, or "dark of the moon," occurs again when the lighted half of the moon is turned away from the earth, as shown in phase 1 of the diagram below. ❷

Turn to the left until the ball becomes a model of a crescent moon. Continue to turn to the left, and watch the crescent moon grow larger. This is called a waxing moon. Notice that the arms, or cusps, of a waxing moon point away from the sun.

Turn more, so that half of the side facing you appears lighted. This is the first quarter moon. Move on, in the same way, to the gibbous moon, and the full moon. At full moon

❷ 

the lighted half of the moon is directly facing the earth, as shown in phase 5 of the diagram at the left below. [2]

Continue turning. The lighted portion of the ball becomes smaller. This represents the waning moon. Model the gibbous moon, the last quarter moon, and the crescent moon. Notice that the cusps of the waning moon also point away from the sun.

No matter where the moon is in its orbit around the earth, it keeps the same side toward us. The moon rotates just once on its axis for each revolution around the earth. This means that we always see the same side of the moon.

Does this mean that the hidden side of the moon is always dark? You can see for yourself by inspecting the diagram on page 223 once more. The historic photograph of the other side of the moon, taken by Lunar Orbiter I spacecraft in 1966, could not have been made without the sun's light. [3]

The Size of the Moon

Hold a new pencil at arm's length. Look at the eraser on the end. Do you think that the moon appears larger, smaller, or about the same size as the eraser? You may be surprised to find that the eraser at arm's length will cover the moon. We somehow think of the moon as much larger in the night sky than

[3]

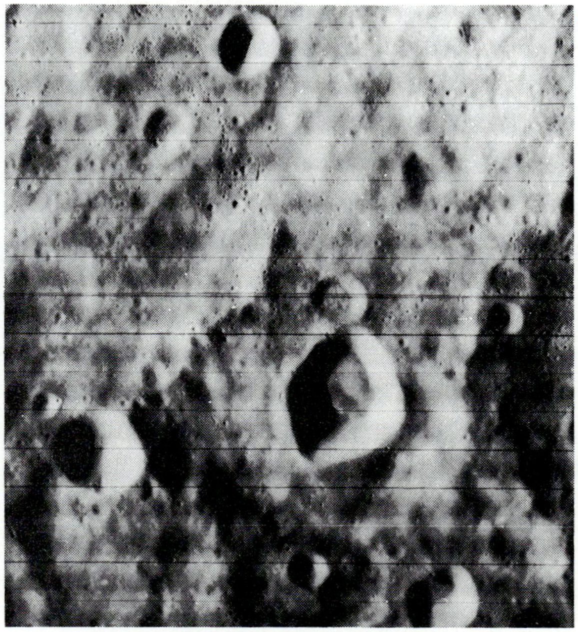

it really is. Here is a circle $\frac{1}{2}$ centimeter ($\frac{1}{5}$ inch) across.

Hold it at a distance of 60 centimeters (2 feet) from your eye. This is the **apparent diameter** of the moon in the sky.

There is a better way of stating the apparent diameter of the moon. The angle that the diameter of an object sighted at a distance makes with your eye, its **angular diameter,** can be measured with a surveyor's transit. [4]

[4]

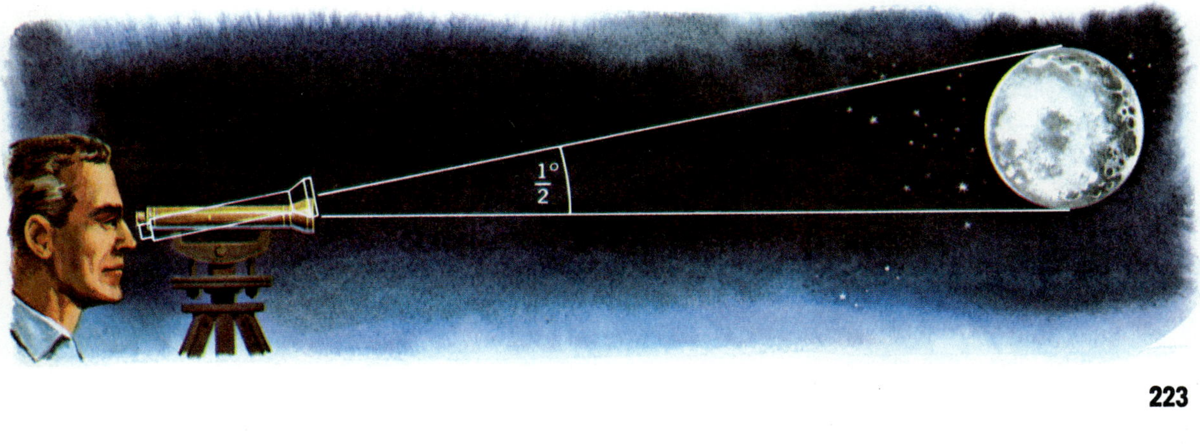

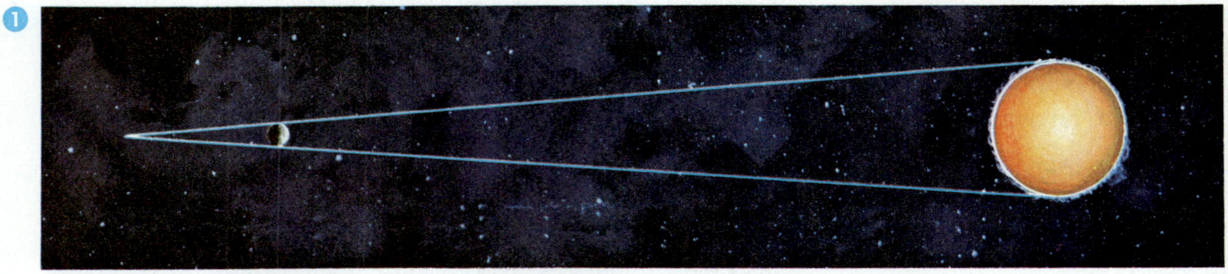

The moon's angular diameter is about $\frac{1}{2}°$. This is the angular diameter of a basketball at a distance of about 30 meters (100 feet). But scientists have determined the *actual* diameter of the moon. Measuring carefully from the earth, they find that the actual diameter is 3,476 kilometers (2,160 miles). The moon's diameter turns out to be a little more than one-fourth that of the earth.

Since the moon's orbit around the earth is not a circle but an ellipse, the distance of the moon from the earth varies. The average distance of the moon from the earth is usually stated as 400,000 kilometers (240,000 miles).

Since the distance of the moon from the earth does vary, the angular diameter of the moon also varies, but by only a small fraction. It is not enough to account for the fact that the moon seen on the horizon appears much larger than when seen overhead. (Scientists have agreed that this is an optical illusion.)

Angular Diameters and Eclipses

The sun is enormously larger than the moon, and also much farther away from the earth, as you know. So it happens that the angular diameter of the sun is about the same as that of the moon—about half a degree. (1)

Because the angular diameters of the sun and the moon are about the same, we are treated to an astonishing spectacle from time to time. The sun's light dims and the sky darkens even in the middle of the day. Birds stop singing, cattle huddle together uneasily, bats and owls awake and fly forth, stars can be seen, and what light there is has a weird tinge. It is a **solar eclipse:** the moon has come between the sun and the earth. (2)

A total solar eclipse, as this is called, does not happen often. There are not more than 50 total solar eclipses in a century, and when one does occur, it can be seen from only a small area. For example, a total solar eclipse was visible in the United States in 1963.

3

One of the longest eclipses of modern times took place on June 20, 1973. (3) The shadow of the moon covered the sun—in some places for over seven minutes. A total solar eclipse lasting this length of time will not take place again until the year 2150. The path of the eclipse started in South America and swept across central Africa. In the northwest United States, a solar eclipse will occur on February 26, 1979. This will be the only solar eclipse visible in the United States for the remainder of this century.

Why is an eclipse visible in a certain area only? Let's look at what happens during a total solar eclipse. The moon comes between the sun and the earth. (4) The shadow that the moon throws on the earth has two parts. The small, dark cone of shadow is called the **umbra.** The large, lighter cone of shadow, surrounding the umbra, is the **penumbra.**

4

1

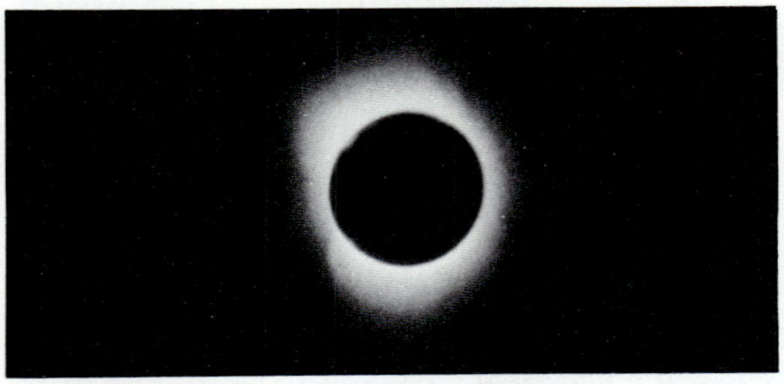

2

People who are within the area of the umbra have the moon directly between them and the sun. The moon covers the disk of the sun completely for them: They see a total solar eclipse. 1

What about people in the penumbra, the light shadow? They do not have the moon directly in line with them and the sun. The moon only partly covers the sun's disk, so in the penumbra there is a partial eclipse. 2

Those people who are outside the penumbra see no eclipse at all. During a total eclipse, the shadow of the moon moves across the surface of the earth along a narrow band.

Since eclipses can provide scientists with invaluable information, astronomers send expeditions that take up positions along this band, when they can, to make observations. Unfortunately, many eclipses are visible only from inaccessible places. And because most total eclipses do not last much more than 3 minutes, and because a stray cloud may spoil the viewing at the critical moment, information is difficult to obtain.

Astronomers do have instruments now that allow them to observe the sun's corona and the solar prominences even when there is no eclipse. However, an eclipse still provides the best conditions for observing these features. So you will still find astronomers packing telescopes, spectroscopes, cameras, and other assorted equipment to go and view an eclipse from some remote spot on the earth.

There was a time when our ancestors cowered in fear as a solar eclipse took place. Today we understand how the relative motions of the earth and the moon and the sun can cause an eclipse. Yet we still feel awe and wonder when we watch an eclipse. Perhaps it is because we understand.

A solar eclipse occurs when the moon's shadow falls on the earth. Things can happen

3

the other way around: the earth's shadow may fall on the moon to cause an eclipse of the moon. Notice that the whole moon may lie within the earth's umbra during a **lunar eclipse,** as it is called. ③ When this happens, the moon sometimes takes on a reddish color at mid-eclipse. The stars that the bright light of the moon would ordinarily hide from us appear around the strange red moon.

REVIEW

1. After Galileo had studied the moon through his "optick tube," he described what he saw. How did his description differ from what people had previously believed?

2. When we can see a thin crescent moon, just as much of the moon's surface is lighted as when we can see a full moon. Explain.

3. Briefly explain the difference between apparent diameter and actual diameter. What is the actual diameter of the moon?

4. What evidence can you observe that supports the conclusion that the moon rotates only once each time it revolves around the earth?

5. Explain the difference between the positions of the sun, moon, and particular locations on earth when there is a total solar eclipse in one place and a partial solar eclipse in another.

NEW VIEW

1. As an astronaut approaches the moon, does the moon's angular diameter change for him? Explain.

2. What uses do astronomers make of the special views of the sun and moon that are available during eclipses of these bodies?

3. When might an astronaut on another planet, or on the moon, see an eclipse of the earth?

4. Make a map of the moon as you see it. Use binoculars or a telescope if you can. Locate on your map some of the areas noted on the map on page 220 in this book.

2. PROBING THE MOON

Armstrong, Aldrin, Conrad, Bean, and other astronauts have been on the moon. Thousands of men and women have built the spaceships and the instruments that made their journeys possible. What joy Galileo and Newton would have felt to see their theories at work—theories some 300 years old. Even before men set foot on the moon, scientists had been making their observations and their inferences based on accurate measurement.

Bouncing Radio Waves

Amazingly accurate measurements of the distance from the earth to the moon have been made by means of radar waves, very short radio waves. A radar set sends a brief burst of radio waves toward the moon. When they hit the moon, the radio waves bounce, somewhat as sound waves do when they hit a wall. Some of the radio waves head back toward the earth. When they arrive, the radar set detects this echo, and measures how long the radio waves took to make the trip to the moon and back.

Suppose, for instance, that the round trip from earth to moon and back took 2.50 seconds. It took the radio waves just half that time, then, to travel from the earth to the moon, or 1.25 seconds. Radio waves travel at the speed of light. In 1.25 seconds, then, the radio waves traveled about 375,000 kilometers (232,500 miles). Radar can measure this distance with amazing accuracy.

In 1957 the distance from the earth to the moon was measured by radar at many points along the moon's orbit. Altogether some 60,000 measurements were made. At the moon's perigee, the point in its orbit nearest the earth, the moon is 356,409 kilometers (221,463 miles) from the earth. At apogee, its

1 

farthest point from the earth, the moon's distance is 406,696 kilometers (252,710 miles). Now that astronauts have been to the moon and left behind a laser beam reflector that reflects laser beams sent from the earth, we will know the distance more accurately. 1 At present, the average distance is determined as 384,375 kilometers (238,840 miles).

Once the distance to the moon was known, the moon's true diameter could be calculated from its angular diameter, as you may remember. The true diameter of the moon is listed in the table below.

Given the moon's diameter, its volume can also be calculated. Here are a few other measurements and calculations about the moon.

SOME MOON MEASUREMENTS

average distance, center of earth to center of moon	384,375 kilometers (238,840 miles)
diameter	3,476 kilometers (2,160 miles)
volume	$\frac{1}{50}$ of earth's volume
mass	$\frac{1}{80}$ of earth's mass
temperature at lunar noon	150°C (300°F)
temperature at midnight	−150°C (−240°F)
gravity	$\frac{1}{6}$ of earth's gravity
escape velocity (average)	8,575 kilometers/hour (5,328 miles/hour)

You may have decided after a quick glance that there is nothing especially interesting about these figures. If you did, you missed something. Look again at the volume and the mass of the moon compared with the earth's.

If the moon's volume is $\frac{1}{50}$ of the earth's volume, why isn't the moon's mass $\frac{1}{50}$ of the earth's? The moon's mass is only $\frac{1}{80}$ of the earth's mass. Why is the moon so much lighter than the earth, volume for volume?

The Density of the Moon

The volume of the moon is about $\frac{1}{50}$ of the volume of the earth. We would expect, if the moon and the earth were made of the same stuff, that the mass of the moon would be about $\frac{1}{50}$ of the mass of the earth. But observations and calculations do not agree with our expectations. The mass of the moon turns out to be much lower than we expected: it is about $\frac{1}{80}$ of the earth's mass. Volume for volume, the moon is lighter than the earth. Or as scientists say, the density of the moon is less than the density of the earth. This is an unexpected clue to what the moon is made of. Let's see what is meant by density. ■

As you could see in the investigation, 1 cc (cubic centimeter) of one kind of wood weighs about 0.7 g (grams). That is, the mass of 1 cc of the wood is 0.7 g. And since density is mass per unit volume, the density of the wood is 0.7 grams/cubic centimeter, usually abbreviated by chemists as g/cc.

Now suppose you had a 2 cc block of the same kind of wood. Its mass would be 2×0.7 g or 1.4 g. But its density would still be the same, 0.7 g/cc, because density is always expressed as the mass of a unit volume.

People are really speaking of density when they say that aluminum is lighter than iron. After all, a large piece of aluminum can be heavier than a small piece of iron. The density

■ AN APPRENTICE INVESTIGATION into Density

What is the length of a side of this cube, in centimeters? ❶ *Note:* there are 10 millimeters (mm) in one centimeter. What is the volume of the cube, in cubic centimeters?

What is the mass of this cube of wood in grams? To find out, weigh the cube on a platform balance. ❷ Here is the result in one trial. ❸

Density is mass per unit volume. The unit of volume used here is the cubic centimeter. What is the density of the wood in grams per cubic centimeter?

$$\text{density} = \frac{\text{mass}}{\text{volume}}$$

❶

❷

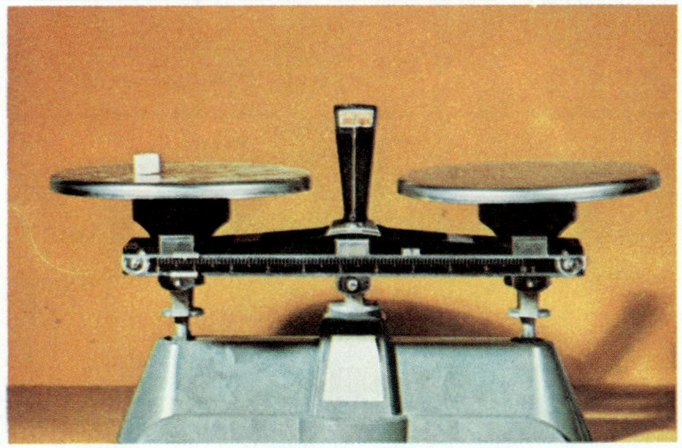

❸

An Investigation On Your Own

How could you find out the density of this rock? ❹ After you have found the density of a rock, find out how you can determine the density of a cork.

❹

of aluminum is always less than the density of iron, however. Here are density values for some common substances.

DENSITIES OF SOME MATERIALS

Material	*Density (in grams per cubic centimeter)*
aluminum	2.7
iron	7.8
wood (rock elm)	0.8
brass	8.5
cork	0.2
magnesium	1.7
paraffin	0.9
water	1.0
olive oil	0.9
alcohol	0.8
glycerin	1.3
carbon tetrachloride	1.6
limestone	2.7
quartz	2.6
sulfur	2.0

The density of the moon leads to some interesting speculations about what the moon is made of. The moon's overall density is about 3.3 grams per cubic centimeter. The average density of the earth is about 5.5 grams per cubic centimeter, so there is a considerable difference between the density of the moon and the density of the earth.

However, the earth's average density of 5.5 grams per cubic centimeter is made up of two main parts. The earth's core is very dense: it has been estimated at about 14.5 grams per cubic centimeter. But the earth's crust, made of rock, has an average density of 2.7 grams per cubic centimeter. This is not very different from the density of the moon. And it suggests to scientists that the moon may be made of the same kinds of rock found in the earth's crust.

Above the Surface

One of the most unfriendly conditions that astronauts will encounter in the environment of the moon is the absence of atmosphere. Moon explorers must take along their own supply of air for breathing. They must talk to one another by radio, since there is no air to carry sound waves between them. The sky will look black even when the sun is shining, for there is no air to scatter the sunlight and produce a blue sky like the earth's.

How do we know that the moon has no atmosphere? There are several kinds of evidence that this is so. For example, we know that the earth's atmosphere causes starlight entering it to be scattered. This is why stars seem to twinkle at night. If the moon had an atmosphere, our telescopes could detect the scattering of starlight passing close to the moon's surface. No scattering is seen. Similarly, it is the scattering of sunlight by our atmosphere that causes twilight after the sun has set. We can observe no twilight on the moon between sunset and night. Night comes quickly. When the moon passes in front of the sun during a solar eclipse, the edge of the moon appears sharp and clear in outline. There is none of the distortion or dimming that an atmosphere on the moon would cause.

If the moon had an atmosphere, it would probably have clouds or mist from time to time. Nothing of the sort has been observed. On the contrary, details of the moon's surface are always perfectly clear.

Why has the moon no atmosphere? Remember that the density of the moon is less than that of the earth, and the diameter of the moon is about $\frac{1}{4}$ the diameter of the earth. So the mass of the moon is much less than the mass of the earth: in fact, the moon's mass is about $\frac{1}{80}$ of the earth's mass, as you may remember.

❶ 

These two things, the diameter and the mass of the moon, affect the moon's gravitation. The result is that the force of gravitation on the moon is only about $\frac{1}{6}$ of the force of gravitation on the earth. As you know, this means that if you were taken to the moon now, suitably protected against its unfriendly environment, you would weigh only $\frac{1}{6}$ of your weight here on earth. You would be able to leap much higher on the moon than you can here, and to lift 6 times the load that you can shoulder here. Being so light, you would have some difficulty in walking at first. Despite their training in special apparatus, astronauts report an unusual sensation when they first walk on the moon. ❶

Forget about these lunar capers for a moment, and consider what the moon's gravitation has to do with the moon's atmosphere, or lack of atmosphere. The moon does not have enough gravitational force to hold an atmosphere.

Because of the moon's low force of gravitation, the escape velocity on the moon is only about 9,000 kilometers (5,400 miles) per hour. This is the speed that an object must have escape from the moon's surface into space. (You may remember that the earth's escape velocity is almost five times this velocity.) The rocket thrust needed to return a spacecraft from the moon to the earth is, fortunately, much less than the thrust needed to send the spacecraft from the earth to the moon. But it also means, does it not, that for this to happen there is no atmosphere on the moon. Is this true?

Theory—and Fact

It is exciting to fashion theories. Much of the life of the scientist is spent in this fascinating work. But it is even more exciting to make observations and determine whether the facts support the theory. Is there any atmosphere on the moon? Men *on the moon* made the final determination. What was it?

REVIEW

1. The moon's orbit is elliptical. What measurements establish this fact?

2. If the weight of an astronaut is 67.5 kilograms (150 pounds) on the earth, what will he weigh on the moon?

NEW VIEW

1. If the volume of an object is 10 ml and its density is 1.2 g/ml, what is its mass in grams?

2. In what ways are surface features of the moon and the earth similar? How do they differ from each other?

3. MAN ON THE MOON

Why go to the moon at all? First and foremost, it is man's insatiable curiosity that made him persevere in the immensely difficult and expensive project of going to the moon.

What can we do on the moon? Why not send instruments? They send back accurate information. A magnificent observatory can be built on the moon: there is no atmosphere to block the electromagnetic radiations that bring information about the universe. In our telescopes on earth, the light from stars twinkles because it passes through our atmosphere. For a telescope on the moon this kind of distortion would not exist. Seen from the moon, the stars shine brighter, clearer, and steadier than when seen from the earth. This idea alone is enough to make an astronomer's mouth water.

The moon is more than a future observatory—it is also a natural space station. It is conveniently situated as a way station for travel to other parts of the solar system. For instance, it is *possible* that people will set out for the planet Mars in your lifetime. They may find it necessary to leave for Mars from the moon because of the lower escape velocity. So the first step for space travelers seems to be the moon.

Landing on the Moon

How did we prepare for the moon landing? Perhaps you remember it took years of preparation. Thousands of scientists and engineers, electricians, carpenters, clerks, typists—all manner of people—worked together.

"Look before you leap" says an old proverb. When the leap is to the moon, it is good advice. A close and careful inspection of the moon was necessary. Telescopes do not bring us close enough, so spacecraft were sent out to get a closer look.

Some of the spacecraft sent back televised pictures of the moon's surface, as well as other information. Most of these probing spacecraft were caught by the moon's gravitational force. They raced with increasing speed toward the moon's surface, and were destroyed by the hard landing. A few spacecraft, however, curved around the moon and then passed on to go into orbit around the sun.

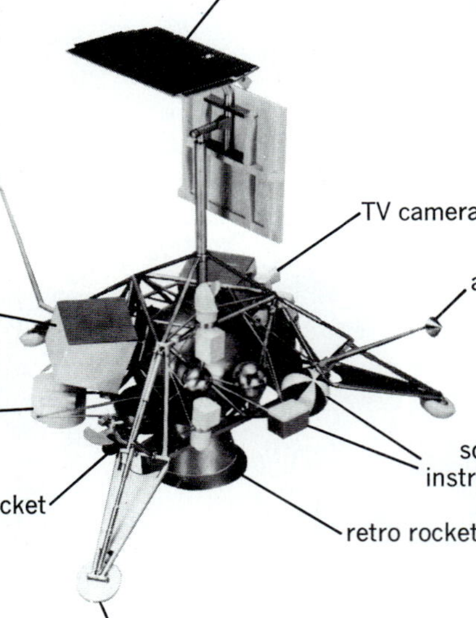

The next phase in exploring the moon's surface was, you realize, to make a "soft landing" on the moon with the unmanned Surveyor spacecraft.1 The soft landing left the craft in one piece so that it could send back information from the surface of the moon. Hurled toward the moon by a Centaur rocket engine, Surveyor was put into orbit. It was then speeded up to escape velocity, so that it traveled away from the earth, slowing down.

When Surveyor came within 100 kilometers (60 miles) of the moon's surface, the retrorockets were fired toward the moon. The retrorockets thrust against the moon's gravitational force to slow down the spacecraft.

When Surveyor's speed had dropped, its guidance rockets steered it into a steep angle of descent. Slowed down to about $\frac{1}{10}$ of its velocity, it settled down gently onto the moon's surface.

One of the tasks that Surveyor accomplished was to examine the nature of the moon's surface. Cameras on the landed spacecraft viewed the lunar surface from close at hand and from different angles. ❷ Television pictures of the surface were sent back to the earth, where they were studied to determine where the moon's surface was strong enough to support a manned spacecraft.

Unmanned spacecraft that made a soft landing on the moon sent back data that helped to answer such questions as these:

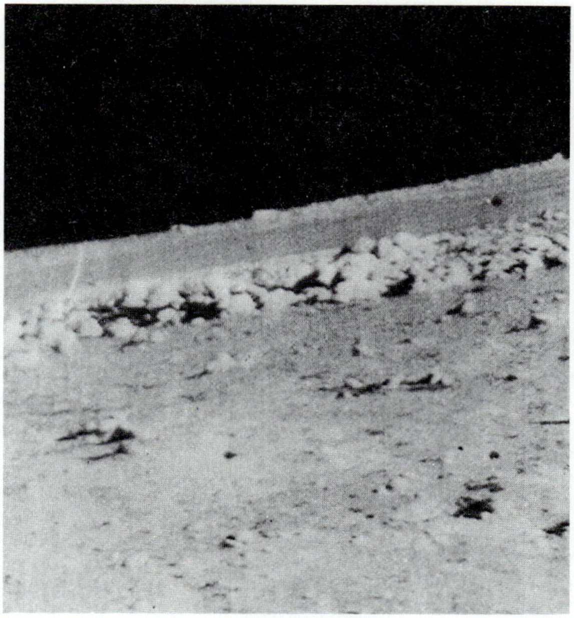
❷

What elements and compounds are to be found on the moon? The unmanned craft did send back to earth an analysis of samples of moon rock.

Is there any life on the moon? Some scientists still think that primitive plants may live in some craters. An unmanned spacecraft can collect material from the surface of the moon, test the material for evidence of life, and radio the results back to earth.

What is the internal temperature of the moon? Does the moon have a molten interior, as some scientists think? Or has it, as others think, a layer of ice under the surface? A temperature probe took the moon's temperature.

There were many more questions that unmanned spacecraft such as Surveyor answered. Does the moon have active volcanoes? Does it have "moonquakes"? And of course, is it safe for men to land on the moon? And what must men do to protect themselves on the moon? Ingeniously designed unmanned space probes, radioing data back to earth, help to answer such questions by sampling the lunar environment. They prepared the way for the next step—sending astronauts to the moon. You know the story of the "first step for mankind."

Astronauts to the Moon

Even before unmanned spacecraft had made a successful soft landing on the moon, the astronauts were learning their jobs. They learned the techniques of launching and landing, they learned to live in their capsules in space, and to perform their tasks there. They learned the effects of weightlessness on human beings. They learned to maneuver their spacecraft so that they could join other astronauts at a rendezvous in space. They learned how to "walk" in space, outside their spacecraft as well as inside it. They learned how to bring two spacecraft together in a docking operation so that a larger spacecraft with all the essential equipment was formed.

1

Project Apollo

You know that the United States program designed to land men on the moon is called Project Apollo. And you know that Apollo 11 was successful. Men walked on the moon—and explored it—and searched it. Perhaps you were watching television as the first astronaut to step on the moon said: "That's one small step for a man, one giant leap for mankind." 1

The Apollo spacecraft can carry three astronauts on a round trip to the moon. The spacecraft is boosted by a three-stage Saturn rocket to the escape velocity needed to leave earth. Just before the third-stage rocket is cast off, two important events take place. First, the panels of the Lunar Module (LM), which is hidden inside the nose of the third-stage rocket, are released. Second, the main spacecraft (the Command Module and Service Module) separates from the third-stage rocket. After turning around to the proper position, the main spacecraft docks with the LM. Once docking is accomplished, the third-stage rocket is abandoned.

As the spacecraft speeds toward the moon, its speed gradually slows down to about $\frac{1}{10}$ of its escape velocity. Yes—the earth's gravitation is continuing to have an effect on the spacecraft. As it approaches the moon, the moon's gravitation exerts a greater force on the spacecraft than the earth's gravitation. The craft gradually speeds up until it approaches the moon at about 9,000 kilometers (5,500 miles) per hour. The astronauts must use the spacecraft's retrorockets to slow it down and go into orbit around the moon. With the drawings on the opposite page, you can follow Apollo's trip.

The LM and main spacecraft are joined together in a way that allows the two astronauts who will walk on the moon to crawl from the main spacecraft into the LM. Now the LM separates from the main spacecraft, which with its one astronaut continues to orbit the moon. The LM, after its retrorockets are fired, descends to the surface of the moon.

The great moment has arrived. The astronauts step onto the moon and explore its surface. When they are ready to leave with their precious samples of the moon's surface, they fire the small but all-important rockets of the LM—and take off. The landing legs of the LM remain behind. The LM goes into orbit around the moon again. Now the astronauts guide it into a rendezvous with the main spacecraft, which, of course, has remained in orbit around the moon. Together again in the main spacecraft, the astronauts leave the LM behind and set a course for the earth. This has now been done several times. There was one failure. Do you remember the heroic flight of Apollo 13?

A
B
C
D
E
F

REVIEW

1. Why is the moon a good place to build an astronomical observatory? What are the disadvantages of this plan?

2. What kinds of information do we get from unmanned soft landings on the moon?

3. Describe the main events of an Apollo moon shot.

NEW VIEW

1. Read a newspaper or magazine account of the most recent manned trip to the moon that is being planned or (perhaps) has already been made. Then answer these questions.
   a. Describe a part of the flight that can be explained by Newton's Law of Inertia.
   b. Describe a part that can be explained by the Law of Action and Reaction.
   c. When is the earth's pull of gravity on the ship greatest during the flight? How is this pull counteracted?

2. Write a report on the qualifications astronauts must have and the training they receive.

4. RELATING THE CONCEPTS

From time immemorial men have studied the earth's natural satellite, the moon. What we have learned about the moon we are now adding to at a tremendous rate. New developments in space technology and new discoveries about the universe are also happening at a tremendous rate.

However, while technology advances and knowledge accumulates at a dizzying pace, the concepts of science remain relatively stable. No matter what new space projects are now underway, the concepts embodied in the laws of gravitation and inertial motion, for instance, will continue to be useful in explaining the motions of the moon and other bodies in space, and the flights of spacecraft.

Reviewing the Concepts

► *The moon's phases are due to its revolution around the earth.* Each phase represents the part of the moon's lighted surface that we can see. Full moon, crescent moon, half moon, gibbous moon, new moon: all these we can explain by the moon's orbit.

► *The angular diameter of an object decreases as the distance to the object increases, although the object's true diameter is unchanged.* The sun's true diameter is much greater than that of the moon. However, the sun is far enough away from us to make its angular diameter nearly the same as that of the moon. Eclipses of the sun and moon are possible because the angular diameters of the sun and the moon are about equal.

► *When an eclipse of the sun occurs, the moon moves between the earth and the sun so that the moon's shadow falls on the earth.* In the dark part of the shadow, a total solar eclipse is seen. In the lighter part, a partial solar eclipse is seen.

► *When an eclipse of the moon occurs, the earth moves between the moon and the sun so that the earth's shadow falls on the moon.* Newton's laws of motion and gravitation describe the motions of the moon around the earth and of the earth around the sun. From these laws the exact positions of these bodies relative to each other at any given time can be predicted. And so the dates and places of eclipses can be predicted with great precision.

► *Density is a measure of mass per unit volume.* The average density of the moon is about the same as the density of rocks in the earth's crust. Thus we have evidence that the moon may be made of material similar to that in the earth's crust.

► *The gravitational force exerted by a body in space depends on the body's mass (its volume times its density).* The escape velocity of an object from a body in space depends on the body's gravitational force. The moon, with its low density, has a low escape velocity —so low that the moon is unable to hold an atmosphere. In other words, if the moon ever had an atmosphere, it "escaped" long ago. The low gravitational force of the moon will make it possible to launch space vehicles from the moon with far less fuel than required to leave the earth—a fact that helps make the moon an ideal space station.

Testing Yourself

1. Describe the shape, size, and surface of the moon as we now believe them to be.

2. How does the appearance of the moon change as we view it from the earth? Account for these changes.

3. What theories have been proposed to explain the craters on the moon?

4. How does a "sea" on the moon compare with a sea on the earth?

5. What is meant by the angular diameter of an object?

6. How do the conditions that result in a lunar eclipse compare to those that result in a solar eclipse?

7. Describe the procedure you would follow to determine the density of an object.

8. How does the weight of an object on the earth compare with its weight on the moon? How is the difference explained?

9. What is some of the evidence that the moon has no atmosphere?

10. Explain why there is a difference between the velocities needed to launch a space vehicle from the earth and from the moon.

11. How does Newton's Law of Inertia help to explain the flight of a spacecraft?

Extending the Concepts

Investigation. Astronomers have several methods of determining distances in the universe. To understand the principle of one of these, hold a pencil about 30 centimeters (1 foot) away from your face. With only one eye open, line the pencil up with some object in the room. Suppose the object is a clock. Now open the other eye and close the one you had open before. What do you observe? The pencil is no longer in line with the clock. What you did was to sight the pencil from two different locations about 8 centimeters (3 inches) apart —that is, the distance between your eyes. The pencil seemed to shift its position in relation to the clock in the background. This shift is known as *parallax*.

Repeat the procedure you have just followed, but this time hold the pencil at arm's length. Now you will observe a smaller shift, or parallax, than before. Generally, the less the object seems to shift, the farther away it is. In other words, the smaller the parallax, the greater the distance.

Devise a way to measure the amount of the shifting, and then make scale drawings of the parallax angle for several sets of conditions.

Suggested Reading

Cooper, S. F., *Moon Rocks*, New York, Dial, 1970. An account of the people and events that surrounded the study of the moon rocks.

Von Braun, W., and F. Ordway, *History of Rocketry and Space Travel*, rev. ed., New York, Crowell, 1969. Written by an authority on rockets.

Wilford, John, *We Reach the Moon*, New York, Bantam Books, 1969. A fully illustrated account of the voyage of Apollo 11.

Unit Four

THE EARTH'S AIR AND WATER

The water from the atmosphere finds its way into soil, rock, rivers, lakes—and the sea. Thus between the water in the atmosphere and the earth's waters there is a strong link.

Living in the atmosphere, you walk at the bottom of an ocean of air. If you equipped yourself with a skindiver's mask and tank of air, you could continue walking—at the bottom of the ocean of water. These two oceans, of air and of water, are continuous, and both cover the land.

In this unit, you observe both oceans—the ocean of air and the ocean of water.

12

Water in the Seas and Oceans

"The sea is many things to many people. To the commercial fisherman it is a sometimes calm, sometimes violent, but usually productive environment from which he derives his livelihood. To the mother of small children at the beach, it may be a terrifying thing of ripping currents and pounding surf, an unknown menace to her offsprings, a threat against which they have no defense. To the economic mineralogist faced with shortages of strategic metals on land, it appears as a veritable treasure trove of untapped mineral wealth. To the artist and poet it is a never-ending source of inspiration, a thing of constantly changing beauty, at times restful and calm, but capable of fits of violence to try the souls of those who love her. To the scientist who studies her—the oceanographer—the sea is a magnificent addiction; once exposed to her complex interrelationships, once made aware of the sheer joy of learning her secrets, of exploring her vast uncharted reaches, he is a willing slave to the pursuit of more knowledge of her."

These words are written by a man who knows the sea well—Dr. Harris B. Stewart, Jr., Chief Oceanographer of the United States Coast and Geodetic Survey, in his book, *The Global Sea.*

1. THE UNKNOWN SEA

We who live on land easily forget that most of the earth's crust is under the sea. The oceans of the world are actually one vast body of water: the Atlantic and Pacific Oceans are simply the sea's largest divisions. (1) Inconsistently, we call some of the smaller divisions seas, such as the Mediterranean Sea and the Caribbean Sea. But notice that such bodies of water as Hudson Bay, the Bay of Biscay, and the Gulf of Mexico are also divisions of the global sea. In all, about 71 percent of the surface of the earth is under the sea. And the land is farther below the sea than above it. The average depth of the sea is about 3,720 meters (12,400 feet), while the average height of the land above sea level is only about 780 meters (2,600 feet).

This means that nearly $\frac{3}{4}$ of the earth's surface, the part that lies under water, has not yet been seen. For men have only just begun to learn how to explore the bottom of the sea. Even so, there has already been an unexpected and astonishing discovery that has come out of mapping the bottom of the sea.

Men had been making accurate maps of the moon long before they even began to map the sea's bottom. Can you think why?

1

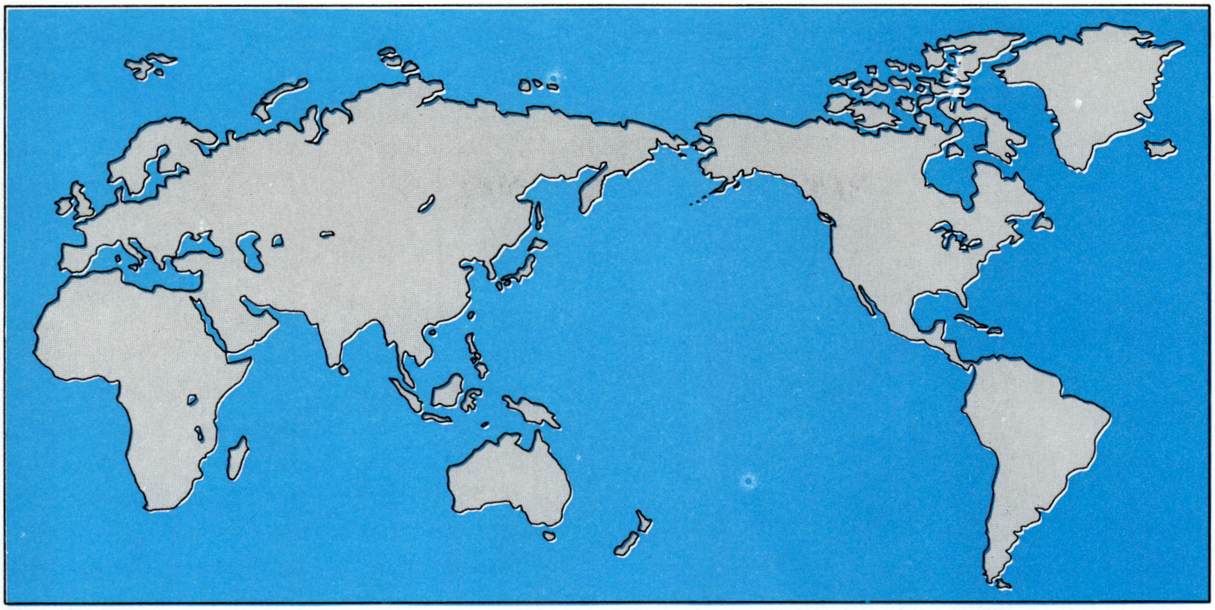

Mapping the Sea Bottom

To map the earth's dry land, or even the face of the moon, is relatively easy, using the reflected light of the sun and photography. But the sea floor is pitch dark. Oceanographers have to use other methods to map the 350 million square kilometers (139 million square miles) of sea bottom.

To map the ocean floor, sound waves are used. As you know, sound is a form of energy that travels through matter. And sound travels at different speeds through different kinds of matter. Sound travels faster through water than through air, for example. In air, sound travels at a speed of about 330 meters (1,100 feet) per second, but in water sound travels more than four times as fast—at about 1,400 meters (4,800 feet) per second. These speeds vary a little with changes in temperature: the warmer it is, the faster sound travels in air or water. There is another interesting difference between sound in air and in water that you may be able to observe. Next time you are in a swimming pool, strike two objects together in air and then under water, while you have one ear submerged. The underwater sound made by the objects will have a higher pitch than the sound in air, because high-pitched sounds are carried better by water than by air.

A high-pitched sound is used to measure the depth of the sea. A sound generator in the bottom of a ship sends out a short, high-pitched burst of sound called a "ping." 2 When it strikes the sea bottom the ping is reflected, and this echo travels back to the

2

❶
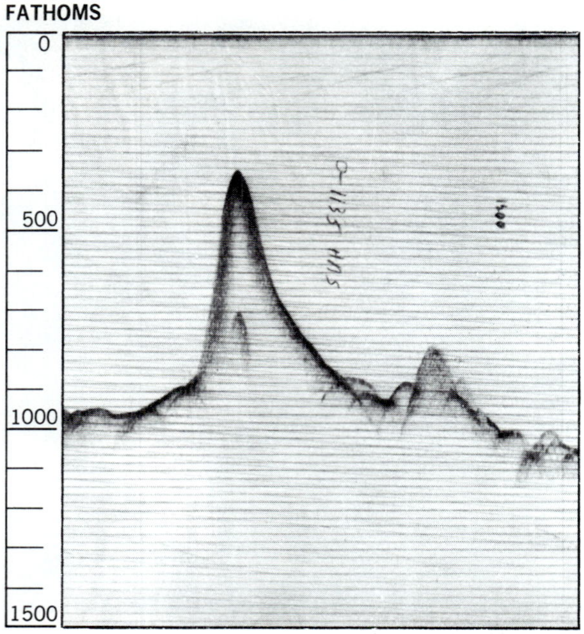

ship. A microphone in the bottom of the ship detects the echo's return, and another instrument measures the length of time taken by the ping to make its round trip, from ship to sea bottom to ship. The time depends on the speed of the sound in the water, which is known, and the distance the sound traveled, which can be calculated. Thus the depth of water below the ship is determined. Actually no calculation is necessary, for this echo-sounding device (sometimes called *sonar*) is set up so that the depth of the water can be read off directly. Or the depth may be recorded on a chart and the echo-sounder made automatic so that depth measurements are continuously made and recorded as the ship steams along. Thus a profile of the sea bottom along a certain course is obtained.❶

Of course to map an area of the ocean floor a great many such profiles are needed. Moreover, a profile is not enough; the oceanographer needs to know just where the ship is positioned at any moment along the profile. Only within the last few years have electronic navigation systems made the desired accuracy possible. However, oceanographers now have enough data of this kind to make, for example, a relief map of the bottom of the Atlantic Ocean. What was once thought to be an uninteresting, uniformly smooth surface turns out to be just the opposite.❷

The Sea's Floor

Mountains, hills, plateaus, valleys, plains, canyons—these features of the earth's dry land seem to be matched by similar formations under the sea. But (in the map on pp. 244–245) notice the great ridge of mountains. The existence of a ridge in the mid-Atlantic has been known for many years; the fact that this ridge extends around the crust of the earth has been discovered only recently. This surprising and very important feature of the earth's crust has been hidden until now by the sea.

Oceanographers and geologists have been able to make out a certain order in the land beneath the sea. Imagine that you could take a walk from the shore straight into the sea and across the sea bottom. The first underwater land you would trudge across is the **continental shelf.** (Find this in the map on the next page.) The shelf is comparatively flat and shallow, and slopes so gently that you would not be aware of it. The shelf descends about 2 meters in a kilometer (12 feet in a mile). You might walk from 50 to 500 kilometers (30 to 300 miles) across the continental shelf, until you reach the **continental slope.** The tilt of the continental slope is only 3 to 6 degrees from the horizontal. The vertical scale of the map has been exaggerated to emphasize the sea bottom features. The continental slope is not smooth; deep canyons have been discovered in it. A canyon in the continental slope off the California coast is as deep as the Grand Canyon. If you keep on walking down the continental slope, you will find yourself in really deep water, perhaps as deep as 3,300 meters (11,000 feet).

A very gentle rise might tell you that you have reached the limit of the continental slope, and you come to the **abyssal plain,** an extremely flat expanse. It may be dotted with the cone-shaped volcanic mountains of the sea known as seamounts. Some of the seamounts have flat tops and are called **guyots.** 2 In general, however, the abyssal plains are extraordinarily flat, flatter than the plains of Kansas or Oklahoma, for example.

In time, if you persisted in your walk, you would reach the mountain range of the Mid-Atlantic Ridge. (If you are walking across the Pacific Ocean, it will be the Mid-Pacific Ridge.) The ridge is a chain of volcanic mountains, higher than any volcanoes on dry land—some of them almost 7 kilometers (4 miles) high, under water.

This mid-oceanic ridge has turned out to be some 67,000 kilometers (40,000 miles) long, extending through the South Atlantic, Indian, and South Pacific Oceans. "Probably the most exciting discovery about our earth in the past twenty years," says one oceanographer. We will see why in a moment.

2

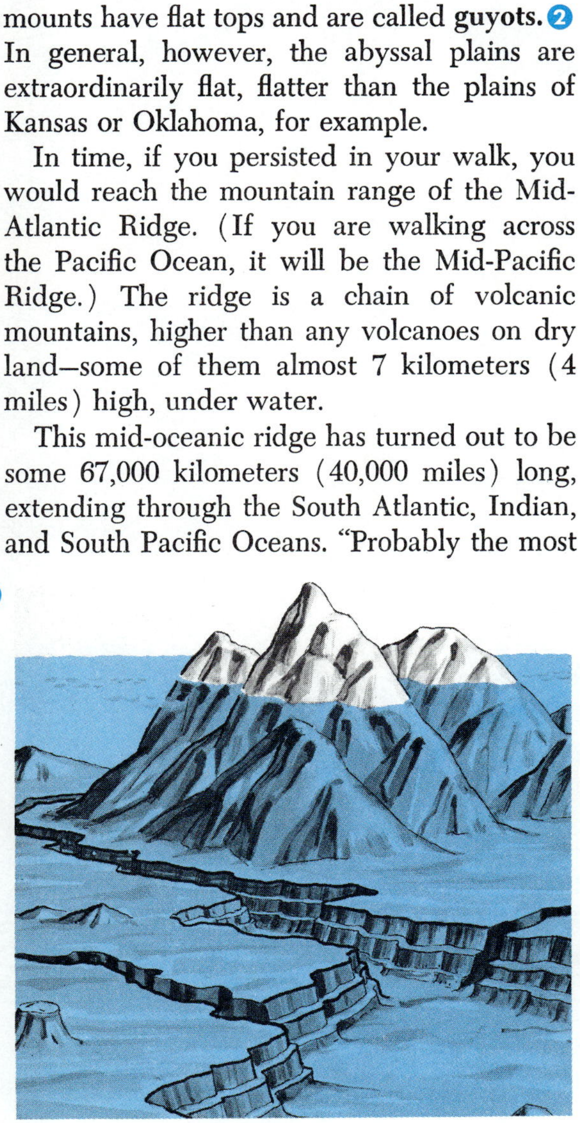

3

Exploring the Depths

The tremendous heights of some of the undersea mountains are rivalled by the depths of some of the long narrow undersea valleys known as **trenches.** In the Marianas Trench near the Mariana Islands in the Western Pacific Ocean is the deepest spot discovered so far, the Challenger Deep, 10,852 meters (36,173 feet) down. Compare this with the height of Mount Everest, about 8,708 meters (29,028 feet). In 1960 Jacques Piccard and Don Walsh descended to the bottom of the Challenger Deep in the *Trieste,* a **bathyscaph.** 3

Oceanographers do more than map the ocean floor. They observe and measure ocean currents. Some of their special instruments measure and record the temperature of ocean water, others collect samples at different depths. Still others collect samples of loose sediment from the ocean floor. Some take samples of rock from the solid ocean floor by drilling holes with special drills. These rock samples, called *cores,* are important in the

THE NORTH ATLANTIC OCEAN FLOOR

This is a portion of the Physiographic Diagram of the North Atlantic Ocean, published by the Geological Society of America. Copyright © 1957 Bruce C. Heezen and Marie Tharp. Adapted with permission.

1

study of the ocean floor. 1 Others make use of the underwater photography and seismology, the study of earthquakes. Although these methods have given oceanographers a good idea of the general features of the sea floor, over 60 percent of the land under the sea has yet to be mapped, and there is much yet to be learned about the ocean waters.

Several small, deep-diving submarines are also being used to explore the ocean floor. One of the most successful is the *Aluminaut*. 2 It carries a crew of six men and can dive to 4,500 meters (15,000 feet). The *Aluminaut* has had an interesting history. In 1966, it participated in the search and successful recovery of a hydrogen bomb that was lost off the coast of Spain.

Vessels like the *Aluminaut* have special instruments to explore beneath the surface. They use "arms" to pick up samples of rock and sediment from the ocean floor. Both submarines and surface vessels use a great variety of instruments to study features below the surface. Still cameras and television cameras, equipped to operate underwater, are used to record sea floor formations or to observe marine life. You may be familiar with the work of some scientists in this field. Recently, the explorations of Captain Jacques-Yves Cousteau and his crew aboard the *Calypso* have revealed valuable information concerning the sea and the life it supports. 3

Samples of water from great depths are obtained with a device known as a Nansen bottle. Special thermometers can be attached to these bottles to record the temperature of the water at which the sample was taken.

A direct way to examine what is below the surface is the use of scuba equipment (self-contained underwater breathing apparatus). With their own oxygen supply, divers can descend to depths of about 60 meters (200 feet).

2

3

During the summer of 1963, five French "oceanauts," divers specially trained to do scientific investigations under water, spent nearly a month below the surface of the Red Sea. These men, directed by Captain Cousteau, lived under water in an air-conditioned steel "house," from which they made repeated dives to depths of 45 meters (150 feet) and more. For their ventures into the deep they donned their scuba equipment. By not returning to the surface, and by living in their underwater house, the divers avoided many of the dangers and difficulties that have beset man's efforts at deep-sea diving in the past.

In 1965, Scott Carpenter, one of our original astronauts, became an "aquanaut." He led two teams of men that lived and worked for 30 days in the U.S. Navy's Sealab II, 62 meters (205 feet) under the Pacific Ocean. Like Captain Cousteau's oceanauts, these American "aquanauts," wearing their Aqua-Lungs, could investigate the sea directly.

The extraordinary successes of the oceanauts and the aquanauts have launched a new era in the exploration of the world under the sea. We think of outer space as a new frontier challenging our ingenuity and courage as explorers. The sea, our "inner space," is a challenge too.

REVIEW

1. What percentage of the earth is covered by the sea?
2. How can sound be used to map the features of the ocean floor?
3. Describe each of these features of the ocean floor: continental shelf, ridge, abyssal plane, trench, continental slope, guyot.
4. What is the Challenger Deep?

NEW VIEW

1. In what ways is mapping the ocean floor similar to mapping the moon's surface? What are the differences?
2. A pulse of sound is sent by an echo sounder (sonar) to the ocean floor and the echo is received 1.5 seconds later. How far is it to the bottom at that point?
3. Many interesting vessels have been used in the exploration of the oceans. Do some library research on the *Alvin, Flip, Trieste,* or the *Hero.* What contributions have they made to our knowledge of the sea?

1

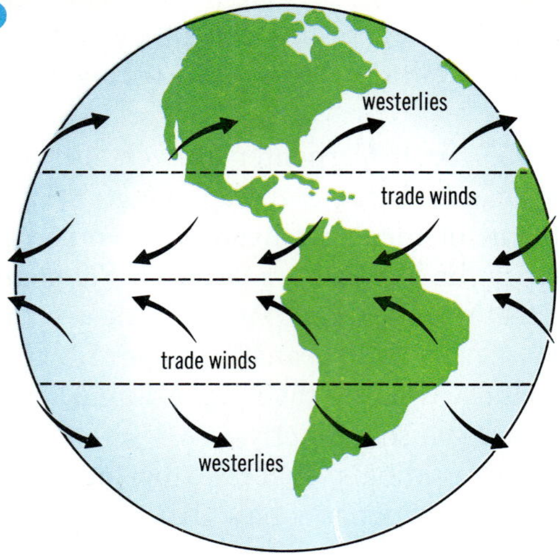

2. OCEAN CURRENTS

A calm sea is a windless sea. A rough sea is a windy one, or has been a windy one not long before. Winds are among the most important causes of the sea's movements, its waves and its currents.

Wind on the Water

Wind moves water by the force of friction, friction between air and water as the air flows in contact with the water's surface. Drifts or currents of water can be created by this frictional force, and it also produces waves, which in turn play a role in producing currents. If you compare the wave action on a windy day at the seashore to that on a relatively windless day, you can easily see the relation between wind and wave. As the wind sweeps over the sea, it raises waves and makes the sea choppy. Then wind pressure against the sides of the waves creates a driving force for currents. Oceanographers have been surprised by evidence that it is not large waves but ripples, the tiny "bumps" of water that give the most force to currents from the wind. Let's look next into the pattern of the sea's currents.

The pattern of ocean currents over the earth is not simple as you can see from the map on page 250. How do winds give rise to the Gulf Stream, and to other currents such as the Brazil current and the Japan current? If winds are a main cause of these currents, then we must look to the pattern of the winds themselves to help explain the pattern of the ocean currents.

You can think of the winds themselves as great currents in our air ocean. In the lower part of the troposphere, the layer of air nearest the ground, there are winds that blow almost always from the same direction. These are called **prevailing winds.** 1

Let's imagine what effect these prevailing winds would have on an ocean. Let's try to take into account as well the effect of the earth's rotation. By using a model ocean we may simplify a complex situation, and see more clearly what forces are at work. After studying the model, we can examine the actual ocean currents and see how well our model explains them. Then we may know if our hypothesis concerning the effect of prevailing winds and the earth's rotation on the ocean currents is useful.

The rectangular area on the model represents either the Atlantic or Pacific ocean, transformed from its actual shape to a shape easier to study. 2 Blowing across this rectangular model ocean are some prevailing winds.

Some Currents in a Model Ocean

Any one of the prevailing winds blowing across our model ocean can push the surface of the ocean along and make a current. In the northern part of the model ocean, for example, the trade winds blow from the east toward the equator, and so tend to move water from the east toward the equator. The

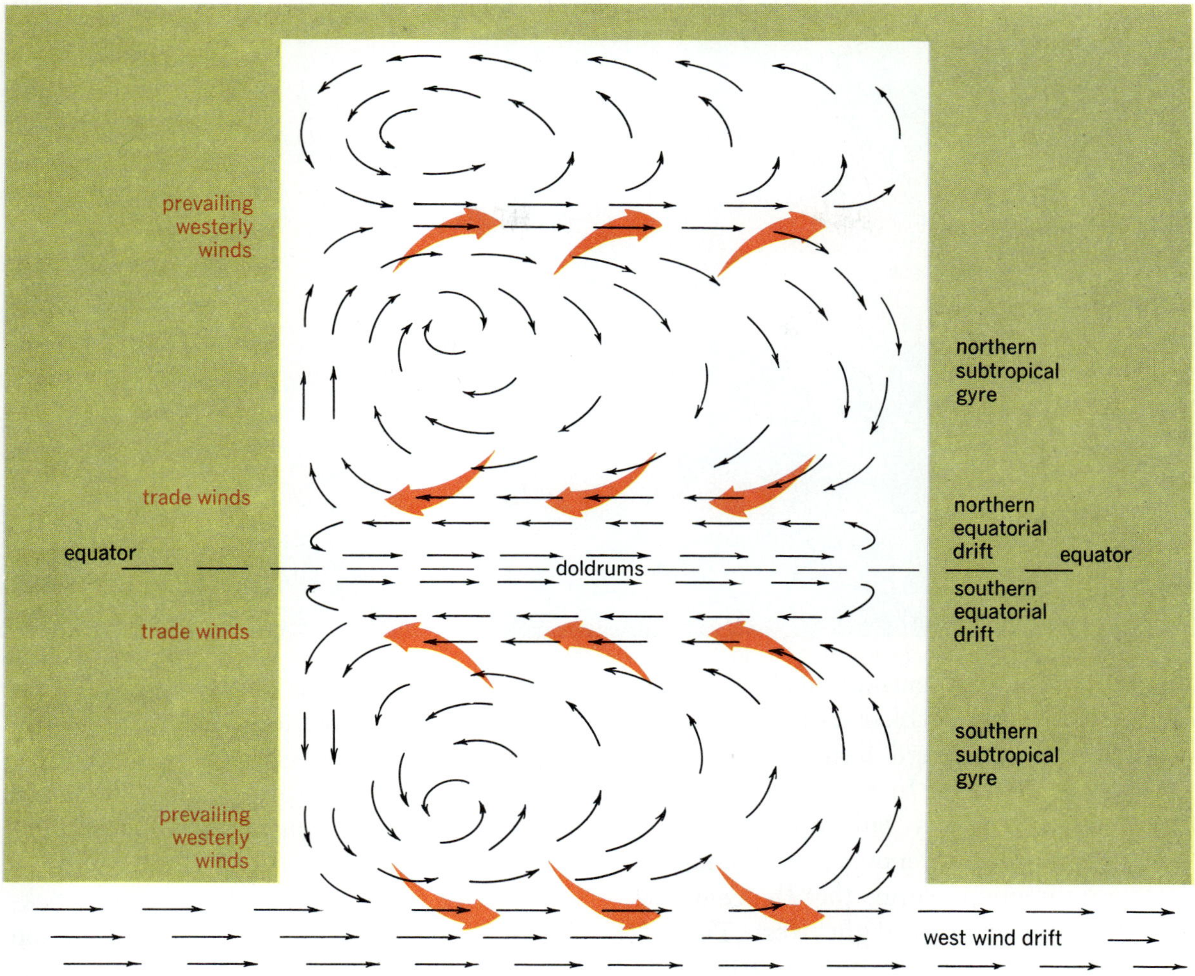

Adapted from "The Circulation of the Oceans" by Walter Munk.

earth's rotation, however, deflects this water movement. The result is that the current of water moves approximately parallel to the equator, or due west. Hence, in the North Atlantic Ocean, the current called the Northern Equatorial Drift moves due west across the ocean, instead of in the southwesterly direction of its driving wind.

The same sort of thing happens in the southern hemisphere. Trade winds in the southern hemisphere blow across the water in a northwest direction. However, the earth's rotation deflects the current so that the water flows nearly parallel to the equator. Thus the current called the Southern Equatorial Drift also moves westward across the ocean.

Both the Northern and Southern Equatorial Drifts flow westward until deflected by the land. Observe how the west shore line forms a barrier forcing the current to change its course.

The combined effects of the prevailing winds, the earth's rotation, and the land masses produce a ring-shaped motion, a kind

① 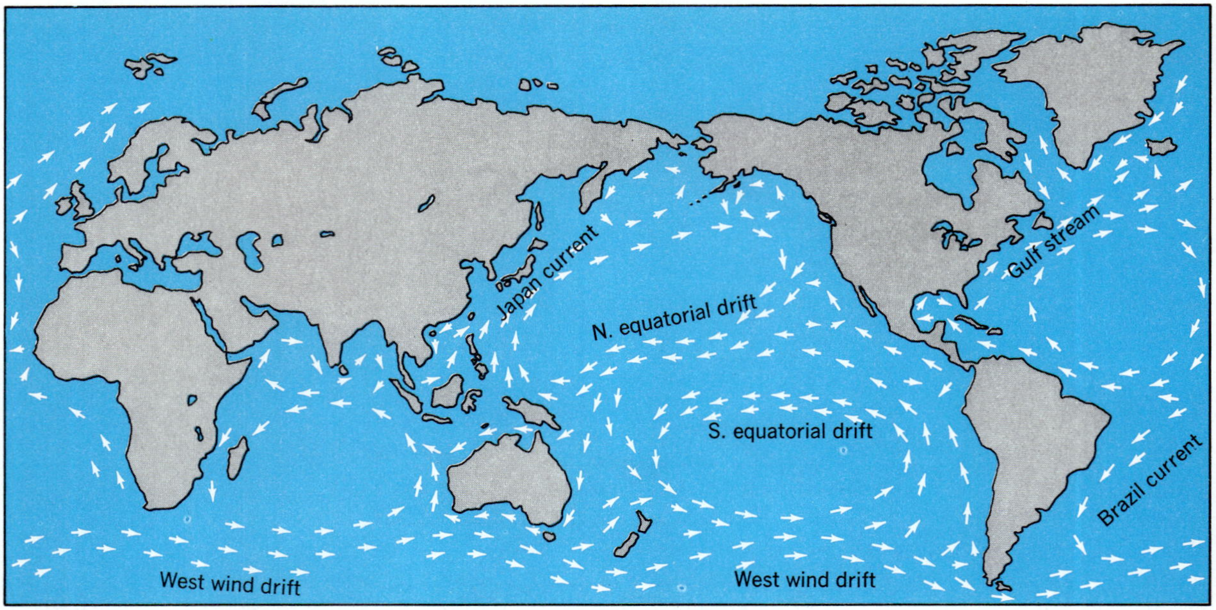

of whirlpool in the current, called a **gyre.** The gyre moves in a clockwise direction in the northern hemisphere, forming the Northern Subtropical gyre. In the southern hemisphere, the Southern Subtropical gyre is formed by a current moving in a counterclockwise direction. Notice that the center of each gyre is over toward the west. This effect is due to the earth's rotation, from west to east.

Observe another feature of the model ocean. In the southern hemisphere the prevailing westerlies blow across the ocean at a point where the water is not bounded by east and west shore lines. In the south near the Antarctic, the shore lines along the ocean boundaries are cut away. A current called the West Wind Drift, or Antarctic Current, is accordingly free to move in a complete circle around the earth.

Testing the Model

Do ocean currents actually move in the way that our model ocean suggests? If they do, then the hypothesis that prevailing winds and the earth's rotation account (in the main) for ocean currents will be acceptable. Look again at the map of the world's main oceans.① Trace the course of the gyres in the North Pacific and North Atlantic. Do the gyres move in the expected direction, clockwise? Trace the course of the gyres in the South Pacific and South Atlantic, to see if they move in a counterclockwise direction. In the four major divisions of the actual ocean the currents do move as predicted by our model ocean.

You may test the model, and the hypothesis, further by tracing the actual course of the West Wind Drift on the map. Notice how the main course of the West Wind Drift travels in a circle all around the earth. Branch currents form when the drift meets land barriers at its northern edge. Thus the West Wind Drift gives rise to smaller currents on the western side of Australia, Peru, and Africa. For simplicity's sake these land barriers were not included in our model. However, the presence of these land barriers is not enough to change the main course of the West Wind Drift. The path of the actual drift in the ocean agrees, in the main, with our model.

It seems, then, that winds do play a role in producing currents. However, a wind works at the surface of the water. A few meters below the surface the effect of a wind is no longer felt. Yet there is evidence that currents do exist below the surface of the water, and in fact very far below the surface. The North American Deep Current, for example, flows at a depth of between 2,100 and 3,900 meters (7,000 and 13,000 feet). It begins at about 60 degrees North latitude and moves south all the way to the shores of Antarctica. For example, again, the Bottom Current of icy water more than 3,900 meters below the surface flows northward from Antarctica until stopped by seamounts at about 40 degrees North. What force drives these currents, below the surface?

Heat and Currents

When a mass of cold water in the ocean comes in contact with a mass of warm water, the cold water sinks and the warm water moves upward. A current flows. Why? Cold water is more dense than warm water, so when cold water is placed in warm water, the cold water tends to sink to the bottom of the warm. Thus cold water above warm water can produce a current. This kind of current, remember, is called a *convection current*.

Scientists think that when the warm waters of the Gulf Stream meet the cold waters of the Arctic in the North Atlantic, a convection current is produced. Cold water sinks to the bottom, just off the coast of Greenland—the northernmost tip of the Gulf Stream—and flows south underneath the Stream's warm water. In this way variations in the temperature of the water may set currents moving below the surface of the sea.

Salt and Currents

The temperature of ocean water can vary; the ocean's salt content, or **salinity,** can vary as well. A difference in salinity means a difference in density of water. The more salt water contains, the more dense the water is.

The greater the percentage of salt in water, the more dense the water. Water with a high salinity thus tends to sink when it is in water that has a lower salinity. Thus a difference in the saltiness of water can also cause a density current.

What makes ocean waters vary in salt content? For example, the Mediterranean Sea, like any body of water, is always exchanging water with the atmosphere. When sea water evaporates, only the water goes into the air as vapor, as you know; the salt remains behind. Thus, as some of the Mediterranean's water enters the air as water vapor, the sea becomes more salty than it was before evaporation.

Rainfall has the opposite effect. When it rains, fresh water is added to the sea and makes the sea less salty than before. The rainfall in the Mediterranean, however, is not great enough to make up for the loss of water by evaporation. So the surface water of the Mediterranean has a relatively high salt content and is heavy enough to sink. As the heavier water sinks it generates a current.

There seem to be, then, two main causes of currents. Horizontal surface currents are mainly wind driven. Density differences, due to variations in temperature and saltiness, cause deep vertical currents. To see how a temperature difference may produce a current, try the investigation on the next page. ■

■ **AN APPRENTICE INVESTIGATION into Warm and Cold Water**

❶

❷

❸

Fill a beaker or tumbler with very cold water. In another beaker, put some very hot water, and add some blue coloring (ink will do). Take up some of this hot, colored water with a medicine dropper. Place the dropper in the cold water. Squeeze a little colored, hot water out of the dropper into the cold water near the bottom of the beaker.❶ What happens to the hot water? Here is what happened in one trial.❷

Now place cold water in hot by squeezing a little colored, cold water out of a dropper into hot water. Here is what happened in one trial.❸ How do you explain the behavior of the colored water in each case?

When you try this investigation, you may find that your observations differ from those shown in the photographs. You may even find the behavior of the colored water confusing and contradictory. But if you set yourself to find out why the colored water behaves as it does, you may find that there is something to be learned from contradictory behavior. A hint: What effect do you think the size of the hole in the dropper has?

Do you notice any similarity between the behavior of the colored water and the behavior of smoke from a chimney? Can you explain this?

An Investigation On Your Own

Predict what the water in the beaker will look like if you continue to add colored, hot water to cold at the bottom. Test your prediction.

The Gulf Stream

One of the early astronauts saw the Gulf Stream from his space capsule as a beautiful light green ribbon of water against the darker background of the surrounding ocean. Where does this famous current begin?

In the North Atlantic Ocean, along the belt of the trade wind, a part of the North Equatorial Drift going west is deflected off the coast of Brazil. You can see this in the map of ocean currents on page 250. Then the current moves northward toward the West Indies, in the Carribean Sea. It enters the Gulf of Mexico, where many rivers and much rainfall swell the current's volume and lighten its color. As the current passes through the Straits of Florida, it moves out into the Atlantic Ocean as the Gulf Stream.

In the Atlantic, the Gulf Stream runs northward all the way past the tip of Greenland, with side branches moving toward the coasts of France, Britain, and Scandinavia. Without these warm waters of the Stream, northern Europe would have a much less favorable climate.

Similar combinations of factors produce the Japan Current and the Brazil Current. Trace the course of these currents on the map on page 250. These currents also affect the environments for living things along the coasts that they bathe.

REVIEW

1. How do winds produce currents?

2. Why are the Northern and Southern Equatorial Drifts deflected?

3. How does temperature affect surface and deep currents?

4. How does salt content affect surface and deep currents?

5. What combination of factors seems to determine the course of the Japan Current?

NEW VIEW

1. Make a map of the Gulf Stream. Indicate on your map points where temperature, salt content, or land masses affect the speed or direction of the flow.

2. In a period of 4 hours, the temperature of a pitcher of water varied from 15°C to 25°C. The temperature of the air, however, varied from 18°C to 34°C during this period.

Consider this and the other factors you have noted in your reading of this section to answer this question:

Why do biologists think of the sea as safer than land for living things?

3. How would the ocean currents be affected if the earth began to rotate from west to east instead of from east to west?

3. THE COASTAL WATERS

Suppose you are standing on a cliff or sea wall overlooking the ocean. What do you see? In addition to a few plants, birds, and people, you surely see a beach of sand, gravel, or larger rocks. Farther out you see long lines of waves. These waves seem to be traveling toward the beach. Let's watch a particular wave as it moves toward the beach. It travels toward the land until it forms a breaker. Then the water from the breaker sweeps up on the beach—and the wave you have been watching is gone.

Ocean Waves

What causes waves on water? If you watch as the wind blows over a swimming pool, a pond, or a lake, you see that small waves, or ripples, form on the surface of the water. The larger the body of water, the larger are the ripples that form. On fairly large bodies of water, the ripples grow into waves. If you observe a large body of water on a day with

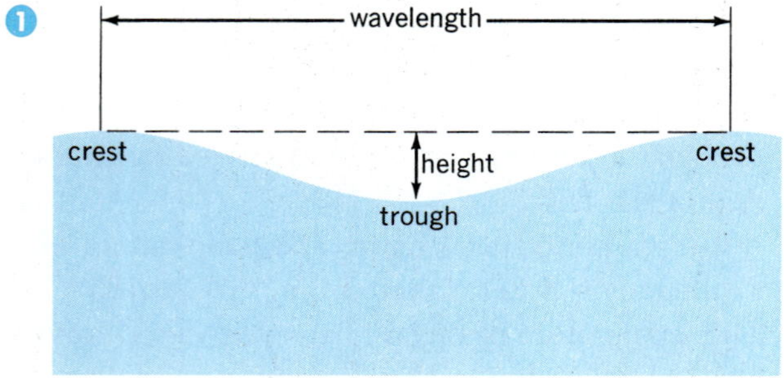

strong winds, you might notice that *stronger winds* cause higher and longer waves. You might also notice that the *longer a wind blows* over the water, the higher and longer the waves become. If you were at sea, you might also observe that the size of a wave depends on the **fetch,** or length of open sea over which the wind blows steadily. The longer the fetch, the higher and longer are the waves that form.

Most of the waves on large lakes and on the ocean are caused by the wind. Because the oceans are so vast, you may not feel the wind that is causing the waves. But somewhere out on the ocean there is an intense storm whose winds are causing the waves you see near the shore. These waves travel out from the storm area like swift messengers. As they travel through the ocean, they become more regular in shape. They also lose much of the energy that was given them by the wind.

How can you describe a wave—in the terms a scientist uses? It doesn't matter whether it is a water wave, a light wave, or a sound wave; the terms he uses are the same. You know from Chapter 7 that a wave has a *crest* (or top) and a *trough* (or bottom). 1 The height of the wave crest above the trough is called the **wave height.** The distance from one wave crest (or trough) to the next is called the **wavelength.** Suppose you were in a lighthouse and measured the time between the crest of one wave and the crest of the next wave. You have measured another property of waves, the **wave period.** Waves produced by the wind have periods of less than 30 seconds.

How fast does a wave travel through the water? Or, as a scientist would ask, what is the **velocity** (speed) of a wave? The velocity of a perfectly formed wave of small height, in deep water, has a definite relationship between its wavelength and period. The velocity of a wave can be determined by dividing the wavelength by the period:

$$\text{velocity} = \frac{\text{wavelength}}{\text{period}}$$

Let's see what this equation tells us. Suppose a wave that is 35 meters long has a period of 5 seconds. What is its velocity? Using the equation above:

$$\text{velocity} = \frac{35 \text{ meters}}{5 \text{ seconds}}$$

$$\text{velocity} = 7 \text{ meters per second}$$

Why not produce some waves and determine their velocity for yourself? ■

The table below gives the results of similar calculations of actual waves in deep water. Copy the table and fill in the missing numbers. *Do not write in this book.*

wave period (seconds)	1	2	5	10	?	30
wave velocity (meters/second)	1.5	?	7.5	15	30	45
wavelength (meters)	1.5	6	37.5	?	600	1,350

A 30-second wave can travel through the deep ocean at a little over 160 kilometers per hour—that is about 100 *miles* per hour!

■ AN APPRENTICE INVESTIGATION into the Velocity of Waves

Fill a large fish tank with water until the water is about 20 centimeters (8 inches) deep.❶ Roll a hand towel around a wire hanger. Then bend the wire hanger and hook it over the far end of the tank so that the towel is just at water level. (If you carry out this investigation at home, use your bathtub instead of the fish tank and a large bath towel instead of the hand towel.) Divide the length of the tank into 5 equal parts and mark the divisions with strips of masking tape.

Place your hand, palm down, just at water level and move your hand up and down a short distance in a rapid but steady rhythm. Did you make any waves? Did you notice the waves move toward the far end of the tank? Estimate the wavelength of the waves by referring to the marks along the tank.❷ What is the wavelength of your waves? Have a partner with a stopwatch count the number of waves that you make in 10 seconds. ***Hint:*** The number of waves is the same as the number of downward palm motions. Divide the number of waves into the time (10 seconds) to find the wave period. What is the period of your waves?

Now that you have determined the wavelength and period of the waves, use the equation you have learned to calculate the velocity of these waves. Calculate their velocity in centimeters or feet per second.

❶

❷

An Investigation On Your Own

Make waves of different periods by moving your hand at a different rate. If you move your hand at a slower rate, how are wavelength, period, and velocity affected? What happens to these wave properties if you move your hand at a faster rate? Are your results similar to the wavelength, period, and velocity of ocean waves? Why? Why not?

How Waves Travel

What does it mean to say that a wave travels through water? Does the water move with the wave? If you are swimming underwater, do you feel the wave passing by? Let's examine these questions. Suppose you are on the beach and there is no wind. If you throw a ball or other floating object out beyond the breakers, what happens? You see the ball rise as every wave crest passes by and fall as every wave trough passes by. Yet the ball stays out beyond the breakers about where it landed. However, you notice that the ball moves up and down.

The water particles are also moving. Each particle of water actually moves in a circular orbit as the wave passes by.❶ Each particle moves up and forward as the crest passes. Then the particle moves down and backward as the trough passes. So the particle of water goes through a complete orbit each time a crest and trough pass by—but the particle ends up almost exactly where it started. This description of the motion of water particles is based on a theory for very simple waves. No one knows exactly how water particles behave in more complex waves. Later on you will see what happens to water particles in a breaking wave.

In a simple wave, a water particle near the surface goes through a very large orbit compared with a particle further below the surface. In fact, for all practial purposes, the water particles do not move at depths that are greater than one-half the wavelength of the wave. For example, if a wave has a wavelength of 6 meters (20 feet), there is no motion of the water particles below a depth of 3 meters (10 feet). If you were swimming at that depth, you would not feel any waves overhead. While surface ships are affected by storm waves, it is very simple for a submarine to submerge below the level of orbital motion and ride out the storm in perfect calm.

❶

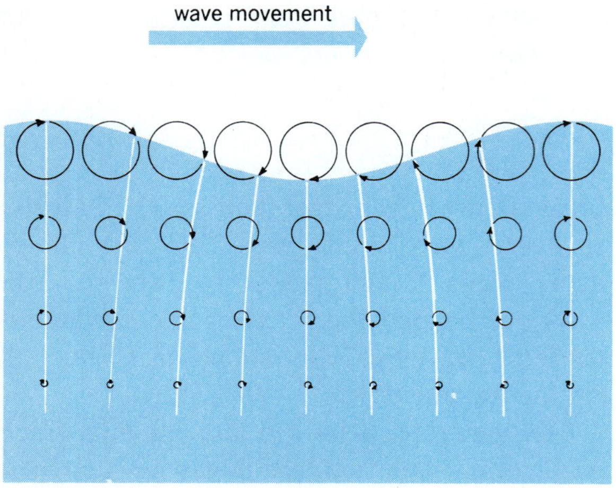

Tsunamis

Thus far, we have been discussing the speed of ocean waves. You may think that 160 kilometers (100 miles) an hour is rather fast for a wave to travel, but it's really slow compared with the velocity of the longest and most destructive waves in the ocean. These waves, remember, are called tsunamis. Tsunamis are produced by underwater landslides and earthquakes. Such waves used to be called tidal waves, but they have nothing to do with the tide. The tsunami is a series of waves, just like wind waves, but these waves have a period of 15 minutes to an hour or more. The velocities and wavelengths of tsunamis depend on the depth of the water.

In the Pacific Ocean, where they are most common, these waves have lengths of several hundred kilometers and may reach velocities of more than 1,000 kilometers (600 miles) per hour. If a tsunami resulted from an earthquake near the Aleutian Islands, the waves from it would spread over the entire Pacific Ocean.❷ They would reach Tokyo, Honolulu, and Vancouver Island, Canada, in $4\frac{1}{2}$ hours. They would reach Valparaiso, Chile, in $18\frac{1}{2}$ hours. If you live along the Pacific Ocean, how long would it take for the waves to reach your city?

Strangely enough, tsunami waves are only about 60 centimeters (2 feet) high as they move through the deep ocean. If you were in a ship, you wouldn't even notice the waves passing by. But when the waves get close to land, they may grow to a height of 30 meters (100 feet) or more. Such waves can destroy whole villages and cities near the coast. In 1896, a tsunami struck Japan and caused the loss of 10,000 homes and the death of 27,000 people. Fortunately, tsunamis do not occur very often. Only 36 tsunamis have been recorded in Hawaii over the past 127 years.

2

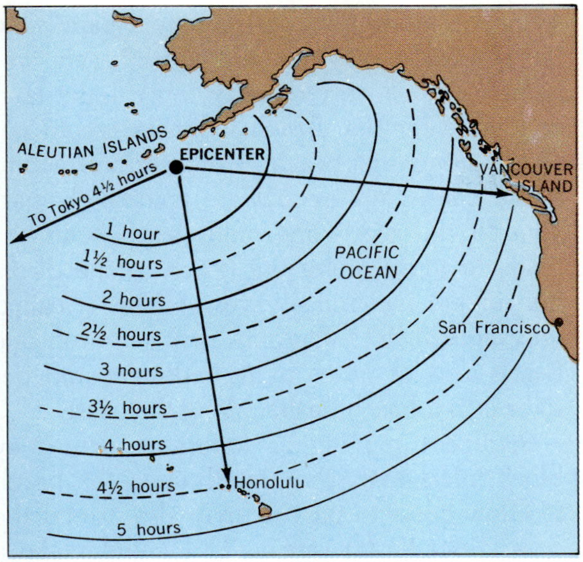

Now there is a warning system that alerts residents of coastal areas of the Pacific Ocean if a tsunami is heading their way. Because it is difficult to tell how high the waves will be when they reach a particular island or continental area, residents must always be prepared for the worst.

Breakers

Ordinary wind waves (just like waves from a tsunami) "peak up" when they are near the beach. As they continue toward a fairly steep shore, they may break as **plunging breakers** that collapse forward on themselves. 3 If the shore slopes gently, **spilling breakers** will probably form. These breakers, the favorites of surfers, begin rather far from the shore and travel for a considerable distance. Spilling breakers are marked by a continuous line of foam that spills forward from the crest of the wave. 4 If you live near the ocean, you have probably observed that waves of longer wavelengths break further offshore than those of shorter wavelengths.

Why do waves break? This is a question that has puzzled scientists for a long time. The problem is so complex that even the best mathematicians have failed to find an answer. One hypothesis goes like this: The orbital motion of the particles of an ideal wave ceases at a depth equal to one-half the wavelength. As the wave gets close to the beach, the water becomes shallower. The water particles can't go through their circular orbits because the water is too shallow. Their orbits become flatter. Close to shore, the orbits are so flat that the water particles in the crest simply cannot follow their orbits. Then the wave breaks.

3

4

Oceanographers used to think that friction with the sea bottom was the most important cause of breakers. They reasoned that friction along the bottom slowed the wave trough more than the wave crest. This caused the crest to move faster than the trough. In shallow water the crest would simply race ahead of the trough and collapse as a breaker. Oceanographers now like the orbit hypothesis better than the friction hypothesis. Perhaps there is a better explanation that no one has thought of yet. Perhaps you will be interested in becoming an oceanographer and doing research on the causes of breakers.

Harbors

Most of the world's population lives near a coast. Major cities like Boston, New York, New Orleans, San Francisco, and San Diego have grown very large because of their fine harbors. Ocean shipping is still the most important means of transporting goods between coastal cities and between continents. How many major cities can you think of that are not near the coast or that are not connected with the ocean by a lake or river? The import and export wealth of the world passes through our major harbors. But wave action can be a problem in harbors. This is especially true when waves from coastal storms and hurricanes enter the harbor and smash against ships and piers. Waves also tend to carry sand and other sediment into the mouths of harbors. This causes the harbors to fill up with sediment that may have to be removed. Let's see how this happens.

Waves often approach the beach at an angle to the main part of the coastline. When these waves enter shallow water, even before they break, the wave crests tend to bend and become parallel to the coastline. ❶ This change in direction of waves is called **refraction.** If refraction made the waves parallel to the beach, the waves would cause beach sediment to move only directly toward the land or toward the sea. Beach sediment would not move *along* the beach. However, refraction rarely causes waves that are completely parallel to the shore line, and beach sediment tends to move along the beach in the direction of the incoming waves. ❷ This is called **longshore drift.** Longshore drift may rob one beach area of much of its sediment and deliver it to a beach farther along the coast.

Sediment moving as longshore drift may block inlets that were cut through the beach to allow boats to pass. It may also extend the beach into harbor areas. This could make a harbor too shallow for boats. Most major harbors require constant dredging of ship channels so ships will not become stuck in the sediment that is being carried into the harbor.

Shifting Sand

The loss of beach sediment, called **beach erosion,** may also cause great financial loss for coastal resort cities. Summer bathers travel to resort cities that have the best beaches. To save its beaches and keep its bathers, the resort city may have sand trucked in from a nearby beach. Or it may hire a dredge to pump sand from the nearby continental shelf. In either case it costs hundreds of thousands of dollars to add sand to the beach.

The famous resort city of Miami Beach is an example of a city with this problem. For the last 30 years Miami Beach has lost enough sand each year to build a beach more than 30 meters (100 feet) wide for a length of 17 kilometers (10 miles) along the coast. To replace the eroded beach sand, it will be necessary to pump sand from off shore. Sand will have to be pumped onto the beach each year to replace what is constantly being lost.

1

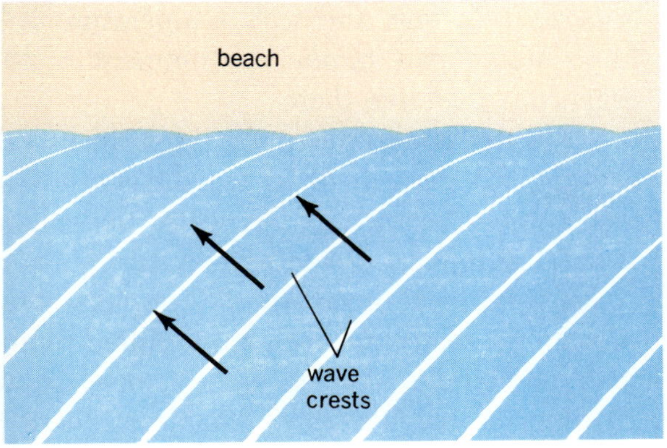

2

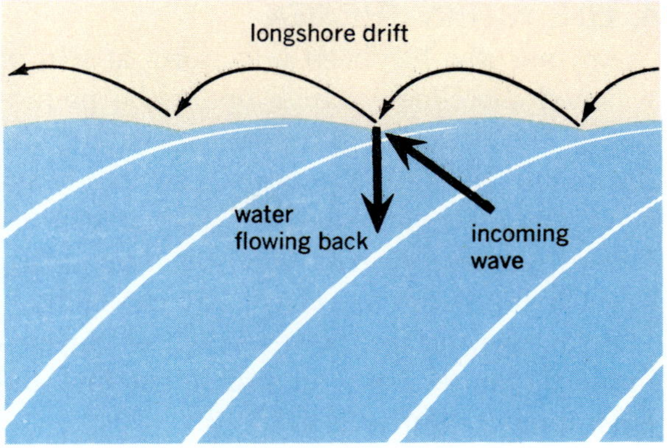

Engineers attempt to stop beach erosion and longshore drift by placing obstructions, called **groins**, in the path of moving sediment. 3 These groins are made of wooden pilings or are built of large piles of rock. They are only partly effective, however. They may stop a particular section of beach from eroding; but because sand is trapped behind the groin, beaches further along the coast will erode faster. Why? Along the stretch of beach protected by a groin, the waves do not pick up as much sediment as they can carry. Therefore, the waves can pick up more sediment as they move further along the beach. You can tell which way the sand is moving along a coast by looking at the groins. Sand builds up on the side of the groin from which the longshore drift is coming.

3

REVIEW

1. What are the three main things that determine the size of an ocean wave?
2. What are the differences between wind waves and tsunami waves?
3. Describe the properties of water waves. How can you determine the velocity of a wave?
4. What changes take place in a wave as it moves into shallow water?
5. Explain why longshore drift of sediment takes place.
6. How do engineers prevent beach erosion?

NEW VIEW

1. The gold, diamonds, iron sands, and tin sands of beaches and continental shelves all have fairly high density. How might this property be used to separate them from sand and gravel?
2. *Breakwaters* are often used to enclose harbor areas. How do they affect wave action and the movement of sediment along the coast?
3. In 1970, newspapers reported that a gigantic "tidal wave" resulting from a cyclone killed thousands and thousands of people in Pakistan. Why was the report technically incorrect?

4. LIFE WITHIN THE SEA

Anyone who has been in a storm at sea, or watched shorelines change under the pounding of the ocean might object to having the sea called "stable." The sea's currents always keep its surface in slow but constant motion. Where surface currents flow, conditions that affect living things are constantly changing.

Below the surface, however, where currents move far more slowly, a fish might find the environment relatively stable.

The Stable Sea

In the main, heat from the sun determines the temperature of the sea. At the equator the average temperature at the surface of the sea is about 26°C, at the polar regions about −2°C. (The freezing point of pure water is 0°C; dissolved salts lower this to about −2°C for sea water.) Water at the bottom of the sea is nearly the same temperature everywhere: about 1°C. In any given region, over a period of time, the sea's temperature is a fairly stable part of the environment of the organisms that live there.

Sea water is also generally stable in its salt content; 3.5 percent of its weight is salt. For four cubic kilometers of sea water this means about 150 million metric tons of salt.

Sea water contains many different dissolved substances, many of which are required by the sea's inhabitants. Water can dissolve about 20 times as much carbon dioxide as there is in the atmosphere. The green plants of the sea depend on this supply of carbon dioxide.

Does relatively warm water dissolve more or less gas than cold water? The solubility of a solid is usually increased when the temperature rises. Is this true for gases? The solubility of gases generally increases as the temperature decreases.

The density of sea water remains fairly stable as well. And at any given depth the pressure within the sea is fairly stable.

1

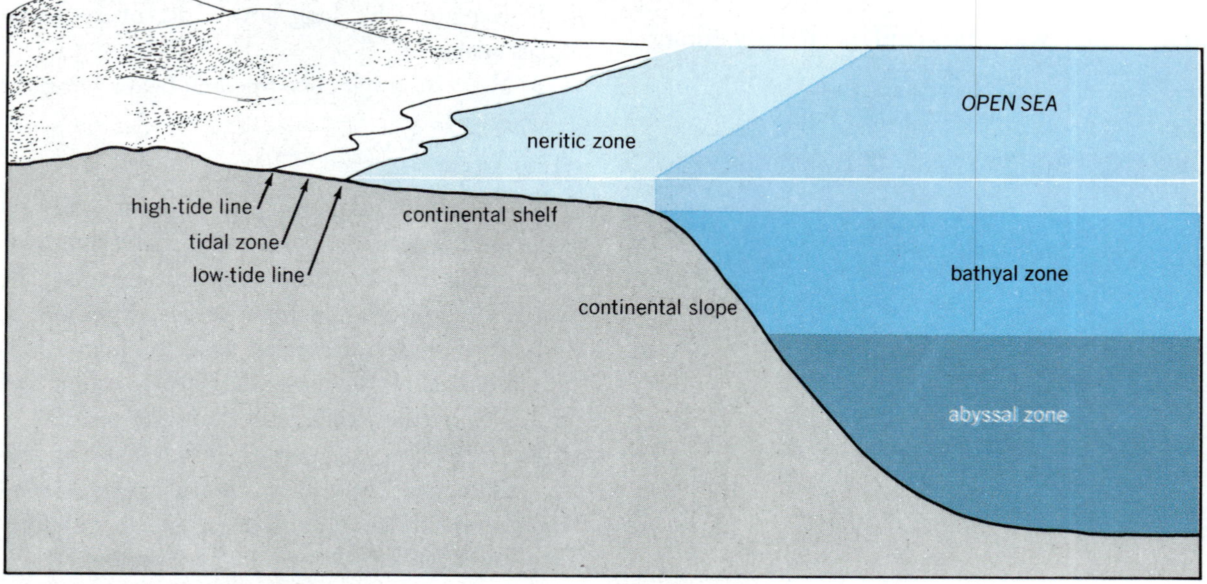

2

3

Life Zones Within the Sea

If you could walk from shore down the continental shelf into the deeps, you would find yourself passing through several *life zones,* each with characteristics that make it a special environment.

Tides, currents, waves, winds, temperature, salinity, evaporation, and pressure vary from one zone to another. In a particular zone, some of these factors may be more important than others for the organisms living there.

The Tidal Zone: Between the low-tide line and the high-tide line is the **tidal zone.** 1 Think of how waves pound the shore, and tides come and go. It is easy to understand why life in the tidal zone is difficult. To keep from being washed out to sea, tidal-zone organisms must be firmly attached, as are certain sea plants and barnacles, or they must live a life partly in burrows, like fiddler crabs and razor clams. 2

The Neritic Zone: From the lowest tide line to the outer edge of the continental shelf is the **neritic zone.** Sunlight penetrates this zone, and the temperature is fairly even. The result is that probably more living things are to be found in a cubic meter of this zone than in any other place on earth. Protozoa, sponges, jellyfish, starfish, clams, crabs, lobsters, snails, and fish abound in the neritic zone. 3 Algae (seaweeds) carpet the bottom. Captain Cousteau's oceanauts had many fascinating adventures in the neritic zone. Life in the shallow inland seas of past geologic ages, it is thought by some scientists, must have occurred under conditions similar to those in the neritic zone.

The Open Sea: If you continued beyond the continental shelf, you would reach the great open sea—the sea of the adventurous sailor, of the whale, and of the huge schools of fish. Some of the life in the open sea floats on the

1

2

surface. There floating life forms are known as **plankton;** they consist mainly of algae, including the diatoms. (1) The quantity of plankton in the sea is immense. Some scientists think that if the plankton were harvested, dried, and turned into a kind of plankton flour, it could help form the food supply of the world.

In the open sea are also the free-swimming life forms of the ocean. These are mainly fish, but include several of the mammals of the sea—the porpoises and the whales.

The Bathyal Zone: In the open sea beyond the continental shelf and between the depths of 180 and 1,800 meters (600 and 6,000 feet) is the **bathyal zone** (see p. 260). The animal population of this zone is quite large, but the plant life is limited to the upper regions, where sunlight penetrates. The animals that live on the bottom of the bathyal zone get their food from dead or dying animals that fall to the bottom. The bottom is covered with a sediment, some of which is **siliceous,** that is, it is made up of silicates. These sediments include the remains of diatoms (algae with shells containing silicates), *Radiolaria,* and the spines of some kinds of sponges. (2)

The cells of organisms of many kinds, plant and animal, not only make living matter from the materials they take in; they also produce various kinds of non-living matter. Plant cells on land, for instance, produce the fibers that make up the woody material in trees. The cotton plant produces these fibers, and we call them cotton.

Similarly, the different kinds of organisms in the sea that make up siliceous sediments have variously shaped spines and shells, all made of silicates. Most of the sediments, however, are not siliceous but **calcareous,** that is, made up of calcium compounds. What animals produce the calcareous sediments?

3

4

Suppose you pour some dilute hydrochloric acid on a bit of the shell of a clam, snail, or oyster. If you collect the gas that bubbles off and test it with limewater, you will observe that a white precipitate forms. From your earlier work with rocks and minerals, you know that this means the shell contains calcium carbonate. Try the same test on such animals as sea urchins and starfish, and the result will be positive. There are, then, a variety of sea animals that add to the calcareous sediment on the sea bottom when their dead bodies reach the floor of the bathyal zone. All this accumulation of sediments, both siliceous and calcareous, is a process that builds land in the bottom of the sea. A more active kind of land building is carried on by living organisms that produce calcareous materials, however. These organisms are the corals, as you shall shortly see. First, let's take an excursion into the sea's deepest life zone.

The Abyssal Zone: Below a depth of 1,800 meters (6,000 feet) is the **abyssal zone,** which has no sunlight. The temperatures in the abyssal zone are nearly freezing; the pressure is greater than one ton on 6 square centimeters. The weight of water overhead produces this tremendous pressure. Yet there is life in the abyssal zone. The animals that live in this incredible environment are highly specialized to withstand the pressure. 3 They depend on the food that settles from the waters near the surface.

Coral Lands

Perhaps you have seen a coral shell with many tiny holes. In each hole once lived a coral animal whose outer body cells deposited calcium carbonate in the shell. 4 Since corals live in colonies, many of their shells grow together and may eventually build rocky land formations known as **coral reefs.**

1

2

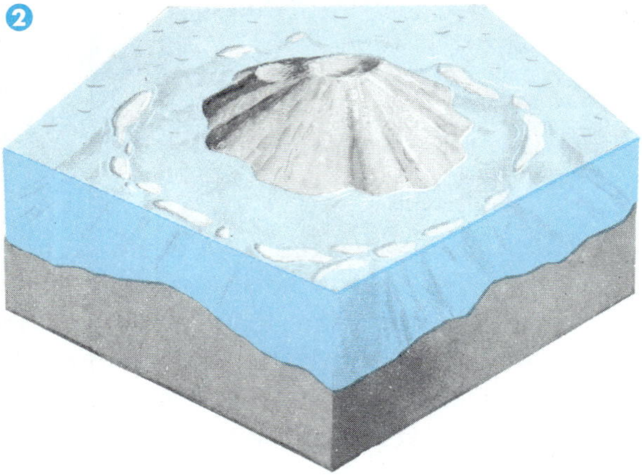

3

The coral reef animals thrive in clear tropical sea water where the temperature is 20°C or above. Waves that aerate the water and bring food, including an abundant supply of calcium salts, also favor the growth of corals.

A coral reef built along the shore of a continent or an island is a **fringing reef.** The fringing reef in this drawing surrounds a volcanic island in a tropical sea. ①

Another kind of coral reef is separated from the land by a shallow channel or *lagoon.* This is known as a **barrier reef.** ② An **atoll** is a ring-shaped reef and completely surrounds a lagoon. ③ Does the appearance of these three kinds of reefs suggest a way in which they may be related to one another?

Charles Darwin, the famous biologist, examined coral reefs of all three kinds and proposed a theory that they are related. What Darwin suggested was that a volcanic island surrounded by a fringing reef might sink. But the organisms in the reef continue to live and grow, so that the reef—now a barrier reef—remains above the surface as the island begins to submerge. Eventually the island disappears below the level of the sea, while the corals grow high enough to remain above water, forming an atoll reef.

Although they are called coral reefs, and the coral animals do help build them, the major calcareous portions of some reefs may be built by plants—the algae. On the coral island of Tinnafute, in the South Pacific, the algae seemed to have formed more of the rock than all the animals combined.

The sea is a marine environment in which plants and animals have a home. The marine environment, like the terrestrial environment, is a place where organisms interact with their surroundings. Organisms everywhere help produce different forms of matter and cause changes in those forms.

REVIEW

1. Distinguish between the tidal zone and the neritic zone.

2. A boy collected some barnacles. In which zone was he?

3. A huge amount of plankton was collected in a fine net. In which zone of the sea was the collection made?

4. Distinguish among fringing reefs, barrier reefs, and atolls. How are they similar?

NEW VIEW

1. Organisms are interdependent with their environment. How is this true of the organisms living in the abyssal zone?

2. In what ways is the hydrosphere similar to the atmosphere?

5. RELATING THE CONCEPTS

Stand on the shore of the ocean, with its waves and currents and tides, and you are likely to be impressed by its constant activity. Think of the multitude of living things that inhabit the sea—moving, reproducing, feeding—and the sea seems even more restless.

This restless sea does more than furnish an evironment for marine life. As one of our planet's great reservoirs of water, the ocean vitally influences the climate and weather that help determine the environment of living things, including ourselves, on the land.

Reviewing the Concepts

► *The floor of the ocean has contours much like those of the dry land.* Probing the solid earth beneath the sea with sound waves, men have begun to map the ocean floor. The structures that they have found—plains and trenches, mountains, and canyons—are strikingly similar to those of the earth's dry lands.

► *Prevailing winds, land masses, and the earth's rotation affect the paths of surface currents in the ocean.* Winds are the main driving force behind the ocean's horizontal surface currents. Thus, the directions in which the prevailing winds generally blow largely determine the directions of the currents they set up in the water. But the paths of these currents are modified by the motion of the earth as it rotates on its axis, and wherever the sea encounters a land mass there is further modification of the currents.

► *Temperature and salinity affect vertical ocean currents.* Warm water is less dense than cold water. Water with low salinity (saltiness) is less dense than water with high salinity. And water that is more dense than the surrounding water tends to sink, while water that is less dense tends to rise. Therefore a vertical current may be produced when masses of water of different densities come in contact with one another. For example, when relatively light warm water from the tropics comes in contact with relatively heavy cold water from arctic regions, the lighter water may rise and the heavier water may sink, thus creating a current.

► *Organisms that live in the sea are adapted to and interdependent with their environment.* The sea is, in a sense, a collection of several different environments for living things. Each of the sea's life zones—the tidal, the neritic, the pelagic, the bathyal, and the abyssal—has its own special characteristics. Living things in the ocean, as on the land, are not only affected by, but also affect, the forms and changes of matter in their surroundings. We see an example of this interaction in a coral reef—a form of land that is itself produced by the life processes of organisms that live within it.

▶ *Winds and underwater earthquakes cause ocean waves that affect the coastal zone.* Winds blowing over the ocean generate waves that travel at speeds up to 160 kilometers (100 miles) per hour. Underwater earthquakes produce tsunami waves that travel at speeds up to about 1,000 kilometers (600 miles) per hour. Wind waves cause damage to beaches and harbors, but the much larger tsunami waves can destroy whole towns along the coast.

Testing Yourself

1. What proportion of the earth's crust is covered by water?

2. Describe some important features of the sea bottom that you might encounter during an imaginary walk across the floor of the Atlantic Ocean.

3. Explain how particles of ocean water move as simple waves pass by.

4. Why do waves break?

5. What is the result of wave refraction?

6. How does longshore drift affect a beach?

7. What do oceanauts and aquanauts do, and why is it important?

8. Describe and explain what wind does to the sea.

9. What are prevailing winds? How are they related to sea currents?

10. Why doesn't an equatorial drift flow in the same direction as a prevailing wind?

11. What are two causes of different densities in water? How can different water densities cause currents?

12. How is it that we can divide the sea into life zones? Give some examples of life zones in your answer.

13. Why don't the living things in the sea move from zone to zone?

Extending the Concepts

Investigation 1. Can you design an investigation to determine how much gas is dissolved in a certain amount of water? Here is a clue: if you can drive off the dissolved gases, they may be collected by downward displacement. Can you think of a way to drive out the gases? If so, try comparing sea water, drinking water, and pond water, for example, for their content of dissolved gases. First try predicting what the results will be.

Investigation 2. Compare the salt content of drinking water, pond water, and (if you can get it) sea water. If 1 ml of a 1 percent solution of silver nitrate ($AgNO_3$) dissolved in distilled water is added to 20 ml of the liquid you want to test, the chlorides or salts in the liquid will be precipitated. Use narrow test tubes and measure the amount of precipitated chlorides with a ruler.

Suggested Reading

Carson, Rachel L., *The Sea Around Us,* New York, Oxford, 1961. A scientific account of the oceans written in an enjoyable, literary style.

Engel, Leonard, and the editors of LIFE, *The Sea* (Life Nature Library), Time Inc., 1969. A picture story of currents, tides, the earth beneath the sea, and the sea's life forms.

Linklater, Eric, *The Voyage of the Challenger,* New York, Doubleday, 1972. Share the trials and the excitement of this historic voyage of discovery.

Sweeney, James, *A Pictorial History of Oceanographic Submersibles,* New York, Crown, 1970. A fascinating account of the vessels that have explored beneath the surface of the seas.

13

The Changing Atmosphere

When we think of the earth's hydrosphere, we usually think of the sea that covers three fourths of the globe. But then, of course, there is the water in the world's lakes, rivers, streams, and glaciers; and there is also the water that has soaked into the soil and the rock of the earth's lithosphere. However, there is another part of the hydrosphere that is small in amount but of great importance to us—the water that is mixed with the earth's atmosphere. Life would not be possible without this water in the air, so we take a great interest in it. Much of this water in the atmosphere is in the form of water vapor.

1. WATER VAPOR IN THE ATMOSPHERE

Water vapor—the gaseous state of that kind of matter we call water—is a tasteless, colorless, and odorless gas. There is certainly some water vapor in the air around you now. In fact, you yourself are a source of water vapor. For example, there is a water vapor in your breath. The water in your perspiration is also evaporating into the air. How can we show that this invisible gas is in the air? Here is some chemical evidence for the presence of water vapor.

Cobalt chloride is an unusual compound that changes from blue to pink in the presence of water, whether the water is a liquid or a vapor. A piece of paper containing the compound is called cobalt chloride paper. Blue cobalt chloride paper exposed to air containing a fairly large amount of water vapor turns pink as the cobalt chloride reacts with the water. What the chemist calls hydrated cobalt chloride—a pink substance—is formed. You may find it helpful to examine the equation for the chemical change that occurs.

$$\underset{\text{(blue)}}{\text{cobalt chloride}} + \text{water} \longrightarrow \underset{\text{(pink)}}{\text{hydrated cobalt chloride}}$$

If the air becomes dry, water leaves the cobalt chloride and the paper changes from pink to blue. The pink hydrated cobalt chloride becomes blue as it loses its water.

$$\underset{\text{(pink)}}{\text{hydrated cobalt chloride}} \longrightarrow \underset{\text{(blue)}}{\text{cobalt chloride}} + \text{water}$$

Thus the color change of cobalt chloride, as it reacts with water vapor, indicates the presence of invisible water vapor in the air. Now see this chemical evidence for yourself in the investigation on the next page. ■

■ AN APPRENTICE INVESTIGATION into a Color Test for Water

❶

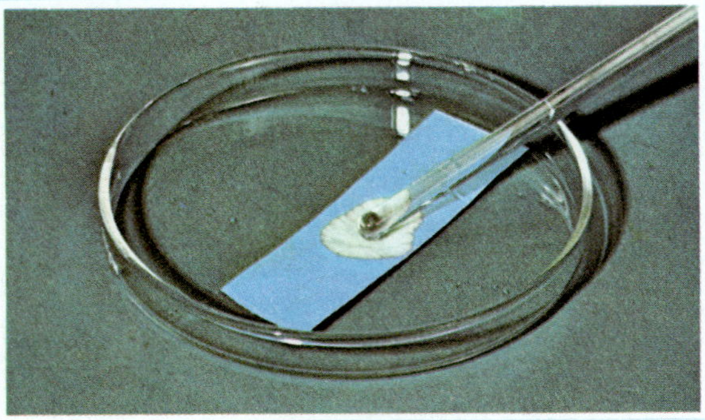

❷

Dissolve about 10 grams of cobalt chloride in 100 ml of water. Soak a strip of filter paper in the solution, then set the wet paper in a warm place to dry. Notice how the paper changes color as it dries.

Place a drop of water on the dry strip. What happens to the color of the paper? Here is what happened in one trial.❶

Will water vapor affect the paper in the same way as liquid water? Place a closed jar with a little water in the bottom in a warm place for several hours. The air in the jar will then be well supplied with water vapor. Place a strip of dry cobalt chloride paper in the air in the jar, do not let the strip touch any liquid water, and cover the jar again. Does the paper change color? Here is what happened in one trial.❷ Does the water vapor in the jar affect the paper?

An Investigation On Your Own

Expose a strip of the dry filter paper to the air in your room for several days. Are any color changes observed? Explain what happens.

There is more evidence of the presence of water vapor in the air around you that also provides a way of determining *how much* water vapor the air is holding. Let's observe how water vapor in the air can be made to condense—that is, become liquid. Then you can make use of this phenomenon to determine how much water there is in the air. Try the investigation on the next page.■

When the side of the can has cooled to a certain temperature, water appears on it. This water comes from the air around the can, as the water vapor in the air surrounding the can changes to a liquid. Why does the water change its state? The water vapor touching the side of the can is cooled by the ice water inside the can. And when water vapor is cooled enough, it condenses to liquid water.

As you can see, the water vapor in the air condenses on the can at a certain temperature. This temperature is called the **dew point**—the temperature to which air must be

■ AN APPRENTICE INVESTIGATION into Water from the Air

Half fill a small, shiny can with lukewarm water. Use a thermometer to take the temperature of the air near the can. Record the air temperature. Here is the reading obtained during one trial. ❶

Put the thermometer in the water in the can, add some ice to the water, and stir with a rod. As the temperature of the water goes down, watch for the appearance of a thin film of water on the shiny surface of the can. The film will dull the shiny surface. ❷ As soon as the film begins to form, read the temperature. This reading was obtained during one trial. ❸

Where does the film of water come from?

An Investigation On Your Own

Try this procedure every day for a week. Do the results vary? Why?

❶

❸

❷

cooled for water vapor in it to condense. In the trial shown in the investigation, for instance, the dew point is 2°C. The air around the can had to be cooled to this temperature to condense its water vapor.

Does this definition of dew point give you a clue to how dew is formed? If the ground is cool enough, the air next to the ground may be cooled to its dew point. Then water vapor in the air will condense on grass and leaves.

The dew point you obtained in your trial was probably different from the dew point obtained above. If you repeat the procedure for finding the dew point daily, for a few days, you will very likely find that the dew point varies from day to day. Let's see why.

Humidity

"It isn't the heat, it's the humidity," you've heard people say to explain how uncomfortable they feel on a hot, sticky summer's day. Probably most people who use the word have only a vague idea of what it means, but for scientists the word *humidity* has a definite meaning. Humidity is the amount of water vapor in the air. You know from experience that the humidity can vary. Let's examine how this may happen.

Imagine that you have before you a large glass box in the shape of a cube, one meter long on each side. Inside the box is completely dry air, containing no water vapor, and a thermometer by which the temperature of the air can be read. There is a device for heating the air in the box, which you can control, and a kind of spray by which water can be added to the air in the box.

Suppose that the cubic meter of air in the box is at a temperature of 20°C. If you add a little water to the air, the water disappears —it evaporates and becomes water vapor. You add more water to the air, it also becomes invisible water vapor. But this does not go on indefinitely. You find that at a certain point the water added to the air ceases to evaporate. The air is holding all the water vapor it can. For a cubic meter of air at 20°C, in fact, the limit is 18.2 grams of water vapor. At this point, when the air is holding all the water vapor it can, the air is said to be **saturated.** A cubic meter of air at 20°C can hold any amount of water vapor up to 18.2 grams, at which point the air is saturated.

What will happen to the amount of water vapor that a cubic meter of air can hold if the temperature of the air is raised? Put a fresh batch of dry air in the imaginary glass box and raise the temperature to 28°C. Add water to the air. You will find that the air will hold *more* water vapor at a higher temperature. Air at 28°C becomes saturated when it contains 25.0 grams of water vapor per cubic meter.

As you might now expect, if the temperature of air is lowered, the air can hold *less* water vapor. Air at 4°C, for instance, can hold only 6.4 grams of water vapor in a cubic meter. To give you an idea of how the amounts vary, the table on page 271 shows how much water vapor is present in saturated air at different temperatures. The colored bands in the table mark the examples we have already mentioned and those we shall mention as we continue.

We have been speaking of saturated air. Usually, however, the air around us is not saturated—it is not holding as much water vapor as it can. A way has been devised to describe this situation in numbers—which, as you know, scientists have a fondness for. Actually you are quite familiar with this measurement: you hear it in weather reports every day.

WATER VAPOR IN SATURATED AIR

Temperature °C	*Grams of water vapor per cubic meter of air*
−3	3.7
−2	4.0
−1	4.4
0	4.8
1	5.2
2	6.0
4	6.4
6	7.5
8	8.1
10	9.3
12	10.7
14	11.4
16	13.0
18	16.0
20	18.2
22	19.4
24	22.0
26	23.5
28	25.0
30	30.0
32	34.0

Suppose, for instance, that the temperature of the air around you is 18°C. How much water vapor can air hold at this temperature? A glance at the table will show you that saturated air can hold 16.0 grams of water vapor per cubic meter at 18°C. But suppose that the air around you is not saturated. Suppose it contains only 8.0 grams of water vapor per cubic meter. Then the air holds only half, or 50 percent, of the water vapor that it could hold at this temperature.

Scientists have a label for this ratio. It is called **relative humidity,** the ratio of the amount of water vapor in the air to the amount that the air could hold at that temperature. Relative humidity is usually given in percent. If the relative humidity of the air around you now is 25 percent, then the air is holding 25 percent of the water vapor that it could hold at that temperature.

If the relative humidity is 100 percent, then the air is holding all the water vapor it can, and is saturated. Oddly enough, this does not happen very often. Even when it is raining the relative humidity is likely to be less than 100 percent.

This formula is helpful for calculating relative humidity.

$$\text{relative humidity} = \frac{\text{amount of water vapor present}}{\text{amount of water vapor for saturation}} \times 100$$

Let's try the formula on an example. If the temperature of the air is 22°C, and the air contains 9.7 grams of water vapor per cubic meter, what is the relative humidity? The table shows that air at 22°C can hold 19.4 grams of water vapor per cubic meter. Substituting the values in the formula, we get:

$$\begin{aligned}\text{relative humidity} &= \frac{9.7 \text{ grams}}{19.4 \text{ grams}} \times 100 \\ &= \tfrac{1}{2} \times 100 \\ &= 50 \text{ percent}\end{aligned}$$

Calculating the relative humidity, then, isn't a very complicated operation.

You may, however, be wondering about one thing: How is the amount of water actually in the air determined? To catch and count the water vapor molecules in a cubic

1

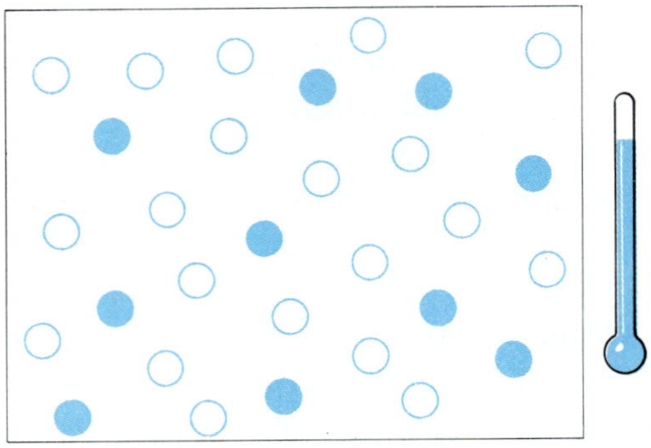

2

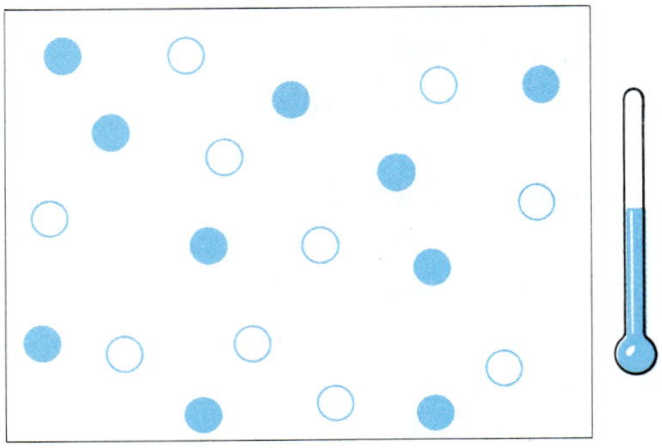

3

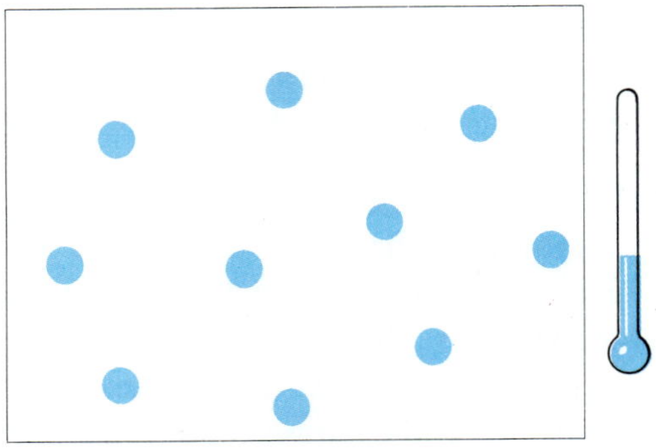

4

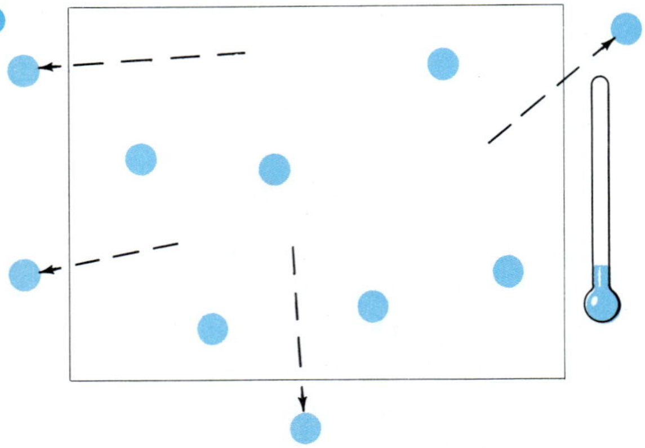

meter of air sounds like a job for an elaborate and expensive instrument. It can be done, though, with the shiny tin can and the other materials that you used in the dew-point investigation.

Dew Point and Relative Humidity

When the can cools to a certain temperature, you recall, water vapor in the air around the can condenses on the can. The temperature at which this takes place is the dew point. Now let's carry the analysis a little farther. Let's ask *why* the water vapor condenses as the air is cooled.

The air around the can contains water vapor but is not saturated—is not holding all the water vapor it can hold. Let's represent the water vapor present by solid blue dots, and the additional amount of water vapor that the air could hold (at this temperature) by blue circles. 1

What will happen if the air is cooled a little? The water vapor in the air is not affected. What is affected is the amount of water vapor that the air can hold. As the temperature decreases, the amount of water vapor that the air can hold decreases. 2 Notice that as the temperature goes down, the relative humidity increases, for the ratio of the amount of water vapor in the air to the amount that the air could hold is increasing.

What happens if the cooling is continued? The amount of water vapor that the air can hold continues to decrease, while the amount of water vapor in the air remains constant. Therefore, the ratio of these amounts, the relative humidity, increases.

A point is reached at which the amount of water vapor in the air is equal to the amount that the air can hold at that temperature. The air is saturated. The relative humidity is 100 percent. 3

What happens now if the cooling is continued? The amount of water vapor that the air can hold decreases further. Since there is more water vapor present than the air can hold at this temperature, the surplus water vapor returns to the liquid state, or condenses.❹ The temperature at which this condensation takes place is the dew point.

In the trial shown in the investigation, the dew point was 2°C. At this temperature the air next to the can was saturated with water vapor. How much water vapor is there in saturated air at 2°C? According to the table on page 271, 6.0 grams per cubic meter. This, then, is the amount of water vapor present in the air before the air was cooled. In the same trial, the temperature of the air was 20°C. At this temperature, according to the table on page 271, 18.2 grams of water vapor are needed for saturation. By using the formula we can now obtain the relative humidity at the time of the investigation.

$$\text{relative humidity} = \frac{\text{amount of water vapor present}}{\text{amount of water vapor for saturation}} \times 100$$

$$\begin{aligned}\text{relative humidity} &= \frac{6.0 \text{ grams}}{18.2 \text{ grams}} \times 100 \\ &= 0.329 \times 100 \\ &= 32.9 \text{ percent}\end{aligned}$$

To be able to calculate the relative humidity, we had to determine the air's temperature and its water vapor content. The water vapor content was read from a table after determining the dew point. These two quantities, the temperature of the air and the temperature at the dew point, vary from time to time and from place to place. They are examples of what scientists call **variables.** Variables are quantities or characteristics that change as the conditions upon which they depend change.

Using the procedure for finding dew point shown in the investigation, you can determine relative humidity. Do so on different days or at different times, when you think that the variables, air temperature and dew point, have changed. The matter in the air, like all matter in our world, is constantly changing.

REVIEW

1. A certain kind of "weather forecaster" is a doll with a blue skirt. When the air is very humid the doll's skirt turns pink. Suggest an explanation.

2. Why is the percentage of water vapor in the air in the Congo often 10 times as high as it is in the air in Alaska?

3. A solution may be saturated with a solute. How is this similar to the saturation of air by water?

4. Suppose the air is 24°C and the dew point is 2°C. Find the relative humidity.

5. What is a variable? Give examples.

NEW VIEW

1. Suppose the relative humidity is 50%. How much water vapor does the air contain if the temperature is 10°C? If the temperature is 30°C? If the temperature is —4°C?

2. Why are summer days in most parts of the United States usually more humid than winter days? In what areas are summer days very dry? Why? Find out why hot, dry days are more comfortable than hot, humid days.

3. Cobalt chloride is a compound that sometimes has water of hydration. What is water of hydration? How was it part of the investigation you did on page 268? (You may also wish to consult a chemistry text.)

4. What are some variables in the consideration of whether a solute will or will not precipitate from a solution?

1 

2 

3 

4 

2. PRECIPITATION

On a cold winter's day you can see your breath. In the cool of a summer morning the grass is wet with dew. A mist forms at the spout of a boiling kettle. A cloud drifts in the sky, a fog hugs the ground. All of these things are the result of the condensation of water vapor from the air, of water changing from the gaseous state to the liquid state. The matter that makes up a cloud (or a fog, or the mist in front of the kettle spout) consists of tiny droplets of liquid water in the air.

Everyone knows that it is the water in clouds that makes rain, snow, sleet, and hail —that is, **precipitation,** the depositing of moisture from the atmosphere on the surface of the earth. How do the clouds form?

Clouds

Look at the sky. Do you see any interesting cloud shapes? How do you think these clouds were formed?

If you have ever taken a walk on a foggy day, you have walked right *through* a cloud. A fog is a cloud that forms on the ground. This is how clouds are started. A mass of air over a body of water carries a large amount of water vapor. When this air moves over the warmer land, the temperature of the air is raised. Warmer air expands and rises. The higher the air rises, the *cooler* it becomes. (You will learn more about this process in the next section.) When the air is below its dew point, the excess water vapor condenses into tiny droplets of water. We see a cloud when large numbers of these droplets come together.

There are three main types of clouds. Highest in the sky are thin, feathery **cirrus** clouds. 1 These are often called "mare's tails." Below the cirrus form low, uniform sheets called **stratus** clouds.❷ Lower still are **cumulus** clouds, thick, fleecy masses.❸ Different cloud shapes are described by adding the prefix *alto* (high) and the word *nimbus* (rain cloud) to these terms. Cumulonimbus clouds bring heavy rain and often thunder and lightning.❹ You may already know them as "thunderheads."

Nuclei for Droplets

But what makes the droplets form? You might expect the answer to be simply that water vapor is cooled to the dew point and condenses to form tiny droplets of water. Surprisingly, however, it turns out that there is more to it than that.

As you know, the lower the temperature of air, the less water vapor it can hold. Lower its temperature by 8°C (18°F), for instance, and the air's water vapor capacity at saturation is roughly halved. The cooling of air until it is saturated with water vapor is the main cause of condensation and the formation of the droplets that make up a cloud. But something more than cooling is usually needed. The air must contain very tiny particles of matter—solid or liquid. It is on these particles that condensation takes place and droplets form. The particles are **condensation nuclei.**

If there are no condensation nuclei present, water vapor must be cooled far below its dew point before it will condense. There is no shortage of condensation nuclei in the air, however—1 cubic centimeter of air may contain from 1,000 to 10,000 particles. Their sizes vary. Some are microscopic, some can be seen without a microscope. You may have observed such particles drifting in a beam of light in a dark room. Smoking chimneys, for instance, add to the air vast quantities of solid smoke particles which can serve as condensation nuclei. Jet planes distribute particles at high altitudes while burning fuel.

Tiny droplets of water, formed by condensation of water vapor on nuclei, can form a cloud. (If this condensation happens at the earth's surface, a fog is formed.) A cloud must form before precipitation can take place, but a cloud does not necessarily produce precipitation.

It takes about a million cloud droplets to make a raindrop. Somehow, then, about a million droplets must combine, to make one raindrop. How do they do it? Scientists are not completely sure, but there is at least one explanation that seems to be supported by a good deal of evidence.

Droplets to Drops

In the upper region of a cloud the temperature may be well below the freezing point of water. Yet the cloud droplets there may remain liquid. Just as water vapor needs condensation nuclei to condense on, liquid water droplets need **freezing nuclei** to form ice on. Ice crystals made from the water of cloud droplets form around the freezing nuclei.

Ice crystals and water droplets cannot exist together. The ice crystals grow at the expense of the water droplets. As the crystals grow, they become heavier, and fall. When a falling crystal touches a droplet, the droplet freezes to the crystal. Droplets merge with falling crystals, but as the crystals descend the temperature rises. The crystals melt and become raindrops. But there are times when the temperature of the air through which the ice crystals fall is so low that they do not melt. Then, as you expect, there is snow.

Sometimes, however, rain falls from clouds that are too warm to have any ice particles in them. How do the droplets become drops in this case? Cloud droplets have different sizes, since their condensation nuclei have different sizes. As large droplets fall, they collide with small ones and collect their water. The bigger they get, the more droplets they collide with, and the faster they grow.

The drops may become so large, in fact, that they break apart. The falling parts grow by colliding with more droplets. A chain reaction is set going, resulting in rain. [1]

Among the condensation nuclei in the air are particles of salt, which seem to be especially effective. Where do these specks of salt come from? The evidence points to the sea. Salt does not evaporate from the sea, however, as water does. How can salt crystals get into the air, then? It seems likely that waves start the process. Bursting bubbles in whitecaps propel small droplets of sea water into the air. The water of these little droplets quickly evaporates, leaving the salt in the air. The wind does the rest: it sweeps the salt high into the atmosphere. Winds arriving over land from the sea may bring salt nuclei to aid in rain-making, and the sea's salt may fall with rain far inland.

[1]

Moving Water

Wherever we find water, we find change. If we consider the role of water in all the changes the earth undergoes from day to day, as well as during long periods of time, we can appreciate the importance of the movement of water in our environment. This all-important movement has three main phases.

1. *Evaporation* from the oceans, lakes, streams, snow-covered fields, glaciers, and the leaves of plants.
2. *Condensation* from the vapor state in the air into clouds, dew, frost, and fog.
3. *Precipitation* from clouds as snowflakes and raindrops, in which freezing and melting, from water to ice and from ice to water, is involved.

This endless, recurring movement of water is called the **hydrologic cycle.**

Water works in other ways. Evaporation from the ocean tends to raise its salt content and lower its temperature, creating conditions that contribute to water movement as ocean currents. Again, water flows from mountains to sea, carrying with it (by erosion over million of years) the very mountains themselves, to make sedimentary rock. Water in the form of the ice in flowing glaciers also does its share of shaping the earth.

Finally, think of how our daily weather involves the movement of water in the atmosphere. Air masses of different pressures, temperatures, and relative humidities bring us different amounts of water. Whether or not condensation and precipitation take place depends on *all* parts of the hydrologic cycle. For to have water vapor in the air there must be evaporation from the earth's supplies of water in the liquid (and sometimes solid) state.

All this—and more—is summed up in the hydrologic cycle. ❷ In studying the diagram, begin with the sea and think of it as the earth's largest reservoir of water. (The diagram is designed to relate the ocean to the other reservoirs of water in the atmosphere and on the land.) Compare the air ocean, the "atmospheric sponge," with the water ocean. The atmosphere, too, holds water, as vapor and as droplets and drops of liquid. On land, snow and glaciers hold water; rivers, lakes, and underground reservoirs of porous rock also hold water.

The hydrologic cycle reminds us that a tremendous amount of matter (water) and energy (especially for change of state) is bound up in this sequence of change. There was a time when we could unthinkingly use up water or dump wastes into it, for the supply of water seemed endless. That time has passed, and now we have to understand how the system of matter and energy described in the hydrologic cycle works. And since our need for water is growing at a tremendous rate, our need to understand the proper conservation of water grows too. What can threaten our supply of water? What can each of us do to conserve water?

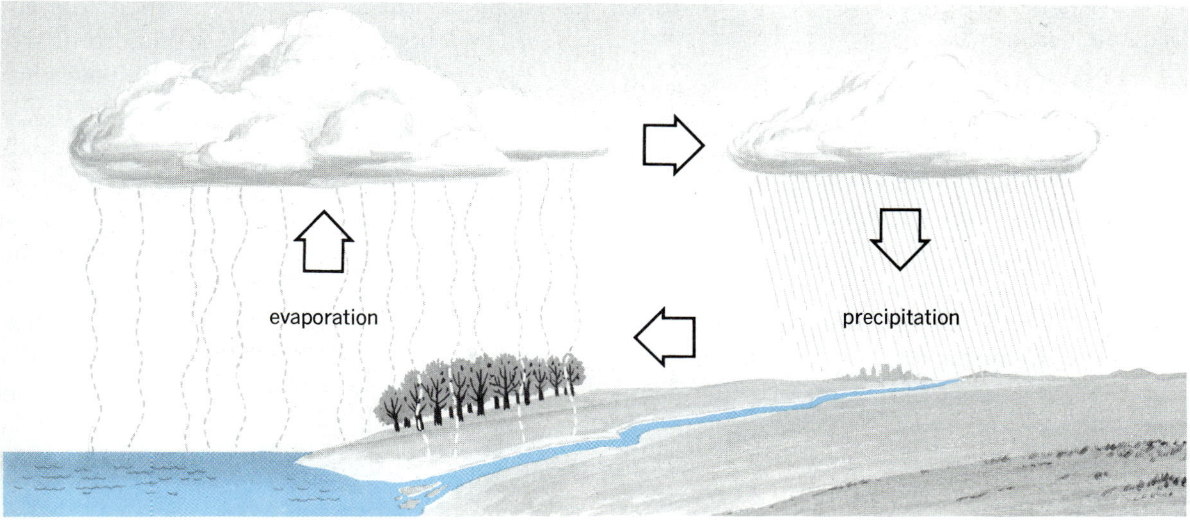

❷

As it rains, or as water falls to the surface of the earth as snow, sleet, or hail, water that had entered the great reservoir of the atmosphere by evaporation, returns to the great reservoir of the earth's surface by precipitation. The movement of water through the cycle of evaporation, condensation, and then precipitation is one more example of the unceasing interaction of matter and energy that makes up the world we live in.

REVIEW

1. What is the primary cause of condensation?
2. How does the formation of an ice crystal in a cloud resemble the formation of a crystal of a mineral?
3. What is the difference between dew, fog, and rain?
4. How does a cloud form? What are the three basic types of clouds?
5. Describe how the water of the land and the sea is involved in the hydrologic cycle.

NEW VIEW

1. Explain how cloud-seeding might be used in making rain.
2. What is one kind of observation you would make if you were seeking evidence for the theory that salt particles form raindrop nuclei?

3. HEAT IN THE AIR OCEAN

We visit the seashore in the summer for many reasons. One of them is to be in the path of a cool breeze. Have you ever noticed how breezes behave at the seashore? During the day, the breeze blows from the sea to the land; during the night it blows from the land to the sea. Why do you think this happens?

Heating the Air

Any wind—and a breeze is a light wind—has energy, for wind is simply air in motion. Motion is a form of energy. Where does the wind get its energy? Radiation from the sun, as you might expect, is the primary source of the wind's energy.

Energy in the form of light travels by radiation from the sun, through space, and penetrates the atmosphere. The surfaces of the land and water absorb much of this energy and are warmed. They then reradiate some of this energy back to the air as infrared radiation. Thus the air above the land receives some heat by radiation from the land.

Some heat may also be given by the process of conduction from the land to the air. Suppose, for example, that at a given time the temperature of the soil at the earth's surface is higher than that of the air just above it. Then heat will be conducted from the particles of soil to the molecules in the air as they bounce against the land. As a result of this transfer of heat, the air is warmed by the land.

High in the air, radiation is the chief means by which heat is transferred. But at the surface, conduction also plays an important role.

Like the land, the sea also reradiates heat and conducts heat to the air above it, but this occurs more slowly. Thus the air above the sea is heated more slowly than is the air above the land. This means, then, that while the sun shines, the air above the land becomes warmer than the air above the sea.

It is because of this difference in air temperatures above sea and land that a wind is started. In the next investigation, you can see how for yourself. ■

■ AN APPRENTICE INVESTIGATION into Air Currents

Place two lamp chimneys over holes in the top of a metal box with a removable glass side, as shown. Put an unlighted candle in the candleholder on the floor of the box at the right-hand side. Now light one end of a piece of folded paper towel and blow out the flame almost at once, so that smoke is produced. Hold the smoking towel just above the left-hand chimney. Which way does the smoke go? ❶

Now light the candle under the right-hand chimney. Again hold the smoking paper towel over the opening of the left-hand chimney. Which way does the smoke go now? ❷

How can you account for this behavior?

The smoke from the paper moves *down* through the left chimney and *up* through the right chimney. The smoke is carried through the box by a current of air, as the air above the candle flame rises. Warm air is less dense than cold air. The cold air moves down as the warm air rises.

❶

❷

An Investigation On Your Own

Predict what is happening to the air above a warm radiator in a room. What must be happening to air below the radiator? Devise a way to test your predictions and show what is happening to the air.

1

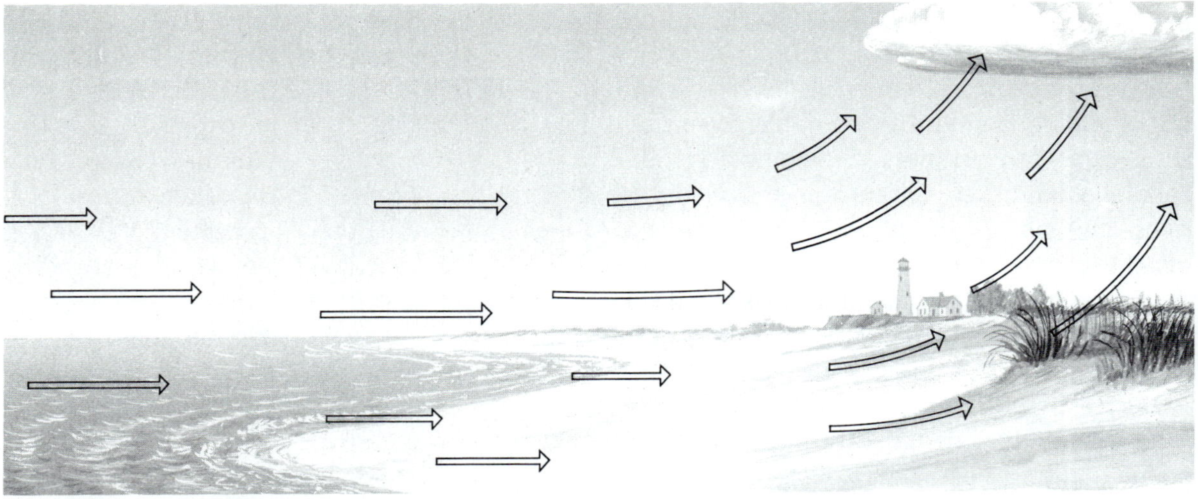

Something similar happens to make a sea breeze, a wind from the sea to the land. During the day, the air over the land becomes warmer than the air over the sea. The warmer, less dense air rises; the colder, heavier air from the sea moves in underneath it. 1 Then this colder air is warmed by the land. Thus a sea breeze is set in motion.

You may recall that, in the ocean, the contact of a mass of more dense water and a mass of less dense water can generate a current called a convection current. In much the same way, a mass of warm air and a mass of cool air may set up a convection current. The winds that are formed as a result of temperature differences, then, are actually convection currents. Moreover, as a mass of warmed air moves upward, heat is carried up, too. Convection, then, is a third way—in addition to radiation and conduction—by which heat is moved in the air.

Here's how a convection current may form at night at the seashore. 2 Can you see why it is called a land breeze rather than a sea

2

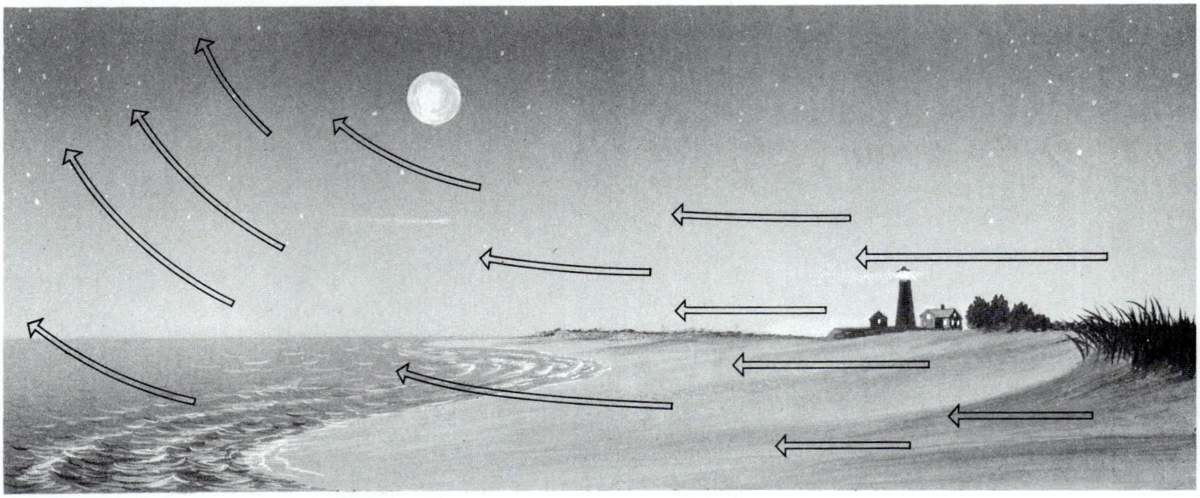

breeze? Can you explain why the breeze flows from the land to the sea, in the opposite direction from the sea breeze in the day time?

After the sun goes down, both the land and the sea cool off. However, the land cools off more quickly than the sea does, leaving the air over the land cooler than the air over the water. This cool, more dense air moves from the land to the sea and flows under the rising warm air above the sea. Thus there is a convection current moving from land to sea, and the direction of the breeze is the reverse of what it was during the day.

Molecules of Expanding Air

Warm air is less dense than cool air, other things being equal. What is the reason? "Because when air is heated it expands," you will very likely answer. You have probably observed a demonstration of the expansion of air, such as this one. 3 As the flask is heated, the air inside it expands. 4

Expanded air is less dense than it was before expansion. Why is this so? We know that air is made up of molecules. What happens to these molecules when air expands?

Suppose the flask with the balloon holds one liter (about a quart) of air at room temperature. When the air is heated, it expands to take up a greater volume. At this higher temperature there is more than one liter of air. The air needs more space but the flask can't expand to make room for this greater volume of air. What happens instead is that some of the expanding air pushes out of the flask and takes up more space in the balloon. No new air has been put into the system, so something must have happened to the air in the flask.

How does air expand? Scientists have concluded, after many investigations, that the way air (or any gas) expands is by *increasing the space between its molecules.* If you have never investigated the expansion of air, you may want to do so now. ■

3

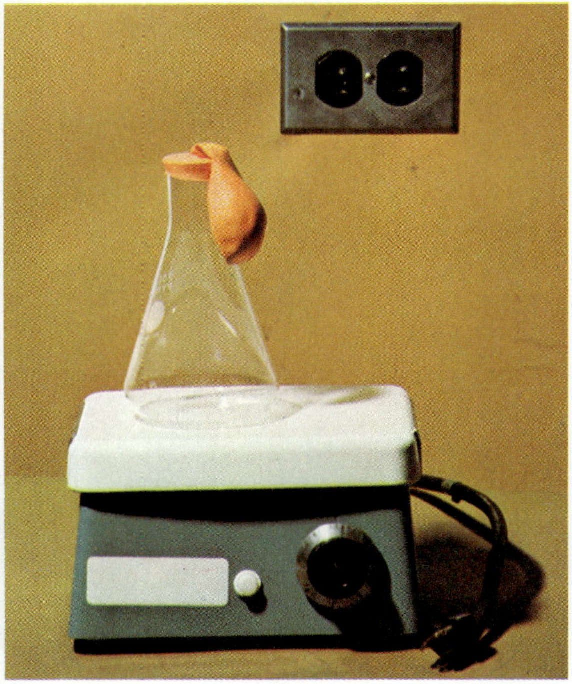

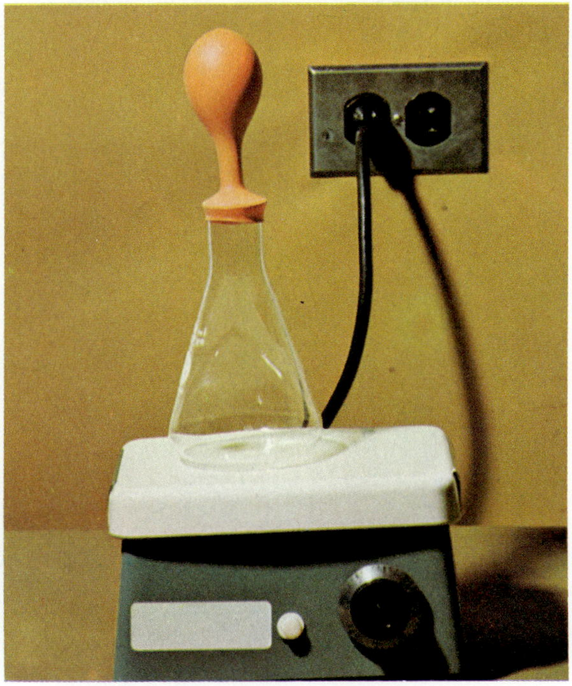

4

■ AN APPRENTICE INVESTIGATION into the Expansion of Air

❶
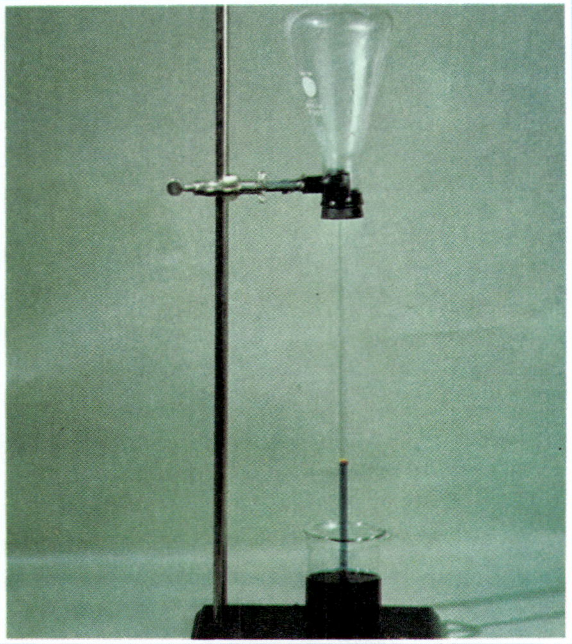

To make an air thermometer, set up a flask, glass tube, and beaker of colored water as shown.❶ Before you insert the tube in the stopper, be sure to moisten the end of the glass and the inside of the stopper.

Adjust the water level so that the water rises part of the way up the tube.❶ Now warm the air in the flask by holding the flask in both hands. What happens to the water in the tube? Here is what happened in one trial.❷ Explain what happens. Devise a way to cool the air in the flask, and again explain the result. Why is this device called an *air* thermometer?

An Investigation On Your Own

Arrange the apparatus as shown, and place colored water in the U-tube.❸ Predict what will happen if you immerse the flask in cold water. Try it. Was your prediction correct?

❷
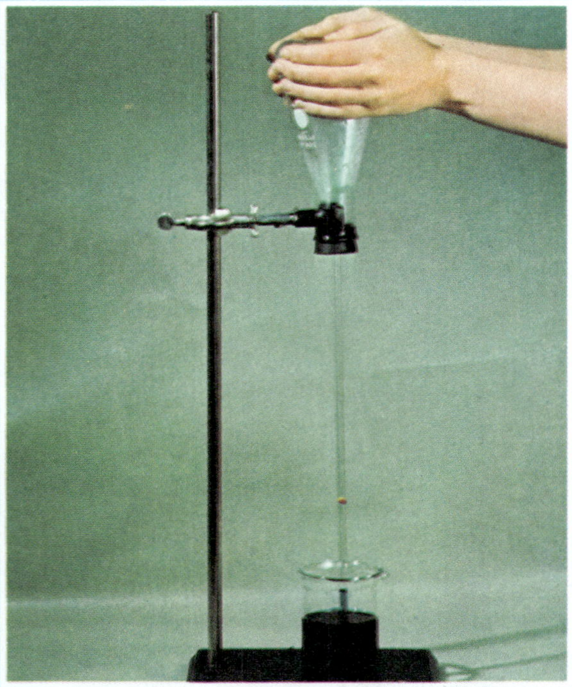

❸
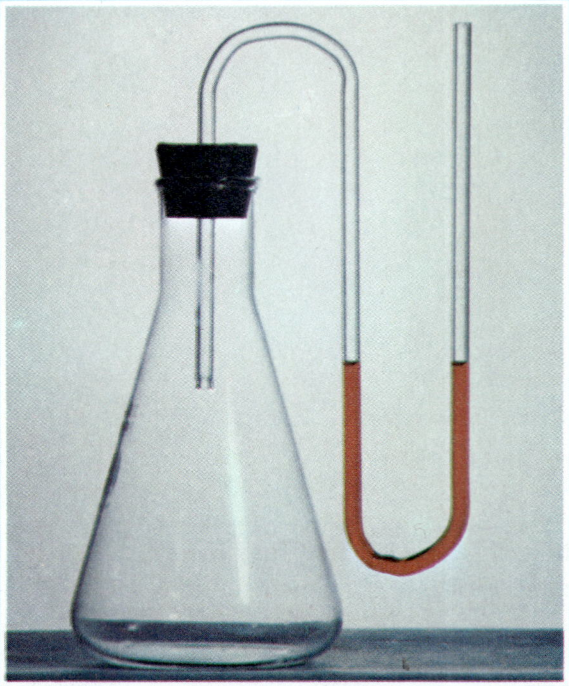

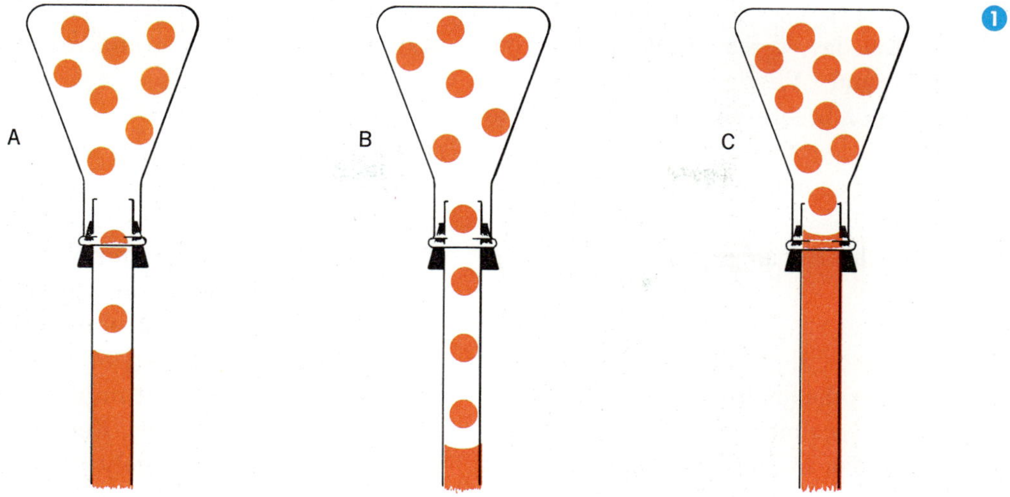

Let's fill 3 imaginary flasks, similar to the one used in the investigation, with imaginary molecules. ❶ Flask A contains 10 molecules and let's say that the temperature of flask A is about room temperature. Note the level of the colored water.

What will happen to the molecules when the flask is warmed? Flask B is flask A after it has been warmed, so that the water indicator has moved down in the tube. ❶ The temperature has gone up. How many molecules of air are in the enclosed part of the apparatus? Still 10.

Heating does not add or subtract any molecules, but merely gives those that are there more energy to move farther away from one another. The spaces between the molecules increase, but the molecules themselves remain the same size.

What happens to the molecules when the air is cooled? Flask C is flask A after it has been cooled somewhat below room temperature. ❶ Observe how the space between the molecules has decreased, and that the number of molecules is still the same.

Now consider the volume of just the flask itself, the volume between the base and the stopper. How many molecules are in flask A? Only 8. The other 2 are in the narrow tube. How many are in the flask at B? Only 7, for expansion has caused the other molecules to move out into the narrow tube. Now look at flask C. All 10 molecules are inside the flask.

You can see that the expanded air contains fewer molecules per liter (or any given volume) than the contracted air contains.

How do the three flasks compare in weight? Molecules, as you know, have weight, because they are made of atoms that have weight. Of the three flasks, clearly the air in C weighs the most, since it has the largest number of molecules. Flask B has the least weight of the three, since it has the fewest molecules. Since the weights of air in the flasks are different, while their volumes are the same, these samples of air trapped in the flasks have different densities.

Because it is less dense than cold air around it, warm air tends to rise. That is, the less dense air is forced up by the greater weight of the more dense air around it. Thus changes in temperature contribute directly to the motion of air, and, therefore, to the origin of winds and clouds.

REVIEW

1. During the day, a sea breeze blows from the sea to the land. Why?

2. When does a breeze blow from the land to the sea? Why?

3. Distinguish among radiation, conduction, and convection.

4. Why does heated air expand?

NEW VIEW

1. In the tropics, there often occurs an area of calm, known as the doldrums. Old sailing ships were indeed "becalmed." Surely there was enough heat in the tropics. Why was there not enough wind?

2. To get circulation of air within a room (to produce an indoor wind), it is often useful to open windows from the top and bottom. Why is this helpful?

4. PRESSURE IN THE AIR OCEAN

We are used to the idea that we live at the bottom of an ocean of air which has weight and exerts pressure. So it is hard for us to realize that there was a time when this was not known, when men argued the question, and even the great Galileo did not believe that air had weight or pressure. It took some solid experimental evidence and hard reasoning to convince men that this was so. Let's look at some evidence, and reasoning.

The Pressure of Air

There is a very simple and striking phenomenon that can be demonstrated with a basin of water and a tumbler. Perhaps you can remember your amazement when you first saw it, and your feeling that something which was not supposed to happen was happening. Submerge the tumbler completely so that it fills with water. Keeping the mouth of the tumbler completely under water, turn the tumbler upside down. Now raise the upside-down tumbler slowly above the water until the mouth is just below the surface. The tumbler remains full: the water does not run out. (1)

We feel that it is somehow unnatural for the water in the tumbler to be standing above the level of the water in the basin, but there it is. How is this phenomenon to be explained? The answer is that it is evidence of the pressure of air. There is no air inside the tumbler, therefore there is no air pressure inside the tumbler. But there is air outside the tumbler, and it has pressure. It is pressing on the water in the basin, and thereby pressing the water up into the tumbler. (2)

(1)

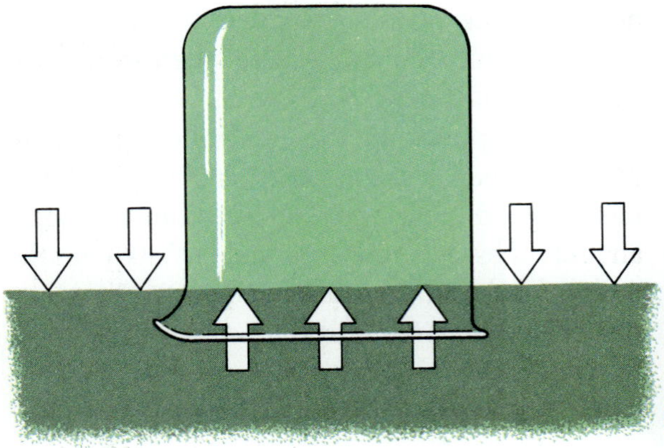

(2)

It is easy to collect further evidence in favor of this explanation. Run one end of a flexible tube into the water in the tumbler, and blow a little air into the tube. By letting a little air in, you let in a little air pressure, and the level of the water in the tumbler drops. Of course, if you lift the mouth of the tumbler above the surface of the water in the basin, air enters the tumbler at once and the water flows out.

The pressure of the air, then, is strong enough to hold up the small amount of water in the tumbler. Just how strong is this pressure? How high a column of water can it hold? About the year 1640, an Italian named Gaspar Berti fastened about 12 meters (40 feet) of lead pipe in a vertical position to an outside wall of his house to try an experiment. Each end of the pipe had a tap, and the lower end was immersed in a cask of water. Berti closed the lower tap and filled the pipe completely with water. Then the upper tap was closed—and the lower tap opened. The level of the water in the cask rose a little, as some of the water ran out of the pipe. Most of the water remained in the pipe, however, to a height of about 10 meters (34 feet) above the water in the cask. The pressure of the air at sea level is about 1,034 grams per square centimeter (14.7 pounds per square inch) of surface. This pressure can support a column of water about 10 meters high.

It was another Italian, Evangelista Torricelli who thought of investigating air pressure with a column of mercury instead of water. Torricelli wanted to "make an instrument which might show the changes of the air, now heavier and coarser, now lighter and more subtle. . . ." He suspected that the pressure of the air changed, and wanted an instrument that would show such changes—what we now call a **barometer.** Let's take a

3

look at the kind of instrument that Torricelli suggested.

Suppose we fill a glass tube that is closed at one end and about 800 millimeters (32 inches) long with mercury. 3 Tapping the tube gently while it is being filled will bring trapped air bubbles to the surface. When the tube is completely filled with mercury, we clamp a thumb tightly over the open end and invert the tube. We put the end (with the thumb still on it) under the surface of a dish of mercury and clamp the tube in a vertical position. What happens to the level of

1

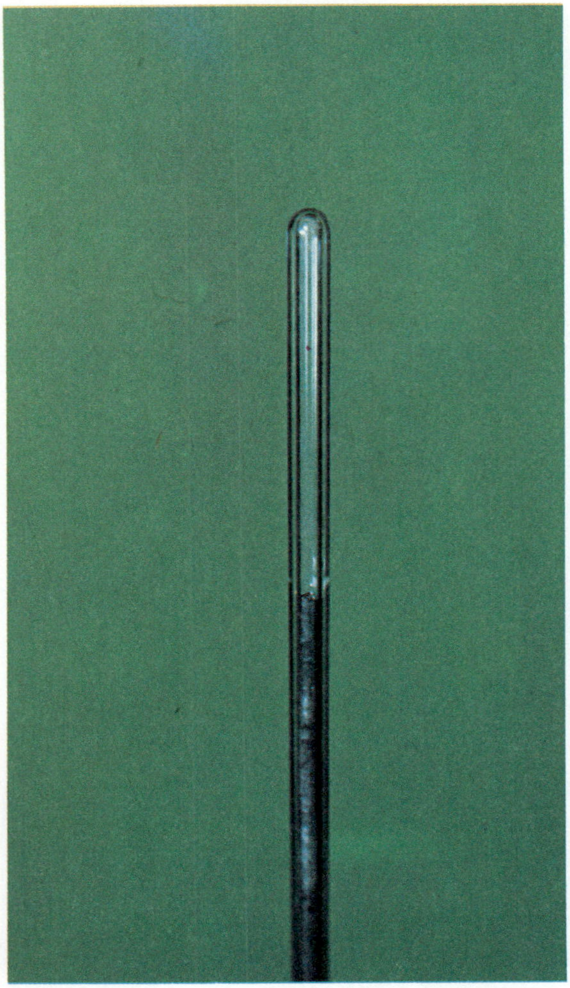

2

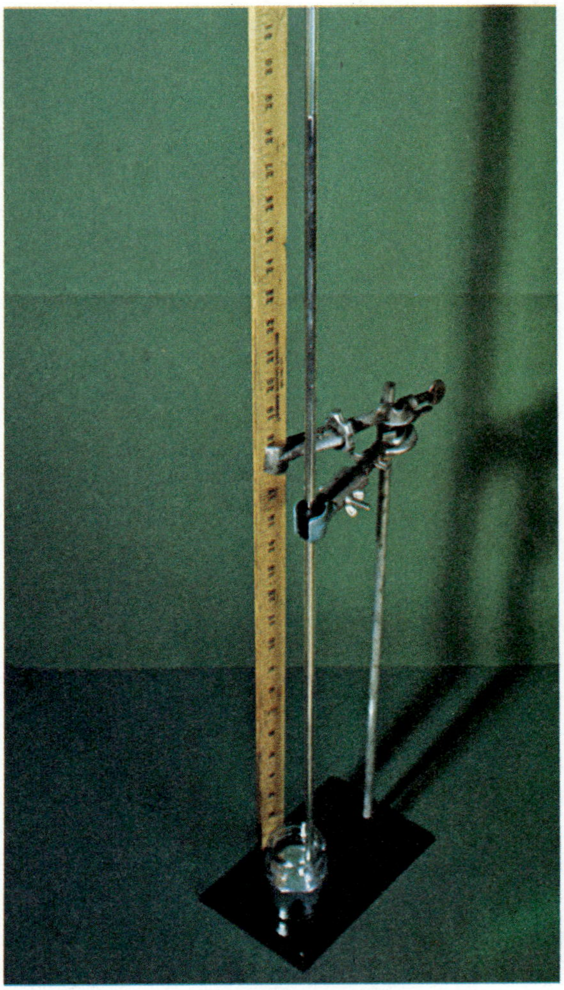

mercury in the tube when the thumb is removed? (1)

In one trial the height of the column of mercury above the surface of the mercury in the dish was 724 millimeters ($28\frac{1}{2}$ inches). (2)

How is it that air pressure supports a long column of water but a short column of mercury? Mercury has a density of 13.6 g/cc (grams per cubic centimeter); water has a density of 1 g/cc. Mercury weighs 13.6 times as much as water, then, volume for volume. The atmospheric pressure can hold up the same weight of mercury and water, but the volume of mercury is smaller than the volume of water because the density of mercury is greater than that of water.

Record your measurements of the height of the mercury column. For the next few days, measure the height of the column every day. You will probably find that the pressure of the air is changing from day to day.

The mercury column is in fact a barometer, an instrument for indicating changes in the pressure of the air—as Torricelli thought it would be. When the pressure of the air decreases, the height of the column decreases;

when the air pressure increases, the column is pushed farther up into the tube and its height increases.

Torricelli and his friends, by the way, were deeply interested in the space that appears between the top of the mercury and the sealed end of the tube when the thumb is removed and the mercury is supported by air pressure. You probably know that this space is a vacuum. In Torricelli's time, however, this was a controversial question. Torricelli believed that the space was a vacuum, but there were scholars who denied that such a thing as a vacuum could exist. After all, they reasoned, a vacuum is *nothing*. How, in the first place, can *nothing* exist? And how, in the second place, can *nothing* be detected, if it does exist? The advance of science is not always smooth, you see.

Heat, Water Vapor, and Pressure

It is easy to observe with a barometer that the atmospheric pressure does change from day to day and even from hour to hour. What makes the pressure change?

(3)

Here is an area of one square centimeter. (3) The air is pressing on this square right now with a force of about 1,000 grams. (Since the air is pressing on the other side of the square with the same force, you don't notice anything.) What causes the pressure? The weight of the one centimeter square column of air resting on the square. Imagine this column of air rising straight up to the outer limits of the atmosphere. (4) This column of air weighs about 1,000 grams. The pressure at its base is 1,000 grams per square centimeter. If the area were one square inch, the column of air

(4)

over the square would weigh 14.7 pounds. The pressure on a one inch square would be 14.7 pounds.

If this pressure changes, then, it must mean that the weight of the column of air resting on the square changes. What could make the weight of air change? One way would be by changing the number of molecules in a given volume of air, or by changing the density, in other words.

You already know one way in which the density of air can be changed: by heating or cooling. When a part of the atmosphere is heated, it expands. Its molecules are, on an average, farther apart, and the density decreases. When a part of the atmosphere is cooled, it contracts; its molecules, on the average, move closer together and the gas becomes more dense. Cool air thus contains more molecules than the same volume of warm air, and weighs more per unit volume. Since the atmosphere is always being heated and cooled, its density and its pressure are always changing.

The weight of the column of air above one square centimeter can change for another reason. Besides having different temperatures, that air can have different amounts of water vapor in it from time to time. Here are two cubes of air containing the same number of molecules. ❶ The air in cube A is perfectly dry. The air in cube B, however, contains some molecules of water vapor, represented in red. Will one cube weigh more than the other, or will they have the same weight? It depends on the total weight of the molecules in A compared with the total weight of the molecules in B.

Now it happens that water molecules are lighter than the molecules of nitrogen or oxygen which they replace in the air. Hence, although both cubes have the same number of molecules, cube B has some lighter molecules than cube A, and so the dry air of cube A weighs more than the humid air of cube B. Air that contains water vapor is *less* dense than dry air, other things being equal.

Atmospheric pressure can be lowered in two ways, then: by increasing the temperature or by increasing the humidity. Atmospheric pressure can be raised by decreasing the temperature or decreasing the humidity.

With a barometer you can observe that the air pressure changes where you are from time to time. If you could collect barometer readings from other regions, however, at the same time, you'd find that the air pressure differs from place to place, too. The air pressure in one region may be higher or lower than the pressure in another region. Now air tends to flow, as you might expect, from a region of high pressure to a region of low pressure, so winds can be understood in terms of differences in air pressure.

We accounted for a sea breeze in terms of warm and cold air, you remember, but it can be described in terms of pressure as well. The cooler, denser air over the sea is a region of higher pressure. The warmer, less dense air over the land is a region of lower pressure. The air tends to move from the high pressure region to the low, from sea to land, resulting in a sea breeze. Since air pressure is easy to measure, this is a convenient way to determine air flow tendencies. One kind of information displayed on weather maps is how air pressure varies across the country. You will study these maps in the next chapter.

❶

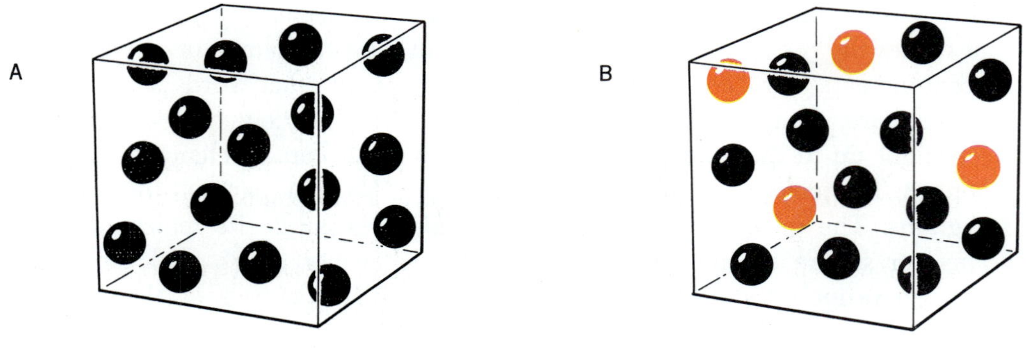

REVIEW

1. Why does the atmosphere have pressure?
2. Why does water have pressure?
3. Does dry air have a higher pressure than moist air? Explain.
4. How does a mercury barometer work?

NEW VIEW

The average pressure of the atmosphere at sea level is 14.7 lbs per square inch. This is known as one atmosphere of pressure. Two atmospheres of pressure would be 29.4 lbs per square inch. To how many lbs per square inch would a person be subjected if he were under pressure of 8 atmospheres?

5. RELATING THE CONCEPTS

You live on the crust of the earth in contact with two "oceans," the atmosphere and the hydrosphere. Both are related in many ways to one another, and to the lithosphere under your feet. Evaporation of water from the sea and the ground results in water vapor in the air. This water vapor in turn condenses to form raindrops, streams, rivers, and glaciers. Water, air, and energy are involved in this continuous cycle of change. Heat from the sun provides the energy for the cycle to take place. Because this system of matter and energy is essential for all living things, it is important that we understand it and help to preserve it.

Reviewing the Concepts

► *The earth's atmosphere, hydrosphere, and lithosphere are continually interacting.* Here the processes of the water cycle—evaporation, condensation, precipitation—play an important part. Water, in solid, liquid, or vapor form, is stored in all three spheres.

► *To set air in motion, energy is required.* Air is matter and has mass. The source of energy for setting this mass in motion is the sun. Some of the energy received as radiation from the sun by the earth is absorbed and reradiated to heat the atmosphere.

► *Heat can produce movement in the air ocean.* Heat causes the air to expand and to become less dense. Warm, less dense air tends to rise when in contact with colder, denser air. The greater pressure of the denser air forces the less dense air upward. Increased humidity causes air to become less dense as well, with the same tendency to rise when in contact with denser air.

► *Horizontal movements of the air ocean are produced by differences in air pressure.* The pressure of the air varies from place to place, and changes with time. Because air has mass, it has weight and exerts pressure; when its density changes, the weight and pressure of the air change. Air flows from a region of high pressure toward a region of low pressure.

Testing Yourself

1. Describe the three methods by which our atmosphere receives heat.
2. Air becomes less dense when heated. How does the molecular theory account for this fact?
3. What evidence and reasoning would you use to convince someone that the air has pressure?
4. Explain how a mercury barometer works.
5. What are two possible causes of a change in atmospheric pressure? How do they work?
6. What has the hydrologic cycle to do with the weather?

7. The temperature of a sample of air is 30°C. If the air holds 24 grams of water vapor per cubic meter, what is the relative humidity?

8. Define the terms condensation nuclei and freezing nuclei. Explain how they are involved in precipitation.

9. What is the difference between a fog and a cloud?

10. Describe and name four types of clouds.

Extending the Concepts

Investigation. How does the rate at which rainwater evaporates compare to the amount that falls over a period of time? You can learn something about this by carrying out a simple investigation.

Obtain 3 large cans with straight sides. Remove one end completely from each of the cans, and clean them.

Dig holes deep enough to bury each can to within 5 centimeters (2 inches) of the open top. Dig two of the holes in open spots where rain can fall unhindered into the cans—one where the can will get a maximum of sunlight, and the other where the can is in the shade. The third can may be placed alongside either of the other cans, or in a place by itself.

When all three cans are in position, pour water into can number three until it is half full. Measure the depth of water as accurately as you can. The other two cans remain empty. Every 24 hours measure the depth of water in each can. Record these measurements on a chart that identifies each can. Of course, if it does not rain, there will be no water in cans 1 and 2. What will happen to the depth of the water in can 3? Be punctual in making your observations and accurate in your measurements, and see whether or not your prediction is correct.

During a period of several weeks, you should be able to draw graphs from which you can see whether the cans have gained or lost water, how much they have gained or lost, and at what rates.

Some questions you can consider are:

a. Of what use is it to begin with a third can partly full of water?
b. How does the rate at which water accumulates compare with the rate at which water is lost?
c. Is there any difference in the rate of loss for the can in the sun and the can in the shade?
d. Did the land around the cans gain or lose water over the period investigated?
e. What practical purpose can such an investigation serve?

Suggested Reading

Berry, Frederick A., and Sidney R. Frank, *Your Future in Meteorolgy*, New York, Rosen, 1962. Describes the work of professional weathermen and how you can become one.

Laird, Charles, and Ruth Laird, *Weathercasting*, Englewood Cliffs, Prentice-Hall, 1955. A complete guide for the beginner who wants to learn weather forecasting as a hobby. Tells how to build your own instruments.

14

Weather and Climate

Yesterday was warm and sunny. You rode your bike, or played basketball, or planted a garden. Today you are on your way to school —you are wearing a jacket and a rain hat! What caused this overnight change in the weather?

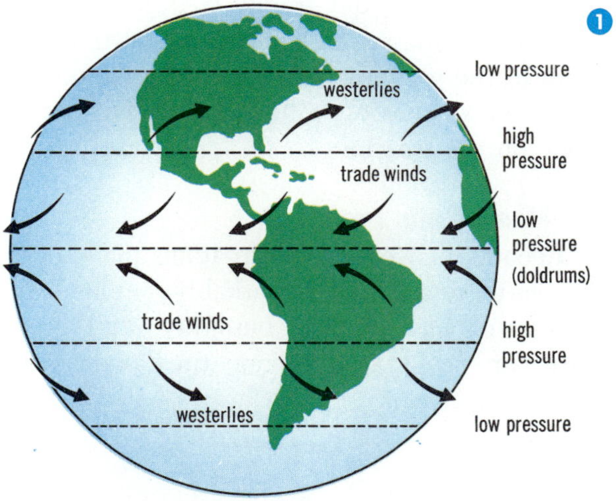

1. WINDS AND WEATHER

The earth is an unevenly heated sphere. The sun's rays strike the equator more directly than they do the middle latitudes and the poles (Chapter 10). So there is a Torrid Zone with warm temperature near the equator, a Frigid Zone with cold temperature near each of the poles, and a Temperate Zone of moderate temperature in between. There is a considerable difference between the average temperatures of the Torrid and Frigid Zones, but the circulation of the air in our troposphere keeps this difference from being even greater.

Prevailing Winds

The pattern of the earth's general air circulation is the pattern of the prevailing winds. Perhaps you recall that the prevailing winds are the main driving source of the earth's major ocean currents (Chapter 12). Since a wind tends to blow from a region of high pressure to a region of low pressure, the earth's air pressure distribution is one factor that determines the direction of prevailing winds. Here is a simplified map of pressure belts and prevailing winds. 1 The arrows indicate the directions of the earth's surface winds, moving from high pressure belts to low pressure belts.

If pressure belts alone determined wind directions, then all winds would blow either due north or due south. However, because the earth is rotating, the winds in the northern hemisphere are deflected to their right, and those in the southern hemisphere are deflected to the left. This deflection is known as the **Coriolis effect.** As an example of the Coriolis effect, notice how the "westerlies," which would blow north if the earth did not rotate, are deflected toward the east.

This pattern of the prevailing winds around the globe is well established, and its relationship to the pressure belts and the earth's rotation is clear. But meteorologists, scientists who study weather, have not yet found a satisfactory explanation for the *origin* of the pattern of pressure belts and wind belts. Yet they do know that many day-to-day weather changes are due to masses of air that move into the path of the westerlies. Let's look at the movements of air masses to understand their influence on the weather.

Air Masses and Fronts

Records of weather observations made over the earth reveal that remarkably similar conditions of temperature, humidity, and pressure can occur at the same time over wide areas. For example, on a day in March the temperature in Little Rock, Arkansas, was 57°F; in Oklahoma City, Oklahoma, 58°F; Kansas City, Missouri, 53°F; Bismarck, North Dakota, 50°F. Barometer readings were likewise similar. Skies were clear and the humidity was low in all these places, yet from Bismarck to Little Rock is about 1,000 miles. (*As the records of the Weather Bureau are kept in the English system, English units will be used throughout this chapter.*) Why does the same weather occur over such a large area? Meteorologists have discovered that giant masses of air move over the earth's surface. Each air mass has a fairly uniform temperature, humidity, and pressure. Each air mass carries its own weather, then, to a large area of land at the same time.

Some of these air masses come from the polar regions, some from tropical regions. Some come from land areas and are called continental air masses. Some come from sea areas and are called martime air masses. (1) Polar air masses (maritime and continental)

(1)
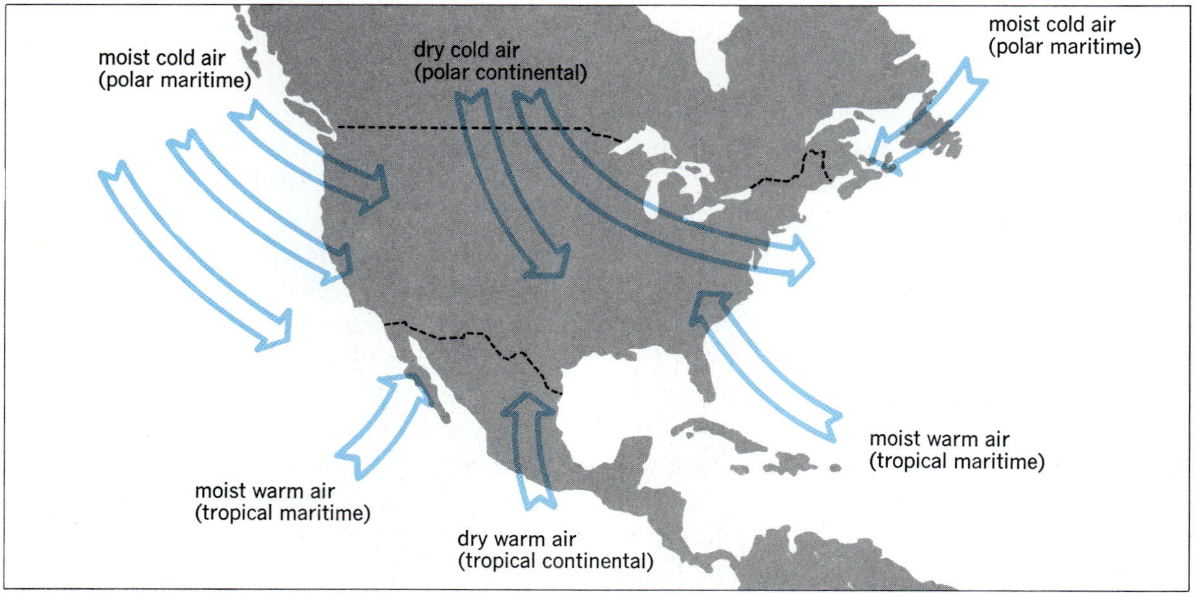

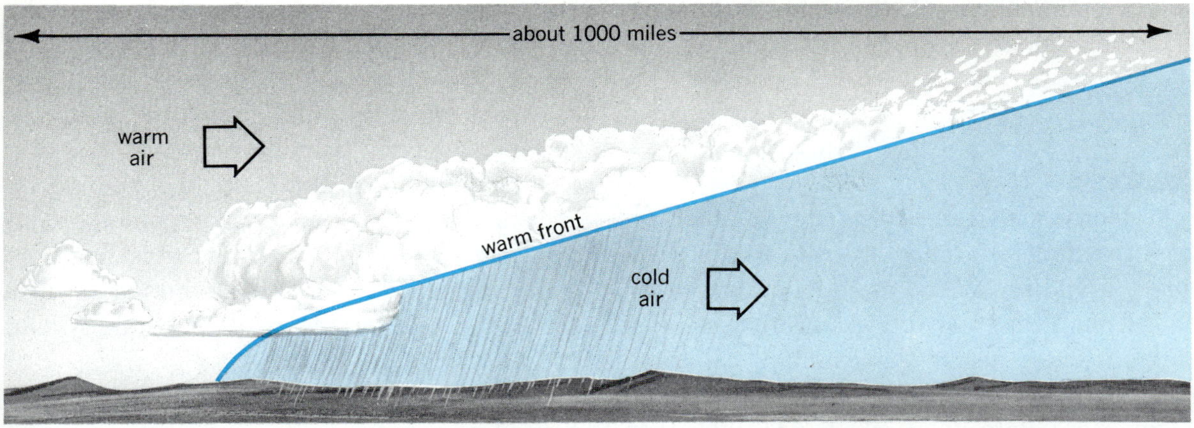

2

migrate from the northwest, and tropical air masses (maritime and continental) from the southwest, in the northern hemisphere.

If you know the characteristics of different air masses, you can form some idea of what will happen when air masses meet. For each air mass, try to answer these questions. (1) Is the air mass warm or cold? (2) Is the air moist or dry? (3) Is the pressure high or low? A tropical maritime air mass would be: (1) warm, (2) moist, and (3) low pressure. What is the answer for polar maritime air, polar continental air, tropical continental air?*

What happens when one air mass meets another? Oddly enough, they do not mix or blend. A boundary forms between the two masses: the boundary formed between air masses is called a **front.** Here is the boundary between a warm air mass and the gradually sloping wedge of a cold air mass. 2 This warm air mass is moving in to replace the cold air mass, which retreats, so the front is called a warm front.

A warm front is accompanied by a series of certain kinds of clouds. The last in the series is *nimbostratus,* a kind of cloud that produces steady and prolonged rain or snow ahead of the front line (Chapter 13).

Here is the wedge of a cold air mass moving against a warm air mass. 3 When a cold air mass advances against a warm air mass that retreats, a cold front is formed. A cold front is accompanied by a series of clouds, ending in *cumulonimbus* clouds, which produce rain. Rain at a cold front is heavy and brief—a thunderstorm, perhaps. If you know the series of cloud types that accompanies a front you can predict the kind of air mass (and weather) flowing toward you.

As you see, air masses influence not only the weather within them but the weather at their boundaries. By identifying air masses

* polar maritime—cold, moist, low pressure
polar continental—cold, dry, high pressure
tropical continental—warm, dry, high pressure

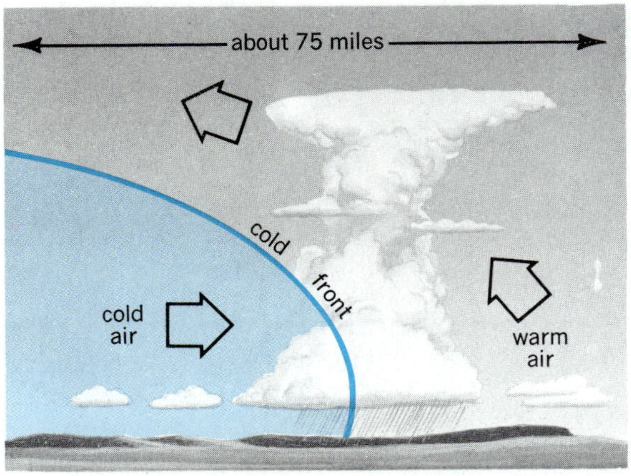

3

and keeping track of them as they move across the country, you can get some idea of the passage of weather across the country.

The Weather Map

Meteorologists forecasting the weather receive readings of the temperature, air pressure, humidity, wind direction, and other data from a vast network of weather stations and observers across the country. All these readings have been made at the same time. From these data they construct a weather map.(1) On the map they can read many of the factors that influence the local weather, including the location of fronts and air masses. By comparing this map with previous ones, they see how air masses, fronts, and pressure distributions are moving.

Notice the symbols on the map for warm fronts and cold fronts. Symbols for two other kinds of fronts of interest to the meteorologist are also on the map—where the front seems to be standing still it is *stationary,* and where masses of cold air have pushed under a warm air mass and raised it from the ground, the front is *occluded.*

Precipitation depends on the amount of moisture in the warm air mass and the temperature of the cold air mass at a front. In other words, rain (or snow) production at a front depends on the relative humidity and the dew point.

The smooth curved lines on the weather map are **isobars.** Isobars connect points of equal pressure to show pressure patterns across the country. These patterns help the meteorologist to determine the regions marked "LOW" and "HIGH" on the map. These are centers of low and high air pressure. A "low" is often associated with cloudy and rainy weather, and a "high" with fair weather. Knowledge of low and high air pressure areas, and of air masses and fronts, is useful in weather forecasting.

(1)

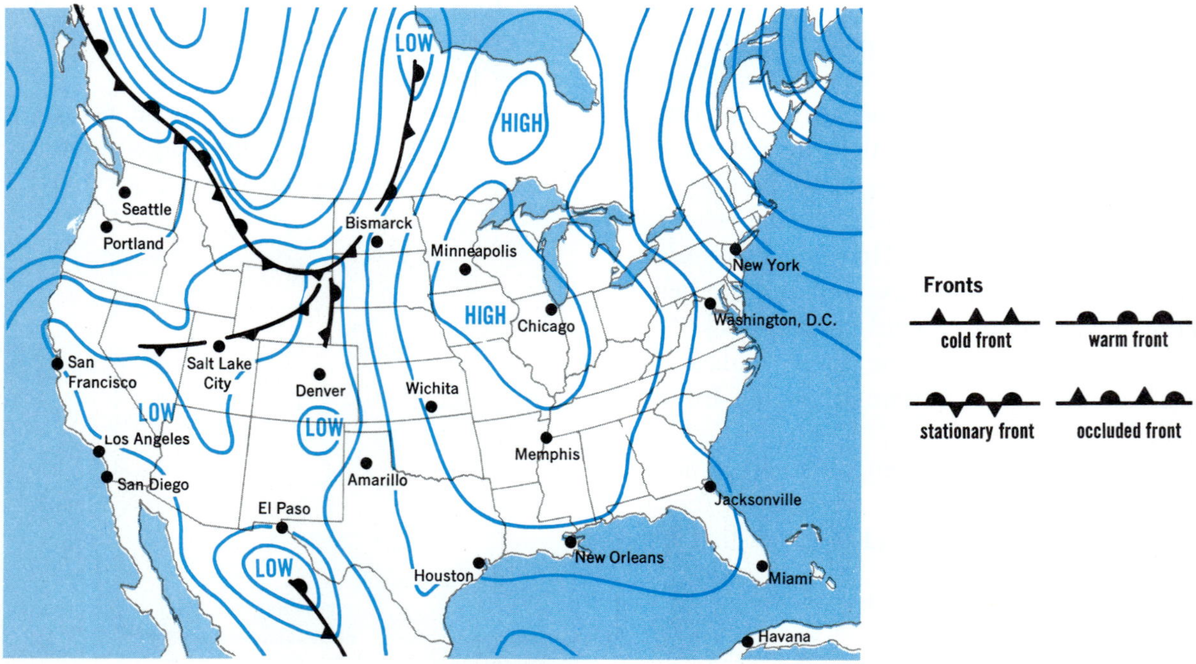

January 19, 1966 1:00 A.M.

2

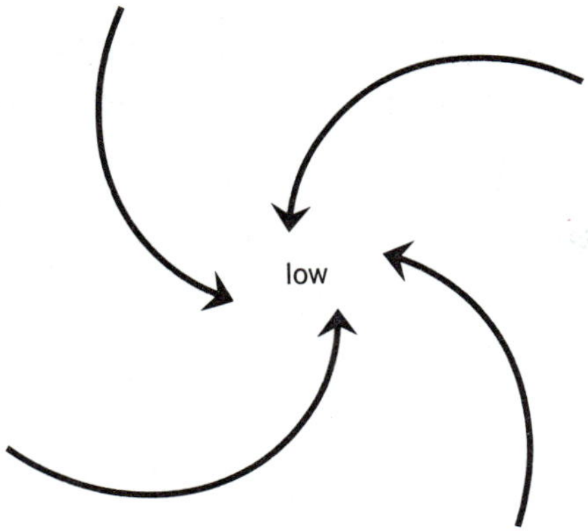

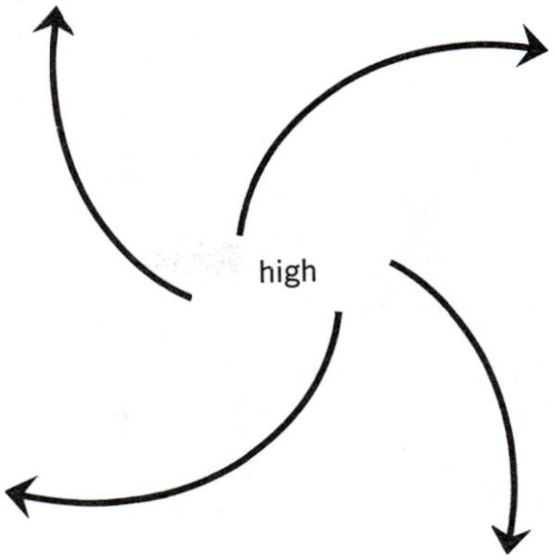

3

Lows and Highs

A low is an area with low barometric pressure, and a high is an area with high barometric pressure. A low also goes by the name **cyclone,** a word suggesting the spiraling motion of its winds. In the northern hemisphere the winds associated with a cyclone or low move in a counterclockwise direction, spiraling into the center. (2) Its opposite is a mass of air with high pressure at its center, with winds spiraling outward from the center in a clockwise direction. (3)

In a "low," winds spiral inward because the center of the low has low pressure, and the outside of the low has relatively high pressure. In a high, winds spiral outward from the central high pressure region to the relatively low pressure outer region. High pressure areas usually have both drier and cooler air than low pressure areas.

Examine item number 5 in the table. Why does the air rise at the center of a low and descend at the center of a high?

The low pressure of the air in the center of a low is due to the fact that this air is lighter than the surrounding air. This being so, the lighter air will be forced up by the heavier air around it, and will rise. As it rises, the air cools. As the air cools to its dew point and below, its water vapor is likely to condense and form clouds. Precipitation of rain or snow may follow. Hence a low usually means cloudy, rainy weather. Where the air pressure in a high is greatest, in the center of the high, the relatively dry and cool air descends, accompanied by bright, clear weather.

On the next page are weather maps for two consecutive days. Examine them and notice how the weather moves across the country.

COMPARISON OF LOW AND HIGH PRESSURE AREAS

Low	*High*
1. Air has lower density.	Air has higher density.
2. Air has lower pressure.	Air has higher pressure.
3. Air has higher moisture content.	Air has lower moisture content.
4. Winds move inward.	Winds move outward.
5. Air rises in the center.	Air descends in the center.

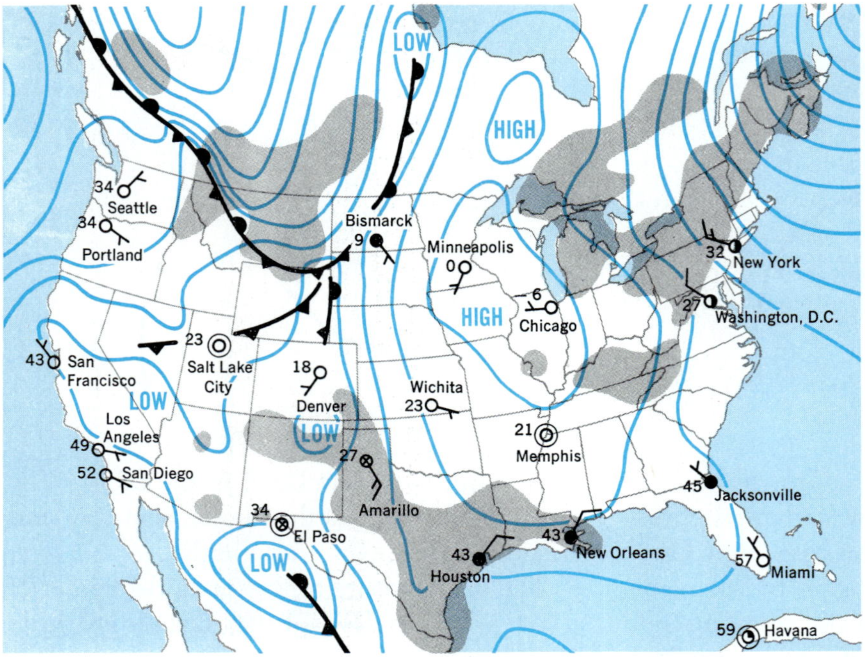

January 19, 1966 1:00 A.M.

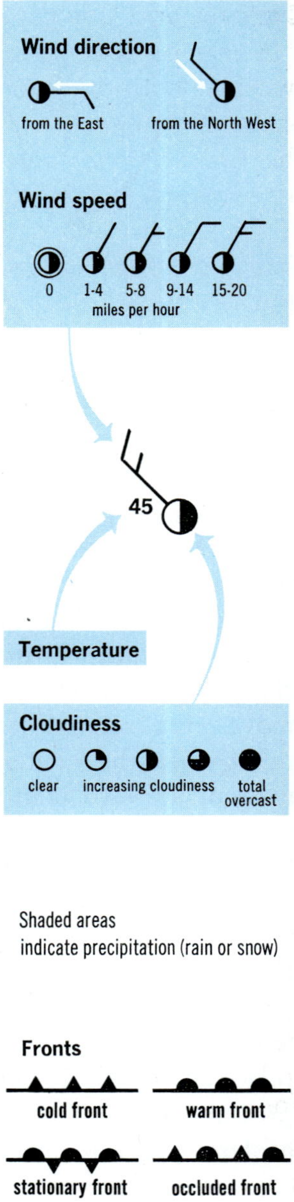

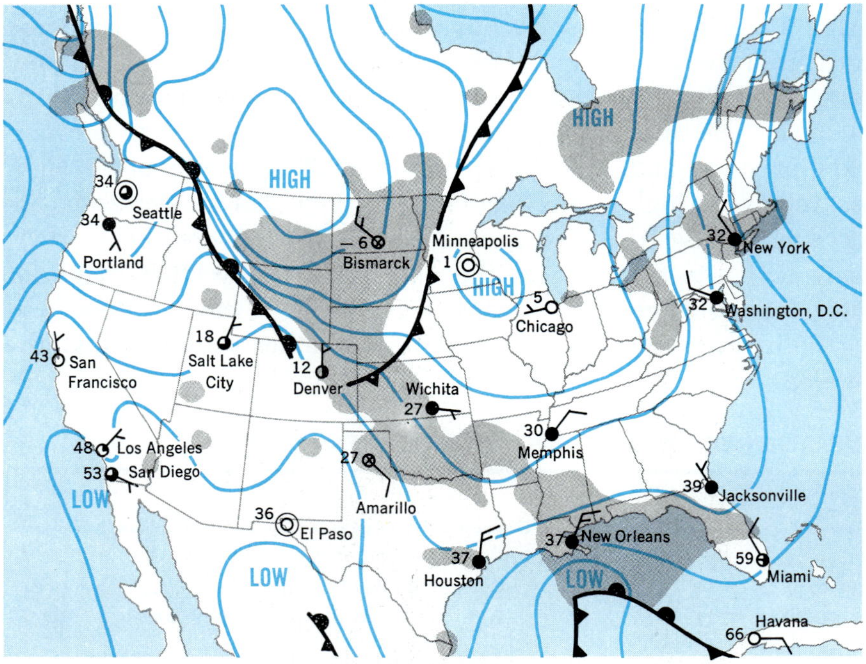

January 20, 1966 1:00 A.M.

Cyclones and Tropical Cyclones

A low pressure area often brings stormy weather, but not all lows are as mild as the ones that move across the United States along the belt of westerlies. Recall that another name for a low is cyclone, and the mild lows of the middle latitudes are typical cyclones. Some lows, named for their origin in the tropics, are destructively violent tropical cyclones. You may know them as **hurricanes.**

Like any low, a tropical cyclone has winds that spiral into a low-pressure center. In the northern hemisphere, the spiral is counterclockwise; in the southern hemisphere the spiral turns clockwise. A typical cyclone often travels along at 20 to 40 miles per hour, carrying stormy weather over an area some 500 to 1,000 miles in diameter. Its winds may reach gale force—40 miles per hour or more. In a tropical cyclone or hurricane, however, winds blow from 75 to 150 miles per hour, and the storm's path is about 200 to 400 miles wide. The hurricane itself may travel slowly, about 5 to 12 miles per hour, while it is near its birthplace in the Caribbean Sea. It speeds up as it reaches the coast line and the middle latitudes, and may travel up to 50 miles per hour if it reaches New England.

Hurricanes can be ruinous. In 1900 at Galveston, Texas, a hurricane took a terrible toll in lives—over 6,000 people were drowned. In 1964, hurricane Dora, a hurricane almost 300 miles in diameter, cut a wide swath of damage across Florida and Georgia, but took no lives. (The Weather Bureau, by the way, favors feminine names for hurricanes.)

A hurricane's devastating winds are accompanied by torrential rains. The storm can continue for weeks before it is spent. Much of the property destruction and loss of life caused by hurricanes is due to flooding, as well as the force of winds.

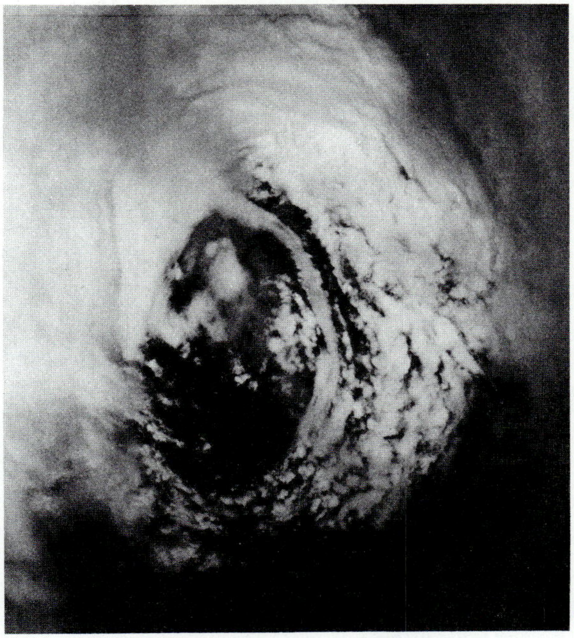

1

A special feature of the tropical cyclone is its center, known as the **eye.** 1 Within the eye is an area of calm, 5 to 20 miles across. Strange to say, the air currents in this small area are descending, rather than rising. There is no wind, no rain, no clouds: the sun shines brightly.

Meteorologists hope that studying hurricanes will lead to some means of controlling them. Just how a hurricane comes into being, and why it develops an eye, is not yet known. The path of a hurricane can, however, be predicted and people warned of its approach. Radar is one method of tracking a hurricane once the hurricane comes into existence. The Hurricane Hunters are courageous U.S. Navy pilots who fly directly into hurricanes, gathering data that will help predict the storm's course as well as help scientists understand the storm's origin. And our Tiros satellites have been highly successful in detecting the beginnings of tropical cyclones and tracking their paths.

Tornadoes

Tornadoes, or "twisters," are the smallest and most violent of all storms. They are also the briefest, lasting less than an hour on the average. A twister is named for its funnel-shaped cloud that develops at the base of a cloud. (1) The funnel twists along near the ground at 25 to 40 miles per hour. Inside the whirling funnel there is an extremely low air pressure. Like a gigantic vacuum cleaner, the funnel sucks up matter in its path. Thus the twister turns black or brown with soil and debris from wrecked buildings. The path of a twister is erratic. Sometimes the funnel rises up in the air and then touches the earth again, or goes around in a circle, stops, and even reverses its direction. The only safe place to be in a tornado is in an underground shelter or cellar.

(1)

Twisters usually come in groups. They have been known to strike in almost every state, but they are most common in the midwestern region of the United States. Twisters frequently form when a cold, dry continental air mass from Canada meets a warm, moist, air mass moving north from the Gulf of Mexico. In a way not yet well understood, the clouds that result from these conditions give rise to the tornadoes that hit the midwest "Tornado Alley." Kansas is most often hit, followed by Iowa, Texas, Oklahoma, Arkansas, and Missouri.

One of the most devastating series of tornadoes ever to hit the midwest ripped through Indiana, Ohio, Michigan, Illinois, and Wisconsin on April 11, 1965. A total of 235 persons were killed and 2,500 injured. Some communities were wiped out, with no buildings that were not destroyed or severely damaged. Property losses ran into millions of dollars. There were 37 separate tornadoes in the area on the same day.

The swiftness with which a tornado strikes once made people feel there was no way to escape the storms. In recent years, however, the Weather Bureau in Kansas City has been able to warn of the approach of tornadoes a few hours before they strike. Without the warnings, the death toll of the 1965 disaster might have been much higher. In 1925, when little was known about how to forecast the storms, tornadoes killed 689 persons in three hours, twisting through Missouri, Illinois, and Indiana.

Tornadoes are still considered largely a mystery by meteorologists, but efforts to learn more about their origin continue. Perhaps, when we know more about the behavior of our atmosphere, man will be able to nip young tornadoes and hurricanes in the bud. Just as medical science can often prevent or cure a disease when its cause is known, it may be possible to prevent or "cure" these violently destructive disturbances. First, however, research in the atmospheric sciences must find the causes of these storms.

REVIEW

1. How are the earth's prevailing winds associated with its low pressure belts?

2. How does the earth's rotation affect the circulation of its atmosphere?

3. What are the main differences between a high and a low?

4. How are hurricanes and tornadoes alike? How are they different from one another?

5. How does the Coriolis effect alter the direction of the trade winds?

NEW VIEW

Refer to the weather maps on page 296 to answer the following:

1. What was the temperature, wind speed and direction, and condition of the sky in the city nearest your home on each of the two days represented in the maps?

2. Did it rain (or snow) where you live on either day?

3. In which direction (east or west) do high and low pressure areas tend to move across the country? Explain in terms of what you know about prevailing winds.

4. What relationship between fronts and precipitation can you see on the maps?

2. ON THE AVERAGE

Most of you have lived in one place long enough to know what to expect of the weather, "on the average," throughout the year. If you live in the northern section of the country, you expect winters to be cold and snowy. If you live in some of the southern states you expect winters to be much like any other season—warm with perhaps occasional rains. But does the record of any one day's weather give us clues to what the weather is like all year round? Can it tell us if there is a long-term pattern of weather? Let's see.

On January 18, 1973, the TV weatherman gave this daily record:

High temperature: 66°F
Low temperature: 46°F
Present temperature: 46°F
Daily average: 56°F

With this information, do you know where the city is located? In New England? on the West Coast? in the South? or in the Mid-West? Actually, this is weather data for New York City. It is a record high for January since records began being kept.

No, the long term pattern of weather of an area, the **climate,** cannot be predicted from any one day's weather. Other types of data are needed to predict climate. What are these data?

Weather Records

Some weather stations have recorded the elements of weather—the temperature, precipitation, winds, and atmospheric pressure for over 100 years. For any one day at any of these stations, over 100 observations for each weather element are made. To handle this enormous amount of data, *climatologists,* scientists who study long term weather patterns, have found it convenient to group the data in special ways. To understand this procedure, you might review some ideas about *averages.*

Suppose you want the average of twelve observations. First add the values of the twelve observations, then divide the total by the number of observations, twelve. The result is an average. You had an example of "average daily temperature" in the previous section. This average was found by adding the highest temperature of the day to the lowest temperature of the day and dividing the result by 2: $(66° + 46° = 112°; 112° \div 2 = 56°)$.

To find the average monthly temperature, add all the daily averages, and divide by the number of days in the month. Finally, an average yearly temperature is obtained by adding the average monthly temperatures and dividing the result by 12. Average monthly precipitation data is obtained by a similar procedure. However, the average yearly total precipitation for the year is simply the sum of all the average monthly precipitation data.

Using the monthly precipitation and temperature data given below, find the average yearly temperature and average total precipitation for Chicago.

Did you find that the average yearly temperature was 49.7°F, while the average total precipitation for the year was 33 inches?

Locations having a similar pattern of temperature and precipitation data have a similar climate. New Haven, Connecticut, for example, has an average yearly temperature of 50°F and an average yearly total precipitation of 46 inches. New Haven and Chicago have similar climates. When such locations are grouped together, a climate classification for large areas can be made. Let's look at these classifications.

Classifying Climates

By 1918, enough weather data had been gathered by Dr. Wladimir Köppen, a university professor in Austria, to map broad areas of the earth into zones having similar climates. His system, still the most widely used classification, uses letters to show climate types. ❶ These climate types are also known by zone names. Let's look at the meaning of each letter and name, and examine a station in North America that illustrates each type.

In *tropical climates,* or A climates, the average temperature of each month is above 64°F. Obviously, there are no winter seasons in A climates. Annual precipitation is high, and plant life grows vigorously. Key West, Florida, is a station located in an A climate. ❷ Locate Key West on the climate map; then find the climate data in the table.

Tropical deserts, or B climates, contain great deserts and the semi-arid areas of the world. Precipitation is generally low, usually less than 10 inches a year. Yuma, Arizona, is located in a B-type climate. ❸ Once again find the city on the climate map and the climate data in the table. What differences do you see between the climate of Key West and that of Yuma?

Warm temperate climates, or C climates, cover almost half of the eastern United States, as well as sections of the west coast. These climates occur where the mean temperature of the coldest month is between 64°F and 27°F.

Station Name: Chicago, Illinois

Elevation: 1,180 ft

	J	*F*	*M*	*A*	*M*	*J*	*J*	*A*	*S*	*O*	*N*	*D*
Temperature (°F)	25	27	36	47	58	67	74	72	65	54	41	30
Precipitation (inches)	2.0	2.0	2.5	3.0	3.5	3.5	3.5	3.0	3.0	2.5	2.5	2.0

1

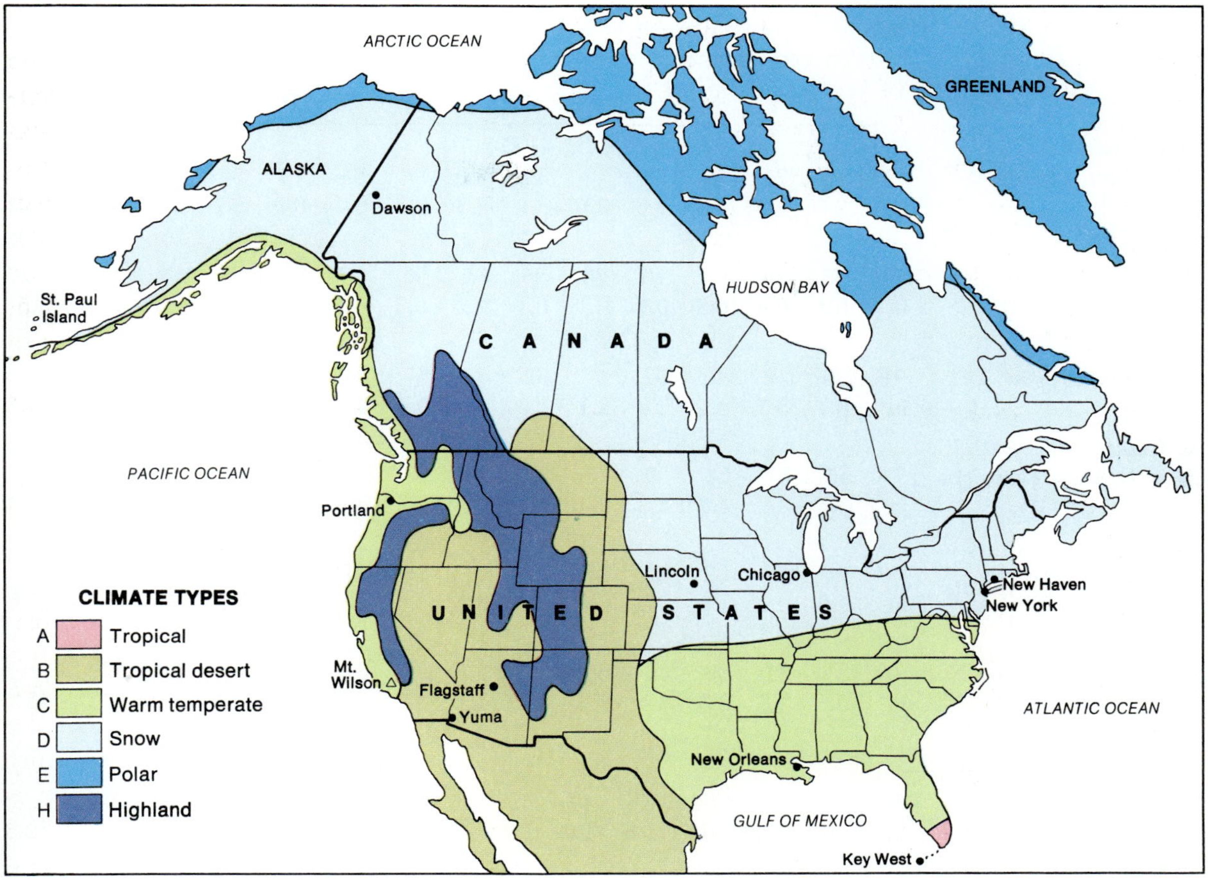
ARCTIC OCEAN
GREENLAND
ALASKA
Dawson
HUDSON BAY
St. Paul Island
CANADA
PACIFIC OCEAN
Portland
Lincoln
Chicago
New Haven
New York
UNITED STATES
CLIMATE TYPES
A Tropical
B Tropical desert
C Warm temperate
D Snow
E Polar
H Highland
Mt. Wilson
Flagstaff
Yuma
ATLANTIC OCEAN
New Orleans
GULF OF MEXICO
Key West

2

3

CLIMATE DATA

		J	F	M	A	M	J	J	A	S	O	N	D	Aver-age	Total
A Climate— Key West, Florida	**°F**	70	71	73	76	79	82	83	84	84	79	74	70	77	
	in	2.0	1.3	1.3	1.3	3.6	4.2	3.3	4.5	6.7	6.0	2.1	1.8		38.1
B Climate— Yuma, Arizona	**°F**	55	59	64	70	76	85	92	95	85	73	63	55	72	
	in	0.4	0.4	0.3	0.1	0.1	0.1	0.2	0.5	0.4	0.3	0.2	0.5		3.5
C Climate— Portland, Oregon	**°F**	39	42	46	52	57	62	67	67	61	55	47	41	53	
	in	6.1	5.1	4.7	2.8	2.1	1.6	0.5	0.6	1.9	3.2	6.2	7.0		41.8
C Climate— New Orleans, Louisiana	**°F**	55	57	68	69	75	81	83	83	80	72	62	56	69.5	
	in	4.5	4.3	4.8	4.8	4.4	5.5	6.6	5.8	4.8	3.5	3.8	4.6		57.4
D Climate— Lincoln, Nebraska	**°F**	24	27	39	52	62	72	77	76	67	55	40	29	51.5	
	in	0.6	0.9	1.2	2.5	4.0	4.1	4.0	3.5	2.9	2.0	1.2	0.8		27.7
D Climate— New York City, New York	**°F**	31	31	39	49	60	69	74	72	67	56	44	34	52	
	in	3.3	3.3	3.3	3.4	2.4	3.4	4.2	4.2	3.4	3.4	3.4	3.3		42
D Climate— Dawson, Yukon Territory, Canada	**°F**	–21	–21	4	28	47	56	60	54	42	26	2	–14	23	
	in	0.8	0.8	0.5	0.5	1.0	1.2	1.5	1.5	1.4	1.2	1.1	1.0		12.5
E Climate— St. Paul, Alaska	**°F**	25	24	24	29	35	42	45	48	45	40	33	29	35	
	in	1.7	1.2	1.2	1.1	1.1	1.2	2.4	3.2	3.4	3.0	2.5	2.0		24.0
H Climate— Mt. Wilson, California	**°F**	42	44	45	50	56	67	73	72	68	58	50	45	55.5	
	in	6.4	6.6	6.0	2.7	1.2	0.2	0.1	0.1	0.5	1.0	2.0	4.4		31.2
H Climate— Flagstaff, Arizona	**°F**	27	31	36	44	50	56	65	64	56	46	37	29	45.5	
	in	2.4	2.2	2.4	1.3	1.0	0.4	3.1	2.7	1.6	1.4	1.4	2.0		21.9

Stations as far apart as Portland, Oregon, and New Orleans, Louisiana, have C climates. ❶

Snow climates, or D-type climates, occur where at least one of the warmest months has an average temperature over 50°F but the coldest month's average is under 27°F. D climates cover most of Canada, as well as northern sections of the United States. Chicago, Illinois, has a D-type climate. ❷ So do Lincoln, Nebraska, and New York City.

1

2

Polar climates, or E climates, include the areas within the Arctic and Antarctic Circles. In these areas, no month has an average temperature over 50° F. 3 St. Paul Island, Alaska, has an E climate.

On the climate map you may have noted regions of North America marked H. These are *highland climates.* Highland climates are found in the mountain and high plateau areas of the earth. 4 The climate of a mountain can vary a great deal, and the climate can be different even a short distance away. Mt. Wilson, California, elevation 5,850 feet, and Flagstaff, Arizona, elevation 6,903 feet, are examples of highland climates.

In what climate zone do you live? What is the average temperature in your area? How can you find out?

3

4

REVIEW

1. What is the difference between weather and climate?

2. Describe a system used to classify climate zones.

3. Select a station in one zone and describe the climate of that station.

4. Describe the climate where you live.

NEW VIEW

1. Obtain climate data for the area in which you live. What type of climate is it? What other areas of the country have a similar climate?

2. Collect local weather data from newspapers for one month. Compare the conditions of that month with the same month's figures in the climate data of question 1. How are they alike? How different?

3. CONTROLLING CLIMATE

How many times have you listened to the weather report? You know that to give you the weather report, meteorologists collect data on temperature, precipitation, winds, and air pressure. All the information about these weather elements tells you the condition of the atmosphere at that time. If you collect the data for a long enough time, you will have a picture of the climate of your area.

These elements that "make" our weather, particularly temperature and precipitation, are the same elements that control climate. But what controls temperature and precipitation?

The Sun and Climate

You know the earth is warmed by the sun. Some of the heat that reaches us evaporates water from the oceans and eventually deposits some of this water on the land. So it is the earth's relationship to the sun that ultimately determines weather and climate.

The regions of the earth near the equator receive more heat than the polar regions. Does this mean that the equatorial regions are getting continually warmer while the polar regions are getting colder? No. Heat is transferred from the warmer regions of the earth to the cooler regions, mainly by the wind system of large storms (cyclones).

The heat that flows from the warmer to the cooler regions maintains an "average" temperature for the earth as a whole. Here is a map showing the average temperature for the northern hemisphere in January. ❶ Observe the lines connecting places having the same temperature. These lines are called **isotherms.** Compare the January map with the July map. ❷ Notice the shift of the isotherms. Do you think this has something to do with the relative positions of the earth and the sun during these months?

Remember that the part of the earth receiving the vertical rays of the sun is warmer than the part that receives the angular rays (Chapter 10). From March 21 through the summer months, the vertical rays of the sun warm areas north of the equator.

From September 21 through the winter months, the vertical rays warm areas south of the equator. Thus some sections of the earth are warmed more than other sections during these times. Do you see how the warming of the earth coincides with the shift of the isotherms?

Latitude

Stand on the sidewalk in front of your school and face the street. Which direction are you facing? Which way do you walk when you go home? to your friend's house? or to the park? That's easy! You can always tell where you are going by orienting yourself to "landmarks"—street signs, buildings, trees, high-

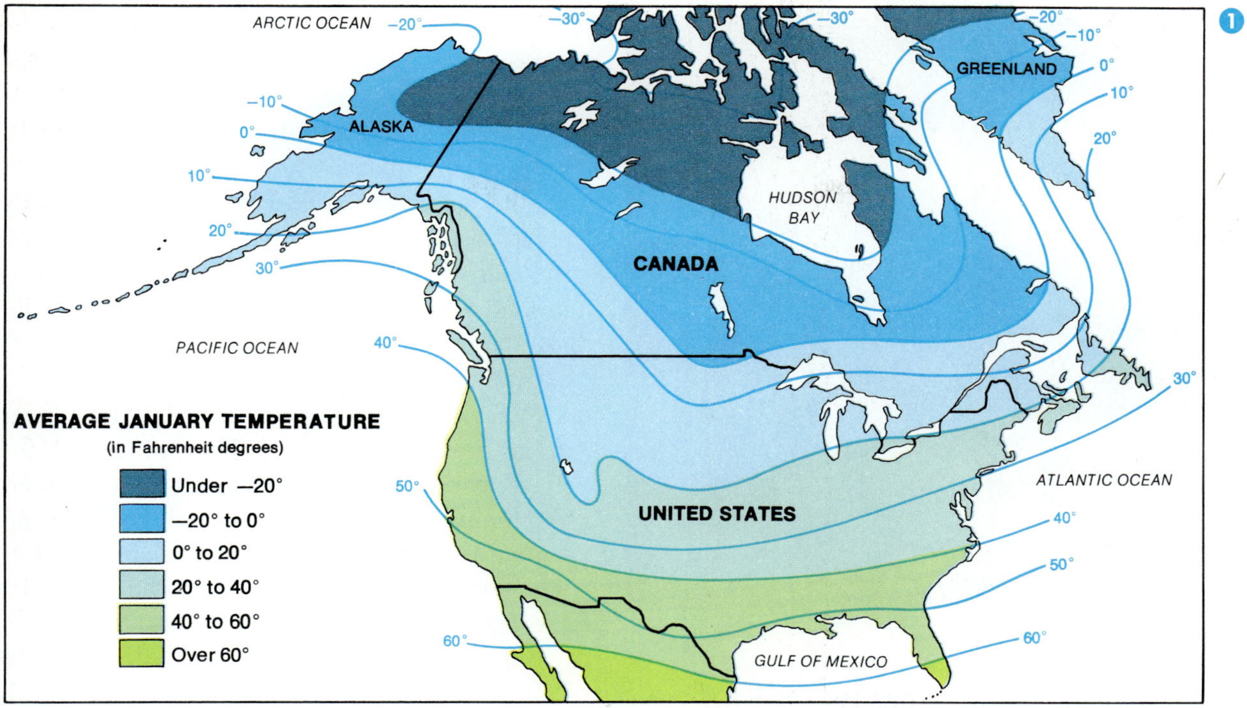
1
ARCTIC OCEAN
PACIFIC OCEAN
ATLANTIC OCEAN
GULF OF MEXICO
HUDSON BAY
GREENLAND
ALASKA
CANADA
UNITED STATES
AVERAGE JANUARY TEMPERATURE
(in Fahrenheit degrees)
Under —20°
—20° to 0°
0° to 20°
20° to 40°
40° to 60°
Over 60°
—30°
—20°
—10°
0°
10°
20°
30°
40°
50°
60°

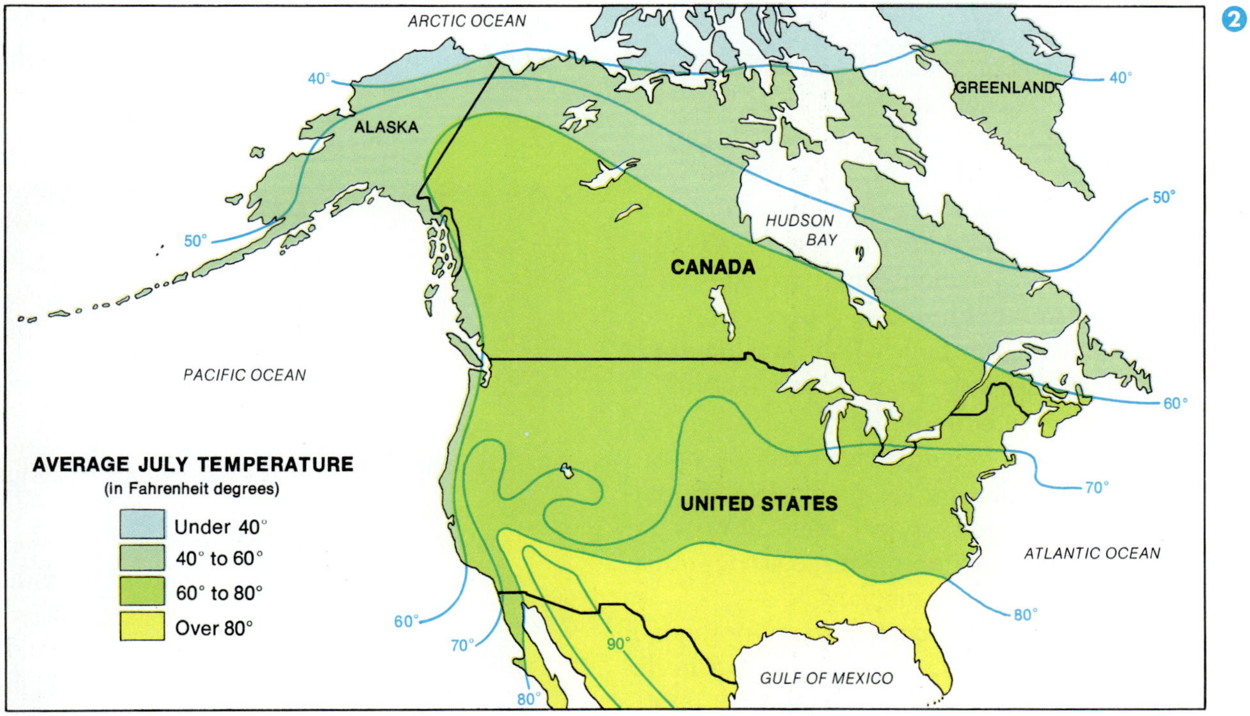
2
ARCTIC OCEAN
PACIFIC OCEAN
ATLANTIC OCEAN
GULF OF MEXICO
HUDSON BAY
GREENLAND
ALASKA
CANADA
UNITED STATES
AVERAGE JULY TEMPERATURE
(in Fahrenheit degrees)
Under 40°
40° to 60°
60° to 80°
Over 80°
40°
50°
60°
70°
80°
90°

1

ways. 1 It even works for long distance trips. But how would you know where you were going if you were at sea, without any landmarks to guide you?

A ship's captain does have some landmarks —the North Pole and the South Pole. But these aren't enough. A model of the earth can be divided by a pattern of intersecting lines, using the Poles as reference points. No doubt you have seen these lines on a globe. 2 They help us locate positions anywhere on earth. The north-south lines that extend from the North Pole to the South Pole are **longitude** lines. The east-west lines drawn parallel to the equator are **latitude** lines.

Latitude and longitude lines can be drawn through any point on the globe. We are particularly interested in locations near or far away from the equator, so let's focus our attention on latitude positions only.

Latitude describes locations north or south of the equator. Latitude values are stated in degrees and vary from 0° at the equator to 90° at the poles. Positions north of the equator have north latitude (N), those south of the equator have south latitude (S). Using a globe with latitude and longitude lines, find the latitude of the place where you live. There is another easy way to find your latitude. Simply measure the angle from the northern horizon to Polaris, the North Star. This angle, measured in degrees, is the latitude of your position.

Latitude and Temperature

What is your latitude position? Are you near or far from the equator? The latitude of the place where you live determines both the average temperature for the year and the daily and annual temperature range. In general, the farther you live from the equator, the lower the average temperature for the year.

Suppose you lived in Cristobal, a city in Panama. Cristobal is located about 10° north of the equator. The average temperature for the year is about 80°F, and the temperature range is only about 2 degrees. The sun shines for about 12 hours every day and the night also lasts about 12 hours. There is a rainy sea-

2

son, with an average annual rainfall of 130 inches, usually occurring between May and December.

If you live in Chicago or New York, your latitude is about 40°N. The average yearly temperature is about 50°F. The average monthly temperature ranges from 25°F to 74°F. The average rainfall is about 33 inches. Winters are cold with about 8 hours of sunlight. Summers are hot with 15 to 16 hours of sunlight.

You can see for yourself how latitude affects temperature. Suppose you lived in Dawson in the Yukon Territory of Canada, at a latitude of 65°N. Predict what the climate is like. Then check your prediction with the data in the table on page 302.

3

Altitude

Latitude is not the only factor that affects the temperature of a location. Even in warm areas, extremely high mountains may be covered with snow for part of the year. 3 Can you explain why? The altitude of the mountain, its height above sea level, is the answer. Temperature decreases at a rate of 3.5°F for every 1,000 feet we ascend. The higher a station is above sea level, the cooler it is. Consider Flagstaff, Arizona, a city we studied on page 303. Flagstaff, at an elevation of about 7,000 feet, has an average annual temperature of 46°F.

If temperature also increases 3.5°F for every 1,000 feet we descend, then Flagstaff could have an average annual temperature of 70°F if it were at sea level (altitude 0 feet). Do you agree?

Oceans and Prevailing Winds

Oceans also influence land areas located some distance inland, particularly where the prevailing winds blow over the water toward the land (onshore). Passing over warm water, these onshore winds carry with them mild, maritime air. Parts of the west coast of the United States have marine west-coast climates. The prevailing westerlies, blowing across the Pacific Ocean, carry moisture onto the land areas.

The prevailing westerlies blow from west to east across the United States. Therefore, there are no strong onshore winds on the east coast.

Ocean Currents and Mountain Ranges

Ocean currents and high mountain ranges also affect the temperature of some regions. Some ocean currents (see page 250) carry warm or cold water far into northern latitudes, while other currents carry cold water into southern latitudes. Winds blowing over these currents can become cooler or warmer than the surroundings and carry this air into neighboring land areas.

Mountain ranges are effective barriers to invading winds. On the west side of the coast ranges of California, the region experiences a

1

2

marine climate with moderate temperatures. On the eastern side, desert regions exist. ① These hot, dry areas are a result of the moisture-free air flowing down over the mountain, becoming warmer as it descends.

Precipitation Controls

The amount of precipitation an area receives also determines the type of climate the area has. What controls the precipitation of any area?

Two principal factors affect the amount of precipitation received in most areas of the United States: mountain barriers and storm tracks. You know that moist air is cooled when it rises. You also know that this cooling is one cause of precipitation. Mountain barriers force air to rise, cool, and condense. Precipitation is the result. The windward side of our Pacific Coast ranges, the side from which the wind blows, is wet. This favorable condition gives rise to some lush vegetation on the western slopes. ② The sheltered, or leeward, side of these mountain chains is a dry area. These areas on the eastern side of the mountains, sometimes called rain shadow deserts, have sparse vegetation.

Storms, or traveling low pressure centers called cyclones, move across the United States from west to east. Recall that these storms are generated by air masses with different temperature and varying amounts of moisture. It is the moisture from such storms—the intense but brief thunderstorm, the quiet summer rain, the heavy snowfalls—that provides the major source of precipitation for most of our country. Study this map showing the average amount of precipitation that the United States receives in a year. ③ How much precipitation does your location receive in any one year?

REVIEW

1. Define the term isotherm. How is shifting of the isotherms related to the motion of the earth and the sun?
2. How does the latitude of a location affect its temperature?
3. In California desert regions are located on the eastern side of coastal ranges. Explain why.
4. Describe the factors that control precipitation.

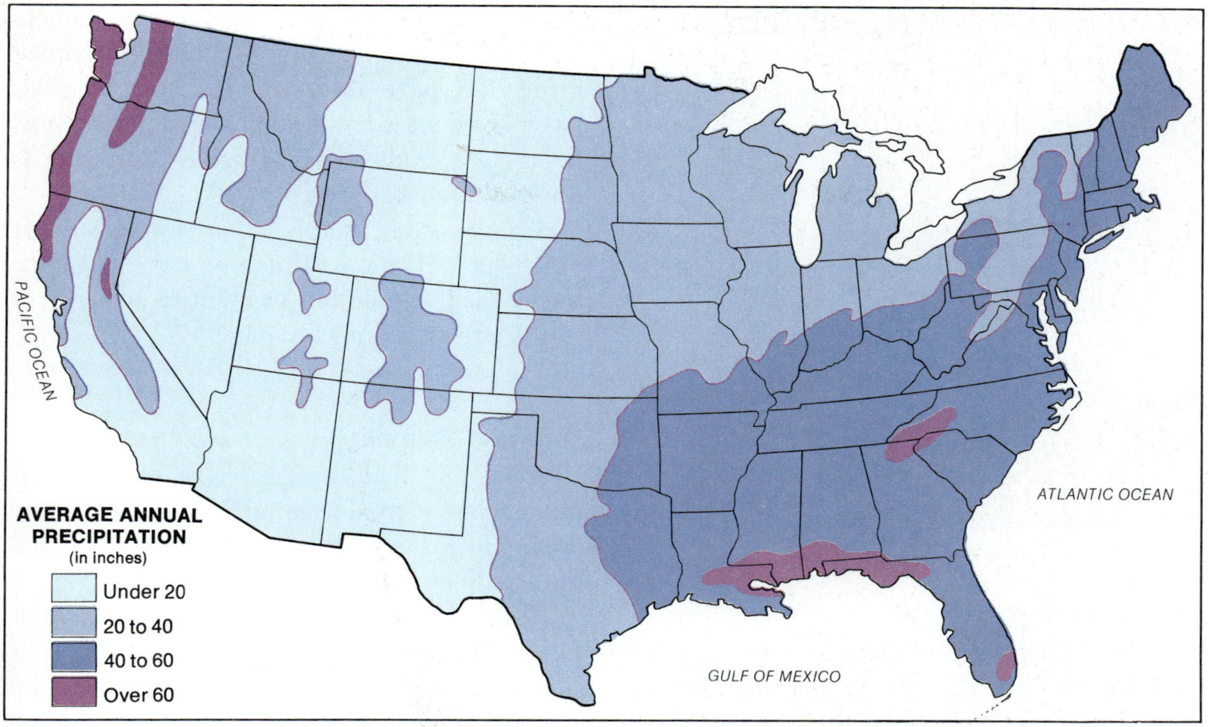

3

NEW VIEW

1. Describe the temperature and precipitation controls that affect the climate in your part of the country.

2. If you are at the North Pole, latitude 90° N, where would you see Polaris? If you are at the equator, latitude 0°, where would you see Polaris?

4. SOIL, CLIMATE, AND PLANTS

Do you know you can raise some of your favorite plants without using soil? 4 **Hydroponics,** growing plants in water, is the interesting technique that makes this possible. Although hydroponics can be used to grow plants without soil, it is the soil that gives us the many forms of vegetation we use every day.

Climate plays a large part in determining the type of soil in a certain place. And soil, in turn, determines the type of vegetation in that area. We use soil for cultivating crops, grazing herds, maintaining forests. Indeed, climate has a direct bearing on our lives through the soil it helps form.

4

1 

Parent Material

As rock decays, sediment is formed. The sediment may become mixed with humus, decayed plant and animal matter, and form a *residual soil.* This residual soil stays where it was formed. On the other hand, sediment may be moved from the place when it is formed. Eroded material, moved by water, wind, or glaciers, may eventually be deposited on other bedrock. Here it becomes mixed with humus and forms a *transported soil.* The soils of New England are transported soils. As glaciers moved over the land, they deposited the sediment that became these soils.

Soil Profiles

If you visit a building site, you may see several layers of exposed soil. 1 What you are looking at is a **soil profile.** Different layers of soil in the profile are known as **soil horizons.**

The upper layer is the **topsoil,** or the A horizon. Topsoil contains humus, which gives it a darker color than the other layers.

The **subsoil,** or B horizon, is the second layer. Rainfall washes down soluble minerals and clay from the A horizon. These substances collect in the subsoil. **Weathered bedrock** forms the next layer, the C horizon. This layer contains rock and minerals but almost no organic material. Below the C horizon is **unweathered bedrock.**

As you can see, soil is not as simple as most of us think. The next time you have a chance to see a soil profile, try to identify as many of of the layers as you can.

Soils and Rainfall

You know that climate is the most important factor in the formation of the soil in any area. How does the climate of the United States affect our soil? 2

In the eastern section of the country, rainfall usually exceeds 25 inches a year. The soils in these states are called **pedalfers.** In the western states, where the rainfall is less than 25 inches a year, the soils are known as **pedocals.** What type of soil do you think is in your section of the country?

The names of these soils describe themselves. The word pedalfer is made up of three parts: *ped*–meaning soil, *al*–for aluminum, and *fer*–indicating iron. We know then that pedalfers contain accumulations of iron compounds and aluminum. Rainfall washes the soluble calcium and magnesium compounds out of the soil. These compounds are carried away in ground water. The aluminum and iron compounds stay behind in the B horizon. Regions that are covered by forests usually have pedalfer soils.

The word pedocal is made up of *ped*–soil, and *cal*–calcium. Pedocals develop in areas with little rainfall. The rain is enough to wash down soluble calcium and magnesium compounds into the B horizon, but the rain is not sufficient to wash these compounds away.

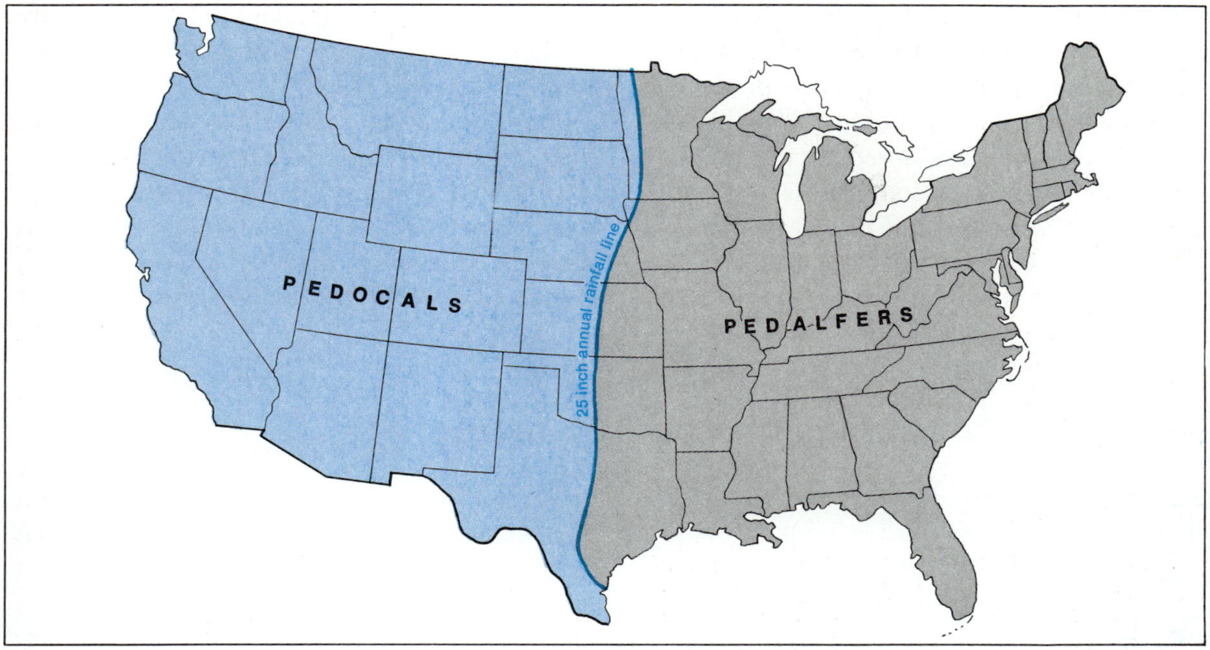

2

Large deposits of calcium and magnesium compounds accumulate and over a period of time they form a hard, white crust called **caliche.** Deposits of caliche make the soil very fertile, but irrigation is needed to make the soil produce good crops. Here is an example of what can be produced when people and nature work together. 3

Water in the Soil

What properties determine the way in which water moves through the soil? Soil is made up of small particles of weathered rock. These particles differ in size. The surfaces of soil particles hold water and dissolved minerals. The smaller the particles, the greater the total surface area, and the greater the amount of water that can wet the surface. Soil scientists call the smallest particles clay, the larger ones silt, and the largest sand. Loam soils have some of the properties of each of these soil types.

The grains, or particles, of a clay soil are very tiny. Between the grains are small spaces called *pores*. Although the pores are extremely small, there are a great many of them. The percentage of space between grains is known as **porosity.** Porosity determines the amount of water a soil can hold.

3

When rain water enters a clay soil, it passes through it very slowly. The rate at which water passes through a material is called **permeability.** Clay soils have low permeability, because water is trapped and stored in the pores of these soils. For this reason, clay is most effective in holding water and dissolved minerals.

Compared to clay soils, sandy soils have larger grain sizes and larger pore spaces. From what you have learned about soil and its ability to hold water, predict how water will move through a sandy soil.

In very fine soils, water may actually move upward toward the surface from the zone where the ground is saturated with water. This upward movement of water through the soil is known as **capillary action.** To see how capillary action works, try this investigation. ■

■ AN APPRENTICE INVESTIGATION into Capillary Action

❶

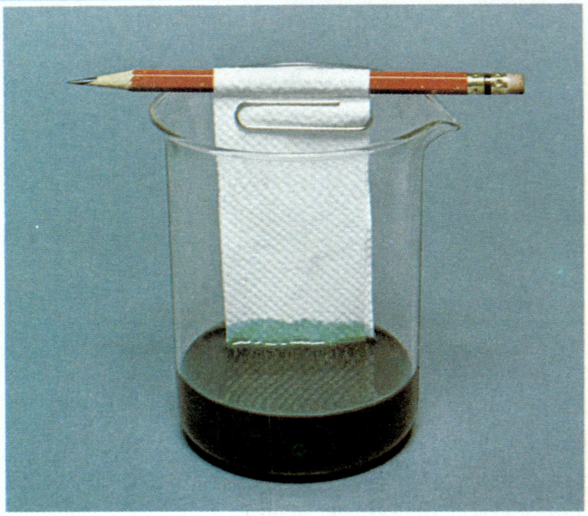

❷

Pour a small amount of colored water into a beaker. Cut a strip of paper toweling about 3 centimeters (1 inch) wide. Suspend this strip in the beaker so that the lower edge is slightly below the surface of the water. After several minutes, note what has happened. ❶

Now take two pieces of glass tubing with different inside diameters. Place both tubes in the beaker of water. Here is the result of one trial. ❷ The water rises in the porous paper and in the narrow tubes because of capillary action. Do you see a relationship between the diameter of the tube and the height that the water rises in the tube?

An Investigation On Your Own

Do different liquids rise to the same height in the same size tube? Try the investigation using alcohol, oil, and water. First make a prediction and then check it!

In your investigation, you saw that capillary action causes water to rise in porous materials and in narrow tubes. The tiny spaces between the soil particles act much like narrow tubes, thus bringing water up to the surface of the soil, against the pull of gravity. The water then enters the thin, hairlike root systems of plants and is carried high into the plants by capillary action.

Plants in the Soil

In what part of the country do you live? Can you find palm trees, cactus, maple trees? The kinds of plants that grow in any area depend on the soil—and soil depends on climate! Now you can see how soil, climate, and vegetation are related.

You already know soil types can be classified. But because vegetation also affects soil formation, soils can be grouped according to the type of vegetation they produce. Soil types in the United States, for example, can be divided into forest, grassland, and desert. (1)

(2)

Compare this vegetation map with the climate map on page 301. In what climate zone does the forest area fall?

Here is a soil profile from a forest area. (2) The surface layer is the topsoil, where humus has accumulated. Rainwater passing through this layer becomes an acid solution. This solution washes out materials from below the topsoil, making it a lighter color. Material from the topsoil is collected in the B horizon.

(1)

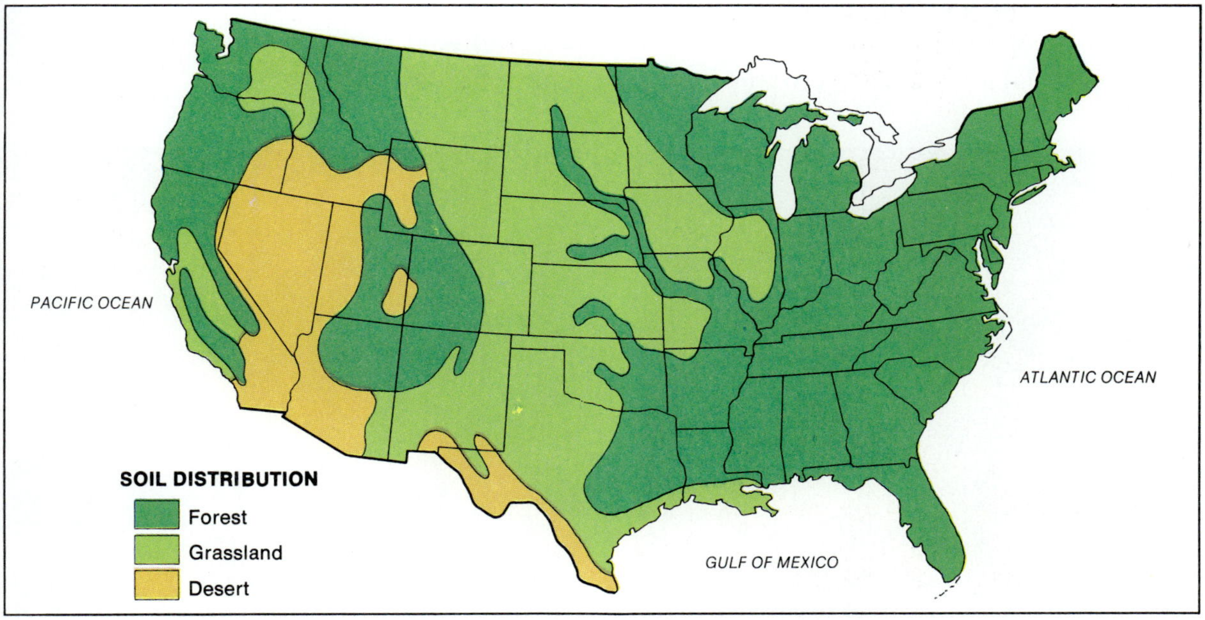

1

2

Vegetation of the forests changes in different sections of the country. In the northern forest you find eastern white pine and white oak,① ponderosa pine and aspen grow in the western forest, while mangrove and mahogany grow in the tropical forests of southern Florida.

Grasslands occupy the central portion of the United States from the Gulf of Mexico to Canada.② On the climate map this area corresponds to the warm temperate, or C, climate.

This is a soil profile of a grasslands area.③ The topsoil layer is usually deep, because the root systems of grasses add organic material to the soil. Soluble minerals are washed down to lower levels of the subsoil, and remain there since rainfall is not great enough to wash them completely out of the soil. For this reason, grasslands are fertile agricultural areas.

Where there is little rainfall, vegetation is sparse and desert soils develop. Compare the soil profile of a desert area with those you have already studied.④ Since there is little rainfall, you would expect that only small amounts of minerals wash down into lower layers. Also, because there is little vegetation, little topsoil is formed. You have seen photographs of a desert.⑤ And you may have wondered what kinds of plants can grow there. In the warm

3

4

5

desert regions of the United States, sagebrush and creosote bushes grow in widely scattered clumps. Deserts at high altitudes have lower temperatures, thus they support different types of vegetation. How many desert plants are you familiar with?

Long ago, early people lived every day of their lives in a wilderness. From the land, they gathered wild plants and fruits. They cut trees to build houses. On the cleared land, they grazed animals. They depended on these animals for meat and clothes.

Today, we still depend on the soil for our food, fibers, and lumber products. Our modern use of soil, however, requires special care. As the amount of space covered by soil becomes smaller, we must increase the number of plants growing on each piece of the soil. The wise use of fertilizer and irrigation systems help us. We also use new strains of plants —types that will be of a higher quality and have a more abundant yield. 6 Using modern farming practices, we can preserve the soil and keep it from eroding away. We do all these things because we understand how much we depend on the earth, how much we depend on the soil.

6

REVIEW

1. What is a soil profile? Briefly describe the layers of a profile.

2. Compare pedalfer and pedocal soils. In what areas of the United States are these soils found?

3. How are soils classified according to vegetation type? Describe the soil profile of one of these types.

4. Define the terms porosity and permeability.

NEW VIEW

1. Soils are often termed mature or immature. Find out what these distinctions mean.

2. What effect does the *leaching* process have on soil?

3. Determine how capillary action affects the formation of desert soils.

5. RELATING THE CONCEPTS

Weather records collected over a long period of time indicate patterns for different parts of the earth. The long-term pattern of weather is called climate.

When locations having similar climates are grouped together, climate classifications for large areas can be made. These climate types are tropical, desert; warm temperate, snow, polar, and highland.

Climate is determined by temperature and precipitation. In turn, temperature is controlled by the earth's relationship to the sun, altitude, nearness to oceans, prevailing winds and mountain ranges. Precipitation is controlled by mountain ranges and the effect of storm tracks on the area.

Climate determines the type of soil found in a particular area. And the vegetation of an area depends on the soil. Climate and soil are two of our most important resources—we must use them wisely.

Reviewing the Concepts

► *The global pattern of prevailing winds is due to air pressure differences.* Winds are horizontal movements of the air ocean produced by air pressure differences. They are influenced by the rotation of the earth as well as by the uneven heating of the earth's surface by the sun.

► *The movement of air masses has an important influence on weather.* An air mass is a large body of air with fairly uniform temperature and humidity, which therefore has fairly uniform weather inside the mass. As an air mass moves across the land, influenced by low pressure and high pressure regions, it carries its own weather. When different air masses meet, fronts that form between them are sources of predictable weather.

► *Climate is the long-term pattern of weather.* The pattern becomes known after weather records have been kept for a long period of time. By examining weather records, it is also possible to find out if the climate of a region is changing. Such changes may be related to increasing pollution of the atmosphere.

► *Average yearly temperature and total yearly precipitation are elements used to classify climates.* Locations with similar patterns of temperature and precipitation can be grouped together into climate classifications.

► *Climate is controlled by a variety of factors.* Temperature is controlled by latitude, altitude, nearness to oceans, prevailing winds and mountain ranges. Precipitation is controlled by mountain ranges and the location of the area in relation to storm tracks. Of course, the ultimate control for both temperature and precipitation is the earth's position relative to the sun and the earth's motion on its axis.

► *Climate determines the type of soil and natural vegetation of an area.* In this respect, climate becomes one of our most valuable natural resources. Today, as in earliest times, most of the world's population is found in areas where the climate is moderate rather than extreme.

Testing Yourself

1. On a weather map, what is a low? a high?

2. Name two factors that affect the direction of a prevailing wind. What effects do they have?

3. What is an air mass? Give one or more examples.

4. What happens when a moving, cold air mass meets a warm air mass that is not moving? What is the effect on the weather?

5. Why is a weather map useful in predicting weather?

6. How are tornadoes and hurricanes alike? How are they different? How are they related to air pressure?

7. Portland, Oregon, is located in a C climate. Describe the climate of Portland. What is another name for a C climate?

8. At the equator, mountains can be covered with snow for part of the year. Explain why this is so.

9. Mountain ranges control temperature and precipitation. Explain.

10. How do cyclones form? What effect do cyclones have on climate?

11. Compare the soil profile of a desert region with that of a forest.

12. What effect does rainfall have on the types of soil found in the United States?

Extending the Concepts

Investigation. What is the weather pattern where you live? Make your own weather observations and you may find out some things about the local weather that most of your friends don't know. You can do as thorough a job as you wish, according to your interest, and the tools with which you work.

A simple set of observations may consist of noting wind direction, temperature, and kind of weather at a given time each day for a couple of weeks. From these observations you may be able to make some generalizations about how wind direction and rainfall are (or are not) related.

More observations, made at closer intervals, might uncover a more definite pattern. Such observations as temperature, wind direction and speed, air pressure, humidity, kinds of clouds, and percent of cloud cover, along with the kind of weather, could be made. These observations should be taken at regular intervals two or more times in each 24-hour period. They should be continued over a period of several weeks.

Perhaps you can borrow some of the needed instruments or make or buy them. It may be that such investigations will help you decide that a meteorologist's career is for you.

Suggested Reading

Findley, Rowe, *American Deserts,* Washington, D.C., National Geographic, 1972. An interesting description of the geological formations of the desert as well as the plant and animal life.

Milgrom, Harry, *Understanding Weather,* New York, Crowell, 1970. The how and why of weather with experiments that you can do.

Unit Five

THE RECORD IN THE ROCKS

What you see here are the petrified remains of trees that grew on the earth hundreds of millions of years ago.

The wood of the trees has long since decayed and been replaced by silica. Thus we have preserved in stone the original size and shape of these ancient trees.

How does petrification take place? What can we learn from the preserved remains of living things from the distant past?

Let's look at earth's history written in stone.

15

Keys to the Past

Every day you walk on planet Earth. How old is the planet you walk on? When did marine animals begin to leave a record of their presence in the rocks? Perhaps you have answers to these questions from your previous work in science or from an encyclopedia or newspaper report. But how do scientists know? Shakespeare wrote the play *As You Like It* in 1599. In it he reported that the earth was 6,000 years old. (1) Almost the same age was used in 1654 by the Anglican Archbishop Ussher who proclaimed that the Earth was created in 4004 B.C. A later scholar went a step further and stated that creation occurred at 9 A.M. on September 17, 4004 B.C.

We now know that these estimates of the age of the earth are in serious error. The scientific path leading to better estimates of the age of the earth has been long and difficult. We still don't have an exact answer, but we're closer to the truth—about 4.6 billion years closer—than Shakespeare was. How has this come about?

1

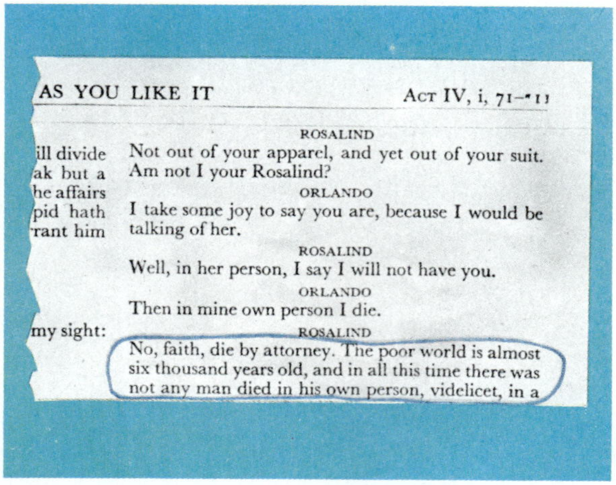

AS YOU LIKE IT — ACT IV, i, 71–111

ROSALIND
Not out of your apparel, and yet out of your suit. Am not I your Rosalind?

ORLANDO
I take some joy to say you are, because I would be talking of her.

ROSALIND
Well, in her person, I say I will not have you.

ORLANDO
Then in mine own person I die.

ROSALIND
No, faith, die by attorney. The poor world is almost six thousand years old, and in all this time there was not any man died in his own person, videlicet, in a

1. DATING THE PAST

The study of dates for events in the earth's past is called **geochronology,** from *geo* meaning "earth" and *chronos* meaning "time." Geochronology has been a major occupation of geologists and chemists over the last hundred years or so. They have developed two basic ways of estimating the age of the earth. These are **relative dating** and **absolute dating.** Absolute dating is based on measuring the atomic decay of natural radioactive elements in rocks and other materials such as shells, wood, and bones. Material can be dated quite accurately by absolute dating. For convenience, any other dating method is called relative dating. Let's look first at some methods of relative dating.

Relative Dating

In 1715, the British astronomer Edmund Halley suggested that the saltiness of the ocean was a clue to the age of the earth. Almost two hundred years later, the Irish geologist John Joly attempted to calculate the age of the earth based on the amount of salt in the ocean. Joly determined the amount of sodium carried into the ocean each year. He divided this into the amount of sodium in the ocean and obtained an age of 90 million years for the earth. Was he right?

Lord Kelvin, a respected British physicist of the nineteenth century, tried a different method. He reasoned that the earth was once molten and was still cooling off. You can't feel the heat escaping from the earth—but it does. Miners feel the earth's heat in deep mine shafts. In fact, it gets so hot that the mines must be air-conditioned for the miners.

Scientists now use sensitive electric thermometers to measure the flow of heat from the earth. Kelvin knew the melting temperature of rocks, and he knew approximately how fast heat was flowing from the earth. He calculated that the earth had taken 20 to 40 million years to cool from its original molten condition. How close was Kelvin to knowing the true age of the earth?

In another relative dating method, geologists used the thickness of sedimentary rocks as a clue to the age of some relatively recent events in the earth's past. They estimated that about 120,000 meters (400,000 feet) of sedimentary rock has been deposited since the first hard-shelled marine organisms appeared on earth. (2) This depth of sedimentary rock was not deposited in one place. Later we'll see how geologists estimate the total thickness of all sedimentary rocks.

In addition to the total thickness, geologists must know how fast sedimentary rock is being formed. According to an early estimate, 30 centimeters (1 foot) of sedimentary rock is formed each 100 years. A simple calculation reveals that the first hard-shelled marine organisms appeared 40 million years ago. This calculation seems to confirm Kelvin's estimate. Was Kelvin right after all?

Absolute Dating

There was no way of knowing if any of these estimates were right until the development of absolute dating techniques. These techniques are based on knowing the rates of decay of radioactive elements. You have already learned about half-life and you probably know that some radioactive isotopes can be used for absolute dating. Within recent years the radioactive isotope potassium-40 has become another important source of dating events in the earth's past.

The drawings and photographs of prehistoric plants and animals in this book are based on reconstructions. The paintings of the environments are the artist's view based on information available.

(2)

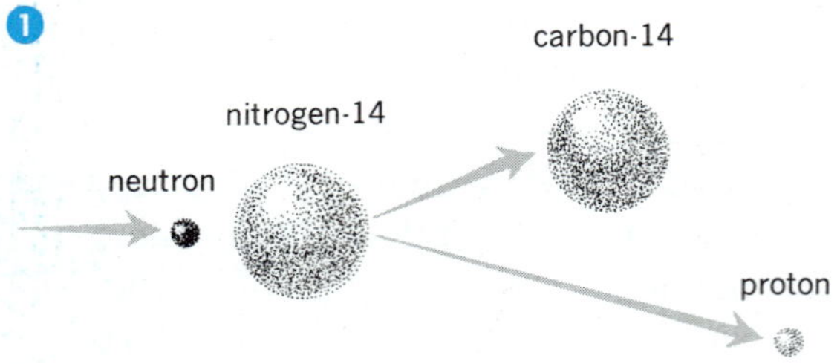

Potassium-40 decays to both argon-40 and calcium-40. Dating is based on the relative amounts of potassium-40 and argon-40 in samples of feldspar, mica, and the green marine mineral glauconite. The half-life of potassium-40 is 1.3 billion years. The potassium-argon method has been used to determine most of the critical dates used in the newest geologic time scale (p. 347). Geologists have refined the methods of chemical analysis for potassium-argon dating so that rocks can be dated if they are 1 million to several billion years old. It has been very helpful to find such a relatively simple dating technique that can be used in dating the oldest rocks as well as some of the youngest.

Carbon-14 Dating

Until 1947 no one knew the precise dates of some fairly recent events. In that year the American chemist Willard F. Libby proposed a dating method based on carbon-14, a radioactive isotope of carbon. Carbon-14 is produced when nitrogen high in the atmosphere is bombarded by neutrons from cosmic radiation. (1) This carbon-14 combines with oxygen to form carbon dioxide. The carbon dioxide quickly reaches the lower atmosphere where it is absorbed by plants. These plants, in turn, are eaten by animals. Therefore, carbon-14 is found as part of the carbon in calcium carbonate that makes up the bones and shells of land and water animals.

When a plant or animal dies, the supply of carbon-14 is cut off. By radioactive decay, the carbon-14 in the plant or animal slowly becomes nitrogen-14 again. The half-life of carbon-14 is 5,760 years. As you can see, this is quite a short half-life compared with the other radioactive isotopes used in absolute dating. To find the age of a sample shell, bone, or piece of wood, the material is burned to produce carbon dioxide or some other form of carbon. The resulting carbon product is placed in a special type of radiation counter, similar to a Geiger counter, to measure the radioactivity remaining in the sample.

While the plant or animal is alive, there is

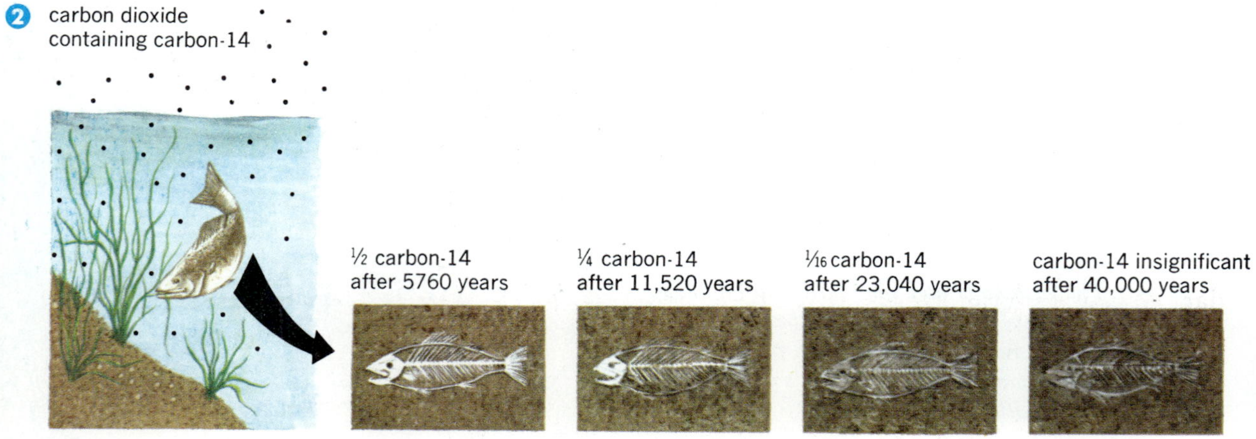

a balance, or ratio, between the amount of carbon-14 and ordinary carbon, carbon-12. New carbon-14 is added as fast as it decays. ❷ But when the organism dies, no new carbon-14 is added. The ratio of carbon-14 to ordinary carbon gradually decreases. The less carbon-14 there is in relation to ordinary carbon, the older the sample is. Carbon-14 dating permits us to date events back to about 40,000 years ago.

How Accurate Is Carbon-14 Dating?

Scientists have ways of checking the accuracy of carbon-14 dating for events of the last few thousand years. For example, if a living tree is cut down, the carbon-14 age of the heartwood should agree with the age found by counting the number of annual rings. As you probably know, the wide, light-colored part of each ring marks the rapid growth of springtime; the dark part marks the slow growth of late summer and fall.

In a similar manner we can count the number of annual layers of sediment in a lake as a check of the carbon-14 dates related to the lake. During the warm months, lakes receive snow meltwater and rainwater that carry large amounts of light-colored sediment into the lake. During the winter, the lake is frozen and only a small amount of fine, dark-colored material suspended in lake water settles to the bottom. These alternately light and dark layers of sediment are called **varves.** ❸ How are they similar to tree rings? When used on living trees and existing lakes, both annual-ring and varve counting give absolute dates for past events.

Another absolute dating tool is the calendar. When historic events have been recorded according to calendars still in use, it is easy to check the results of carbon-14 dating against the true dates. By using the calen-

❸

dar, annual rings, and varves, geologists have improved the accuracy of carbon-14 dating techniques. The method can now be used with confidence for dating relatively recent events where no other method is available.

We can now investigate such interesting questions as when men first migrated to the Americas. Wood from their campfires tells us the route these men followed across our continent. Shells tell us where they had their meals of marine shellfish and where the beaches were at that time. The beginning and end of ancient civilizations have also been dated by the carbon-14 technique.

REVIEW

1. How does absolute dating differ from relative dating?
2. Why is the potassium-argon method more useful to geologists than some other methods of radioactive dating?
3. How is carbon-14 formed in the atmosphere? Why is carbon-14 important in radioactive dating?
4. In what ways are varves and tree rings similar? How are they used for geologic dating?

NEW VIEW

1. There are many thick layers of salt in sedimentary rocks on land. These were precipitated from ocean water when parts of the continents were submerged. How do these salt layers affect the calculation of the age of the earth based on the saltiness of the ocean?

2. The radiocarbon dating method assumes that carbon-14 has been produced at a constant rate over the last 40,000 years or so. What would happen to the apparent age of samples dated by carbon-14 if the amount of cosmic radiation has been greater or less at times in the past?

2. FOSSILS

Suppose you are trying to follow someone across an open stretch of land without letting him know. If there are few places to hide, you have to stay far behind so you won't be seen. Suddenly you realize you've lost him. Which way did he go? You hurry ahead and search for clues. As you walk quickly over the bare rock surface, you find nothing. Then in a sandy patch you see footprints leading off toward a tree-lined valley. But the wind is blowing the sand and making the footprints disappear. Now you really hurry toward the valley. You reach a muddy area, and there you find more footprints. These are sharp and clear. They lead toward a wide, shallow stream that flows into a lake. You follow these footprints to the edge of the stream, and then they disappear. Which way did the man go?

Footprints That Survive

You have seen variations of this plot many times on television and in the movies. For the geologist this little drama is quite real—but he plays it with animals and plants that lived hundreds of millions of years ago. These animals and plants migrated across continents and shallow seas. The only clues they left of their journeys are footprints, imprints of leaves, shells, or other **fossil** evidence. (1) You probably know that fossils are the remains or evidence of remains of an organism that lived long ago.

1

Our story illustrates some of the difficulty scientists have in finding evidence of past life. No footprints are left on bare rock surfaces. Any footprints made in the sediment of a stream bed are quickly washed away by the stream. Is there a chance that any of the footprints in our story could be preserved as fossils? Remember, the footprints in the sand were disappearing. The wind was smoothing them out. But those in the mud near the stream remained clear. Could they be preserved as fossils? What would have to happen?

If the wind continued to blow, the mud would dry and become very hard. Now there would be hard impressions of the footprints. These impressions are called **molds.** Later on, the wind might blow a layer of fine sand over the area. The fine sand would fill the mold of each footprint and make a solid mold, or **cast,** of each print. Then the stream might rise and cover the sand. Fine sediment carried by the stream would be deposited layer upon layer over the footprints. Then, as time passed slowly, the mud and fine sediment would harden into shale under the weight of the layers of sediment above them.

Perhaps ground water containing calcium carbonate, silicon dioxide, or iron oxide would move through the sandy layer. The mineral matter would precipitate on the sand grains and slowly cement them together to form sandstone. Thousands of years later the shale and sandstone layers might be uplifted and partly eroded. The footprints might now be part of a small hill lying in the path of some new construction. As workmen cut away the rock layers, one man might notice the mold and cast of a footprint. Perhaps the story spreads, and geologists come to examine the fossil footprint of an ancient man who once crossed a patch of muddy ground.

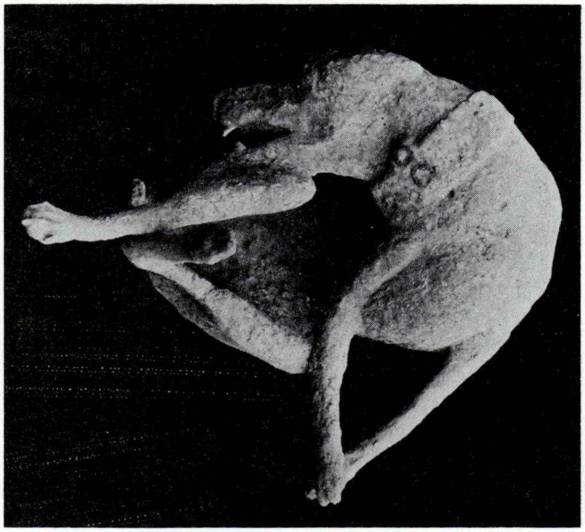

3

More Evidence of Life

You could substitute many different "players" for the man who left his footprint. Tracks might have been left by a bird, a prehistoric horse, a woolly mammoth, or a dinosaur. 2 And, of course, these events could happen any time from the appearance of the first land animals in the distant past into the distant future.

2

If preserving and discovering fossils seems extraordinary, you're right. Scientists estimate that more than 99 percent of all life on earth has disappeared without leaving a trace. Now you have some idea why fossils are rare. Fossils of marine animals, however, are not as rare as those of land animals. There are great numbers of marine animals, and their burial by sediment is usually much faster and more certain.

Rapid burial can also occur on land when a mudflow sweeps along a canyon at 30 kilometers (20 miles) an hour and buries everything in its path. Volcanic eruptions can lay down thick layers of ash that have the same effect. When Mt. Vesuvius erupted in A.D. 79, it buried the nearby town of Pompeii in stifling gases and hot ash. Animals died almost instantly as the ash surrounded them. Their bodies decayed long ago; but before that happened, the ash hardened and formed perfect molds of their bodies. 3

❶ 

Producing Molds and Casts

When a marine animal with a shell is buried, its soft body decays, and its shell may be dissolved by ground water, leaving a hole in the rock. This too would be a fossil—a mold in the exact shape of the outside of the animal. If the mold were filled with mineral matter from ground water, a cast would form in the exact shape of the original animal. You can investigate the properties of such molds and casts. ■

❷ 

A marine animal with two shells, say a clam or an oyster, might die and only its soft inner parts decay. This inner cavity might then act as a mold. Mineral matter filling this mold would form a cast of the inside of the shell. Because molds and casts have formed of both the inside and outside of ancient marine animals, we have some excellent fossil records of their size, shape, and internal structure.

Some Unusual Fossils

Fossil plants sometimes show marvelous detail of the structure of the original plant. In many instances the plant has been preserved as a film of carbon on the surrounding rock. We can see much of the original detail in the carbon remains of this fossil fern. ❶ Fossils of some soft-bodied animals such as starfish have also been found as thin films of carbon. In other cases, silicon dioxide from ground water has replaced each molecule of cellulose in a plant while the plant was being buried by mud and sand. Many of the tree trunks in the Petrified Forest of Arizona still show annual growth rings and bark preserved as hardened silicon dioxide. ❷

Is it ever possible to find fossils that still have their original shells, bones, and tissue? By now you'll probably agree that the chances are not good. Actually, ground water may not have had a chance to replace the original shell or bone material of some fossils from fairly recent times. The fossil land animals and birds from the Rancho La Brea tar pits of Los Angeles are an excellent example of this. The bones of these creatures have become impregnated with tar. The tar has preserved the bones and given geologists an excellent record of the horses, camels, birds and

■ AN APPRENTICE INVESTIGATION into the Formation of a Fossil

If you have a seashell or the shell of a snail, you can make a "fossil." Use a small paint brush to coat one side of the shell with vaseline. Then press the coated side of the shell into a block of modeling clay about twice as long and wide as the shell. ❶ What type of fossil impression have you made?

Mold a thin rim of clay around the top edge of the block. Remove the shell from the clay. Then paint vaseline on the top of the block and inside the rim. Next, mix water and plaster of Paris. Add water until you have a thick, soupy mixture that you can pour into the fossil mold. (The vaseline should prevent the plaster of Paris from sticking to the clay.) Fill the mold to the top of the rim with plaster. ❷ Predict what type of fossil impression will be formed when the plaster hardens.

Let the plaster harden for about half an hour. A 24-hour drying time is even better. Gently peel off the rim, and then remove the block of clay from the plaster. ❸ Do you have a perfect plaster cast of one side of the shell? You can trim the edges of the plaster with a dull knife, chisel, or small hand saw to produce a perfect "fossil."

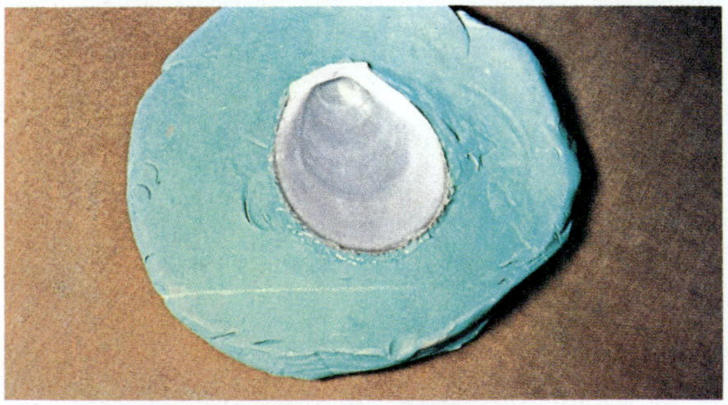

❶

❷

❸

An Investigation On Your Own

You can make a plaster cast of a complete shell by pressing the shell between two blocks of clay. Be sure to coat the entire shell with vaseline if necessary. Also coat the surfaces of the block of clay that join together. Try to have only half of the shell impression in each block. Otherwise, a poor cast may result.

Separate the blocks and remove the shell. Place the blocks together again, and if necessary hold them tightly together with several rubber bands. Cut a funnel-shaped hole in the top of the blocks so you can pour plaster into the mold. Mix the plaster and pour it into the mold. Tap the mold gently on the table top to remove air bubbles from the mold, and add more plaster if necessary. Let the plaster harden. If plaster escapes from the edges of the mold, press the clay blocks together at that point. Open the mold and trim the cast of your fossil. Did you get a perfect cast?

1 

saber-toothed cats that once lived in the area. 1

Remarkable examples of preserved animals and plants have been found in *amber* from the southern coast of the Baltic Sea. Amber is a fossil resin that hardened from the sap of pine trees. As this resin dropped to the floor of the pine forest, many insects and plants became trapped in it. Later on, the sea covered the forest and buried the amber in bluish-gray clay. This clay layer is now covered by the shallow water of the Baltic Sea. Waves erode the amber from the clay, and the amber floats ashore to be picked up from the beaches by collectors. A perfectly preserved insect in 35-million-year-old Baltic Sea amber is an example of the rich plant and animal life of the forest. 2

In a Deep Freeze

Completely preserved fossils of recent animals are fairly common. You don't think it unusual to go to the freezer for a steak bought at the store last month. How would you like a steak that has been in a freezer for a few thousand years? A large part of the world has been a huge "freezer" for the last two million years or so. This natural freezer began operating at the beginning of the ice ages—and it's still operating today! You find it in the icecaps of Antarctica and Greenland. You also find it in the permanently frozen ground of Siberia, northern Europe, Canada, and Alaska. These permanently frozen regions are called **permafrost** regions.

Woolly mammoths and hairy rhinoceroses roamed these permafrost regions during the ice ages. 3 Some were trapped when they fell into crevasses in the glacial ice. Some sank into soft mud at the edge of the ice. They were frozen quickly and remain frozen today. Occasionally a complete carcass with hair, skin, and vital organs intact is exposed by the erosion of streams. Some are on display in refrigerated cases at museums. Wolves and sled dogs have eaten the meat of these animals without harm. Thousands of their tusks have been sold for ivory.

We have seen several ways that fossils are formed. These remains of ancient life are important because they give us clues to the past history of plants and animals on earth. But as we shall soon see, they are also im-

2

3

portant clues to physical events in the earth's past.

REVIEW

1. Describe how several different kinds of fossils are formed.

2. What conditions are needed for the formation of fossils?

3. Why are fossils of marine animals more common than fossils of land animals?

4. How is ground water important in fossil formation?

NEW VIEW

1. You are walking on a layer of fairly hard sandstone. Suddenly you see several bones projecting out of the sandstone in a dry stream bed. How would you remove those bones and search for others nearby? (A trip to the museum may be helpful.)

2. Carnotite, a yellow oxide of uranium, is a valuable source of radioactive compounds. It is often found concentrated in fossil tree trunks. How did it get there?

3. LAYERS AND LAYERS OF ROCK

Consider again the geologist's estimate of the thickness of sedimentary rock that has been deposited since the appearance of the first hard-shell marine animals (p. 321). It amounts to about 125 kilometers (76 miles)! Where would you go to find this thickness of sedimentary rock?

Unfortunately, you couldn't visit any one place on earth to find all this rock. The average thickness of the earth's crust is only about 34 kilometers (20 miles). Sedimentary rocks are only a thin cover for the igneous and metamorphic rocks that make up 95 percent of the earth's relatively thin crust. Over much of the earth, igneous and metamorphic rocks are found at the surface, without any cover of sedimentary rocks. In other places, thousands to tens of thousands of centimeters of sedimentary rock cover the other rocks of the earth's crust. The deepest oil well that has ever been drilled went through about 7,500 meters (25,000 feet) of sedimentary rocks, but such thicknesses are unusual. How then did geologists determine the total thickness of sedimentary rock?

A Giant Jigsaw Puzzle

Geologists have had to piece together the rock record to find the total thickness of sedimentary rock. You know the rules for piecing together a jigsaw puzzle. What rules do geologists use to piece together the sedimentary rock record?

Before the work of Nicholas Steno and James Hutton, among others, there were no rules. Steno was a Danish clergyman and amateur geologist. In 1669 he stated three concepts for understanding the relationships between sedimentary rocks. These concepts, which are often called geologic laws, are simple but quite fundamental. Steno's first concept is the **law of superposition.** According to the law of superposition, younger rocks are deposited on top of older rocks. So when we look at a cross section of undisturbed sedimentary rock layers, we find the oldest layers on the bottom and the youngest layers on top.

1

Steno's second concept is the **law of original horizontality.** In effect, the law of original horizontality states that sedimentary rocks are deposited in approximately horizontal layers. If we find them in some other position, we know they have been rearranged by the action of forces within the earth. (1) We shall call Steno's third concept the **law of maximum extent.** The law of maximum extent states that if a sedimentary layer does not cover the entire earth, it must either thin out at its edges or meet other deposits.

The Present Is the Key to the Past

James Hutton was a Scotsman who studied to be a physician, but he never practiced medicine. He became interested in geology and summarized thirty years of observations in a two-volume geology book published in 1795. The concept of **uniformitarianism** (yōō′nə·fôr′mə·târ′ē·ən·iz′əm) is one of the fundamental new observations in his writings. A simple statement of this concept is *the present is the key to the past*. That is, the geologic processes in operation today have been in operation throughout the history of the earth.

These geologic processes include the upward or downward movement of the earth's crust, the erosion of mountains, and the formation of sedimentary rock. Using the concept of uniformitarianism, geologists are confident that sedimentary rock has been deposited throughout all geologic time. All they need do is find the sedimentary rocks so they can piece together the record of the rocks. The concept also tells geologists they can interpret what they find in the record of the rock by referring to the geologic events that are taking place around them today. Without this concept, geologists could not have come to many conclusions about the past history of the earth.

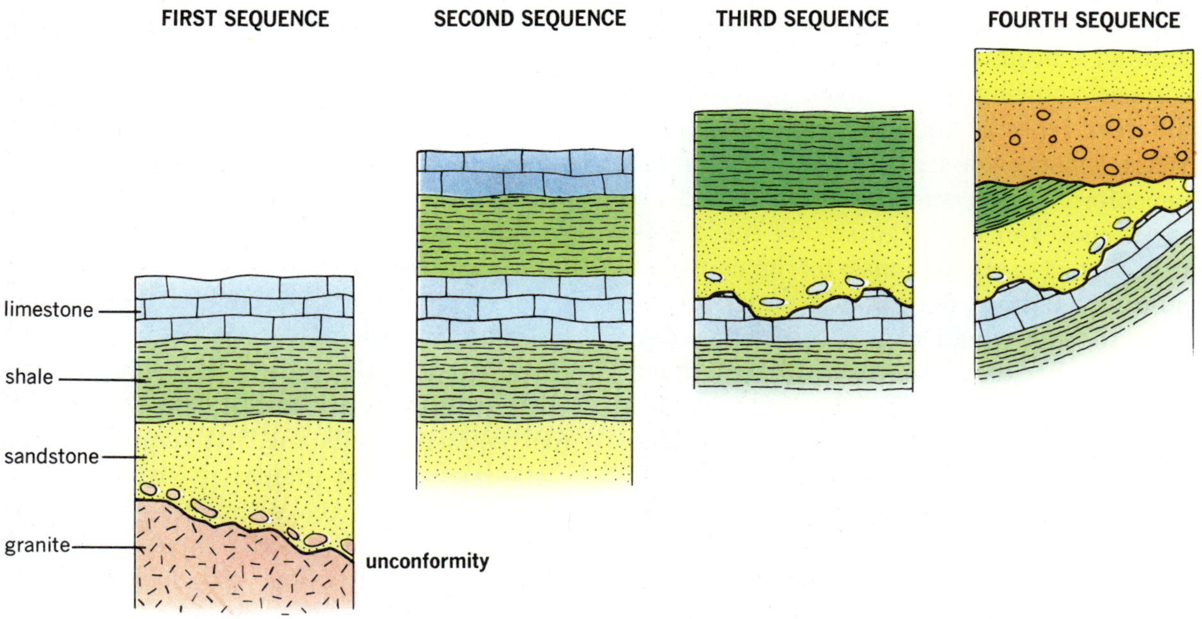

Unconformities in the Rocks

Now you know some of the concepts necessary for understanding relationships in sedimentary rocks. You can also see how geologists might go about the job of piecing together the total thickness of sedimentary rock. Let's look at a simple example of the procedure. ❷ Suppose you find several layers, or a sequence, of rocks like that on the left side of the diagram. The vertical sequence is an easy way to show how the rocks would appear if you drilled a hole or dug a mine shaft straight down into the earth. A cross section composed of three sedimentary rock layers is shown in the first sequence. Standard geologic symbols and colors are used for each type of rock.

According to the law of superposition, the limestone at the top is the youngest sedimentary rock in the sequence. The sandstone at the bottom is the oldest. A layer of shale is shown in between. Now look at the granite underneath the sandstone. Is the granite older or younger than the sandstone?

In the photograph, which was taken in Colorado, you see an actual example of a layer of granite beneath a layer of sandstone. ❸

Here a sedimentary rock is found in contact with an igneous rock, granite. Such a buried surface, showing the contact between two different types of rock, is an **unconformity.** What is the evidence for the origin of this unconformity between the granite and the sandstone? You might guess that the granite was part of a molten mass of igneous rock pushing up from deep in the crust. If this were so, you would expect the sedimentary rocks to be disturbed from their original position. They aren't. You might also expect the structure of the sandstone to have been affected by the presence of the mass of molten igneous rock that cooled to form granite. The sandstone should show some metamorphism. But it doesn't. Therefore, you can assume that the igneous rock was already in position *before* the sedimentary rocks were deposited.

There is other evidence that the granite was present before the sedimentary rocks were deposited. The lower part of the sandstone contains large, rounded fragments of the underlying granite. If the granite were being weathered and eroded while the sandstone was being deposited, you would expect to find pieces of weathered granite in the sandstone—and you do.

All three lines of evidence lead you to conclude that the granite is the oldest rock in the cross section. Why wasn't the use of the law of superposition alone sufficient to reach this conclusion? Remember you were dealing with nonsedimentary as well as sedimentary rocks.

Correlating Rock Layers

Geologists attempt to relate their study of the rocks in one small area to a broader region. They attempt to match rocks deposited in one area with rocks deposited during the same time span in another area. This procedure is called **correlation.** One of the best ways of demonstrating that rock layers are continuous from one place to another is simply to follow one distinctive layer until it disappears. A rock layer may disappear by thinning out at its edges, or it may be lost from view deeper in the earth.

The second rock sequence in the diagram on page 331 shows a series of rock layers found some distance away from the first sequence. How can you correlate this second rock sequence with the first sequence? You don't know if the granite is present below the sandstone in the second sequence. But you do recognize that the three lower rock layers are the same age and thickness as in the first sequence. By applying the law of superposition, you know that these lower rock layers have been covered by younger shale and even younger limestone. You have correlated these two rock sequences.

Look at the diagram once again. In the third sequence of rock layers, you find one original shale layer on the bottom and only the lower part of the limestone layer. The upper part of the limestone layer must have been removed by erosion. How do you know that erosion took place? The rounded fragments of limestone in the overlying sandstone resulted from erosion. Here there is an unconformity between parallel layers of sedimentary rock. The lower layer was partly eroded before the next layer was deposited on top of it.

Observe that a shale layer is the uppermost and youngest layer. But wait a minute! In the previous cross section, shale and limestone were overlying the older limestone layer. Now you have sandstone and shale overlying the older limestone layer. What happened? You can find out for yourself. ■

■ AN APPRENTICE INVESTIGATION into the Formation of a Layer of Sediment

Dig up about 500 grams of soil composed of particles of *different* sizes. If this type of soil is not available, you can make "soil" by combining sand used by builders with powdered clay. Moisten the soil by mixing it with just enough water to wet all the particles. Bank this wet soil against the short end of a rectangular metal tray.❶ The tray should be at least 25 centimeters long. (You can also use a shoe box lined with plastic, aluminum foil, or waxed paper). Cut a *small* hole in the opposite end of the tray. Then close the hole with a stopper or with clay. Use a grease pencil to mark on the sides of the tray the height of the edge of the mound of soil.

Fill a container with about one liter of water. Holding the container close to the top of the soil, pour the water at a moderate rate while moving the container from side to side over the entire mound of soil.❷ Allow the particles to settle for a few minutes. Be sure all the fine particles have settled. Now remove the clay and allow all the water to drain from the tray. What does the bottom of the tray look like? Is there any obvious difference in the size of the sediment from one end of the tray to the other?

Run your index finger through the sediment on the far side of the tray.❸ Start at the end of the tray farthest away from the original soil, and stop when you feel the sediment becoming sandy in texture. Mark the spot by making a scratch with your fingernail. Repeat this procedure along the center of the pan, and then at the near side of the tray. Connect the points where the sediment becomes sandy. This con-

❷

❶

❸

❶ 

sand. Draw a line along the edge of the original mound of soil. Is the region of fine sand wider or narrower than the clay region? Is the region of coarse sand wider or narrower than the region of fine sand? Explain any differences in width.

necting line represents the boundary between the clay and the fine sand. ❶

In the same way, draw a line to represent the boundary between the fine sand and the coarse

An Investigation On Your Own

Use the grease pencil to mark on the sides of the tray the boundaries in the investigation you have just completed. Remove the soil from the tray. Mix the soil again or use a new batch of moist soil. Repeat the investigation, but pour the water more rapidly. Mark the new boundaries on the sides of the tray. How do they compare with those from the previous trial? What happens if you fill the tray half full of water and repeat the procedure?

From Sediment to Sedimentary Rock

Did you observe in the investigation that the finer the sediment the farther it is deposited from the original "land"? Similarly in a large lake or inland sea, the finer sediments are deposited farther from the shore. In one sedimentary layer you might find coarse sand and gravel near the shore, finer sand farther out, and silt or clay even farther out in the body of water. ❶ When changed to sedimentary rock, these would become conglomerate, sandstone, and shale, respectively. If a geologist found this new deposited sedimentary layer either before or after it had changed to rock, he would observe the change in size of the sediment in each part of the layer.

These zones of different composition over the length of a sedimentary layer are called **facies** (fā′shēz). A geologist labels each part

❶ 

2

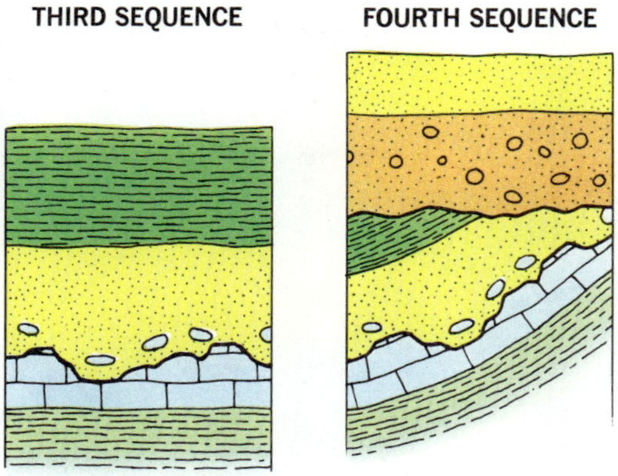

of the layer as a separate facies. In sequence from shore, these are the coarse sand and gravel facies, the fine sand facies, and the silt or clay facies. By noting the change in facies, a geologist interprets the way in which this layer was formed.

Now consider the third sequence of rock layers on page 331 once again. (It is repeated at the left in the diagram above.) 2 You wanted to determine how sandstone and shale were found above the eroded limestone. Perhaps after the limestone eroded, the land sank, a lake formed, and sediment was deposited in the lake. In time, sandstone was formed from the fine sand facies of one sedimentary layer. Somewhat later, shale was formed from a silt or clay facies of another sedimentary layer. Would this account for the present sequence of rock layers?

A Disturbance in the Rocks

In the fourth, and last, sequence of rock layers, a disturbance has taken place. 2 The older limestone and the younger sandstone and shale have been turned upward. There is an irregular contact between these layers and the layers of younger conglomerate and sandstone above. Can you interpret this change? First the three lower rock layers were tilted upward. Then erosion of the new surface took place. Finally the two upper rock layers were formed. As a result, there is contact between the older, tilted sedimentary rocks and the younger, horizontal sedimentary rocks above. The result is another type of unconformity, an example of which you see below. 3

You have seen how geologists determine the relative age of rocks, how they attempt to correlate rocks, how they interpret sedimentary facies, and how they study the contacts between rock layers. One more step is needed before you can start adding up the total thickness of sedimentary rocks.

If you move hundreds of miles away to another sedimentary rock sequence, or even to another continent, how will you know where the new sedimentary rocks fit together with the rocks you have been studying? Are the new rocks older, younger, or the same age? That is, should you add their thickness to what you already have, or should you simply substitute their thickness for the thickness of the rocks in the place you have been studying. You certainly can't add thicknesses of rocks deposited during exactly the same time in different places.

3

You might be able to use a radioactive dating technique to find out the ages of two different rock sequences. Fossils may also give the answer you've been seeking. Let's see how.

REVIEW

1. State Steno's three laws related to sedimentary rocks. Why is each important?
2. What does the concept of uniformitarianism indicate about events in the earth's past?
3. If a geologist is piecing together the sequence of rocks, why is it important that he identify an unconformity?
4. What are facies? How do they form in a rock layer?
5. How does a geologist use correlation?

NEW VIEW

1. Suppose you have been tracing a horizontal layer of sandstone. After tracing it for some distance, you find that the layer turns upward and stands as a vertical ridge. Resting against the sandstone is a vertical layer of shale, and resting against the shale is a vertical layer of limestone. Which layer is the oldest? (*Hint:* Draw a cross section of the earth to show the layers.) Why?
2. Imagine you have taken a dive in a research submarine and located the boundaries of facies on the continental shelf as you moved away from shore. If the sea level rose, how would the boundaries of the facies shift as new sediments were deposited?

4. FOSSILS, ROCKS, AND TIME

When a geologist is trying to correlate rock layers in widely separated areas, he cannot physically trace a distinct rock layer or sequence of layers. Nor can he always rely on radioactive dating to tell him when different rock sequences were deposited. In

1

fact, all the major rock sequences around the world were worked out long before radioactive dating was developed. How did geologists do it? Fossils in sedimentary rocks provided the necessary clues to the age of the rocks in different areas.

From Simple to Complex

The law of superposition guides geologists in studying sequence of rock layers. In a similar way the concept of **faunal succession** guides geologists in understanding the sequence of fossils in rock layers. The concept of faunal succession states that life has evolved from simple to complex organisms over the span of geologic time. Therefore, we can use the relative complexity of fossil organisms as a guide to the age of rock layers. In practice, the geologist picks a group of organisms and studies how their characteristics changed over a long time span.

Fossils—and Engineers

One of the first men to use faunal succession as a tool for correlating rock layers was the Englishman William Smith. He was a self-trained surveyor, civil engineer, and geologist. While supervising the digging of a canal in England, he noticed that certain rock layers contained characteristic fossils. He also studied fossil succession in different areas and found that the sequence of fossils remained the same even if the rock layers changed. His studies were of practical value to him as a canal-builder, because he could predict the types of rock that would be found in digging a canal. Knowing the types of rock, he could estimate how difficult it would be to dig each section of the canal.

If someone asked you to dig a trench three feet deep across the school yard, you'd want to know at what depth rock layers are found and how hard the rock is. With this information you would know if the job could be done with a shovel or whether jack-hammers would be needed. You could then predict how long the job would take and how much help you would need. These are the kinds of information Smith was trying to develop through the correlation of rocks containing fossils.

As a result of his correlations, Smith was able to list the sedimentary layers according to their relative ages. In 1815, at his own expense, he published a geological map of England and Wales showing the geographic distribution of rock layers. His pioneering work led to the development of a more complete sequence of rock layers for Europe and England.

Sir Charles Lyell, a Scotsman, studied to be a lawyer, but he adopted geology as a profession. 1 In 1833 he used the work of Smith and others to construct the first complete **geologic column.** A geologic column is a sequence of rock layers of all ages in proper order from youngest to oldest. You will learn more about geologic columns in the next chapter.

Index Fossils

After Lyell, geologists continued to study how fossils could be used to correlate rocks in areas that had not been studied before. They noticed that certain marine animals left fossil remains in rocks over a wide geographic area. And some fossils could be found in different types of sedimentary rocks. Moreover, the shells of some of these widely distributed fossil animals had distinctive forms. In fact, the forms of their shells are an important characteristic in identifying certain fossil groups.

The evidence indicates that groups of marine animals with distinctive fossil remains seemed to appear suddenly, exist for a short time, and suddenly disappear. Geologists coined the term **index fossil** for these animals that ranged over a wide area, left distinctive fossil remains, and existed as a group for only a relatively short time in geologic history.

Free-swimming marine animals make the best index fossils. They lived in the shallow seas that often covered large areas of the continents. The animals died in all parts of these seas and left their shells in the sediment facies. Among the marine animals, *trilobites* make the best index fossils for correlation of the early sedimentary rocks, perhaps 400 to 600 million years ago. 2 The trilobites were

2

1

arthropods, animals with jointed legs. They were somewhat like our present-day lobsters and horseshoe crabs.

Brachiopods and *ammonites* make excellent index fossils for somewhat later sedimentary rocks. 1 2 Brachiopods had top and bottom shells resembling modern scallops and clams. Brachiopods reached their climax 230 to 400 million years ago. The ammonites were among the largest marine invertebrates, animals without backbones, ever known. Their soft bodies were protected by a coiled shell. One type had a shell 4 meters (13 feet) long. Their modern-day relatives are the squid, octopus, and pearly nautilus.

2

Horses and Camels

Rocks formed on land also contain index fossils. Horses make an excellent index fossil for the young sedimentary rocks deposited in North America during the last 50 million years or so. Fossil evidence indicates that the earliest horse, *Eohippus,* roamed the western plains at about this time. *Eohippus* was the size of a fox terrier and had four toes. 3 In your earlier work in science, you may have studied the sequence of fossil horses that is often interpreted to mean that this small animal evolved into our present one-toed horse, *Equus.*

Many other sequences of land animals, such as the rhinoceros and the camel, have also been used as index fossils. The camel evolved in North America at the same time as the horse. Although you are probably not familiar with the fossil sequence of the camel, the evolution of the camel is similar to the evolution of the horse. The first camel of some 50 million years ago was about the size of a tiny lamb and had four toes.

By 30 million years ago, camels walked on only two toes, as they do today. By 20 million years ago, several groups of camels had developed. One group, *Procamelus,* evolved into the camels we know today. Another group, *Alticamelus,* were long-necked "giraffe" camels that died out. Can you identify the *Alticamelus* and the three-toed horses in the drawing of the plains of Nebraska? 4 (The animals at the lower left are Asiatic antelopes; those in the center are rhinoceroses.)

Camels and horses lived in North America through several ice ages, but they died out mysteriously before man arrived. However,

3

both the camel and the horse had migrated to South America and Asia, where they survive today.

The Search Continues

The presence of an index fossil or a succession of fossils does not necessarily prove a correlation between rock layers in different areas. Sometime animals similar to the index fossil but not identical with it have developed at a different time in a different place. Fossil remains are never complete. There are many animals living in every environment that leave no fossil record. Because of the incomplete fossil record, geologists like to have many lines of evidence pointing to the similarity in age of the rock layers they are trying to correlate.

Now you know about some of the tools of the geologist. Radioactive dating, correlation by type of rock, and correlation by fossils are some of the methods he uses to learn about events in the distant past. With these tools we can return to the job of adding up the thickness of sedimentary rock layers deposited since the first marine animal with a hard shell swam in the ocean. But even after we have done all this, we still have not discovered the true age of the earth.

What of the billions of years before life evolved on this planet? Can we ever know

4

all the physical changes that occurred? Geologists continue to search for new tools to develop new concepts that will help them to understand the history of the earth from its very beginning. Perhaps we will find some clues to the earth's history on the moon and the other planets of the solar system. Perhaps not. But scientists will continue to probe, to make observations, and to make inferences based on their observations.

Scientists try to put all these observations and their thinking about these observations into a theory. They have formed a theory called "the theory of organic evolution." The theory is based on the observations and facts now accepted by scientists working in the field of evolution. There are two main hypotheses:

a) all life now on earth came from a much smaller number of life forms in the past;

b) the many different forms of life now on earth developed slowly over the ages as their heredity and the environment changed.

As you now know, the observations and facts of life you have been studying in this book are explained in terms of a theory of evolution. Through the theory of evolution, scientists explain the development of simple and complex forms of life. At present this theory is the best scientific explanation scientists working in the field of evolution have developed.

REVIEW

1. What is faunal succession? Why is it important in relative dating?

2. How do scientists construct a geologic column?

3. What are the various characteristics of index fossils that make them important in dating rock layers?

NEW VIEW

1. Many groups of fossil animals and plants became extinct at the end of certain spans of time. How could the absence of a group of fossil animals or plants be used to correlate rock layers? Is the absence of fossils good evidence of correlation? Why?

2. Faunal succession indicates that complex animals and plants evolved from simpler organisms. Are the horse and camel evidence of faunal succession? Why? Why not?

5. RELATING THE CONCEPTS

Geologists have tried to estimate the age of the earth by many techniques. The discovery of radioactivity led to dating techniques that give fairly accurate time estimates. The half-lives of radioactive isotopes used in dating are quite different, allowing us to date a broad range of geologic events.

The types and thicknesses of sedimentary rocks give clues to the history of the earth. The correct interpretation of these clues is based on the concept that the same kinds of geologic processes we see today were at work in the past.

By tracing distinctive rock layers, geologists can find breaks in the record of earth history. By correlating rock layers and by studying unconformities and the succession of rocks, the geologist hopes to piece together a complete record of earth history. Unfortunately, no one geographic area has a complete set of sedimentary rocks. But by correlating rocks of the same age from one area with those in another area, geologists build new sequences that show which layers were missing from old sequences. This correlation of rock layers is a difficult task that requires matching by type of layer, fossil content, and radioactive date. Index fossils, animals that left distinctive remains over wide geographic areas, are particularly valuable aids in the correlation of rock layers.

Correlations allow us to interpret and understand a part of earth history. A complete geologic column has been developed for the last 600 million years, the time since marine animals first began to leave an extensive fossil record in the rocks. The sequence of events for much of the earlier part of earth history remains a mystery. Will it always remain so? Perhaps not. Perhaps new techniques will be developed to give us clues to older events —even to the time of the earth's formation.

Reviewing the Concepts

► *Absolute dating techniques give reasonably accurate dates for events in the history of the earth.* Rates of decay for naturally occurring radioactive isotopes allow geologists to date rocks, bones, and plants containing these elements. Potassium-argon dating and carbon-14 dating are particularly useful. *Relative dating* techniques do not give accurate dates. Such relative dating techniques as estimating the age of the earth based on rates of cooling, saltiness of the ocean, and the thickness of sedimentary rocks have given inaccurate results.

► *Younger sedimentary rocks are deposited in horizontal layers above older sedimentary rocks.* The geologist at work uses Steno's law of superposition, that younger rocks are deposited on top of older rocks, and his law of original horizontality, that sedimentary rocks are deposited in nearly horizontal layers. Thus, he can analyze fairly easily the relative ages of sedimentary rocks and any tilting or bending of the rocks.

► *The same geologic processes in operation today have been in operation throughout the history of the earth.* This concept of uniformitarianism is fundamental to understanding changes that have occurred in the earth in the past. Confident that the present is the key to the past, geologists interpret clues in rock layers as evidence of such events as the uplift or erosion of mountains.

► *An unconformity is a buried surface showing evidence of a lack of steady and continuous depositing of sediment.* In sorting out the relationships between rocks, it is important to recognize times and places where the formation of sedimentary rock has been interrupted. Some unconformities reveal evidence of erosion between sedimentary layers; other unconformities occur between sedimentary and nonsedimentary layers. In still other unconformities, there is contact between tilted and horizontal sedimentary layers.

► *Fossils are evidence of prehistoric life.* Footprints, shells, bones, plants, and other organic materials may be preserved as fossils. In rare cases the original animal or plant may be preserved without change. A group of fossil organisms that ranged over a wide area, had a short existence, and left distinctive remains make good index fossils. These index fossils are important in correlating rock layers deposited over a short span of geologic time.

► *Sedimentary rock layers in one area can be correlated with rock layers of the same age in distant areas.* In correlating rock layers, rocks deposited in one area are matched with rocks deposited during the same time span in another area. Geologists establish the relative ages of rock layers by tracing distinctive layers and by studying the fossil content of the layers. Correlations are possible even though facies changes occur along the length of a rock layer.

1

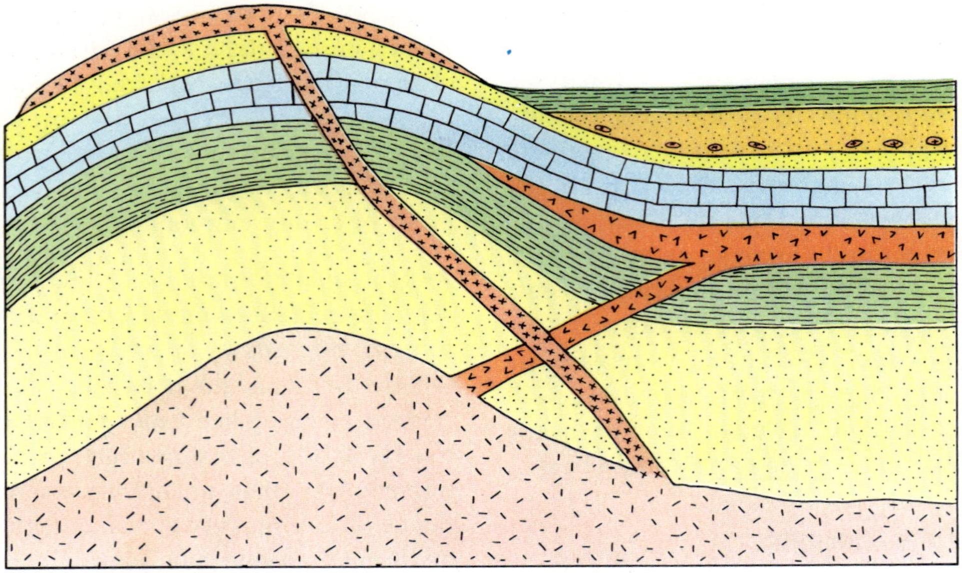

Testing Yourself

1. Why is the potassium-argon dating method an important new tool for the geologist?

2. What is the relationship between the half-life of a radioactive element and the length of geologic time that can be dated by it?

3. Describe the importance of carbon-14.

4. Why is it difficult to know how much sedimentary rock has been formed on earth?

5. Explain the fundamental relationships between sedimentary rock layers as developed by Steno.

6. What is the principle of uniformitarianism? Why is it important to geologists?

7. What is an unconformity? Draw and label one example of an unconformity.

8. Describe briefly how rock layers are correlated.

9. How are facies formed in a large lake or inland sea?

10. Describe several different ways in which a fossil can be formed.

11. Why are some animals found as fossils, while others are not?

12. What special conditions are needed to preserve animal tissue in a fossil?

13. What is the principle of faunal succession?

14. Why are index fossils important in correlating rocks in areas not studied previously?

15. How do index fossils and the succession of fossils aid geologists in the correlation of rock layers?

16. Why do we know more about the last 600 million years of earth history than we do about the much longer time since the earth was formed?

Extending the Concepts

Investigation. You may want to try unraveling another geologic cross section. Use what you have learned about the relative ages of sedimentary layers, unconformities, and so forth. In addition, you will need to use three "rules" we have not discussed before about the formation of igneous rocks.

Rule of uplifting: If a large, igneous mass pushes toward the earth's surface, the igneous mass will bend and tilt the rock layers above it.

Rule of crosscutting: A tubular mass, such as a dike, is younger than any rock it cuts through. (Dikes solidify from molten igneous material that shoots into cracks in existing rocks.)

Rule of baked contacts: 1. The heat from a molten igneous mass will bake any rocks around it. 2. If molten igneous material forces its way between existing rock layers, the rocks above and below will be slightly baked. (This type of igneous rock, remember, is a sill.) 3. If molten igneous material pours out on the earth's surface, only the soil or rock beneath it will be baked.

Now that you know more about the formation of igneous rocks, try to analyze the geologic cross section. ❶

List the first geologic event and each successive event in the order in which they occurred. (*Hint:* First the sedimentary rocks were deposited in horizontal layers.)

Suggested Reading

Eicher, Don L., *Geologic Time,* Englewood Cliffs, New Jersey, Prentice-Hall, 1968. An excellent discussion of the concepts of earth history, correlation, and radioactive dating.

Stirton, Ruben A., *Time, Life and Man,* New York, Wiley, 1963. A well-rounded account of life through geologic ages.

Dunbar, Carl and Karl Waage, *Historical Geology,* 3rd ed., New York, Wiley, 1969. The latest revision of a distinguished introduction to historical geology.

Moore, Raymond C., *Introduction to Historical Geology,* 2nd ed., New York, McGraw–Hill, 1958. An informative and well-illustrated text.

16

The Biography of North America

Has North America always had its present shape and size? Why may our descendants someday be forced to move far south or perish under enormous layers of ice?

Historical geologists spend their lives seeking answers to such questions—questions about the origin and development of the earth; questions about ancient climates, ancient geography, and ancient life.(1) They attempt to provide us with a special type of history book—a book that contains an orderly arrangement of the events that took place on the earth long before there was anyone to observe and record them. How do they go about this type of work? What have they learned?

1 

1. A SPECIAL "HISTORY BOOK"

Imagine a very deep hole in the earth at a time when the earth was very young. Into this hole a giant shovel begins to scoop materials from the earth's surface. Occasionally samples of living things, plants and animals, are included in these "scoops." Year after endless year, as time moves toward the present, the hole is filled.

Suppose you have a chance to examine this long column of the earth's material, layer by layer. On the basis of relative dating, you can determine that the uppermost layers are the youngest and the lower layers are the oldest. You have established an order of occurrence, a sequence of events as it were. Moreover, absolute dating permits you to determine the age of the layers in thousands or millions of years.

A Geologic Column

The layers in this imaginary column provide far more information than just the time when they were deposited. Consider the type of "rock" in the layers. Since the material formed on or near the surface, you can limit your study to sedimentary rocks. Suppose you observe where sedimentary rocks of various types are forming today. Then, from the concept of uniformitarianism, you can assume that similar rocks probably formed in similar places in the past. Using this concept, you can predict whether the giant shovel sampled surface material from a fresh inland lake or a shallow bay, from a desert basin or an ocean floor. After all, you know the types of rock deposited in each of these environments today.

The layers in this imaginary column give still more information. Suppose you find fossils preserved in these layers. From an examination of the entire column, you observe that fossil groups generally differ from layer to layer. But the changes in the fossils seem to follow a pattern. Fossils from the oldest layers are least like plants and animals alive today; fossils from the younger layers tend to resemble modern plants and animals. You observe that some species disappeared, or became extinct, in older layers. You also observe that new species of plants and animals appeared in younger layers. These observations provide evidence that living things have a long history and that groups of organisms can be traced to organisms of the past—that organisms have evolved from one another.

Fossils in the various layers also provide clues to ancient climates. Most corals, for example, thrive only in water whose temperature is near 21°C. Deposits of coral limestone, therefore, indicate a warm, tropical climate. 2

Finally, imagine that you have not one column to examine, but hundreds of columns from all over the world. The layers of rock in each column provide clues to the past history of the earth for that area: clues that tell of life, and climate, and geography that were very different in the past.

2

A Record of Earth History

You know, of course, that we don't find a continuous layer-by-layer rock record of earth history. In the past, environmental conditions such as temperature and moisture and natural processes such as mountain building were probably much like those today. Material was being deposited in some areas and erosion was occurring in others. Because of constant changes, no rock layers cover entire continents. No one place contains a complete succession of all rock layers ever deposited.

But the historical geologist has found a way to piece together layers from widely separated places. Using radioactive dating, correlation by type of rock, and correlation by fossils, he can trace and recognize similar rock layers, even though the layers may be quite far apart. By correlating rock sequences from all over the world, geologists have pieced together a continuous column of rock representing the history of the earth, layer by layer. Geologists have summarized their observations and interpretations of physical changes in the earth's surface and changes in the organisms on the earth in the **geologic time scale** (on page 347).

The Geologic Time Scale

As you can see by studying the geologic time scale, the largest divisions of geologic time are represented by five *eras*. The Archeozoic era, or era of primitive life, represents the oldest period of time, from about 4.6 billion years ago to about 1.5 billion years ago. The Proterozoic era, or era of early life, extends from about 1.5 billion years ago to about 600 million years ago. Often these eras are referred to as the Precambrian. The rocks laid down during these two eras are, of course, Precambrian rocks. Notice that these two eras, about which very, very little is known, represent about 90 percent of the history of the earth. Scientists have fairly good evidence about life on earth and changes in the physical environment for only the last 10 percent of the earth's history.

The time extending from 600 million years ago to 230 million years ago is known as the Paleozoic era, or era of ancient life. This 370-million-year period represents about 6 percent of the earth's history. The Mesozoic era, or era of middle life, lasted about 170 million years, from 230 million years ago to 63 million years ago. This era represents about 3 percent of the history of the earth. The remaining 1 percent of the earth's history, extending from about 63 million years ago to the present, is called the Cenozoic era, or era of recent life.

The division of rock layers of the geologic column into five sections is the basis for dividing the time scale into these five eras. Each section, of course, represents a certain amount of time during which the rock layers were deposited. The very names of the eras reflect the abundance of certain groups of animals whose fossil remains predominate in that era. The early part of the Paleozoic era is known as the *Age of Invertebrates.* 1 The middle part is the *Age of Fishes*. The last part is the *Age of Amphibians*. The Mesozoic era is known as the *Age of Reptiles,* while the Cenozoic era is the *Age of Mammals*.

1

GEOLOGIC TIME SCALE

Era	*Period*	*Epoch*	*Approximate Time*	*Physical Features*	*Climates*	*Organisms*
CENOZOIC	**Quaternary**	**Recent**	11 thousand years ago	Glaciers melt. Uplift of western coastal area continues.	Changes of seasons and climate zones as we know them today.	Modern man dominant. Insects abundant. Herbaceous plants dominant.
		Pleistocene	2 million years ago	Ice ages. Cascades and Pacific Coast ranges rise. Sierra Nevadas re-elevate.	Cold climates alternate with moderate ones several times.	Early man. Many large mammals (horse and camel in North America) extinct. Decrease of trees.
	Tertiary	**Pliocene**	13 million years ago	Uplift of mountains in midwest. Carving of Grand Canyon proceeds.	Cooler climates well-established away from equator.	Mammals abundant. Herbaceous plants numerous. Grasslands on increase.
		Miocene	25 million years ago	North America joined to Asia. Columbia Plateau rises.	Climates cooling and becoming less humid.	Increase of mammals. Forests shrinking. Beginnings of grasslands.
		Oligocene	36 million years ago	Coastal ranges of California rise.	Warm and humid climates still prevalent.	Appearance of modern mammals. Tropical forests throughout world.
		Eocene	58 million years ago	Volcanic activity in western United States.	Climate zones established.	Primitive horses, camels, and other mammals. Spread of angiosperms.
		Paleocene	63 million years ago	Uplift continues in west. Great Plains formed.	Climate zones first appear.	Expansion of mammals. First primates. Rise of angiosperms.
				Rocky Mountain Revolution		
MESOZOIC	**Cretaceous**		135 million years ago	Last marine invasion covered half of North America. Appalachian Mountains eroded.	Generally warm and humid climates, but some variation.	Climax of dinosaurs, later extinct. First modern bony fish. Many ammonites. Spread of flowering plants.
	Jurassic		180 million years ago	Sierra Nevadas rise. Uplift and folding of Rocky Mountain geosyncline.	Worldwide warm and humid climates.	First bird, mammals, and flowering plants. Giant dinosaurs, gymnosperms, and cycads dominant.
	Triassic		230 million years ago	Erosion in eastern United States. Redbeds and lava beds formed.	Worldwide tropical and subtropical climates.	First dinosaurs. Mammal-like reptiles appear. Increase of gymnosperms. First cycads.
				Appalachian Revolution		
PALEOZOIC	**Permian**		280 million years ago	Shallow seas evaporate, leaving salt and gypsum.	Variable climates. Glaciers in Southern hemisphere.	Expansion of reptiles. Seed ferns and many marine invertebrates extinct. Ancient plants decrease.
	Carboniferous		345 million years ago	Much of continent submerged. Uplift and folding of Appalachian geosyncline.	Climate warm and humid throughout world.	First reptiles. Amphibians dominant. Expansion of insects. Primitive gymnosperms. Tropical fern forests.
	Devonian		405 million years ago	Eastern geosyncline welded to continent. White Mountains rise.	Quite warm uniform climate, but some drying out.	First amphibians. First insects. Age of Fishes. Sharks abundant. Vascular land plants spread.
	Silurian		425 million years ago	Geosynclines continue to fill. Shallow seas dry up.	Cooling and drying toward end of period.	Extensive spread of invertebrates. First known land plants.
	Ordovician		500 million years ago	Taconic and Green Mountains raised. Much of continent submerged.	Uniformly warm climate.	Marine invertebrates dominant. Earliest known fishes. No known land plants. Many marine algae.
	Cambrian		600 million years ago	Filling of eastern and western geosynclines.	Climate becoming warmer.	Many marine invertebrates; trilobites and brachiopods abundant. Marine algae and fungi.
PROTEROZOIC	**PRECAMBRIAN**		1,500 million years ago	Metamorphism, uplift and erosion, volcanoes.	Cool climate with glaciers earlier.	Primitive marine invertebrates. Earliest fossil algae.
ARCHEOZOIC			? ? ?	Oldest rocks of Canadian Shield.	? ? ?	Evidence of life, but no recognizable fossils.

The Paleozoic, Mesozoic, and Cenozoic eras are divided into smaller divisions of geologic time called *periods*. In piecing together the geologic column, historical geologists noted that certain sequences of rock layers could be grouped into a section composed of several layers. These larger sections of rock layers were given special names that reflect either certain characteristics in the rocks, or the area where they were first studied, or an area where a large section of the layers can be easily seen. The name "Cambrian," for example, applies to rock sequences that were first studied in *Cambria*, the Latin name for Wales. Whenever rocks with these same characteristics are found, they are called rocks of the Cambrian period. ❶

Look once again at the geologic time scale. Do you see that the periods of the Cenozoic era are subdivided into *epochs*? In the Cenozoic era, the Tertiary period includes the epochs from the Paleocene through the Pliocene. The Quaternary period is divided into two epochs: the Pleistocene and the Recent. The beginning of the Pleistocene marks the time when large glaciers, or ice sheets, covered much of North America and other continents. The beginning of the Recent epoch, some 11,000 years ago, is about the time when these great glaciers receded. Much of the land once again became a home for the thousands of kinds of plants and animals we know today.

❶

Evidence for the Time Scale

At first, the division of geologic time into eras and periods was based on unconformities (see Chapter 15). Some of these unconformities in different parts of the world could be correlated. This led to the conclusion that major changes, such as the uplift of mountains, occurred throughout the world at various intervals. Therefore these changes seemed to be a reasonable basis for dividing the geologic time scale.

Closer investigation by thousands of geologists has revealed that this method is unsatisfactory. Major changes at some locations occurred in the middle of a period; in other locations, a similar change occurred at another time during the period. Some other basis had to be selected for separating the geologic time scale into eras, periods, and epochs. Today scientists agree that marked differences in fossils and in the number of certain kinds of fossils found in different rock layers are the most important bases for determining the divisions of the geologic time scale.

Layers of rocks, the fossils they contain, geosynclines, unconformities—these are the raw materials used in reconstructing the early history of the earth. Now let's examine some of the physical and biological data "inscribed" on the pages of the past. Since we have neither the time nor the space to probe the earth history of the entire world, we will limit our study to the continent of North America.

REVIEW

1. What is the geologic time scale? Why is it important to scientists?

2. How do eras, periods, and epochs differ from one another?

3. How has the basis for dividing geologic time changed since the first geologic time scale was developed?

4. Predict the order in which you would find the main types of animal fossils if you could examine the entire geologic column.

NEW VIEW

1. How does material deposited in a fresh inland lake differ from material deposited on the ocean floor?

2. How do fossils provide clues to ancient climates? Give several examples of living plants and animals that might provide clues to specific climates someday in the distant future.

3. How were the various "periods" named? (You will find a historical geology text helpful.)

4. The Carboniferous period is divided into two periods by some geologists. What are the names of these periods?

2. THE PRECAMBRIAN

Platforms of rock—dreary gray and brown—rise above oceans of clear water. Above a harsh landscape, the sky darkens. Thunder and lightning announce yet another storm. The winds howl, the rain falls. Streams gather themselves into raging rivers and roar toward the basins of water. Waves generated by strong winds crash against the land. Inland, a rock tumbles down a steep slope; elsewhere, lifeless silence. Devoid of life for eons of time, young planet Earth must have presented a strange array of such sights and sounds. For almost 4,000 million years, no plants clothed the landscape in green; no animals made their home on land, in the air, or in the water.

The Beginning of the Continent

The first abundant fossils of plants and animals are found in rock layers of the Cambrian period, 600 million years ago. Below the rocks of the Cambrian period are many other layers of rock, older rocks deposited before the Cambrian. These are rocks of the Archeozoic and Proterozoic eras, the Precambrian rocks.

Precambrian rocks are exposed in many of the world's ranges and cover large areas of the continents. These continental areas are broad, flat regions called **shields.** Geologists believe that shields are the eroded cores of ancient mountains. These shields apparently supplied material to the surrounding geosynclines. Mountains, remember, were raised from these geosynclines. These mountains attached themselves rigidly to the adjacent shields. In turn, they supplied material to other synclines. In this way, continents seemed to have "grown."

Extensive areas of Precambrian rock are exposed in Canada. This area, called the Canadian Shield, has apparently remained above sea level since its formation. (2) The

(2)

❶ 

Canadian Shield probably represents an ancient eroded mountain core upon which the continent of North America grew to its present size and shape. In this and the other maps in this chapter, land areas are shown in brown, areas covered by water are shown in blue. You notice quickly how little the shape of the Precambrian land area resembles the present continent (whose outline is shown in black).

Although the rocks of the Precambrian include rocks of all types, many of them have undergone great changes. It is very difficult to decipher the original rock types. Thus, geologists can make only rough approximations in reconstructing an outline of North America for these early eras. Other continents have similar Precambrian shield areas and histories of growth.

Evidence of Life

There is an almost complete lack of distinct fossils in the Precambrian rocks. The absence of fossilized shells and the hard parts of animals is particularly surprising, since fossil evidence for animal life begins so abruptly in the Cambrian period. Also, the first abundant animal fossils are not simple, primitive forms, but somewhat advanced invertebrates. The remains of primitive plants, however, have been found in rocks over 2 billion years old.

Fossils in the Precambrian rocks are of two types: chemical traces of living organisms, and preserved parts or impressions of living organisms. Chemical traces include structures of calcium carbonate or silica. These deposits are similar to those made today by blue-green algae. ❶ Another important chemical trace is graphite (carbon). Graphite is probably evidence of some life process in a simple animal or plant during the Precambrian.

In addition to chemical traces, there appear to be a few fossils of soft-bodied organisms in Precambrian rocks. Fossils resembling present-day bacteria and algae have been found in the Precambrian rocks of Minnesota and Ontario. Within these fine-grained rocks are filaments and fragments that represent the oldest known plants. No distinct Precambrian animal parts have been found. However, impressions of ancient animals resembling modern earthworms and jellyfish have been discovered in Precambrian sandstone rock in Australia. ❷

There is little biological and physical data for the Archeozoic and Proterozoic eras. Therefore an accurate reconstruction of these early periods of earth history is very difficult. What a difference in the amount of physical and biological data as we examine the Paleozoic, Mesozoic, and Cenozoic eras.

REVIEW

1. What is a shield area? Why is the Canadian Shield important in the geology of North America?

2. How are geosynclines important to the "growth" of a continent?

3. Describe briefly the evidences of life found in Precambrian rocks.

4. A geologist finds a Precambrian rock. What is the oldest it can be? the youngest?

NEW VIEW

1. Shields probably are eroded cores of mountains that were once deep underground. How were these cores exposed?

2. "Greenstone" rocks, metamorphosed lava, are among the earliest rocks of the Canadian Shield. With this added data, try to describe the early geologic processes of this shield.

2

3. THE PALEOZOIC ERA

The rock layers of the Paleozoic era record a strange geography for North America. As the era began 600 million years ago, only one extensive land area is thought to have existed, an area in eastern Canada. Elsewhere, water covered the land that was to become the United States. (Here and in sections that follow, *United States* refers to the adjacent forty-eight states.) As the era progressed, seas receded and additional land areas were formed. Mountain building and volcanic action provided land areas that rose above the ancient seas.

Climates were as varied as the landscape throughout the different periods of the Paleozoic. At times, warm, humid climates favored the growth of swamps and tropical forests. At other times, very cold climates caused ice to cover much of the land.

The fossils in the rock layers of the Paleozoic era record the first abundant evidence of ancient life. Early in this era, marine invertebrates dominated the waters. Later, vertebrate animals—from fishes to amphibians—made their way out of the water and onto the land. Marine plants gave rise to land plants, and the landscape of the Paleozoic era was covered with the first forests. The water, land, and air of planet Earth were rapidly being filled with a variety of living forms. Now let's examine the biological and physical record of the Paleozoic era in more detail.

How a Continent Grows

There are three main features to the framework of any continent: a stable, central nucleus, or *shield;* a *platform* of nearly horizontal rock surrounding the shield; and *geosynclines* surrounding the platform. In North America, the Canadian Shield is the stable nucleus. During the Paleozoic era the Precambrian shield contributed sediment to the surrounding platforms and geosynclines. Our present mountain systems evolved from these geosynclines. Therefore the evolution of continents from geosynclines becomes the major focus in reconstructing land-sea relationships. In the United States, the east and west coasts are the sites of these former geosynclines.

The Continent Changes Slowly

Now examine the map showing the general land-sea relationships of North America for the Cambrian, Ordovician, and Silurian, the

1

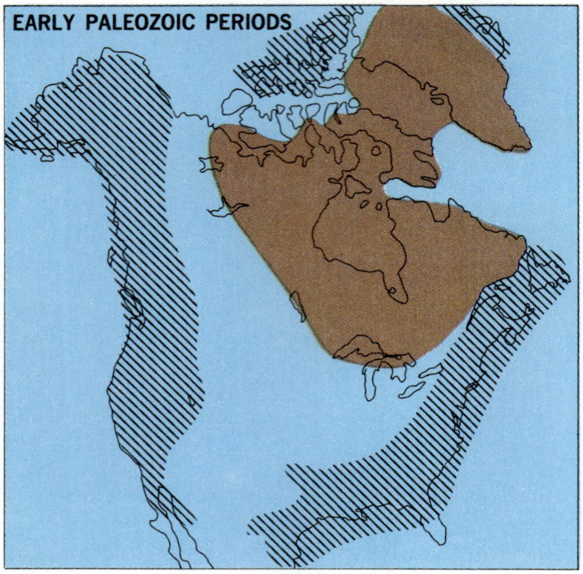

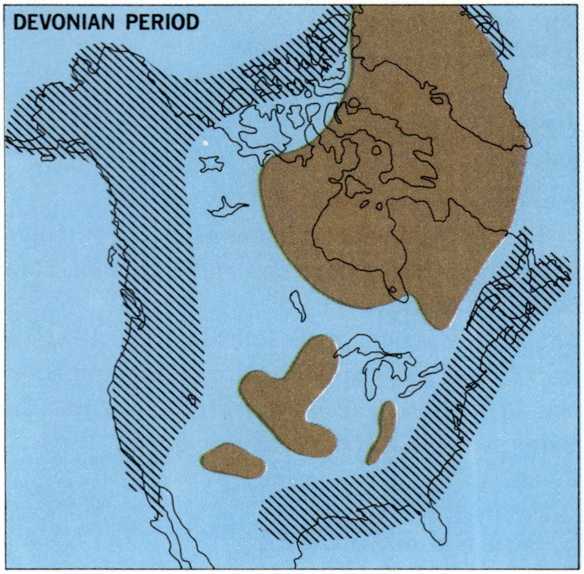

2

first three periods of the Paleozoic era. 1 The shield area covers most of northeastern Canada. Broad seas cover the surrounding platforms throughout the central part of the continent. Surrounding the platforms are two major geosynclines. Geosynclines are indicated on the map by a diagonal, striped pattern over the blue water. Throughout these periods, the geosynclines received sediment from the continental shield and platform. They also received sediment from volcanoes or volcanic islands within the geosynclines themselves.

Before the middle of the Ordovician period, a great change took place in the eastern geosyncline. Such a mountain building process over a small area of the earth's surface is called a **disturbance.** A continuous mass of rock was uplifted to form a range of mountains from Nova Scotia and New England through North Carolina. The Green Mountains of Vermont and the Taconics of western New York were raised at this time. These new uplands contributed a great deal of sediment to the eastern geosyncline. Previously the inner shield area had supplied the sediment. This event of earth history is called the Taconic disturbance.

During the Silurian period, some parts of North America were covered by warm, shallow seas. Corals are found in Silurian rocks as far north as Greenland—an indication of an extremely warm climate. As the shallow seas slowly evaporated under a hot, drying sun, thick beds of salt and gypsum were deposited from New York to Michigan.

More Mountains Rise

During the Devonian period a few areas of land existed within the region that is now the United States; but most of the Central platform of North America was still covered by broad seas. 2 During the Devonian period, uplift in the eastern geosyncline welded this entire part of North America to the continental shield. Since that time, this welded area has acted as part of the rigid continental shield.

A new mountain chain was raised from Newfoundland to the southern Appalachians.

The White Mountains of New Hampshire were formed as a result of the Devonian disturbance. In the western geosyncline, the depositing of sediment that began in the Cambrian period continued.

Mountains and Shallow Seas

Now study the map of the next period, the Carboniferous. (3) Do you observe that the eastern geosyncline no longer exists? Rather, a series of highlands are present throughout the area. Mountain building also occurred in the southern part of North America. The Wichita Mountains of Oklahoma and Texas were formed at this time. Sediment continued to be deposited in the western geosyncline, although small portions of the geosyncline were uplifted.

During a great part of the Carboniferous period, the interior of the United States was covered by shallow inland seas and large fresh-water swamps. At the same time, a warm and humid climate favored the growth of magnificent tropical plants. The buried remains of these tropical plants became the valuable coal deposits found today throughout many of our states.

The Appalachian Mountains Rise

The Permian period is the last period of the Paleozoic era. (4) During this period major mountain building activity occurred throughout the eastern and southern geosynclines. This was the time when the Appalachian Mountains were formed. So great and widespread was this major uplift that it is called a **revolution**—the Appalachian revolution.

Many volcanoes erupted in the southwestern United States, yet much of the central portion of the continent was still covered by shallow seas. Toward the end of the Permian, particularly in Oklahoma and Texas, large deposits of gypsum and halite (rock-salt) were deposited as these seas evaporated in a hot, dry climate. These physical events laid the foundation for further development of the continent during the Mesozoic and Cenozoic eras. But the biologic events that unfolded during the Paleozoic were just as dramatic.

(3)

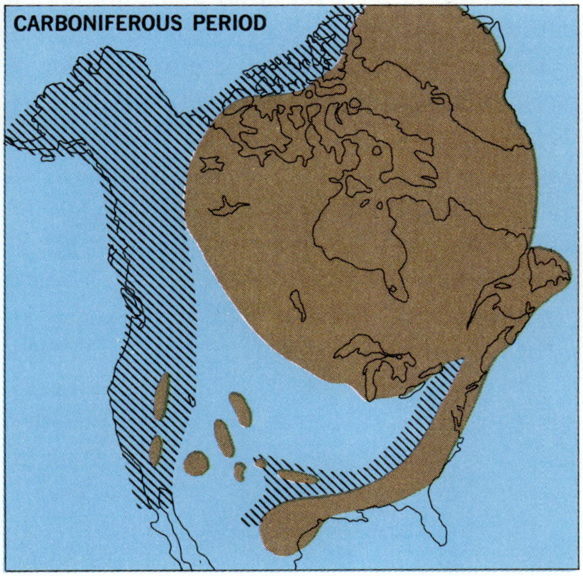

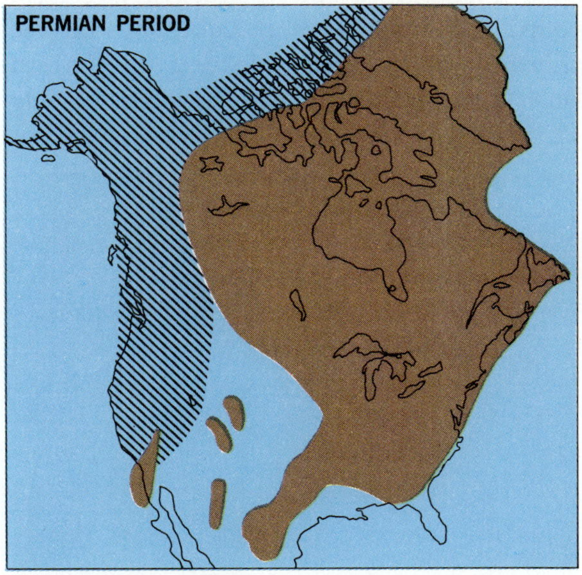

(4)

Life in the Early Seas

Fossil remains of the Cambrian period indicate that the seas were filled with many kinds of animals and plants, but there are no traces of life on land. The marine animals were all invertebrates. The Cambrian seas contained sponges, snails, jellyfish, trilobites, and brachiopods (see page 337). Trilobites, recall, are extinct crab-like animals; brachiopods are tiny shellfish resembling clams. They were very widespread and dominated life in the seas. Marine plants included a variety of seaweeds and algae. As these algae died, they left circular deposits of calcium carbonate on the rock layers (page 350).

In the Ordovician period, marine animals included those found in the Cambrian seas as well as clams, corals, and *graptolites*. The graptolites are extinct marine invertebrates whose remains resemble pencil lines on the layers of shale in which they are found. ❶

Many kinds of mollusks, animals with soft bodies and protective shells, also flourished in Ordovician seas. The *nautoloids* were among the largest and most highly developed mollusks of the period. Some were coiled and some were straight, such as the animal with tentacles extended on the sea floor in the scene on page 346. Today only one close relative, the modern chambered nautilus, survives. Other relatives, the squid and octopus, are fairly common today.

One animal in the Ordovician seas almost escaped notice. Only a few fossil fragments of bones and scales remain. But these fossil remains are extremely important. Why? They were the first animals with a backbone—primitive, bony, jawless fish called *ostracoderms* (äs·trək'ō·derms). ❷ Here you see a fossil as well as a model of an *ostracoderm*.

Marine plants were similar to those found in the Cambrian seas. No trace of land animals or plants has yet been discovered in the rocks of this period.

The Land is Invaded

The Silurian period saw a great change take place. ❸ It is theorized by paleontologists that the first plants and animals left the sea and invaded the land. The fossil record of land plants includes mosses and lichens. Animals on land included scorpions, spiders, and various other insects. Marine animals, particularly primitive fishes and giant sea-scorpions called *eurypterids* (yor'ip'tor·odz), abounded in the seas. ❸

In the Devonian period, many varieties of marine plants existed. Some marine animals,

❶

❷

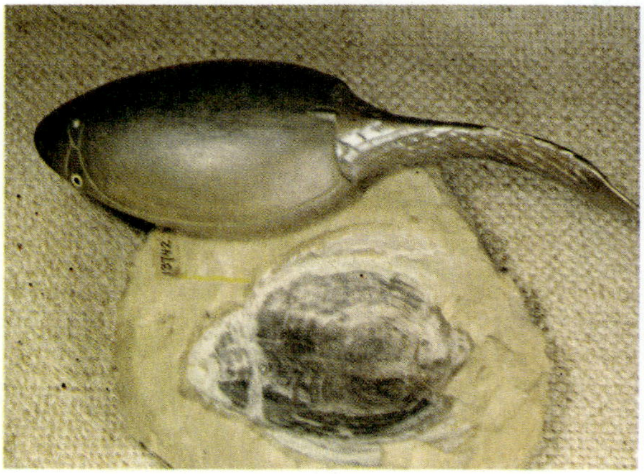

3

such as the brachiopods, flourished and reached a climax. Others, such as the trilobites and graptolites, began to decline. Sharks and giant armored fish were common during this Age of Fishes. Lungfish and lobe-finned fish, two groups that have lunglike organs, made their appearance.

All the evidence is not yet in; but most scientists believe that the lobe-finned fish, plodding along on their heavy fins, were the first vertebrates to take to the land.4 Perhaps some 370 million years ago—and that's not very long in the history of the earth—the ancient lobe-finned fish gave rise to the first primitive amphibians. These amphibians were the first vertebrates, except for the lobe-finned fish, to live on land. They were to give rise to many vertebrates that dominate the earth today. The early amphibians probably crawled through the first forests—forests of large ferns, a few primitive conifers (cone-bearing plants or evergreens), and rushes.

The Coal Forests

In the Carboniferous period, many species of marine and land plants developed and thrived. In the marine world, trilobites continued to decline and graptolites died out. Foraminifera (the tiny protozoans that secrete lime shells), brachiopods, and fishes were abundant. Among the invertebrates,

4

1 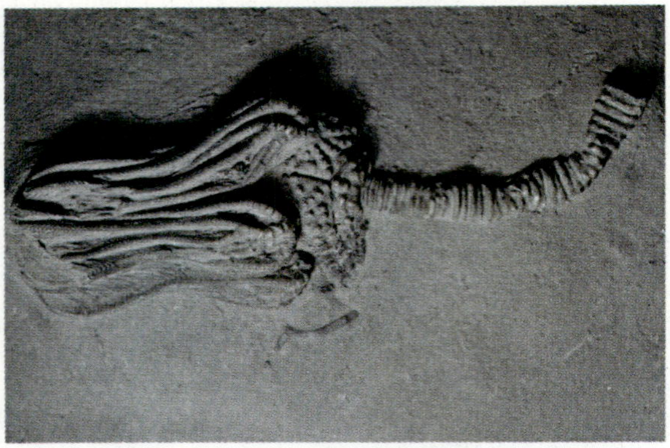

crinoids were prominent. 1 These animals, commonly called sea lilies, have feather-like arms and live attached to the sea floor. Don't be fooled. Yes, they are animals, not plants. Their distant relatives include the starfish. Among the land animals, amphibians were developing rapidly.

But the major event of the Carboniferous period was the evolution of the first all-land vertebrate, a lizard-like reptile. One important way in which amphibians differ from reptiles is that amphibians lay their eggs in water while reptiles lay their eggs on land.

Insects, especially cockroaches and giant dragonflies, were abundant. They crawled or flew in swampy forests. The forests were typical fern forests, including club mosses and horsetails among the giant seed ferns. 2 Seed ferns, unlike the ferns of today, reproduce by seeds rather than by spores. These forests are often called "coal forests," because their condensed remains are mined as coal.

The Permian period witnessed the disappearance of the trilobites and several other groups. Among the land animals, the amphibians declined, while reptiles and insects evolved rapidly. In the forests, the true conifers developed, while the seed ferns declined and finally disappeared. The Permian period saw the end of numerous plant and animal groups and marks the end of the Paleozoic era.

REVIEW

1. Compare the length of the Paleozoic era with the lengths of the Archeozoic and Proterozoic eras.

2. Briefly describe the three main features in the formation of a continent. Using these features, describe how a continent grows.

3. Using the maps of the different periods of the Paleozoic era as a guide, briefly describe the physical events that took place in your state during the Paleozoic.

4. How did the Applachian revolution differ from the disturbances of the earlier periods?

5. What is the importance of each of the following: trilobites, ostracoderms, lobe-finned fish, mosses and lichens?

NEW VIEW

1. What evidence indicates that during the Paleozoic era broad seas covered much of the interior of the United States?

2. The remains of the fern forests of the Carboniferous period are mined as coal. How did the change from plants to coal take place?

3. Present all the evidence you can that at different times during the Paleozoic era much of the land was covered by tropical forests or by ice sheets.

4. THE MESOZOIC ERA

The geography of North America during the Mesozoic era was shaped by two major events. The formation of the Appalachian Mountains at the end of the Paleozoic had provided a highland in the east. This highland was steadily eroded throughout the Mesozoic. In the west, depositing of sediment in the shallow seas of the geosyncline ended when mountain building processes

2

produced the Rocky Mountains. This revolution marks the end of the Mesozoic era.

Geologists now know that locating various landforms of the Mesozoic, particularly those in the west, is important economically. Many valuable mineral resources occur in Mesozoic deposits: copper, zinc, and silver in the Rockies; gold in the Sierra Nevadas; uranium in the vicinity of the Colorado Plateau; petroleum in Texas; coal in many western states.

The fossil record of the Mesozoic era provides evidence of a wide variety of animal and plant life occupying land, water, and air. This was the time of the terrible dinosaurs, the giant sea lizards, and strange flying reptiles and birds. Under a consistently mild climate, flowering plants and hardwood trees evolved along with evergreens to fill the Mesozoic forests. Now let's examine some of the physical and biological records of the Mesozoic in more detail.

The Continent Changes

During the early Paleozoic, geosynclines existed in the eastern and western sections of the continent. This distribution around the central shield and platform changed dramatically in the Mesozoic. The eastern geosyncline became attached to the continental nucleus as a highland area. Immediately this highland began to undergo erosion. In the western geosyncline, the depositing of sediment continued.

Examine the land-sea relationships of North America during the Triassic, the first period of the Mesozoic era. 3 In the eastern section of the country, erosion was the pri-

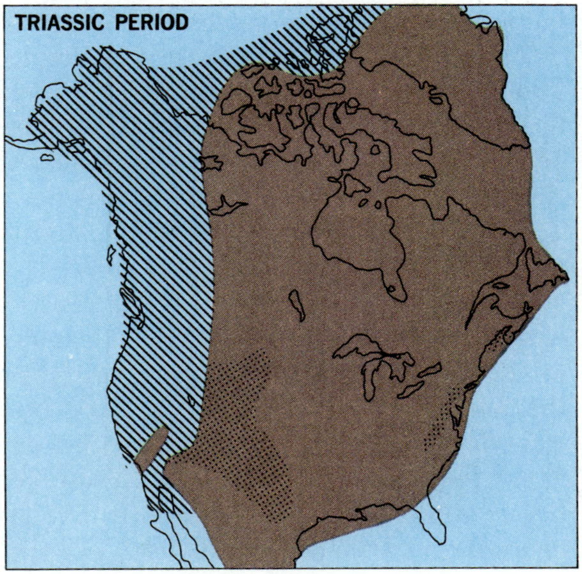

3

❶

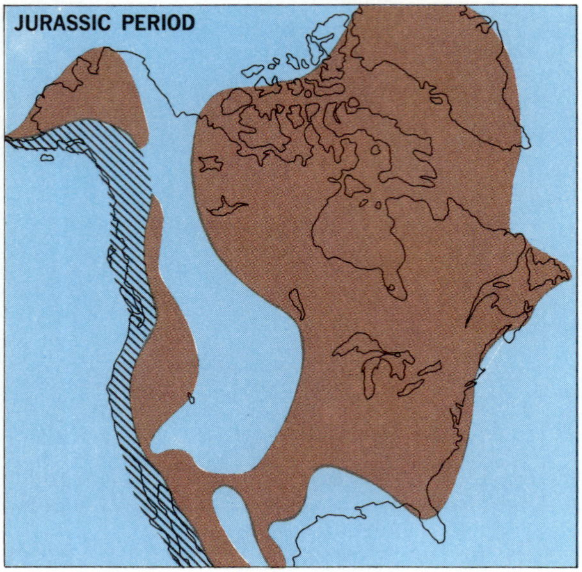

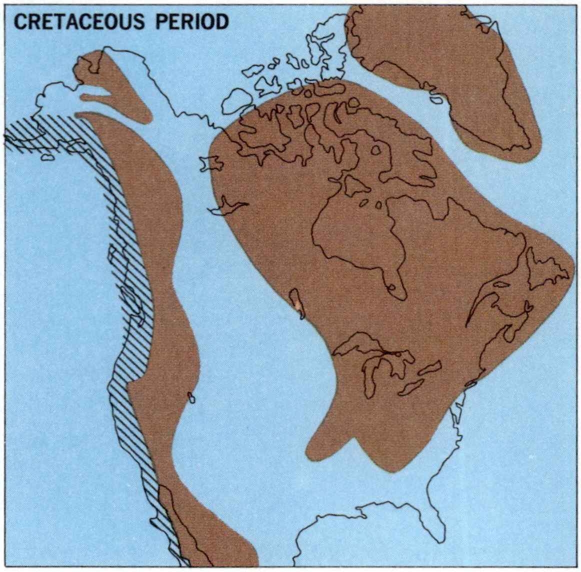

❷

mary event; this highland was reduced to an almost level area. In the north-south direction throughout this eroded area, huge faults produced basins, hollows or depressions that contained water. These basins were quickly filled with sediment. Lava that poured from many volcanoes helped fill the basins between the times sediment was being deposited. After the basins were filled, uplifting and faulting exposed many of these deposits.

Large beds of red sandstone were formed from stream deposits. (See the location of these redbeds, indicated by the dotted areas on the map of the Triassic.) The Watchung Ridges of New Jersey are ancient lava flows. The Palisades on the west side of the Hudson River is an exposed sill (see Chapter 5).

The geosyncline of western North America was covered by shallow seas that continued to accumulate marine sediments. Throughout the midwest, however, additional red beds were deposited in lowland areas by wind and rivers from adjacent highlands. These red beds are extremely important since they are an excellent source of uranium ores.

An Inland Sea Forms

The Jurassic, recall, is the second period of the Mesozoic era. As you study the map of the Jurassic, you see that large areas of central North America were again covered by an inland sea.❶ Observe that the sea covers the area formerly occupied by the western geosyncline and much of the interior platform. Uplift also produced a chain of mountains along the entire western coast. The beautiful Sierra Nevada range of California was also formed at this time.

The Rocky Mountains Rise

Examine the map of the Cretaceous period, the last period of the Mesozoic.❷ The most obvious feature is the enormous extent of the inland seas that appear to divide North America into two large "islands." This was the last great marine invasion of the continent.

In the east, the original Appalachians were washed into the sea, and water spread over much of the land that was once a highland of splendid peaks. In the western section of the continent, the geosyncline was being uplifted in the largest mountain building event the world has ever known. The magnificent Rocky Mountain system that extends from Alaska to Mexico and also includes the Andes in South America was formed. This Rocky Mountain revolution brought the physical events of the Mesozoic era in North America to a dramatic close.

Then Came the Reptiles

By mid-Triassic time, marine plants included representatives of several types of algae, bacteria, and diatoms that still exist today. Land plants of the Triassic included spore-bearing ferns and seed plants that do not flower. Among these nonflowering plants were ginkos, conifers, and cycads, plants much like palm trees. The great conifers, resembling modern pine trees, are found as petrified logs in the Petrified Forest of Arizona.

Marine invertebrates included many corals and many varieties of mollusks: oysters, mussels, snails, clams, lobsters, and ammonites. The ammonites were the dominant invertebrate of the Mesozoic seas. Insects dominated the land invertebrates. Grasshoppers, flies, termites, and many other groups appeared and flourished.

The development of the vertebrate animals of the Mesozoic is dramatic and complex. In the Paleozoic, recall, lobe-finned fish apparently gave rise to the first primitive amphibians, which in turn gave rise to the early reptiles. By the beginning of the Mesozoic, the first "mammal-like" reptiles had appeared. These mammal-like reptiles were the ancestors of the mammals. Other primitive reptiles gave rise to the birds and the many Mesozoic reptiles—including the *flying reptiles* and the terrible reptiles of the land, the *dinosaurs*.

The fossil record of the Triassic contains evidence of tiny animals that probably indicate the arrival of the first mammals—an especially important event. Footprints in Triassic rock also indicate the existence of early dinosaurs.

The Age of Dinosaurs

Into the Jurassic, animal and plant life continued to flourish. On land, Jurrasic plants resembled those of the Triassic. Cycads and conifers continued to dominate the forests. But many new kinds of animals were evolving. Mammals continued to develop. The first bird, *archeopteryx* (är′kē·op′ter·iks), complete with feathers, teeth, and wings that ended in claws, made its appearance. ❸ Joining the early birds in the air was another strange animal, a flying reptile. This reptile, called *pterosaurus* (ter′o·sôr′us), flew by means of a thin layer of skin stretching from its body to its arms.

❸

In the sea the dominant reptiles were *ichthyosaurs* (ik′thē·o·sôrz′), reptiles that looked something like dolphins. (1) Marine reptiles grew especially large; and giant *plesiosaurs* (plē′sē·ō·sôrz′), with their long necks and paddlelike limbs, preyed upon other marine life.

The dominant reptiles of the Jurassic, however, were the dinosaurs. Often called the Age of Dinosaurs, the Jurassic landscape teemed with large numbers and various kinds of these beasts. Although dinosaurs originated in the Triassic period, three of their best-known representatives first appeared in the Jurassic. Although the word *dinosaur* comes from the Greek term for "terrible reptile," you may be surprised to know that not all dinosaurs were huge. Some were not much larger than chickens. No doubt you have studied about dinosaurs before, so we will name only a few.

Brontosaurus (bron′tō·sôr′əs) was a giant four-footed, plant-eating dinosaur, the largest animal that ever lived on land. Fossil remains indicate that Brontosaurus was almost 21 meters (70 feet) long and may have weighed over thirty tons. *Stegosaurus* (stəg′ō·sôr′əs) was a "plated" dinosaur. (2) With plates on his back and spikes on his tail, this large animal probably roamed the Jurassic forest without too much annoyance from the other animals. *Allosaurus* (al′ō·sôr′əs) was a giant meat-eating dinosaur who walked and ran on his hind legs. A huge skull with massive jaws, long teeth, and sharp claws made *Allosaurus* an excellent hunter and killer.

(1)

Life in the Cretaceous

A variety of animal life existed in the Cretaceous seas. Invertebrates included the sponges, corals, crabs, and mollusks. Giant ammonites were still abundant in early Cretaceous seas. (3) By the close of the period, they were extinct. Sharks and bony fishes represented the vertebrates. The many swimming reptiles included the ichthyosaurs and plesiosaurs, as well as huge sea-turtles and giant sea-serpents over 22 meters (75 feet) long.

The greatest evolution of all time among land plants took place during the Cretaceous. The first flowering plants, the angiosperms, may have appeared earlier, but now they expanded rapidly. Very soon they were competing with the earlier trees and shrubs. Broad-leaved trees developed rapidly. The magnolia, fig, and willow arrived first. Later came familiar trees of today—the oak, maple, and chestnut. By the end of this period, the flowering plants had replaced most other kinds of land plants. They dominated the landscape just as they do today.

During the Cretaceous, animal life on land was dominated by the insects and the reptiles. Bees, butterflies, and other insects were probably as numerous as the 800,000 species that exist today. New varieties of dinosaurs evolved among the reptiles.

Tyrannosaurus rex (ti·ran′ō·sôr′əs reks) was the last and largest of the two-legged meat-eaters. 4 Fossil remains indicate that *Tyrannosaurus* was over 13 meters (45 feet) long and weighed over eight tons. With gigantic teeth this beast must have been a ferocious hunter and killer. *Anatosaurus* (ən·ət′ō·sôr′əs) was a "duck-billed" dinosaur. These reptiles had strong tails, webbed limbs, and ducklike jaws. Primarily plant-eaters, they lived along the shores of rivers and lakes. *Triceratops* (trī·ser′ə·täps), another plant-eater was a "horned" dionsaur. 4 A thick bony plate protected its neck. On either side of this plate were two immense horns, and above the nose was a third smaller horn.

2

3

Dinosaurs Die Out

By the close of the Mesozoic, most of these animals had disappeared. The dinosaurs, the flying reptiles, the swimming reptiles, all became fossils to be seen only in museums as a reminder of a strange time long ago. Today only turtles, alligators, snakes, and small lizards survive from this once great group of animals.

4

What caused these many different types of giant reptiles to become extinct? Some geologists believe that uplift of the land and changes in climate may have destroyed the environment of land and vegetation to which the reptiles were adapted. Others suggest that the evolution of a different type of plant life may have caused starvation among the plant-eating dinosaurs. As the plant-eating dinosaurs died, so did the meat-eaters who depended on them for food. Finally, some scientists suggest that the small evolving mammals may have caused the extinction of the dinosaurs by destroying their huge eggs. Whatever the explanation, the giant reptiles were gone. In their place, the mammals developed; they dominate the last era of earth history, the Cenozoic.

REVIEW

1. How does the length of the Mesozoic era compare with the lengths of the three previous eras?

2. Describe briefly the physical changes in North America during the three periods of the Mesozoic era.

3. Using the maps of the Mesozoic era as a guide, describe briefly the physical events that took place in your state during the Mesozoic.

4. List several mineral resources found in Mesozoic deposits.

5. Briefly describe the various kinds of plants that evolved during the Mesozoic era.

6. How does the animal record of the Triassic differ from the animal record of the Cretaceous?

NEW VIEW

1. Name an animal that is becoming extinct today. Why is it becoming extinct? How does this reason compare with the reasons given for the extinction of the dinosaurs?

2. How did the changing climate affect the plant and animal life during the Mesozoic? Give specific examples.

3. In the United States, Triassic fossils are found only in the western regions. Why?

5. THE CENOZOIC ERA

The Cenozoic era, the era in which we are living today, is divided into two periods. The Tertiary period was approximately 61 million years long. The Quaternary period includes the past 2 million years of life. The continent of North America, particularly the landscape and landforms of the United States as we know them today, unfolded in the 63

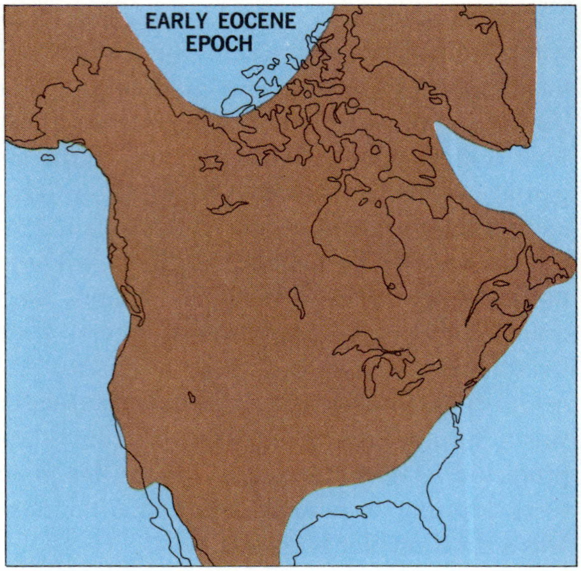

1

million years of the Cenozoic. The three major physical features of any country—mountains, plains, and coast lines—developed during this time.

The record of the plant and animal life that evolved during the Cenzoic is filled with a variety of forms. Plants included many kinds of grasses and grains. Common invertebrates and fishes, including sharks, filled the seas. Life on the land included amphibians, small reptiles, insects, and many kinds of birds. Above all, however, the Cenozoic is the Age of Mammals.

The fossil record supports the concept that mammals evolved from reptiles in much the same way as reptiles evolved from amphibians. Throughout most of the Mesozoic, tiny, primitive mammals existed along with the dinosaurs. They were, of course, very inconspicuous at this time. Nevertheless, by the beginning of the Cenozoic, mammals became the dominant group inhabiting every environment abandoned by the dying reptiles. From mouse-like animals to man, the mammals continue to dominate the earth.

The Present Continent Takes Shape

Examine the map showing the land-sea relationships of the early Cenozoic.❶ Observe that the shape and size of North America are very much the same as today. Throughout this era, the eastern and western seacoasts were covered and uncovered several times by the seas. Other parts of the continent remained above sea level.

In the east, the Appalachian Mountains were reduced to a low plain by the time the Mesozoic era came to a close. Throughout the Cenozoic, these same mountains were gently uplifted, tilted, and eroded to produce the present scene. Much of the sediment from this ancient upland is now part of the Atlantic Coastal Plain. Examine the map of the United States showing the present location of these and other physical features as you continue your study.❷

In the west, the Rocky Mountains were eroding; the sediment was slowly deposited as the Great Plains. In the southwest, uplift around the Colorado River produced a high plateau. At the same time, a river carved its way into the rising rock layers to form the Grand Canyon. The Basin and Range Province was created as faulting and uplift produced the mountains of this area. In the northwest, volcanic activity occurred. Lava that flowed from volcanoes produced the Columbian Plateau; at the same time volcanic cones were formed along the Cascade Mountains.

The ranges of the west coast—the Rocky Mountains, the Sierra Nevadas, the Cascade system, and the Pacific Coastal Ranges—are still involved in the process of uplift that began in the Cenozoic. The earthquakes that occurred in California in 1971 (in Peru in

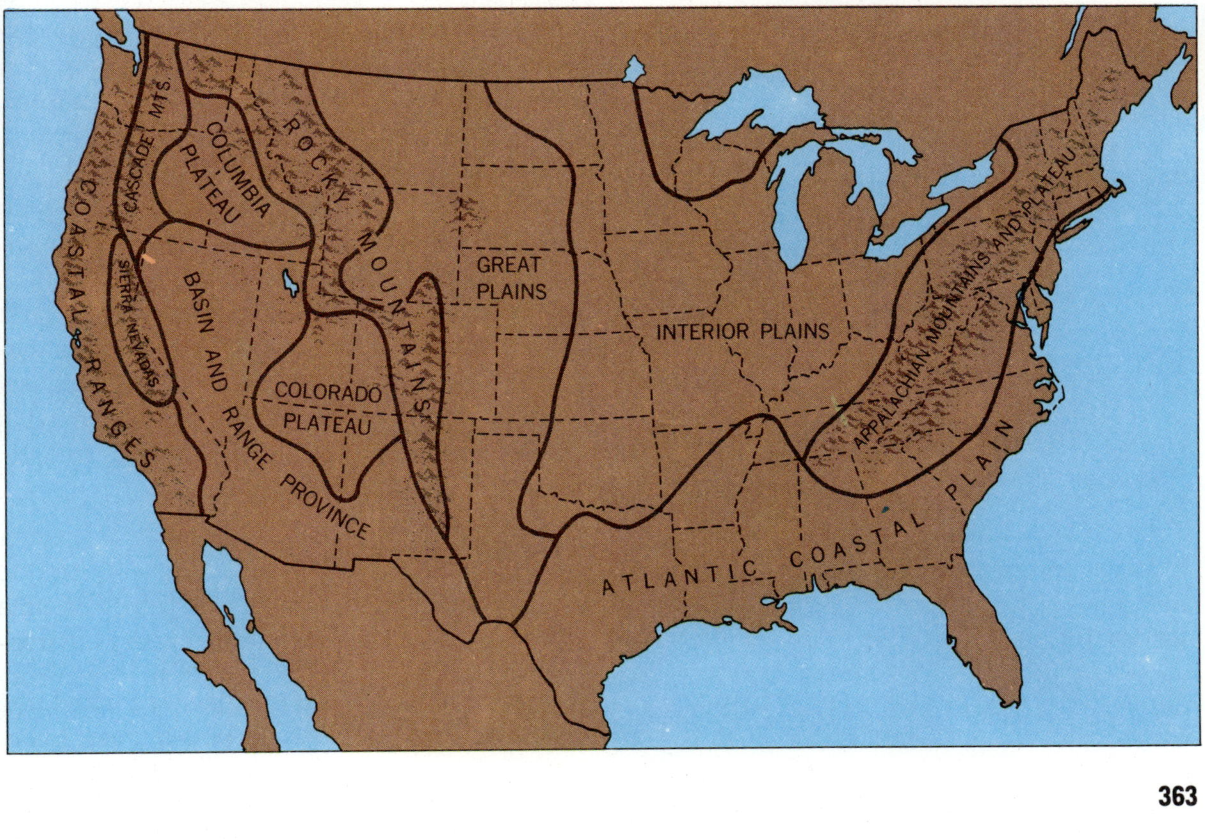

❷

1970) and in Alaska in 1964 testify to the continuing restlessness of this region.[1]

The peninsula of Florida was shaped when an island attached itself to the mainland. The continental shelf along the southern coast of the United States represents a modern geosyncline. Here sediment from the central United States is being deposited in a gradually sinking basin.

The Ice Ages

In the Pleistocene epoch of the Cenozoic, the climate changed radically. Temperatures dropped, and large masses of ice formed. On four different occasions glaciers extended themselves over many sections of our country. Four times the ice spread over the land, and four times it receded. Carefully study the map showing the greatest extent of ice in the United States.[2] Was the place where you now live once covered by ice?

The Pleistocene Ice Age was the last major episode in the earth's history. As the ice

1

2

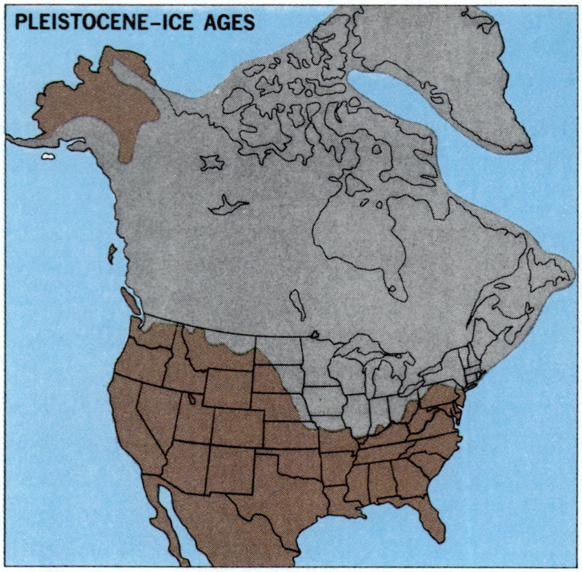

sheets, particularly the last one, advanced and withdrew, they left many conspicuous marks on the landscape of North America. As glaciers moved forward, solid particles of rock frozen into the ice scraped the underlying bedrock. Where the particles were very fine, the rock was smoothed and polished. Larger rock fragments produced long, parallel scratches called striae in the bedrock (see page 134).[3] Larger pebbles and boulders gauged out long, parallel grooves in the rock, particularly if the bedrock was soft.

Wherever glaciers move, they leave marks on the rock that record their passing. Examine again the map showing the greatest extent of ice in the United States. In what states would we be likely to find smooth, striated, or grooved bedrock?

The Work of Glaciers

As glaciers moved southward, they frequently followed the course of river valleys. As the glaciers moved forward, they deepened these valleys. As the glaciers melted, the water often filled these deepened areas. Lakes were formed in front of the glacial debris deposited by the retreating masses of ice. Through a combination of erosion and the depositing of sediment, many lakes were formed in the northern United States and throughout Canada. Lake George and the Great Lakes were formed as rivers that flowed north were dammed by glacial deposits.

Since the retreat of the glaciers, the drainage from the Great Lakes has been eastward into the St. Lawrence River. The flow of water through the Niagara River between Lake Erie and Lake Ontario has created Niagara Falls—the most impressive waterfall in the eastern United States. The falls began as melted glacial water poured into Lake Ontario over the 60-meter (200-foot) high Niagara **escarpment,** a long, high cliff of layers of sedimentary rock. Since that time, erosion of the bed rock under the river has caused Niagara Falls to recede a distance of 12 kilometers (7 miles) back toward Lake Erie.

3

Because of its scenic attraction, engineers are attempting to prevent the falls from receding further by forcing part of the water of the river to flow through tunnels. They have also diverted the water temporarily while strengthening the face of the falls. 4

4

The last retreat of these glaciers probably occurred less than 11,000 years ago—the Recent epoch had begun. Large ice masses on Greenland and Iceland are the remains of this unusual phenomenon. Where this ice reaches the oceans, sections break off to form icebergs. 1 In fact, some scientists believe that we are now in a temporary warm period that will be followed by yet another ice age.

Today the process of erosion, depositing of sediment, uplift, volcanic action, and earthquakes continually change the physical features of the earth. Indeed, we find no feature of this planet is permanent. The earth is in constant change.

Life in the Cenozoic

As the Cenozoic progressed, our familiar grasses appeared and spread over large parts of the land. These grasses were important because they provided rich food for the grazing animals, such as horses and camels, that developed. In addition, these grasses gave rise to our common grains—wheat, oats, barley, corn, and rice.

Invertebrate animals in the Cenozoic seas were much like those we find today. Clams, oysters, snails, crabs, sponges, corals, and starfish thrived. On land, many new kinds of insects continued to develop.

Marine vertebrates included many types of fishes. In particular, extremely large sharks were present in the Cenozoic waters. Frogs and salamanders represented the amphibians. Snakes, lizards, and turtles were common reptiles. Birds developed into the many species we find today—but above all, the mammals. Let's examine their development epoch by epoch.

The Age of Mammals Begins

At the beginning of the Paleocene epoch, animal life on land was scarce. Except for a few turtles, alligators, and snakes, the mighty reptiles were gone. As the Paleocene unfolded, however, a few mammal-like animals, mostly small insect-eaters, made their way out of the trees and onto the land left vacant by the Mesozoic giants. Before the Paleocene came to a close, the first primates, the group of mammals including man, had appeared. The animals of the Paleocene included both meat-eaters and plant-eaters. Among the latter were the ancestors of the hoofed animals.

1

2 

The Changing Scene

Through much of the Paleocene and the early Eocene, North and South America were connected by a land bridge. Consequently, various kinds of animals that evolved on one continent moved easily to another. During the Eocene, however, rising waters divided the continents. In time, several types of mammals that thrived and continued to develop in South America became extinct in North America. Among the North American mammals, the early primates such as the lemurs were extinct by the end of the Eocene, although their relatives survived in South America.2 Not until the coming of early man did our country see another primate.

Small-sized ancestors of the horse and camel were, you remember, among the first of the modern hoofed animals. The Eocene also saw the increase of rodents, as well as many cat-like and dog-like meat-eaters. Perhaps the most unusual animal was a bird called *Diatryma*, which stood seven feet tall. This huge turkey-like running bird had powerful legs and a large, beaked head.3

Modern Mammals Appear

As the Oligocene epoch began, the climate became cooler and subtropical forests began to retreat southward. Now grasses and hardwood trees were everywhere—an ideal environment for the development of many types of mammals.

Rodents of all types continued to evolve; beavers, rabbits, gophers, rats, and mice were abundant. The hoofed plant-eaters included the horse, camel, zebra, rhinoceros, sheep, pig, and giraffe. Meat-eating pack dogs grew in number. And many giant mammals, doomed to extinction, also appeared.

A Land Bridge Long Ago

In the Miocene the climate became even cooler. The plains, or prairies, with their many grasses became the dominant environment for a variety of grazing animals. Miocene horses and camels flourished on the prairie grasses. For a time, several varieties of rhinoceroses also thrived; but they were doomed to extinction in America. A host of other animals roamed the forests that fringed the plains: weasels, skunks, bears, racoons, primitive deer, and killer cats.

Finally, the first mastodon, a giant elephant-like animal, rumbled onto the Miocene

 3

plains of North America. This giant, called *Gomphotherium* (gŏm′fō·thir′ēəm), had developed in the Middle East. Century after century, the mastodons made their way across Asia and over the land bridge across the Bering Sea that connected Asia and Alaska some 20 million years ago. ①

During the Pliocene, the last epoch of the Tertiary period, the climate continued to grow colder. Pliocene life was marked by a variety and abundance of even larger mammals. These included huge dogs and mastodons that had evolved in America. The horse and camel now closely resembled their present-day descendants.

Ice Age Mammals

As the Pliocene ended and the Pleistocene Ice Age began, hearty breeds of animals dominated the frigid environment. Beavers the size of bears and six-foot wolves roamed the land. *Smilodon,* the saber-toothed cat, hunted his prey with deadly weapons—enormous fangs (see page 328). Giant mastodons now shared the land with other giants—the woolly mammoths. Like the mastodons, they entered America from Asia.

The durable musk ox survived the cold and is still present in the Arctic. However the horse and camel died out in North America. Our present horses are descendants of horses returned to America on Spanish ships four hundred years ago.

Like the dinosaurs before them, the mastodons, woolly mammoths, saber-toothed cats and other large mammals vanished as the Pleistocene neared its end. Over much of the continent, only smaller mammals and bison remained.

As the last mass of ice melted, but before the rising waters covered the land bridge to Asia, one mammal had trekked cautiously into North America. Man had arrived in the Western Hemisphere.

①

REVIEW

1. What were the main physical changes in North America during the Quaternary period of the Cenozoic era?

2. Describe briefly the physical setting of your state at the beginning of the Cenozoic era.

3. What physical evidence of Pleistocene glaciers is found in rocks?

4. How did the great glaciers of the Pleistocene affect the animal life of the continent? Give specific examples.

5. How did the development of grasses and grains affect the animal life of the Cenozoic era?

NEW VIEW

1. List several fossils found only in Cenozoic rocks. Are all these fossils mammals?

2. What is the difference between a plain, a plateau, and a mountain? Which of these is found in the area where you live?

3. How did the land bridges between North America and South America and between North America and Asia affect life on these continents?

6. RELATING THE CONCEPTS

Man has recorded a history of his civilization in pictures and in words for the past several thousand years. This is a very direct record of the past. More recently, however, man has developed another type of history book—a book that contains the orderly arrangement of events that have taken place on the earth long before there was anyone to observe and record them. This geologic history book provides information on the origin and evolution of the earth and of life on the earth. As one of the single greatest achievements of mankind, this record provides answers to questions about the age of the earth, ancient life, ancient climates, and ancient geography.

Earth scientists have had considerable success in interpreting clues found in sequences of layered rock. The sedimentary rocks indicate where land and water areas were located in the past. They also contain fossils that provide evidence of past plant and animal life and of changes in climate.

As the present is the key to the past, so is the past a key to understanding the present. Our familiar landscapes are the products of geological events that have occurred over the millions of years since the earth came into existence. In a somewhat similar way, complex plants and animals are the successors of earlier living organisms.

Reviewing the Concepts

► *The rock layers of the geologic column provide clues to the past history of the earth.* Through fossil and rock correlation, geologists have related sequences of rock layers to form a continuous geologic column. Layer by layer, the column tells of changes in life, climate, and geography as they occurred through time.

► *The geologic time scale is a summary of the major physical and biological events of the past.* It is hard to imagine the enormous length of geologic time. The oldest rock found on earth has an age of about 3.5 billion years. Other evidence suggests that the earth's crust is about 4.6 billion years old. Abundant fossil remains do not appear in the rock record until about 600 million years ago. However, some simple plant and animal remains are found in rocks over 2 billion years old.

The geologic time scale is divided into eras, periods, and epochs. The two earliest eras, the Archeozoic and the Proterozoic, extend from about 4.6 billion years ago to about 600 million years ago. These two eras represent almost 90 percent of the earth's history. Little is known about this time. The Paleozoic era extends from 600 million years ago to about 230 million years ago; the Mesozoic from 230 to 63 million years ago; the Cenozoic era from 63 million years ago to the present.

► *The earth is in constant change.* The rock layers of the geologic column record a continuous history of change. Land-sea relationships have changed in the past and continue to change. Our present landscapes are temporary physical features upon the surface of the earth. Mountains rise, volcanoes erupt, glaciers advance and recede. Indeed, no feature of the planet is permanent.

► *Living things have a long past history.* Fossils found in the rock layers of the geologic column indicate that certain groups of living organisms dominated life on earth at various times in the past. The Paleozoic era began with the age of Invertebrates, passed through the Age of Fishes, and ended in the Age of Amphibians. The Mesozoic era is known as the Age of Reptiles, while the Cenozoic era is the Age of Mammals.

Testing Yourself

1. How has the geologist pieced together sequences of rock layers from many places to form a continuous column?

2. What kinds of information are provided by the types of rock found in the geologic column?

3. What kinds of information provided by fossils in the geologic column are useful in preparing a geologic time scale?

4. Why is there little evidence of life in Precambrian rocks?

5. Describe briefly the dominant physical changes in North America during the Paleozoic era.

6. During which era did plant and animal life first appear on land? Why is this event so important?

7. What organisms dominated the seas and the land during the Paleozoic, Mesozoic, and Cenozoic eras?

8. How does a shield area differ from a platform area?

9. Describe briefly the physical changes that have occurred in the Appalachian mountain region since Paleozoic times.

10. Describe briefly the geologic history of the Rocky Mountains.

11. Using the maps of the various periods, show how geosynclines have formed part of the North American continent.

12. Using the maps of the appropriate periods, describe the physical changes in North America during the Mesozoic era.

13. In rocks from which period would you probably find the first fossils of: lobe-finned fish, graptolites, conifers, algae, "mammal-like" reptiles, mammals?

14. How are the histories of the primates, the horses, and the camels in North America similar? How are they different?

15. Give several reasons why various kinds of plants and animals have become extinct in the last 600 million years. Apply your reasons to one specific example.

16. What evidence do scientists have that large areas of the northern part of the United States were covered by glaciers during the Pleistocene epoch?

17. What geologic evidence indicates that the mountain ranges of the west coast of the United States are presently in the process of uplift?

18. What information in the rock layers of the geologic column supports the theory that complex plants and animals evolved from simple plants and animals?

Extending the Concepts

Investigation 1. From as many sources as you can, gather information about a single fossil specimen. Then try to answer the following questions. Is it plant or animal? Did it live in the water, on the land, or both? How old is it? What did it look like when it was alive? How did it become a fossil? Does it have any living relatives? What was the environment where it lived? What other living things existed in the same environment? When did it first appear in the rock record? Did it become extinct? If so, why? Do any descendants survive today?

Investigation 2. In the library, investigate the geologic history of several land formations in Europe. You might consider the Chalk Cliffs of Dover, the Rock of Gibraltar, or the Alps.

Suggested Reading

Colbert, Edwin H., *Evolution of the Vertebrates,* 2nd ed., New York, Wiley, 1969. Shows how animals have developed through the millions of years of earth history.

Kurten, Björn, *The Age of the Dinosaurs,* New York, McGraw-Hill, 1968. An informative and well-illustrated account of life in past ages, with emphasis on the dinosaurs.

Rhodes, F., H. Zim, and P. Shaffer, *Fossils: A Guide to Prehistoric Life,* New York, Golden Press, 1962. A guide to identifying fossils you might find on a field trip.

Unit Six

RESOURCES OF THE LAND AND SEA

People once believed that our planet was made up of just four things: earth, water, air, and fire. These four elements formed four spheres, one within the other. The inner sphere of solid earth was surrounded by a layer of water, then by a layer of air, and finally by a layer of fire—which appeared as lightning when the outer sphere was disturbed.

Today this idea seems strange to us. We have been able to examine the earth and discover the elements it is composed of. Now let's look at some of these elements more closely. Let's discover the value of the stores of earth—and what we can do to preserve them.

17

Resources of the Sea and Air

The growing world population is constantly increasing its demand for raw materials. Coal, gas, and oil are needed for fuels. Ores of iron, copper, and aluminum are needed for refining into metals. Children go to bed hungry each night in many parts of the world. This increased demand for raw materials has led to greater exploration for minerals on land. It has also led to better use of the land for food production through soil conservation, use of fertilizers, and crop rotation.

In our search for new sources of food, we have begun to study our environment—our land, sea, and air—more closely. Because of its huge area and staggering wealth of resources, we have been drawn back to the sea—a sea from which we have always obtained food in the form of fish and shellfish.(1) And ocean water itself is a valuable raw material. It contains huge quantities of dissolved minerals. It can be processed to yield fresh water for drinking and for irrigation. It holds a fantastic population of fish. And beneath ocean waters lie sediments and rocks rich in minerals and fuels.

1. MINING SEA WATER

There are about 1,280 million cubic kilometers (320 million cubic miles) of sea water. Every 4 cubic kilometers (1 cubic mile) contains an average of 150 million metric tons of

(1)

dissolved salt and other minerals. (A metric ton equals 2,204.6 pounds.) These dissolved substances are extremely valuable. But can you get them out of sea water and make a profit doing it? The gold in only 4 cubic kilometers of sea water, for example, is worth $20,000. Unfortunately, it would cost you $50,000 to remove it from the sea water if you used our present techniques. Perhaps you would be wiser to extract some of the other minerals. Every natural element is dissolved in sea water to some extent. You might even consider sea water as a thin liquid ore. Yet only nine elements account for over 93 percent of the dissolved substances in the sea, as shown in the table below. Chlorine and sodium combine to form salt (sodium chloride), the chief mineral.

ELEMENTS IN SEA WATER

Element	*Percent*
chlorine	54.23
sodium	30.17
magnesium	3.63
sulfur	2.51
calcium	1.14
potassium	1.09
bromine	0.19
carbon	0.08
strontium	0.04
all others	6.92

Salt from the Sea

In practice a few important minerals, although present in land deposits, can be more easily extracted directly from sea water. The simplest extraction process is **solar evaporation,** which is used to mine table salt (NaCl) from sea water. Four cubic kilometers of sea water contain 108 million metric tons of table salt. Chinese writings dating from 2200 B.C. mention the use of salt from sea water, but man was probably using salt from the sea long before this. In the solar evaporation process, sea water is passed into large, shallow basins, or settling basins. Here the sun's energy is allowed to evaporate most of the water to form **brine,** a strong solution of sodium chloride. As more and more water evaporates, calcium carbonate, magnesium carbonate, and finally calcium sulfate precipitate and settle to the bottom of the basin. Now the remaining brine is transferred to new settling basins where the sodium chloride precipitates and settles out as a layer of 99.6 percent pure salt. This highly purified salt is scraped up and processed for further purification.

2

The largest solar evaporation salt plant in the world is located in the salt marshes of San Francisco Bay, California. 2 Here salt basins yield 1 million metric tons of salt each year.

Magnesium from Sea Water

If you wanted to buy a light-weight ladder, you might decide to buy an aluminum ladder. But it wouldn't be pure aluminum; it would probably contain magnesium. The ladder would be made of an **alloy,** a combination of metals. Although magnesium itself is not strong, in some way it adds strength and hardness to alloys without increasing their weight. In fact, magnesium is the lightest structural metal in common use.

Because 4 cubic kilometers of sea water contain 5.2 billion kilograms ($11\frac{1}{2}$ billion pounds) of magnesium, we have turned to the sea for our supply of this metal. Most magnesium is obtained from sea water by the electrolytic method begun in Germany in 1866. The method was first used in the United States in 1916. The use of magnesium in aircraft production became extremely important during World War II. In 1939, for example, the United States produced 3 million kilograms (6.7 million pounds) of magnesium. By 1943 our production had jumped to over 50 times that amount.

To produce magnesium, natural gas is needed to turn oyster shells into lime. The lime is then combined with sea water in huge tanks to form milk of magnesia. (1) Hydrochloric acid (HCl) converts this milk of magnesia to magnesium chloride, which is then dried and placed in electrolytic cells. In the electrolytic cells, electricity converts the powder into molten magnesium, which is cast into molds. At the same time, chlorine gas is produced. The chlorine is used in producing hydrochloric acid to replace the acid used earlier in the process. Because of the need for natural gas, lime, ocean water, and electric energy, magnesium extraction plants must be located in coastal regions (near an ocean) where all the raw materials are available at reasonable cost.

In addition to table salt and magnesium, the elements sulfur, calcium, potassium, and bromine are extracted commercially from ocean water. At present, the United States gets 80 percent of its bromine and all of its magnesium from sea water.

Fresh Water from the Sea

Most of the world's population lives in areas where fresh water is limited. Where does your town or city get its fresh water? Has your area had a drought recently? During severe droughts the amount of rainfall is not sufficient to supply fresh water for drinking and for industry. In times of drought, the water supply must be rationed. In fact, 26 percent of the earth's land area is arid (dry) or semiarid. For the people who live in these areas, there is never enough water. Every year is a drought year! As world population increases, the amount and quality of fresh water may become more limited for everyone.

But there is hope. Scientists may discover how to get more rain out of clouds by new cloud-seeding techniques. One system that makes use of both the atmosphere and the oceans has been developed. It could be used on islands that lie in the path of moist, tropical winds. A pump would bring up cold water from deep in the ocean. The cold water would pass through special pipes and then back to the ocean surface. The wind blowing over these pipes contains large amounts of moisture, and the moisture would condense on the pipes. This condensed moisture would then be piped to the place where fresh water was needed. An additional benefit of this system is that the deep ocean water contains mineral nutrients needed for the growth of

(1)

algae and other plankton. Fish would thrive on the plankton. A whole new fisheries resource might then be created in regions where fishing has never been much of an industry.

It has even been suggested that masses of ice from the ice shelves of Antarctica might be towed through the ocean to the dry coastal areas of Australia, South America, and Africa. Once delivered, the ice would be allowed to melt in special artificial basins. The relatively fresh melted water would then be pumped to where it is needed. All this could be accomplished at a cost that is about equal to that of obtaining fresh water by other means in these areas.

Unfortunately, the two sources of fresh water we have discussed will not meet the need for fresh water around the world. Where fresh water is not available from nature, man has devised means for desalting ocean water, that is, removing the salt from the water. The most practical method is the distilling of sea water. You can investigate **distillation** for yourself. ■

■ AN APPRENTICE INVESTIGATION into the Distillation of Salt Water

Place about 5 grams of table salt (NaCl) in a clean Pyrex or Kimax flask. Pour water into a graduated cylinder until it just reaches the 150 milliliter (ml) mark.❶ Pour the water into the flask and shake the solution well. Put a drop of the solution on your tongue. How does it taste? **Remember, never taste a chemical substance without your teacher's permission.**

Clamp the flask to a ringstand. Insert one end of a long, clean glass tube into a one-hole

❶

❷

rubber stopper in the flask. Place a beaker under the other end of the tube.❷ Boil the solution gently until all the liquid collects in the beaker. ***Lower*** the flame under the flask when very little water remains in it. How does the liquid in the beaker taste? What is it?

❶

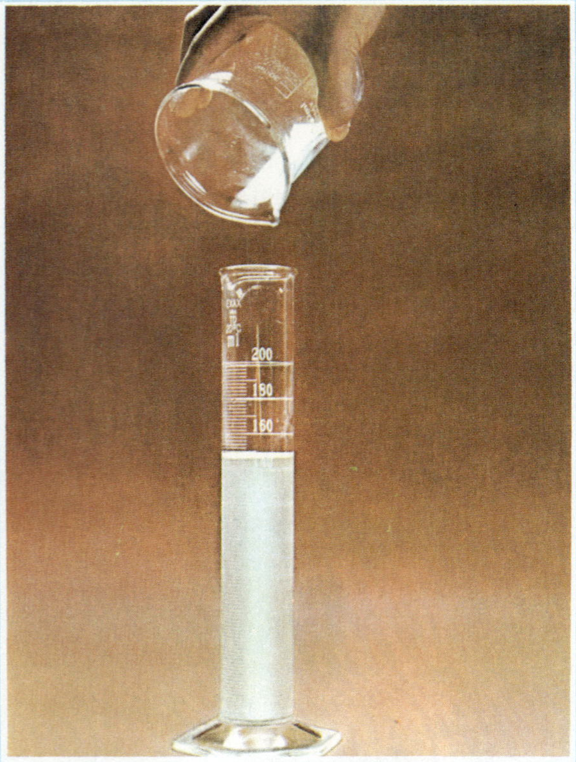

In the graduated cylinder, measure the amount of water that collected in the beaker.❶ What percent of the water in the original salt solution did you recover in the beaker? Study the sample calculation below made by two students.

salt water in flask	= 150 ml
distilled water in beaker	= 146 ml
percent of water recovered	$= \frac{146 \text{ ml}}{150 \text{ ml}} \times 100$
percent of water recovered	= 97%

Now determine the percent of water recovered as distilled water. What might have happened to the water that was "lost"?

What has happened to the salt (sodium chloride) in the solution? Perhaps you can verify the presence of the sodium ion by a flame test and the presence of the chloride ion by using silver nitrate (page 16).

An Investigation On Your Own

Repeat the investigation, but place the beaker in ice water or use a water-jacket type of distillation tube. Did you recover a greater percent of the water in the original salt solution? Why? Why not?

You observed a whitish substance on the inside of the flask as the water boiled away. Could you identify the substance as the salt (and other minerals) dissolved in the water? These minerals have formed a *scale*. If we tried to distill large quantities of sea water, the scale would become very thick and prevent heat from reaching the water being distilled. Then it would take longer and require more heat to distill the same amount of water.

Flash Distillation

To solve the problem of the formation of scale, engineers have developed a sea water distillation procedure that allows the water to evaporate before it reaches normal boiling temperature. This is called the **flash distillation process.** In this process warm water is sprayed into a chamber whose pressure is slightly lower than normal air pressure. At this lower pressure, the water boils at a lower temperature and does not leave a scale inside the chamber. Study the diagram to see how a flash distillation plant operates.❶

Sea water flows through three (or more) chambers before it reaches the main heating unit. The heated water now enters chamber 3 again. In this chamber, where pressure is reduced, the water that boils—or flashes—into steam condenses on the cooling coil and is

1

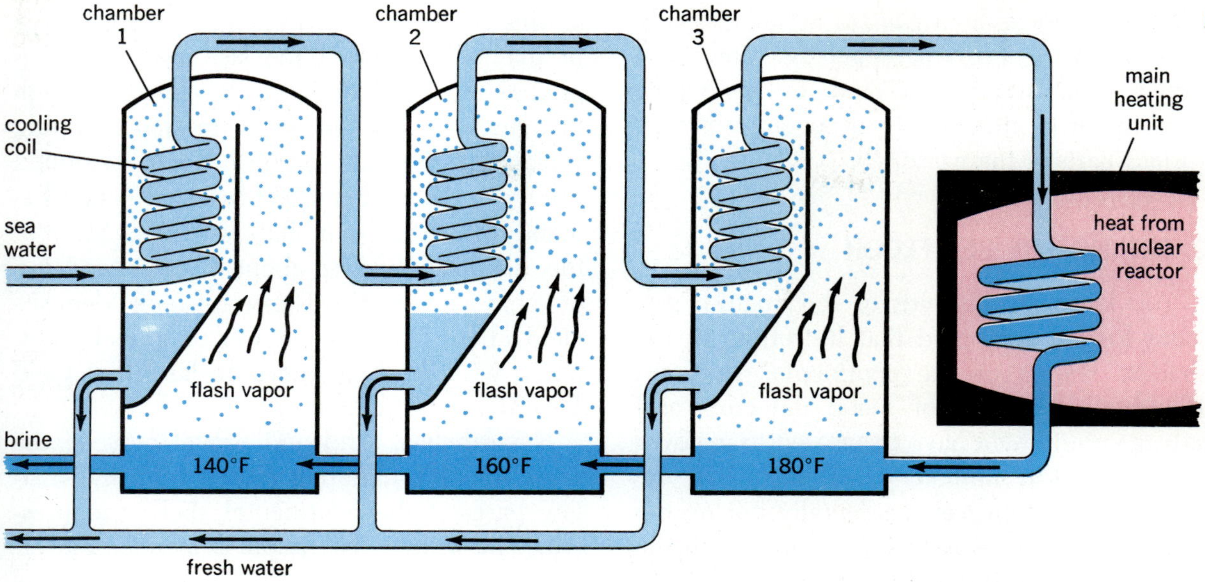

piped away. The sea water is now piped from chamber 3 to chamber 2. Here the water, slightly cooled and at a lower pressure, again flashes into water vapor. It condenses on the cooling pipes and is piped away. This procedure is repeated in the next chamber. The sea water brine that remains after the third distillation flows back to the ocean.

Where nuclear power plants have been built in coastal areas, they can be tied in with distillation plants. This procedure reduces the cost of desalting water. The liquid used to cool the nuclear reactor can be used to heat sea water in the heating unit of the flash distillation plant. The cost of generating electric power is also reduced because no special cooling system is needed for the nuclear reactor.

All desalting systems that produce more than 95,000 liters (25,000 gallons) of fresh water each day use the flash distillation process. The city of Key West, Florida, obtains most of its fresh water from a distillation plant that can produce 10 million liters (2.6 million gallons) each day. A new desalting plant in Kuwait (Arabia) is the largest in the world. It can produce about 10 times this amount of fresh water each day. When even larger plants are built, the cost of producing fresh water by distillation may drop to 9 cents per thousand liters. Why are such plants important even though the cost of fresh water from natural sources is only about 4 cents for each thousand liters?

REVIEW

1. Why is ocean water sometimes called a liquid ore?

2. Describe briefly the process of obtaining large amounts of common salt from sea water by solar evaporation.

3. Why are magnesium extraction plants located in coastal regions?

4. How does the flash distillation process for obtaining fresh water from the ocean differ from ordinary distillation?

NEW VIEW

1. What factors might affect the location of a new solar distillation plant? In which parts of the world would such a plant be most successful?

2. The average salinity of the ocean is usually given as $35\ ^{0}/_{00}$, or 35 parts per thousand. How would such factors as climate or geographic location affect the salinity of ocean water in various parts of the world?

2. MINING THE SEA FLOOR

You know the legends of the Spanish galleons loaded with gold that lie rotting in the shallow waters of the continental shelf off Florida. New types of metal detectors and salvage equipment have been used to uncover treasure worth millions of dollars. But the treasure that man has accidentally put on the continental shelves is tiny compared with the wealth that nature has put there. This wealth is in the form of diamonds, gold, iron ore, tin ore, and chromium ore, washed into the sea from the continents. In addition, chemical precipitation from ocean water has formed valuable mineral deposits on the continental shelves. These deposits include calcium carbonate, used to make lime, and phosphates, used in making fertilizer.

On the Continental Shelves

In southwest Africa, diamond-bearing gravels have been carried to the continental shelf by the Orange River. The coastal desert of this region has always been a rich source of diamonds. Within the last few years, experimental dredging has revealed enough diamonds in shallow water to make mining worthwhile. ❶ At present, one diamond dredge is recovering 1,000 carats of small diamonds per day from shallow water. Most of the diamonds weigh about $\frac{1}{3}$ carat and are of gem quality. ❷ These offshore deposits yield about 5 carats per ton of gravel, compared with the best mines on land that yield 1 carat per ton of ore!

Nevertheless, sand and gravel may be the most valuable materials mined from the shallow parts of the continental shelves at present. The mining operation is simple. Powerful pumps on a dredge suck sand and gravel from the shelves and send it through large pipes to the shore. On shore the sand and gravel may be spread out to form new land for parks or building sites. Sand and gravel are also mixed with cement to form concrete that is needed for constructing roads and buildings. In the United States, the construction industry uses over 450 million metric tons of marine sand and gravel each year. Much more sand and gravel is mined from the land; but as these supplies become exhausted, more will have to be pumped from the continental shelves.

❶

❷

Offshore Drilling for Oil

So far we have been talking about valuable materials on the surface of the continental shelves. What of the resources within the rocks of continental shelves? What types of rocks make up the continental shelves? What types of resources could we expect to find in them?

Geologists have found that the rocks of the continental shelves are the same types as the rocks of the continents. That is, igneous, metamorphic, and sedimentary rocks are all found in continental shelves. Geologists who found oil and gas in sedimentary rocks near the edge of the land reasoned that oil and gas would also be found in sedimentary rocks of the continental shelves. Drilling platforms have been built on the shallow continental shelves of the world to explore for oil and gas. ❸ Drilling at one location goes on for months at a time. Food and equipment are brought to the drillers by boat and helicopter.

The discovery of huge quantities of oil and gas in the Gulf of Mexico and other areas has been the reward for such difficult operations. It is estimated that 172 billion metric tons of oil are located in the rocks of the continental shelves. At present the maximum practical depth of water in which drilling can be done is about 192 meters (640 feet). No doubt improvements in drilling and diving techniques will allow drilling of oil and gas wells in even deeper water.

Petroleum deposits in rocks of the continental shelf of the Gulf of Mexico have resulted from upward movement of large masses of salt. These masses are called **salt domes.** ❹ As the salt moved upward, it pushed the surrounding rocks upward and finally punched through them. The oil and gas in these rocks moved toward the edge of the rocks that had been bent upwards. Because the oil and gas were unable to push through the salt domes, both oil and gas collected at the edges of the domes. Therefore, geologists try to locate the exact edges of salt domes so they can drill wells into the oil and gas deposits.

❸

Oil Pollution

The success in drilling for oil in coastal waters has brought with it some serious problems. One of the most serious is *oil pollution* caused by accidents and carelessness. Actually, the largest amount of oil pollution

❹

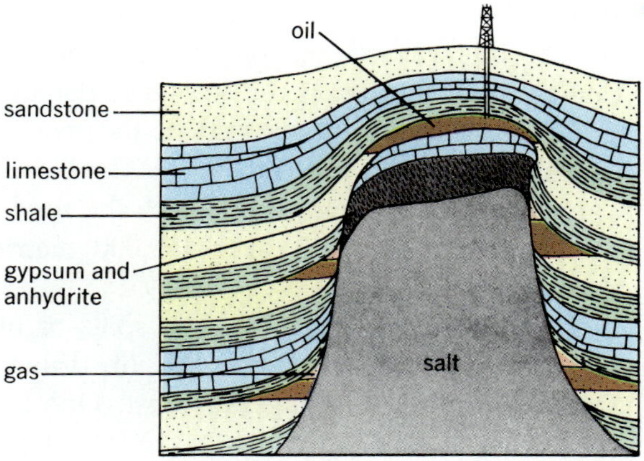

①

comes from tankers. After discharging their loads of oil, they fill their tanks with sea water. The sea water acts as ballast to keep the ships low in the water. Then the ships steer and handle better in waves and currents. This sea water and any oil left in the tanks is usually pumped overboard when the ship nears the port where its next cargo is to be picked up. It is estimated that about 2 million metric tons of oil are pumped overboard by tankers each year. This oil ends up as messy black clumps found on almost every beach.

Tanker accidents have caused serious local disasters. In 1967 the tanker Torrey Canyon ran aground in a storm and broke up near the southwest tip of England. It was carrying about 100,000 metric tons of crude oil. Much of this oil washed up on the beaches of England and France. It did immense damage to the recreation industry and to the marine animal population. And remember, the Torrey Canyon is small in comparison with the supertankers that may soon carry 450,000 metric tons of crude oil.

In our own country, two large spills of oil have recently occurred because of drilling accidents in waters along the coast. One accident happened near Santa Barbara, California. Drilling operations there caused oil to escape from the sea floor. The oil blackened the nearby beaches and was a disaster to recreation and marine life. A more recent oil spill was caused by failure of an unmanned oil platform off the coast of Louisiana. These disasters have made the public more aware of the need for better laws and stronger penalties against those who pollute the waters.

Some progress has been made in various methods of cleaning up these oil spills. At present, the best method of handling major oil spills is simply to bulldoze the oily sand off the beach and cart it away. Some mechanical and chemical methods have been partly effective against floating oil. One method involves putting a long, floating collar around the oily area. The oil is then recovered by pumping it onto a barge. The French treated oil from the Torrey Canyon spill with powdered chalk. The chalk caused the oil to form into clumps and sink.

In another method the floating oil is burned while on the surface of the water. Because it is difficult to get much of the oil to burn, a silica powder has been developed that results in almost complete burning.① However, the billowy black smoke from burning oil could cause an air pollution problem in coastal areas. Detergents and other chemical agents have also been sprayed on floating oil. These cause the oil to break up into small droplets that can be attacked by ocean bacteria. But these chemicals may harm marine life in the area. The solution might be worse than the problem.

Mining the Deep Ocean Floor

We have discussed minerals in sea water and those of the continental shelves. Are

2 

there any other mineral resources in the ocean? The answer is a definite yes! Much of the ocean's mineral wealth is in a type of deposit found only on the deeper ocean floor. These deposits are the light brown to black lumps called **manganese nodules.** 2 Some manganese nodules are microscopic in size. But the nodules of interest to mining engineers vary from the size of a pea to the size of a small potato. Usually they are found in water from 1,500 to 5,400 meters (5,000 to 18,000 feet) deep. In some parts of the Pacific Ocean, there are more than 40 kilograms of manganese nodules on each square meter of ocean floor (8 pounds per square foot).

Scientists think that the minerals in manganese nodules are precipitated from sea water. The nodules are made of layers surrounding a sand grain, a shark's tooth, or other particle on which the minerals first began to precipitate. However, nodules formed near underwater volcanoes may have resulted from direct precipitation of minerals formed from the volcanic rocks. These nodules do not seem to have a particle in the center around which precipitation occurred.

Manganese nodules are found where there are strong bottom currents and very little sediment. The currents shift the nodules so precipitation takes place on all sides. Little sediment reaches these deep ocean areas, and nodules grow larger without being buried. Apparently, it takes several thousand years to grow a nodule the size of a small potato.

Most manganese is used in making steel. The United States must import almost all of its manganese. But we might be able to mine manganese from the ocean floor close to the continent. The cobalt, nickel, and copper ores in the nodules may be more important than the manganese itself. The mineral ores are present in much smaller quantities than manganese or iron, as you see in the table below. However, they may be recovered as by-products of processing the nodules. Most of the by-products are worth more than manganese or iron.

One problem remains. How do we get the manganese nodules off the ocean floor? At present, no practical method exists.

Recently an entirely unexpected type of mineral deposit was found on the floor of the Red Sea. In a deep rift (crack) running down the center of the Red Sea, oceanographers found a thick layer of metallic ore. One layer

MANGANESE NODULES FROM THE PACIFIC OCEAN

Element	*Average percent by weight*
manganese	24.2
iron	14.0
cobalt	0.4
nickel	1.0
copper	0.54
zirconium	0.06
molybdenum	0.05
silicon and other nonmetals	59.75

of this deposit is estimated to be 90 meters (300 feet) thick. It contains rich ores of iron, manganese, zinc, copper, gold, and silver. It is the richest concentration of underwater ores ever found. Perhaps the ores were formed from gases and solutions escaping through cracks in the floor of the Red Sea. Could there also be rich ore deposits in such places as the rift valleys of the mid-ocean ridges? Perhaps so, but this wealth can't be recovered until engineers have figured out some way of mining deep beneath the Red Sea.

REVIEW

1. Why is dredging important to our supply of valuable materials from the continental shelves?
2. What may occur in the continental shelves when rocks containing oil and gas are penetrated by salt domes?
3. How can oil pollution be prevented or controlled?

NEW VIEW

1. Why are dredging operations currently limited to relatively shallow water?
2. Could ordinary suction pumps be used to obtain manganese nodules from the ocean floor? Why or why not?

3. FOOD RESOURCES OF THE OCEAN

The coastal zone has an important influence on plant and animal life in the ocean. Many marine (sea) animals spend at least part of their lives in the marshes and mouths of rivers along the coast. Clams, oysters, and other shellfish live out their lives in the sediment of shallow water along the coast. We are just learning about the large numbers of plants and animals that live in the ocean. We are learning that the idea of an unlimited supply of food from the ocean may *not* be true. But we are also learning that better management of fishing and hunting in the oceans may increase the long-range supply of marine animals. We are also learning to grow seaweeds we can eat. These seaweeds can add to the inadequate supply of food from the land.

World Population and the Food Supply

World population is increasing at an astonishing rate.(1) Between 1970 and 1980, it is expected to increase from 3,632,000,000 to 4,457,000,000. In fact, in the single year from 1967 to 1968, world population increased 2.7 percent. World food production during the same time increased by 3 percent. Why then should anyone in the world be hungry? The answer is that we are considering the *world averages* of population growth and growth of food supply. These averages hide serious problems in certain areas of the world. For example, in Africa (except South Africa) the increase in food supply was exactly balanced by the growth in population. In Latin America (both Central and South America) there was a 5 percent *loss* in the food supply available for each person. Severe droughts in these regions were mainly responsible for the poor food crop.

(1)

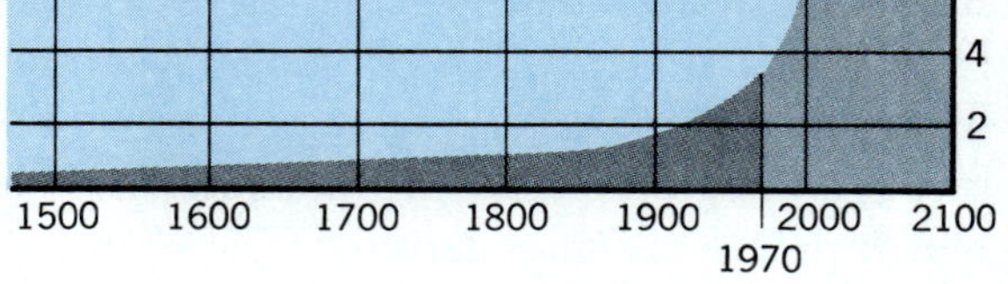

That still isn't the whole story. The developed nations of the Northern Hemisphere have large stocks of surplus food that can be used if food production drops because of droughts, floods, or other disasters. The developing nations of the Southern Hemisphere do not have such surpluses. So if the crop yield is poor or if the crops fail because of floods or other disasters, hunger and famine will be widespread.

These world averages also hide another important problem. Does the available food provide a balanced diet for the world's population? You know that a balanced diet of protein, carbohydrate, and fat is essential for good growth and health. There was a continuing increase in the supply of carbohydrates and fats between 1967 and 1968. However, the world's meat production increased only 2 percent during the same period. You can see that the supply of meat protein did not increase as fast as the population. Animal protein is important because it is usually richer in essential amino acids than proteins derived from grains, nuts, and other sources. Can the oceans help man in his urgent need for food, especially his need for protein?

In our country the average daily diet supplies 3,200 calories; in Latin America the daily diet supplies 2,300 calories. A little over 70 percent of our protein comes from animals (including fish). In Central and South America slightly less than 40 percent of the protein in the diet comes from animals. Other developing nations have much the same diet. Now do you see how the oceans can help both the quantity and quality of the food supply? There is a one-word answer: *Fish*. More fish means more calories in the diet. More fish means more protein in the diet. More animal protein means a stronger and healthier population.

2

Increased Supply of Fish

In the ten-year period from 1958 to 1968, the catch of fish and other marine animals was almost doubled. In the table below, observe that the most dramatic increase took place in South America. Peru and Chile are the two countries responsible for most of the increase. The anchovy is the one fish that accounts for most of the increased supply. 2 This fish is abundant in the cold waters of the Humboldt Current that moves northward along the coast of Chile and Peru. It has been relatively simple for these countries to make use of this important food resource. The entire

CATCH OF FISH AND OTHER MARINE ANIMALS

Regions	*Thousands of metric tons* 1958	1968
Africa	2,130	4,220
North America	3,990	4,570
South America	1,630	12,880
Asia	14,950	24,250
Europe	7,740	11,820
Oceania	110	210
USSR	2,620	6,080
Total	33,170	64,030

fish is ground up as food for cattle, and it is also used as fertilizer.

Notice the slight increase in the fish catch in North America. One reason for the only slight increase is that the catch of fish in the United States dropped by almost 10 percent over the ten-year period.

How much food can the oceans provide? With the present state of fishing technology, the oceans can yield at least 100 to 200 million tons of fish every year. This means that the catch could at least double, just as it did in the last 10 years. And then what?

One way of further increasing the catch would be to improve fishing techniques. This means building newer and larger ships with better equipment for locating fish. As you know, sonar equipment was first used to help a ship's navigator know how deep the water was under his ship. This prevented his steering the ship into shallow water and jagged rocks. Soon it was discovered that schools of fish showed up on a ship's sonar receiver. Within a short time more powerful sonar equipment was being used to locate schools of fish. Other improvements in fishing techniques are being developed. These include luring the fish toward the ship with chemicals, sound, light, or electricity.

Aquaculture

It may be possible to get larger and larger catches of a popular fish over a long period of years and yet not cause that special fish to become extinct (die out). This will require a change in our attitude toward the food resources of the ocean. At present, man is no more than a hunter of marine animals. On land, we gave up hunting as the main method for obtaining our supply of animal food. Now we herd the animals, such as steers and sheep, that we use for food. We protect them from drought, hunger, disease, and natural enemies. The time has come to make man a herder of marine animals. This management of marine animal resources is called **aquaculture,** or sea farming. Aquaculture includes the production of edible seaweeds and other plants, as well as the management of marine animals.

Some "farmers" are already involved in aquaculture on a small scale. Algae, oysters, clams, mussels, lobsters, shrimp, eels, trout, salmon, and many other fishes are raised in sea farming operations. Some of the animals, such as trout and salmon, are raised in hatcheries where water conditions are carefully controlled. Others, like clams and oysters, are placed in a natural **estuary,** an area where the ocean extends into the mouth of a river. Here pollution is a constant threat to their survival. If we can prevent the continuing oil, chemical, insecticide, and sewage pollution of our coastal waters, these food resources may be greatly increased.

Most of the marine animals currently involved in aquaculture programs are the luxury varieties of sea food. These include such animals as shrimp, clams, oysters, trout, and salmon that bring good market prices. Because many of these animals live in estuary areas that can be protected from poachers, the sea farmer has a chance to profit from his effort.

Lobster Farming

One of the newest sea farming ventures is the lobster hatchery program of Massachusetts. Female Maine lobsters are brought from the ocean to the hatchery tanks. (1) Clean sea water is circulated constantly in the tanks and the lobsters are fed a carefully controlled diet of fish and shellfish. Here the lobster completes the many months required

from the fertilization of the eggs to the hatching of the lobster fry (larvae).

In the ocean the 60,000 eggs that each female lays would result in the growth of only 60 adult lobsters. Most of the lobster fry would be eaten by birds, fish, and by one another; or currents might sweep them out to sea, where they would perish. In the hatchery, the fry are separated so that they cannot attack each other. Over 40 percent of the lobster fry survive in the hatchery. The larvae are released once they change from the free-swimming stage to the stage where they crawl along the ocean floor. By this hatchery technique, fishermen hope to increase the population of lobsters in New England waters.

Some people have opposed the building of nuclear power reactors because they think the sea water used to cool them would be heated and this heated water might bring disaster to marine life. However, the lobster hatchery experimentation has shown that maximum growth occurred when sea water in the tanks was between 15°C and 20°C. Ocean temperature in lobster fishery areas is not that high. Therefore, nuclear power plants and desalinization plants discharging heated sea water may help the lobster industry. It has also been found that the rates of growth in oysters, clams, shrimp, and some hatchery fish increase in heated sea water.

Aquaculture of the Future

Scientists are also investigating other types of aquaculture. It may be possible to grow seaweed for food on a large scale in shallow coastal waters. Another plan that has been proposed is to grow dense crops of plant plankton (microscopic marine plants). The plankton could be strained from sea water and processed into food for man. This is not as far-fetched as it might seem, because most of the photosynthesis on earth occurs in plants that grow in the ocean in the form of plankton. Still another plan is to use bubbles rising from perforated hoses on the ocean bottom as fences for fish herding. When the fish grow to mature size, they could be removed easily. Would you like to be a sea farmer?

A New Food

The real benefits of aquaculture lie in the future. But there is something going on right now that promises to bring a quick increase in our food production from the oceans. This is the use of fish to make *fish flour* (fish protein concentrate). Every commercial catch of fish includes many varieties of fish that are not eaten directly by man. These "trash fish"

① 

include menhaden and hake. They make up about half of the catch of our commercial fishermen. Until now the menhaden and hake have been ground up as animal feed. But if they were converted into fish flour, they could be a valuable source of animal protein in our diet.

The production of fish flour also solves the important problem of fish spoilage. This is especially important in underdeveloped countries, where lack of adequate refrigeration prevents fish from being widely used. One of the successful processes of producing fish flour uses the whole fish and converts hake into lightly flavored flour containing 70 percent protein. At present, fish flour plants are in the pilot stage.① It may be a while before fish flour plays a major role as a protein supplement in the human diet.

The earth, you remember, is made up of three spheres—lithosphere, hydrosphere, and atmosphere. What valuable resources can we find in our atmosphere? Next, let's examine the air we breathe.

REVIEW

1. What types of food for man are obtained from the ocean?
2. How has the catch of marine animals changed during the last 10 years?
3. What limits the catch of marine animals at present?
4. How may aquaculture increase the food resources of the ocean?
5. Why will fish flour be an important food product from the ocean?

NEW VIEW

1. How might an increase in plant plankton production increase the animal resources of the ocean?
2. Why are the most productive fishing areas found in cold currents near the continents?
3. What are the chief pollutants in estuaries and coastal waters? How do they affect fish and shellfish populations?

4. LAZY ELEMENT—LIVELY COMPOUNDS

Do you recall what happens to the oxygen you inhale? Much of it is chemically changed into carbon dioxide, which you exhale. What happens to the nitrogen you breathe? Practically nothing. Unlike oxygen, the nitrogen you inhale is not chemically changed in the body. (Perhaps a tiny bit of nitrogen does get absorbed into the blood, but it simply stays in the blood as uncombined nitrogen.) Virtually all the nitrogen you inhale, you exhale again.

From what we know about the chemical make-up of the human body, this is a strange fact, for proteins, which make up the greatest part of the body's tissues—muscle, blood, skin, nerve, and so on—are compounds of nitrogen. Of course your food contains proteins that were built in the bodies of plants or animals that depend on plants. But this seems a roundabout way for the body to get its essential nitrogen when there is such a plentiful supply of nitrogen in the air. Our bodies do, after all, take in and use the free oxygen of the air. Why is nitrogen different? Why, we might say, is nitrogen so chemically lazy? Let's take a look at the lazy element nitrogen, which you can prepare in this investigation. ■

■ AN APPRENTICE INVESTIGATION into Nitrogen from the Air

Do this investigation only in the presence of your teacher. Float two thin pieces of cork on water. On one cork, place about 1 gram of red phosphorus. Invert a tall cylinder over each cork.❶ Lift the cylinder over the phosphorus, ignite the phosphorus with a hot wire, and quickly replace the cylinder.❷ After several minutes compare the level of the water in the two cylinders.❸ Carefully remove both cylinders, with rubber (or glass) squares over their mouths, and set them upright. Thrust a burning wood splint into each cylinder.❹

An Investigation On Your Own

Test the solution in the cylinder with litmus. Explain the result.

❶
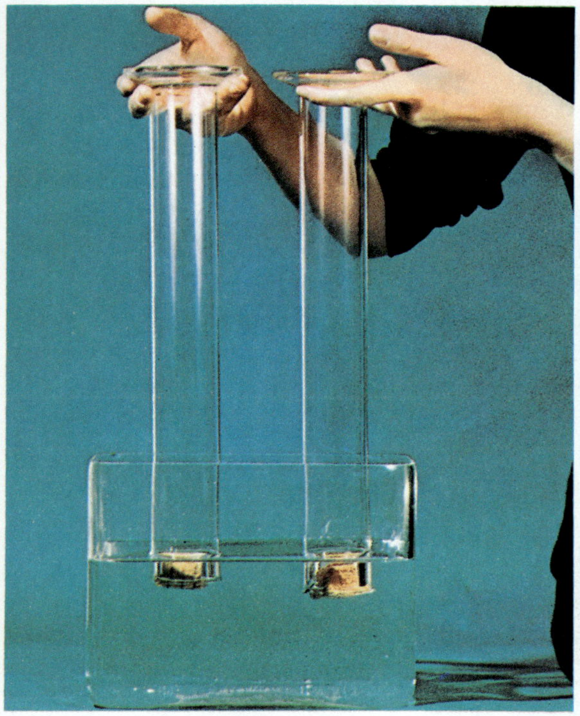

❷
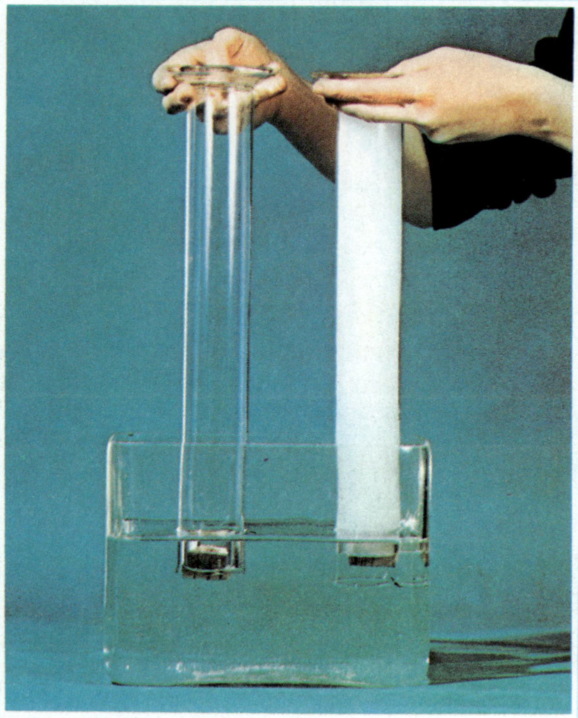

❸

❹
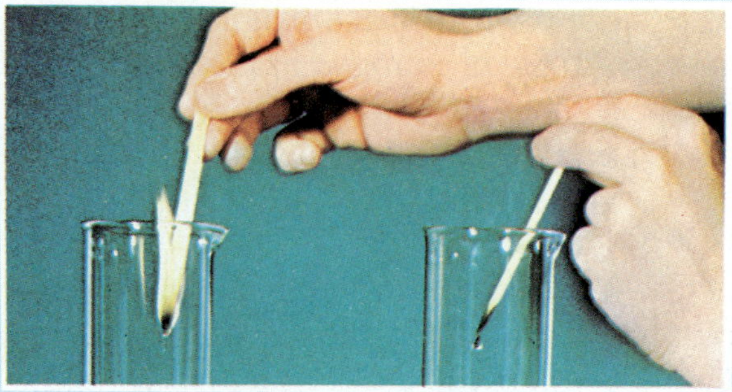

When phosphorus burns in air, dense clouds of phosphorus pentoxide form.

phosphorus + oxygen ⟶ phosphorus pentoxide

When the oxidation of the phosphorus is completed, the smoke clears away as the phosphorus pentoxide dissolves in the water. The level of the water in the cylinder rises about $\frac{1}{5}$ of the way into the cylinder, leaving the cylinder about $\frac{4}{5}$ full of air from which oxygen has been removed. Nearly all of this air is nitrogen. Thrust a burning splint into a cylinder of air and it continues to burn. Thrust a burning splint into a jar of nitrogen, and the splint goes out.

Oxygen in the air easily combines with many substances, as you know. Think of the rusting of iron, the burning of fuel gas, and other oxidation reactions you have observed. Because oxygen combines readily with other elements, chemists say it is an *active* element.

Nitrogen, however, does not combine easily with other elements. We've called it a "lazy" element; the chemist would say nitrogen is relatively *inactive.* But this does not mean nitrogen never combines with other elements. We have evidence that nitrogen does sometimes combine with other elements. The compounds that can be made, once nitrogen atoms react, are of such value and importance that chemists have a special name for the combining of the air's nitrogen to form compounds —**nitrogen fixation.** The combining of nitrogen with magnesium to make magnesium nitride is one example of nitrogen fixation. Let's take a look at some other ways by which nitrogen can be fixed.

Fixing Nitrogen

Did you know it can—and sometimes does—rain nitric acid? True, there is only a little of the acid in a great deal of rainwater. Still, it does happen. Whenever there is a thunderstorm, a little nitric acid may come down with the rain.

How does this happen? Ordinarily the nitrogen and oxygen in the air do not react with one another. There isn't enough energy available to break apart the bonds of the nitrogen molecules. However, the lightning in a thunderstorm may furnish enough energy, in the form of electricity, to break apart some of the nitrogen molecules. Then a nitrogen-fixation reaction can take place between nitrogen and oxygen in the air. The product is nitric oxide (NO). The nitric oxide formed in a thunderstorm combines with more oxygen and with some of the rainwater to make a weak solution of nitric acid (HNO_3). This acid falls to the earth along with the rain, and when it reaches the ground, the nitric acid combines with minerals in the soil to form nitrates. Plants absorb nitrates and build them into complex molecules of proteins. Thus, strange as it seems, lightning actually helps fertilize the soil.

Suitable catalysts (those substances that can help a reaction along but remain unchanged at the end of the reaction) also bring about nitrogen fixation. Catalysts in the cells of living things are called **enzymes.** Certain bacteria, known as nitrogen-fixing bacteria, have enzymes that can catalyze nitrogen fixation. These bacteria can take free nitrogen from air mixed in the soil, and change this nitrogen into compounds. Nitrogen-fixing bacteria live in nodules on the roots of plants such as clover, peanuts, and beans. ❶ A plant that has these nodules has a sort of built-in nitrogen-fixing factory that furnishes the plant with the nitrates it needs to build proteins.

There are, as you have seen, two main ways in which nitrates are formed by nitrogen fixation in nature. These nitrates are of vital importance to the plants we grow for food. But

1

the amount of natural nitrogen fixation is not enough to supply all the nitrates needed by all the world's food crops. So man has to add nitrate fertilizers, and the manufacture of these fertilizers depends on artificial processes of nitrogen fixation.

Nitrogen Compounds

We have called nitrogen a lazy element. Some of its synthetic compounds are anything but lazy, however. Dynamite, TNT, and gunpowder are among the most chemically active inventions of chemists. All of these contain nitrogen compounds. Less dramatic but still very important are the synthetic fertilizers, dyes, plastics, and drugs that contain nitrogen compounds.

For large-scale production of nitrogen compounds, the starting point is atmospheric nitrogen. Finding an efficient and cheap way to combine nitrogen with hydrogen to make ammonia (NH_3) was a major technological achievement. Once nitrogen is "fixed" in the compound ammonia, it is relatively easy to use ammonia as a reactant in making many other nitrogen compounds. One of the most useful compounds derived from ammonia is nitric acid. Ammonium nitrate (NH_4NO_3) and ammonium sulfate $[(NO_4)_2SO_4]$—made from ammonia and nitric acid—are both used as fertilizers. Explosives such as gunpowder, dynamite, and TNT are made from compounds derived from nitric acid. And the dyes we use for paints, textiles, and plastic materials are also synthetic nitrogen compounds derived from ammonia or nitric acid.

Nitrogen and the Air

You know that nitrogen is only one of the substances of which air is composed. About 20 percent of air is oxygen—a gas that is vital for our existence. The small amount of carbon dioxide in the air is essential to plants. Green plants use carbon dioxide and return oxygen to the atmosphere. The other components of air are elements that chemists call the rare gases. Helium is a rare gas. Because it is lighter than air, helium delights children by making balloons float in the air. The U.S. Navy and weather stations use helium for blimps and weather balloons.

Argon is another of the rare gases. Pure argon is used to fill ordinary electric light bulbs. Xenon, krypton, radon, and neon are the other rare gases. Neon is probably the one that most people are familiar with. Signs (and even some modern works of art) made of neon lights come in a variety of brilliant colors. Only the reddish tubes are filled with

❶ 

neon, the other colors are produced by other gases, sometimes mixed with neon. ❶ Very small amounts of neon and most of the other rare gases are present in the air.

Today there is an increasing need to investigate new sources of food and energy. We want to learn how plants use the nitrogen of the air. We need to learn more about the distribution of marine plant and animal life and the relation of these different organisms to each other. We also need to investigate the relation of marine life to such things as ocean currents, salt and mineral content, and temperature. In this way we will be better prepared to manage the resources of the sea and air.

REVIEW

1. What is nitrogen fixation? Give an example.
2. Name some products derived from nitrogen and nitrogen compounds.
3. Give two reasons why nitrogen is essential to man.

NEW VIEW

What class of compounds essential to life always contain the element nitrogen? You may want to read about these compounds in a biology textbook.

5. RELATING THE CONCEPTS

If we look out over the ocean, we see tankers, freighters, passenger liners, and a host of small boats of every description. These ships and boats are evidence of the importance of the ocean for commerce and recreation. This same ocean water is also important because it can be processed to yield badly needed fresh water. Moreover, it contains a wealth of dissolved salts and minerals. Hidden from view by ocean water are rich deposits of gold, diamonds, sand, gravel, and metal ores on the floor of the ocean. Oil and gas deposits in the rock layers of the ocean floor are becoming more important in man's search for fuel.

The ocean is of greatest importance to man as a source of food. The fishing procedures we have used to obtain marine animals may soon be replaced by scientific management of the ocean's food resources. Meanwhile, increased fishing and conversion of fish into edible protein could help end hunger and famine on the earth.

About four-fifths of our air supply is nitrogen. This gas forms many compounds that are important to our daily life. And nitrogen itself is of vital importance to the world's food crops.

Reviewing the Concepts

► *Sea water is a good source of minerals and fresh water.* Some of the tons of salts and minerals dissolved in ocean water can be extracted cheaply. Common salt and magnesium metal, among others, are obtained in this way. In dry coastal areas, fresh water can be obtained from sea water by distillation and other processes.

► *Valuable mineral deposits are found on the continental shelves and the ocean floor.* Gold, diamonds, and other mineral deposits have reached the continental shelves because of land erosion. Manganese nodules on the deep ocean floor result from chemical precipitation. Large deposits of oil and gas are found in sedimentary rocks of the continental shelves.

► *Pollution of marine waters harms ocean life and makes beaches useless.* Oil spills from tankers and oil leaks from offshore wells are especially harmful. Marine animals, especially the birds and shellfish that inhabit the coastal zone, have been harmed by oil pollution. Some beaches can no longer be used for recreation. The best solution to these problems is to prevent oil spills and leaks.

► *Marine animals and plants are an important source of food for man.* Marine animals are caught primarily as food for man or for animal feed. An increased catch of fish can help meet the world's need for animal protein in the diet. Fish flour (fish protein concentrate) may simplify the task of making more protein available to those who need it. Microscopic marine algae and small animals serve mainly as food for the larger marine animals.

► *Scientific management of marine animals will increase the food resources of the ocean.* At present the maximum yearly catch of marine animals may be limited to about twice the current catch. However, scientific management of the oceans, or aquaculture, may greatly increase the food resources of the ocean.

► *The properties of an element determine certain procedures for its manufacture into useful forms.* The properties of nitrogen are a case in point. Nitrogen is relatively inactive. But its compounds are very active, as they serve us in dynamite and in ammonia and nitrates used in fertilizers. And proteins, the nitrogen compounds our bodies cannot make from the air's nitrogen but must get from foods, are the very stuff of which most of the tissues of our bodies are constructed.

Testing Yourself

1. Which salts and minerals are presently obtained in large quantities from sea water?

2. List several valuable substances from sea water. From the continental shelves.

3. Describe one way in which oil and gas deposits form in the rocks of the continental shelves.

4. How do oil tankers and offshore oil wells affect the coastal zone?

5. How do manganese nodules form on the deep ocean floor?

6. Why is it sometimes necessary to produce fresh water in large quantities by desalting sea water?

7. What is the importance of flash distillation of sea water?

8. How does the present catch of marine animals compare with the amount available in the ocean?

9. Why is fish protein so important in many areas of the world?

10. What is aquaculture? How is it related to an increasing world population?

11. Compare the increasing world population with the increasing food supply. How does this comparison hide a serious food shortage?

12. Why is nitrogen fixation important to us?

Suggested Reading

Behrman, Daniel, *The New World of the Oceans,* Boston, Little, Brown, 1969. A survey of the newer developments in oceanography.

The Ocean, Scientific American Book, San Francisco, Freeman, 1969. A beautifully illustrated review of our modern knowledge of the sea.

Yasso, Warren E., *Oceanography,* New York, Holt, Rinehart and Winston, 1965. A survey of marine sciences, with emphasis on how we study the ocean and its resources.

18

Resources of the Land

Now let's take a closer look at some of the rocks of earth. Certain rocks are quite special. These rocks contain compounds that are important sources of certain metals. Look at the sample of cassiterite. (1) Cassiterite is usually reddish-brown to black in color. Contrast the color of the cassiterite with the shiny, silvery cylinder of metal next to it. The metal, which is tin, is extracted from the cassiterite. Cassiterite is tin oxide, a compound of the elements tin and oxygen. Geologists call cassiterite and the other rocks shown here ores. An ore, you will remember, is a rock that is the source of a metal.

Now look at the sample of malachite ore. (2) Its color ranges from bright green to black. Can you identify the metal cylinder next to it as copper? Malachite is the compound copper carbonate; it contains copper, carbon, and oxygen.

Look at the sample of another ore, *galena.* (3) Its lead-gray color is fairly similar to the color of the lead cylinder next to it. Galena is the compound lead sulfide; it contains the element sulfur in addition to lead.

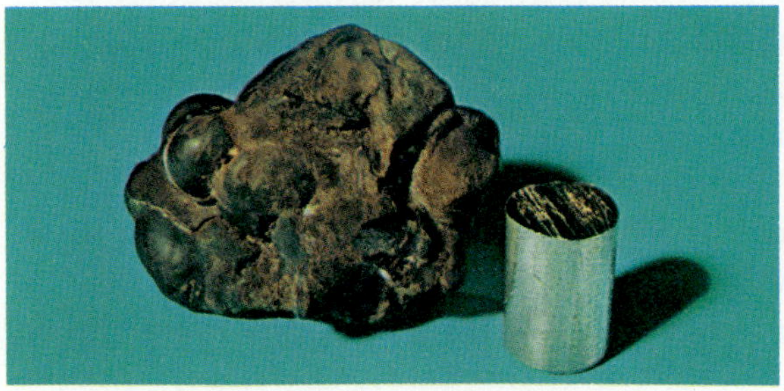

(1)

(2)

(3)

1

Finally, look at the sample of *bauxite.* 1 Contrast this ore, which may be white, yellow, brown, or reddish in color, with the shiny metal cylinder next to it. Could you predict that bauxite is a source of aluminum, the most abundant metal of the earth? Bauxite is an unusual compound. It is aluminum oxide, a combination of aluminum and oxygen.

In studying these four rocks (ores), you have been studying samples of matter from the earth. These samples of matter contain chiefly the metals lead, tin, copper, aluminum, and zinc, and the nonmetals sulfur, carbon, oxygen, and hydrogen. All these substances are important resources of the land. How do we find these valuable substances and how do we use them?

1. THE ELEMENT OF CIVILIZATION

Man first learned to extract iron from its ores and fashion it into tools and weapons about the year 1000 B.C. 2 This marked the beginning of the Iron Age: ever since, iron has been the dominant metal in civilization. Not until about the nineteenth century, however, did iron begin to be used on a large scale to construct such different things as railroads and farm machinery, bridges and rockets, automobiles and baby carriages.

Iron from the Earth

Perhaps the best known of the different kinds of iron ore is the mineral hematite. Hematite consists mainly of iron oxide (Fe_2O_3). Another well-known and particularly interesting iron ore is the mineral magnetite. As you can readily see, magnetite gets its name from its property of magnetism. 3 Hematite, magnetite, and many other iron ores are abundant in the earth's crust. Most of the iron ore mined in the United States is hematite, and it comes from the open-pit mines in the Mesabi range in Minnesota. 4 As the deposits in the Mesabi range are showing signs of becoming exhausted, the steel industry has developed ways of separating particles of iron oxide from low-grade ores, called *taconite.*

After mining, the iron is separated from its ore. Chemically, the separation process used today is similar to the method used by the ancients. Early man extracted iron from iron oxide by heating the ore with carbon. During the reaction that takes place, oxygen is removed from iron oxide.

2

3

4

The ore which early man heated was not *pure* iron oxide; it was rock containing iron oxide mixed with various other substances such as sand or silica. Early man's source of carbon—wood charcoal—contained other substances, too. However, early man had no way of knowing just what amounts of iron ore and carbon to heat together. So instead of pure iron being left at the end of the reaction, there was left iron mixed with silica and excess carbon and other impurities present in the original mixture. Early man's inability to control these impurities limited the usefulness of the iron he made. The advances in technology by which man has learned to remove undesirable impurities and—strange to say—add desirable "impurities" to iron have resulted in many uses of the metal undreamed of by the ironmakers of the ancient Iron Age.

Steel and Its Uses

Only rarely has iron been prepared in a pure form, even in the laboratory. Not only in ancient times but in modern times, chemically pure iron has never been produced on a commercial scale. The reason is not hard to see: iron must be impure to have the properties that make it a useful metal. Unless mixed with other substances (including traces of carbon), iron is too soft and chemically active to serve as a structural metal. When mixed with proper amounts of certain other elements, however, iron becomes steel. It would be more correct to say "steels," for there are many different kinds of steel, each one of them an alloy of iron. An alloy, you recall, is a combination of two or more elements which has metallic properties.

There are three general classes of steel; they are grouped according to carbon content: low carbon steel, medium carbon steel, and high carbon steel. Low carbon steel contains less than 0.2 percent carbon, and is used in such products as fence wire, nuts, and bolts. Medium carbon steel contains from 0.2 to 0.6 percent carbon, and is used for rails, girders, and other structural shapes. High carbon steel contains from 0.6 to 1.6 percent carbon, and is used for razor blades, surgical instruments, and drills. In the chart on the next page are a few of the many kinds of steel produced by adding other elements. Are you surprised that there are so many kinds of steel?

SOME KINDS OF STEEL

Name	*Elements present*	*Properties*	*Uses*
manganese steel	iron manganese carbon	exceedingly hard	crushing and grinding machinery, safes
stainless steel	iron chromium nickel carbon	resists rusting	cutlery, machinery, and equipment for handling food
silicon steel	iron silicon carbon	easily magnetized and demagnetized	cores of motors and transformers; electromagnets
molybdenum steel	iron molybdenum carbon	strong and tough	automobile parts

Making Steel

Steel production in the United States begins in the **blast furnace.** (1) The blast furnace makes crude iron on an industrial scale and is designed to operate continuously. A *charge* of iron ore, coke, and limestone is periodically dumped into the opening at the top. Hot air is piped in from the sides, near the bottom. Also near the bottom, two products of the furnace are drawn off: molten iron and slag, a lavalike substance consisting mainly of molten calcium silicate. Hot gases produced in the furnace are piped off near the top.

The crude iron that comes out of the blast furnace is known as pig iron. Castings of iron from an early model of the furnace were supposed to look like a litter of pigs, hence the name. The blocks of pig iron, known as "pigs," contain various impurities, including about 4 percent carbon. This amount is considerably higher than the percentage in any kind of finished steel. As a result, pig iron does not

(1)

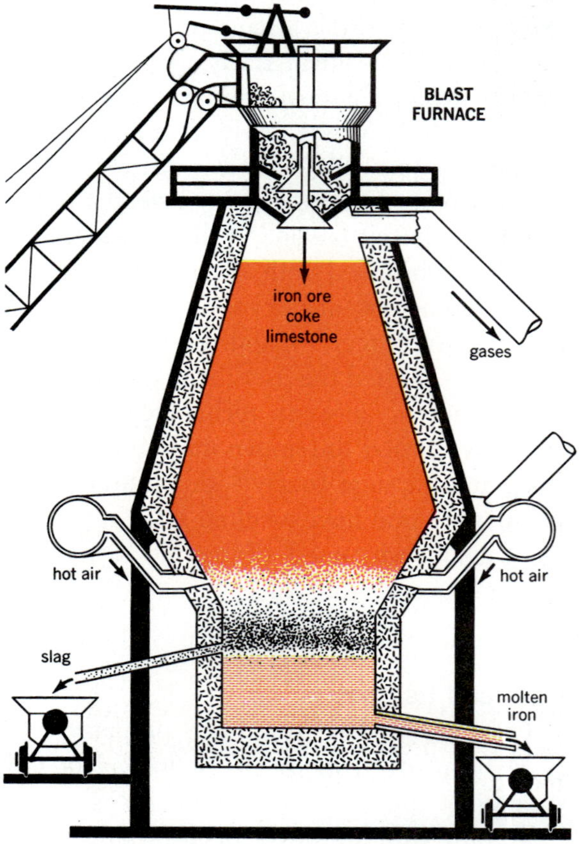

2

have some desirable metallic properties. When melted and cast into various shapes, however, pig iron becomes cast iron, which is used for machinery and hardware of many kinds.

During the nineteenth century the demand for steel grew. The invention of the first commercially successful steel-making process, the **Bessemer process,** was named after one of its developers, the Englishman Henry Bessemer. In a Bessemer converter, molten pig iron is refined by burning away impurities. The Bessemer process is inexpensive and fast, but most of the steel it produces must be further refined.

Most of the iron that comes from blast furnaces and Bessemer converters is further refined in **open hearth** furnaces. Here excess carbon is burned away by the oxygen in a blast of hot air that plays over the surface of the iron. During this process impurities are burned away, the carbon content is reduced to the desired amount, and other elements are added to make the desired kind of steel. Then the open hearth furnace is tapped: a spectacular sight. 2

Special alloys and steels that must meet exacting requirements can be further refined in an electric furnace. For example, these sections

1

of the hull of the Centaur rocket, which boosted Surveyor to the moon, are made from a special stainless steel prepared in the electric furnace. 1

Steel is in fact a main part of the life stream of modern civilization. In 1810 the total production of steel in the United States was about 900 metric tons. By 1850 production had risen to almost 5,400 metric tons a year. The work of Bessemer and the discovery of rich iron ore deposits in the Lake Superior region helped the United States to become the world leader in steel production. In 1950, for every person living in the United States, more than 540 kilograms (1,200 pounds) of steel was produced. In 1965, world production of steel reached 450 *million* metric tons.

Steel frames transport us, and steel beams support us. The steel age began long ago, but steel will continue to be important to us for a long time to come.

Some Sidelights

Interest in reactions involving iron goes far. It has been estimated, for instance, that as much as 20 percent of the steel manufactured yearly is used to replace loss by corrosion—commonly known as rusting. 2 In their efforts to learn how to control corrosion, chemists have investigated the chemical properties of iron very extensively. But strange to say, chemists still do not understand fully the rusting process.

One thing that the results of investigation do suggest is that iron may not rust in absolutely dry air. Rusting occurs faster in the presence of acids, certain other metals, and of rust itself. And strains in the metal may make it rust faster.

Several effective methods of preventing rust are in common use. Among these are plating with other metals (such as zinc for galvanized fence wire, tin for tin cans, and chromium for

2 

automobile trim), painting, and oiling. In all these examples the metal is prevented from contact with either oxygen or water by a coating.

We have discussed the chemistry of iron as it applies to steel—but many compounds of iron have useful properties. Blueprints, for example, are made by a chemical process that makes use of iron compounds. And there is scarcely anything that could be more important to you than your blood. Blood depends on the presence of hemoglobin, a compound of iron, for its redness and for its ability to carry oxygen. Another colorful compound of iron, often used in paints, is the oxide Fe_2O_3, which may be dark yellow, reddish-brown, or yellowish-brown, depending on the size of its particles.

REVIEW

1. What is the most common ore from which iron is extracted?
2. What element besides iron is always found in steel?
3. What are the ingredients of the charge of a blast furnace? What are the products?
4. What factors seem to contribute to rusting?

NEW VIEW

1. Gold and silver are two of the many metals that are used in alloys, not in their pure forms. Explain.
2. What are some reasons why modern steelmakers can control impurities better than could men of the ancient Iron Age?
3. How is the percentage of carbon in steel related to the hardness of the product?

2. SULFUR: A NONMETALLIC ELEMENT

You may find it hard to believe, but sulfur, a nonmetal, was once rare and expensive. For thousands of years most of the sulfur used by man was gathered from the ground in volcanic regions. This sulfur had solidified after being ejected as gas from erupting volcanoes. The demand for sulfur was always much greater than this supply. Then in 1867 vast underground deposits of sulfur were discovered in Texas and Louisiana. As it turned out, just as important as the discovery of these deposits was the discovery of a way to mine them.

Mining Sulfur

The sulfur in the Texas and Louisiana deposits, about 180 meters (600 feet) below the surface, is mixed with rock. The obvious thing to do to reach the sulfur was to dig, but in this case digging didn't work. Before they got to the sulfur, the diggers ran into a layer of quicksand which put a stop to their efforts.

Then a Philadelphia pharmacist, Herman Frasch, came on the scene. As a pharmacist, Frasch had learned a good deal about sulfur. In 1891 he switched his interest from pharmacy to chemical engineering and put what was eventually to be named the **Frasch process** to work. His process depended on a knowledge of the properties of sulfur. You can see for yourself how a knowledge of the properties of sulfur aided in mining the precious substance. ■

■ AN APPRENTICE INVESTIGATION into Some Physical Properties of Sulfur

❶

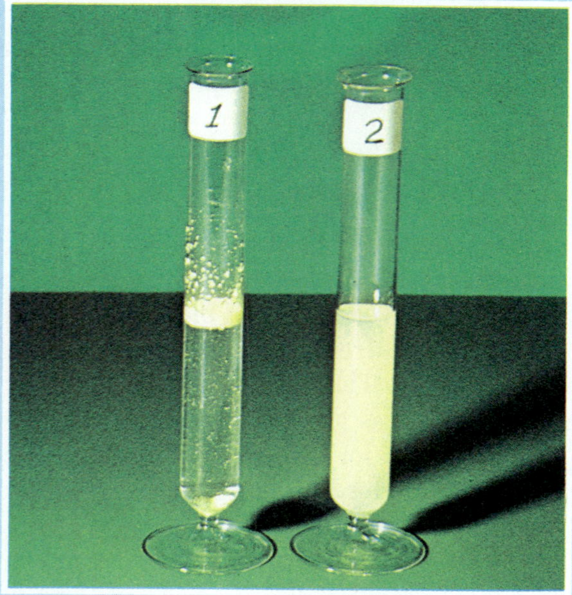

❷

❸

Place a small amount of sulfur in one test tube about half full of water, and the same amount of sulfur in a second test tube about half full of carbon tetrachloride. Stopper both tubes and shake thoroughly. Clearly sulfur does not dissolve in water but does dissolve in carbon tetrachloride. ❶ Pour the solution of sulfur in carbon tetrachloride into a watch glass and place it under a fumehood to evaporate. (***Caution:*** Do not breathe vapors of carbon tetrachloride. They are poisonous.) Examine the crystals of sulfur that form and sketch their shape. ❷ Sulfur with crystals like this is known as rhombic sulfur.

Now, determine the melting point of sulfur. Half fill a Pyrex, Kimax, or porcelain dish with powdered sulfur, insert a thermometer, and heat very gently on a hot plate. ❸ Record the temperature at which the sulfur just begins to melt. (A handbook gives the melting point of sulfur as 112.8°C. Why might the melting point you observe not be exactly 112.8°?)

An Investigation On Your Own

Pour some of the melted sulfur into a beaker of cold water. What form does the sulfur take?

In the investigation you have seen that one physical property of sulfur is its insolubility in water. You have seen that sulfur *does* dissolve in carbon tetrachloride, and that well-formed crystals of rhombic sulfur can be prepared when a solution of the element in carbon tetrachloride is evaporated.

The familiar yellow powdered sulfur and glossy yellow chunks of roll sulfur that are commonly used in chemical laboratories are both rhombic sulfur. They are made up of crystals of the rhombic form, but usually the crystals are too small or too broken up to be seen easily. If you dissolve powdered or roll sulfur in carbon tetrachloride, however, and allow the liquid to evaporate, you may obtain well-shaped rhombic crystals.

Another physical property of sulfur you have seen is the element's relatively low melting point. (As you shall see shortly, this low melting point is important in the mining of sulfur.) Suppose we now allow some just-melted sulfur to cool until it solidifies, and then examine it with a magnifying glass before it cools all the way to room temperature. What we see are the transparent, needle-shaped crystals known as monoclinic sulfur. (1) Now wait several minutes and look at the sulfur again. As the sulfur cools further, these clear crystals of monoclinic sulfur become opaque, and they soon turn back into a mass of yellow sulfur. (2)

When rhombic sulfur is melted and then cooled a bit, monoclinic sulfur forms. Soon after it forms, its transparent needlelike crystals begin to change back into opaque, yellow rhombic sulfur. This is because monoclinic sulfur can only exist at certain temperatures—between 96°C (about 205°F) and 119°C (246°F). When the crystals first form, they are at 119°C, but as soon as the warm crystals cool below 96°C they begin to change into rhombic sulfur.

Just-melted sulfur is pale yellow, but if it is heated to the boiling point, its color darkens to a reddish brown. Suppose a test tube of

1
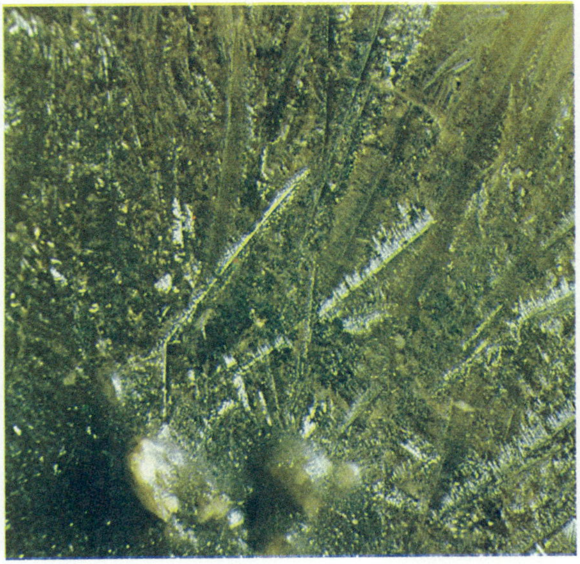

2

1

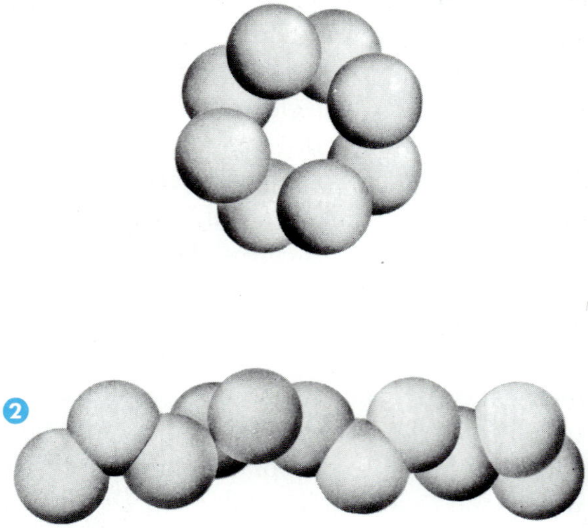
2

liquid sulfur were brought to the boiling point, then poured into a beaker of cold water. 1 The result would be a dark rubbery mass, known as amorphous sulfur. Like monoclinic sulfur, amorphous sulfur is unstable, for soon after it is formed, it begins to turn brittle and yellow again. Amorphous sulfur eventually changes back into rhombic sulfur.

It seems as if any form of sulfur, if left alone, sooner or later becomes rhombic sulfur. And so it does. Rhombic sulfur is the only form of sulfur that is stable under ordinary conditions for more than a short time. Yet the other forms of sulfur do exist, forms whose properties are distinctly unlike those of rhombic sulfur.

How can sulfur exist in so many forms, each so different from the other? You have already met one element that had different forms, or **allotropes.** This element, you may recall is oxygen, and its two allotropic forms are ordinary oxygen (O_2) and ozone (O_3). (Recall that ozone is formed in the earth's stratosphere.)

Ordinary oxygen consists of molecules made up of two atoms of oxygen each. Ozone consists of molecules made up of three atoms of oxygen each. Like these allotropes of oxygen, the allotropes of sulfur have molecules arranged in different ways. A molecule of rhombic sulfur is a ring made up of eight sulfur atoms. The other allotropes of sulfur are made up of chains of various numbers of sulfur atoms. 2 Even though sulfur molecules usually have eight or more atoms, chemists use the symbol S to represent any of the allotropic forms of sulfur.

As we've said, the element sulfur melts at a relatively low temperature and does not dissolve in water. Herman Frasch ingeniously made use of these properties to solve the problem of mining sulfur. Let's turn now to Frasch's invention.

Frasch's Invention

The sulfur Frasch wanted to mine was mixed with calcite rock. This kind of rock melts at about 800°C. Sulfur, however, melts at about 113°C. So Frasch sought a way to supply enough heat to melt the sulfur only. Then, in a liquid state, the sulfur could flow to the surface through a pipe. To melt the sulfur, Frasch decided to use hot water, but the water had to be raised to a temperature *above* its normal boiling point of 100°C to melt sulfur at 113°C. The best temperature of the water for melting sulfur and keeping it liquid was about 165°C.

Since it ordinarily boils at 100°C, how can water be heated to 165°C? If you know how a pressure cooker works, you have a clue. A pressure cooker makes short work of cooking because it boils water at a higher temperature than usual. The boiling point of water *rises* with the increasing pressure. So Frasch put the hot water under pressure, to raise its temperature.

In the Frasch process three pipes reach down to the sulfur-bearing calcite rock. Here's how the pipes are arranged. 3 A stream of hot water under pressure is forced down the outermost pipe. The heated water melts the sulfur, but does not dissolve it, since sulfur is insoluble in water. As a pool of melted sulfur forms, hot air is forced down the innermost pipe. The hot compressed air helps keep the sulfur hot enough to stay melted and forces it to rise in a bubbly froth through the middle pipe. When this froth emerges at the surface, the air escapes, the water drains off, and the sulfur is allowed to solidify in large wooden bins. Thus, Herman Frasch succeeded not only in mining sulfur, but managed also to get sulfur of high quality. Sulfur mined by the Frasch process is over 99 percent pure.

3

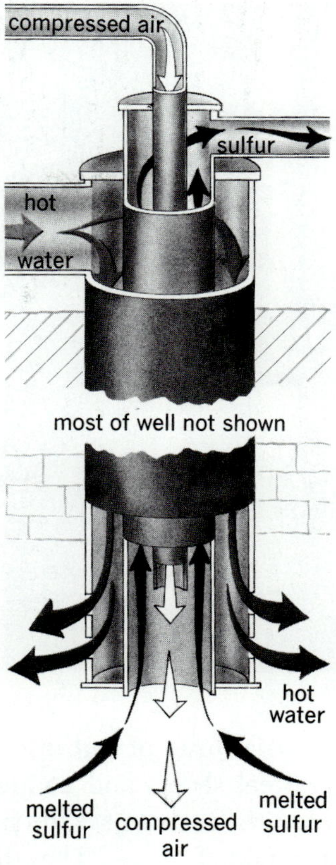

"The King of Chemicals": H_2SO_4

Most of the sulfur mined by the Frasch process goes into useful compounds. Sulfur, oxygen, and water are the basic raw materials for making sulfuric acid (H_2SO_4).

Sulfuric acid is an essential ingredient in an amazing variety of manufacturing procedures. It is, in fact, used to convert raw materials into so many different finished products that it is sometimes called "the king of chemicals." Let's consider some of the things we have through the use of sulfuric acid.

Crops that depend on fertilizers come first. In the United States a greater amount of sulfuric acid is used in making phosphate fertilizers than for any other purpose. The second

1

largest industrial use of sulfuric acid is in metallurgy. Steel sheets and copper wire, for example, require treatment with sulfuric acid during their manufacture. The third largest industrial use of sulfuric acid is in petroleum refining. 1 Think how different your life would be without things made from petroleum —gasoline, oil, and the asphalt used to pave streets.

Many more things depend on sulfuric acid—plastics, dyes, drugs, leather, insecticides, ink, storage batteries, textiles, dynamite . . . the list is almost endless. Even so, sulfuric acid accounts for only part of the importance of sulfur to civilization.

Other Uses of Sulfur and Its Compounds

Everything that depends on the use of paper depends on sulfur. You know that paper is made from trees. To separate the substance, the fibrous cellulose that makes up paper, from other substances in wood, logs from trees are shredded and made into chips. Then the wood chips are cooked in large vats in a solution of a sulfur compound. This process makes sulfite pulp, which is rolled into sheets that make the kind of paper suitable for writing and printing. 2 Another important use of sulfur is in **vulcanization.** In vulcanization, rubber is heated with sulfur. The process of vulcanization transforms natural rubber from a soft, sticky mass into a strong and pliable material suitable for making tires and hundreds of other articles.

REVIEW

1. Describe briefly how the Frasch process makes use of some of the properties of sulfur.

2. Why is sulfuric acid called the "king of chemicals"?

3. An automobile's body, fuel, tires, lubrication, and (often) the pavement it rides on, depend on sulfur. Explain.

NEW VIEW

1. Sulfur dioxide is often produced by volcanoes. Find out how sulfur dioxide reacts with water and how acids act on limestone. Then account for the chemical weathering of limestone in volcanic regions.

2

2. Compounds of sulfur are major factors in air and water pollution. Find out how these compounds enter the environment. What steps are being taken to prevent this type of pollution?

3. THE ELEMENT OF LIFE

Carbon is another nonmetal you are familiar with. Coal, soot, and charcoal, for instance, are forms of carbon that you have probably seen. Perhaps you also know that complex molecules containing carbon are the main "building blocks" of all organisms. So would it surprise you to find out that the element carbon is not very abundant in the earth's crust? At the same time, carbon is one of the basic architectural units of the earth's living things. Let's examine this important element, and the compounds it makes, more closely.

Forms of Carbon

Burn some wood, cotton, toast, steak, or nearly any matter that was once alive. What happens to the matter? It chars. Have you noticed that the word "char" is included in the word "charcoal"? Charcoal is a form of carbon made by heating wood or bones in a special way. Coal, another form of carbon, is a kind of sedimentary rock made from the remains of ancient plants. Soot is carbon that comes from burning certain substances that have their origin in living things, substances such as oil, paraffin, coal, and natural gas. Life and the element carbon are closely associated. Now let's get better acquainted with some different forms of the element carbon itself.

Investigating Forms of Carbon

One form of carbon is probably right on your desk in front of you. Do you know what it is? The "lead" in your pencil is made up of the form of carbon we call graphite, mixed with clay. If you can rub some pure graphite between your fingers, you'll notice its greasy feel. Because of this slippery quality, graphite is often used as a "dry" lubricant for such things as locks and bicycles. If you rub your pencil lead between your fingers, does it feel greasy, too? Compare the look and feel of the mark made on a piece of paper by pure graphite and by a pencil lead—the softer the pencil, the better. Which do you think has a larger proportion of graphite compared to clay, a "hard" or a "soft" pencil? The same slippery quality that makes graphite a good lubricant makes your pencil glide smoothly across the paper as you write.

Let's look at another form of carbon. Hold a cold, white dish in a candle flame, or a yellow flame from a burner. The soot that collects on the dish is a form of carbon known as lampblack. Rub a bit of soot between your fingers. Like graphite, soot has a greasy feel. Graphite and soot have this in common: both are nearly pure forms of carbon. Of the two, however, graphite is the more pure.

Diamond is a pure form of carbon. Not all diamonds are big enough or perfect enough to be used for jewels. Diamonds have other uses that do not depend on beauty. If you can, try the scratch test with a commercial-grade diamond on some minerals or rocks, provided you don't mind your specimens getting scratched. As you probably remember, diamond is at the top of the hardness scale of minerals. No substance is harder than diamond. Just one other substance can match diamond in hardness, so far, and that is *borazon,* a synthetic compound of boron and nitrogen.

Let's go to the laboratory and investigate yet another form of carbon. ■

■ AN APPRENTICE INVESTIGATION into a Form of Carbon

❶

Heat some broken wood splints in a test tube connected to a jet tube for the escape of gases. Watch the changes that occur as the heating proceeds.❶ When a liquid begins to form in the cooler part of the tube, hold a lighted match at the tip of the jet. What happens?❷

In one trial, a tarry substance was formed in the cool end of the tube, and gas escaping through the jet burned with a smoky yellow flame. This is what was left of the wood.❸

An Investigation On Your Own

Using the same equipment, heat some bits of soft coal in the same way. What form of carbon is produced?

❷
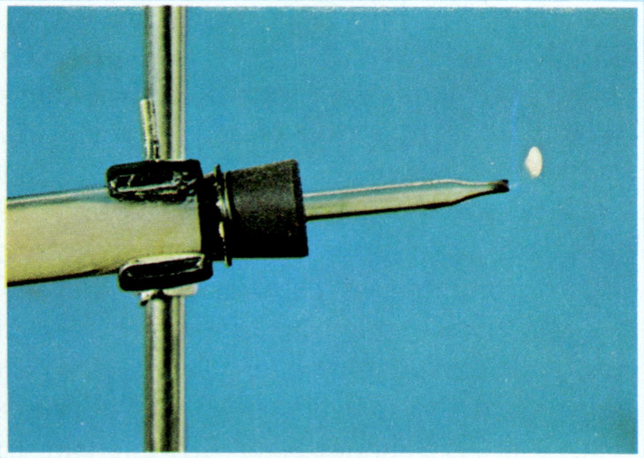

❸

As you can see in the investigation, wood breaks down when heated in a closed tube with a limited supply of air. Chemists call this **destructive distillation.** When wood is destructively distilled it is chemically changed into several products. Some of these (the gaseous and liquid products) are driven away from the wood. What remains is wood charcoal. Something similar happens when bones are destructively distilled, that is, heated in a limited supply of air. Animal charcoal, or boneblack, forms as other substances are driven out of the container in which the bones are heated.

After heating bones or wood this way for a certain amount of time, no more liquids or

❶

gases are driven off. But this does *not* mean that the black substance left—wood charcoal or boneblack—is pure carbon. For if either of these kinds of charcoal is completely burned in open air, white or gray ashes are left behind (the carbon oxidizes to carbon dioxide). These ashes contain mineral substances that do not burn. This is evidence that charcoal is a relatively impure form of carbon, compared to soot, graphite, or diamond.

Chemists recognize two crystalline forms of the element carbon. One of these is diamond, whose origin from coal is suggested by the way the precious stones are found in the earth. ❶ It isn't quite so obvious that the other crystalline form of carbon is graphite. One clue is its shiny look. Have you noticed that crystals are generally shiny? Even though graphite is crystalline, it is very unlike diamond. Graphite and diamond are, in fact, two allotropes of carbon. Recall that oxygen and sulfur are other elements that have allotropes—two or more forms of the same element with different properties.

What about the forms of carbon we call charcoal, boneblack, soot, and coke? As you know, none of these is nearly as pure as diamond or graphite. It was some time before chemists discovered that these forms are not amorphous or "without shape" (like some of the allotropes of sulfur), but that all forms of carbon except diamond have the same basic crystalline structure as graphite.

The differences in properties between the allotropes of carbon—graphite and diamond—are striking. Graphite is grayish-black, diamond is clear. Graphite is soft and greasy, diamond is exceptionally hard. Yet chemists know that both substances are composed of nothing but carbon atoms. When either graphite or diamond is heated in pure oxygen, just one product forms: carbon dioxide. (It was Lavoisier, by the way, who first reported that a diamond forms carbon dioxide when burned.)

Both diamond and graphite contain only atoms of carbon. How, then, can we account for the differences between them? To answer this, we must examine the arrangement of their atoms in molecules. Let's begin with a look at the make-up of the atoms themselves.

Structure of Carbon Allotropes

When we examine an electron-shell diagram of an atom of carbon, we see that there are 4 electrons in the outermost shell. ❷ Since the outer shell of an atom has a capacity of 8 electrons, an atom of carbon can share 4 electrons with other atoms of carbon. In other words, then, a carbon atom can form 4 chemical bonds. To see how a carbon atom forms bonds,

❷

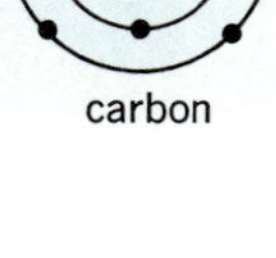

carbon

1

2

a ball-and-stick model is useful. 1 The ball represents the atom, and a stick represents an electron that can be shared to make a bond.

In diamond, 5 carbon atoms join together so that one of the carbon atoms is surrounded by the other 4. 2 Each of these 4 atoms, in turn, shares electrons with 4 more carbon atoms. This pattern repeats itself, so that the entire crystal is one big molecule, a **macromolecule,** made up of an enormous number of atoms. Only a small part of a macromolecule of diamond is shown in this model. 3 Since there are billions and billions of carbon atoms in a single diamond, and all the atoms in any one diamond form one huge macromolecule, we can't show a model of an entire macromolecule of carbon!

In the diamond macromolecule, the atoms are packed very close together. The bonds are very strong and, as a result, diamond is exceptionally hard. It is the pattern of the carbon atoms that gives crystals of diamond their characteristic shape.

The carbon atoms in graphite do not form the same patterns as they do in diamond. Instead, the carbon atoms in graphite are arranged in *layers.* 4 Within each layer the atoms have strong bonds connecting them with their neighboring atoms. But the bonds from one layer to the next are weak bonds. Thus graphite is somewhat like a stack of notebook paper. Each sheet of paper is one layer. It is easy to slide the sheets over each other, but a relatively strong force is needed to tear the sheets themselves. The weak bonds between layers of atoms in graphite account for the slippery quality of this form of carbon. The strong bonds between the atoms that make up any one layer give graphite an essentially crystalline nature.

How do diamonds come to be formed in the earth? Scientists aren't sure. Some think that diamonds come about by the metamorphosis of graphite subjected to great heat and

3

4

pressure. In 1955, the first synthetic diamonds were produced from graphite by using extraordinarily high pressures. Synthetic diamonds do not have gem quality, but because of their hardness they are used industrially. The fact that diamonds can be made from graphite is a bit of evidence in support of the hypothesis that diamonds originate from graphite in the earth.

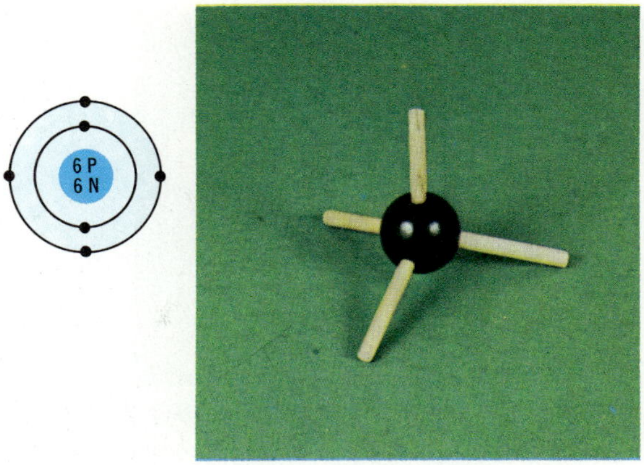

5

Carbon in Chains

What kinds of matter are found in living things and their products—things like apples, wood, bones, cotton, silk, and meat? It will hardly come as a surprise to you, yet it is really remarkable: Most of the substances that make up organisms and most of the substances that organisms make, are complex compounds of carbon and several other elements. Because these compounds are closely related to organisms, the chemist calls them **organic compounds.** *All* organic compounds contain carbon. But why is *carbon* the element that is special to organisms? After all, living things do contain hydrogen, oxygen, nitrogen, and at least a dozen other elements. But of all the elements, only carbon has atoms that can bond together in chains long enough to make possible the tremendous complexity and great variety of molecules that make up living matter.

To investigate organic compounds, however, you do not need to start with anything complex. On the contrary, you can start with a group of compounds that are very simple. These simple organic compounds are made up of only two elements, carbon and hydrogen. Chemists call them **hydrocarbons,** which, as you shall see, make up many familiar substances such as fuel gas, gasoline, and wax.

Structures of Some Hydrocarbons

How are carbon and hydrogen combined in a hydrocarbon? Here are an electron-shell diagram and a ball-and-stick model: each stands for an atom of carbon. 5 Chemists also use this symbol to stand for a carbon atom:

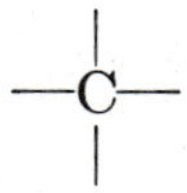

Notice that each of the 4 dashes in this symbol is like a stick in the model. The sticks stand for the 4 electrons that the carbon atom is able to share for a possible chemical bond with another atom.

A hydrogen atom has just 1 electron it can share. Therefore the symbol H— may stand for an atom of hydrogen. The dash in the symbol stands for the 1 electron that the hydrogen atom is able to share.

How many hydrogen atoms will combine with 1 carbon atom? The carbon atom tends to share 4 electrons, and each hydrogen atom tends to share 1. Thus 4 atoms of hydrogen can combine with 1 atom of carbon. The result is a molecule with the formula CH_4. The name of the compound CH_4 is methane. As you may

1

know, methane is a gas. It is one of the substances that make up the fuel gas used in many kitchen stoves and in laboratory burners. Because methane is made up of the two elements hydrogen and carbon, it is a hydrocarbon.

Another way to represent the methane molecule is:

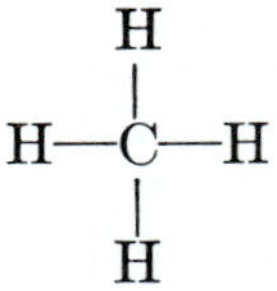

This is the **graphic formula** for methane, a kind of picture of the arrangement of atoms within the molecule. Compare the graphic formula for methane with the ball-and-stick model. 1

The short formula for methane, CH_4, is sometimes called its **molecular formula.** The molecular formula for a substance tells how many of each kind of atoms the substance has. For methane, the molecular formula CH_4 stands for 1 atom of carbon combined with 4 atoms of hydrogen.

Chemists have discovered that there are hundreds of different hydrocarbons, compounds containing only carbon and hydrogen, each with a different formula. How can this be? What are the structures of all these other hydrocarbons? You already have one clue from what you know about the structures of diamond and graphite, which are made up of carbon atoms *bonded to one another.* In somewhat the same way, carbon atoms bond with small or large numbers of other carbon atoms. At the same time, they also bond with atoms of hydrogen.

With diagrams and models you can easily see how carbon atoms bond together in a hydrocarbon containing two carbon atoms. Make an electron-shell diagram of two carbon atoms sharing one pair of electrons. 2 Each atom now has 5 electrons in its outer shell, and each needs 3 more electrons to make its outer shell complete.

How many hydrogen atoms will be needed to complete the outer shells of both carbon atoms? Suppose we construct a ball-and-stick model for two carbon atoms sharing a pair of

2

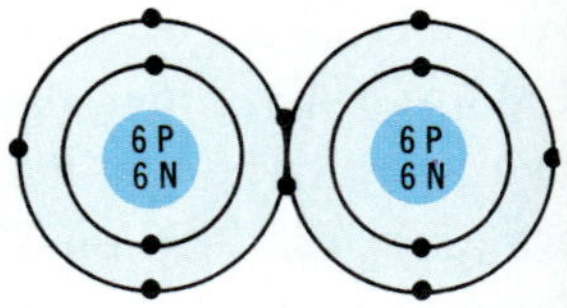

3

4

electrons. ❸ Now it is easy to see that each atom of carbon will bond with three hydrogen atoms, so that altogether there will be six hydrogen atoms in the molecule. A model of the molecule of ethane looks like this. ❹ Like its close relative methane, ethane is a gas that may also be used as a fuel. Here is the graphic formula for ethane:

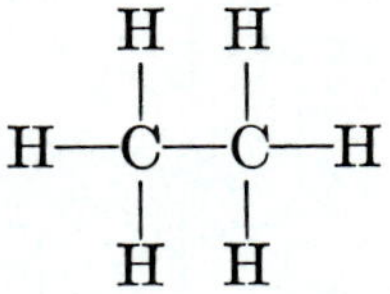

The molecular formula for ethane is C_2H_6.

Structures of More Hydrocarbons

Let's write the graphic formula for propane, C_3H_8. Propane is a gaseous hydrocarbon that has 3 carbon atoms joined together the same way the 2 carbon atoms in ethane are joined together.

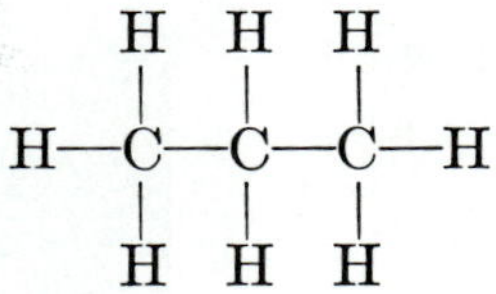

Butane (C_4H_{10}), another gas often used as a fuel, is a hydrocarbon with 4 carbon atoms

SOME HYDROCARBONS

Name	*Graphic formula*	*Molecular formula*	*Physical state*	*Use*
methane	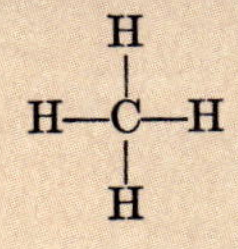	CH_4	gas	fuel gas
ethane	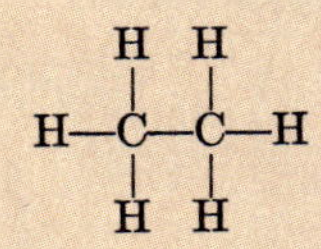	C_2H_6	gas	fuel gas
propane	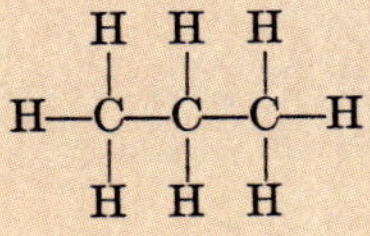	C_3H_8	gas	fuel gas
butane	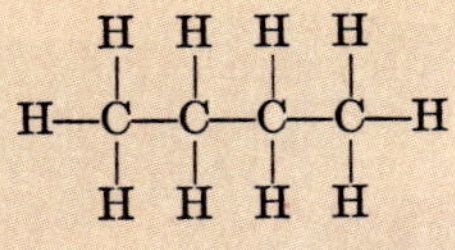	C_4H_{10}	gas	fuel gas
octane	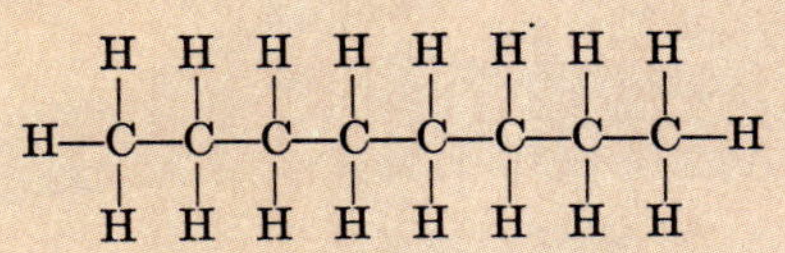	C_8H_{18}	liquid	gasoline
heptodecane	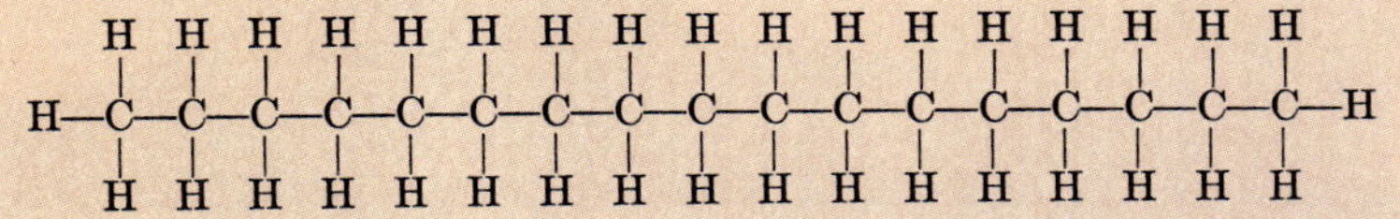	$C_{17}H_{36}$	solid	wax

STAGES IN THE FORMATION OF ONE TYPE OF PETROLEUM DEPOSIT

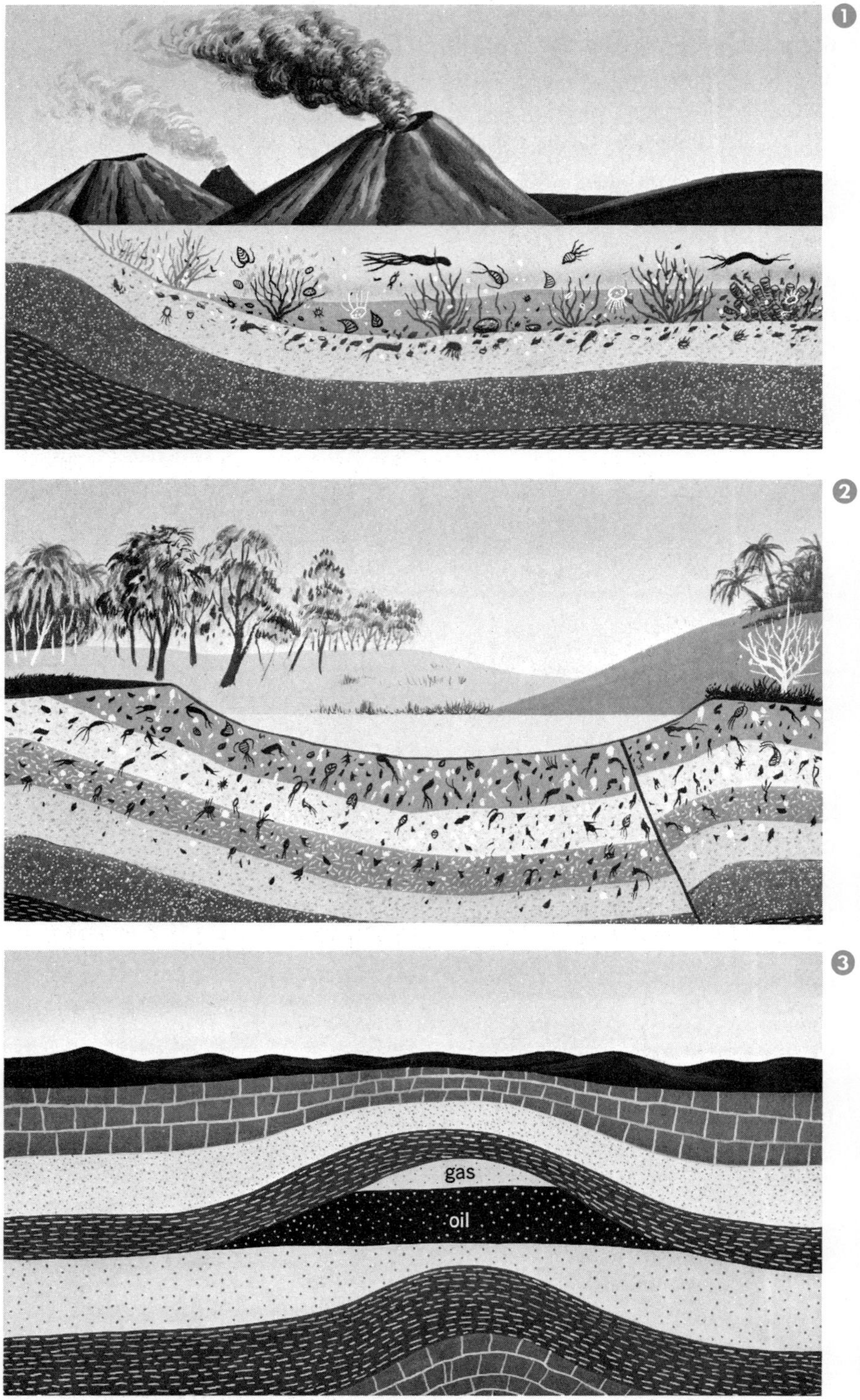

joined in the same kind of chain. Try to write on your own a graphic formula for butane. Then check your result against the formula in the chart on page 413.

The hydrocarbons in the chart (p. 413) belong to a large group of compounds known as the **methane series** of hydrocarbons. The series is named after its first member, methane. There are hundreds of compounds in the methane series alone, and there are several other series of hydrocarbons besides, each of them with large numbers of compounds composed of only carbon and hydrogen.

Source of Hydrocarbons

Natural gas is about 90 percent methane, and petroleum is mainly a mixture of members of the methane series. What is the origin of natural gas and petroleum?

Some scientists believe they were formed from the bodies of billions of microscopic organisms that lived in the sea millions of years ago.❶ When these tiny plants and animals died, they fell to the bottom of the sea. In time, layers of sediment covered the remains of these organisms.❷ As the sediment turned into sedimentary rock, these remains were transformed into gas and droplets of oil. After millions of years, the undersea sediment was uplifted. Water, gas, and oil seeped into the pores of rock such as sandstone. In the type of petroleum deposit shown here, the gas, oil, and water were trapped by a layer of impermeable shale.❸ The so-called "gas pockets" and "oil pools" are actually saturated layers of sandstone.

Hydrocarbons as Fuels

Natural gas and petroleum furnish us with a variety of fuels: gas for home cooking and heating; oils for diesel engines and jets; gasoline for automobiles and planes. The United States consumes far more oil than it produces, and we are searching constantly for new sources of petroleum. In 1968, perhaps the largest oil fields in North America were located along the Arctic shores of Alaska.❹ Although reaching the oil through frozen ground and shipping it through ice-bound waters is a real problem, the fields will undoubtedly help meet our tremendous demand for petroleum products.

❹

The value of petroleum fuels, substances used to produce heat, depends upon the combustibility—the ability to burn—of their hydrocarbons. How does the substance in a fuel change when the fuel burns? Try this investigation. ■

■ AN APPRENTICE INVESTIGATION into Burning Gas

Reduce the air supply to a Bunsen burner until the flame is quiet. Support a large, cold, Pyrex or Kimax flask over the tip of the flame and watch carefully for the condensation of water droplets inside the flask. ❶

Keep the flame under the flask for about five minutes. Turn off the flame, set the flask on the table, and pour a little limewater into the flask. Stopper the flask and mix the limewater and condensed water. What happens? ❷

❶

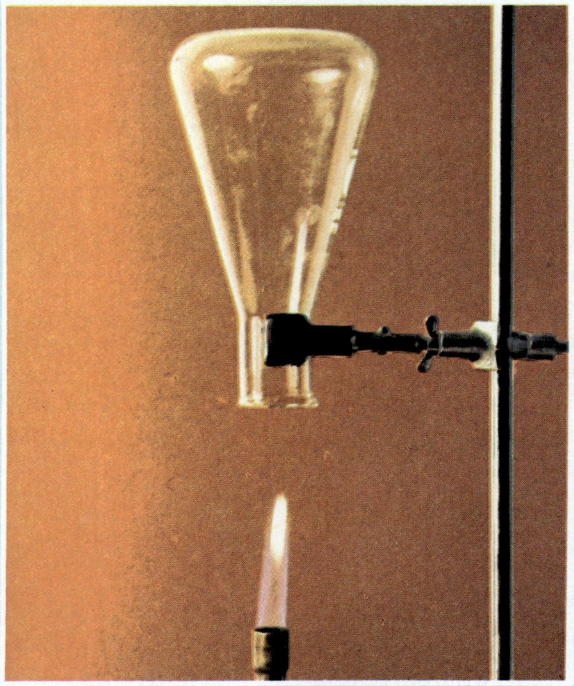

❷

One product of the combustion of fuel gas is water. The fact that limewater turns milky is evidence of another product of the combustion —carbon dioxide. How do we explain the formation of water and carbon dioxide? Fuel gas contains several hydrocarbons, among them methane and ethane.

methane + oxygen ⟶ carbon dioxide + water + energy

ethane + oxygen ⟶ carbon dioxide + water + energy

When these substances are burned, the carbon from the hydrocarbon combines with oxygen to form carbon dioxide, and hydrogen combines with oxygen to form water. The reactions for complete combustion of all hydrocarbons follow the same pattern.

A Curious Event

On April 18, 1973, strange events began to take place in Williamsburg, Michigan. Small geysers of natural gas suddenly erupted at the edge of a stream. ❶ Within days, hundreds

1 

of geysers—both large and small—sprang up throughout the area. All the residents were evacuated and precautions were taken to prevent the explosion of the gas.

What was the cause of this unusual occurrence? An oil well outside of town was the prime suspect. If the well was damaged, gas could have escaped into porous layers of rock and be forced to the surface by the pressure underground.

The well was plugged up—and both scientists and townspeople waited. Meanwhile tons of clay pushed up by the gas were pouring into streams that feed Lake Michigan. Even after the geysers stopped, life could not return to normal immediately.

What damage was done to the environment of Williamsburg, Michigan? Are we concerned—are you to be concerned—with the environment of Williamsburg, Michigan? Of course. Just multiply the Williamsburgs over the United States, no—over the world—and you will begin to have the proper concern.

True, life today is better for the vast majority of people than it was, say, 150 years ago. For example, the life span of the average American was near 40 years of age. Today it is near 75 years of age.

But many would agree that today we are making the environment unfit for life and living. At the center of the conflict—the combustion engine using fossil fuels. If we were wise enough to invent so wonderful a device, are we not wise enough to invent a way of controlling it? Of course. Are we willing to do so? Are you?

REVIEW

1. Why is the element carbon associated with living things?

2. Write a graphic formula for:
   a. methane (CH_4)
   b. ethane (C_2H_6)
   c. propane (C_3H_8)

3. What is believed to be the origin of natural gas and petroleum?

4. What is the product of the burning of the hydrocarbon propane?

5. Describe the structures of two different crystalline allotropes of carbon. How do these structures explain the differences in properties between these two forms of the element?

NEW VIEW

1. Gas, gasoline, kerosene, light oil, lubricating oil stocks, and "bottoms" are among the various *fractions* of petroleum. What products do we obtain from each of these fractions?

2. The methane series of hydrocarbons is only one of several large groups of compounds made up only of carbon and hydrogen. Find out the names, formulas, and uses of some hydrocarbons of other series, such as the acetylene series and the benzene series.

3. Scientists think diamond may be formed by the metamorphosis of graphite in the earth. What is the origin of deposits of the graphite?

4. RELATING THE CONCEPTS

We sometimes speak of science as though it had two "divisions"—basic or "pure" science, and technology or "applied" science; and these are thought of as being closely interrelated. Basic science is sometimes described as *discovery*, and applied science as the *uses of discovery*. Indeed, technology grows out of basic research, and then, in turn, advances in technology spur further basic research. Thus, our knowledge of the particulate nature of matter, or the principles of chemical change in matter, and of the properties that characterize individual elements, leads to our use of this knowledge in the manufacture of the many thousands of products that make our civilization possible.

In this chapter we have singled out, by way of example, three of the earth's elements for which we have found many valuable uses. We have considered certain technological advances that have resulted from the application of our knowledge of the properties of these elements—sulfur, carbon, and iron—and their compounds. And from our study we may single out some concepts that apply also to the chemistry of many other substances.

Reviewing the Concepts

► *The properties of an element determine certain techniques for its mining.* Sulfur has a low melting point and is insoluble in water; these properties are decisive for the method of its mining by the Frasch process.

► *The properties of an element determine certain procedures for its manufacture into useful forms.* Iron occurs in nature in the form of iron oxide, for example, mixed with silicate rocks. The facts that iron oxide can be reduced by carbon, and that silicates can be converted into slag, determine the method of refining in the blast furnace. And since only "impure" iron (containing some carbon) has the properties that make the metal practically useful, the retention of some of the carbon is essential to the making of steel.

► *The two allotropic forms of elemental carbon have marked differences in properties which reflect the difference in their molecular structures.* Most of the familiar forms of carbon—charcoal, soot, pencil "lead," and so on—have the same basic structure that characterizes pure crystalline graphite: layers of carbon atoms that have strong bonds within the layers, with weak forces of attraction between the layers.

Diamond is the other allotrope of carbon. In this form the atoms of carbon are joined together in a macromolecule with bonds of equal strength in three dimensions. As a result of its molecular structure, graphite is soft, black, and slippery. Diamond, on the other hand, has a molecular structure that results in crystals that are frequently colorless, exceptionally hard, and lustrous.

► *Because of the ability of carbon atoms to bond with one another, carbon is found combined in a great variety of compounds made up of molecules of many different sizes and degrees of complexity.* In the methane series of hydrocarbons, for example, there are hundreds of different compounds composed of the element carbon and just one other element, hydrogen.

Testing Yourself

1. Three allotropes of sulfur are rhombic, monoclinic, and amorphous.

a. How do they differ from one another?
b. How are they similar?

2. Describe briefly the uses of sulfur and its compounds.

3. In what ores is iron usually found?

4. What properties of iron make it undesirable to use as a pure metal?

5. Describe the factors that contribute to the rusting process.

6. Explain why carbon can form so many different compounds.

7. What is the molecular formula for octane? the graphic formula?

8. What elements are present in all hydrocarbons?

9. Describe the different properties of diamond and graphite and account for these differences.

Extending the Concepts

Investigation 1. You have read that sulfur is added to rubber in the process of vulcanization. Use the reaction between silver and the sulfur in rubber to demonstrate a test for sulfur that you may then apply to different kinds of foods and other materials. What product will form if sulfur reacts with silver? Scrub a silver coin with detergent and steel wool until it is shiny. Wrap a rubber band around the coin and let it stand for a few days. What happens? Look up the reaction in a high school chemistry text to see if you correctly predicted the product. Then use a clean silver coin in the same way to test egg white, egg yolk, and other substances.

Investigation 2. A major use of iron compound is in making inks and blueprints. You can make blueprints from the iron compounds potassium ferricyanide and ferric citrate (or ferric ammonium citrate), obtained from a supply house. In one beaker, dissolve 10 grams of potassium ferricyanide in 50 ml of water, and in another beaker dissolve 10 grams of ferric citrate in 50 ml of water. In a darkened room, mix the two solutions and pour the mixture into a shallow pan. Dip a sheet of well-sized (bond) paper in the solution in the pan, and allow the paper to dry in a dark place. Place a key or some other object on the dried paper, then expose to the light for 2 to 10 minutes. Wash the paper under running water, then dry. Determine for yourself the time exposure to light of different intensities that gives the best results.

Suggested Reading

Asimov, Isaac, *The World of Carbon*, New York, Abelard-Schuman, 1958. An excellent introduction to the field of organic compounds.

Parr, J. Gordon, *Man, Metals and Modern Magic*, New York, Macmillan, 1963. The story of ancient and modern metallurgy.

Strahler, Arthur and Alan Strahler, *Environmental Geoscience*, Santa Barbara, Hamilton, 1973. Discusses the principles of earth science you need to know to understand environmental problems.

Finding Your Way

1. READING ROAD MAPS

The major features of the land—the mountains and the hills, the valleys and the rivers, the plains and the plateaus—are too large to see completely at any one time. We can examine only a small part of each of them. The earth scientist has solved this problem by using *maps*. Not one kind of map, but hundreds of different maps! They come in many sizes and show different amounts of the earth's surface. Now let's learn how to read a map.

Using Map Symbols

This illustration is part of a road map of New York State. **1** You will probably find similar features on a map of your own state. Find the section on your map that shows the *map symbols*. **2** This part of the map is called the **map legend.** Most map legends show types of roads by color and symbol, the population of cities and towns by bold or lighter print, points of interest by special markings, and other information. Study the symbols in the legend and find examples on the map.

1

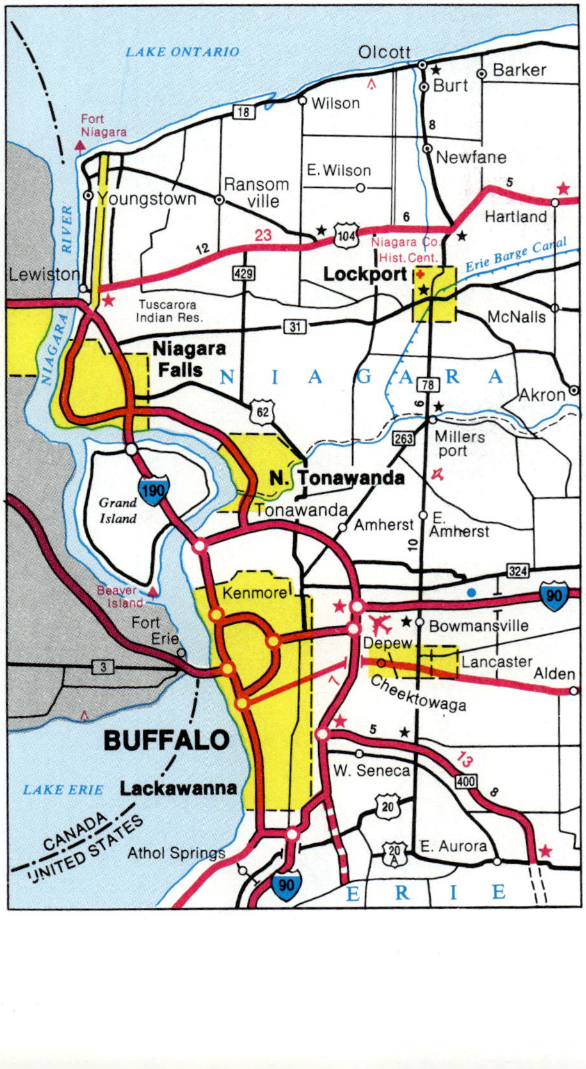

2

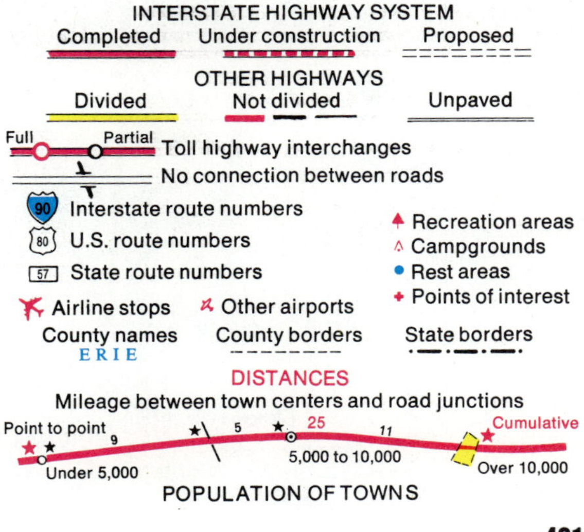

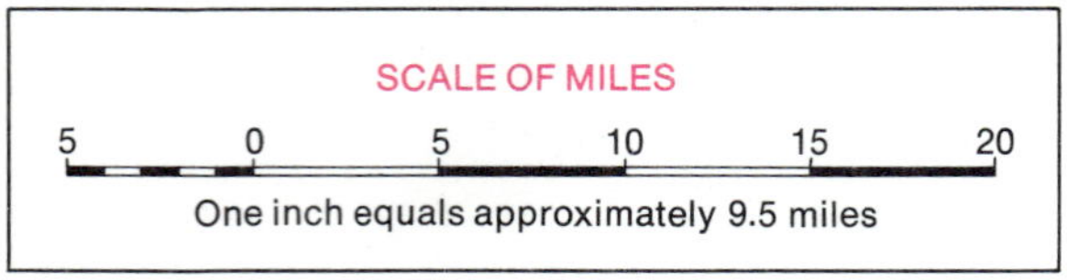
SCALE OF MILES
5 0 5 10 15 20
One inch equals approximately 9.5 miles

1

N
W
E
S

2

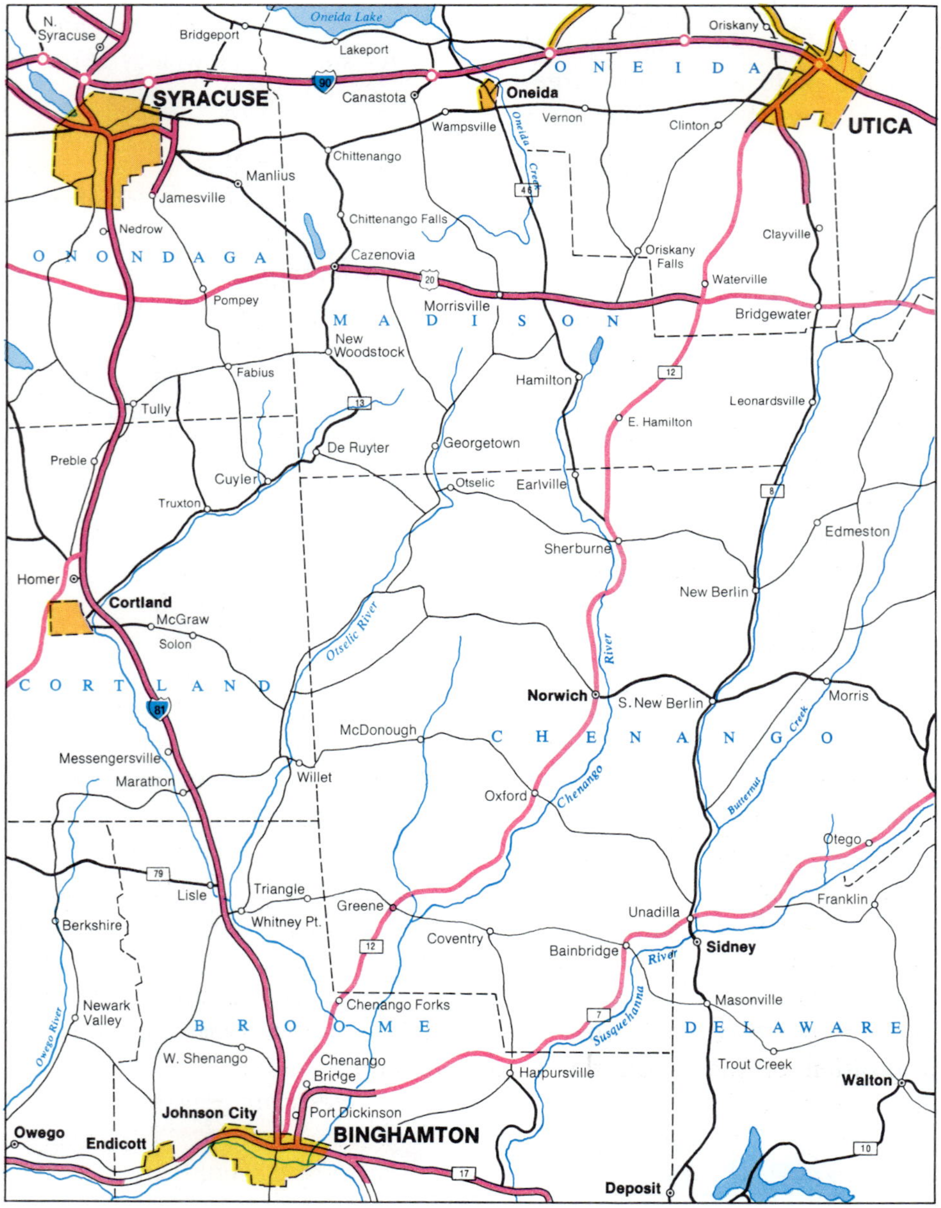
Oneida Lake
N. Syracuse
Bridgeport
Lakeport
Oriskany
SYRACUSE
90
Canastota
Oneida
O N E I D A
UTICA
Vernon
Clinton
Wampsville
Oneida Creek
Chittenango
Manlius
Jamesville
46
Chittenango Falls
Nedrow
Oriskany Falls
Clayville
O N O N D A G A
Cazenovia
20
Waterville
Pompey
Morrisville
Bridgewater
M A D I S O N
New Woodstock
Fabius
Hamilton
12
Leonardsville
13
Tully
E. Hamilton
De Ruyter
Georgetown
Preble
Cuyler
Otselic
Earlville
8
Truxton
Edmeston
Sherburne
Homer
Cortland
New Berlin
McGraw
Solon
Otselic River
River
C O R T L A N D
Norwich
S. New Berlin
Morris
81
McDonough
C H E N A N G O
Messengersville
Butternut Creek
Willet
Marathon
Oxford
Chenango
Otego
79
Triangle
Lisle
Greene
Franklin
Unadilla
Berkshire
Whitney Pt.
Coventry
12
Bainbridge
Sidney
River
Masonville
Chenango Forks
Newark Valley
7
Susquehanna
B R O O M E
D E L A W A R E
Owego River
W. Shenango
Chenango Bridge
Trout Creek
Harpursville
Walton
Johnson City
Port Dickinson
Owego
Endicott
BINGHAMTON
10
17
Deposit

3

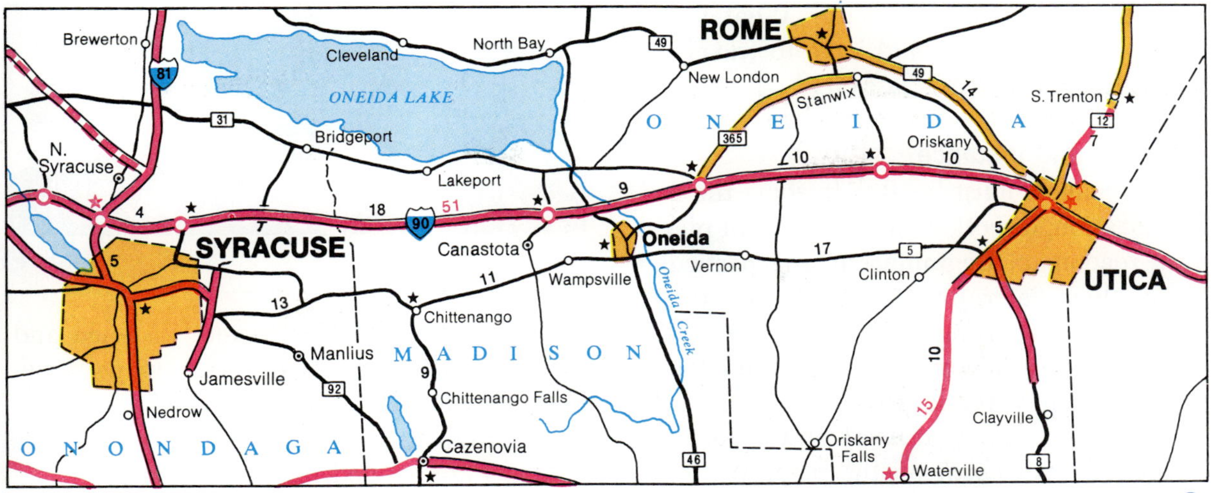

❹

How far apart are places on the map? To answer this question, examine the **map scale.** ❶ Because almost every map is a representation of a much larger portion of the earth's surface, the map scale tells you how much *real* ground distance is represented by one unit of scale distance. Usually the map scale shows distance by a numbered line, called a **graphic scale.** In this road map, one inch on the graphic scale equals twelve miles of real ground distance. Get a map of your state. Find the scale on your map. (At present, road maps and maps prepared by the U.S. Geological Survey use the English system of measurement. For this reason, only the English system is referred to in this section.)

Somewhere on a road map you will find a "north arrow" or picture of a compass similar to this one. ❷ If you hold the map so that the north arrow is pointing north, you know the correct position of places on the map *relative to your location.* Try this example. ❸ Suppose you were in Syracuse, New York, and had the map turned, or oriented, correctly. To get to Utica, New York, you would travel east. To get to Binghamton, New York, you would travel south. How far is it from Syracuse to Binghamton?

True Distance—Actual Distance

If you were flying from one place to another, you could use the graphic scale to find the straight line distance or *true ground distance* between two cities. Unfortunately, most roads are not laid out in straight lines. Therefore, we usually want to find the *actual ground mileage* between two places on a map. Most maps have this mileage recorded in small numbers next to the roads that connect various towns and cities. ❹ Use the graphic scale to determine the straight-line distance from Syracuse to Utica. Compare the straight-line distance with the mileage marked on the road between these two cities. How are they different? Why?

On a map of your state, trace a line that connects five cities. What is the distance and direction you would have to travel to move from the first to the last city? What is the actual mileage you would have to travel between the first and the last city?

Direction and Distance

Map makers must be able to show the correct location, direction and distance, of places on a road map. Beginning at any particular place, they determine the direction to another place by using a compass. Try it for yourself. Suppose you were at position A and wanted to know the location of position B. (1) Place a compass so that *north* on the compass is aligned with *north* on the map. Wouldn't you walk due east to get to position B? Direction, then, is easy to find—just use a compass.

To determine how far you must travel to get to position B, measure the distance. Distances are measured in feet or miles, meters or kilometers. If the distance is not too great and the land surface is smooth between A and B, you can measure the distance directly. This is similar to measuring the length or width of a room.

You know, of course, that the earth is not a smooth surface. Yet road maps show measurements as if the earth were smooth—as if there were no mountains or valleys. Road maps are examples of **planimetric maps.** Planimetric maps show the correct distance and direction between places. Such maps, however, *do not* give information on the height of the land from place to place. Other types of maps are needed for this purpose.

(1)

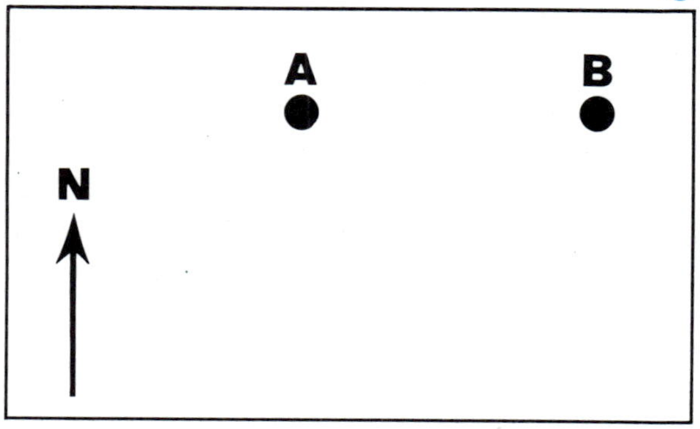

(2)

2. READING TOPOGRAPHIC MAPS

The height of the land—its hills and valleys, mountains and plateaus—is usually called the **topography** of the earth. *Topographic maps* show the heights of various features of the landscape. These maps will tell you the elevation of the land, its height above sea level.

Showing Elevation—Pictures and Color

On topographic maps there are many ways to show the relief features of the earth's surface. One of the earliest methods was pictorial. (2) Find an elevation of one of the peaks in the mountain chain. Such an elevation is known as a spot elevation, since it gives only the elevation of certain point, or *spot.*

Color bands are often used to show elevation. These color bands represent different ranges of elevation above sea level. When bands are used, the map is known as an *altitude tint map.* (3) On this map, the land within the tan band rises to 100 feet above sea level. The medium brown shows land that is between 100 and 200 feet above sea level. A legend for this map would include the meaning of the other colors.

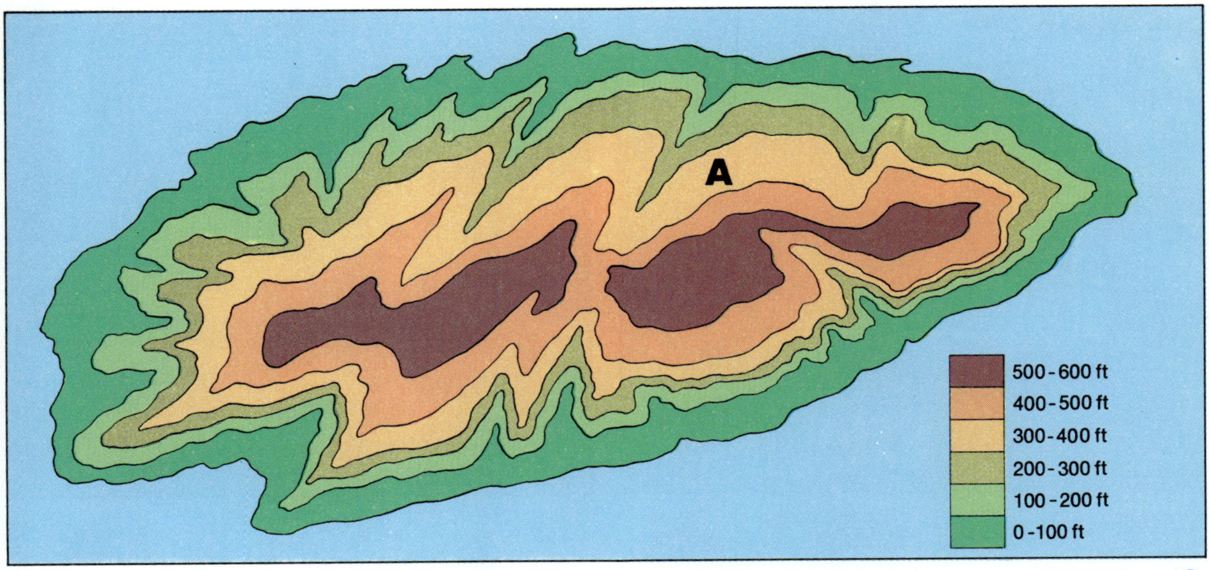

3

What do you know about the elevation of point A on the map? Only that it is more than 300 feet high and less than 400 feet high. If you needed the exact elevation of point A the map maker would have to provide a spot elevation at that point because there is no way you can determine it from the altitude tint map.

Contour Maps

To give more information on topography, the map maker developed **contour lines.** On a map, contour lines connect points having the same elevation above sea level. No matter where you are on a given contour line, the land surface has the same elevation. Let's study a simple diagram. 4 The upper part of this picture shows a small island rising over 80 feet above sea level. The lower part of this picture shows a contour map of this island. On the contour map, the contour line marked "0" indicates the shoreline of the island. This contour line traces out the shape of the island. The next contour line—marked 20—is 20 feet above sea level. Anywhere on this line,

4

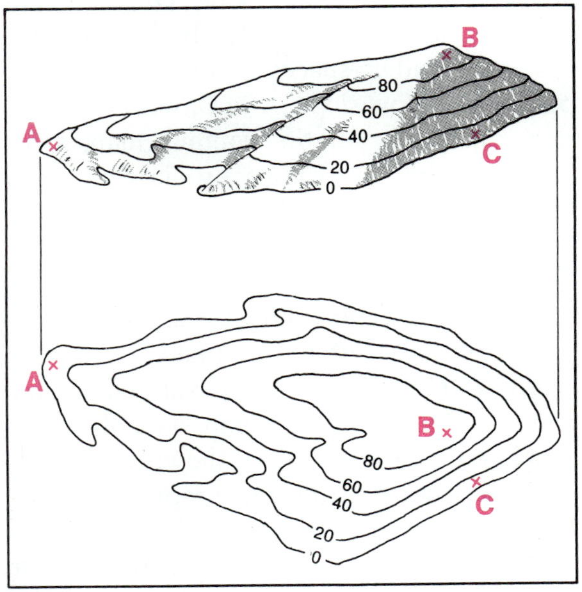

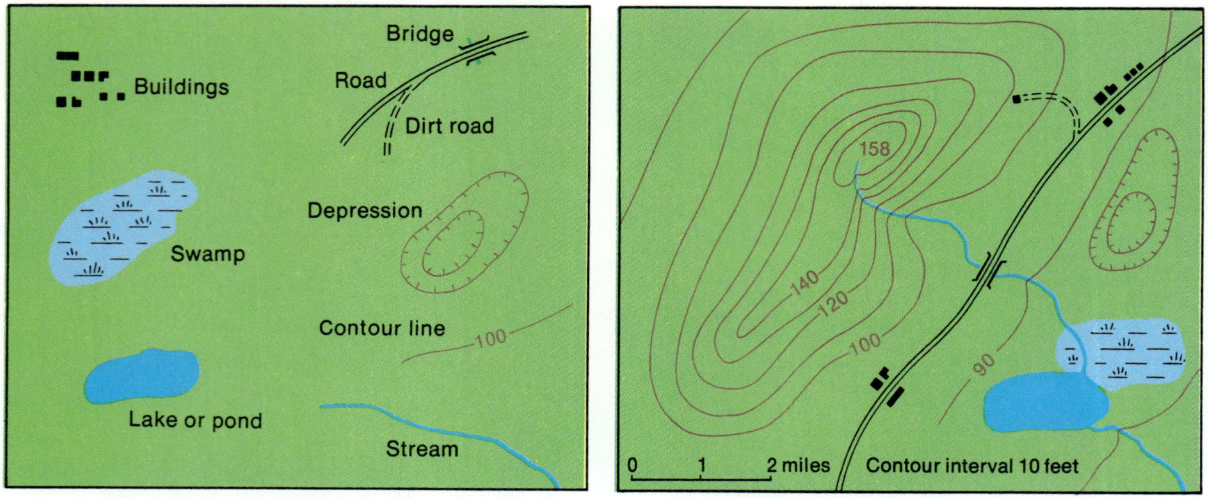

1

the elevation is 20 feet. The difference in elevation between contour lines is called the **contour interval.** In the diagram, the contour interval is 20 feet. Each contour line differs from the next by 20 feet.

Now find points A, B, and C. To go from point A to the top of the island, point B, we want to climb a gentle slope. On a contour map, gentle slopes or relatively flat areas are shown by widely-spaced contour lines. Compare the shallow slope, A to B, with the steep slope, B to C. On the contour map, steep slopes or cliffs are shown by closely spaced contour lines.

Topographic Maps

Topographic maps show the shape and elevation of the land by contours. By special symbols, they point out artificial and natural features. Some common map symbols and a simplified contour map are shown in the diagram. 1 To read this topographic map we have to understand the symbols.

The symbols shown in the diagram are from a list of topographic map symbols produced by the U.S. Geological Survey. (By writing to the U.S. Geological Survey, Washington, D.C., you can get a free publication called "Topographic Maps," which lists all of the topographic map symbols.) The symbols for buildings, bridges, lakes, swamps, roads, and streams are easy to identify. The *depression* symbol, however, needs some explanation.

A topographic depression is a basin or lowered section of land between elevated parts of the earth. These basins are shown by closed contour lines with short slashes pointing toward the inside of the basin. On the topographic map, a depression is shown next to the 90-foot contour line. The outer circle of the depression would also be at an elevation of 90 feet. The inner circle would have an elevation of 80 feet since the contour interval is 10 feet.

Interpreting Topographic Maps

Let's find out what else we can learn about topographic maps. Each of the following questions can be answered by referring to the map pictured here.

What area is shown on the map? Using the map scale, we find that the map represents an area about 6½ miles long by 8 miles wide, or 52 square miles (6½ × 8).

What is the highest and lowest point on the map? The highest point is 158 feet above sea level. The lowest point is in the depression contour, 80 feet above sea level.

What is the contour interval of the map? The contour interval is 10 feet.

How would you describe the land between contour lines 90 and 100? The land slopes very gently. Wide spacing of the contour lines indicates a gradual slope. The slope of the land is steepest where the lines are closest together.

Why do the contour lines bend "upstream" where the stream crosses them? As contour lines approach a valley, they bend upstream to stay at the elevation they represent. You can also observe the bending of the contour lines in the detailed section. ②

What does the closed circle around position "158" represent? This is the 150-foot contour line. It outlines the top of the mountain.

Note the long, closed oval-shaped contour lines stretching towards the bottom of the map. *What do these contour lines represent?* These lines indicate a long and narrow ridge.

We have learned quite a bit from this map. But there is still one more thing we can learn. We can make a *profile* of the land surface from such a topographic map. A profile allows you to see a "side view" of the land feature.

To construct a profile, draw a horizontal line, AB, through a contour map. ③ Be sure that the horizontal line crosses all the contour lines. Place the top edge of a piece of graph paper along the horizontal line. Draw a horizontal line, AB, as near to the top of the graph paper as possible. Then place a dot along this line (AB) whenever a contour line on the map crosses the line AB on your graph paper.

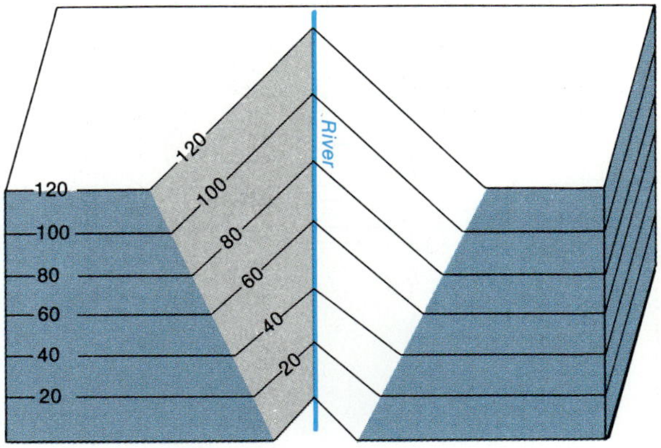

②

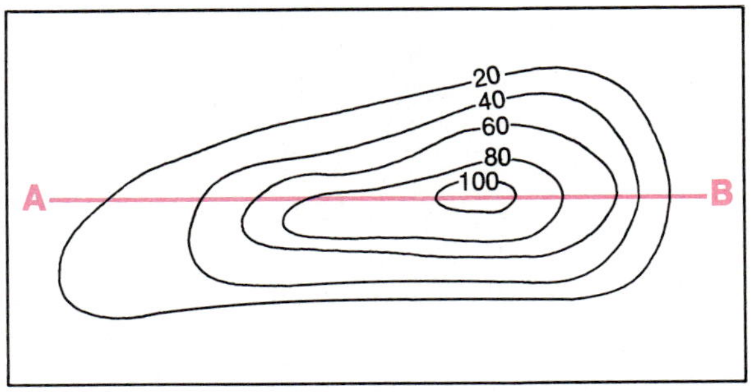

③

On the graph paper, draw another horizontal line A′B′ about three inches below line AB. Label this line with the number that represents the *lowest* contour line on the map (for example, 20). Above line A′B′ draw additional horizontal lines equal distances apart to represent all of the contour lines (for example, 40, 60, 80, and 100). Now draw a *vertical* line from each dot on the top horizontal line to the appropriate horizontal line at the bottom of the graph. (For example, draw a vertical line from the dot on the 40 contour line to the horizontal line labeled 40.) Connect the points at the end of each

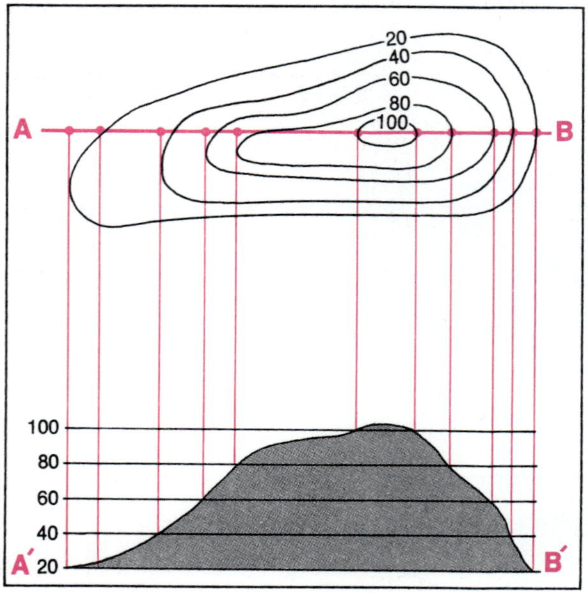

❶

vertical line. Then shade the area under the curved line you have just drawn. The result is a profile. ❶

Can you draw a profile from the topographic map along a straight line extending through the road, the top of the mountain, and the depression? Try it!

As you continue your study of earth science, you will examine topographic maps published by the U.S. Geological Survey. A portion of such a map is shown here. ❷ On these maps, you can find all the types of information you have been considering: direction, distance, scale, contours, and spot elevations. You can use the information you have learned to interpret such maps.

Maps have been closely related to many important events of our history. Why not learn about how maps developed?

❷

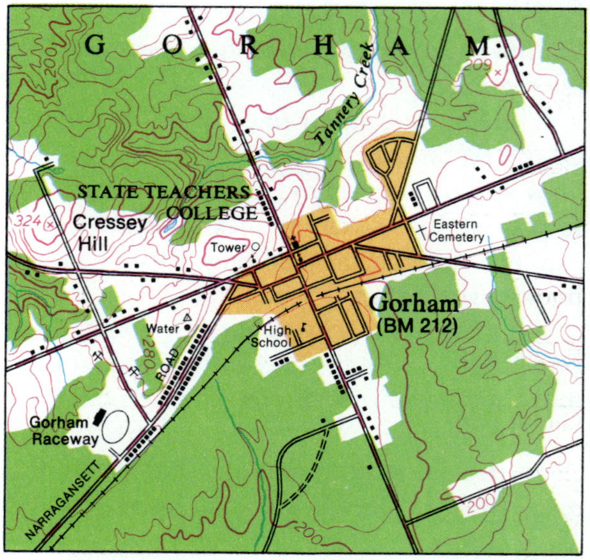

PROPERTIES OF SOME MINERALS

Mineral	*Hardness*	*Breakage*	*Streak*	*Luster*	*Usual color*	*Specific Gravity*	*Special characteristics*
Bauxite* (aluminum ore)	1–3		varies	dull to earthy	white to gray	2–2.5	claylike odor
Calcite*	3	3 cleavages no right angles	white	glassy to earthy	white to colorless	2.7	effervesces in HCl
Cassiterite (tin ore)	6.0–7.0	uneven fracture	whitish-gray	glassy	brown to black	6.8–7.1	brittle
Feldspar*	6	2 cleavages at right angles	white	glassy	white, gray, pink	2.5^+	
Galena* (lead ore)	2.5	perfect cubic cleavage	lead gray	bright metallic	lead gray	7.6	very dense
Garnet	6.5–7.5	poor cleavage	scratches plate	glassy	red	3.5–4.3	brittle, 8-sided crystals
Graphite	1–2		black	metallic to dull earthy	black	2.1^+	marks paper easily, greasy
Gypsum*	2	cleavage in 3 directions	white	glassy to silky	colorless to white, gray	2.3	
Halite	2.5	perfect cubic cleavage	white	glassy	colorless to white	2.1^+	salty taste
Hematite*	5.5–6.5	uneven fracture	red-brown	metallic	reddish brown to black	5.2^+	
Hornblende*	5–6	2 cleavages	green to black	glassy	dark green to black	3.2	
Kaolinite	2^+	1 cleavage	white	dull, earthy	white	2.6^+	
Limonite	5–5.5	shell-like fracture	yellow brown	glassy	dark brown to black	3.6^+	
Magnetite*	6		black	metallic	black	5.1^+	strongly magnetic
Malachite* (copper ore)	3.5–4		light green	silky	green	3.9–4	
Mica*	2.5^+	1 perfect cleavage	white	glassy	dark green, black, brown	2.8^+	
Pyrite	6–6.5		greenish to brownish black	metallic	pale brass yellow	4.8^+	sometimes mistaken for gold and called "fool's gold"
Quartz*	7	shell-like fracture	white or colorless	glassy	colorless, variety	2.6^+	6-sided crystals
Smithsonite (zinc ore)	5	3 cleavages, no right angles	white	dull	white to yellowish brown	4.5–5.0	brittle
Sphalerite* (zinc ore)	3.5–4		yellow-brown	resinous	white to green	3.9^+	sometimes black or red
Talc	1	no cleavage	white	greasy	apple green, gray, white	2.7	feels soapy

* See pictures on pages 57–58.

SOME COMMON ROCKS

Rock	*Composition*	*Characteristics*
Igneous		
Granite*	Quartz, feldspar, and often mica	Coarse grain, light color, low density
Gabbro*	Feldspar, pyroxene, sometimes olivine	Coarse grain, dark color, high density
Basalt*	Feldspar	Fine grain, dark color, low density, cavities lined with olivine are frequent
Felsite*	Biotite, feldspar, quartz	Fine grain with very fine crystals, light in color
Pumice*	Component minerals not visible	Glassy, porous, silky fibers, usually a light color, floats in water
Obsidian*	Component minerals not visible	Glassy, dark color, fractures in shell-like manner
Sedimentary		
Conglomerate*	Cemented, rounded gravel with sand	Coarse particles cemented together
Sandstone*	Cemented sand grains, usually quartz	Porous and gritty, does not usually react with hydrochloric acid, color varies
Shale*	Compact mud or clay particles (kaolinite)	Earthy smell, brittle, waterproof, usually does not bubble with hydrochloric acid
Limestone*	Compact limey mud (calcite)	Color varies, bubbles with hydrochloric acid
Dolomite	A carbonate of calcium and magnesium	Less bubbling with hydrochloric acid than limestone
Coquina*	Shells and shell fragments	Loosely consolidated material that bubbles with hydrochloric acid
Metamorphic		
Gneiss*	Quartz, feldspar, mica or hornblende	Minerals structured in coarse, parallel bands; formed from granite and resembles granite
Schist*	Mica, quartz, hornblende, garnet	Minerals arranged in thin, parallel bands; can be split; has wavy, uneven surface; formed from sedimentary or igneous rocks
Anthracite*	Carbon	Formed from soft coal, which originated from plant life
Slate*	Clay minerals	Slaty cleavage; splits into smooth, flat surfaces; red, gray, green, or purple; formed from shale
Quartzite*	Quartz	Very crystalline, hard, dense; formed from sandstone
Marble*	Calcite	Crystalline, granular, bubbles with hydrochloric acid, white or gray or streaked with colors due to impurities (iron, carbon)

* See pictures on pages **74–75**.

Glossary

The terms and meanings in this listing apply to their use in this text. Many of the words have other or additional meanings and uses in advanced work in science. The page reference next to an entry generally indicates the place in the text where the term appears in boldface type and is first discussed or illustrated. For additional pages on which the term is used, consult the index. A few terms whose meanings you probably know from earlier work in science do not have page references.

PRONUNCIATION KEY

SYMBOL	KEY WORDS	SYMBOL	KEY WORDS	SYMBOL	KEY WORDS
a	add, map	ī	ice, write	th	thin, both
ā	ace, rate	o	odd, hot	u	up, done
â(r)	care, air	ō	open, so	û(r)	urn, term
ä	palm, father	ô	order, jaw	y	yet, yearn
e	end, pet	oi	oil, boy	ə	an unstressed vowel
ē	even, tree	o͞o	pool, food		as in the words above,
i	it, give	o͝o	took, full		sicken, clarity, focus

absolute dating, estimating the age of the earth on the basis of the measurement of decay of natural radioactive isotopes, 320

abyssal (ə•bis′əl) **plain,** an extremely flat expanse of land on the ocean floor, 243

abyssal (ə•bis′əl) **zone,** the area of the sea below a depth of 1,800 meters, or 6,000 feet, 263

acid, a compound whose water solution contains hydrogen ions (H+) and turns blue litmus to pink

air mass, a large body of air having uniform temperature, pressure, and humidity throughout, 292

allotropes (al′ə•trōps), two or more forms of an element with different properties, 404

alloy, a combination of metals, or of metals and other elements, that has the properties of a metal, 375

alpha particle, atomic particle consisting of two protons and two neutrons, 90

alpha radiation, a stream of particles consisting of 2 protons and 2 neutrons from an atomic nucleus, 90

altitude tint map, a map in which colored bands represent different ranges in height above sea level, 424

amu, see **atomic mass unit,** 33

angular diameter, the angle that the diameter of an object sighted at a distance makes with the eye, 223

anticline, upfolded layers of rock, 102

apogee (ap′ə•jē), the point, in the orbit of a satellite, which is at the greatest distance from the earth, 214

apparent diameter, the diameter that an object appears to have when sighted at a distance; see **angular diameter,** 223

apparent magnitude, the brightness of a star as it appears to an observer on earth, 170

aquaculture, sea farming, or the wise management of marine animals and plants to increase the food supply, 386

asteroid (as′tə•roid), one of a number of small bodies revolving around the sun, in orbit between Mars and Jupiter, 188

astronomical unit (A. U.), the average distance between the earth and the sun, about 150 million kilometers, or 93 million miles, 202

atmosphere (at′məs•fir), the gaseous layer surrounding the earth, made up of the mixture of substances known as air, 5

atoll, a ring-shaped coral reef that completely surrounds a shallow channel or lagoon, 264

atom, the particle of matter of which elements are made up, 23

atomic mass unit (amu), the unit of atomic weight (or mass) defined as 1/12 the weight (or mass) of an atom of carbon-12, 33

atomic number, the number of protons (or electrons) in an atom of an element, 33

atomic weight, the relative weight of an element, in atomic mass units, compared to an atom of carbon-12, 33

A. U., see **astronomical unit, 202**

barometer (bə•rom′ə•ter), an instrument for measuring the pressure of the atmosphere, 285

barrier island, sand mass separated by water from the shore, 136

barrier reef, a coral reef separated from nearby land by a shallow channel or lagoon, 264

base, a compound whose water solution contains hydroxide ions (OH^-) and turns pink litmus to blue

batholith (bath′ə•lith), a massive plutonic rock formation that flares outward with depth, 109

bathyal (bath′ē•əl) **zone,** the area of the sea beyond the continental shelf, between the depths of 120 and 1,800 meters, or 400 and 6,000 feet, 262

bathyscaph (bath′ə•skaf), a vessel designed and equipped for exploring the deepest parts of the ocean floor, 243

bedrock, the rock that lies just below the soil in the earth's crust, 81

Bessemer (bes′ə•mər) **process,** a process in which pig iron is refined by burning away impurities, 399

beta radiation, a stream of high-speed electrons from the nucleus of an atom, 90

blast furnace, a type of furnace in which iron ore is converted into pig iron, 398

blowout, a shallow basin produced by wind erosion, 135

blue giant, a relatively large, bright, and hot star, blue-white in color, 173

blue shift, a shift to shorter wavelengths of the light from stars and galaxies moving toward the earth, 178

breccia, an igneous rock composed of slivers of volcanic glass, pumice, mineral fragments, and fragments of volcanic rock cemented together, 72

bright-line spectrum, a spectrum made up of colored lines, indicating the presence of certain wavelengths of light, against a black background, 150

brine, a strong solution of salt (sodium chloride), 375

butte, small, elevated land area where a plateau has been washed away; usually the height is equal to the width, 111

calcareous (kal•kâr′ē•əs) **sediments,** sediments made up of calcium compounds, principally calcium carbonate, 262

caliche, a hard white crust formed by the accumulation of calcium and magnesium compounds in the soil, 311

capillary action, upward movement of water through the thin tubes of a material, 312

carbon-14 dating, dating of a relatively recent substance of organic origin based on the proportion of carbon-14 to carbon-12 it contains, 322

cast, a replica of an organism produced by a substance filling a mold of the organism, 324

catalyst (kat′ə•list), a substance that changes the speed at which a reaction occurs, but which itself remains unchanged, 390

cell, the smallest living unit of structure and function in an organism

cepheid (sef′ē•id) **variable,** a star that periodically changes its output of energy, and therefore its luminosity, 172

chemical bonding, the combining of two or more elements to form a compound, 35

chemical change, *see* **chemical reaction**

chemical formula, *see* **formula,** 25

chemical property, a property of a substance that refers to a chemical reaction, usually with another substance, that the substance undergoes, 43

chemical reaction, a change in a substance resulting in another substance with different chemical properties

cirque (sûrk), a circular basin, on a mountain side, formed by a glacier, 133

cirrus clouds, thin and feathery clouds at high altitudes, 275

clastic (klas′tik) **rock,** sedimentary rock formed from fragments of preexisting rocks, 68

cleavage, the breaking up of a mineral, when struck, into pieces of a characteristic shape for that mineral, 48

climate, the long term pattern of weather of an area, 299

cloud chamber, an instrument that makes visible the paths of atomic particles, 91

collision hypothesis, the hypothesis, that the planets originated from matter knocked loose when the sun collided with another star, 200

comet, an object in space revolving around the sun, generally in a very elongated orbit, 188

compound, a substance made up of two or more elements chemically combined, 15

condensation nuclei, particles of solid or liquid matter on which condensation of water vapor into droplets takes place in the air, 275

constellation, a pattern of stars to which a name has been given, as Orion, Big Dipper, Sagittarius, Cepheus, 163

continental drift, the theory that the continents were originally joined together and in some time past broke up and slowly drifted apart, 94

continental glacier, a vast sheet of ice that spreads in all directions, 133

continental shelf, a shelf of undersea land extending 50 to 500 kilometers, or 30 to 300 miles out to sea from the shoreline, 242

continental slope, the sloping undersea land that connects the continental shelf with the abyssal plain, 242

continuous spectrum, the smooth rainbow of colors, produced by a glowing solid, in which light of every visible wavelength is present, 150

contour line, on a map, the line connecting points having the same elevation above sea level, 425

control, the part of an experiment that includes all the conditions (variables) except the condition (variable) being investigated

convection (kən•vec′shən) **current,** (1) in water: a current caused by the upward movement of a mass of warmer water in contact with a mass of cold water that is moving downward, 251; (2) in air: the flow of air caused by the upward movement of a mass of warm air in contact with a mass of downward moving cold air, 280; (3) in the earth's mantle: a current caused by the flow, under the ocean crust, of hot mantle rock from a mid-ocean ridge toward the land, 98

coral reef, a rocky land formation made up principally of the shells of colonies of coral animals, 263

core, the innermost region of the earth, 82

Coriolis effect, the deflection of the winds to the right in the northern hemisphere, and to the left in the southern hemisphere because of the rotation of the earth, 292

corona, the outer part of the sun's atmosphere, visible as a glow during a total eclipse of the sun, 154

correlation, matching of rocks deposited in one area with rocks deposited during the same time span in another area, 332

cosmic radiation, consists of extremely short electromagnetic waves from outer space, 146

crest, top of a wave, 145

crystal, geometrical solid with plane faces and definite angles, 44

cumulus clouds, thick, fleecy masses of clouds, 275

cyclone, *see* **low,** 295

dark-line spectrum, a spectrum made up of black lines against a background of a continuous spectrum, 150

decay, the breakdown of an atomic nucleus, in which radiation is given off, 90

deferent (def′ər•ənt), a circle around the earth about which a planet, or its epicycle, was supposed to move in the Ptolemaic system, 183

delta, fan-shaped deposits of sediment formed where the mouth of a stream meets a body of water, 131

density, the mass per unit volume, often measured in grams per cubic centimeter (g/cc) or grams per milliliter (g/ml), 229

destructive distillation, the heating of a substance, such as wood or coal, in a limited supply of air, with the result that the substance changes chemically into several products, 408

dew point, the temperature to which air must be cooled for water vapor in it to condense, 268

diatomic (dī′ə•tom′ik) **molecule,** a molecule made up of two like atoms, 31

diffraction grating, a piece of transparent plastic, ruled with very fine parallel lines very close together, which breaks light into its component wavelengths, 150

dike, the igneous rock formation, often table-shaped, that originates when molten rock cuts across existing layers of rock, 109

distillation (water), the process of producing fresh water from water containing chemical impurities, by evaporating and condensing the water, 377

disturbance, a mountain building process over a small area of the earth's surface, 352

dome mountains, mountains in which rock layers are gently folded over a local area of uplift, 110

Doppler (dôp′lər) **effect,** the apparent change in wavelength due to the relative motion of the wave source and the observer, 176

drumlin (drum′lin), a loaf-shaped hill of debris left behind by a retreating glacier, 134

eclipsing binary, a pair of stars, one bright and one dim, which revolve around each other so that the dim one periodically blots the bright one from view, 165

electrolysis (i•lek′trol′ə•sis), a process in which a substance, such as water, is decomposed by electric energy, 23

electromagnetic (i•lek′trō•mag′nə•tik) **spectrum,** the arrangement of electromagnetic waves of all wavelengths in order of their wavelengths, 147

electromagnetic waves, radiant energy, both electric and magnetic in nature, given off by the stars and other glowing objects, and by radioactive elements, 147

electron (i•lek′tron), the negatively charged particle revolving around the nucleus of an atom, 32

electron-shell diagram, diagrams that show how electrons are arranged in each element, 32

element, a substance made up of just one kind of atom, 15

energy, the ability to do work

enzymes (en′zīms), the catalysts in living cells, 390

epicycle (ep′ə•sī′kəl), a circle whose center moves along the circumference of a larger circle; used to explain the motions of planets in the Ptolemaic system, 183

erosion, the gradual removal of the surface of the land by water, winds, or glaciers, 126

escape velocity, the minimum velocity required for an object to overcome the gravitational attraction of the earth, moon, or other body in space, 214

escarpment (es•kärp′mənt), a long, high cliff of layers of sedimentary rock, 365

estuary, area where the ocean extends into the mouth of a river, 386

evaporation, the change from a solid or a liquid to a gas

exosphere (eksō•fir), the outermost layer of the earth's atmosphere, a region with hardly any air, 7

experiment, an investigation carried out under carefully planned conditions in which known variables are carefully controlled

extrusive rock, fine-grained, igneous rocks that cool quickly at the surface, 65

eye, the calm, low-pressure center of a hurricane, around which high-speed winds move, 297

facies (fā′shi·ēz), zones of different composition over the length of a sedimentary layer, 334

fall equinox (ē′kwə•noks), the time of year in the fall, on or about September 22, when daylight and darkness are of equal length, 206

fault, a break in layers of rock resulting from pressure, and causing a shift in a section of the earth's crust, 86

fault-block mountains, mountains formed from large masses of rock broken by faults, 110

faunal succession, concept that life has evolved from simple to complex organisms over the span of geologic time, 336

fetch, length of open sea over which wind blows steadily, 254

flash distillation, a process by which drinking water is produced from sea water by evaporation below its normal boiling temperature, 378

flood plain, the flat area which is flooded by a nearby stream, 131

foci (fō′sī), two points inside an ellipse, the sum of whose distance to any point on the ellipse is always the same, 186

fold mountains, long belts of mountains from highly bent and broken rocks, 110

foliated rock, metamorphic rock that can break into layers, 70

formula, a chemical notation showing (1) for a molecular substance, the kinds and numbers of atoms that are bonded in a molecule of that substance, as H_2O,NH_3; (2) for an ionic substance, the proportion in which the atoms are bonded, as NaCl, $MgBr_2$, Al_2O_3, 25

fossil, remains or evidence of remains of an organism that lived long ago, 324

fracture, the breaking up of a mineral that does not break along cleavage surfaces when struck with a hammer, 48

Frasch (fräsh) **process,** a method of mining sulfur from underground beds, 401

freezing nuclei, particles of solid matter onto which water droplets freeze, 275

frequency, the number of vibrations per second of a compression wave, 84

fringing reef, a coral reef built along the shore of a continent or island, 264

front, the boundary formed between two air masses, 293

fumaroles, cracks or holes in the earth's surface through which steam erupts, 128

fusion, *see* **nuclear fusion,** 159

galaxy, a grouping of millions of stars and nebulae, such as the Milky Way, 166

gamma radiation, waves of electromagnetic energy with very short wavelengths, 80

gas, a state in which matter is able to spread out equally in all directions to take the shape of a closed container

geochronology (jē′ō•krə•nol′ə•je), study of dates of events in the history of the earth, 320

geologic column, sequence of rock layers of various ages in order from youngest at the top to oldest at the bottom, 337

geologic time scale, a vertical sequence of events of earth history arranged in order of time, 345

geologist, scientist who specializes in study of earth

geosyncline (jē′ō•sin′klīn), a large depression or trough, running parallel to a continent, in the earth's crust, 114

geysers, hot springs that erupt and give off their water as a fountain, 127

gram, the basic unit of weight in the metric system

graphic formula, the formula for a substance that pictures the arrangement of atoms within a molecule of that substance, 412

graphic scale, a numbered line showing real distance represented by one unit of scale distance, 423

gravitation (grav′ə•tā′shən), a force that attracts all objects (masses) in the universe to one another; each mass tends to pull every other mass toward itself, 209

gravity (grav′ə•tē), commonly refers to the attraction of the earth for another object, 208

groin, obstruction built on a beach to prevent movement of sand, 258

ground water, the water that collects in porous rock layers underground, 126

guyot (gī′ōt), a seamount with a flattened top, 243

gyre (jīr), a whirlpool that moves clockwise in the northern hemisphere and counter-clockwise in the southern hemisphere, 250

half-life, the period of time it takes for half of the radioactive atoms in a substance to decay, 91

high, an air mass of high pressure, 295

humidity, the amount of water vapor in the air, 271; *see also* **relative humidity,** 295

humus (hyōō′məs), decaying plant and animal matter in the soil, 310

hurricane, a violent, cyclonic storm originating in the tropics, and sometimes called a tropical cyclone, 297

hydrocarbons (hī′drə•kär′bənz), a class of compounds, each of which is made up of carbon and hydrogen, 411

hydroponics, the technique of growing plants with water and nutrients, rather than soil, 309

hydrosphere (hī′drə•sfir), the liquid layer of the earth, made up of the earth's waters, 5

hypothesis (hī′poth′ə•sis), a possible explanation of an object or event that can form the basis for planning the design of an investigation

igneous (ig′nē•əs) **rock,** the kind of rock that is formed by the cooling and solidification of a hot liquid substance, 64

index fossil, an organism that ranged over a wide area, left distinctive fossil remains, and existed for only a relatively short time in geologic history, 337

inertia (in•ûr′shə), the tendency of a body in motion to keep moving, or of a body at rest to stay at rest, 208

infrared radiation, radiation beyond the red end of the visible spectrum, and longer in wavelength, 146

insolation, solar radiation that reaches the earth, 9

intrusive rock, coarse-grained, igneous rock that cools slowly underground, 64

ion (ī′ən), an electrically charged atom or group of atoms, whose charge results from the atom or group of atoms gaining or losing one or more electrons, 7

ionic (ī•on′ik) **bond,** a chemical bond between the positive and negative ions of an ionic compound formed by the transfer of electrons, 35

ionic compound, a compound consisting of ions formed by the transfer of electrons, 35

ionosphere (ī•on′ə•sfir), the layer of the earth's atmosphere containing electrically charged particles (ions), located between the chemosphere and erosphere, 7

isobars, a line on a weather map connecting places with the same atmospheric pressure, 294

isostasy (ī•sos′tə•sē), the theory that the earth maintains a balance among its parts, 117

isotherm, a line on a weather map connecting places with the same temperature, 304

isotopes (ī′se•tōps), atoms of the same element that differ in the number of neutrons in the nucleus, 91

laccolith (lak′ə•lith), a mushroom-shaped plutonic rock formation spread between rock layers, 109

lava, molten rock (magma) that flows from an erupting volcano, 106

law of maximum extent, if a layer of sedimentary rock does not cover the entire earth, it either thins out at the edges or meets other deposits, 330

law of original horizontality, sedimentary rocks are deposited originally in approximately horizontal layers, 330

law of superposition, in an undisturbed section of sedimentary rock layers, the oldest layers are at the bottom and the youngest layers are at the top, 330

light-year, a unit of length equal to the distance traveled by light in one year, equivalent to about 10 trillion kilometers, or 6 trillion miles, 166

liquid, a state in which matter takes the shape of the container in which it is placed

lithification (lith′ə•fə′kā′shən), the compression and cementing together of material in a sediment until it turns into rock, 68

lithosphere (lith′ə•sfir), the solid layer of the earth, sometimes called the earth's crust, 5

longshore drift, movement of beach sediment in the direction of the incoming waves, 258

low, an air mass of low pressure, 295

luminosity (lo͞o′mə•nos′ə•tē), the intensity of light actually being given off by a light source, 171

lunar eclipse, the darkening of the moon that occurs when the earth passes between the sun and the moon so that the earth's shadow is cast on the moon, 227

macromolecule (mak′rə•mol′ə•kyo͞ol), a huge molecule made up of an enormous number of atoms, as a macromolecule of diamond made up of billions of carbon atoms, 410

magma (mag′mə), the molten mixture of minerals found below the earth's surface, 66

magnetosphere (mag•net′ə•sfir), the region in space that encloses the earth's magnetic field, 8

magnitude, the degree of brightness of a star; the lower the magnitude the brighter the star, 170

manganese nodules, small lumps of manganese on the ocean floor, 383

mantle, the layer of plastic rock just beneath the earth's crust in the earth's interior, 81

marine terraces, flat areas carved in rock by breaking waves, 104

mass, the amount of matter in an object

matter, anything that takes up space and has mass, 25

mesa, small elevated land area where a plateau has been washed away; its width and length are greater than its height, 111

mesosphere, the layer of the earth's atmosphere in which a sudden drop in the temperature occurs; between stratosphere and thermosphere, 7

metamorphic (met′ə•môr′fik) **rock,** rock that has undergone change from its first form, 64

meteor, a particle of solid matter that enters the earth's atmosphere from outer space, 188

meteorite (mē′tē•ə•rīt′), a meteor that has hit the surface of the earth, 188

meteoroid (mē′tē•ə•roid′), a bit of solid matter moving through space, 188

methane series, a series of hydrocarbons, including the compounds methane, ethane, propane, butane, and many more, 415

metric system, a system of measurement in which each unit is multiplied by 10 to obtain the next larger unit, or divided by 10 to obtain the next smaller unit; the basic unit of length is the meter; the basic unit of weight is the gram; and the basic unit of volume is the liter

mineral, any naturally occurring solid substance in the earth's crust, 39

mixture, a substance in which different substances are present, a mixture has no definite composition, 17

mobile zone, an area of the earth where volcanoes and earthquakes are most frequently located, 88

Moho, the boundary between the earth's crust and mantle, 87

mold, an impression or open space that preserves the form of an object in rock or other solid material, 324

molecular (mə•lek′yə•lər) **bond,** the kind of chemical bond formed when electrons are shared to make a molecule of a substance, 36

molecular compound, a compound consisting of molecules formed by the sharing of electons between two or more elements, 36

molecular formula, the formula for a substance that tells how many of each kind of atom the substance has, 412

molecule (mol′ə•kyo͞ol), the smallest particle of an element or molecular compound that has all the properties of that element or compound, 22

moraine (mə•rān′), a deposit of gravel, sand, sediment, rocks, and boulders left behind when a glacier melts and retreats, 134

neap tides, the tides that occur when the moon and sun make a right angle with the earth, and their gravitational pulls work against each other, 212
nebula (neb′yə•lə), a cloud of dust or gas in interstellar space, 166
nebular (neb′yə•lər) **hypothesis,** the hypothesis that the solar system began as a cloud of dust and gas in space, 198
neritic (ni•rit′ik) **zone,** the area of the sea that extends from the lowest tide line to the outer edge of the continental shelf, 261
neutron (no͞o′tron), a particle in the nucleus of an atom, having no electrical charge, 32
nimbus cloud, a rain cloud, 275
nitrogen fixation, the combining of the air's nitrogen to form compounds, 390
nova, a star that suddenly explodes and becomes many times brighter, and then slowly fades, 174
nuclear fusion, a nuclear reaction in which atomic nuclei join together, 159
nuclear reaction, a change in matter involving changes in the make-up of the nuclei of atoms, 158
nucleus (no͞o′klē•əs), the center of an atom, 32

open hearth (furnace), a furnace in which steel is made from iron mixed with certain other elements, 399
orbit, the path of one body around another, as a satellite around the earth or the earth around the sun
ore, a mineral or rock that is the source of a metal, 395
organic compound, any compound containing the element carbon, with a few exceptions, 411
organism, any living thing that carries on life functions
ox-bow lake, a lake formed when a channel is cut off from the main flow, 131
oxidation reaction, one type of oxidation consists of the combining of oxygen with another substance, 18
ozone (ō′zōn), an allotropic form of oxygen made up of triatomic molecules, (O_3), 6

paleomagnetism, study of the direction of the magnetic field "frozen" in a rock mass when the rock was formed, 93
pedalfer, soil receiving more than 25 inches of rain a year, 310
pedocal, soil receiving less than 25 inches of rain a year, 310
penumbra (pi•num′brə), during an eclipse of the sun, the partly lighted area, surrounding the umbra, in which a partial eclipse of the sun is seen, 225
perigee (per′ə•jē), the point in the orbit of an earth satellite at which it is nearest the earth, 214
permafrost, permanently frozen ground, 328
permeability, the rate at which water passes through a material, 312
physical change, any change in matter that does not change its chemical composition
physical properties, the properties of a substance that can be observed without changing the chemical make-up of the substance, 40
planet, any one of the 9 major bodies that move in nearly circular orbits around the sun, 181
planetoid (plan′ə•toid), see **asteroid,** 188
planimetric map, map showing correct distances and directions between places, 424
plankton (plangk′tən), the organisms that float with currents and waves in the sea, 262
plasticity (plas•tis′ə•tē), the ability of some solids to bend or flow, 82
plate tectonics, a model that describes motion of pieces of the earth's crust, 95
plateau, raised area of horizontal rock layers, 111
platform, an area of nearly horizontal rock surrounding a continental shield, 351
plutonic rock, see intrusive rock, 64
porosity, percentage of space between grains determining the amount of water a soil can hold, 311
precipitate (pri•sip′ə•tāt), a solid that forms when two clear solutions react, 16
precipitation (pri•sip′ə•tā′shən), (1) in meteorology, the depositing of moisture from the atmosphere on the surface of the earth, 274; (2) in chemistry, the formation of a precipitate
pressure wave, a kind of seismic wave that causes the particles of a substance it passes through to be alternately squeezed together and pushed apart, 84
prevailing winds, the winds in the lower troposphere that generally flow from the same direction, as the prevailing westerlies, 248
product, a substance formed as a result of a chemical reaction, written on the right side of the arrow in a chemical equation, 23
prominence, a tonguelike cloud of glowing-hot gas coming from and extending beyond the sun's surface, 154
proper motion, apparent change in position of a star, 175
proton (prō′ton), a particle in the nucleus of an atom, having a positive charge, 32
protoplanet (prō′tə•plan′it), a body of condensed matter that later became a planet, according to one hypothesis of the origin of the solar system, 201

quasar (kwā′zar), a very distant, fast, and energetic object in space that is a powerful source of radio and light energy, 179

radar (*ra*dio *d*etection *a*nd *r*anging), a device used for the detection of objects by radio waves, 227
radiation pressure, the slight pressure exerted by sunlight or other radiation, 201
radioactivity (rā′dē•ō•ak′tiv′ə•tē), the spontaneous breaking down of the nuclei of certain unstable atoms, such as those of radium, uranium, and thorium, 91
radioactive isotope, a form of an element whose nucleus decays and, in doing so, yields radioactive particles, 91

radio telescope, a radio receiver, often dish-shaped, designed to receive radio waves from outer space, 148

radio waves, the electromagnetic waves used for communication, with wavelengths longer than infrared radiations, 146

reactant (rē•akt′ənt), a substance entering into a chemical reaction, written on the left side of the arrow in a chemical equation, 23

red dwarf, a relatively faint, cool, and small star, reddish in color, 173

red giant, a relatively large, faint, and cool star, reddish in color, 173

red shift, a shift to longer wavelengths of the light from stars and galaxies moving away from the earth, 178

refraction (wave), change in direction of a wave, 258

relative dating, estimating the age of the earth on the basis of geologic events that have occurred throughout the earth's history, 320

relative humidity, the ratio of the amount of water vapor in the air to the amount that the air could hold at that temperature, 271

revolution, a great, mountain building process over a widespread region of the earth's surface, 353

root-pry, the process by which cracks in rock or pavement are enlarged by the force of the growing roots of plants, 124

salinity (sə•lin′ə•tē), the degree of saltiness of a salt solution, especially applied to ocean water, 251

salt dome, large masses of salt that have pushed upward, moving and punching through surrounding rock layers; often oil and gas are trapped at edges of a salt dome, 381

saturated air, air that is holding all the water vapor it can hold at a given temperature, 270

saturated solution, a solution containing as much dissolved substance as can dissolve at a given temperature, 46

sea arch, *see* sea stack, 136

sea cave, *see* sea stack, 136

sea cliff, steeply sloping land surface descending into the water formed by water erosion, 136

sea-floor spreading, the spreading apart of the mid-ocean ridge system, 94

seamount, a volcanic mountain that rises from the ocean floor and has its top under water, 105

sea stack, a feature formed by the erosion of waves against a rock mass extending into the water, 136

sediment, rock particles, formed by weathering and removed by erosion, that settle in low-lying areas, 67

sedimentary rock, the rock formed when sediments are compressed together and lithified, 64

seismic (sīz′mik) **wave,** a compression wave caused by movements in the earth's crust, 84

seismograph (sīz′mə•graf), an instrument used to detect vibrations in the earth, 83

selenologist (sel′ə•nol′ə•jist), scientist who specializes in the study of the moon, 221

shear wave, a kind of seismic wave that causes particles of a substance it passes through to slide past each other crosswise, 84

shield, an extensive, broad, flat region that is the stable, central nucleus of a continent, 349

silicate (sil′i•kāt), one of many substances made up of silicon, oxygen, and other elements, 52

siliceous (si•lish′əs) **sediment,** a sediment made up of silicates, 262

sill, an igneous rock formation in between, and parallel to, preexisting layers of rock, 109

soil horizon, a layer of soil in a soil profile, 310

soil profile, layers of exposed soil showing topsoil, subsoil, and bedrock, 310

solar eclipse, the blotting from view of the sun from the earth that occurs when the moon passes directly between the earth and sun, 224

solar evaporation, the process of removing salt from sea water by allowing the sun to evaporate the water from shallow basins, 375

solar flare, a bright spot on the sun that releases enormous amounts of energy, 154

solar wind, a shower of atomic particles emitted by the sun, 154

solid, a state of matter in which a substance has a definite size and shape and well-defined surfaces that separate it from all other matter

solute, *see* **solution**

solution, a mixture of two substances, one of which is dissolved in the other. The dissolved substance is called the solute.

sonar, a device to detect underwater objects by the reflection of sound waves from them, 242

space lattice, the arrangement of particles within a crystal, 49

specific gravity, the weight of an object compared with the weight of an equal volume of water, 41

spectroscope (spek′trə•skōp), an instrument that separates light into the wavelengths that make it up, 149

spring equinox (ē′kwə•noks), the time of year in the spring, on or about March 21, when daylight and darkness are of equal length, 206

spring tides, the tides that occur when the sun and moon pull in the same direction on the earth, 211

stable isotope, a nonradioactive form of an element, 91

stalactite, an "icicle" of calcium carbonate hanging down from the roof of a cave, 128

stalagmite, a deposit of calcium carbonate pointing upward from the floor of a cave, 129

star cluster, a group of stars that appear together and seem to have properties such as distance and motion in common, 105

stratosphere (strat′ə•sfir), the layer of the earth's atmosphere in which temperature and weather change very little; between troposphere and chemosphere, 6

stratus clouds, low, uniform sheets of clouds, 275

striae (strī′ē), long, parallel scratches made in a rock surface by fragments embedded in the underside of a glacier, 134

submarine canyon, deep channel on the ocean floor through which sediment flows, 87
subsoil, second layer, or B horizon, of soil; soluble minerals washed down from the top soil collect in this layer, 310
summer solstice (sōl'stis), the time when the sun is at its highest point in the sky at noon; on or about June 21 in the northern hemisphere, 206
sunspot, a dark, relatively cool patch on the sun, believed to be an eruption of the sun's surface, 154
supernova (sōō'pər·nō'va), an unusually brilliant flare-up of a large star, 174
surface runoff, rain water that runs off the surface of the ground, carrying various materials with it, 129
symbol, a capital letter, or a capital letter and a small letter, that represents an element; for example, C for carbon, Cl for chlorine, Fe for iron, 24
syncline, downfolded layers of rock, 102

talus (tā'ləs), a sloping pile of rock fragments at the bottom of a cliff, 124
temperature, the measurement of hotness or coldness; that is, the average kinetic energy of the molecules in a substance, measured in degrees
terminal moraine (mə'rān), a crescent-shaped ridge of debris left when the front edge of a glacier retreats, 134
theory, a reasonable explanation of a set of related observations
thermonuclear (thûr'mō·nōō'klē·ər) **reaction,** a fusion reaction between the nuclei of atoms, in which a very large amount of energy is released, 158
thermosphere, the layer of the earth's atmosphere above the mesophere in which the air particles are widely spaced, 7
tidal zone, the area on the seashore between the low-tide line and the high-tide line, 261
top soil, upper layer, or A horizon, of soil's containing humus, 310
topographic map, various kinds of maps showing elevation of land in relation to sea level, 424
tornado, a violent storm characterized by funnel-shaped clouds, high-speed winds, and great destructiveness over a short path and a small area, 298
troposphere (trop'ə·sfir), the lowest layer of the earth's atmosphere, in which the phenomena of weather take place, 6
trough, bottom of a wave, 254
tsunami (tsōō·nä'mē), a seismic sea wave caused by an earthquake in the land under the sea, 87

ultraviolet radiation, radiation beyond the violet end of the visible spectrum, and shorter in wavelength, 146
umbra (um'brə), the dark cone of shadow thrown on the earth by the moon during a solar eclipse, 225
unconformity, a buried surface showing the contact between two different types of rock layers, 332
unfoliated rock, metamorphic rock that does not form sheets or layers when broken, 71
uniformitarianism (yōō'nə·fôr'mə·târ'ē·ən·iz'əm), concept that geologic processes in operation today have been in operation throughout the history of the earth, 330

valley glacier, a mass of moving ice that flows through a valley, 133
Van Allen belt, a zone of radiation around the earth, 8
vapor, the gaseous state of a substance that usually exists as a solid or liquid, 26
variable, a quantity or characteristic that changes as the conditions upon which it depends change, 273
varves, alternately light and dark layers of sediments beneath a lake, 323
velocity, speed with which a wave moves in a given direction; velocity of a wave equals wavelength divided by wave period, 254
volcanic rock, igneous rock that solidifies above the earth's surface, 65
volcanic mountains, mountains formed from the accumulation of volcanic material, 110
volume, the measurement of the space occupied by a substance
vulcanization (vul'kən·i·zā'shən), a process in which rubber is heated with sulfur so that the rubber becomes strong and pliable, 406

water table, the level at which saturation of porous rock with water below ground begins, 126
wave height, height of wave crest above trough, 254
wavelength, the distance from the crest of one wave to the crest of the next, 254
wave period, time between the crest of one wave and the crest of the next wave, 254
weathering, the breaking down of rock due to exposure to the atmosphere, 122
weight, a measure of the pull of gravitation on an object
white dwarf, a relatively small, cool, and dim star, with a very high density, 174
winter solstice (sōl'stis), the time when the sun is at its southernmost point in the sky at noon; on or about December 21 in the northern hemisphere, 206

X rays, electromagnetic waves with short wavelengths, beyond the ultraviolet radiations in the electromagnetic spectrum, 146

Index

A page reference in **boldface** type indicates an illustration.

B

C

F

G

H

I

J

K

N

O

P

Q

R

S

T

U

V

W

X

Y

Z

Picture Credits

Illustrators: Diamond Art Studio, Joseph Ferruzzi Associates, Henri Fluchere, Harbrace art staff, Howard Koslow, Don Spaulding, John Paul Trembley, and SN Studios, Inc.

FRONTISPIECE: David Muench.

KEY: (t) top; (c) center; (l) left; (r) right; (b) bottom.

INTRODUCTION: Page x, California Institute of Technology and Carnegie Institute of Washington; all others, Harbrace.

HARBRACE: Pages 5, 11, 14-16, 18, 22-28, 31, 41-44(t); 46, 47, 51(t); 52(b); 53, 54(bl); 57, 58, 61, 62, 67, 69(t); 71, 74, 75, 83, 84, 103(l col); 122, 123, 124(b); 126(b); 145, 149, 151, 171, 186, 188(t); 203, 207, 213, 229, 252, 255, 268, 279, 281, 282, 284-286, 306, 312, 320, 327, 333, 334, 377, 378, 389, 395, 396(t); 397(l); 401-404, 408, 409, 410-412, 416.

UNIT ONE: Page 2, John H. Gerard, Natl. Aud. Soc.; 4, NASA; 9, Wide World Photo; 19, Wallace Litwin, Photo Trends; 39, American Museum of Natural History; 44(b), Lincoln Nutting, Natl. Aud. Soc.; 48, Dr. E. R. Degginger; 49, Picker Corporation; 51 (second from t), George Whiteley, Photo Researchers, (second from b); Dr. E. R. Degginger; (b), John H. Gerard, Natl. Aud. Soc.; 52(t), University Museum, University of Pennsylvania; 54(tl), John H. Gerard, Natl. Aud. Soc.; (tr), Breck P. Kent; (br), Dr. E. R. Degginger; 55(tl), John H. Gerard, Natl. Aud. Soc.; (tr), George Whiteley, Photo Researchers; (cr), Breck P. Kent; 56(t), Dr. E. R. Degginger; (b), De Beers Consolidated Mines, Ltd.; 64(t), Shostal; (b), American Museum of Natural History; 65(t), A. W. Ambler, Natl. Aud. Soc.; (c), American Museum of Natural History; (b), Dr. E. R. Degginger; 66(tl), Mike Lewis, Peter Arnold; (tr), Marando, DPI; (bl), Dr. J. Weissberg, Photo Researchers; (br), Grant Heilman; 68, Grant Heilman; 69(b), Lawrence Pringle, Photo Researchers; 70, Jim Theologos; 72(t and br), C. L. and M. A. Fenton; (bl), Office of Public Information, Colorado School of Mines; 73, NASA.

UNIT TWO: Page 78, American Museum of Natural History; 80, N.Y. Public Library, Picture Collection; 88, MacDougall, DPI; 91, Brookhaven National Laboratory; 96, Icelandic Information Office; 101(l), Mimi Forsyth, Monkmeyer; (r), Marco Foote; 102(t), Martin Vanderwall, DeWys, Inc.; (b), G. R. Roberts; 103(br), R. J. Witkind, U.S. Geological Soc.; 104(tr), Grant Heilman; (b), Dolores McCutcheon Brown, Monkmeyer; 105, W. K. Waterfall; 106, Hjalmar R. Bardarson; 111(tl), Grant Heilman; (tr), John Gajda, DPI; 112, Alan Pitcairn, Grant Heilman; (b), Shostal; 113, Philip Hyde; 114, Marion Bernstein; 121, Earl Roberge, Photo Researchers; 124(t), C. L. and M. A. Fenton; 126(t), Grant Heilman; 127(b), Karen Collidge; 128(t), Karen Collidge; (b) Carlsbad Cavern National Park; 129(t), Grant Heilman; (b), C. L. and M. A. Fenton; 130(t), C. L. and M. A. Fenton; (b), David Muench; 131(t), Shostal; (c), Grant Heilman; (b), G. R. Roberts; 132, Lawrence Lowry, Rapho Guillumette; 133, Ray Atkeson; 134, American Museum of Natural History; 135(t), David Muench; (b), Grant Heilman; 136(l), Grant Heilman; (r), Hal Harrison, Grant Heilman; (b), Dennis Brokaw, Natl. Aud. Soc.; 137, Laurence Lowry, Natl. Aud. Soc.

UNIT THREE: Page 140, Calif. Inst. of Technology and Carnegie Inst. of Washington; 142, Istituto e Museo de Storia della Scienza, Florence; 143, Mount Wilson and Palomar Observatories; 144, Maria Mitchell Observatory; 147, Bell Telephone Laboratories; 148, Australian News and Information Bureau; 152(t), Lick Observatory; (b), Mount Wilson and Palomar Observatories; 153, Mount Wilson and Palomar Observatories; 155(t), High Altitude Observatory, Boulder, Colorado; (bl), Perkin Elmer Corp.; 155(br), Mount Wilson and Palomar Observatories; 160, Acme Pictures; 163, American Museum of Natural History; 165, Mount Wilson and Palomar Observatories; 166(l), Lick Observatory; (r), Mount Wilson and Palomar Observatories; 167, Harvard College Observatory; 168, 169, 174, Mount Wilson and Palomar Observatories; 175, American Museum of Natural History; 176, Yerkes Observatory; 178, Mount Wilson and Palomar Observatories; 181, NASA; 182, 184, Jean Arlaud; 185, Staatsbibliothek Berlin, Bildarchir Handke; 188(b), Mount Wilson and Palomar Observatories; 210, National

Film Board of Canada; 214, 216, NASA; 219, 220, Lick Observatory; 221, Josef Muench; 223, NASA; 225, Wide World Photo; 226(t), NASA; (b), American Museum-Hayden Planetarium; 228, 231-234, NASA.

UNIT FOUR: Page 238, Ray Atkeson; 242, Woods Hole Oceanographic Institution; 243, Official U.S. Navy photographs; 246(t), Donald Baird; (b), Reynolds Metals Co.; 247, Paris Match, Pictorial Parade, Inc.; 257, Josef Muench; 259, Marvin B. Winter; 274(t), Paul W. Nesbit, Natl. Aud. Soc.; (second from t), Edna Bennett, Photo Researchers; (second from b), Russ Kinne, Photo Researchers; (b), Cal Harbert, Natl. Aud. Soc.; 297, USAF; 298, ESSA, U.S. Dept. of Commerce; 301(bl), Runk/Schoenberger, Grant Heilman; (br), Josef Muench; 303(tl), Feily, Monkmeyer; (tr, bl), Shostal; (br), Arizona Photographic Assoc. Inc.; 307, Eric G. Carle, Shostal; 308(l), David Muench; (r), Josef Muench; 309, Grant Heilman; 310, G. R. Roberts; 311, 313, Alan Pitcairn, Grant Heilman; 314(tl), Karales, Peter Arnold; (tr), Shostal; (bl), Grant Heilman; (br), U.S. Dept. of Agriculture, Soil Conservation Service; 315(t), Shostal; (b) Joe Rychetnik, Photo Researchers.

UNIT FIVE: Page 318, Josef Muench; 323, American Museum of Natural History; 324, Donald Baird; 325(bl), Peabody Museum of Natural History, Yale University; (tr), The Bettmann Archive; 326(t), Donald Baird; (b), Josef Muench; 328(t), American Museum of Natural History; (b), Frank M. Carpenter; 329, American Museum of Natural History; 330, Donald Baird; 331, Darton N.H., U.S. Geological Survey; 335, Donald Baird; 336, Culver Pictures Inc.; 337, American Museum of Natural History; 338, Donald Baird; 339, American Museum of Natural History; 344, Donald Baird; 345, Field Museum of Natural History; 346, American Museum of Natural History; 348, Geological Survey of Canada; 350, Marvin B. Winter; 351, M. F. Glaessner, University of Adelaide; 354, Donald Baird; 355(t), Smithsonian Institution; (b), American Museum of Natural History; 356, Donald Baird; 357, American Museum of Natural History; 359, Donald Baird; 360, 361, American Museum of Natural History; 364, Steve and Dolores McCutcheon; 365(t), American Museum of Natural History; (b), New York State Power Authority; 366, F.P.G.; 367(t), National Audubon Society; (b), American Museum of Natural History; 368, American Museum of Natural History.

UNIT SIX: Page 372, Douglass Baglin, Natl. Aud. Soc.; 374, Dr. Georg Gerster, Rapho Guillumette; 375, Leslie Salt Company; 376, Merck & Co., Inc.; 380, N. W. Ayer and Son Inc.; 381, Design Photographers International Inc.; 382, Cabot Corporation; 383, Deep Sea Ventures Inc.; 385, Steinhart Aquarium; 387, U.S. Department of Interior; 388, U.N.F.A.O.; 391, The Nitragin Co., Inc.; 392, Rainbow Neon Sculpture by Billy Apple, 1965; 396(b), American Museum of Natural History; 397(r), Shostal; 399, U.S. Steel; 400, Convair, a division of General Dynamics Corp.; 406(t), E. R. Degginger; (b), Paper Trade Journal; 415, Steve and Dolores McCutcheon; 417, Dann Perszyk.